Mike Holt's Illustrated Guide to

UNDERSTANDING NEC® REQUIREMENTS FOR
BONDING AND GROUNDING

BASED ON THE
2020 NEC®

Mike Holt Enterprises
888.NEC.CODE (632.2633) • www.MikeHolt.com

NOTICE TO THE READER

The text and commentary in this book is the author's interpretation of the 2020 Edition of NFPA 70®, the *National Electrical Code*®. It shall not be considered an endorsement of or the official position of the NFPA® or any of its committees, nor relied upon as a formal interpretation of the meaning or intent of any specific provision or provisions of the 2020 edition of NFPA 70, *National Electrical Code*.

The publisher does not warrant or guarantee any of the products described herein or perform any independent analysis in connection with any of the product information contained herein. The publisher does not assume, and expressly disclaims, any obligation to obtain and include information other than that provided to it by the manufacturer.

The reader is expressly warned to consider and adopt all safety precautions and applicable federal, state, and local laws and regulations. By following the instructions contained herein, the reader willingly assumes all risks in connection with such instructions.

Mike Holt Enterprises disclaims liability for any personal injury, property or other damages of any nature whatsoever, whether special, indirect, consequential or compensatory, directly or indirectly resulting from the use of this material. The reader is responsible for relying on his or her personal independent judgment in determining safety and appropriate actions in all circumstances.

The publisher makes no representation or warranties of any kind, including but not limited to, the warranties of fitness for particular purpose or merchantability, nor are any such representations implied with respect to the material set forth herein, and the publisher takes no responsibility with respect to such material. The publisher shall not be liable for any special, consequential, or exemplary damages resulting, in whole or part, from the reader's use of, or reliance upon, this material.

Mike Holt's Illustrated Guide to Understanding NEC® Requirements for Bonding and Grounding, based on the 2020 NEC®

First Printing: January 2020

Author: Mike Holt
Technical Illustrator: Mike Culbreath
Cover Design: Bryan Burch
Layout Design and Typesetting: Cathleen Kwas

COPYRIGHT © 2019 Charles Michael Holt
ISBN 978-1-950431-03-8

Produced and Printed in the USA

All rights reserved. No part of this work covered by the copyright hereon may be reproduced or used in any form or by any means graphic, electronic, or mechanical, including photocopying, recording, taping, or information storage and retrieval systems without the written permission of the publisher. You can request permission to use material from this text by e-mailing Info@MikeHolt.com.

For more information, call 888.NEC.CODE (632.2633), or e-mail Info@MikeHolt.com.

NEC®, NFPA 70®, NFPA 70E® and *National Electrical Code*® are registered trademarks of the National Fire Protection Association.

 This logo is a registered trademark of Mike Holt Enterprises, Inc.

If you are an instructor and would like to request an examination copy of this or other Mike Holt Publications:

Call: 888.NEC.CODE (632.2633) • Fax: 352.360.0983

E-mail: Info@MikeHolt.com • Visit: www.MikeHolt.com/Instructors

You can download a sample PDF of all our publications by visiting www.MikeHolt.com/products.

I dedicate this book to the
Lord Jesus Christ, *my mentor and teacher.*
Proverbs 16:3

"For All Your Electrical Training Needs"

www.MikeHolt.com

We Care...

Since the day we started our business over 40 years ago, we have been working hard to produce products that get results, and to help individuals in their pursuit of learning how to be successful in this exciting industry. I have built my business on the idea that customers come first, and that everyone on my team will do everything they possibly can to take care of you. I want you to know that we value you, and are honored that you have chosen us to be your partner in electrical training.

I believe that you are the future of this industry and that it is you who will make the difference in years to come. My goal is to share with you everything that I know and to encourage you to pursue your education on a continuous basis. I hope that not only will you learn theory, code, calculations or how to pass an exam, but that in the process you will become the expert in the field and the person who others know to trust.

We are dedicated to providing quality electrical training that will help you take your skills to the next level and we genuinely care about you. Thanks for choosing Mike Holt Enterprises for your electrical training needs.

God bless and much success,

Exam Preparation | Continuing Education | Apprenticeship Products | In-House Training | & more

"...as for me and my house, we will serve the Lord." [Joshua 24:15]

TABLE OF CONTENTS

About This Textbook..x

Additional Products to Help You Learn.............................xiii

How to Use the *National Electrical Code* 1

SECTION I—ELECTRICAL FUNDAMENTALS 7

Unit 1—Matter 9
1.1 Atomic Theory..9
1.2 Electrostatic Force...11
1.3 Atomic Charges...12
1.4 Charged Material (Static Charge)............................12
1.5 High-Voltage Electrostatic Discharge......................13
1.6 Lightning..14
1.7 Lightning Protection 15

Unit 1—Practice Questions.. 17

Unit 2—Electron Theory... 21
2.1 Electron Orbitals..21
2.2 Valence Electrons..21
2.3 Freeing Electrons from an Atom..............................22
2.4 Conductance..22

Unit 2—Practice Questions.. 25

Unit 3—Sources, Uses, and Dangers of Electricity........... 27
3.1 Electrical Power Source 27
3.2 Electric Current Flow (Electricity).............................27
3.3 Electricity 28
3.4 Dangers of Electricity 29
3.5 *National Electrical Code* 31

Unit 3—Practice Questions.. 33

Unit 4—Circuit Protective Devices 37
Part A Overcurrent Protection Devices 37
4.1 Overcurrent Protection..37
4.2 Clearing Faults..38
4.3 Overcurrent Protective Device Types......................39
4.4 Fuses...39
4.5 Circuit Breaker Trip Elements 40

Part B Ground-Fault Circuit Interrupters (GFCIs).......... 40
4.6 Ground-Fault Circuit Interrupters (GFCIs)...............40
4.7 Neutral-to-Case Detection......................................41
4.8 Line-to-Neutral Shock Hazard.................................41
4.9 GFCI Fails—Circuit Remains Energized 42
4.10 GFCI Test Button 42

Unit 4—Practice Questions.. 43

SECTION II—*NEC* RULES FOR BONDING AND GROUNDING... 47

Article 90—Introduction to the *National Electrical Code* 49
90.1 Purpose of the *NEC*..49
90.2 Scope of the *NEC* 50
90.3 *Code* Arrangement..52
90.4 Enforcement 53
90.5 Mandatory Requirements and Explanatory Material 55
90.7 Examination of Equipment for Product Safety........55

Article 90—Practice Questions... 57

CHAPTER 1—GENERAL RULES 59

Article 100—Definitions... 61
100 Definitions...61

Article 110—Requirements for Electrical Installations...... 83
110.1 Scope..83
110.2 Approval of Conductors and Equipment.................83
110.3 Examination, Identification, Installation, Use, and Product Listing (Certification) of Equipment 84
110.5 Conductor Material 84
110.6 Conductor Sizes 84
110.7 Wiring Integrity..85
110.8 Suitable Wiring Methods...85
110.11 Deteriorating Agents...85
110.14 Conductor Termination and Splicing.......................86

Chapter 1—Practice Questions... 91

Article 250 | Table of Contents

CHAPTER 2—WIRING AND PROTECTION 97

Article 250—Grounding and Bonding 99

Part I. General 99
- 250.1 Scope 99
- 250.4 Performance Requirements for Grounding and Bonding 100

Earth Shells 104
- 250.6 Objectionable Current 106

Objectionable Current 107

Dangers of Objectionable Current 108
- 250.8 Connection of Grounding and Bonding Connectors 110
- 250.10 Protection of Ground Clamps and Fittings 110
- 250.12 Clean Surfaces 110

Part II. System Grounding and Bonding 111
- 250.20 Systems Required to be Grounded 111
- 250.21 Ungrounded Systems 112
- 250.24 Grounding 112
- 250.25 Grounding for Supply Side of the Service Disconnect 116
- 250.28 Main Bonding Jumper and System Bonding Jumper 117
- 250.30 Separately Derived Systems 118

Special Section 250.30 Separately Derived Systems 125
- 250.32 Buildings Supplied by a Feeder 127
- 250.34 Generators—Portable and Vehicle- or Trailer-Mounted 129
- 250.36 High-Impedance Grounded Systems 130

Part III. Grounding Electrode System and Grounding Electrode Conductor 131
- 250.50 Grounding Electrode System 131
- 250.52 Grounding Electrode Types 131
- 250.53 Grounding Electrode Installation Requirements 134

Measuring the Contact Resistance of Electrodes to Earth 138

Soil Resistivity 139
- 250.54 Auxiliary Grounding Electrodes 139
- 250.58 Common Grounding Electrode 140
- 250.62 Grounding Electrode Conductor 141
- 250.64 Grounding Electrode Conductor Installation 141
- 250.66 Sizing Grounding Electrode Conductor 145
- 250.68 Grounding Electrode Conductor and Bonding Jumper Connection to Grounding Electrodes 146
- 250.70 Grounding Electrode Conductor Termination Fittings 148

Part IV. Enclosure, Raceway, and Service Cable Connections 149
- 250.80 Service Raceways and Enclosures 149
- 250.86 Other Enclosures 149

Part V. Bonding for Fault Current 149
- 250.90 General 149
- 250.92 Bonding Equipment Containing Service Conductors 149
- 250.94 Bonding Communications Systems 152
- 250.96 Bonding Other Enclosures 153
- 250.97 Bonding Metal Parts Containing 277V and 480V Circuits 154
- 250.98 Bonding Loosely Jointed Metal Raceways 155
- 250.102 Neutral Conductor, Bonding Conductors, and Bonding Jumpers 155
- 250.104 Bonding of Piping Systems and Exposed Structural Metal 157
- 250.106 Lightning Protection Systems 161

Part VI. Equipment Grounding and Equipment Grounding Conductors 162
- 250.109 Metal Enclosures 162
- 250.114 Equipment Connected by Cord and Plug 162
- 250.118 Types of Equipment Grounding Conductors 163
- 250.119 Identification of Equipment Grounding Conductors 167
- 250.120 Equipment Grounding Conductor Installation 168
- 250.121 Restricted Use of Equipment Grounding Conductors 168
- 250.122 Sizing Equipment Grounding Conductors 168

Part VII. Methods of Equipment Grounding Conductor Connections 172
- 250.134 Equipment Connected by Permanent Wiring Methods 172
- 250.136 Equipment Secured to Grounded Metal Supports 173
- 250.138 Cord-and-Plug-Connected 173
- 250.140 Frames of Ranges, Ovens, and Clothes Dryers 173
- 250.142 Neutral Conductor for Effective Ground-Fault Current Path 174
- 250.146 Connecting Receptacle Grounding Terminal to an Equipment Grounding Conductor 175
- 250.148 Continuity and Attachment of Equipment Grounding Conductors in Boxes 178

Chapter 2—Practice Questions 181

CHAPTER 3—WIRING METHODS AND MATERIALS 193

Article 300—General Requirements for Wiring Methods and Materials 197
- 300.1 Scope 197
- 300.3 Conductors 198
- 300.10 Electrical Continuity 200
- 300.20 Induced Alternating Currents in Ferrous Metal Parts 200

Article 314—Outlet, Device, Pull, and Junction Boxes; Conduit Bodies; and Handhole Enclosures 203
- 314.1 Scope 203
- 314.3 Nonmetallic Boxes 203
- 314.4 Metal Boxes 203

Part II. Installation 204
- 314.25 Covers and Canopies 204
- 314.28 Sizing Pull and Junction Boxes 204
- 314.30 Handhole Enclosures 205

Article 320—Armored Cable (Type AC) 207
- 320.1 Scope 207

| 320.2 | Definition | 207 |
| 320.108 | Equipment Grounding Conductor | 208 |

Article 330—Metal-Clad Cable (Type MC) ...209
330.1	Scope	209
330.2	Definition	209
330.108	Equipment Grounding Conductor	210

Article 334—Nonmetallic-Sheathed Cable (Type NM) ...211
334.1	Scope	211
334.2	Definition	211
334.108	Equipment Grounding Conductor	211

Article 348—Flexible Metal Conduit (Type FMC) ...213
348.1	Scope	213
348.2	Definition	213
348.60	Equipment Grounding and Bonding Conductors	213

Article 350—Liquidtight Flexible Metal Conduit (Type LFMC) ...215
350.1	Scope	215
350.2	Definition	215
350.60	Equipment Grounding and Bonding Conductors	215

Article 352—Rigid Polyvinyl Chloride Conduit (Type PVC) ...217
352.1	Scope	217
352.2	Definition	217
352.60	Equipment Grounding Conductor	217

Article 356—Liquidtight Flexible Nonmetallic Conduit (Type LFNC) ...219
356.1	Scope	219
356.2	Definition	219
356.60	Equipment Grounding Conductor	219

Article 358—Electrical Metallic Tubing (Type EMT) ...221
358.1	Scope	221
358.2	Definition	221
358.42	Couplings and Connectors	222
358.60	Equipment Grounding Conductor	222

Article 362—Electrical Nonmetallic Tubing (Type ENT) ...223
362.1	Scope	223
362.2	Definition	223
362.60	Equipment Grounding Conductor	223

Article 386—Surface Metal Raceways ...225
386.1	Scope	225
386.2	Definition	225
386.60	Equipment Grounding Conductor	226

Article 392—Cable Trays ...227
392.1	Scope	227
392.2	Definition	227
392.60	Equipment Grounding Conductor	227

Chapter 3—Practice Questions ...229

CHAPTER 4—EQUIPMENT FOR GENERAL USE ...231

Article 404—Switches ...233
404.1	Scope	233
404.9	General-Use Snap Switches, Dimmers, and Control Switches	233
404.12	Grounding of Enclosures	234

Article 406—Receptacles and Attachment Plugs (Caps) ...235
406.1	Scope	235
406.3	Receptacle Rating and Type	235
406.4	General Installation Requirements	236
406.6	Receptacle Faceplates	238
406.11	Connecting Receptacle Grounding Terminal to Equipment Grounding Conductor	238

Article 408—Switchboards and Panelboards ...239
| 408.1 | Scope | 239 |
| 408.40 | Equipment Grounding Conductor | 239 |

Article 410—Luminaires, Lampholders, and Lamps ...241
Part I. General ...241
| 410.1 | Scope | 241 |
| 410.30 | Supports | 241 |

Part V. Grounding (Bonding) ...242
410.40	General	242
410.44	Equipment Grounding Conductor	242
410.46	Equipment Grounding Conductor Attachment	242

Part XVI. Special Provisions for Horticultural Lighting Equipment ...242
| 410.182 | Grounding | 242 |

Article 440—Air-Conditioning and Refrigeration Equipment ...243
| 440.1 | Scope | 243 |
| 440.9 | Grounding and Bonding | 243 |

Article 450 | Table of Contents

Article 450—Transformers 245
450.1   Scope 245
450.10   Grounding and Bonding 245

Chapter 4—Practice Questions 247

CHAPTER 5—SPECIAL OCCUPANCIES 251

Article 501—Class I Hazardous (Classified) Locations 253
Part I. General 253
501.1   Scope 253
501.30   Grounding and Bonding 253

Article 502—Class II Hazardous (Classified) Locations 255
502.1   Scope 255
502.30   Grounding and Bonding 255

Article 503—Class III Hazardous (Classified) Locations 257
503.1   Scope 257
503.30   Grounding and Bonding 257

Article 517—Health Care Facilities 259
517.1   Scope 259
517.2   Definitions 259
517.12   Wiring Methods 260
517.13   Equipment Grounding Conductor for Receptacles and Fixed Electrical Equipment in Patient Care Spaces 260
517.16   Isolated Ground Receptacles 262

Article 525—Carnivals, Circuses, Fairs, and Similar Events ... 265
525.1   Scope 265
525.31   Equipment Grounding 265
525.32   Portable Equipment Grounding Conductor Continuity ... 265

Article 547—Agricultural Buildings 267
547.1   Scope 267
547.2   Definitions 267
547.5   Wiring Methods 268
547.10   Equipotential Planes 269

Article 555—Marinas, Boatyards, and Docking Facilities ... 271
555.1   Scope 271
555.13   Bonding of Non-Current-Carrying Metal Parts 271
555.37   Equipment Grounding Conductor 271

Chapter 5—Practice Questions 273

CHAPTER 6—SPECIAL EQUIPMENT 277

Article 600—Electric Signs and Outline Lighting 279
600.1   Scope 279
600.7   Grounding and Bonding 280

Article 645—Information Technology Equipment 283
645.1   Scope 283
645.15   Equipment Grounding and Bonding 283

Article 680—Swimming Pools, Spas, Hot Tubs, Fountains, and Similar Installations 285
Part I. General Requirements for Pools, Spas, Hot Tubs, and Fountains 285
680.1   Scope 285
680.2   Definitions 285
680.6   Bonding and Equipment Grounding 289
680.7   Bonding and Equipment Grounding Terminals 289
Part II. Permanently Installed Pools 289
680.21   Pool Motors 289
680.23   Underwater Pool Luminaires 290
680.24   Junction Box, Transformer, or GFCI Enclosure 291
680.25   Feeders 291
680.26   Equipotential Bonding 292
Part IV. Spas, Hot Tubs, and Permanently Installed Immersion Pools 295
680.40   General 295
680.42   Outdoor Installations 296
680.43   Indoor Installations 296
Part V. Fountains 296
680.50   General 296
680.54   Connection to an Equipment Grounding Conductor ... 297
680.55   Methods of Equipment Grounding 297
Part VII. Hydromassage Bathtubs 297
680.70   General 297
680.74   Equipotential Bonding 297
Part VIII. Electrically Powered Pool Lifts 298
680.80   General 298
680.83   Bonding 298

Article 690—Solar Photovoltaic (PV) Systems 299
Part I. General 299
690.1 Scope 299
690.2 Definitions 300
Part IV. Wiring Methods and Materials 300
690.31 Wiring Methods 300
Part V. Grounding and Bonding 301
690.43 Equipment Grounding and Bonding 301
690.45 Size of Equipment Grounding Conductors 303
690.47 Grounding Electrode System 303

Chapter 6—Practice Questions 305

CHAPTER 8—COMMUNICATIONS SYSTEMS 309

Article 800—General Requirements for Communications Systems 311
Part I. General 311
800.1 Scope 311
800.100 Cable and Primary Protector Bonding and Grounding 311
800.180 Grounding Devices 314

Article 810—Radio and Television Satellite Equipment 315
810.1 Scope 315
810.4 Community Television Antenna 315
810.6 Antenna Lead-In Protectors 316
810.7 Grounding Devices 316
810.15 Metal Antenna Supports—Grounding 316
810.20 Antenna Discharge Unit 316
810.21 Bonding Conductor and Grounding Electrode Conductors 317
Part III. Amateur and Citizen Band Transmitting and Receiving Stations—Antenna Systems 319
810.57 Antenna Discharge Units—Transmitting Stations 319
810.58 Bonding Conductors and Grounding Electrode Conductors—Amateur and Citizen Band Transmitting and Receiving Stations 319

Article 820—Community Antenna Television (CATV) and Radio Distribution Systems (Coaxial Cable) 321
Part I. General 321
820.1 Scope 321
Part III. Protection 321
820.93 Grounding of the Outer Conductive Shield of Coaxial Cables 321
Part IV. Grounding Methods 322
820.100 Bonding and Grounding Methods 322

Chapter 8—Practice Questions 323

Final Exam A—Section II Straight Order 325

Final Exam B—Section II Random Order 335

INDEX 345

About the Author 349

About the Illustrator 350

About the Mike Holt Team 351

ABOUT THIS TEXTBOOK

Mike Holt's Illustrated Guide to Understanding NEC® Requirements for Bonding and Grounding, based on the 2020 NEC®

This textbook covers Article 250 Grounding and Bonding, as well as the *Code* rules contained in the *National Electrical Code*® that relate to bonding and grounding. Grounding and Bonding is the most important and possibly least understood article in the *NEC*®. Surveys have repeatedly shown that a high percentage of electrical shocks and power quality problems are due to poor bonding or grounding (not to mention the hazards) created from the misapplication of the *NEC* rules.

The text clears up misconceptions about bonding versus grounding and breaks down each of the *Code* articles that deal with this topic. Mike's ability to explain these rules and their practical application in real-world settings will help you to fully understand the "why" behind these rules, helping to ensure you know how to apply the *NEC* every day.

Mike's writing style is informative, practical, easy to understand, and applicable for today's electrical professional. Just like all of Mike Holt's textbooks, this one is built around hundreds of full-color illustrations and photographs that show the requirements of the *National Electrical Code* in practical use. The graphics show current flow in both normal and fault conditions, illustrating what is happening, helping you visualize *Code* rules as they're applied to electrical installations.

This textbook also contains cautions regarding possible conflicts or confusing *NEC* requirements, tips on proper electrical installations, and warnings of dangers related to improper electrical installations. Sometimes a requirement seems confusing and it might be hard to understand its actual application. When this occurs, we will point out the situation in an upfront and straightforward manner to provide context. We apologize in advance if that ever seems disrespectful, but our intention is to help the industry understand the current *NEC* as best as possible, point out areas that need refinement, and encourage *Code* users to be a part of the change process that creates a better *NEC* for the future.

Keeping up with requirements of the *Code* should be the goal of everyone involved in electrical safety—whether you're an installer, contractor, inspector, engineer, or instructor. This textbook is the perfect tool to help you do that.

The Scope of This Textbook

1. Bonding vs. Grounding. What's the difference between grounding and bonding? Is there a difference? Many in our industry are confused when trying to disseminate the distinct differences between these terms. This textbook will define those differences and help you to finally understand just what each is and its essential function in electrical systems.

2. Based on the 2020 *NEC*. This textbook covers the bonding and grounding requirements contained throughout the *NEC* that are a key component to ensuring the safest possible electrical installations.

3. Conductor Material. Conductors are considered copper, unless aluminum or copper-clad aluminum is identified or specified.

4. "Article 680." You may notice a particular emphasis on Article 680 and you'd have to agree that when it comes to grounding and equipotential bonding, that emphasis is well justified.

5. "Grounded." The term "grounded" has been replaced with the more appropriate, "connected to an equipment grounding conductor" in the *NEC* which is reflected throughout this textbook.

How to Use This Textbook

This textbook is to be used along with the *NEC* and not as a replacement for it. Be sure to have a copy of the 2020 *National Electrical Code* handy. You'll notice that we've paraphrased a great deal of the *NEC* wording, and some of the article and section titles appear different from the text in the actual *Code* book. We believe doing so makes it easier to understand the content of the rule, so keep this in mind when comparing this textbook to the actual *NEC*.

Always compare what's being explained in this textbook to what the *Code* book says. Get with others who are knowledgeable about the *NEC* to discuss any topics that you find difficult to understand.

This textbook follows the *Code* format, but it doesn't cover every requirement. For example, it doesn't include every article, section, subsection, exception, or Informational Note. So, don't be concerned if you see that the textbook contains Exception 1 and Exception 3, but not Exception 2.

Cross-References. *NEC* cross-references to other related *Code* requirements are included to help you develop a better understanding of how the *NEC* rules relate to one another. These cross-references are indicated by *Code* section numbers in brackets, an example of which is "[90.4]."

Informational Notes. Informational Notes contained in the *NEC* will be identified in this textbook as "Note."

Exceptions. Exceptions contained in this textbook will be identified as "Ex" and not spelled out.

As you read through this textbook, allow yourself sufficient time to review the text along with the outstanding graphics and examples, to give yourself the opportunity for a deeper understanding of the *Code* as it relates to bonding and grounding.

Technical Questions

As you progress through this textbook, you might find that you don't understand every explanation, example, calculation, or comment. Don't become frustrated, and don't get down on yourself. Remember, this is the *National Electrical Code*, and sometimes the best attempt to explain a concept isn't enough to make it perfectly clear. If you're still confused, visit www.MikeHolt.com/forum, and post your question on our free *Code* Forum. The forum is a moderated community of electrical professionals.

Textbook Corrections

We're committed to providing you with the finest product with the fewest errors and take great care to ensure our textbooks are correct. But we're realistic and know that errors might be found after printing. The last thing we want is for you to have problems finding, communicating, or accessing this information, so any adjustments to the text are listed on our website.

To check for known errors, visit www.MikeHolt.com/corrections.

If you believe that there's an error of any kind (typographical, grammatical, technical, etc.) in this textbook or in the Answer Key, and it's not listed on the website, send an e-mail that includes the textbook title, page number, and any other pertinent information to corrections@MikeHolt.com.

Key Features

The layout and design of this textbook incorporate special features and symbols designed to help you navigate easily through the material, and to enhance your understanding.

 A **QR Code** under the section number can be scanned with a smartphone app to take you to a sample video clip to see Mike and the video panel discuss this rule. For a complete list of all the videos that accompany this product call 888.632.2633.

Caution, Warning, and Danger Icons

These icons highlight areas of concern.

 Caution: An explanation of possible damage to property or equipment.

 Warning: An explanation of possible severe property damage or personal injury.

 Danger: An explanation of possible severe injury or death.

Formulas

$$P = I \times E$$

Formulas are easily identifiable in green text on a gray bar.

Modular Color-Coded Page Layout

Chapters are color-coded and modular to make it easy to navigate through each section of the textbook.

Key Features | About This Textbook

Author's Comments. These comments provide additional information to help you understand the context.

Code Change text. Underlined text denotes changes to the *Code* for the 2020 *NEC*.

Examples. These practical application questions and answers are contained in framed yellow boxes.

If you see an ellipsis (• • •) at the bottom of the example, it is continued on the following page.

Additional Background Information Boxes. Where the author believes that information unrelated to the specific rule will help you understand the concept being taught, he includes these topics, easily identified in boxes that are shaded gray.

Code Rule Headers. The Code rule being taught is identified with a chapter color bar and white text.

ADDITIONAL PRODUCTS TO HELP YOU LEARN

Bonding and Grounding Videos, based on the 2020 NEC

One of the best ways to get the most out of this textbook is to use it in conjunction with the corresponding videos. Mike Holt's videos provide a 360° view of each topic with specialized commentary from Mike Holt and his panel of industry experts. Whether you're a visual or an auditory learner, watching the videos will enhance your knowledge and understanding.

To order a copy of the videos that accompany this textbook at a discounted price, call our office at 888.632.2633.

Changes to the National Electrical Code Training Program

Don't let the scale of the changes to the Code intimidate you. This package will get you up to speed on the most essential 2020 NEC changes. The book is well-organized, easy to follow, and the full-color illustrations and photos bring the material to life. The videos bring together a group of experts from the field to discuss the changes and how they apply in the real world.

- Changes to the NEC 2020 textbook
- Changes to the NEC 2020 DVDs (4)

To order a Code product visit www.MikeHolt.com/products or call 888.632.2633.

Understanding the NEC Complete Training Library

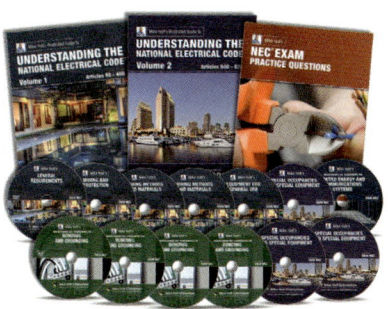

When you really need to understand the NEC, there's no better way to learn it than with Mike's NEC Complete Training Library. It takes you step-by-step through the NEC, in Code order with detailed illustrations, great practice questions, and in-depth analysis on the videos. This library is perfect for engineers, electricians, contractors, and electrical inspectors.

- *Understanding the National Electrical Code—Volume 1* textbook
- *Understanding the National Electrical Code—Volume 2* textbook
- *NEC Exam Practice Questions* workbook
- *General Requirements* DVD
- *Wiring Methods and Materials* DVDs (2)
- *Bonding and Grounding* DVDs (4)
- *Wiring and Protection* DVD
- *Equipment for General Use* DVD
- *Special Occupancies and Special Equipment* DVDs (3)
- *Limited Energy and Communications Systems* DVD

2020 Code Book and Tabs

The ideal way to use your Code book is to tab it for quick reference—Mike's best-selling tabs make organizing the NEC easy. If you're using your Code book for an exam, you'll need to confirm with your testing authority that a tabbed Code book is allowed into the exam room.

Notes

HOW TO USE THE *NATIONAL ELECTRICAL CODE*

The original *NEC* document was developed in 1897 as a result of the united efforts of various insurance, electrical, architectural, and other cooperative interests. The National Fire Protection Association (NFPA) has sponsored the *National Electrical Code* since 1911.

The purpose of the *Code* is the practical safeguarding of persons and property from hazards arising from the use of electricity. It isn't intended as a design specification or an instruction manual for untrained persons. It is, in fact, a standard that contains the minimum requirements for an electrical installation that's essentially free from hazard. Learning to understand and use the *Code* is critical to you working safely; whether you're training to become an electrician, or are already an electrician, electrical contractor, inspector, engineer, designer, or instructor.

The *NEC* was written for qualified persons; those who understand electrical terms, theory, safety procedures, and electrical trade practices. Learning to use the *Code* is a lengthy process and can be frustrating if you don't approach it the right way. First, you'll need to understand electrical theory and if you don't have theory as a background when you get into the *NEC*, you're going to struggle. Take one step back if necessary and learn electrical theory. You must also understand the concepts and terms in the *Code* and know grammar and punctuation in order to understand the complex structure of the rules and their intended purpose(s). The *NEC* is written in a formal outline which many of us haven't seen or used since high school or college so it's important for you to pay particular attention to this format. Our goal for the next few pages is to give you some guidelines and suggestions on using your *Code* book to help you understand that standard, and assist you in what you're trying to accomplish and, ultimately, your personal success as an electrical professional!

Language Considerations for the *NEC*

Terms and Concepts

The *NEC* contains many technical terms, and it's crucial for *Code* users to understand their meanings and applications. If you don't understand a term used in a rule, it will be impossible to properly apply the *NEC* requirement. Article 100 defines those that are used generally in two or more articles throughout the *Code*; for example, the term "Dwelling Unit" is found in many articles. If you don't know the *NEC* definition for a "dwelling unit" you can't properly identify its *Code* requirements. Another example worth mentioning is the term "Outlet." For many people it has always meant a receptacle—not so in the *NEC*!

Many *Code* articles use terms unique to that specific article, and the definitions of those terms only apply to that given article. Definitions for them are usually found in the beginning of the article. For example, Section 250.2 contains the definitions of terms that only apply to Article 250—Grounding and Bonding. Whether definitions are unique to a specific article, or apply throughout the *NEC*, is indicated at the beginning of the definitions (xxx.2) section of the article. For example,

Article 690 contains definitions (in 690.2) that apply ONLY to that article while Article 705 introduces definitions (in 705.2) that apply throughout the entire *Code*.

Small Words, Grammar, and Punctuation

Technical words aren't the only ones that require close attention. Even simple words can make a big difference to the application of a rule. Is there a comma? Does it use "or," "and," "other than," "greater than," or "smaller than"? The word "or" can imply alternate choices for wiring methods. A word like "or" gives us choices while the word "and" can mean an additional requirement must be met.

An example of the important role small words play in the *NEC* is found in 110.26(C)(2), where it says equipment containing overcurrent, switching, "or" control devices that are 1,200A or more "and" over 6 ft wide require a means of egress at each end of the working space. In this section, the word "or" clarifies that equipment containing any of the three types of devices listed must follow this rule. The word "and" clarifies that 110.26(C)(2) only applies if the equipment is both 1,200A or more and over 6 ft wide.

Grammar and punctuation play an important role in establishing the meaning of a rule. The location of a comma can dramatically change the requirement of a rule such as in 250.28(A), where it says a main bonding jumper shall be a wire, bus, screw, or similar suitable conductor. If the comma between "bus" and "screw" was removed, only a "bus screw" could be used. That comma makes a big change in the requirements of the rule.

Slang Terms or Technical Jargon

Trade-related professionals in different areas of the country often use local "slang" terms that aren't shared by all. This can make it difficult to communicate if it isn't clear what the meaning of those slang terms are. Use the proper terms by finding out what their definitions and applications are before you use them. For example, the term "pigtail" is often used to describe the short piece of conductor used to connect a device to a splice, but a "pigtail" is also used for a rubberized light socket with pre-terminated conductors. Although the term is the same, the meaning is very different and could cause confusion. The words "splice" and "tap" are examples of terms often interchanged in the field but are two entirely different things! The uniformity and consistency of the terminology used in the *Code*, makes it so everyone says and means the same thing regardless of geographical location.

NEC Style and Layout

It's important to understand the structure and writing style of the *Code* if you want to use it effectively. The *National Electrical Code* is organized using twelve major components.

1. Table of Contents
2. Chapters—Chapters 1 through 9 (major categories)
3. Articles—Chapter subdivisions that cover specific subjects
4. Parts—Divisions used to organize article subject matter
5. Sections—Divisions used to further organize article subject matter
6. Tables and Figures—Represent the mandatory requirements of a rule
7. Exceptions—Alternatives to the main *Code* rule
8. Informational Notes—Explanatory material for a specific rule (not a requirement)
9. Tables—Applicable as referenced in the *NEC*
10. Annexes—Additional explanatory information such as tables and references (not a requirement)
11. Index
12. Changes to the *Code* from the previous edition

1. Table of Contents. The Table of Contents displays the layout of the chapters, articles, and parts as well as the page numbers. It's an excellent resource and should be referred to periodically to observe the interrelationship of the various *NEC* components. When attempting to locate the rules for a specific situation, knowledgeable *Code* users often go first to the Table of Contents to quickly find the specific *NEC* rule that applies.

2. Chapters. There are nine chapters, each of which is divided into articles. The articles fall into one of four groupings: General Requirements (Chapters 1 through 4), Specific Requirements (Chapters 5 through 7), Communications Systems (Chapter 8), and Tables (Chapter 9).

> Chapter 1—General
> Chapter 2—Wiring and Protection
> Chapter 3—Wiring Methods and Materials
> Chapter 4—Equipment for General Use
> Chapter 5—Special Occupancies
> Chapter 6—Special Equipment
> Chapter 7—Special Conditions
> Chapter 8—Communications Systems (Telephone, Data, Satellite, Cable TV, and Broadband)
> Chapter 9—Tables–Conductor and Raceway Specifications

3. Articles. The *NEC* contains approximately 140 articles, each of which covers a specific subject. It begins with Article 90, the introduction to the *Code* which contains the purpose of the *NEC*, what is covered and isn't covered, along with how the *Code* is arranged. It also gives information on enforcement, how mandatory and permissive rules are written, and how explanatory material is included. Article 90 also includes information on formal interpretations, examination of equipment for safety, wiring planning, and information about formatting units of measurement. Here are some other examples of articles you'll find in the *NEC*:

> Article 110—Requirements for Electrical Installations
> Article 250—Grounding and Bonding
> Article 300—General Requirements for Wiring Methods and Materials
> Article 430—Motors, Motor Circuits, and Motor Controllers
> Article 500—Hazardous (Classified) Locations
> Article 680—Swimming Pools, Fountains, and Similar Installations
> Article 725—Remote-Control, Signaling, and Power-Limited Circuits
> Article 800—General Requirements for Communications Systems

4. Parts. Larger articles are subdivided into parts. Because the parts of a *Code* article aren't included in the section numbers, we tend to forget to what "part" an *NEC* rule is relating. For example, Table 110.34(A) contains working space clearances for electrical equipment. If we aren't careful, we might think this table applies to all electrical installations, but Table 110.34(A) is in Part III, which only contains requirements for "Over 1,000 Volts, Nominal" installations. The rules for working clearances for electrical equipment for systems 1,000V, nominal, or less are contained in Table 110.26(A)(1), which is in Part II—1,000 Volts, Nominal, or Less.

5. Sections. Each *NEC* rule is called a "*Code* Section." A *Code* section may be broken down into subdivisions; first level subdivision will be in parentheses like (A), (B),..., the next will be second level subdivisions in parentheses like (1), (2),..., and third level subdivisions in lowercase letters such as (a), (b), and so on.

For example, the rule requiring all receptacles in a dwelling unit bathroom to be GFCI protected is contained in Section 210.8(A)(1) which is in Chapter 2, Article 210, Section 8, first level subdivision (A), and second level subdivision (1).

Note: According to the *NEC Style Manual*, first and second level subdivisions are required to have titles. A title for a third level subdivision is permitted but not required.

Many in the industry incorrectly use the term "Article" when referring to a *Code* section. For example, they say "Article 210.8," when they should say "Section 210.8." Section numbers in this textbook are shown without the word "Section," unless they're at the beginning of a sentence. For example, Section 210.8(A) is shown as simply 210.8(A).

6. Tables and Figures. Many *NEC* requirements are contained within tables, which are lists of *Code* rules placed in a systematic arrangement. The titles of the tables are extremely important; you must read them carefully in order to understand the contents, applications, and limitations of each one. Notes are often provided in or below a table; be sure to read them as well since they're also part of the requirement. For example, Note 1 for Table 300.5 explains how to measure the cover when burying cables and raceways and Note 5 explains what to do if solid rock is encountered.

7. Exceptions. Exceptions are *NEC* requirements or permissions that provide an alternative method to a specific rule. There are two types of exceptions—mandatory and permissive. When a rule has several exceptions, those exceptions with mandatory requirements are listed before the permissive exceptions.

Mandatory Exceptions. A mandatory exception uses the words "shall" or "shall not." The word "shall" in an exception means that if you're using the exception, you're required to do it in a specific way. The phrase "shall not" means it isn't permitted.

Permissive Exceptions. A permissive exception uses words such as "shall be permitted," which means it's acceptable (but not mandatory) to do it in this way.

8. Informational Notes. An Informational Note contains explanatory material intended to clarify a rule or give assistance, but it isn't a *Code* requirement.

9. Tables. Chapter 9 consists of tables applicable as referenced in the *NEC*. They're used to calculate raceway sizing, conductor fill, the radius of raceway bends, and conductor voltage drop.

10. Informative Annexes. Annexes aren't a part of the *Code* requirements and are included for informational purposes only.

> Annex A. Product Safety Standards
> Annex B. Application Information for Ampacity Calculation
> Annex C. Raceway Fill Tables for Conductors and Fixture Wires of the Same Size
> Annex D. Examples
> Annex E. Types of Construction
> Annex F. Critical Operations Power Systems (COPS)
> Annex G. Supervisory Control and Data Acquisition (SCADA)
> Annex H. Administration and Enforcement
> Annex I. Recommended Tightening Torques
> Annex J. ADA Standards for Accessible Design

11. Index. The Index at the back of the *NEC* is helpful in locating a specific rule using pertinent keywords to assist in your search.

12. Changes to the *Code*. Changes in the *NEC* are indicated as follows:

- Rules that were changed since the previous edition are identified by shading the revised text.
- New rules aren't shaded like a change, instead they have a shaded "N" in the margin to the left of the section number.
- Relocated rules are treated like new rules with a shaded "N" in the left margin by the section number.
- Deleted rules are indicated by a bullet symbol "•" located in the left margin where the rule was in the previous edition. Unlike older editions the bullet symbol is only used where one or more complete paragraphs have been deleted. There's no indication used where a word, group of words, or a sentence was deleted.
- A Δ represents text deletions and figure/table revisions.

How to Locate a Specific Requirement

How to go about finding what you're looking for in the *Code* book depends, to some degree, on your experience with the *NEC*. Experts typically know the requirements so well that they just go to the correct rule. Very experienced people might only need the Table of Contents to locate the requirement for which they're looking. On the other hand, average users should use all the tools at their disposal, including the Table of Contents, the Index, and the search feature on electronic versions of the *Code* book.

Let's work through a simple example: What *NEC* rule specifies the maximum number of disconnects permitted for a service?

Using the Table of Contents. If you're an experienced *Code* user, you might use the Table of Contents. You'll know Article 230 applies to "Services," and because this article is so large, it's divided up into multiple parts (eight parts to be exact). With this knowledge, you can quickly go to the Table of Contents and see it lists the Service Equipment Disconnecting Means requirements in Part VI.

> **Author's Comment:**
>
> ▸ The number "70" precedes all page numbers in this standard because the *NEC* is NFPA Standard Number 70.

Using the Index. If you use the Index (which lists subjects in alphabetical order) to look up the term "service disconnect," you'll see there's no listing. If you try "disconnecting means," then "services," you'll find that the Index indicates the rule is in Article 230, Part VI. Because the *NEC* doesn't give a page number in the Index, you'll need to use the Table of Contents to find it, or flip through the *Code* book to Article 230, then continue to flip through pages until you find Part VI.

Many people complain that the *NEC* only confuses them by taking them in circles. Once you gain experience in using the *Code* and deepen your understanding of words, terms, principles, and practices, you'll find it much easier to understand and use than you originally thought.

With enough exposure in the use of the *NEC*, you'll discover that some words and terms are often specific to certain articles. The word "solar" for example will immediately send experienced *Code* book users to Article 690—Solar Photovoltaic (PV) Systems. The word "marina" suggests what you seek might be in Article 555. There are times when a main article will send you to a specific requirement in another one in which compliance is required in which case it will say (for example), "in accordance with 230.xx." Don't think of these situations as a "circle," but rather a map directing you to exactly where you need to be.

Customizing Your *Code* Book

One way to increase your comfort level with your *Code* book is to customize it to meet your needs. You can do this by highlighting and underlining important *NEC* requirements. Preprinted adhesive tabs are also an excellent aid to quickly find important articles and sections that are regularly referenced. However, understand that if you're using your *Code* book to prepare to take an exam, some exam centers don't allow markings of any type. For more information about tabs for your *Code* book, visit www.MikeHolt.com/tabs.

Highlighting. As you read through or find answers to your questions, be sure you highlight those requirements in the *NEC* that are the most important or relevant to you. Use one color, like yellow, for general interest and a different one for important requirements you want to find quickly. Be sure to highlight terms in the Index and the Table of Contents as you use them.

Underlining. Underline or circle key words and phrases in the *Code* with a red or blue pen (not a lead pencil) using a short ruler or other straightedge to keep lines straight and neat. This is a very handy way to make important requirements stand out. A short ruler or other straightedge also comes in handy for locating the correct information in a table.

Interpretations

Industry professionals often enjoy the challenge of discussing, and at times debating, the *Code* requirements. These types of discussions are important to the process of better understanding the *NEC* requirements and applications. However, if you decide you're going to participate in one of these discussions, don't spout out what you think without having the actual *Code* book in your hand. The professional way of discussing a requirement is by referring to a specific section rather than talking in vague generalities. This will help everyone involved clearly understand the point and become better educated. In fact, you may become so well educated about the *NEC* that you might even decide to participate in the change process and help to make it even better!

Become Involved in the *NEC* Process

The actual process of changing the *Code* takes about two years and involves hundreds of individuals trying to make the *NEC* as current and accurate as possible. As you advance in your studies and understanding of the *Code*, you might begin to find it very interesting, enjoy it more, and realize that you can also be a part of the process. Rather than sitting back and allowing others to take the lead, you can participate by making proposals and being a part of its development. For the 2020 cycle, there were 3,730 Public Inputs and 1,930 comments. Hundreds of updates and five new articles were added to keep the NEC up to date with new technologies and pave the way to a safer and more efficient electrical future.

Here's how the process works:

STEP 1—Public Input Stage

Public Input. The revision cycle begins with the acceptance of Public Input (PI) which is the public notice asking for anyone interested to submit input on an existing standard or a committee-approved new draft standard. Following the closing date, the committee conducts a First Draft Meeting to respond to all Public Inputs.

First Draft Meeting. At the First Draft (FD) Meeting, the Technical Committee considers and provides a response to all Public Input. The Technical Committee may use the input to develop First Revisions to the standard. The First Draft documents consist of the initial meeting consensus of the committee by simple majority. However, the final position of the Technical Committee must be established by a ballot which follows.

Committee Ballot on First Draft. The First Draft developed at the First Draft Meeting is balloted. In order to appear in the First Draft, a revision must be approved by at least two-thirds of the Technical Committee.

First Draft Report Posted. First revisions which pass ballot are ultimately compiled and published as the First Draft Report on the document's NFPA web page. This report serves as documentation for the Input Stage and is published for review and comment. The public may review the First Draft Report to determine whether to submit Public Comments on the First Draft.

STEP 2—Public Comment Stage

Public Comment. Once the First Draft Report becomes available, there's a Public Comment period during which anyone can submit a Public Comment on the First Draft. After the Public Comment closing date, the Technical Committee conducts/holds their Second Draft Meeting.

Second Draft Meeting. After the Public Comment closing date, if Public Comments are received or the committee has additional proposed revisions, a Second Draft Meeting is held. At the Second Draft Meeting, the Technical Committee reviews the First Draft and may make additional revisions to the draft Standard. All Public Comments are considered, and the Technical Committee provides an action and response to each Public Comment. These actions result in the Second Draft.

Committee Ballot on Second Draft. The Second Revisions developed at the Second Draft Meeting are balloted. To appear in the Second Draft, a revision must be approved by at least two-thirds of the Technical Committee.

Second Draft Report Posted. Second Revisions which pass ballot are ultimately compiled and published as the Second Draft Report on the document's NFPA website. This report serves as documentation of the Comment Stage and is published for public review.

Once published, the public can review the Second Draft Report to decide whether to submit a Notice of Intent to Make a Motion (NITMAM) for further consideration.

STEP 3—NFPA Technical Meeting (Tech Session)

Following completion of the Public Input and Public Comment stages, there's further opportunity for debate and discussion of issues through the NFPA Technical Meeting that takes place at the NFPA Conference & Expo®. These motions are attempts to change the resulting final Standard from the committee's recommendations published as the Second Draft.

STEP 4—Council Appeals and Issuance of Standard

Issuance of Standards. When the Standards Council convenes to issue an NFPA standard, it also hears any related appeals. Appeals are an important part of assuring that all NFPA rules have been followed and that due process and fairness have continued throughout the standards development process. The Standards Council considers appeals based on the written record and by conducting live hearings during which all interested parties can participate. Appeals are decided on the entire record of the process, as well as all submissions and statements presented.

After deciding all appeals related to a standard, the Standards Council, if appropriate, proceeds to issue the Standard as an official NFPA Standard. The decision of the Standards Council is final subject only to limited review by the NFPA Board of Directors. The new NFPA standard becomes effective twenty days following the Standards Council's action of issuance.

Temporary Interim Amendment—(TIA)

Sometimes, a change to the *NEC* is of an emergency nature. Perhaps an editing mistake was made that can affect an electrical installation to the extent it may create a hazard. Maybe an occurrence in the field created a condition that needs to be addressed immediately and can't wait for the normal *Code* cycle and next edition of the standard. When these circumstances warrant it, a TIA or "Temporary Interim Amendment" can be submitted for consideration.

The NFPA defines a TIA as, "tentative because it has not been processed through the entire standards-making procedures. It is interim because it is effective only between editions of the standard. A TIA automatically becomes a Public Input of the proponent for the next edition of the standard; as such, it then is subject to all of the procedures of the standards-making process."

Author's Comment:

▶ Proposals, comments, and TIAs can be submitted for consideration online at the NFPA website, www.nfpa.org. From the homepage, look for "Codes & Standards," then find "Standards Development," and click on "How the Process Works." If you'd like to see something changed in the *Code*, you're encouraged to participate in the process.

SECTION 1

ELECTRICAL FUNDAMENTALS

Introduction to Section 1—Electrical Fundamentals

In order to understand the bonding and grounding of electrical systems, you need to understand electrical fundamentals—the how and why electricity does what it does. This understanding is crucial to correctly apply the *National Electrical Code*'s rules for bonding and grounding. Knowing that the movement of electrons is what generates current flow helps you better understand the capabilities of electricity and, more importantly, the dangers of such a powerful force.

The fundamentals covered in this section break down and examine the core principles of electricity and should be considered a vital component of being a successful electrical professional.

Notes

UNIT 1

MATTER

Introduction to Unit 1—Matter

Just what is matter, and why is understanding it so important to professionals in the electrical industry? Matter is everything that has weight. You will learn about the atomic structure of matter in this unit, including what electrons and protons are and how they interact with each other.

We will also review electrostatic charge (static electricity) and lightning. As we do, we will focus on what can be done to reduce the hazards of each.

The best electrical professionals understand that everything having to do with electricity begins with matter. They also recognize the importance of understanding what is contained in its atomic structure because this is the "why" and the "how" electricity does what it does. Everything you will encounter in the field is built on these important fundamentals.

1.1 Atomic Theory

Atoms contain three types of subatomic particles: protons, neutrons, and electrons. The central part of the atom is called the "nucleus," and is made up of protons and neutrons. The nucleus of an atom is surrounded by electrons existing in orbits around the nucleus. ▶Figure 1-1

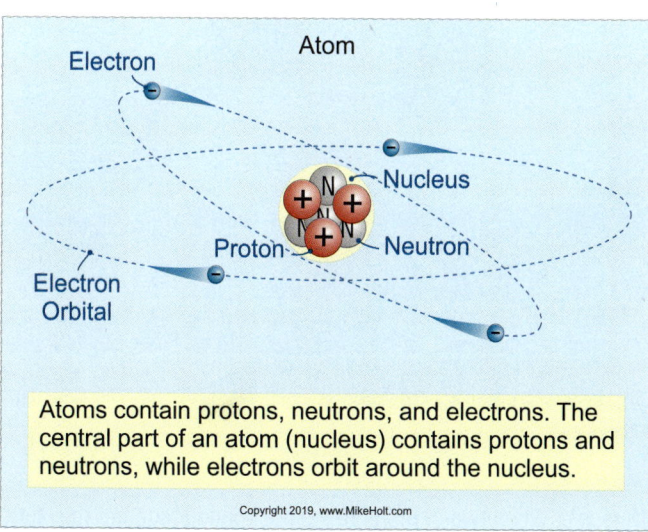

▶Figure 1-1

Protons. Protons have a positive electrostatic charge which exits the protons.

Author's Comment:

▸ Protons and neutrons are the two components in the nucleus of an atom. They are both the same size, have nearly the same mass, and remain stationary in the center of an atom. The number of protons (positive charge) in the nucleus determines the number of electrons (negative charge) in the atom's orbit. ▶Figure 1-2

Neutrons. Neutrons have no electrostatic charge. ▶Figure 1-3

Electrons. Electrons are the smallest particles of an atom and have a negative electrostatic charge which enters the electron from its "line of force" inward from all directions." ▶Figure 1-4

Author's Comment:

▸ The "lines-of-force" for protons and electrons are not actual lines. They simply represent the inward or outward direction of the electrostatic force of the particle.

Atomic Theory | Matter

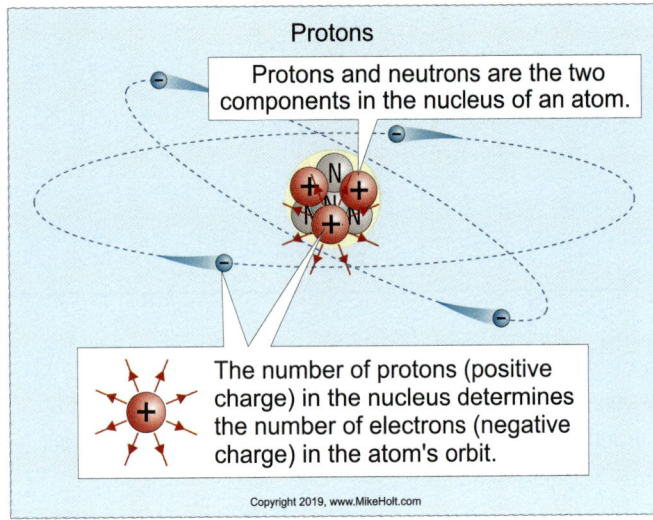
▶Figure 1–2

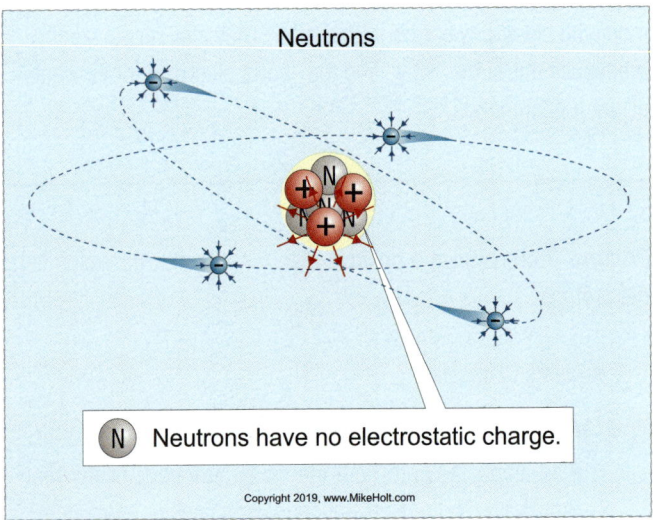
▶Figure 1–3

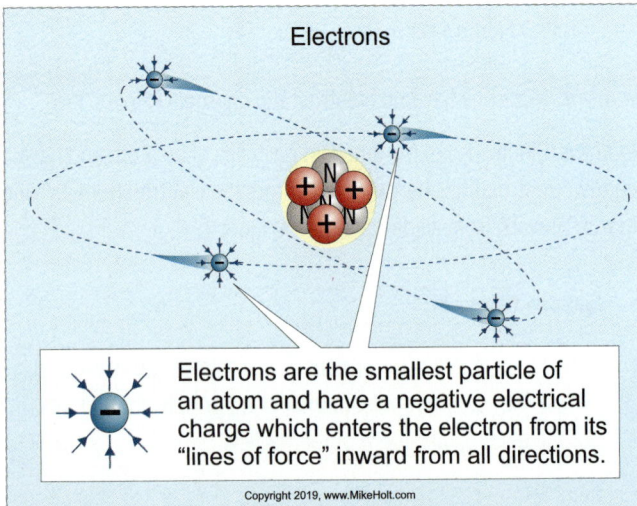
▶Figure 1–4

Electrons are much smaller than either protons or neutrons, and about 1,800 times lighter. Because of their light weight, they can easily be separated from an atom when energy is applied to the electron. As a result, they actively participate in the transfer of energy. ▶Figure 1–5

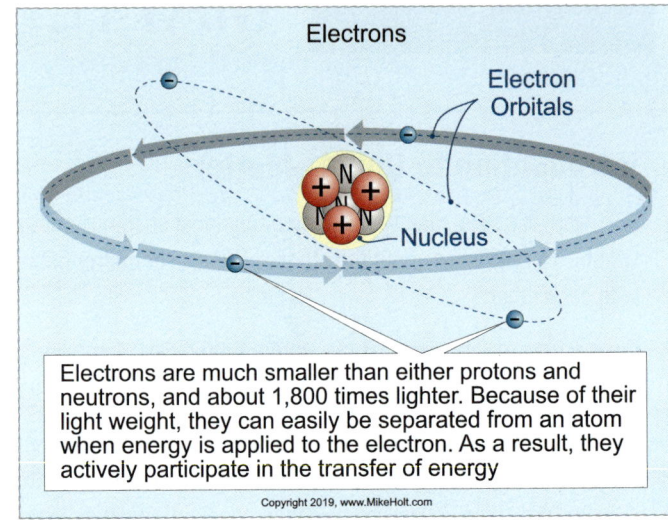
▶Figure 1–5

Element. When matter is made of a single type of atom, it is called an "element." They are listed on the "Periodic Table of Elements" in numeric order by the number of protons each contains. Common elements important in the electrical industry include gold, silver, copper, aluminum, and iron. ▶Figure 1–6

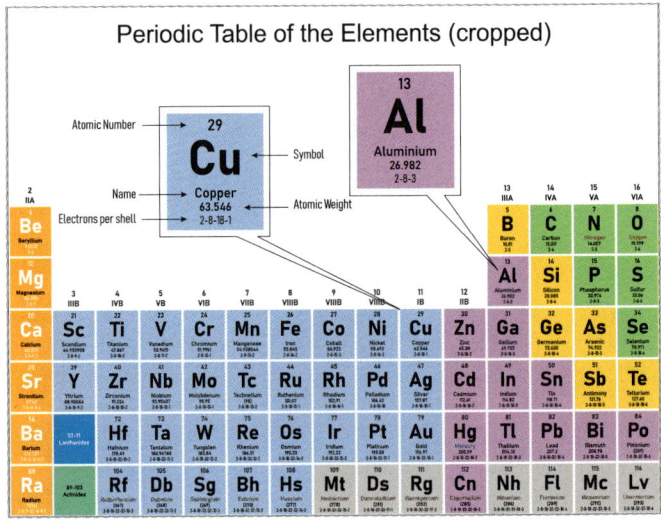
▶Figure 1–6

Molecule. When two or more atoms are bonded together they form a "molecule." The element hydrogen, for example, naturally occurs as the molecule H_2, which consists of two hydrogen atoms bonded together by their shared electrons.

If one atom of the element oxygen shares an electron with two atoms of the element hydrogen, H_2O is formed and creates the compound molecule called "water." ▶Figure 1–7

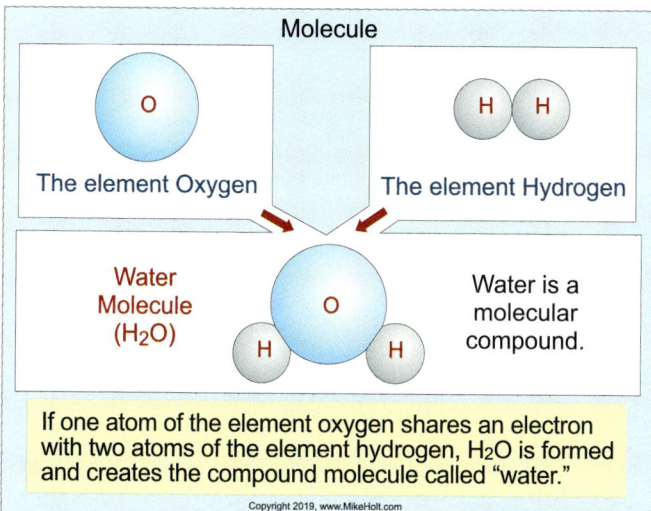
▶Figure 1–7

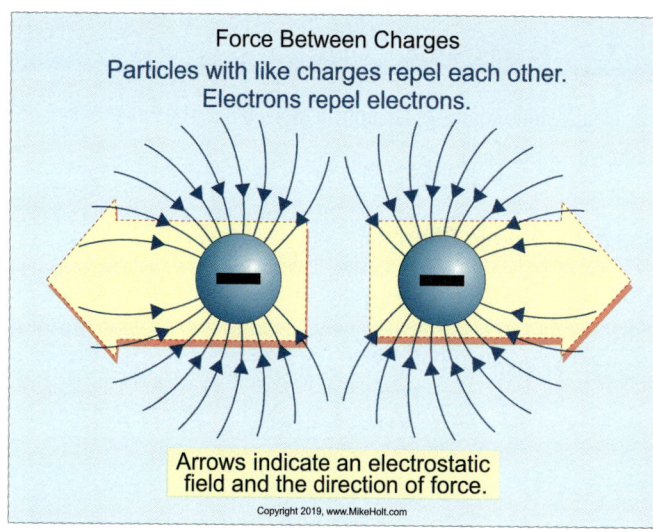
▶Figure 1–8

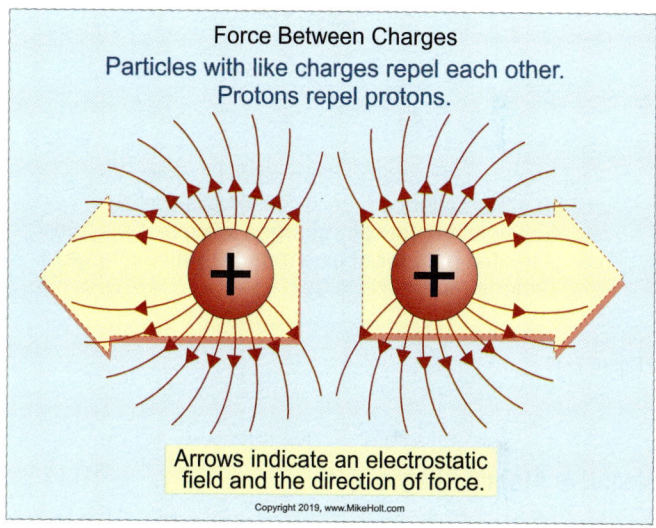
▶Figure 1–9

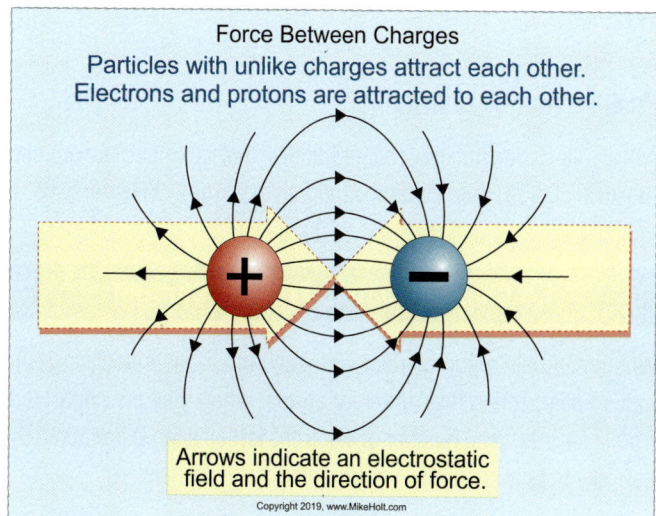
▶Figure 1–10

1.2 Electrostatic Force

In 1785, Charles Coulomb discovered a way to describe the force that exists between negatively and positively charged subatomic particles. His discovery became known as "Coulomb's Law." He explained mathematically that particles with like charges repel each other, and particles with unlike charges attract each other.

For example, electrons (negative electrostatic charge) will repel electrons (negative electrostatic charge), and protons (positive electrostatic charge) will repel protons (positive electrostatic charge). But electrons will attract protons.

This attracting and repelling force between electrons and protons is called the "electrostatic field." ▶Figure 1–8 ▶Figure 1–9, and ▶Figure 1–10

Atomic Charges | Matter

1.3 Atomic Charges

The electrostatic charge of an atom or molecule will be either balanced, negative, or positive.

Balanced Atomic Charge

A balanced electrostatically charged atom or molecule has an equal number of electrons (negative charge) and protons (positive charge). ▶Figure 1–11

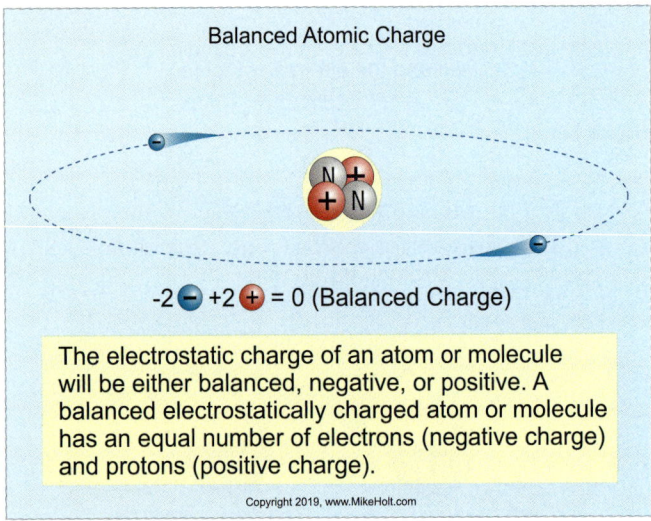
▶Figure 1–11

Negative Atomic Charge

A negatively electrostatically charged atom or molecule will have more electrons (negative charge) than protons (positive charge). ▶Figure 1–12

Positive Atomic Charge

A positively electrostatically charged atom or molecule has more protons (positive charge) than electrons (negative charge). ▶Figure 1–13

1.4 Charged Material (Static Charge)

When materials are in contact with each other, their electrons can move freely among their different atoms. When they are separated from each other, the number of electrons left on each is impacted by how electrically conductive or insulative the materials are.

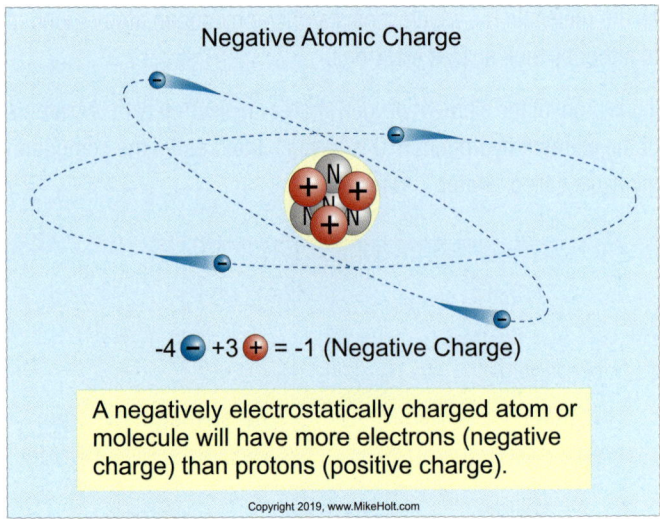
▶Figure 1–12

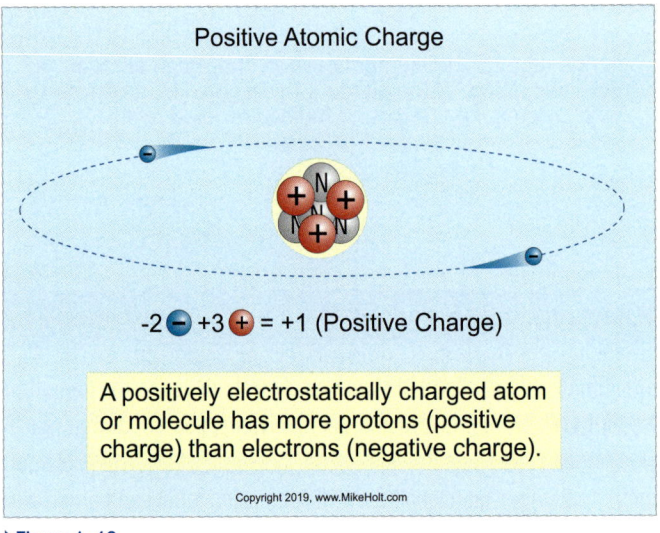
▶Figure 1–13

Electrically Conductive Materials

When conductive materials are in contact with each other, electrons in the atoms of the materials will move among their different atoms. When the conductive materials are quickly separated, the electrons can easily transfer and the materials will have a balanced electrostatic charge.

Insulative Materials

When insulative materials are in contact with each other, electrons in the atoms of the materials will move among their different atoms. However, when they are quickly separated, the electrons cannot easily transfer, thus preventing the materials from having a balanced electrostatic charge. One will be left with more electrons than protons (a negative charge), and the other will have fewer electrons than protons (a positive charge).

The human body can accumulate an electrostatic charge of tens of thousands of volts simply by walking because of contact between shoes and surfaces like carpet, a trampoline, or a floating plastic dock. ▶Figure 1–14

For example, a person walking across a carpet in a low-humidity environment can pick up enough high-voltage electrostatic charge to reach tens of thousands of volts and have a high-voltage electrostatic discharge arc to the positively charged metal doorknob. ▶Figure 1–15

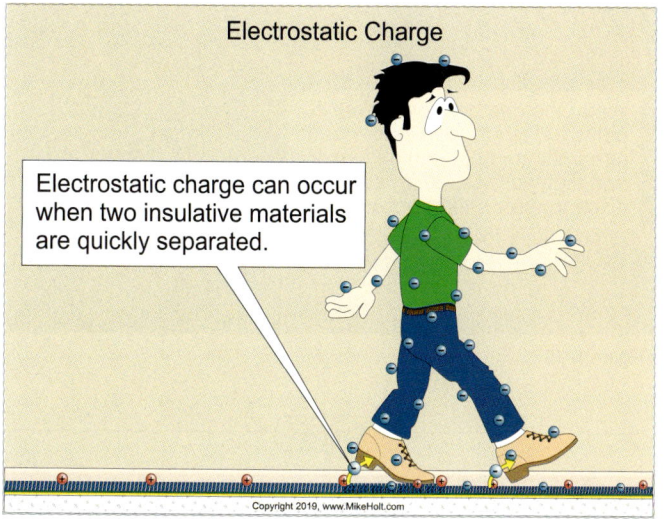

▶Figure 1–14

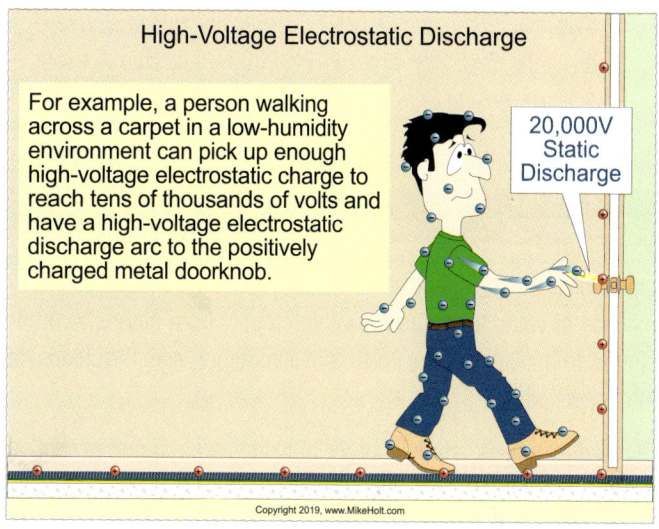

▶Figure 1–15

Static Charge

The electrostatic charge developed on an insulated surface is related to its number of deposited and stored electrons compared to the number in its surroundings. An electrostatic charge can accumulate on an insulating surface under the influence of continuous charge. If leakage of charge from the surface of the insulating surface is not rapid enough, a discharge voltage can be reached, and a high-voltage static discharge can occur.

1.5 High-Voltage Electrostatic Discharge

To reduce electrostatic charge between objects (static electricity), a conductive path must be provided for the electrons and protons to become equalized. Cotton clothing, ion generators, humidifiers, and antistatic furniture, walls, and flooring are all used to assist in creating the conductive path necessary to reduce electrostatic charge between objects.

If a conductive path is not provided, the buildup of a high-voltage electrostatic charge can discharge when an object comes close to a positively charged or uncharged object. It will quickly transfer electrons to the other object, and a high-voltage electrostatic discharge arc is sometimes seen and/or felt. The distance a high-voltage electrostatic discharge arc might travel is a function of the voltage between the two objects; it takes about 20,000V for an arc to move ¼ in.

> **Danger**
>
> A high-voltage electrostatic discharge can:
>
> ▸ Ignite flammable or explosive liquids, gases, dusts, or fibers.
>   ▶Figure 1–16
> ▸ Damage sensitive electronic equipment.
> ▸ Cause the loss of electronically stored data.

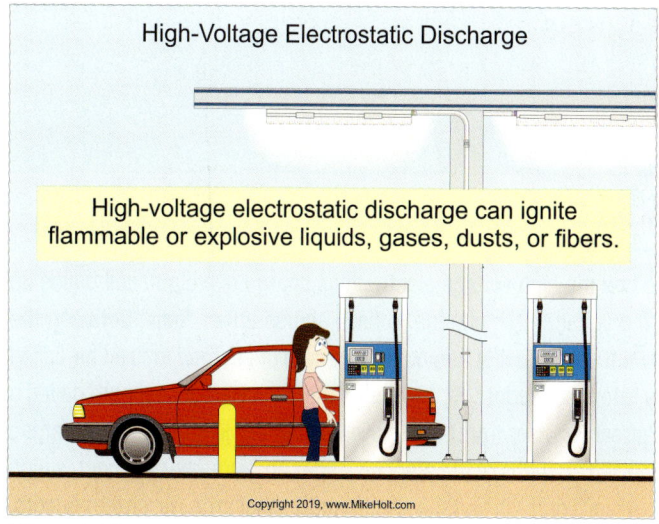

▶Figure 1–16

Lightning | Matter

Author's Comment:

▸ For more information on solving problems associated with static electricity (electrostatic charge), see IEEE 142, *Recommended Practice for Grounding of Industrial and Commercial Power Systems (Green Book)*; NFPA 77, *Recommended Practice on Static Electricity*; and API RP 2003, *Protection Against Ignitions Arising Out of Static Lightning and Stray Currents*.

1.6 Lightning

Lightning is a high-voltage electrostatic discharge consisting of many millions of volts. It can occur within clouds, from clouds to other clouds, from clouds to the Earth, and sometimes even the clouds up into outer space.

High-voltage electrostatic charges in clouds are a result of friction caused by the movement of air within the cloud. These high-voltage, electrostatic, negatively charged cells in the clouds are attracted to positively charged objects in other clouds or on the Earth. ▸Figure 1–17

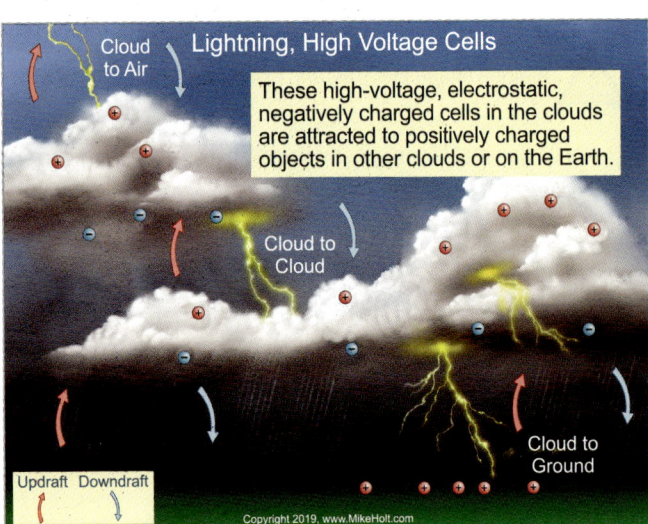

▸Figure 1–17

When the high-voltage electrostatic charge of a cloud cell builds up to a voltage high enough to flash across an air "gap" between the cloud and object, it begins down a path of charged ionized air called a "stepped leader." At the same time, a similar ionized path called a "streamer" rises from the positively charged objects. When the charged ionized air paths of the stepped leader and streamer connect, a high current and high voltage electrostatic discharge (or strike) occurs. This lightning strike temporarily neutralizes the positive and negative electrostatic charges between the objects. ▸Figure 1–18

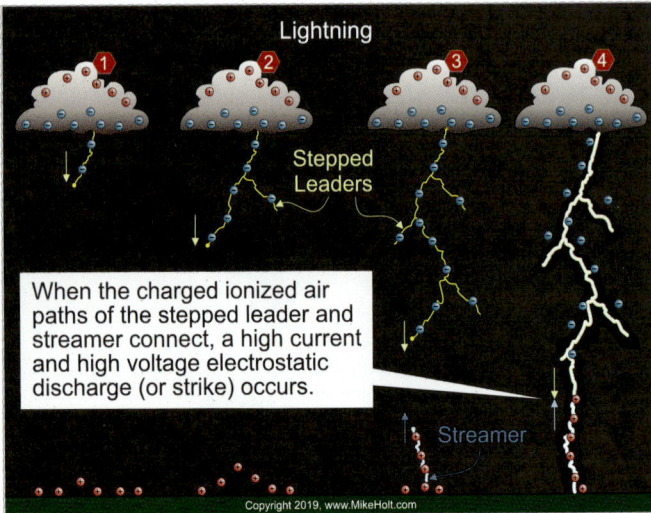

▸Figure 1–18

Caution: Any point of, or on, the Earth can form a streamer when subjected to a strong electrostatic field from a storm cloud. Lightning generally strikes a point of relatively higher elevation, such as a tree, a building, a transmission line, or a human in an open field; however, it can strike an object at a relatively lower elevation instead. Contrary to popular belief, lightning strikes both metallic and nonmetallic objects with the same frequency.

Lightning striking a high resistance point on a building or structure will produce a high temperature at the termination point and can be hot enough to crack concrete or ignite combustible materials on its way down to the Earth. ▸Figure 1–19

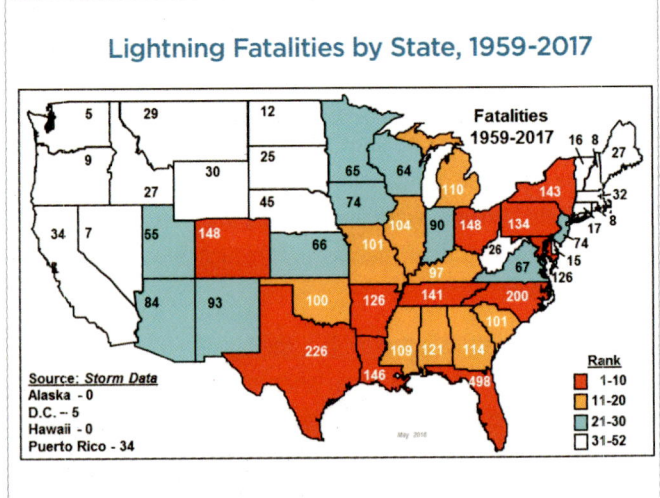

▸Figure 1–19

> **Danger**
>
> Each year, lightning strikes cause many deaths and injuries, and billions of dollars in property damage in the United States. Lightning can have a voltage charge as high as thirty million volts (30,000,000V), and a current discharge of over fifty thousand amperes (50,000A).

1.7 Lightning Protection

To protect property against direct lightning strikes, a lightning protection system must be installed to direct its current flow around nonconductive structures or buildings down into the Earth. Strike termination devices (air terminals or lightning rods) are placed on top of the structure to be protected. They are connected to each other by large wires and attached to ground rods or other electrodes in the Earth. For proper protection, the lightning protection system should be installed in accordance with the requirements contained in NFPA 780, *Installation of Lightning Protection Systems*. ▶Figure 1–20

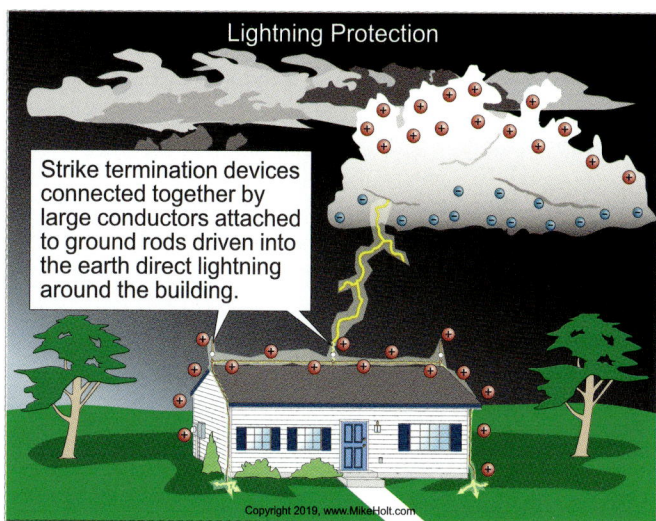
▶Figure 1–20

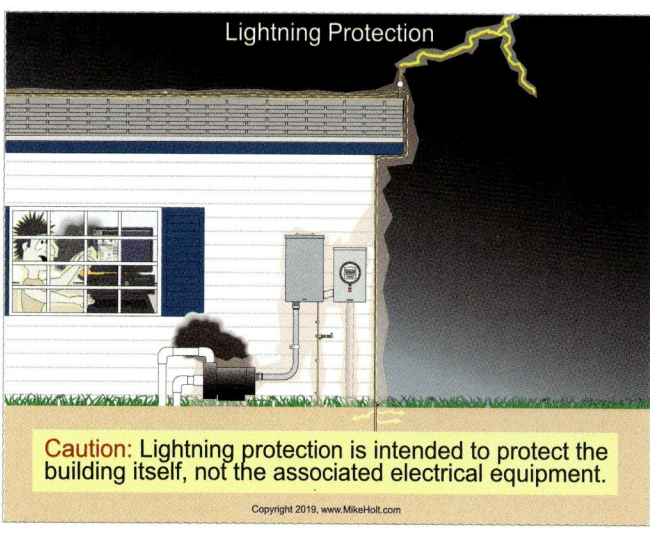
▶Figure 1–21

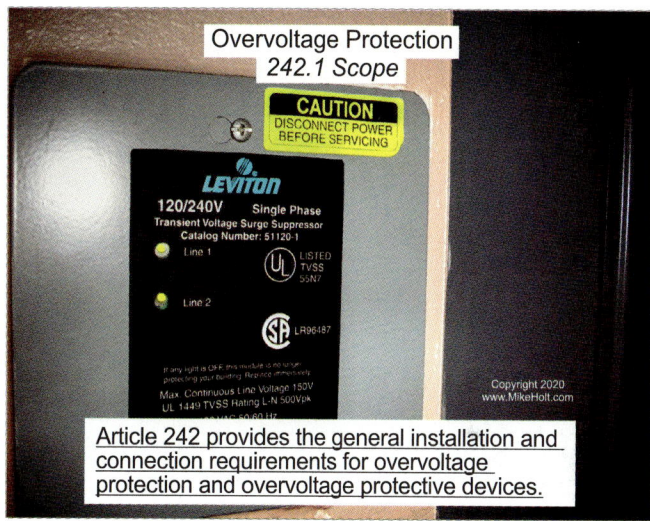
▶Figure 1–22

> **Caution**
>
> The lightning protection system is intended to protect the building or structure, not the associated electrical equipment inside. To reduce damage to electrical equipment from a nearby lightning event, surge protection devices (SPDs) must be installed on the electrical system in accordance with manufacturer's instructions and the *National Electrical Code*. ▶Figure 1–21 and ▶Figure 1–22

Notes

UNIT 1 PRACTICE QUESTIONS

UNIT 1—MATTER

Introduction to Unit 1—Matter

1. Matter is everything that has weight.

    (a) True
    (b) False

1.1 Atomic Theory

2. Atoms contain subatomic particles called _____.

    (a) protons
    (b) neutrons
    (c) electrons
    (d) all of these

3. The central part of an atom is called the "_____."

    (a) core
    (b) nucleus
    (c) center mass
    (d) shell

4. The central part of an atom is made up of _____.

    (a) neutrinos
    (b) electrons
    (c) protons and neutrons
    (d) protons and electrons

5. The nucleus of an atom is surrounded by _____.

    (a) static electricity
    (b) electrons
    (c) antimatter
    (d) shells

6. Electrons exist in orbits around the _____ of an atom.

    (a) core
    (b) nucleus
    (c) center mass
    (d) shell

7. Protons have a _____ electrostatic charge.

    (a) positive
    (b) negative
    (c) neutral
    (d) balanced

8. Neutrons have _____ electrostatic charge.

    (a) a balanced
    (b) a positive
    (c) no
    (d) a variable

9. _____ are the smallest particles of an atom.

    (a) Protons
    (b) Neurons
    (c) Neutrinos
    (d) Electrons

10. Electrons have a _____ electrostatic charge.

    (a) balanced
    (b) positive
    (c) negative
    (d) variable

11. Electrons are _____ protons and neutrons.

    (a) much smaller than
    (b) much larger than
    (c) the same size as
    (d) much heavier than

12. _____ can easily be separated from an atom when energy is applied. As a result, they actively participate in the transfer of energy.

    (a) Protons
    (b) Neurons
    (c) Neutrinos
    (d) Electrons

Unit 1 | Practice Questions

13. When matter is made of a single type of atom, it is called a(n) "_____."

    (a) compound
    (b) mixture
    (c) element
    (d) singular

14. Elements are listed on the "Periodic Table of Elements" in numeric order by the number of _____ each contains.

    (a) Protons
    (b) Neurons
    (c) Neutrinos
    (d) Electrons

15. Common elements important in the electrical industry include gold, silver, copper, aluminum, and iron.

    (a) True
    (b) False

16. When two or more atoms are bonded together, they form a _____.

    (a) molecule
    (b) mixture
    (c) compound
    (d) particle

17. If one atom of the element oxygen shares an electron with two atoms of the element hydrogen, H_2O is formed and creates the compound molecule called "_____."

    (a) salt
    (b) hydrogen peroxide
    (c) water
    (d) hydrochloric acid

1.2 Electrostatic Force

18. "Coulomb's Law" explains that particles with unlike charges _____ each other.

    (a) repel
    (b) neutralize
    (c) balance
    (d) attract

19. The attracting and repelling force between electrons and protons is called the "_____ field."

    (a) electrostatic
    (b) attraction
    (c) repulsion
    (d) electromagnetic

1.3 Atomic Charges

20. The electrostatic charge of an atom or molecule will be _____.

    (a) balanced
    (b) negative
    (c) positive
    (d) any of these

21. A balanced electrostatically charged atom or molecule has an equal number of _____.

    (a) electrons and neutrons
    (b) electrons and protons
    (c) ions
    (d) protons and neutrons

22. A negatively electrostatically charged atom or molecule will have more _____.

    (a) electrons than ions
    (b) protons than neutrons
    (c) electrons than protons
    (d) magnetic force

23. A positively electrostatically charged atom or molecule has more _____.

    (a) electrons than ions
    (b) protons than electrons
    (c) electrons than protons
    (d) magnetic force

1.4 Charged Material (Static Charge)

24. When materials are in contact with each other, their electrons can _____.

    (a) move freely
    (b) attract each other
    (c) repel each other
    (d) bond together

25. When materials are separated from each other, the number of electrons left on each is impacted by how electrically _____ the materials are.

    (a) attracted
    (b) repelled
    (c) conductive or insulative
    (d) similar

26. When conductive materials are in contact with each other, electrons in the atoms of the materials will _____ their different atoms.

    (a) attract
    (b) move among
    (c) repel
    (d) duplicate

27. When the conductive materials are quickly separated, the electrons can easily _____ and the materials will have a balanced electrostatic charge.

    (a) increase
    (b) decrease
    (c) develop
    (d) transfer

28. When insulative materials are quickly separated, the electrons cannot easily transfer, thus preventing the materials from having a(n) _____ electrostatic charge.

    (a) negative
    (b) positive
    (c) balanced
    (d) excessive

29. The human body can accumulate an electrostatic charge of tens of thousands of _____ simply by walking because of contact between shoes and surfaces like carpet, a trampoline, or a floating plastic dock.

    (a) protons
    (b) electrons
    (c) volts
    (d) amperes

30. The electrostatic charge developed on an insulated surface is related to its number of deposited and stored _____ compared to the number in its surroundings.

    (a) protons
    (b) electrons
    (c) volts
    (d) neutrons

31. An electrostatic charge can _____ on an insulating surface under the influence of continuous charge.

    (a) accumulate
    (b) dissipate
    (c) become magnetic
    (d) start a fire

32. If leakage of charge from the surface of the insulating surface is not rapid enough, a discharge voltage can be reached, and a high-voltage static discharge can occur.

    (a) True
    (b) False

1.5 High-Voltage Electrostatic Discharge

33. To reduce electrostatic charge between objects (static electricity), a(n) conductive path must be provided for the electrons and protons to become _____.

    (a) effective
    (b) attractive
    (c) conductive
    (d) equalized

34. _____ and antistatic furniture, walls, and flooring are all used to assist in creating the conductive path necessary to reduce electrostatic charge between objects.

    (a) Humidifiers
    (b) Ion generators
    (c) Cotton clothing
    (d) all of these

35. If a(n) _____ path is not provided, the buildup of a high-voltage electrostatic charge can discharge when an object comes close to a positively charged or uncharged object.

    (a) effective
    (b) conductive
    (c) grounded
    (d) reactive

36. The distance a high-voltage electrostatic discharge arc might travel is a function of the voltage between the two objects; it takes about 20,000V for an arc to move ¼ in.

    (a) True
    (b) False

Unit 1 | Practice Questions

1.6 Lightning

37. Lightning is a high-voltage electrostatic discharge consisting of many millions of volts.

    (a) True
    (b) False

38. Lightning can occur within clouds, from clouds to other clouds, from clouds to the Earth, and sometimes even the clouds up into outer space.

    (a) True
    (b) False

39. High-voltage electrostatic charges in clouds are a result of _____ caused by the movement of air within the cloud.

    (a) thunder
    (b) up drafts
    (c) friction
    (d) photons

40. High-voltage, electrostatic, positively charged cells in the clouds are attracted to positively charged objects in other clouds or on the Earth.

    (a) True
    (b) False

41. When the high-voltage electrostatic charge of a cloud cell builds up to a _____ high enough to flash across an air "gap" between the cloud and object, it begins down a path of charged ionized air called a "stepped leader."

    (a) ampacity
    (b) capacity
    (c) resistance
    (d) voltage

42. A lightning strike temporarily _____ positive and negative electrostatic charges.

    (a) amplifies
    (b) intensifies
    (c) neutralizes
    (d) magnetizes

43. Lightning striking a high resistance point on a building or structure will produce a high temperature at the termination point, hot enough to crack concrete.

    (a) True
    (b) False

44. Lightning can have a voltage charge as high as thirty million volts (30,000,000V), and a current discharge of over fifty thousand amperes (50,000A).

    (a) True
    (b) False

1.7 Lightning Protection

45. To protect property against direct lightning strikes, a lightning _____ must be installed to direct its current flow around nonconductive structures or buildings down into the Earth.

    (a) ground rod
    (b) ground ring
    (c) protection system
    (d) copper mesh

46. Strike termination devices (_____ or lightning rods) are placed on top of the structure to be protected.

    (a) air rods
    (b) lightning crowns
    (c) free rods
    (d) air terminals

47. Strike termination devices are connected _____ by large wires and attached to ground rods or other electrodes in the Earth.

    (a) to each other
    (b) in series
    (c) in parallel
    (d) in tandem

48. A lightning protection system is intended to protect the building or structure and the associated electrical equipment inside.

    (a) True
    (b) False

49. To reduce damage to _____ from a nearby lightning event, surge protection devices (SPDs) must be installed on the electrical system.

    (a) electrical equipment
    (b) the building contents
    (c) the building's structure
    (d) metal piping systems

UNIT 2

ELECTRON THEORY

Introduction to Unit 2—Electron Theory

This unit focuses on electrons and the theory of electricity. It begins by exploring where electrons exist in an atom, then moves on to how and why electrons do what they do. Next, it covers how electricity is produced, and the properties that make an object a good conductor or insulator of electricity. Semiconductors and compound molecules, and their importance as a foundation to understanding electrical concepts, round out the topics covered here.

2.1 Electron Orbitals

Electrons exist in "orbitals" that surround the nucleus of an atom and the electrostatic attraction between the electrons and the protons in the nucleus hold the atom's subatomic particles together. ▶Figure 2–1

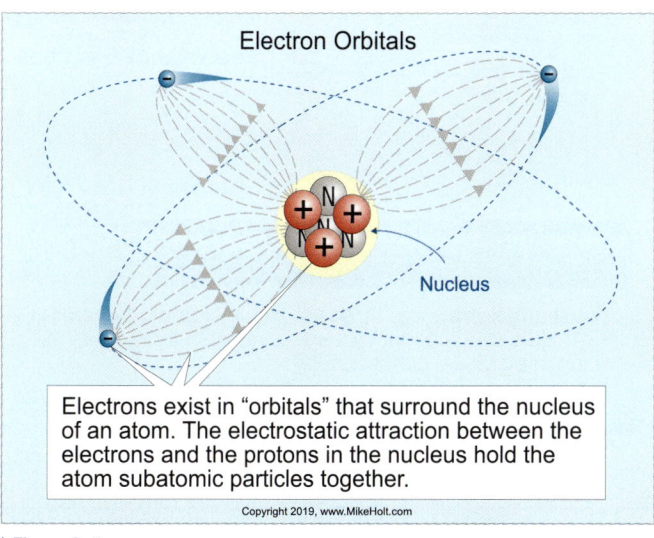

▶Figure 2–1

Orbitals are not circular like those of a planet's orbit; instead, they have more complex shapes. However, for the sake of simplicity, our graphics will show them as orbits around the nucleus of an atom.

2.2 Valence Electrons

The number of electrons in each orbital of an atom is dependent on the atom type. Each orbital can contain multiple electrons that follow a different path around the nucleus. The outermost orbital (shell) of an atom is called the "valence shell," so the electrons in this orbital are called "valence electrons." ▶Figure 2–2

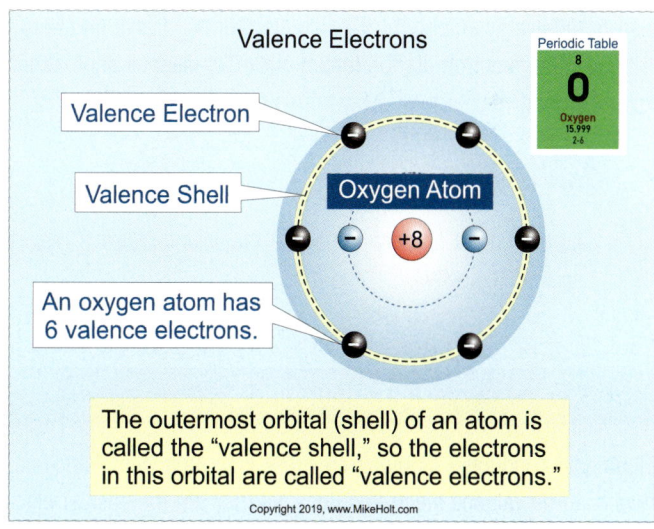

▶Figure 2–2

Freeing Electrons from an Atom | Electron Theory

2.3 Freeing Electrons from an Atom

According to Coulomb's Law, the strength of the electrostatic field between the protons and electrons of an atom decreases as its distance from the nucleus increases. This means that the electrons in the orbitals closest to the nucleus of the atom are not as easily separated from the atom as the electrons farther from the nucleus. ▶Figure 2-3

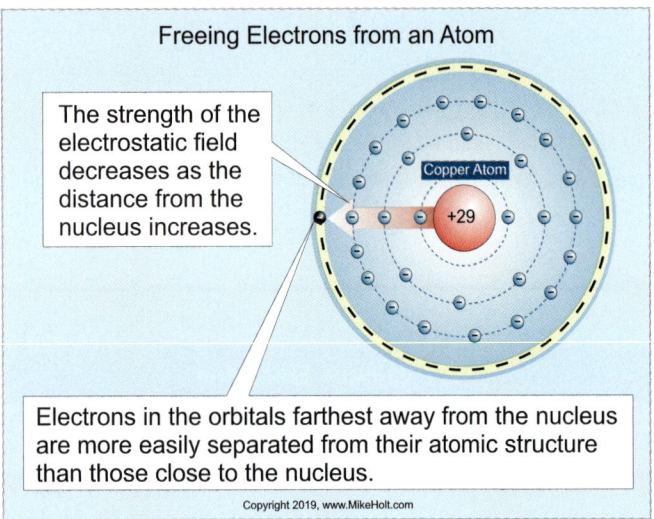

▶Figure 2-3

When energy is applied to the valance electrons of an atom, it will be distributed evenly among the valence electron(s). If enough energy is applied, an electron can be forced out of its valence shell either toward a positive charge or away from a negative charge.

Author's Comment:
▸ The movement of electrons out of the valance shell is the basis of electricity.

2.4 Conductance

Electrically conductive materials are made of an atom containing one, two, or three valence electrons. Because they are the easiest electrons to move in conductive materials, they actively participate in the flow of electricity. Elements with atoms containing only one valance electron (such as silver, copper, and gold) are the most conductive. ▶Figure 2-4

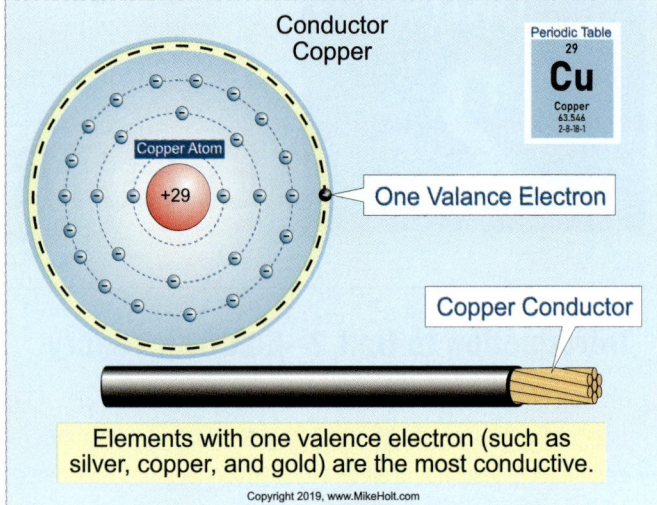

▶Figure 2-4

Aluminum atoms have three valence electrons; therefore, aluminum is considered a conductor and is suitable to be used for wiring in electrical construction. ▶Figure 2-5

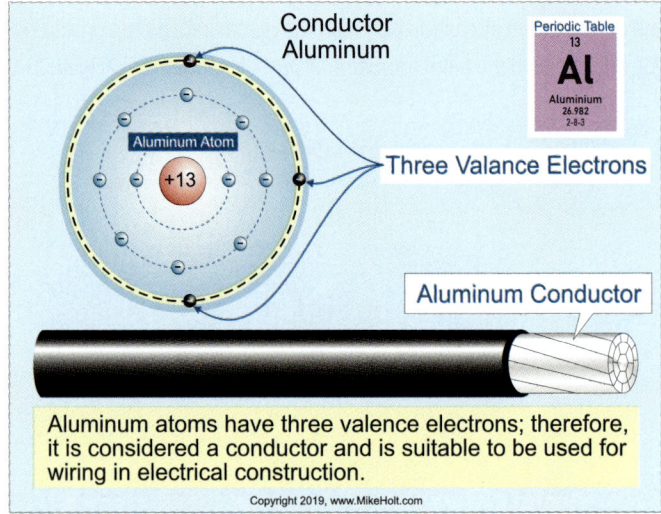

▶Figure 2-5

Copper atoms have only one valence electron, making copper a better electrical conductor than aluminum. When energy is applied to the single valance electron of a copper atom, all of it is focused toward the single valance electron which allows the valance electron to break free from the copper atom. ▶Figure 2-6

When the same amount of energy is applied to the three valance electrons of an aluminum atom, the energy is distributed evenly between them. It is therefore more difficult to cause the valence electrons to break free from the aluminum atom than it is to cause them to break free from the copper atom. ▶Figure 2-7

Electron Theory | **Conductance**

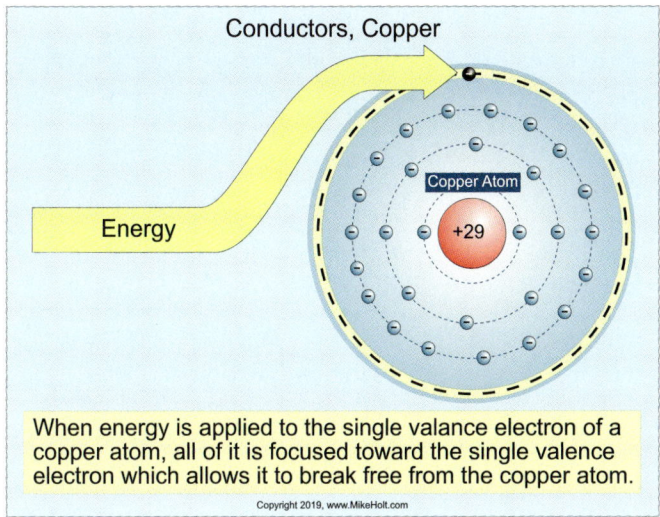

▶Figure 2–6

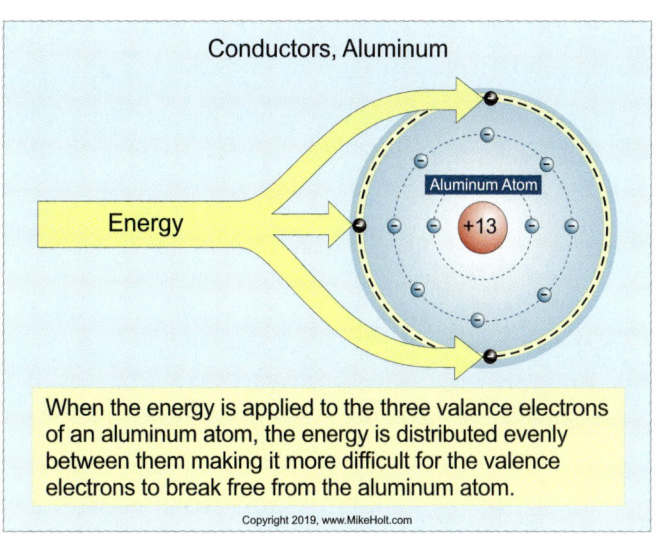

▶Figure 2–7

Even though aluminum is not as good of a conductor as copper, its light weight and low cost offer practical advantages that justify its use as wiring in the electrical industry.

Notes

UNIT 2 PRACTICE QUESTIONS

UNIT 2— ELECTRON THEORY

2.1 Electron Orbitals

1. Electrons exist in "_____" that surround the nucleus of an atom.

    (a) groups
    (b) orbitals
    (c) shells
    (d) none of these

2. The electrostatic attraction between the electrons and the protons in the nucleus hold the atom's subatomic particles together.

    (a) True
    (b) False

3. Orbitals are circular like those of a planet's orbit.

    (a) True
    (b) False

2.2 Valence Electrons

4. The _____ orbital (shell) of an atom is called the "valence shell," so the electrons in this orbital are called "valence electrons."

    (a) static
    (b) innermost
    (c) outermost
    (d) dynamic

2.3 Freeing Electrons from an Atom

5. According to Coulomb's Law, the strength of the electrostatic field between the protons and electrons of an atom _____ as its distance from the nucleus _____.

    (a) increases, increases
    (b) decreases, decreases
    (c) increases, decreases
    (d) decreases, increases

6. The electrons in the orbitals closest to the nucleus of the atom are not as easily separated from the atom as the electrons farther from the nucleus.

    (a) True
    (b) False

7. When energy is applied to the valance electrons of an atom, it will be distributed evenly among the _____.

    (a) neutrons
    (b) valence electrons
    (c) nuclei
    (d) protons

8. If enough energy is applied, an electron can be forced out of its valence shell either toward a positive charge or away from a negative charge.

    (a) True
    (b) False

2.4 Conductance

9. Electrically _____ materials are made of an atom containing one, two, or three valence electrons.

    (a) balanced
    (b) insulative
    (c) conductive
    (d) capacitive

10. Elements with atoms containing _____ valence electron(s) (such as silver, copper, and gold) are the most conductive.

    (a) one
    (b) two
    (c) three
    (d) four

Unit 2 | Practice Questions

11. Aluminum atoms have _____ valence electron(s) therefore, aluminum is considered a conductor and is suitable to be used for wiring in electrical construction.

    (a) one
    (b) two
    (c) three
    (d) four

12. Copper atoms have _____ valence electron, making copper a better electrical conductor than aluminum.

    (a) one
    (b) two
    (c) three
    (d) four

13. When energy is applied to the single _____ of a copper atom, all of it is focused toward the single valence electron which allows the valance electron to break free from the copper atom.

    (a) neutron
    (b) valence electron
    (c) orbital
    (d) proton

14. When the same amount of energy applied to a copper atom is applied to the three valance electrons of a(n) _____ atom, the energy is distributed evenly between them and more difficult for the valence electrons to break free.

    (a) gold
    (b) silver
    (c) zinc
    (d) aluminum

15. Even though aluminum is not as good of a conductor as copper, its light weight and low cost offer practical advantages that justify its use as wiring in the electrical industry.

    (a) True
    (b) False

UNIT 3
SOURCES, USES, AND DANGERS OF ELECTRICITY

Introduction to Unit 3—Sources, Uses, and Dangers of Electricity

When an energy source is applied to the atoms contained in an electrical circuit, the energy source's electrons will repel electrons away from the energy source. Protons within the energy source will attract electrons back into the source from the electrical circuit.

3.1 Electrical Power Source

Batteries, generators, and solar panels are all sources of energy. When one of these devices is placed in a circuit, they supply the energy needed to move electrons out of their orbitals. This causes electrons to flow away from, and then back toward, the power source. The energy needed to move electrons through the circuit can come from mechanical devices, chemical activity, magnetic attraction or repulsion, photovoltaic exposure (light), or even heat or pressure. This movement of electrons within an electrical circuit is known as "electron current flow," "electrical current," or simply "electricity."

3.2 Electric Current Flow (Electricity)

In an electrical circuit, an energy power source pushes and pulls electrons through the wires of the circuit. Electricity is the movement (or flow) of electrons through an electrically conductive path; from the power source, to an appliance or piece of equipment, and then back again to the power source. The conductive path these electrons take is called an "electrical circuit." ▶Figure 3–1

The direction of electron current flow through an electrical circuit is explained by one of two theories—the "Conventional Flow Theory" based on Benjamin Franklin's early writings, or the "Electron Flow Theory" as discovered by J.J. Thompson.

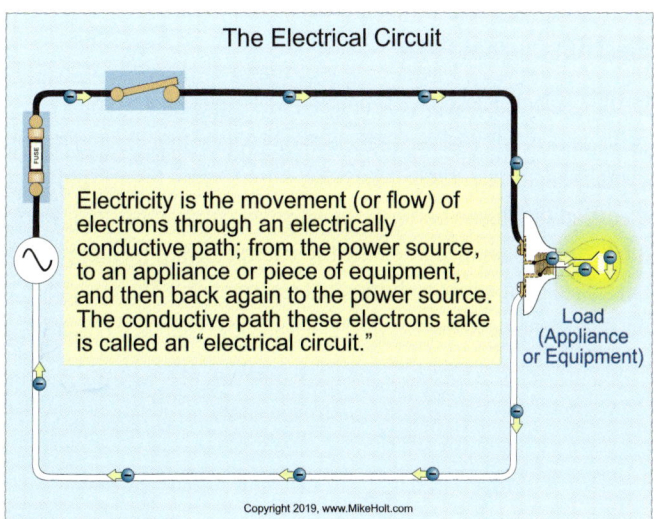
▶Figure 3–1

Conventional Current Flow

During an experiment in 1752, Benjamin Franklin discovered that an electric charge could move from one object to another (from wax to wool in this case). Not knowing an atom even existed, he assumed that electricity was fluid and flowed from the point of excess which he called "positive," to the point of deficiency which he called "negative." Needing some way to explain what he thought was the movement of the "electrical fluid," he developed his "Conventional Flow Theory" which is based on the concept that electrons flow from positive to negative. ▶Figure 3–2

Electricity | Sources, Uses, and Dangers of Electricity

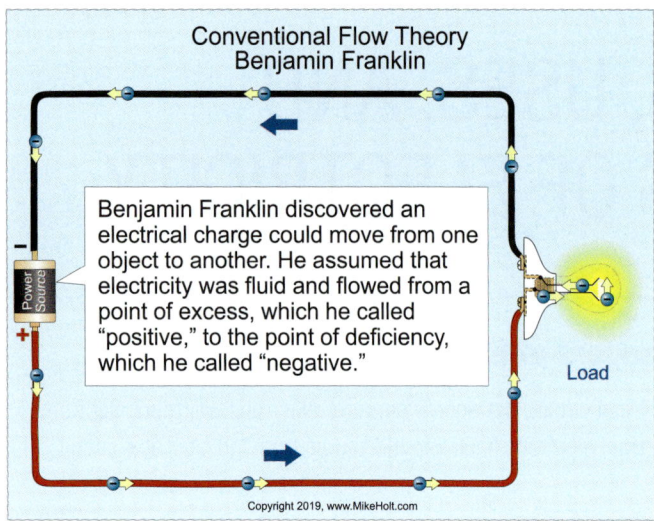
▶Figure 3–2

Electron Current Flow

In 1897, scientist Joseph J. Thompson was exploring the properties of cathode rays and realized that electricity was in fact, the movement of many negatively charged particles much smaller than an atom. He theorized that these particles, being small parts of an atom, would move from an atom with a negative charge toward an atom with a positive charge. His hypothesis (that electrons flow from negative to positive) became known as the "Electron Flow Theory." ▶Figure 3–3

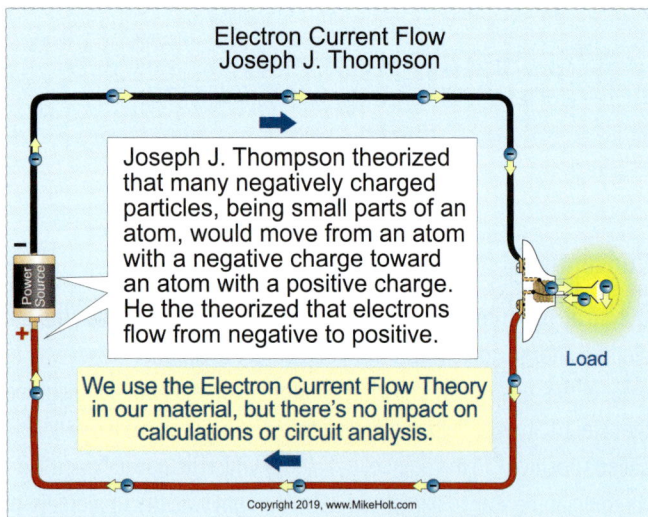
▶Figure 3–3

For the 145 years before Thompson's realization, the notations and symbols used in science and engineering had been based on Franklin's conventional flow theory. Thompson's electron flow theory is contrary to Franklin's, yet it accurately describes the physical movement of electrons and current flow.

Electron or Conventional Flow Theory?

Since the direction of direct current flow has no effect on the physical or mathematical analysis of a circuit, many still write, teach, and use the Conventional Flow Theory (positive to negative). Those who want to describe the physical movement of electrons within a direct-current circuit use the Electron Flow Theory (negative to positive).

Author's Comment:

▸ In this textbook we use the Electron Flow Theory (negative to positive) for direct-current circuits because it represents the electrons' direction of current flow.

3.3 Electricity

To cause electrons to flow through a circuit, energy must be applied to its electrons so they will leave their atoms, move away from the energy power source, move through the load, and then return to the energy power source. This energy needed at the power source can be supplied by mechanical devices, chemical activity, magnetism, light, heat, or pressure. ▶Figure 3–4

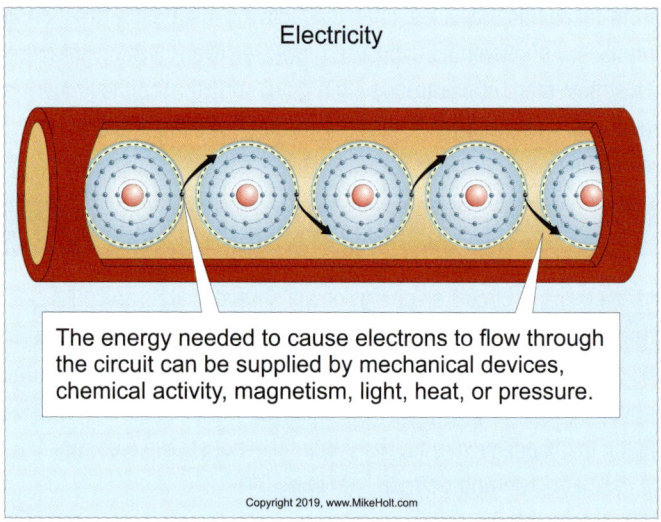
▶Figure 3–4

Magnetism (Magnetoelectricity)—Generators and Transformers

Magnetoelectricity is where electrons within an electrical circuit are forced to move in a given direction by either moving a magnetic field through a wire, or by moving a wire through a magnetic field. The direction of current flow through the circuit is relative to the direction of the movement of the magnetic field to the wire. ▶Figure 3–5

Sources, Uses, and Dangers of Electricity | **Dangers of Electricity**

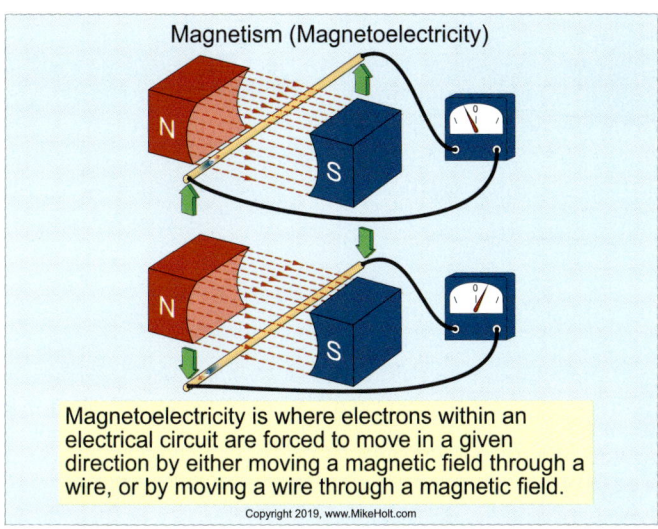
▶Figure 3-5

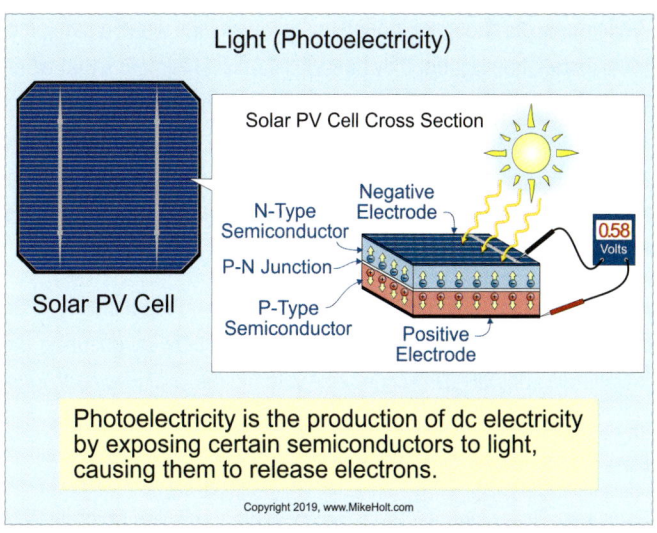
▶Figure 3-6

When the movement of the magnetic field relative to the wire is one direction, then the current flow on the wire will be in the same direction. When the movement of the magnetic field relative to the wire is in the opposite direction, then current flow on the wire will be in the opposite direction. The alternating movement of the magnetic field causing current to flow in opposite directions is known as "alternating current" (ac).

Nikola Tesla pioneered much of the innovation in magnetoelectricity thereby improving alternating-current generators, motors, and transformers. Without his work, and the widespread adoption of alternating-current power, it is extremely doubtful our society would have advanced as rapidly as it has in the last one hundred years.

Light (Photoelectricity)

Photoelectricity (photoelectric effect) is the conversion of light energy into electrical energy. When photons (light) strike certain semiconductors they cause electrons to flow from one semiconductor to the other, creating the energy necessary to move electrons within a circuit. This is the basis of the photovoltaic (PV) cell. ▶Figure 3-6

A photovoltaic (PV) system is the combination of all components and subsystems that convert solar energy into electric energy. As the production costs of photovoltaic cells and batteries decrease, and efficiencies increase, the initial costs of these PV systems are being substantially reduced. ▶Figure 3-7

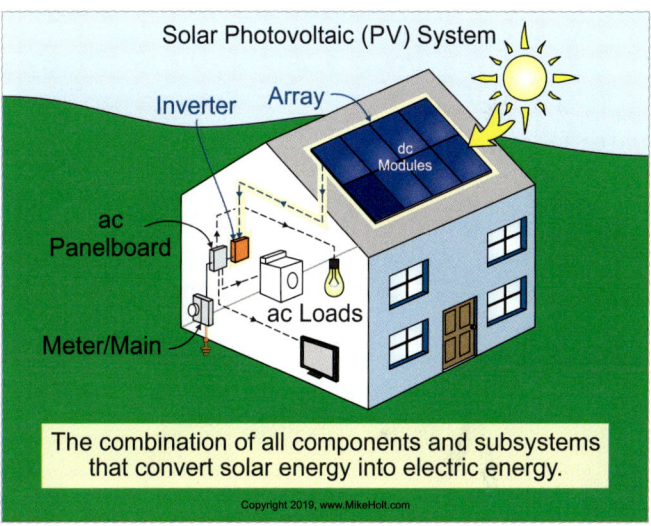
▶Figure 3-7

3.4 Dangers of Electricity

The dangers of electricity include electric shock, electrocution (death), arc flashes, and fire. Even though electricity is very useful, we must be very careful in the design, installation, inspection, and maintenance of electrical systems. According to the National Safety Council, approximately 300 people in the United States die each year from being shocked by electricity and thousands receive treatment for injuries.

Dangers of Electricity | Sources, Uses, and Dangers of Electricity

While many products are judged on how well they work, a safe electrical installation is judged by how well it fails. This means that when the system fails, the installation is designed and installed to protect against electric shock, electrocution, fire, and arc flash. Dangerous arc flashes (explosions spewing molten metal and extreme temperature flashes) are possible when equipment and safeguards are not properly installed and used.

People working in the electrical industry have a responsibility to be sure electrical installations are as safe as possible by ensuring the installation is installed in accordance with the *National Electrical Code*.

Fire

Each year, fires from electrical faults result in the loss of many lives and billions of dollars in property damage. Electrical fires are primarily caused when electrical energy heats an object above its ignition temperature. ▶Figure 3–8

▶Figure 3–9

▶Figure 3–8

Excessive heat resulting in a fire can be generated when wires are not terminated properly, or not properly sized and the load exceeds the rating of the circuit's components. ▶Figure 3–9

> **Author's Comment:**
> ▸ For more information on the causes of electrical fires, search the web. There are some great articles and videos out there. Electrical forensic investigation is an amazing career that specializes in the many causes and effects of damage and injury caused by electricity.

Electric Shock

For electrical current to flow there must be a power source and a path for electrons to leave that power source and return to that power source. People and animals can be shocked or electrocuted when electrons flow through their bodies, especially when those electrons flow through their hearts. ▶Figure 3–10

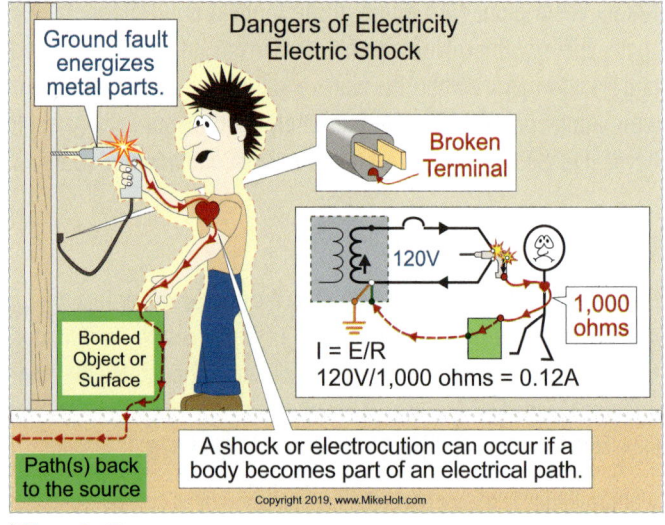
▶Figure 3–10

Tragically, individuals can become electrocuted from electrical current when as little as 50/1,000 of an ampere connects with them. This can disrupt the heart's electrical signal. When that occurs, the heart goes into a rapid ineffective heartbeat of over 350 beats per minute. This is called "ventricular fibrillation" and prevents blood from circulating through the body. Death can result in a matter of minutes, particularly when blood circulation to the brain is hindered.

Electric shock or electrocution is dependent on the current flowing through the body and is impacted by both the contact voltage and the contact resistance. The effects of electrical current on an average human include electrical sensation, pain, inability to "let-go," and ventricular fibrillation. ▶Figure 3–11

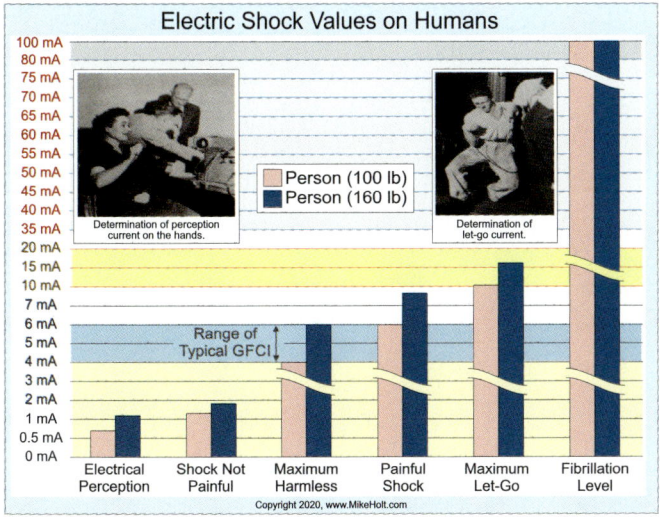

▶Figure 3–11

Author's Comment:

▶ Ventricular fibrillation (VF) is a life-threatening condition. To avoid serious injury or death, the person must be treated with a defibrillator immediately. Cardiopulmonary resuscitation (CPR) provides some extra time, but defibrillation is essential for surviving ventricular fibrillation. ▶Figure 3–12

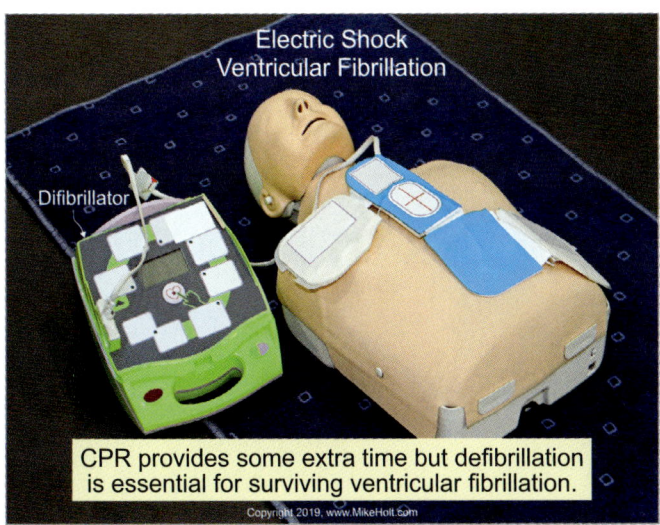

▶Figure 3–12

3.5 National Electrical Code

It is vitally important for all wiring to be installed in accordance with the *National Electrical Code* (at a minimum) to ensure the practical safeguarding of persons and property from the dangers of electricity. The *NEC (Code)* contains rules, that when followed, result in electrical installations essentially free from electrical hazards. ▶Figure 3–13

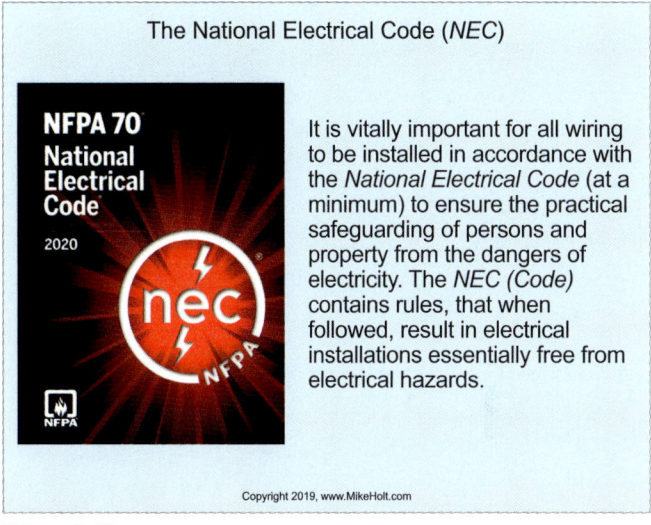

▶Figure 3–13

Notes

UNIT 3 PRACTICE QUESTIONS

UNIT 3—SOURCES, USES, AND DANGERS OF ELECTRICITY

Introduction to Unit 3—Sources, Uses, and Dangers of Electricity

1. When an energy source is applied to the atoms contained in an electrical circuit, the energy source's electrons will repel electrons away from the energy source.

    (a) True
    (b) False

2. When an energy source is applied to the atoms contained in an electrical circuit, protons within the energy source will attract electrons back into the source from the electrical circuit.

    (a) True
    (b) False

3.1 Electrical Power Source

3. Batteries, generators, and solar panels are all sources of energy that can supply the energy needed to move electrons out of their orbitals.

    (a) True
    (b) False

4. The energy needed to move electrons through a circuit can come from mechanical devices, chemical activity, magnetic attraction or repulsion, photovoltaic exposure (light), or even heat or pressure.

    (a) True
    (b) False

5. The movement of electrons within an electrical circuit is known as "_____."

    (a) electron current flow
    (b) electrical current
    (c) electricity
    (d) all of these

3.2 Electric Current Flow (Electricity)

6. In an electrical circuit, an energy power source _____ electrons through the wires of the circuit.

    (a) forces
    (b) pushes
    (c) pulls
    (d) pushes and pulls

7. Electricity is the movement (or flow) of _____ through an electrically conductive path.

    (a) protons
    (b) atoms
    (c) electrons
    (d) neutrons

8. "Conventional Flow Theory" is based on the concept that electrons flow from _____.

    (a) positive to positive
    (b) positive to negative
    (c) negative to negative
    (d) negative to positive

9. "Electron Flow Theory" is based on the concept that electrons flow from _____.

    (a) positive to positive
    (b) positive to negative
    (c) negative to negative
    (d) negative to positive

10. To describe the physical movement of electrons within a direct-current circuit, use the Electron Flow Theory (negative to positive).

    (a) True
    (b) False

Unit 3 | Practice Questions

3.3 Electricity

11. To cause electrons to flow through a circuit, energy must be applied to its electrons so they will leave their atoms, move away from the energy power source, move through the load, and then return to _____.

    (a) ground
    (b) the energy power source
    (c) the neutral
    (d) the protective device

12. The energy needed at the power source to cause electrons to flow can be supplied by mechanical devices, chemical activity, magnetism, light, heat, or pressure.

    (a) True
    (b) False

13. Magnetoelectricity is where electrons within a(n) _____ are forced to move in a given direction by either moving a magnetic field through a wire, or by moving a wire through a magnetic field.

    (a) orbital
    (b) valence shell
    (c) electrical circuit
    (d) atom

14. The direction of current flow through a(n) _____ is relative to the direction of the movement of the magnetic field to the wire.

    (a) element
    (b) circuit
    (c) valence shell
    (d) atom

15. When the relative movement of a magnetic field to a wire is one direction, then the current flow on the wire will be in the same direction.

    (a) True
    (b) False

16. The alternating movement of the magnetic field causing current to flow in opposite directions is known as "_____."

    (a) oppositional current
    (b) bi-directional current
    (c) alternating current
    (d) an electromagnetic field

17. Photoelectricity (photoelectric effect) is the conversion of _____ energy into electrical energy.

    (a) light
    (b) random
    (c) turbine
    (d) magnetic

18. When photons (light) strike certain semiconductors they cause electrons to flow from one semiconductor to the other, creating the energy necessary to move electrons within a circuit. This is the basis of the photovoltaic (PV) cell.

    (a) True
    (b) False

19. A photovoltaic (PV) system is the combination of all components and subsystems that convert _____ into electric energy.

    (a) atoms
    (b) solar energy
    (c) chemicals
    (d) metallic elements

3.4 Dangers of Electricity

20. The dangers of electricity include electric shock, electrocution (death), arc flashes, and fire.

    (a) True
    (b) False

21. While many products are judged on how well they work, a safe electrical installation is judged by _____.

    (a) passing inspection
    (b) the costs to install
    (c) how well it fails
    (d) how long it lasts

22. When a system fails it means that the installation was designed and installed to protect against electric shock, electrocution, fire, and arc flash.

    (a) True
    (b) False

23. People working in the electrical industry have a responsibility to be sure electrical installations are as safe as possible by ensuring the installation is installed in accordance with the _____.

    (a) OSHA guidelines
    (b) *National Electrical Code*
    (c) UL standards
    (d) installers expertise

24. Excessive heat resulting in a fire can be generated when wires are not terminated properly, or not properly sized and the load exceeds the rating of the circuit's components.

    (a) True
    (b) False

25. For electrical current to flow there must be a power source and a path for _____ to leave that power source and return to that power source.

    (a) protons
    (b) atoms
    (c) neutrons
    (d) electrons

26. People and animals can be shocked or electrocuted when electrons flow through their bodies, especially when those electrons flow through their hearts.

    (a) True
    (b) False

27. In as little as _____ second(s), individuals can become electrocuted from electrical current when as little as 50/1,000 of an ampere connects with them.

    (a) one
    (b) two
    (c) three
    (d) four

28. Electric shock or electrocution is dependent on the current flowing through the body and is impacted by both the contact voltage and the contact resistance.

    (a) True
    (b) False

29. The effects of electrical current on an average human include electrical sensation, pain, inability to "let-go," and ventricular fibrillation.

    (a) True
    (b) False

3.5 *National Electrical Code*

30. It is vitally important for all wiring to be installed in accordance with _____.

    (a) OSHA guidelines
    (b) the *National Electrical Code*
    (c) UL standards
    (d) the designer's specifications

31. Wiring installed in accordance with the *NEC* helps to ensure the practical safeguarding of persons and property from the dangers of electricity.

    (a) True
    (b) False

32. The *NEC (Code)* contains _____, that when followed, result in electrical installations essentially free from electrical hazards.

    (a) suggestions
    (b) advice
    (c) guidance
    (d) rules

Notes

UNIT 4
CIRCUIT PROTECTIVE DEVICES

Introduction to Unit 4—Circuit Protective Devices

Current flow and the path(s) electricity takes back to its source are very important to its safe use. This unit explains overcurrent and why overcurrent protection is an important part of every circuit. It is the low resistance of the fault current return path that permits the circuit overcurrent protective device to de-energize the circuit.

The primary function of an overcurrent protective device is to prevent excessive current flow from damaging wires and equipment. Different types of overcurrent protection serve different purposes so study this unit carefully. Topics such as overloads, faults, how a fuse differs from a circuit breaker, and how fuses and circuit breakers work, will all be covered.

Part A Overcurrent Protection Devices

4.1 Overcurrent Protection

The purpose of overcurrent protection is to protect wires and equipment against excessive or dangerous temperatures due to the presence of current in excess of the rated ampacity of equipment or wires. ▶Figure 4–1

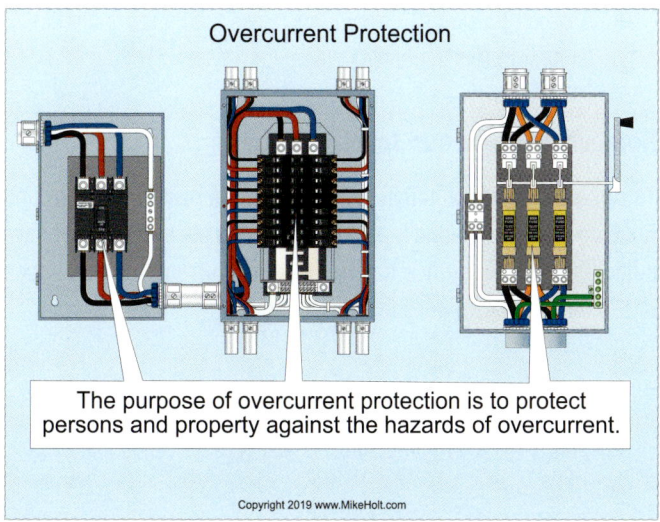

▶Figure 4–1

Overcurrent conditions might result from an overload, short circuit, or ground fault [*NEC* Article 100 Definition].

Overload

An overload is a condition where equipment or wires carry current in excess of their rated ampacity. ▶Figure 4–2

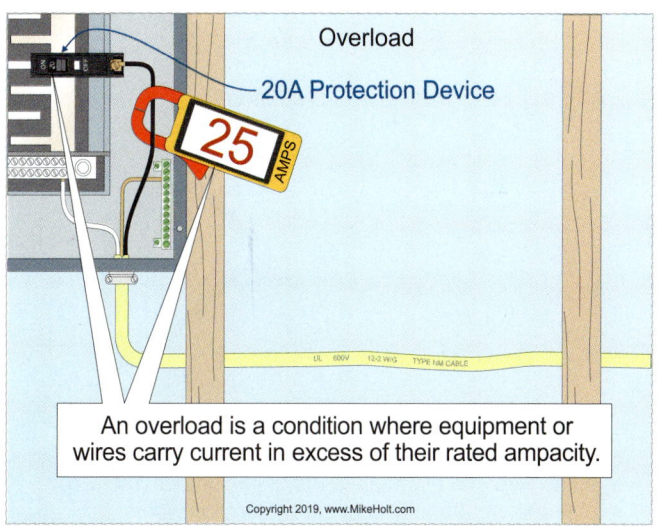

▶Figure 4–2

Short-Circuit

A short circuit is an unintentional electrical connection between two current-carrying wires of the electrical system such as line-to-line or line-to-neutral. ▶Figure 4–3

Clearing Faults | Circuit Protective Devices

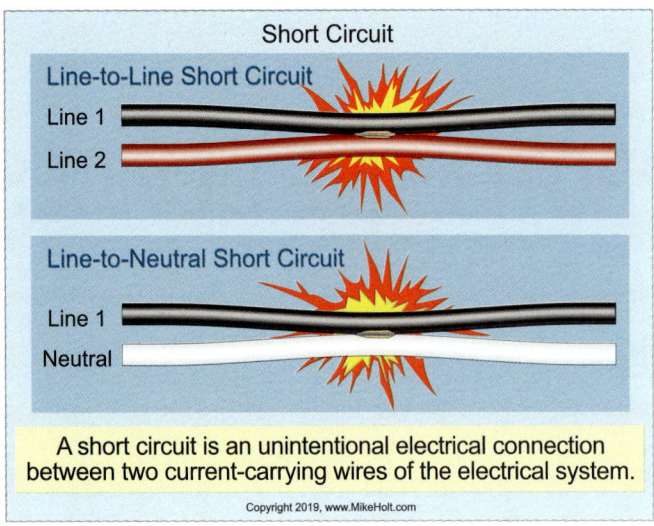

▶Figure 4–3

Ground Fault

The *Code* defines a ground fault as an unintentional, electrically conductive connection between a phase wire and the metal parts of enclosures, raceways, equipment, or normally noncurrent-carrying wires. During a ground fault, and while the circuit is still energized, dangerous voltages and large currents exist on one or more of the wires making up the circuit. The proper protective device will quickly and safely clear this condition by opening the circuit. ▶Figure 4–4

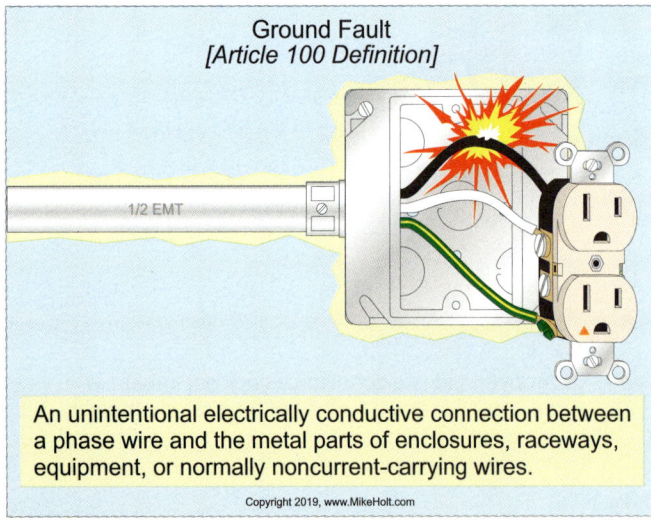

▶Figure 4–4

4.2 Clearing Faults

To protect against electric shock from dangerous voltages on metal parts, and to prevent a fire due to an overload, ground fault, or short circuit they must be quickly removed by the opening of the circuit's overcurrent protective device.

Time-Current Curves

The opening time for an overcurrent protective device is inversely proportionate to the magnitude of the current. This means that the greater the fault current returning to the source, the less time it will take for the protective device to open and clear the fault.

For example, a 20A circuit breaker with an overload of 40A (twice the device rating) will trip within 25 to 150 seconds. If the overload is five times the rating of the breaker (100A) it will trip in 5 to 20 seconds. ▶Figure 4–5

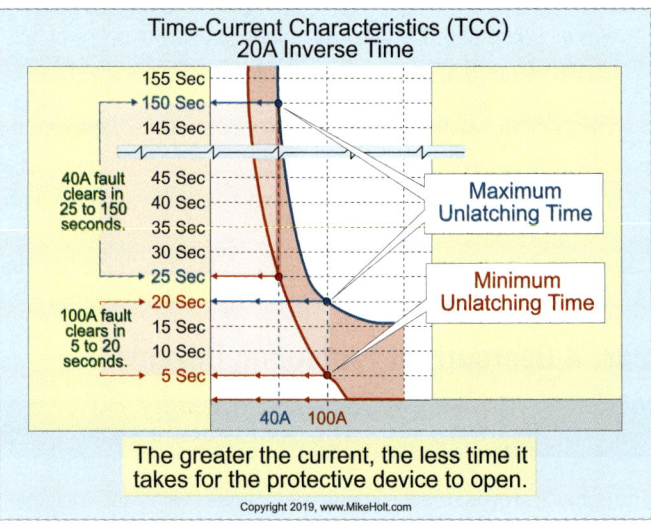

▶Figure 4–5

Author's Comment:

▶ A circuit breaker can trip in much less than a second if the fault current is ten times its ampere rating.

Removing Dangerous Touch Voltage

To remove dangerous touch voltage on metal parts from a ground fault, an effective ground-fault current path to the source must have sufficiently low resistance to allow the fault current to quickly open or trip the circuit overcurrent device.

▶ **Example**

Question: The approximate ground-fault current for the following is _____.

- Phase circuit wires—200 ft of 3 AWG (0.05 ohms)
- Equipment bonding wire—200 ft of 8 AWG (0.156 ohms)

▶Figure 4–6

(a) 100A   (b) 200A   (c) 600A   (d) 800A

Circuit Protective Devices | Fuses

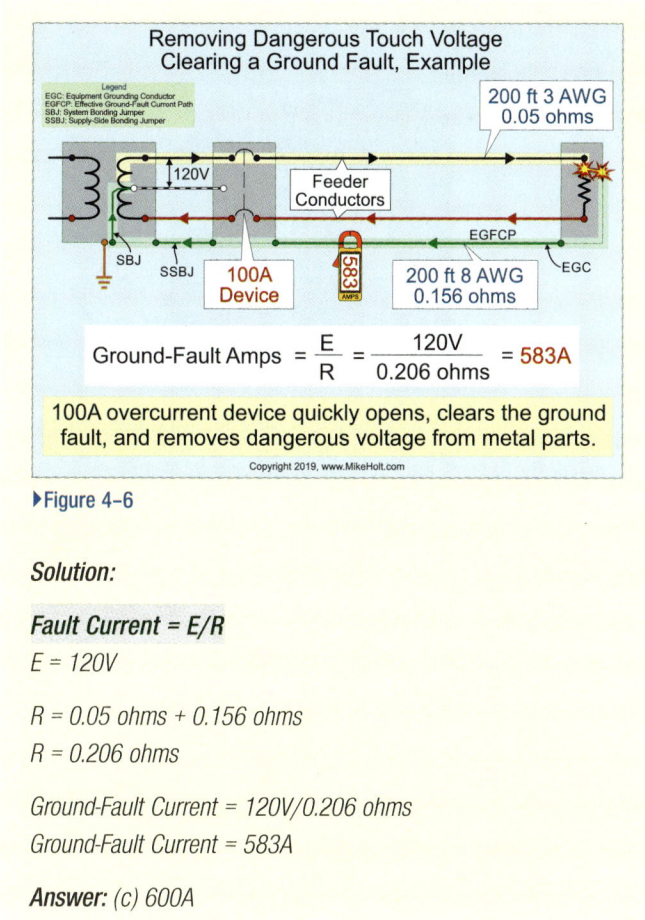
▶Figure 4–6

Solution:

Fault Current = E/R

E = 120V

R = 0.05 ohms + 0.156 ohms

R = 0.206 ohms

Ground-Fault Current = 120V/0.206 ohms

Ground-Fault Current = 583A

Answer: (c) 600A

4.3 Overcurrent Protective Device Types

The most common types of overcurrent protective devices are fuses and circuit breakers. They are available in a variety of configurations, ampere ratings, and voltage ratings. ▶Figure 4–7

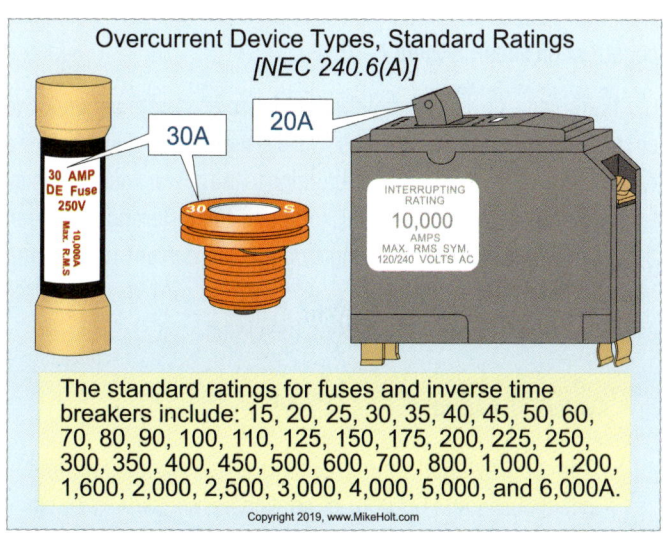
▶Figure 4–7

4.4 Fuses

A fuse is an overcurrent device that includes an element designed to melt and open a circuit when an overload, short circuit, or ground fault exists.

Construction

Fuses consist of a conductive element, and each fuse is enclosed in a tube surrounded by nonconductive filler material. ▶Figure 4–8

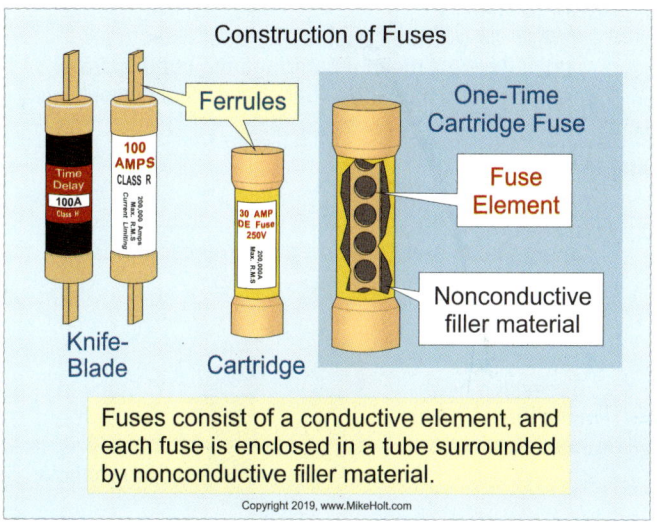
▶Figure 4–8

Fuse Overload Protection

When current flows through the conductive element of a fuse, the current generates heat based on the fuse element's resistance. During normal operation, the filler material surrounding the conductive element absorbs the heat from the current flow. When an overload occurs, the heat rises to a point where it melts a portion of the conductive element and stops the flow of electrical current. ▶Figure 4–9

Short-Circuit and Ground-Fault Protection

When a short circuit or ground fault occurs, the fault current through the fuse can be in the thousands of amperes. This high current flow on the conductive element of the fuse causes multiple segments of the conductive element to melt and stops the flow of electrical current. Fuses are typically designed to open a circuit to clear short-circuit and ground-fault current in less than one cycle of the waveform (1/60th of a second). ▶Figure 4–10

Circuit Breaker Trip Elements | Circuit Protective Devices

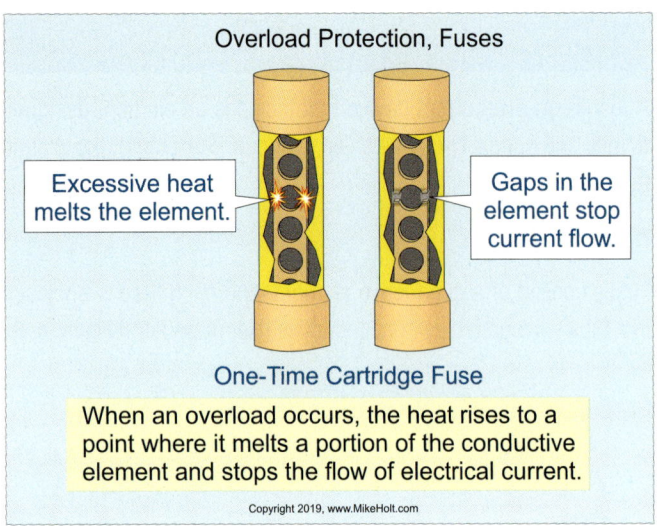

▶Figure 4–9

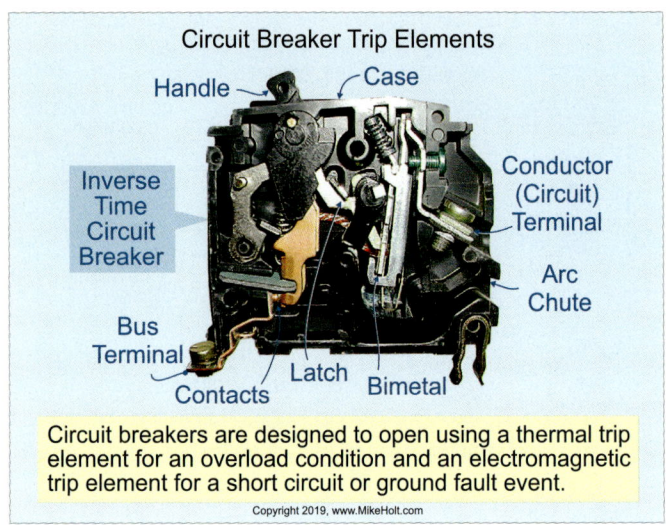

▶Figure 4–11

Magnetic Trip Element

An electromagnetic trip device within a circuit breaker responds to short circuit and ground-fault events by operating on the solenoid principle. A movable core, called a slapper, is held with a spring and moves when an electromagnetic field is created from high fault current due to a short circuit or ground fault. The solenoid is designed to have enough electromagnetic force to activate the trip mechanism when the current level reaches about ten times the rating of the circuit breaker.

Part B Ground-Fault Circuit Interrupters (GFCIs)

4.6 Ground-Fault Circuit Interrupters (GFCIs)

A ground-fault circuit interrupter (GFCI) is designed to protect people against electric shock. GFCI-protective devices for building wiring include GFCI-circuit breakers or GFCI-type receptacles. There are also GFCI devices for temporary use to protect workers in places like construction sites. ▶Figure 4–12

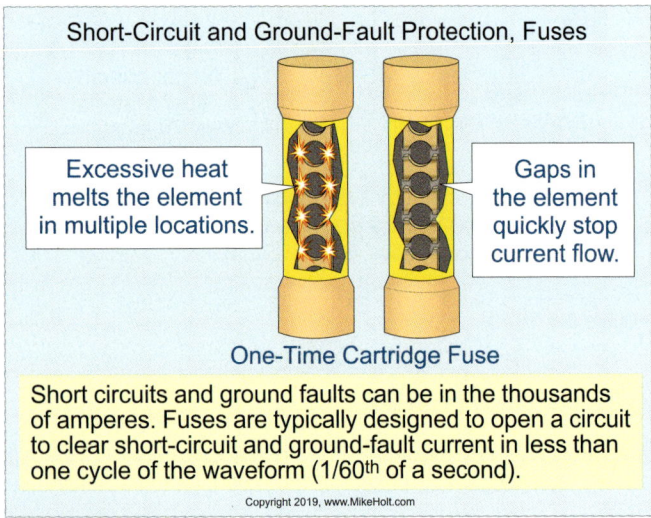

▶Figure 4–10

4.5 Circuit Breaker Trip Elements

Circuit breakers, like fuses, are designed to be installed in series with the circuit wires being protected. Circuit breakers are designed to open using a thermal trip element for an overload condition and an electromagnetic trip element for a short circuit or ground-fault event. ▶Figure 4–11

Thermal Trip Element

The thermal trip device within the circuit breaker responds to temperature rise due to increased current flow by using a bimetal thermal sensing element. In an overload condition, excessive current flow mechanically activates the circuit breaker's thermal trip mechanism to open the circuit.

GFCI-protective devices detect the imbalance of current between the circuit's phase and neutral wires. During the normal operation of a typical 2-wire circuit, the current returning to the power source is equal to the current leaving the power source. If the difference between the current leaving and returning through the current transformer of the GFCI-protective device exceeds 5 mA (± 1 mA), the solid-state circuitry in the GFCI device will open the circuit.

Author's Comment:

▸ The abbreviation "mA" (used above) stands for one one-thousandth (1/1,000) of an ampere, so 5 mA is equal to 5/1,000 of an ampere or 0.005A.

Circuit Protective Devices | **Line-to-Neutral Shock Hazard**

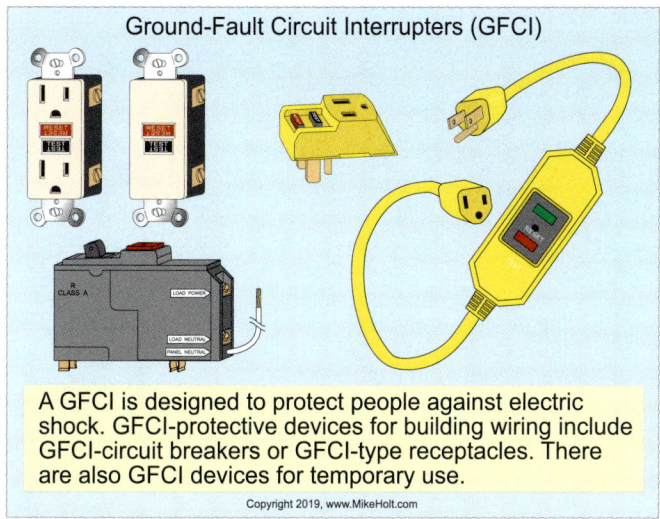
▶Figure 4–12

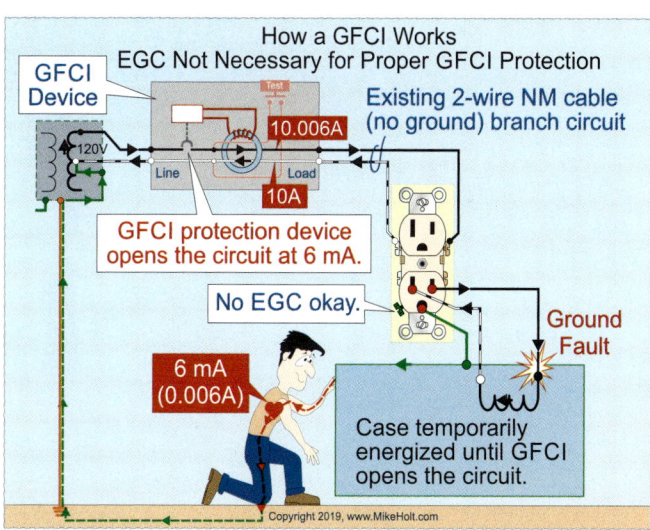
▶Figure 4–14

For example, a GFCI opens the circuit when the unbalanced current has a value of 6 mA or higher but does not do so when the unbalanced current is less than 4 mA. ▶Figure 4–13

If one is present, the GFCI-protective device's sensors detect it and prevent the GFCI-protected device from being turned on. This feature can give the appearance of a "defective" GFCI because it trips when the circuit is energized, even with no loads on or connected to the circuit. ▶Figure 4–15

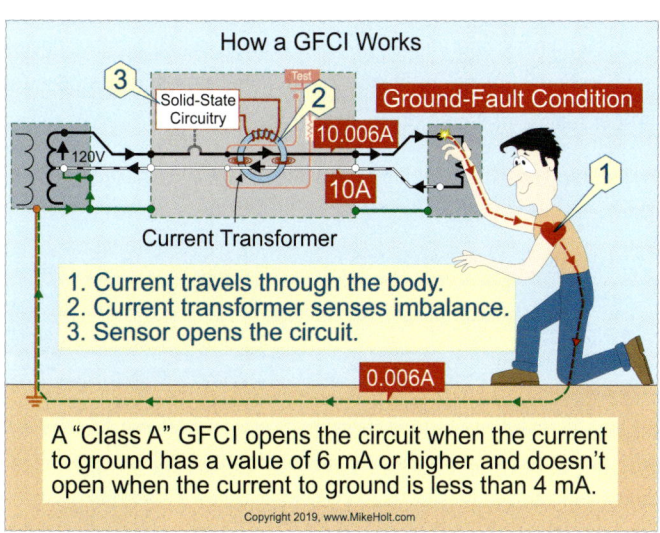
▶Figure 4–13

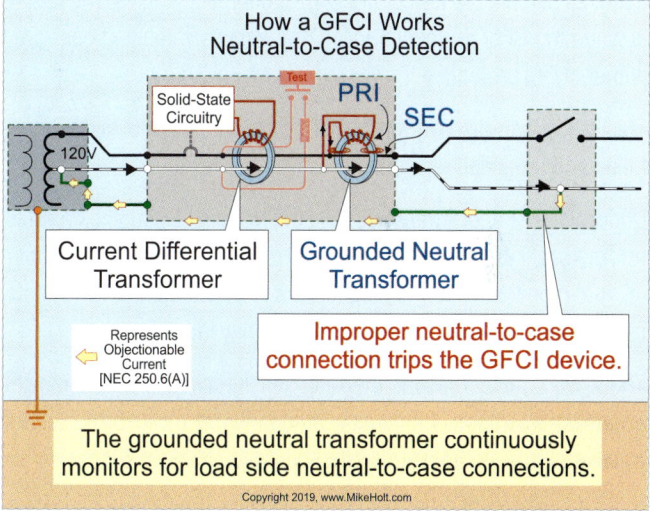
▶Figure 4–15

An interesting point about GFCIs is that despite their name, they operate based on unbalanced circuit conductor current, not ground. This means that they will operate on a circuit with or without an equipment grounding conductor. ▶Figure 4–14

4.8 Line-to-Neutral Shock Hazard

Warning

⚠️ Severe electric shock or death can occur if someone touches the phase and neutral wires at the same time, even if the circuit is GFCI protected. Under this condition, the current between the conductors is balanced within the GFCI and considered a normal load because there is no unbalance between the phase and neutral wires within the GFCI. ▶Figure 4–16

4.7 Neutral-to-Case Detection

Another function of a GFCI is to detect downstream (load side) improper neutral-to-case connections between the neutral wire and an equipment grounding conductor. An electronic circuit in the GFCI continuously monitors its load side for neutral-to-case connections.

Mike Holt Enterprises • www.MikeHolt.com • 888.NEC.CODE (632.2633) | **41**

GFCI Fails—Circuit Remains Energized | Circuit Protective Devices

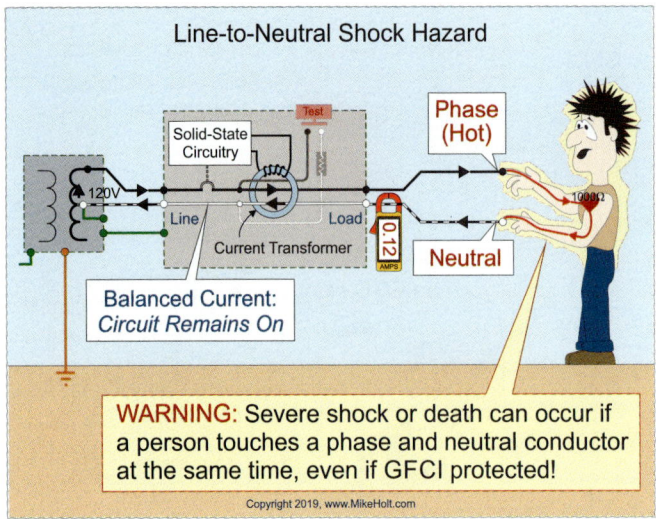

▶Figure 4–16

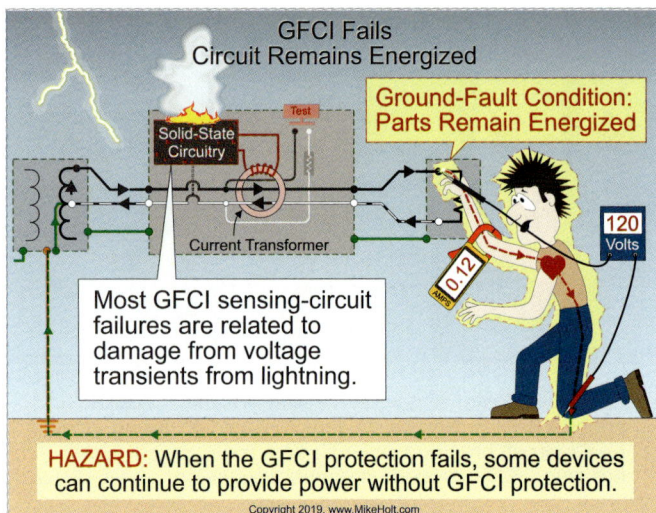

▶Figure 4–17

4.9 GFCI Fails—Circuit Remains Energized

According to a GFCI field test survey report, about 11 percent of the GFCI-circuit breakers protecting indoor receptacles failed, as did about 20 percent of those protecting outdoor receptacles. The hazard is when the GFCI protection failed, the circuits remained energized without GFCI protection.

This study also discovered that eight percent of GFCI receptacles failed and remained energized.

Underwriters Laboratories (UL) and the National Electrical Manufacturers Association (NEMA) responded to these findings by calling for an auto-monitoring/self-testing feature to be added to GFCI receptacles to force them to de-energized once they fail.

There were many reasons the GFCI-sensing circuits failed, but the greatest percentage of failures related to damage caused by voltage transients from lightning and other sources. ▶Figure 4–17

Since the UL 943, *Standard for Ground-Fault Circuit-Interrupters* update in 2015, manufacturers are required to produce 15A, 125V, GFCI receptacles that cannot be reset if the GFCI-protected circuit no longer provides ground-fault protection. As an added safety improvement, some GFCI receptacles have a built-in line/load reversal protection feature that prevents the receptacle to power up if the installer mistakenly reverses the line and load connections on the receptacle. However, this does not apply to GFCI circuit breakers.

4.10 GFCI Test Button

Pressing a GFCI's test button is the only way to confirm the sensing circuit within it is operational. Do not assume a GFCI-protective device is operational unless you follow the manufacturer's instructions for proper testing of the product. ▶Figure 4–18

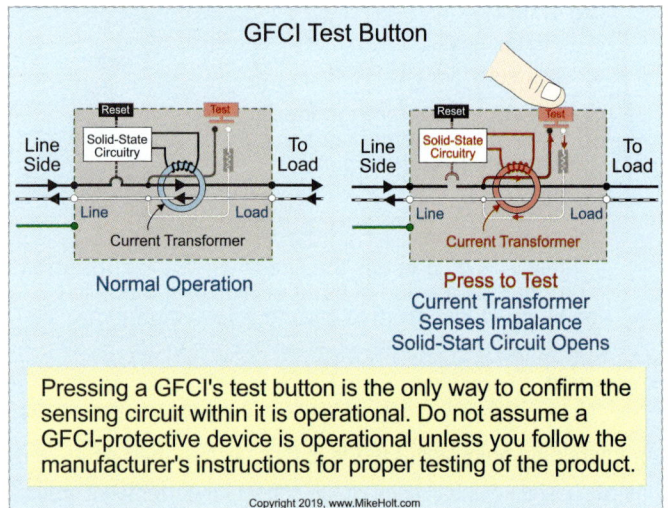

▶Figure 4–18

Author's Comment:

▸ There are plug-in type GFCI receptacle testers available that can identity whether it is providing power and is properly wired for safe operation; however, you must follow the manufacturer's testing instructions to see if the device is functioning as it should.

UNIT 4

PRACTICE QUESTIONS

UNIT 4—CIRCUIT PROTECTIVE DEVICES

Introduction to Unit 4—Circuit Protective Devices

1. The primary function of an overcurrent protective device is to prevent excessive voltage flow from damaging wires and equipment.

    (a) True
    (b) False

4.1 Overcurrent Protection

2. The purpose of _____ protection is to protect wires and equipment against excessive or dangerous temperatures due to the presence of current in excess of the rated ampacity of equipment or wires.

    (a) overcurrent
    (b) ground fault
    (c) surge
    (d) fire

3. Overcurrent conditions might result from a(n) _____.

    (a) overload
    (b) short circuit
    (c) ground fault
    (d) any of these

4. An overload is a condition where equipment or wires carry current in excess of their rated _____.

    (a) voltage
    (b) ampacity
    (c) capacity
    (d) resistance

5. A short circuit is an unintentional electrical connection between two current-carrying wires of the electrical system such as line-to-line or line-to-_____.

    (a) metal enclosure
    (b) ground
    (c) neutral
    (d) water

6. The *Code* defines a ground fault as an unintentional, electrically conductive connection between a phase wire and the metal parts of enclosures, raceways, equipment, or normally noncurrent-carrying wires.

    (a) True
    (b) False

7. During a _____, and while the circuit is still energized, dangerous voltages and large currents exist on one or more of the wires making up the circuit.

    (a) thunderstorm
    (b) short circuit
    (c) power surge
    (d) ground fault

4.2 Clearing Faults

8. To protect against electric shock from dangerous voltages on metal parts, and to prevent a fire due to an overload, ground fault, or short circuit they must be quickly removed by the opening of the circuit's overcurrent protective device.

    (a) True
    (b) False

9. The opening time for an overcurrent protective device is _____ to the magnitude of the current.

    (a) proportional
    (b) inversely proportional
    (c) relative
    (d) irrelevant

Unit 4 | Practice Questions

10. The greater the fault current returning to the source, the less time it will take for the protective device to open and _____ the fault.

    (a) compensate for
    (b) improve
    (c) clear
    (d) decrease

11. A 20A circuit breaker with an overload of 40A (twice the device rating) will trip within 25 to 150 seconds. If the overload is five times the rating of the breaker (100A) it will trip in _____.

    (a) 1 to 10 seconds
    (b) 5 to 20 seconds
    (c) 6 to 60 seconds
    (d) 12 to 75 seconds

4.3 Overcurrent Protective Device Types

12. The most common types of overcurrent protective devices are _____ and circuit breakers.

    (a) GFCIs
    (b) AFCIs
    (c) fuses
    (d) shunt trips

13. Fuses and circuit breakers are available in a variety of configurations, ampere ratings, and voltage ratings.

    (a) True
    (b) False

4.4 Fuses

14. A fuse is an overcurrent device that includes an element designed to _____ and open a circuit when an overload, short circuit, or ground fault exists.

    (a) flash
    (b) explode
    (c) evaporate
    (d) melt

15. Fuses consist of a _____ element, and each fuse is enclosed in a tube surrounded by nonconductive filler material.

    (a) limiting
    (b) conductive
    (c) capacitive
    (d) reactive

16. When an overload occurs, the heat rises to a point where it _____ a portion of a fuse's conductive element and stops the flow of electrical current.

    (a) disintegrates
    (b) explodes
    (c) evaporates
    (d) melts

17. When a short circuit or ground fault occurs, the fault current through the fuse can be in the thousands of amperes.

    (a) True
    (b) False

4.5 Circuit Breaker Trip Elements

18. Circuit breakers, like fuses, are designed to be installed in _____ with the circuit wires being protected.

    (a) parallel
    (b) tandem
    (c) series
    (d) alignment

19. Fuses are designed to open using a thermal trip element for an overload condition and an electromagnetic trip element for a short circuit or ground-fault event.

    (a) True
    (b) False

20. The thermal trip device within a circuit breaker responds to _____ due to increased current flow by using a bimetal thermal sensing element.

    (a) current rise
    (b) voltage rise
    (c) nonsinusoidal waves
    (d) temperature rise

21. An electromagnetic trip device within a circuit breaker responds to short circuit and ground-fault events by operating on the _____.

    (a) solenoid principle
    (b) current flow theory
    (c) electron flow theory
    (d) time curve

22. The solenoid in a circuit breaker is designed to have enough electromagnetic force to activate the trip mechanism when the current level reaches about _____ times the rating of the circuit breaker.

    (a) two
    (b) five
    (c) ten
    (d) 20

4.6 Ground-Fault Circuit Interrupters (GFCIs)

23. A ground-fault circuit interrupter (GFCI) is designed to protect people against _____.

    (a) loss of electricity
    (b) electric shock
    (c) fires
    (d) overloads

24. GFCI-protective devices for building wiring include GFCI-circuit breakers or GFCI-type receptacles.

    (a) True
    (b) False

25. There are GFCI devices available for temporary use to protect _____ in places like construction sites.

    (a) tools
    (b) workers
    (c) buildings
    (d) electric supply sources

26. GFCI-protective devices detect the _____ of current between the circuit's phase and neutral wires.

    (a) presence
    (b) loss
    (c) imbalance
    (d) inrush

27. During the normal operation of a typical 2-wire circuit, the current returning to the power source is equal to the current leaving the power source.

    (a) True
    (b) False

28. If the difference between the current leaving and returning through the current transformer of a(n) _____-protective device exceeds 5 mA (± 1 mA), the solid-state circuitry in the _____ device will open the circuit.

    (a) circuit breaker
    (b) fuse
    (c) AFCI
    (d) GFCI

29. A GFCI opens the circuit when the unbalanced current has a value of 6 mA or higher but does not do so when the unbalanced current is less than 4 mA.

    (a) True
    (b) False

4.7 Neutral-to-Case Detection

30. Another function of a GFCI is to detect downstream (load side) improper neutral-to-case connections between the neutral wire and a(n) _____.

    (a) equipment grounding conductor
    (b) second neutral conductor
    (c) phase conductor
    (d) grounding electrode conductor

31. An electronic circuit in the GFCI continuously monitors its load side for neutral-to-case connections. If one is present, the GFCI-protective device's sensors detect it and prevent the GFCI-protected device from being turned on.

    (a) True
    (b) False

Unit 4 | Practice Questions

4.8 Line-to-Neutral Shock Hazard

32. Severe electric shock or _____ can occur if someone touches the phase and neutral wires at the same time, even if the circuit is GFCI protected.

    (a) fires
    (b) ground faults
    (c) death
    (d) power surges

33. If someone touches the phase and neutral wires at the same time, the current between the conductors is balanced within the GFCI and considered a normal load because there is no unbalance between the phase and neutral wires within the GFCI.

    (a) True
    (b) False

4.9 GFCI Fails—Circuit Remains Energized

34. According to a GFCI field test survey report, about 11 percent of the GFCI-circuit breakers protecting indoor receptacles _____.

    (a) exceeded expectations
    (b) failed
    (c) caught fire
    (d) were redesigned

35. When GFCI protection fails, the circuits can remain energized without GFCI protection.

    (a) True
    (b) False

36. There are many reasons GFCI-sensing circuits fail, but the greatest percentage of failures related to damage caused by _____ from lightning and other sources.

    (a) excessive current
    (b) excessive heat
    (c) voltage transients
    (d) arcing

37. Since the UL 943, *Standard for Ground-Fault Circuit-Interrupters* update in 2015, manufacturers are required to produce 15A, 125V, GFCI receptacles that cannot be reset if the GFCI-protected circuit no longer provides ground-fault protection.

    (a) True
    (b) False

4.10 GFCI Test Button

38. Pressing a GFCI's test button is the only way to confirm the sensing circuit within it is operational.

    (a) True
    (b) False

SECTION II

NEC RULES FOR BONDING AND GROUNDING

Introduction to Section II—*NEC* Rules for Bonding and Grounding

Now that you have a better understanding of the "how and why" electricity does what it does, you're prepared to understand the *NEC* rules related to Bonding and Grounding. Section II of this book covers Article 250—Grounding and Bonding with a complete examination and explanation of not only every concept contained within Article 250, but also the rules for bonding throughout the other articles of the *NEC*.

From the pertinent definitions in Article 100 all the way to the bonding of communication systems in Chapter 8, the rules for (and differences between) bonding and grounding are explained in depth, all in an effort to ensure that electrical installations achieve the number one priority; and that is an "effective ground-fault current path" to maintain as safe an installation as possible!

Notes

ARTICLE 90 — INTRODUCTION TO THE *NATIONAL ELECTRICAL CODE*

Introduction to Article 90—Introduction to the *National Electrical Code*

Article 90 opens by saying the *National Electrical Code* (*NEC*/*Code*) is not intended as a design specification or instruction manual. It has one purpose only, and that is the "practical safeguarding of persons and property from hazards arising from the use of electricity." That does not necessarily mean the installation will be efficient, convenient, or able to accommodate future expansion; just safe. The necessity of carefully studying the *Code* rules cannot be overemphasized, and the step-by-step explanatory design of a textbook such as this is designed to help in that undertaking. Understanding where to find the requirements in the *NEC* that apply to the installation is invaluable. Rules in several different articles often apply to even a simple installation.

Article 90 then goes on to describe the scope and arrangement of the *NEC*. The balance of it provides the reader with information essential to understanding the *Code* rules.

Most electrical installations require an understanding of the first four chapters of the *NEC* (which apply generally) and have a working knowledge of the Chapter 9 tables. That understanding begins with this article. Chapters 5, 6, and 7 make up a large portion of the *Code* book, but they apply to special occupancies, special equipment, or special conditions. They build on, modify, or amend the rules in the first four chapters. Chapter 8 contains the requirements for communications systems, such as radio and television equipment, satellite receivers, antenna systems, twisted pair conductors, and coaxial cable wiring. Communications systems are not subject to the general requirements of Chapters 1 through 4, or the special requirements of Chapters 5 through 7, unless there is a specific reference to a rule in the previous chapters.

90.1 Purpose of the *NEC*

(A) Practical Safeguarding. The purpose of the *National Electrical Code* is to ensure electrical systems are installed in a manner that protects people and property by minimizing the risks associated with the use of electricity. The *NEC* is not a design specification standard nor is it an instruction manual for the untrained and unqualified. ▶Figure 90–1

> **Author's Comment:**
> ▸ The *Code* is intended to be used by those who are skilled and knowledgeable in electrical theory, electrical systems, building and electrical construction, and the installation and operation of electrical equipment.

The purpose of the *NEC* is the practical safeguarding of persons and property from hazards arising from the use of electricity. This *Code* is not intended as a design specification or an instruction manual for untrained persons.

▶Figure 90–1

90.2 | Introduction to the National Electrical Code

(B) Adequacy. The *NEC* contains the requirements considered necessary for a safe electrical installation. If one is installed in compliance with the *Code*, it is considered essentially free from electrical hazards.

The requirements contained in the *NEC* are not intended to ensure an electrical installation will be efficient, convenient, adequate for good service, or suitable for future expansion. ▶Figure 90–2

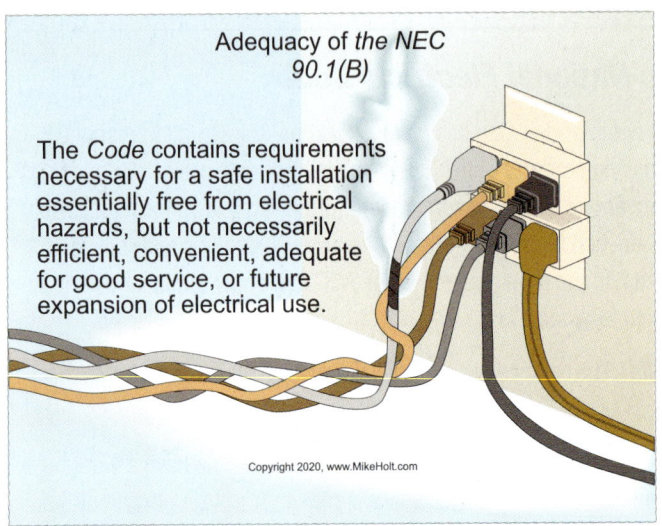

▶Figure 90–2

Author's Comment:

▸ Electrical energy management, equipment maintenance, power quality, or suitability for future loads are not issues within the scope of the *Code*.

Note: Hazards often occur because the initial wiring did not provide for increases in the use of electricity and therefore wiring systems become overloaded. ▶Figure 90–3

Author's Comment:

▸ The *NEC* does not require electrical systems to be designed or installed to accommodate future loads. However, the electrical designer (typically an electrical engineer) is concerned with not only ensuring electrical safety (*Code* compliance), but also with ensuring the electrical system meets the customers' needs; both for today and in the near future. To satisfy their needs, electrical systems are often designed and installed above the minimum requirements contained in the *NEC*.

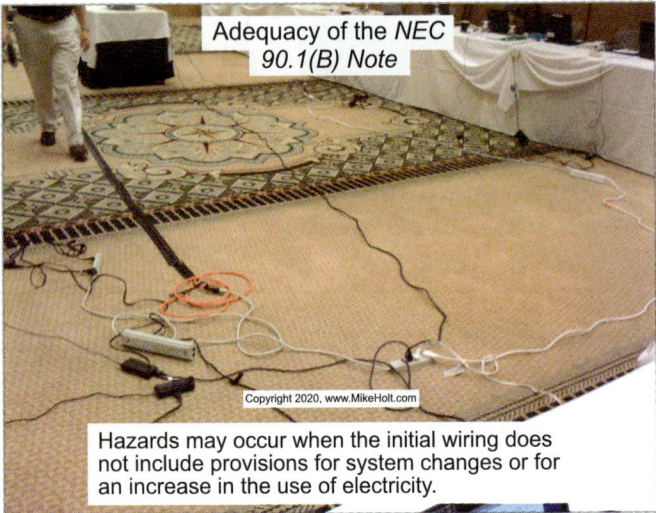

▶Figure 90–3

(C) Relation to International Standards. The requirements of the *NEC* address the fundamental safety principles contained in the International Electrotechnical Commission (IEC) Standard, including protection against electric shock, adverse thermal effects, overcurrent, fault currents, and overvoltage. ▶Figure 90–4

▶Figure 90–4

90.2 Scope of the NEC

(A) What is Covered by the NEC. The *NEC* covers the installation and removal of electrical conductors, equipment, and raceways; signaling and communications conductors, equipment, and raceways; and optical fiber cables and raceways for the following: ▶Figure 90–5

Introduction to the *National Electrical Code* | 90.2

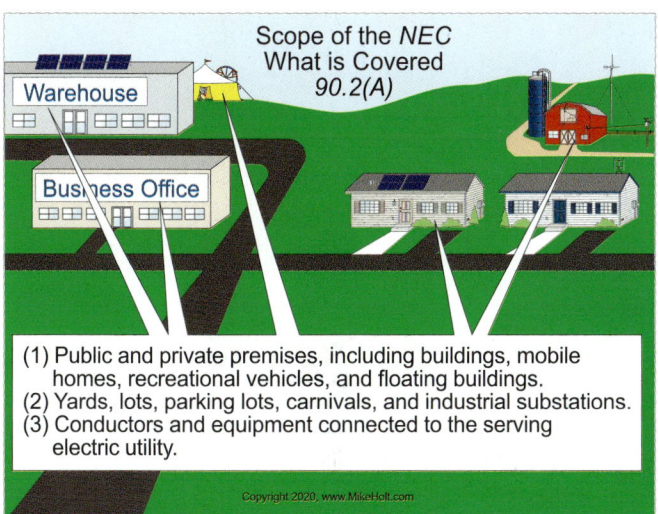
▶Figure 90-5

▶Figure 90-7

(1) Public and private premises including buildings, mobile homes, recreational vehicles, and floating buildings.

(2) Yards, lots, parking lots, carnivals, and industrial substations.

(3) Conductors and equipment connected to the serving electric utility.

(4) Installations used by a serving electric utility such as office buildings, warehouses, garages, machine shops, recreational buildings, and other electric utility buildings that are not an integral part of a utility's generating plant, substation, or control center. ▶Figure 90-6

Author's Comment:

▸ The new item in the scope, 90.2(A)(5), appears to include the power cable between the pedestal and the boat in the scope of the *NEC*, but there are no specific rules in Article 555 covering that power-supply cord.

▸ The text in 555.35(B) requires leakage detection equipment to detect leakage current from boats and applies to the load side of the supplying receptacle.

(6) Installations used to export electric power from vehicles to premises wiring or for bidirectional current flow. ▶Figure 90-8

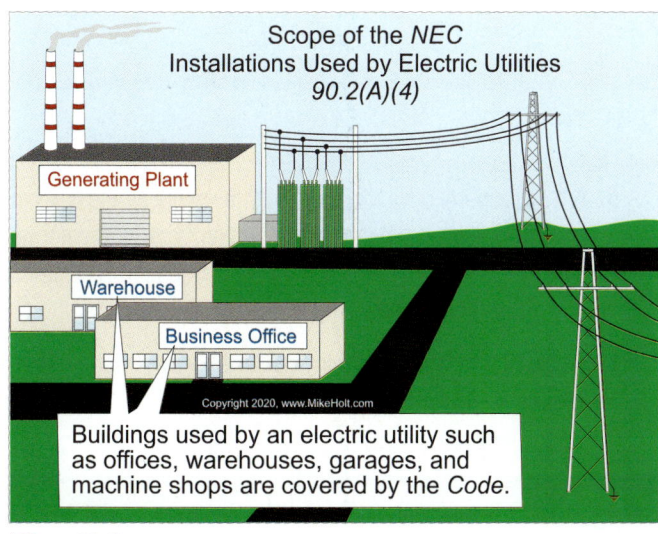
▶Figure 90-6

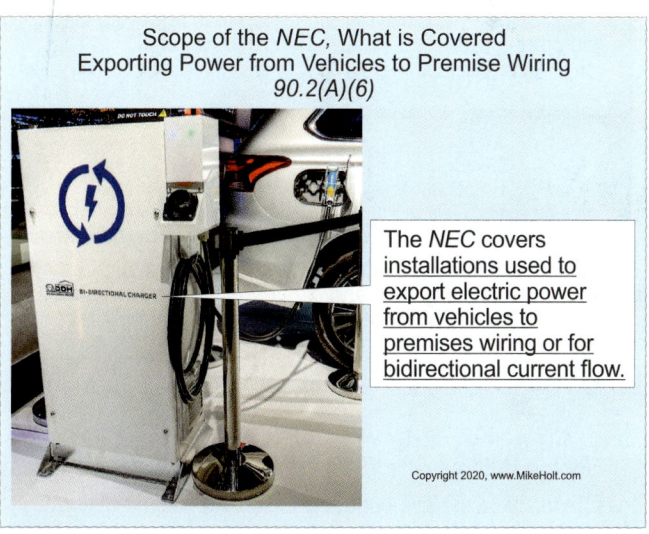
▶Figure 90-8

(5) Installations supplying shore power to watercraft in marinas and boatyards, including monitoring of leakage current. ▶Figure 90-7

90.3 | Introduction to the *National Electrical Code*

Author's Comment:

▸ The battery power supply of an electrical vehicle can be used "bidirectionally" which means it can be used as a backup or alternate power source to supply premises wiring circuits in the event of a power failure. The rules for this application can be found in Article 625.

(B) What is not Covered by the *NEC*. The *Code* does not apply to the installation of electrical or communications systems for:

(1) Transportation Vehicles. The *NEC* does not apply to installations in ships and watercraft other than floating buildings, and automotive vehicles other than mobile homes and recreational vehicles.

(2) Mining Equipment. The *Code* does not apply to installations underground in mines, and in self-propelled mobile surface mining machinery and its attendant electrical trailing cables.

(3) Railways. The *NEC* does not apply to railway power, signaling, energy storage, and communications wiring.

(4) Communications Utilities. The *Code* does not apply to installations under the exclusive control of the communications utility located in building spaces used exclusively for these purposes or located outdoors. ▸Figure 90–9

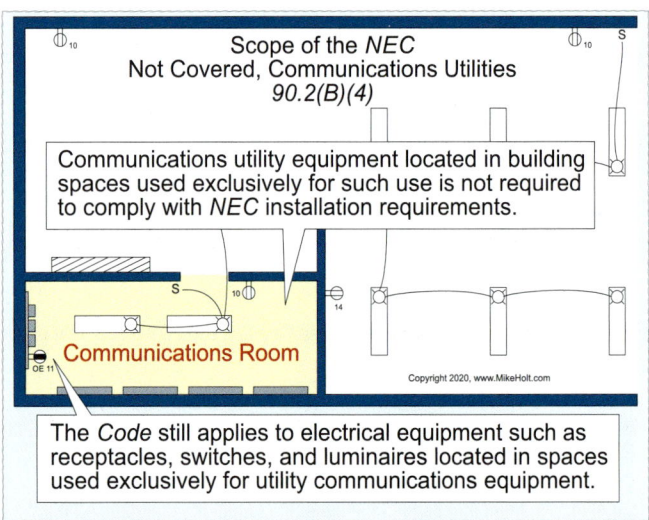
▸Figure 90–9

(5) Electric Utilities. The *NEC* does not apply to electrical installations under the exclusive control of a serving electric utility where such installations: ▸Figure 90–10

a. Consist of service drops or service laterals and associated metering, or ▸Figure 90–11

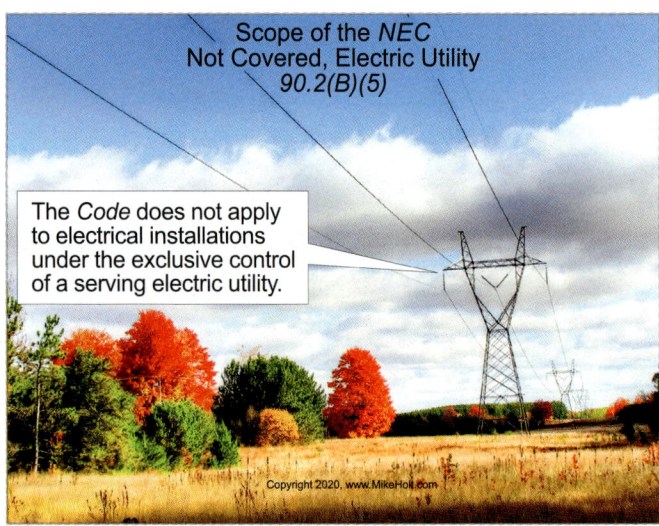
▸Figure 90–10

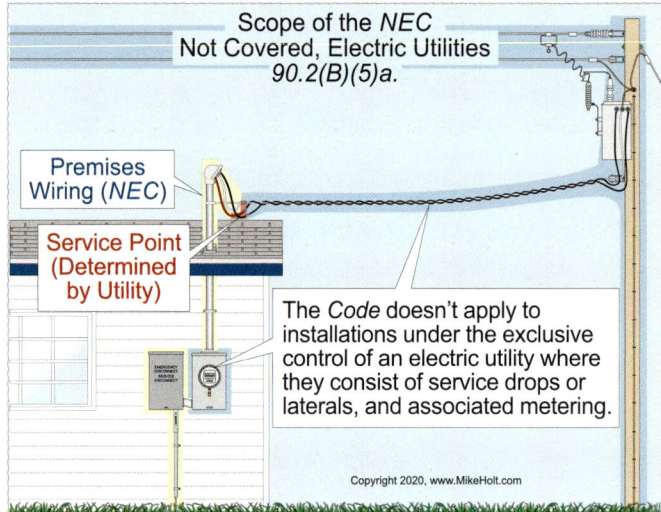
▸Figure 90–11

b. Are on property owned or leased by the utility for the purpose of communications, metering, generation, control, transformation, transmission, energy storage, or distribution of electrical energy, or ▸Figure 90–12

c. Are located in legally established easements or rights-of-way ▸Figure 90–13

90.3 *Code* Arrangement

General Requirements. The *Code* is divided into an introduction and nine chapters followed by informative annexes.

Chapters 1, 2, 3, and 4 are general conditions. ▸Figure 90–14

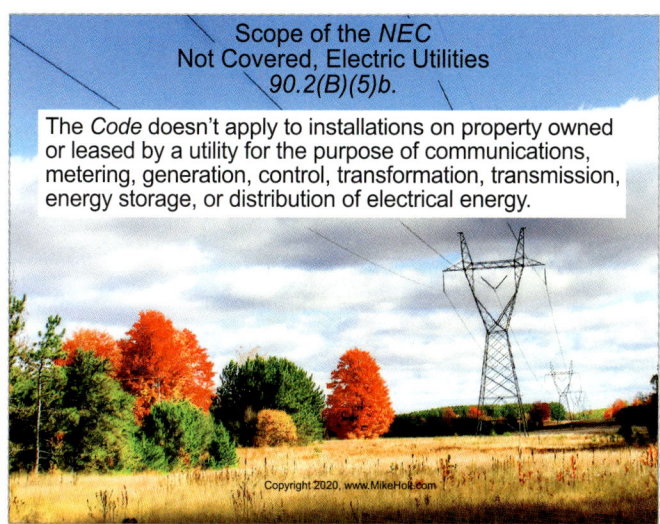
▶ Figure 90-12

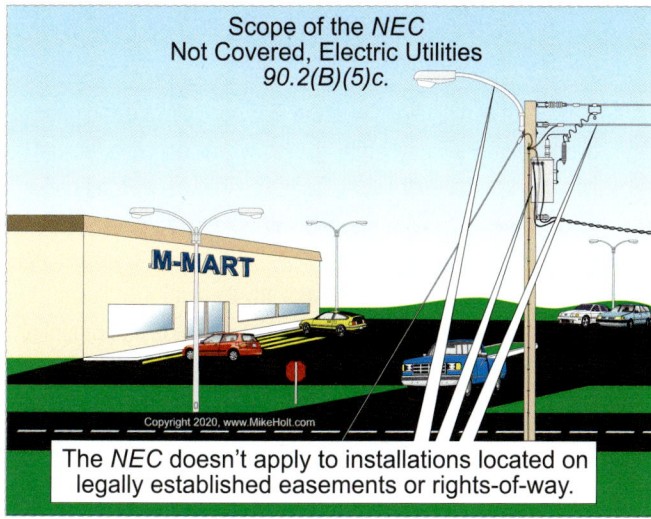
▶ Figure 90-13

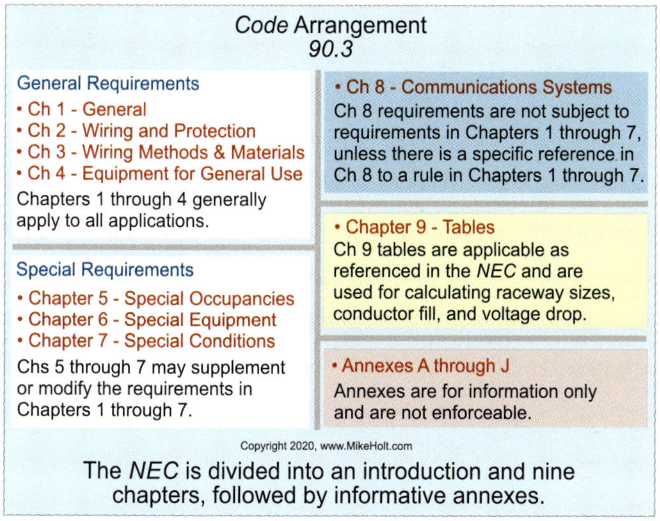

The requirements contained in Chapters 5, 6, and 7 apply to special occupancies, special equipment, or other special conditions, which may supplement or modify the requirements contained in Chapters 1 through 7; but not Chapter 8.

Chapter 8 contains the requirements for communications systems (twisted wire, antennas, and coaxial cable) which are not subject to the general requirements of Chapters 1 through 4, or the special requirements of Chapters 5 through 7, unless a specific reference in Chapter 8 is made to a rule in Chapters 1 through 7.

Chapter 9 consists of tables applicable as referenced in the *NEC*. The tables are used to calculate raceway sizing, conductor fill, the radius of raceway bends, and conductor voltage drop.

Annexes are not part of the requirements of the *Code* but are included for informational purposes. There are ten annexes:

- ▶ Annex A. Product Safety Standards
- ▶ Annex B. Application Information for Ampacity Calculation
- ▶ Annex C. Raceway Fill Tables for Conductors and Fixture Wires of the Same Size
- ▶ Annex D. Examples
- ▶ Annex E. Types of Construction
- ▶ Annex F. Critical Operations Power Systems (COPS)
- ▶ Annex G. Supervisory Control and Data Acquisition (SCADA)
- ▶ Annex H. Administration and Enforcement
- ▶ Annex I. Recommended Tightening Torques
- ▶ Annex J. ADA Standards for Accessible Design

90.4 Enforcement

The *NEC* is intended to be suitable for enforcement by governmental bodies that exercise legal jurisdiction over electrical installations for power, lighting, signaling circuits, and communications systems such as: ▶ Figure 90-15

Signaling circuits include:

- ▶ Article 725. Remote-Control, Signaling, and Power-Limited Circuits
- ▶ Article 760. Fire Alarm Systems
- ▶ Article 770. Optical Fiber Cables

Communications systems which include:

- ▶ Article 810. Radio and Television Equipment (Satellite Antenna)
- ▶ Article 820. Community Antenna Television and Radio Distribution Systems (Coaxial Cable)

▶ Figure 90-14

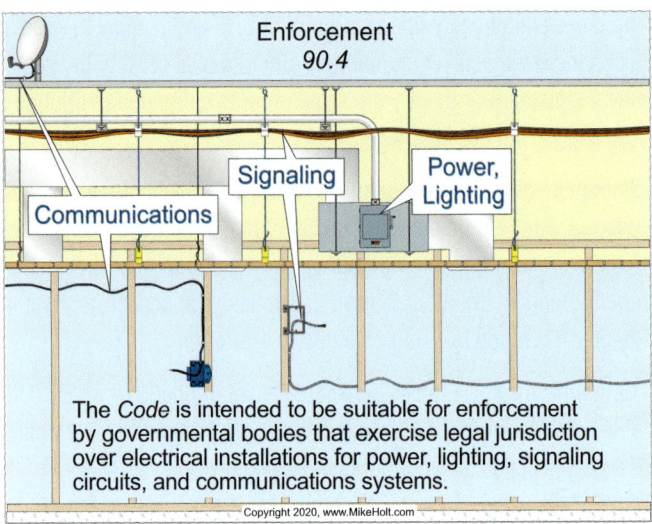
▶Figure 90–15

Author's Comment:

▸ Once adopted (in part, wholly, or amended), the *National Electrical Code* becomes statutory law for the adopting jurisdiction and is thereby considered a legal document.

Enforcement. The enforcement of the *NEC* is the responsibility of the authority having jurisdiction, who is responsible for interpreting requirements, approving equipment and materials, waiving *Code* requirements, and ensuring equipment is installed in accordance with listing instructions. ▶Figure 90–16

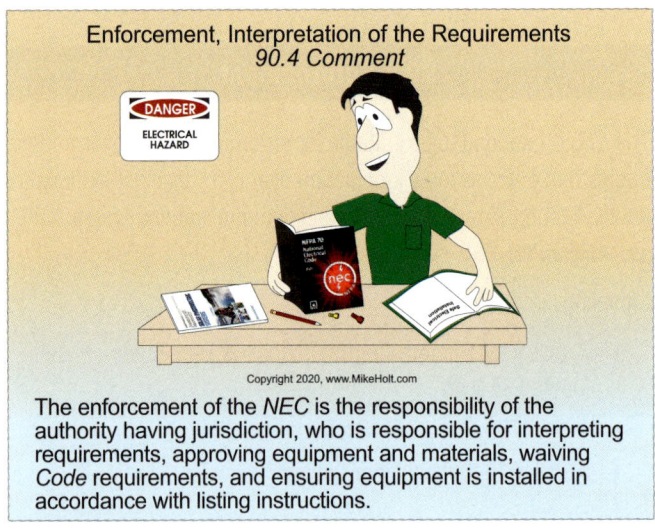
▶Figure 90–16

Author's Comment:

▸ "Authority Having Jurisdiction (AHJ)" is defined in Article 100 as the organization, office, or individual responsible for approving equipment, materials, an installation, or a procedure. See 90.4 and 90.7 for more information.

▸ "Approved" is defined in Article 100 as acceptable to the authority having jurisdiction; usually the electrical inspector.

Interpretation. The authority having jurisdiction is responsible for interpreting the *NEC*.

Author's Comment:

▸ The authority having jurisdiction's decisions must be based on a specific *Code* requirement. If an installation is rejected, the AHJ is legally responsible for informing the installer of the specific *NEC* rule that was violated.

▸ The art of getting along with the AHJ consists of doing good work and knowing what the *Code* says (as opposed to what you think it says). It is also useful to know how to choose your battles when the inevitable disagreement does occur.

Approval of Equipment and Materials. Only the authority having jurisdiction has the authority to approve the installation of equipment and materials. ▶Figure 90–17

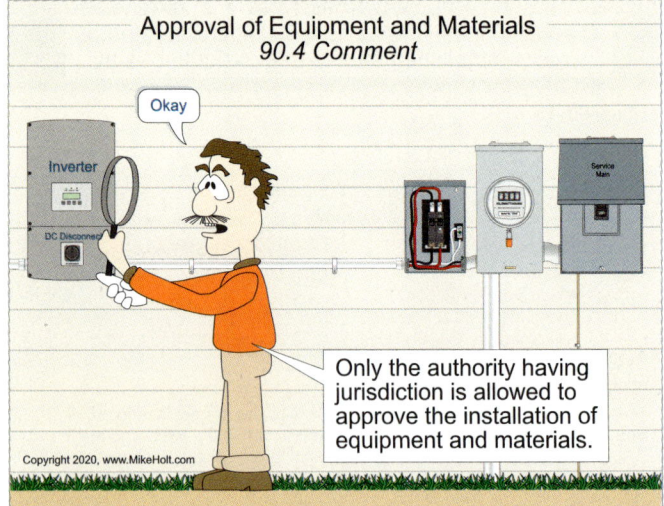
▶Figure 90–17

Author's Comment:

▸ Typically, the AHJ will approve equipment listed by a product testing organization such as Underwriters Laboratories, Inc. (UL). The *NEC* does not require all equipment to be listed, but many state and local authorities having jurisdictions do. See 90.7, 110.2, and 110.3 and the definitions for "Approved," "Identified," "Labeled," and "Listed" in Article 100.

▸ According to the *Code*, the authority having jurisdiction determines the approval of equipment. This means he or she can reject an installation of listed equipment and can approve the use of unlisted equipment. Given our highly litigious society, approval of unlisted equipment is becoming increasingly difficult to obtain.

Approval of Alternate Means. By special permission, the authority having jurisdiction may approve alternate methods where it is assured equivalent safety can be achieved and maintained.

Author's Comment:

▸ "Special Permission" is defined in Article 100 as the written consent of the AHJ.

Waiver of Product Requirements. If the *Code* requires products, constructions, or materials that are not yet available at the time the *NEC* is adopted, the authority having jurisdiction can allow products that were acceptable in the previous *Code* to continue to be used.

Author's Comment:

▸ Sometimes it takes years for testing laboratories to establish product standards for new *NEC* product requirements; then it takes time before manufacturers can design, manufacture, and distribute those products to the marketplace.

90.5 Mandatory Requirements and Explanatory Material

(A) Mandatory Requirements. The words "shall" or "shall not" indicate a mandatory requirement.

Author's Comment:

▸ For greater ease in reading this textbook, we will use the word "must" instead of "shall."

(B) Permissive Requirements. When the *Code* uses "shall be permitted" it means the action is permitted, but not required. Permissive rules are often contained in exceptions to the general requirement.

Author's Comment:

▸ For greater ease in reading, the phrase "shall be permitted" (as used in the *NEC)*, has been replaced in this textbook with the phrase "is permitted" or "are permitted."

(C) Explanatory Material. References to other standards or information related to a *Code* rule are included in the form of "Informational Notes." Such notes are for informational purposes only and are not enforceable as an *NEC* requirement.

For example, Informational Note No. 3 in 210.19(A)(1) recommends that the voltage drop of a circuit not exceed 3 percent; this is a recommendation—not a *Code* requirement.

Author's Comment:

▸ For convenience and ease in reading this textbook, "Informational Notes" will simply be identified as "Note."

Caution

⚡ Informational notes are not enforceable but notes to tables are. Within this textbook, we will call notes contained in a table a "Table Note."

(D) Informative Annexes. Informative annexes contained in the back of the *Code* book are for information only and are not enforceable as requirements of the *NEC*.

90.7 Examination of Equipment for Product Safety

Product evaluation for *Code* compliance, approval, and safety is typically performed by a nationally recognized testing laboratory in accordance with the listing standards.

Except to detect alterations or damage, listed factory-installed internal wiring of equipment that has been processed by a qualified testing laboratory does not need to be inspected for *NEC* compliance at the time of installation. ▸Figure 90-18

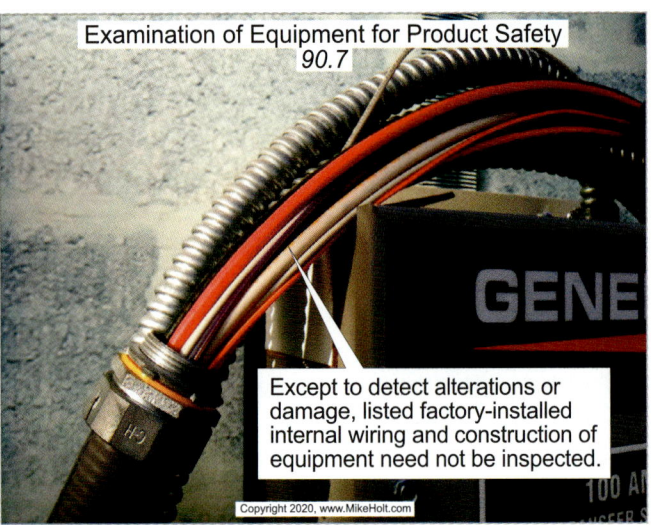

▶Figure 90-18

Note 1: The requirements contained in Article 300 do not apply to the integral parts of electrical equipment, see 110.3(B).

Note 2: "Listed" is defined in Article 100 as equipment or materials included in a list published by a testing laboratory acceptable to the authority having jurisdiction. The listing organization must periodically inspect the production of listed equipment or material to ensure it meets appropriate designated standards and is suitable for a specified purpose.

ARTICLE 90 PRACTICE QUESTIONS

Please use the 2020 *Code* book to answer the following questions.

Article 90—Introduction to the *National Electrical Code*

1. The *NEC* is _____.

   (a) intended to be a design manual
   (b) meant to be used as an instruction guide for untrained persons
   (c) for the practical safeguarding of persons and property
   (d) published by the Bureau of Standards

2. Compliance with the *Code* and proper maintenance result in an installation that is essentially _____.

   (a) free from hazards
   (b) not efficient or convenient
   (c) not adequate for good service or future expansion
   (d) all of these

3. Installations used to export electric power from vehicles to premises wiring or for _____ current flow are covered by the *NEC*.

   (a) emergency
   (b) primary
   (c) bidirectional
   (d) secondary

4. The *NEC* does apply to installations in _____.

   (a) floating buildings
   (b) mobile homes
   (c) recreational vehicles
   (d) all of these

5. The *Code* covers underground mine installations and self-propelled mobile surface mining machinery and its attendant electrical trailing cable.

   (a) True
   (b) False

6. Installations of communications equipment that are under the exclusive control of communications utilities and located outdoors or in building spaces used exclusively for such installations _____ covered by the *NEC*.

   (a) are
   (b) are sometimes
   (c) are not
   (d) may be

7. Chapters 1 through 4 of the *NEC* apply _____.

   (a) generally to all electrical installations
   (b) only to special occupancies and conditions
   (c) only to special equipment and material
   (d) all of these

8. Chapters 5, 6, and 7 of the *NEC* apply to _____.

   (a) special occupancies
   (b) special equipment
   (c) special conditions
   (d) all of these

9. Installations shall comply with the material located in the *NEC* Annexes because they are part of the requirements of the *Code*.

   (a) True
   (b) False

Article 90 | Practice Questions

10. The _____ has the responsibility for deciding on the approval of equipment and materials.

    (a) manufacturer
    (b) authority having jurisdiction
    (c) testing agency
    (d) the owner of the premises

11. If the *NEC* requires new products that are not yet available at the time a new edition is adopted, the _____ may permit the use of the products that comply with the most recent previous edition of the *Code* adopted by that jurisdiction.

    (a) electrical engineer
    (b) master electrician
    (c) authority having jurisdiction
    (d) permit holder

12. When the *Code* uses "_____," it means the identified actions are allowed but not required, and they may be options or alternative methods.

    (a) shall
    (b) shall not
    (c) shall be permitted
    (d) shall or shall not

13. Nonmandatory Informative Annexes contained in the back of the *Code* book are _____.

    (a) for information only
    (b) not enforceable as a requirement of the *Code*
    (c) enforceable as a requirement of the *Code*
    (d) for information only and not enforceable as a requirement of the *Code*

CHAPTER 1

GENERAL RULES

Introduction to Chapter 1—General Rules

Before you can make sense of the *NEC*, you must become familiar with its general rules, concepts, definitions, and requirements. Chapter 1 consists of two topics; Article 100 which provides definitions that help ensure consistency when *Code*-related matters are discussed, and Article 110 which supplies the general requirements needed to correctly apply the *NEC*.

After gaining an understanding of Chapter 1, some of the *Code* requirements that might be confusing to many, will become increasingly clear to you. *NEC* requirements will make more sense because you will have the foundation from which to build upon your comprehension and application of the rules.

▶ **Article 100—Definitions.** Article 100 is organized into three parts. Part I contains the definitions of terms used throughout the *Code* for systems that operate at 1,000V, nominal, or less. The ones in Part II apply to systems operating at over 1,000V, nominal, and are not within the scope of this textbook. Part III contains definitions applicable to the "Hazardous (Classified) Locations" covered in Chapter 5 of the *NEC*.

The definitions here only cover terms used in more than one article, but not standard ones such as volt, voltage drop, ampere, impedance, and resistance. If the *NEC* does not define a term, then a dictionary or building code acceptable to the authority having jurisdiction should be consulted.

Definitions are sometimes located at the beginning of an article. When this occurs, those terms only apply to that given article. There is uniformity in the location of the definitions specific to an article in that the article number will be followed by ".2." For example, definitions specific to solar photovoltaic (PV) systems are found in 690.2.

▶ **Article 110—Requirements for Electrical Installations.** This article contains the general requirements applicable to all electrical installations.

Notes

ARTICLE 100 DEFINITIONS

Introduction to Article 100—Definitions

Have you ever had a conversation with someone only to discover that what you said and what he or she heard were completely different? This often happens when people have different definitions or interpretations of the words being used and is why the definitions of key *NEC* terms are located at the beginning of the *Code* (Article 100), or at the beginning of each article. If we can all agree on important definitions, then we speak the same language and avoid misunderstandings. Words taken out of context have created more than their fair share of problems. Because the *NEC* exists to protect people and property, it is very important for you to be able to convey and comprehend the language used. Review and study Article 100 until you are confident you know the definitions presented.

100 Definitions

Scope. This article contains definitions essential to the application of this *Code*; it does not include general or technical terms from other codes and standards. In general, only those used in two or more articles are defined in Article 100.

Definitions are also found in the XXX.2 sections of other articles.

Part I of this article contains definitions intended to apply wherever the terms are used throughout the *NEC*.

Accessible (as applied to equipment). Capable of being reached for operation, renewal, and inspection.

Appliance [Article 422]. Electrical equipment, other than industrial equipment, built in standardized sizes. Examples of appliances are ranges, ovens, cooktops, refrigerators, drinking water coolers, and beverage dispensers.

Approved. Acceptable to the authority having jurisdiction; usually the electrical inspector. ▶Figure 100–1

> **Author's Comment:**
>
> ▶ Product listing does not mean the product is approved, but it can be a basis for approval. See 90.4, 90.7, 110.2, and the definitions in this article for "Authority Having Jurisdiction," "Identified," "Labeled," and "Listed."

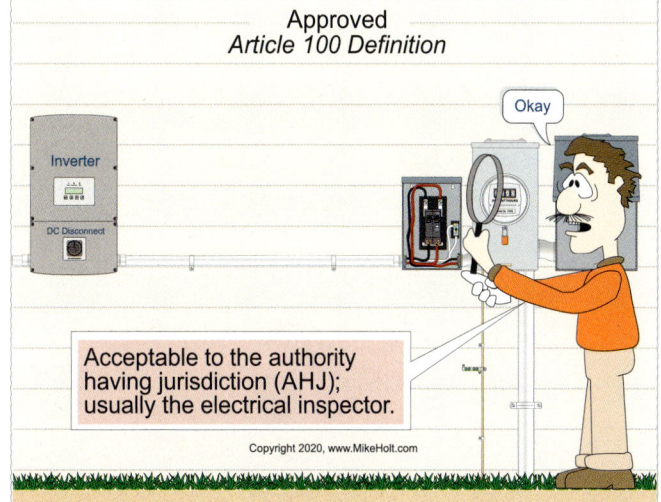

▶Figure 100–1

Attachment Fitting. A device that, by insertion into a locking support and mounting receptacle, establishes a connection between the conductors of the attached utilization equipment and the branch-circuit conductors connected to the locking support and mounting receptacle.

Note: An attachment fitting is different than an attachment plug, because no cord is associated with the fitting. An attachment fitting in combination with a locking support and mounting receptacle secures the associated utilization equipment in place and supports its weight.

100 | Definitions

Attachment Plug (Plug Cap), (Plug). A wiring device at the end of a flexible cord intended to be inserted into a receptacle in order to make an electrical connection. ▶Figure 100–2

> **Author's Comment:**
>
> ▶ Either the term "Bonding Conductor" or "Bonding Jumper" can be used. They can be short or several feet long and are typically used to ensure electrical conductivity between two metal objects.

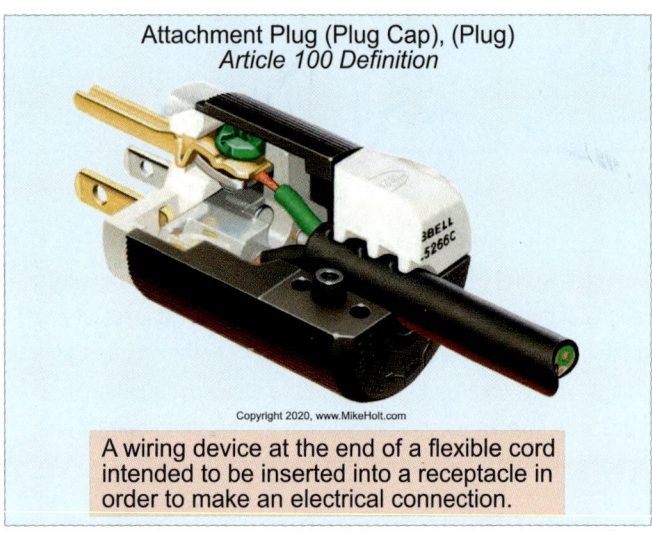

▶Figure 100–2

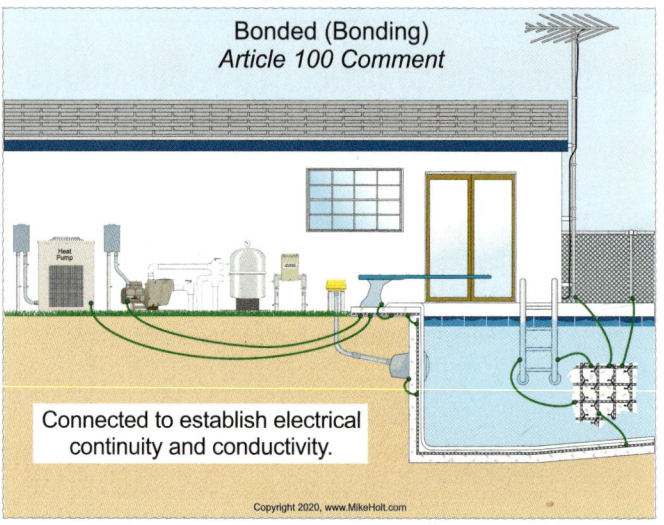

▶Figure 100–4

Bonded (Bonding). Connected to establish electrical continuity and conductivity. ▶Figure 100–3 and ▶Figure 100–4

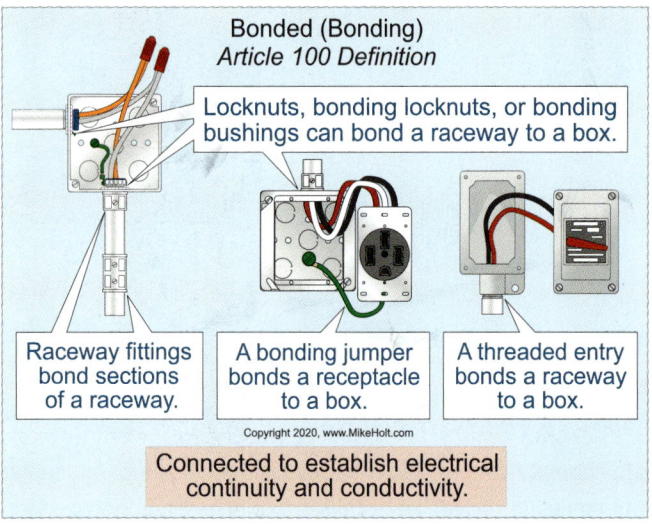

▶Figure 100–3

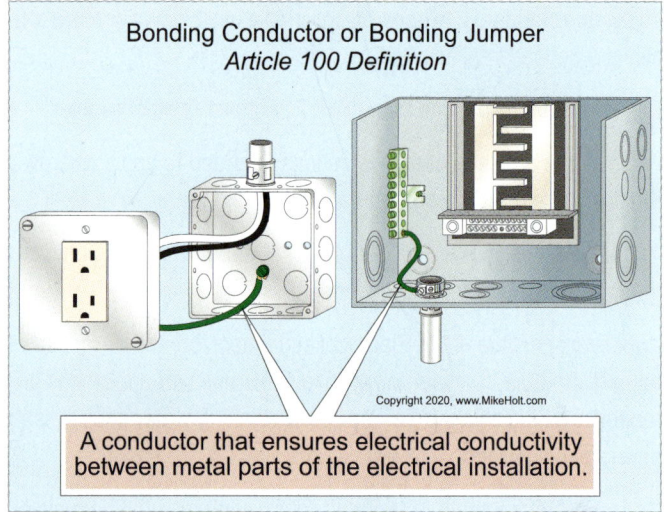

▶Figure 100–5

Bonding Conductor or Bonding Jumper. A conductor that ensures electrical conductivity between metal parts of the electrical installation. ▶Figure 100–5

Bonding Jumper, Equipment. A connection between two or more portions of the equipment grounding conductor. ▶Figure 100–6

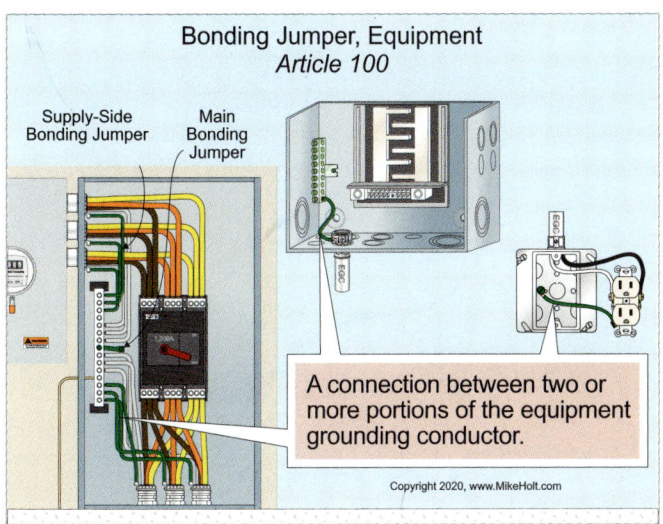
▶Figure 100-6

Author's Comment:

▶ Equipment bonding jumpers are used where the mechanical or electrical path for the effective ground-fault current path would be compromised or interrupted. ▶Figure 100-7

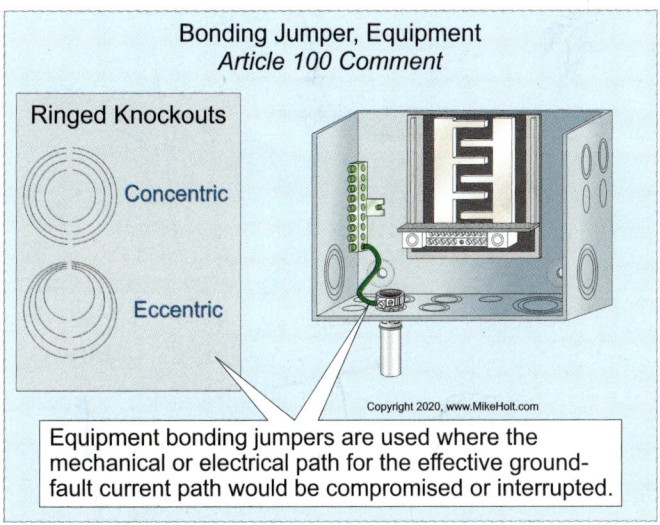
▶Figure 100-7

Bonding Jumper, Main. A conductor, screw, or strap used to connect the circuit equipment grounding conductor to the neutral conductor or to the supply-side bonding jumper at the service equipment in accordance with 250.24(B). ▶Figure 100-8 and ▶Figure 100-9

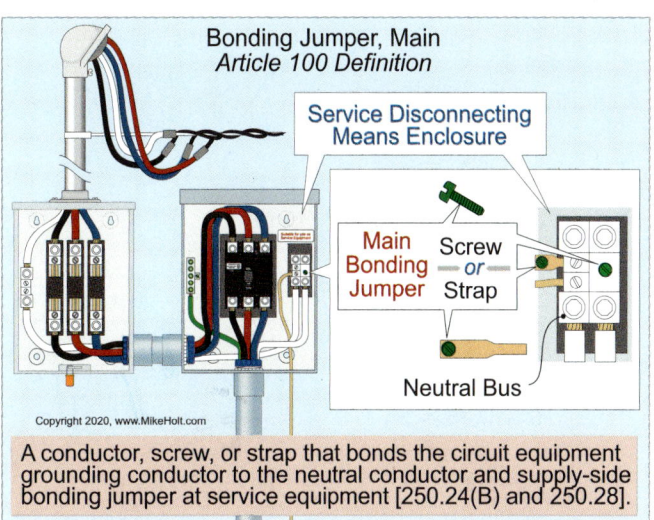
▶Figure 100-8

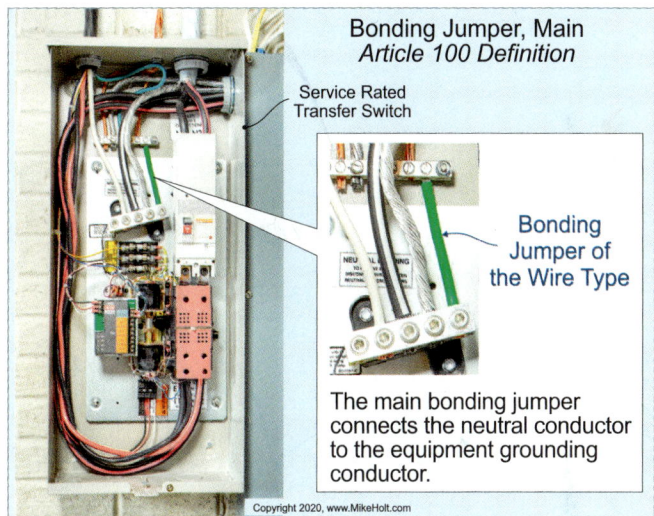
▶Figure 100-9

Bonding Jumper, Supply-Side. The conductor installed on the supply side of a service or separately derived system that ensures electrical conductivity between metal parts. ▶Figure 100-10, ▶Figure 100-11, and ▶Figure 100-12

Bonding Jumper, System. The connection between the neutral conductor or grounded-phase conductor and the supply-side bonding jumper or equipment grounding conductor, or both, at a transformer. ▶Figure 100-13

Building. A structure that stands alone or is separated from adjoining structures by fire walls. ▶Figure 100-14

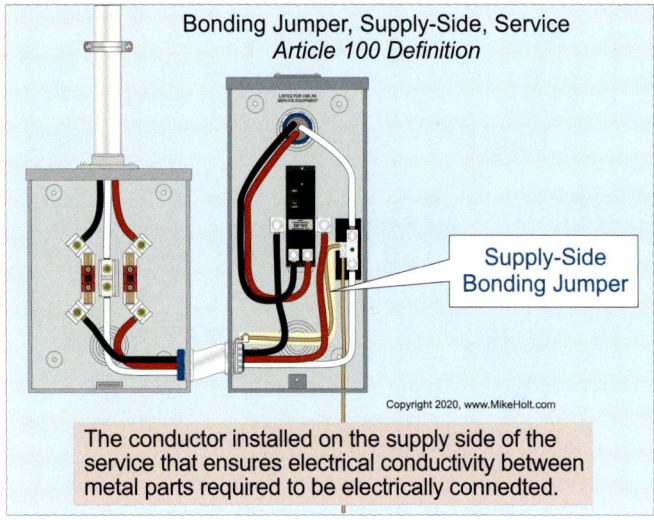
▶Figure 100–10

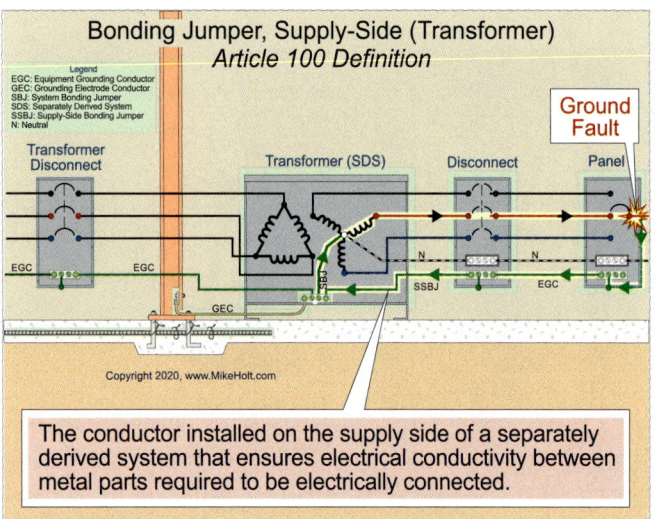
▶Figure 100–11

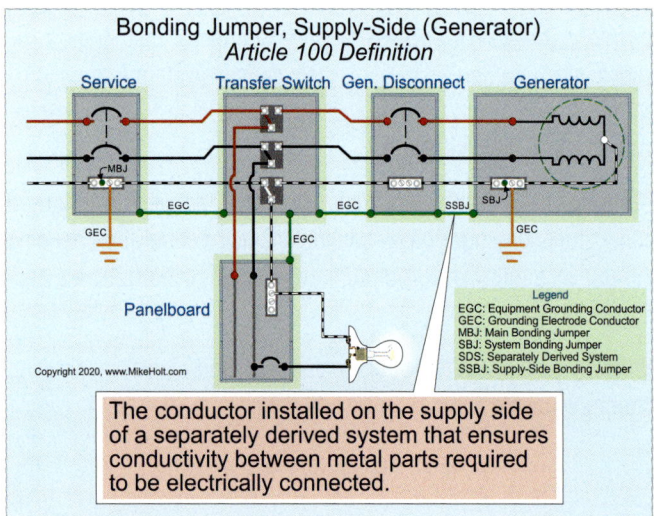
▶Figure 100–12

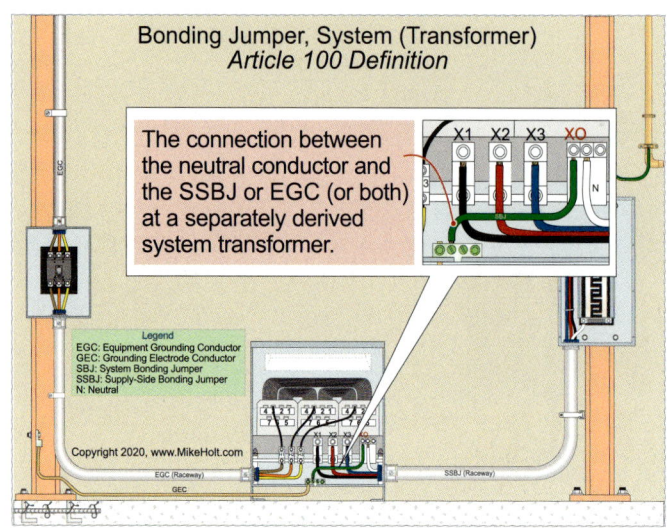
▶Figure 100–13

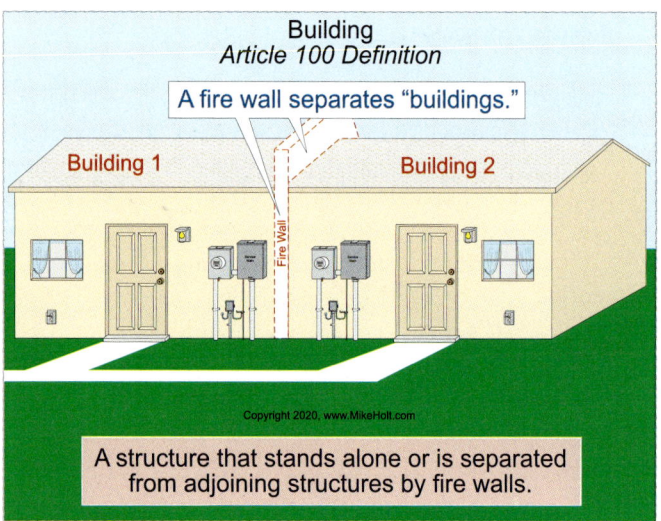
▶Figure 100–14

Cabinet. A surface-mounted or flush-mounted enclosure provided with a frame in which a door can be hung. ▶Figure 100–15

Cable, Coaxial. A cylindrical assembly containing a conductor centered inside a metallic shield, separated by a dielectric material, and covered by an insulating jacket. ▶Figure 100–16

Concealed. Rendered inaccessible by the structure or finish of the building. ▶Figure 100–17

Note: Conductors in a concealed raceway are considered concealed, even though they may be made accessible by withdrawing them from the raceway.

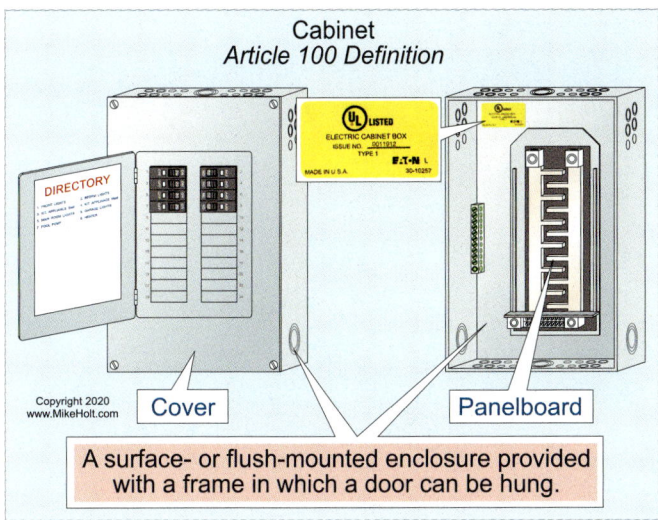

▶Figure 100-15

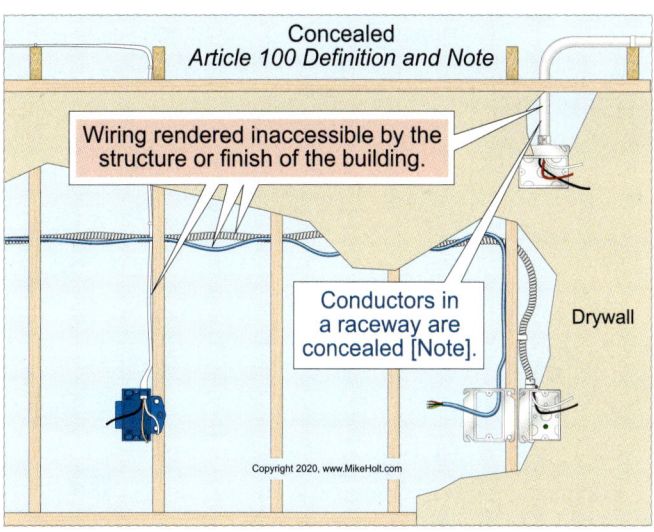

▶Figure 100-17

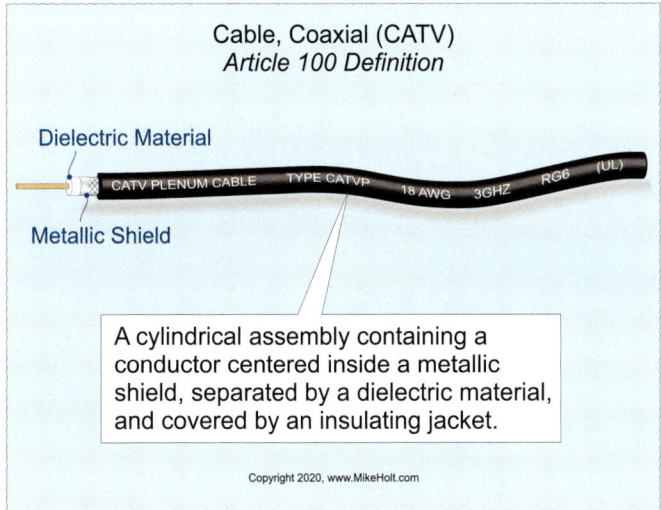

▶Figure 100-16

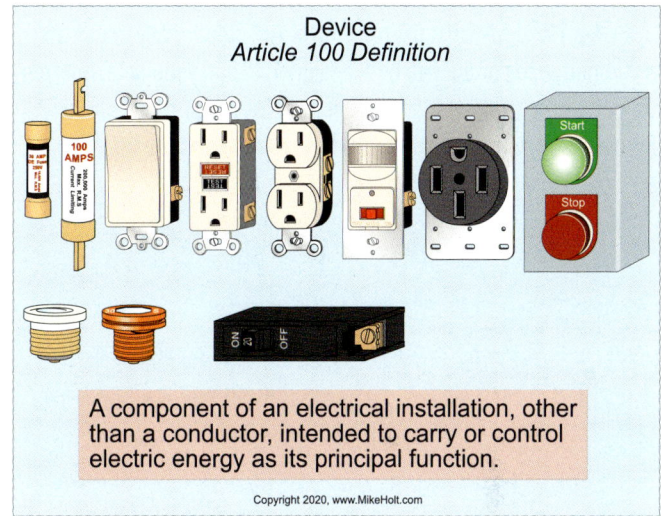

▶Figure 100-18

Author's Comment:

▸ Wiring behind panels designed to allow access, such as removable ceiling tile and wiring in accessible attics, is not considered concealed; it is considered exposed. See the definition of "Exposed (as applied to wiring methods)."

Device. A component of an electrical installation, other than a conductor, intended to carry or control electric energy as its principal function. ▶Figure 100-18

Author's Comment:

▸ Devices generally do not consume electric energy and include receptacles, switches, illuminated switches, circuit breakers, fuses, time clocks, controllers, attachment plugs, and so forth. Some (such as illuminated switches, contactors, or relays) consume very small amounts of energy and are still classified as a device based on their primary function.

Disconnecting Means (Disconnect). A device that disconnects the circuit conductors from their power source. Examples include switches, attachment plugs, and circuit breakers. ▶Figure 100-19

100 | Definitions

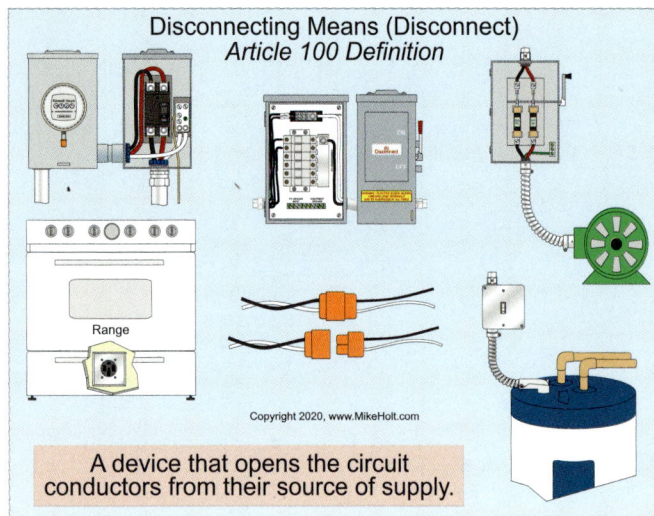
▶Figure 100–19

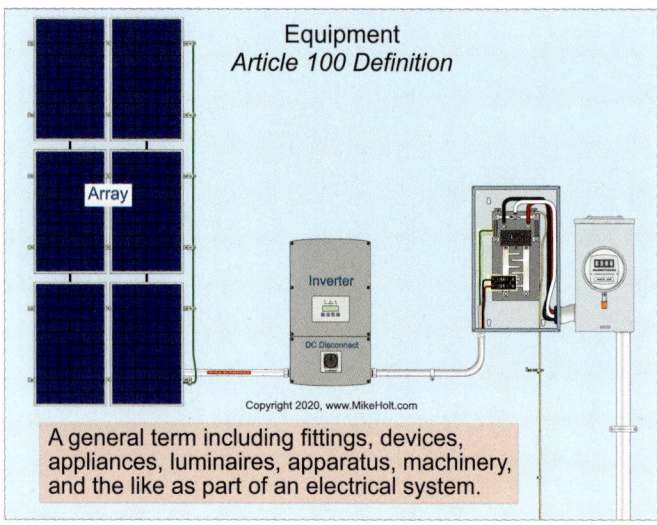
▶Figure 100–21

Effective Ground-Fault Current Path. An intentionally constructed low-impedance conductive path designed to carry fault current from the point of a ground fault to the source for the purpose of opening the circuit overcurrent protective device. ▶Figure 100–20

Equipotential Plane. Accessible conductive parts bonded together to reduce voltage gradients in a designated area. ▶Figure 100–22

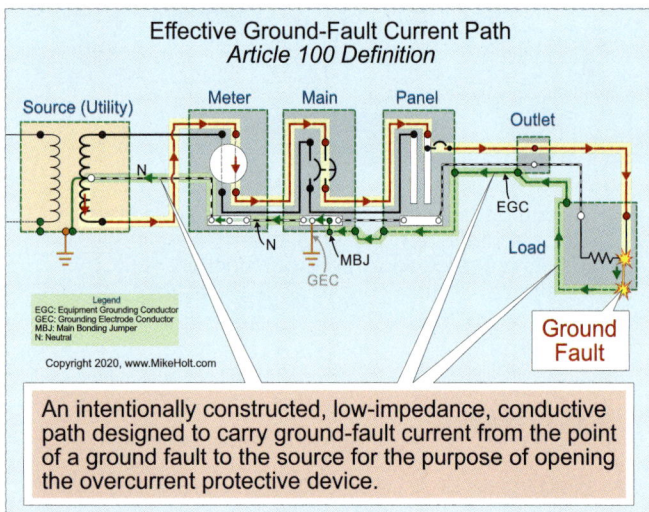
▶Figure 100–20

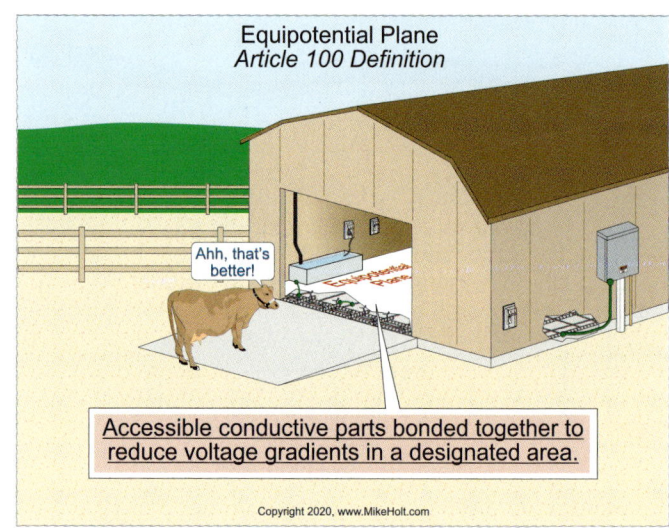
▶Figure 100–22

Author's Comment:

▸ The effective ground-fault current path is intended to help remove dangerous voltage from a ground fault by opening the circuit overcurrent protective device.

Equipment. A general term including fittings, devices, appliances, luminaires, machinery, and the like as part of (or in connection with) an electrical installation. ▶Figure 100–21

Author's Comment:

▸ See 547.10 for equipotential bonding in agricultural facilities, 680.26 for pools, 680.42 for outdoor spas and hot tubs, 680.43 for indoor spas and hot tubs, and 680.74 for hydromassage bathtubs.

Exposed (as applied to live parts). Capable of being accidentally touched or approached nearer than a safe distance. ▶Figure 100–23

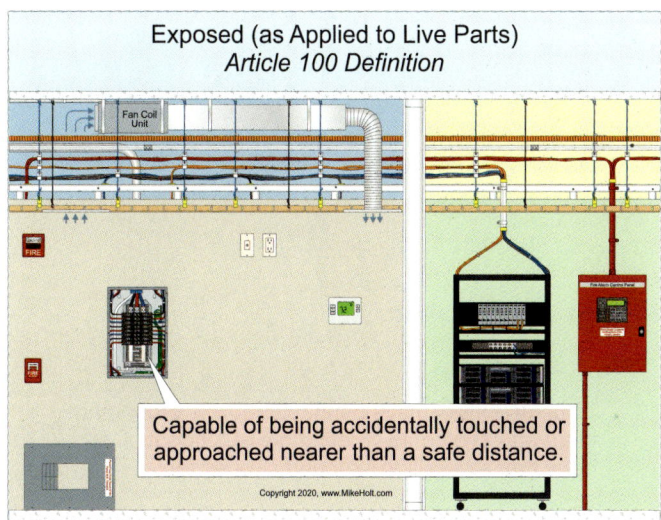
▶Figure 100-23

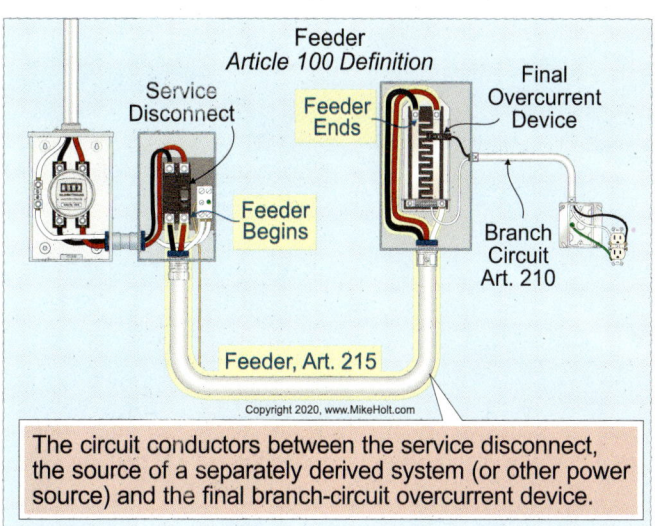
▶Figure 100-25

Note: This term applies to parts that are not suitably guarded, isolated, or insulated for the condition such as line-side lugs in a meter socket or panelboard.

Fault Current. The current delivered at a point on the system during a short-circuit condition. ▶Figure 100-24

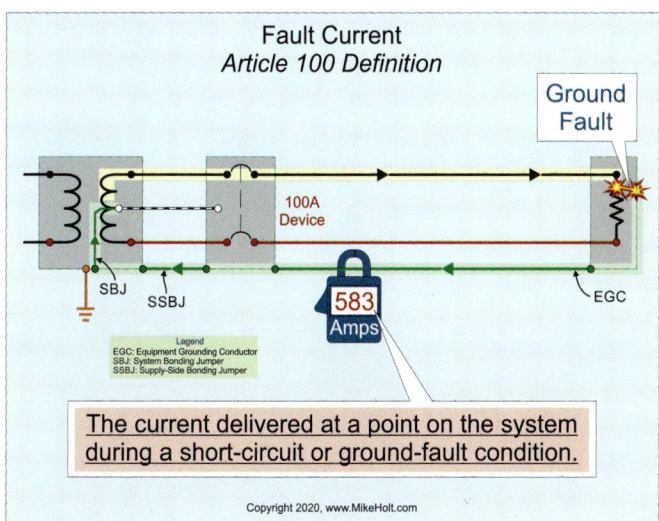
▶Figure 100-24

Feeder. The conductors between the service disconnect, a separately derived system (typically a transformer), or other power supply source and the final branch-circuit overcurrent device. ▶Figure 100-25

Author's Comment:

▸ An "other power supply source" includes solar PV systems or generators. ▶Figure 100-26

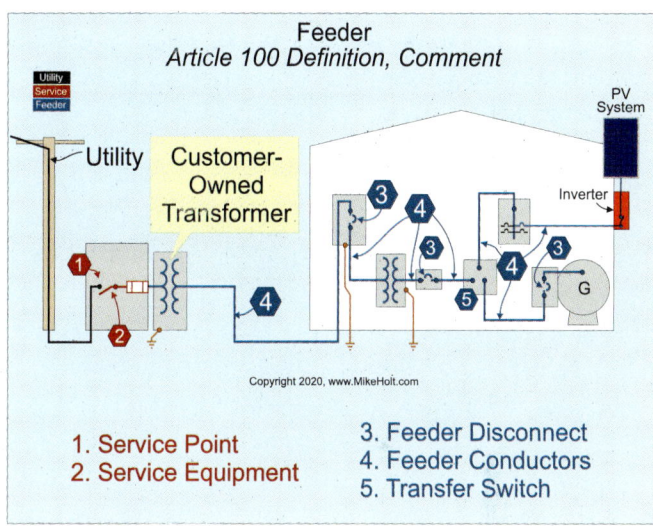
▶Figure 100-26

Fitting. An accessory such as a locknut, bushing, or other part of a wiring system that is primarily intended to perform a mechanical rather than an electrical function. ▶Figure 100-27

Ground. The Earth. ▶Figure 100-28

Ground Fault. An unintentional electrical connection between a phase conductor and normally noncurrent-carrying conductors, metal parts of enclosures, raceways, or equipment. ▶Figure 100-29

Grounded (Grounding). Connected to the Earth (ground) or to a conductive body that extends the Earth connection. ▶Figure 100-30

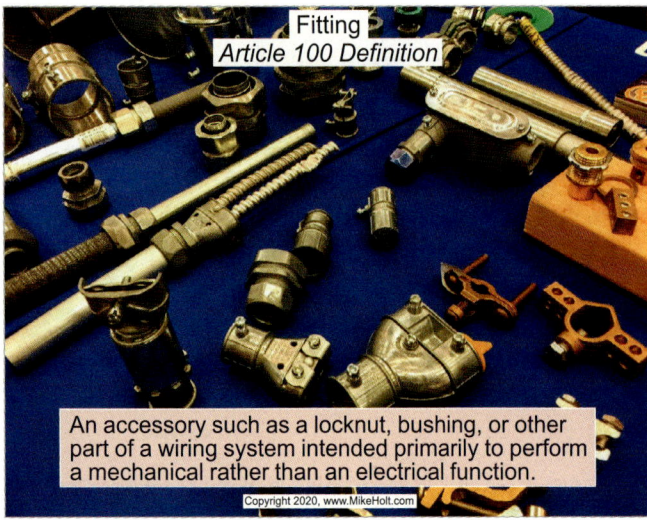
▶Figure 100-27

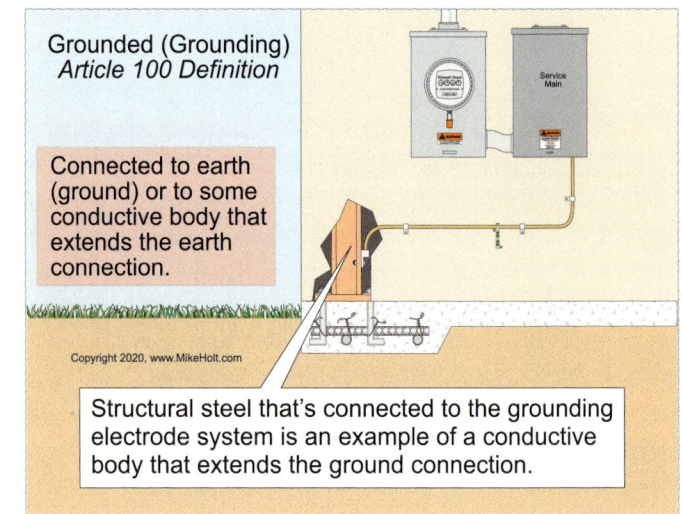
▶Figure 100-30

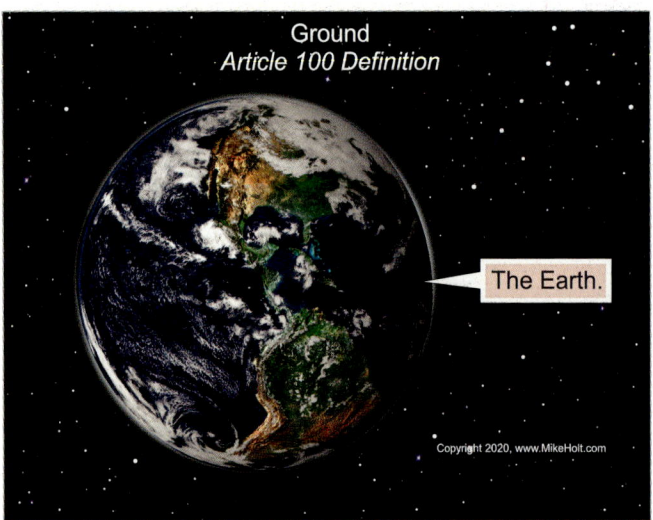
▶Figure 100-28

Author's Comment:

▶ An example of a "body that extends the ground (earth) connection" is a termination to structural steel that is connected to the Earth either directly or by the termination to another grounding electrode in accordance with 250.52.

Grounded Conductor. The system or circuit conductor that is intentionally connected to the Earth (ground). ▶Figure 100-31

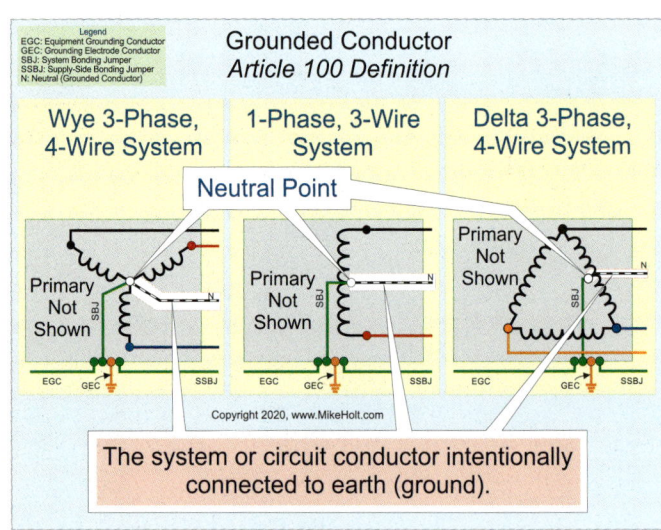
▶Figure 100-31

Note: Although an equipment grounding conductor is grounded, it is not considered a grounded conductor.

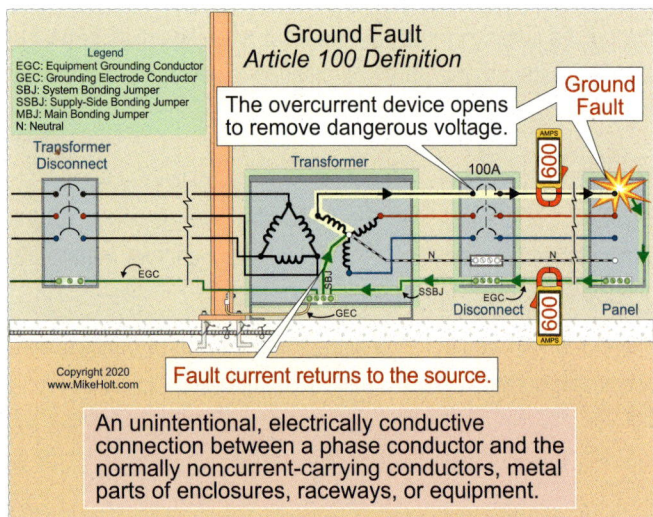
▶Figure 100-29

Definitions | 100

Author's Comment:

▸ There are two types of grounded conductors; neutral conductors and grounded-phase conductors. A system where the transformer secondary is wye connected with the neutral point grounded will have a neutral. ▸Figure 100-32

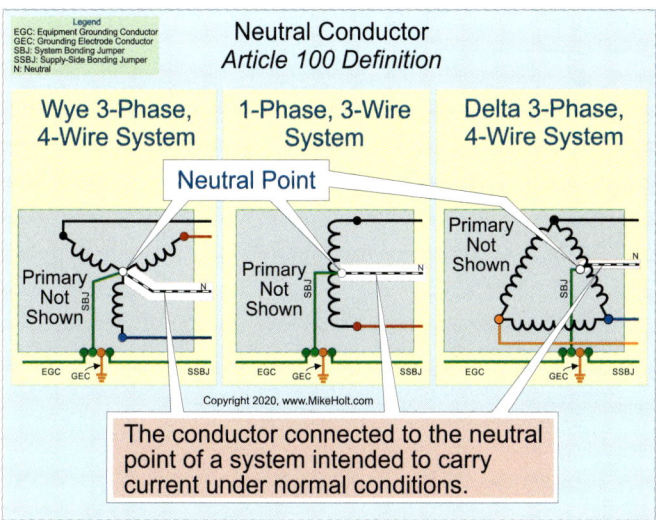

▸Figure 100-32

Author's Comment:

▸ A system where the transformer secondary is delta connected with one corner winding grounded will have a grounded-phase conductor. ▸Figure 100-33

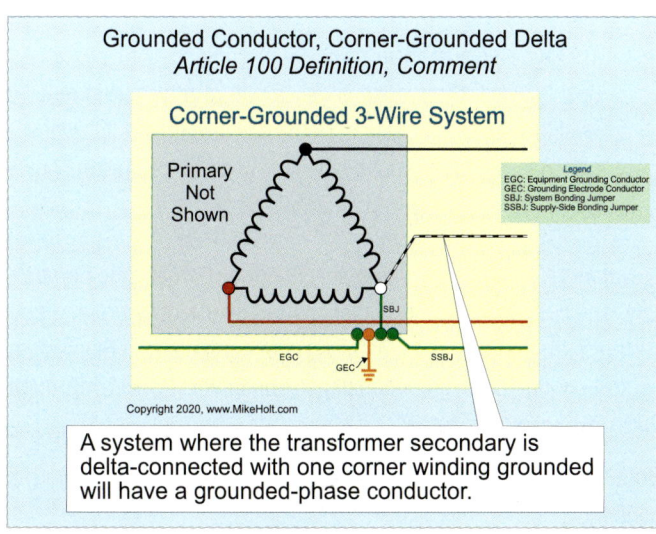

▸Figure 100-33

Grounded, Solidly (Solidly Grounded). Connected to ground (earth) without inserting any resistor or impedance device. ▸Figure 100-34 and ▸Figure 100-35

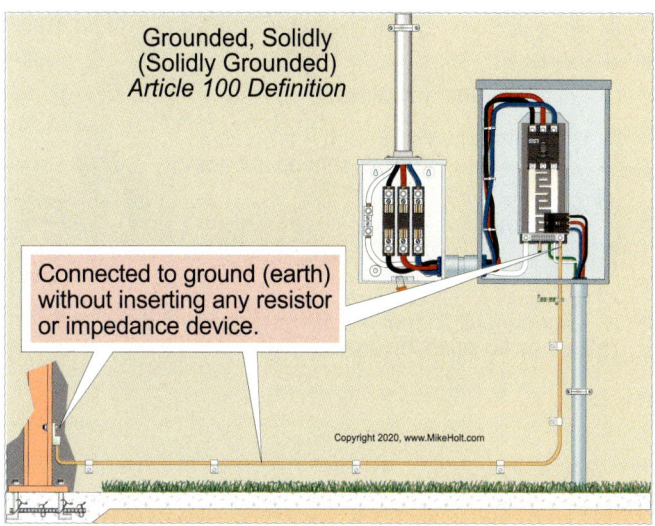

▸Figure 100-34

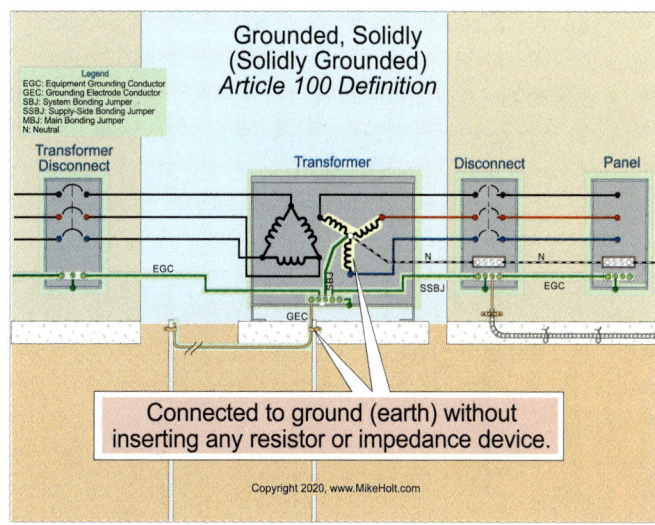

▸Figure 100-35

Ground-Fault Circuit Interrupter (GFCI). A device intended to protect people by de-energizing a circuit when ground-fault current exceeds the value established for a "Class A" device.

Note: A Class A ground-fault circuit interrupter opens the circuit when the ground-fault current is 6 mA or higher and does not trip when the ground-fault current is less than 4 mA. ▸Figure 100-36

100 | Definitions

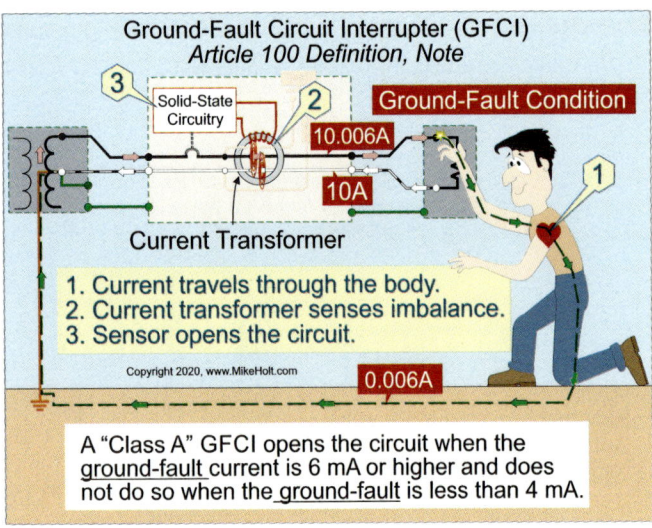
▶Figure 100-36

Author's Comment:

▸ A GFCI-protection device operates on the principle of monitoring the unbalanced current between the current-carrying circuit conductors. On a 120V circuit, the GFCI will monitor the unbalanced current between the phase and neutral conductors; on 240V circuits, monitoring is between all circuit conductors. Receptacles, circuit breakers, cord sets, and other types of devices that incorporate GFCI protection are commercially available. ▶Figure 100-37

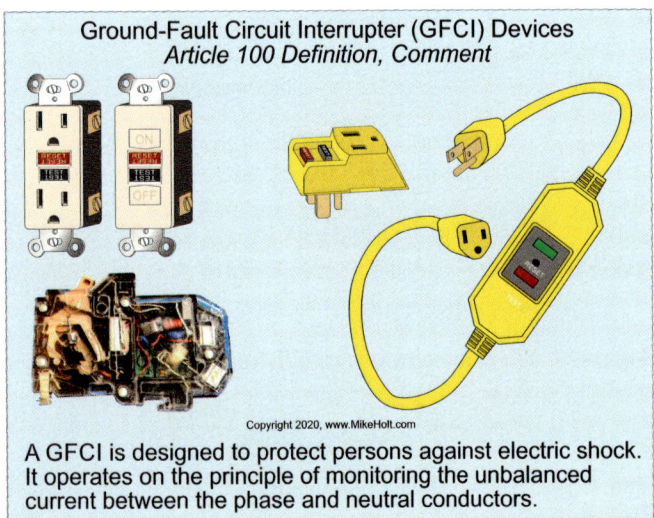
▶Figure 100-37

Ground-Fault Current Path. An electrically conductive path from the point of a ground fault on a wiring system through normally noncurrent-carrying conductors, neutral conductors, equipment, or the Earth to the electrical supply source. ▶Figure 100-38

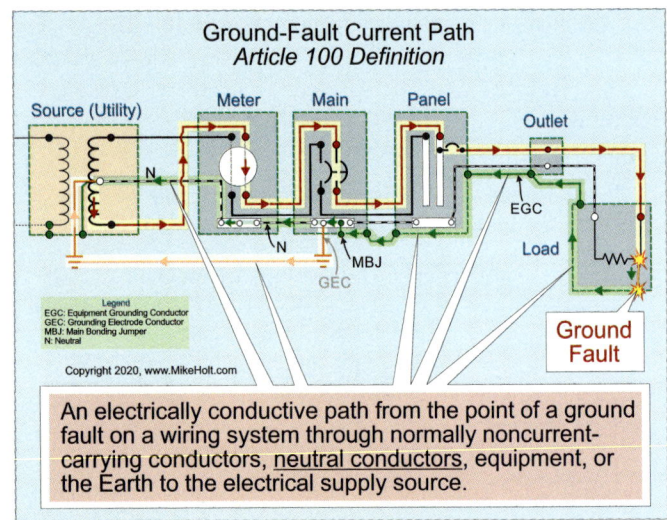
▶Figure 100-38

Ground-Fault Protection of Equipment. A system intended to provide protection of equipment from damaging ground-fault currents by opening all phase conductors of the faulted circuit. This protection is provided at current levels less than those required to protect conductors from damage through the operation of a supply circuit overcurrent device [215.10, 230.95, and 240.13].

Author's Comment:

▸ This type of protective device is not intended to protect people since it trips (opens the circuit) at a higher current level than that of a "Class A" GFCI-protective device. It is typically referred to as ground-fault protection for equipment, or GFPE; but should never be called a GFCI.

Grounding Conductor, Equipment (Equipment Grounding Conductor). The conductive path(s) that is part of an effective ground-fault current path and connects metal parts of equipment to the system neutral conductor or grounded-phase conductor [250.110 through 250.126]. ▶Figure 100-39

Note 1: The circuit equipment grounding conductor also performs bonding.

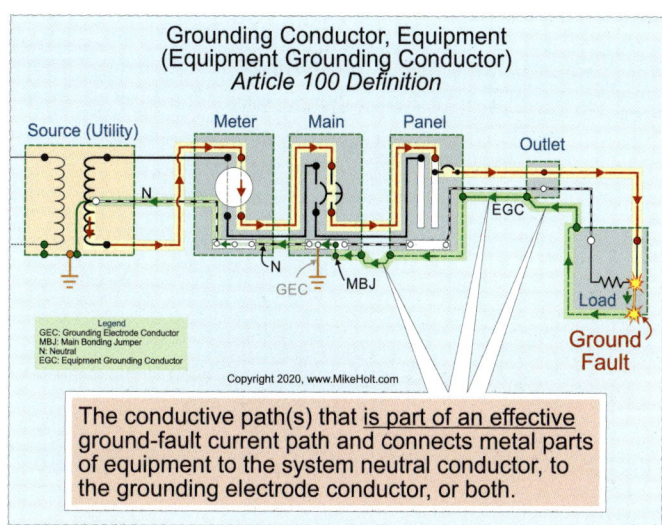
▶Figure 100-39

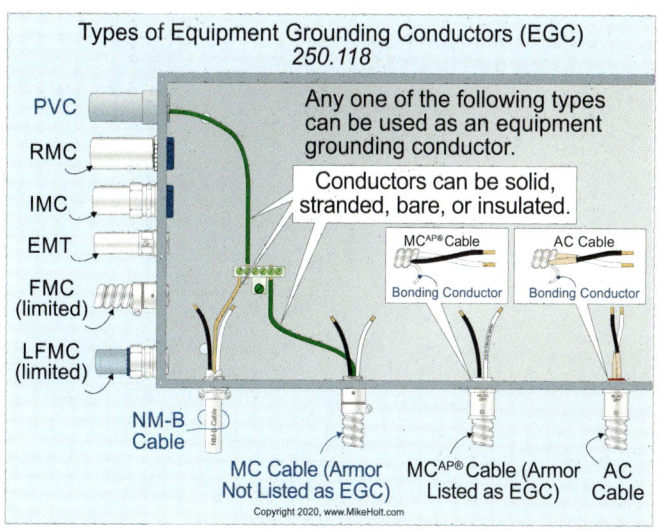
▶Figure 100-41

Author's Comment:

▶ To quickly remove dangerous touch voltage on metal parts from a ground fault, the equipment grounding conductor (EGC), must be connected to the system neutral conductor or grounded-phase conductor at the source and have low enough impedance so fault current will quickly rise to a level that will open the circuit's overcurrent protective device [250.4(A)(3)]. ▶Figure 100-40

Author's Comment:

▶ Equipment grounding conductors include:

▶ A bare or insulated conductor
▶ Rigid metal conduit
▶ Intermediate metal conduit
▶ Electrical metallic tubing
▶ Listed flexible metal conduit as limited by 250.118(5)
▶ Listed liquidtight flexible metal conduit as limited by 250.118(6)
▶ Armored cable
▶ The copper metal sheath of mineral-insulated cable
▶ Metal-clad cable as limited by 250.118(10)
▶ Metal cable trays as limited by 250.118(11) and 392.60
▶ Electrically continuous metal raceways listed for grounding
▶ Surface metal raceways listed for grounding
▶ Metal enclosures

Grounding Electrode. A conducting object used to make a direct electrical connection to the Earth [250.50 through 250.70]. ▶Figure 100-42

Grounding Electrode Conductor. The conductor used to connect the system neutral conductor or grounded-phase conductor, or the equipment to the grounding electrode system. ▶Figure 100-43

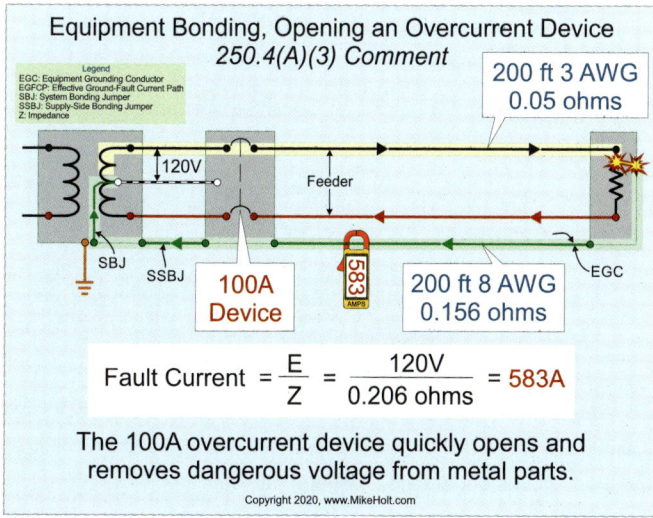
▶Figure 100-40

Note 2: An equipment grounding conductor can be any one or a combination of the types listed in 250.118. ▶Figure 100-41

100 | Definitions

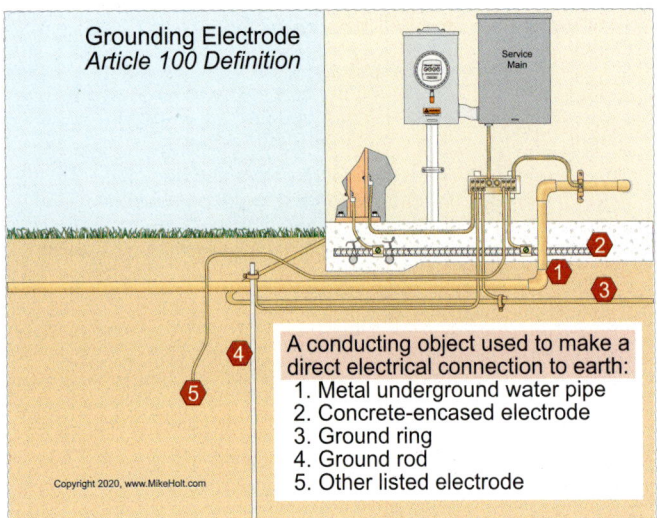
▶Figure 100-42

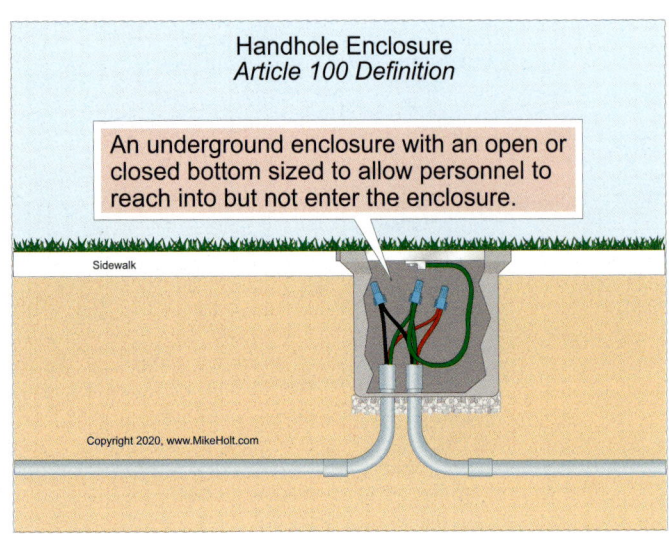
▶Figure 100-44

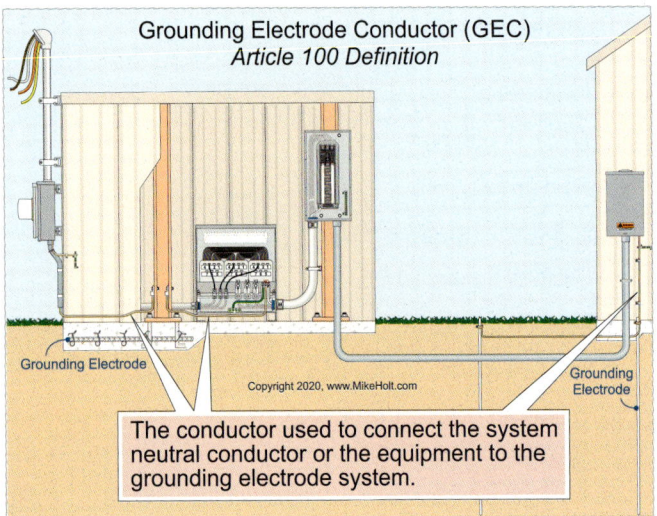
▶Figure 100-43

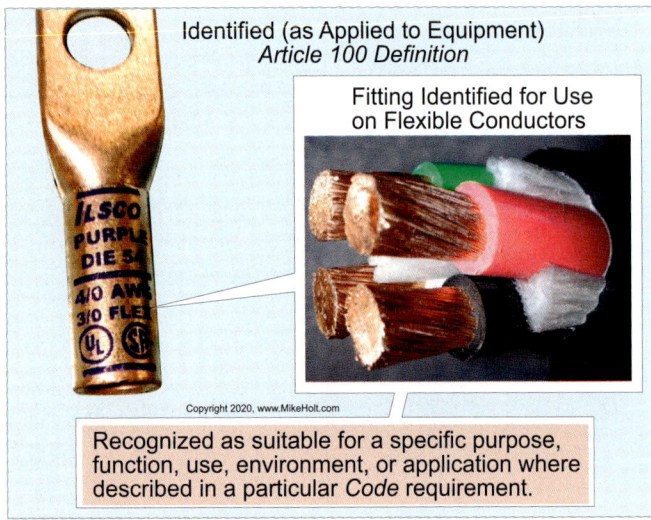
▶Figure 100-45

Handhole Enclosure. An underground enclosure with an open or closed bottom that is sized to allow personnel to reach into but not enter the enclosure. ▶Figure 100-44

Author's Comment:

▸ See 314.30 for the installation requirements for handhole enclosures.

Identified (as applied to equipment). Recognized as suitable for a specific purpose, function, use, environment, or application where described in a Code requirement. ▶Figure 100-45

Author's Comment:

▸ See 90.4, 90.7, and 110.3(A)(1), and the definitions for "Approved," "Labeled," and "Listed" in this article.

Information Technology Equipment (ITE). Equipment used for the creation and manipulation of data, voice, and video. It does not include communications equipment. ▶Figure 100-46

Intersystem Bonding Termination. A device that provides a means to connect intersystem bonding conductors for communications systems (twisted wire, antennas, and coaxial cable) to the grounding electrode system, in accordance with 250.94. ▶Figure 100-47

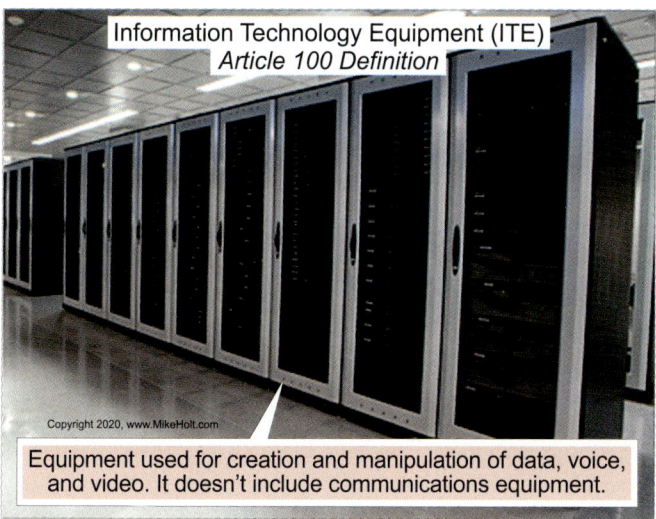

▶Figure 100-46

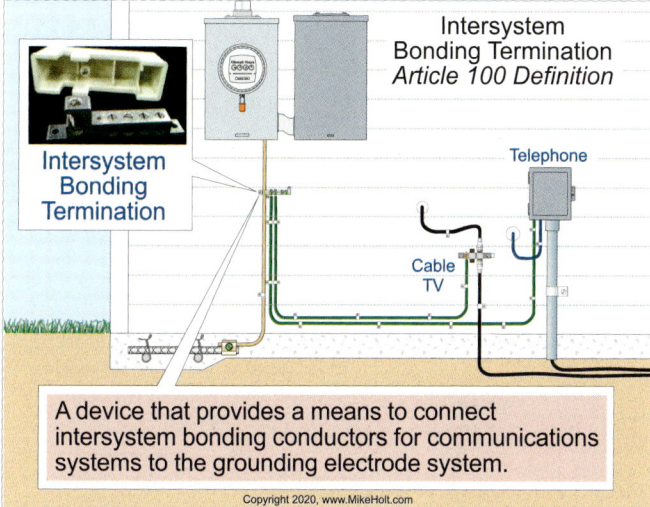

▶Figure 100-47

Author's Comment:

▸ Overcurrent protective devices have two current ratings, "rated current" and "fault current." Rated current protects circuits under normal conditions and the rating is labeled on the handle of the circuit breaker. The fault current rating or "ampere interrupting capacity" (AIC) is the amount of current the device can safely handle during a ground fault or short circuit. Fault current ratings range up to the tens, or even hundreds, of thousands of amperes!

▸ For more information, see 110.9 in this textbook.

Labeled. Equipment or materials that have a label, symbol, or other identifying mark in the form of a sticker, decal, printed label, or with the identifying mark molded or stamped into the product by a recognized testing laboratory acceptable to the authority having jurisdiction. ▶Figure 100-48

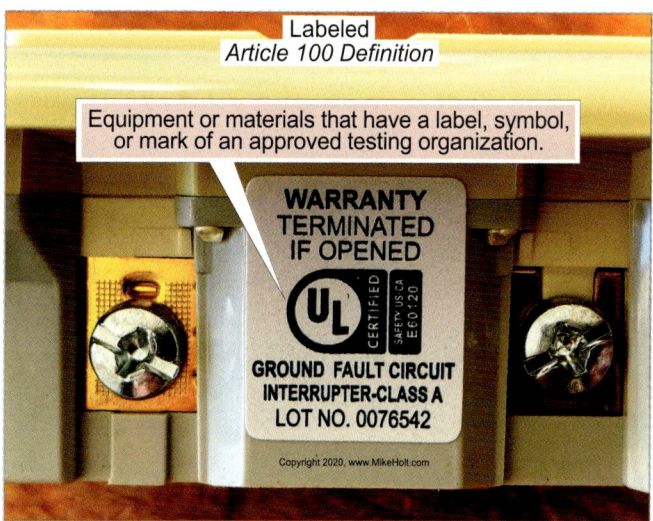

▶Figure 100-48

Author's Comment:

▸ Labeling and listing of equipment typically provides the basis for equipment approval by the authority having jurisdiction [90.4, 90.7, 110.2, and 110.3].

Note: When a listed product is of such a size, shape, material, or surface texture that it is not possible to legibly apply the complete label to the product, it may appear on the smallest unit container in which the product is packaged.

Listed. Equipment or materials included in a list published by a recognized testing laboratory acceptable to the authority having jurisdiction. The listing organization must periodically inspect the production of listed equipment or material to ensure they meet appropriate designated standards and are suitable for a specified purpose.

Note: Examples of nationally recognized testing laboratories (NRTLs) are Underwriters Laboratory (UL) and Canadian Standards Association (CSA). Both are accepted in either the United States or Canada and most electrical equipment is marked by both agencies. Always look for at least one of these seals and accept no imitations or counterfeits.

Author's Comment:

▸ The *NEC* does not require all electrical equipment to be listed, but some *Code* requirements do specifically call for product listing. Organizations such as OSHA are increasingly requiring listed equipment to be used when such equipment is available [90.7, 110.2, and 110.3].

100 | Definitions

Luminaire. A complete lighting unit consisting of a light source with its parts designed to position the light source and connect it to the power supply. Parts to distribute the light may also be included. ▶Figure 100-49

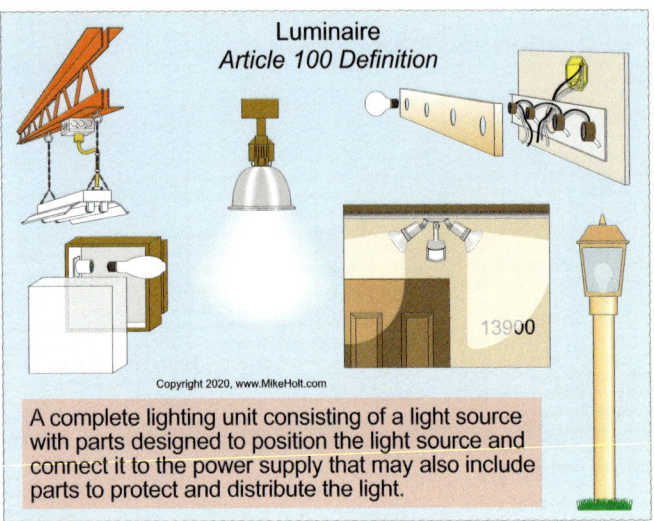

▶Figure 100-49

Neutral Conductor. The conductor connected to the neutral point of a system that is intended to carry current under normal conditions. ▶Figure 100-50

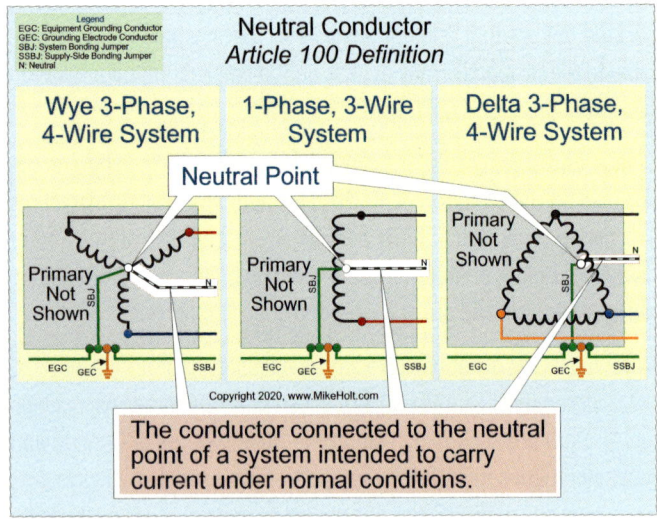

▶Figure 100-50

Neutral Point. The common point of a 4-wire, three-phase, wye-connected system; the midpoint of a 3-wire, single-phase system; or the midpoint of the single-phase portion of a three-phase, delta-connected system. ▶Figure 100-51

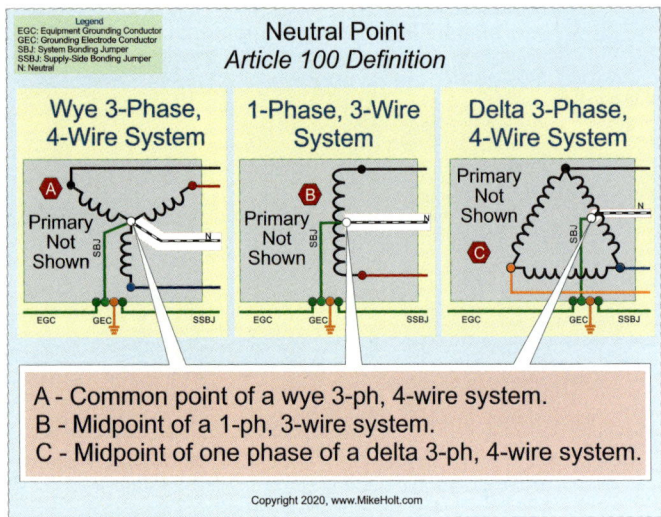

▶Figure 100-51

Outline Lighting. An arrangement of an electrically powered light source used to outline or call attention to building features such as the shape of a building or the decoration of a window.

Overcurrent. Current in excess of the equipment's current rating or a conductor's ampacity caused by an overload, short circuit, or ground fault. ▶Figure 100-52

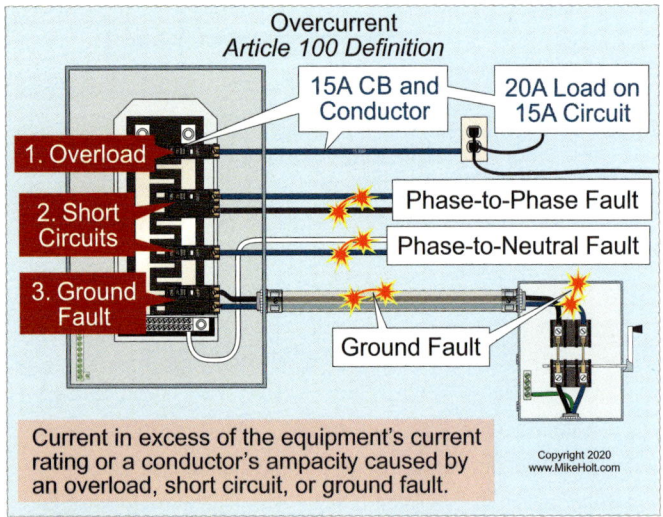

▶Figure 100-52

Panelboard. A distribution point containing overcurrent protective devices and designed to be installed in a cabinet. ▶Figure 100-53

Definitions | 100

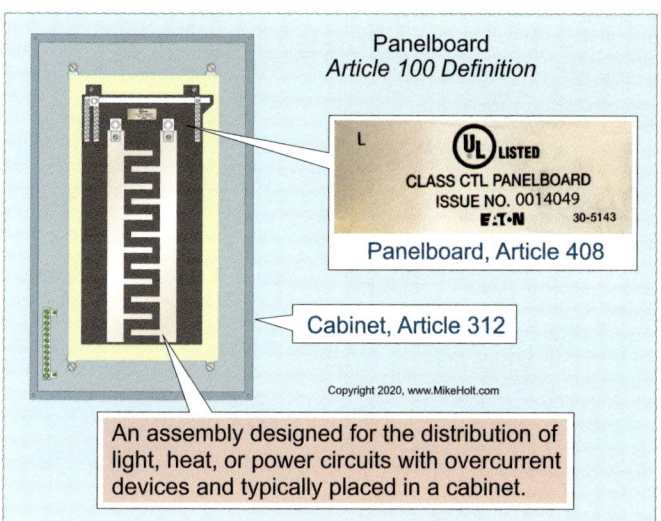
▶Figure 100-53

Author's Comment:

▸ See the definition of "Cabinet" in this article.

▸ The slang term in the electrical field for a panelboard is "the guts." This is the interior of the panelboard assembly and is covered by Article 408, while the cabinet is covered by Article 312.

Photovoltaic (PV) System. The combination of all components and subsystems, including the PV system disconnecting means, that convert solar energy into electric energy for utilization loads. ▶Figure 100-54

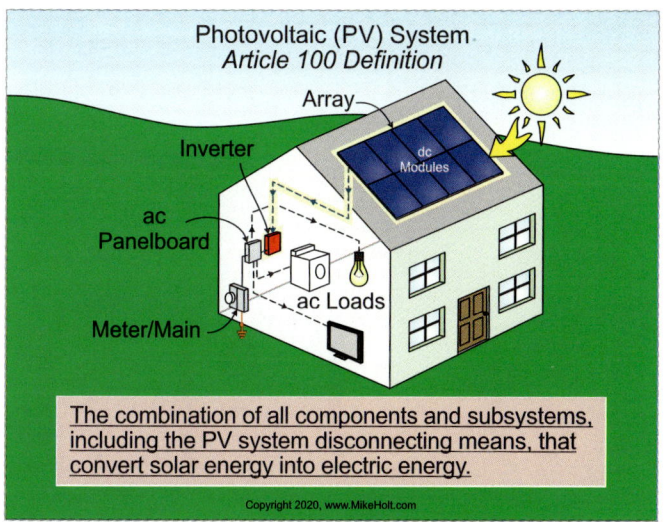
▶Figure 100-54

Premises Wiring. The interior and exterior wiring including power, lighting, control, and signaling circuits, and all associated hardware, fittings, and wiring devices. This includes permanently and temporarily installed wiring from the service point to the outlets. Where there is no service point, it is the wiring from and including the electric power source (such as a generator, transformer, or PV system) to the outlets. ▶Figure 100-55

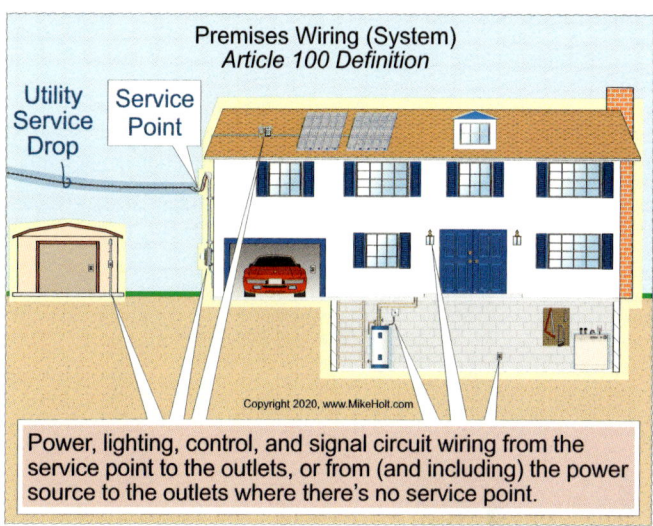
▶Figure 100-55

Premises wiring does not include the internal wiring of electrical equipment and appliances such as luminaires, dishwashers, water heaters, motors, controllers, motor control centers, air-conditioning equipment, and so on [90.7 and 300.1(B)]. ▶Figure 100-56

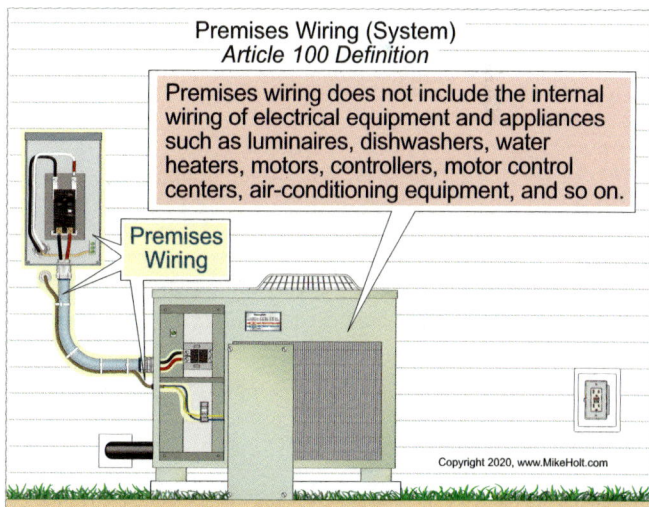
▶Figure 100-56

Note: Electric power sources include (but not limited to) interconnected or stand-alone batteries, PV systems, other distributed generation systems, and generators.

100 | Definitions

Raceway. A channel designed for the installation of conductors, cables, or busbars.

> **Author's Comment:**
> - A cable tray system is not a raceway; it is a support system for cables and raceways [392.2].

Receptacle. A contact device installed at an outlet for the connection of an attachment plug, or for the direct connection of equipment designed to mate with the contact device (SQL receptacle). ▶Figure 100-57

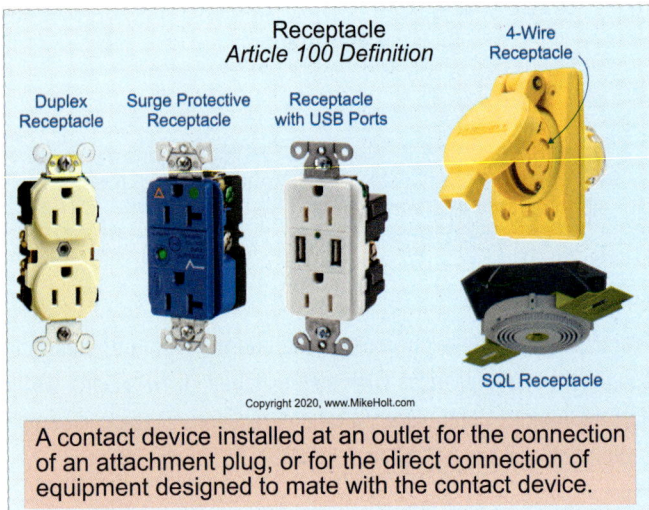

▶Figure 100-57

> **Author's Comment:**
> - For additional information about listed locking support and mounting receptacles, visit www.safetyquicklight.com.

A single receptacle contains one contact device on a yoke or strap; a multiple receptacle has more than one contact device on the same yoke or strap. ▶Figure 100-58

> **Author's Comment:**
> - A yoke (also called a "strap") is the metal mounting structure for such items as receptacles, switches, switches with pilot lights, and switch/receptacles. ▶Figure 100-59 and ▶Figure 100-60

Note: A duplex receptacle is an example of a multiple receptacle with two receptacles on the same yoke or strap.

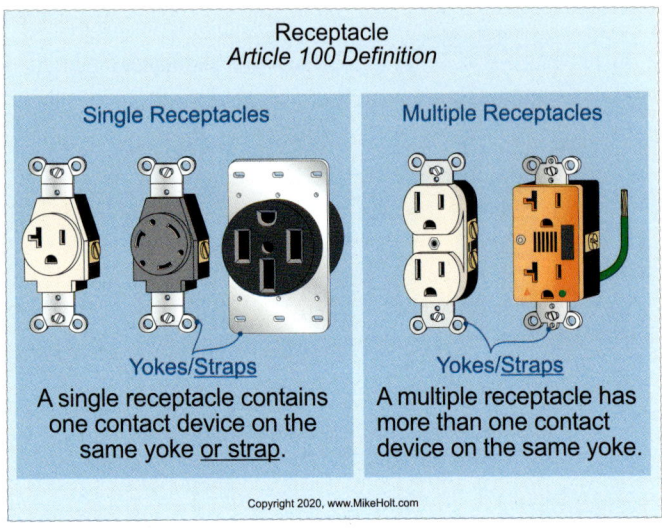

▶Figure 100-58

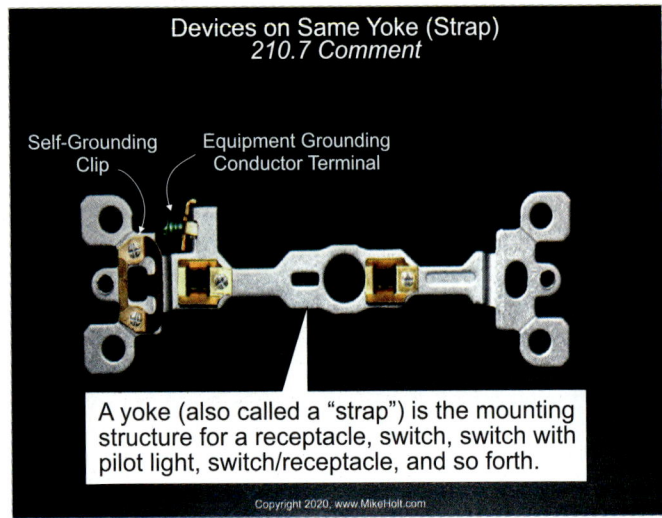

▶Figure 100-59

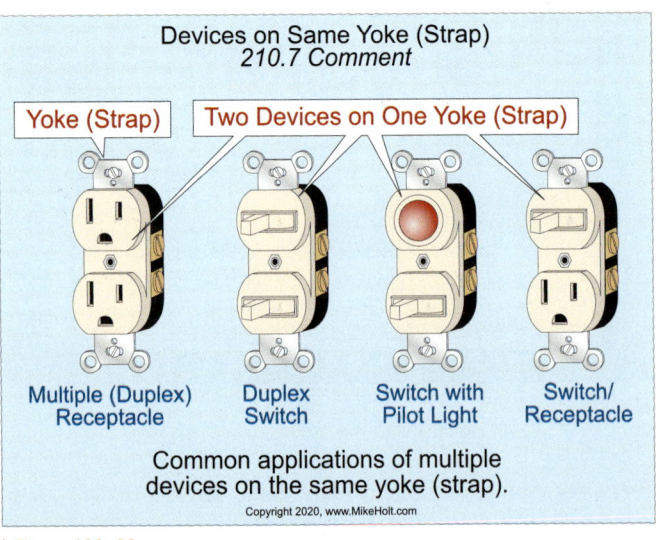

▶Figure 100-60

Definitions | 100

Separately Derived System. An electrical source, other than a service, having no direct connection(s) to the circuit conductors of any other electrical source other than those established by grounding and bonding connections. ▶Figure 100-61, ▶Figure 100-62, and ▶Figure 100-63

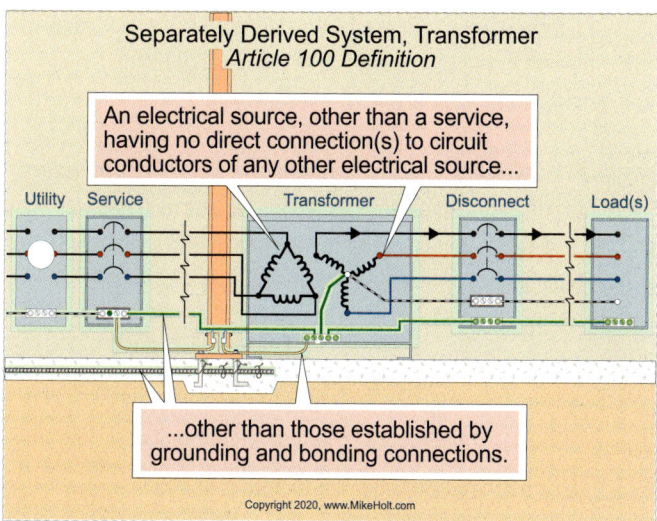

▶Figure 100-61

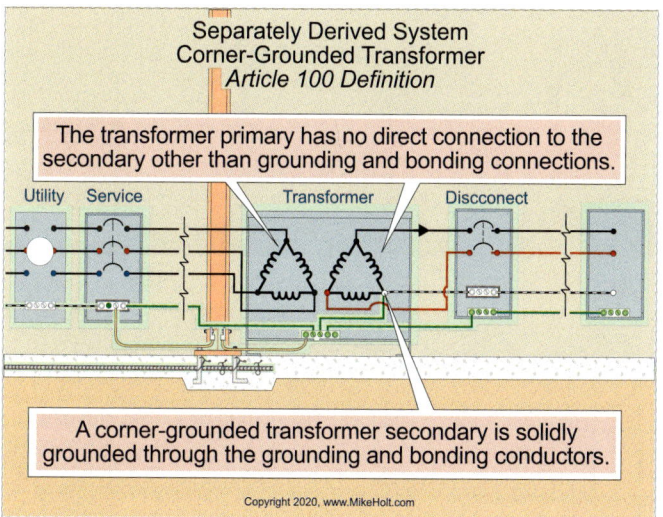

▶Figure 100-62

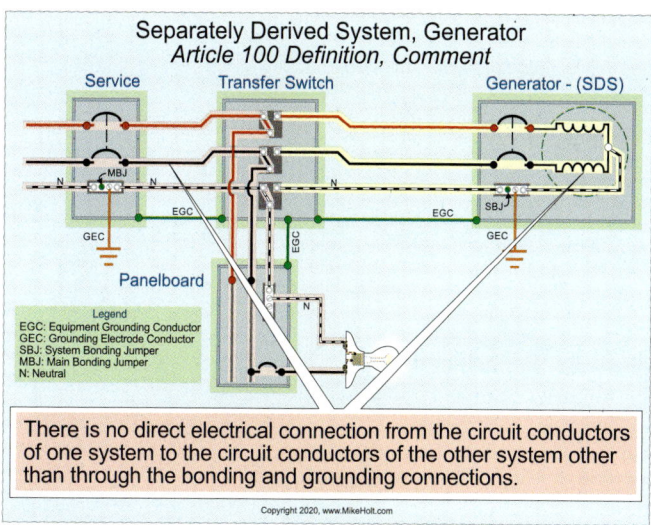

▶Figure 100-63

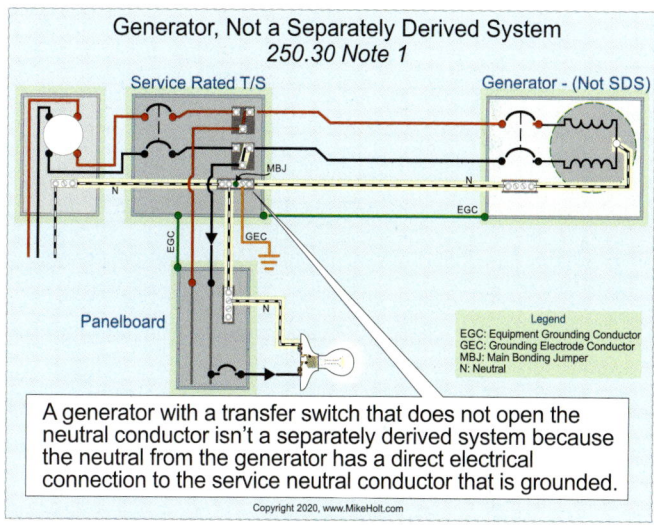

▶Figure 100-64

Author's Comment:

▸ A generator is not a separately derived system if the neutral conductor is solidly interconnected to a service-supplied system neutral conductor. An example is a generator provided with a transfer switch that includes a neutral conductor that is not switched. ▶Figure 100-64

▸ Separately derived systems are much more complicated than the *Code*'s definition suggests and understanding them requires additional study. For more information, see 250.30.

Service [Article 230]. The conductors and equipment <u>connecting</u> the serving electric utility to the wiring system of the premises served. ▶Figure 100-65

100 | Definitions

▶Figure 100–65

Author's Comment:

▸ A service can only be supplied by the serving electric utility. A service is not covered by the *NEC*. If power is supplied by other than the serving electric utility, the conductors and equipment are part of a feeder and covered by the *Code*.

▸ Conductors from UPS systems, solar PV systems, generators, and transformers are not service conductors. See the definitions of "Feeder" and "Service Conductors" in this article.

Service Conductors. The conductors from the serving electric utility service point to the service disconnect. ▶Figure 100–66

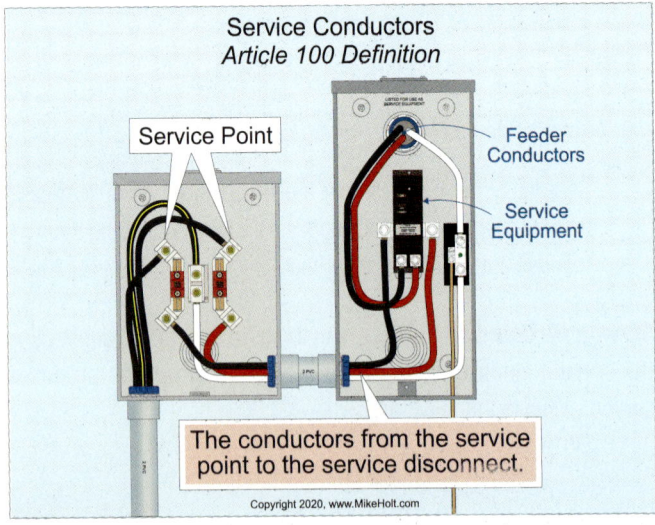
▶Figure 100–66

Author's Comment:

▸ Service conductors can include overhead service conductors, overhead service-entrance conductors, and underground service conductors. These conductors are not under the exclusive control of the serving electric utility, which means they are owned by the customer are covered by the requirements in Article 230.

Service Conductors, Overhead (Overhead Service Conductors). Overhead conductors between the serving electric utility service point and the first point of connection to the service-entrance conductors at the building. ▶Figure 100–67

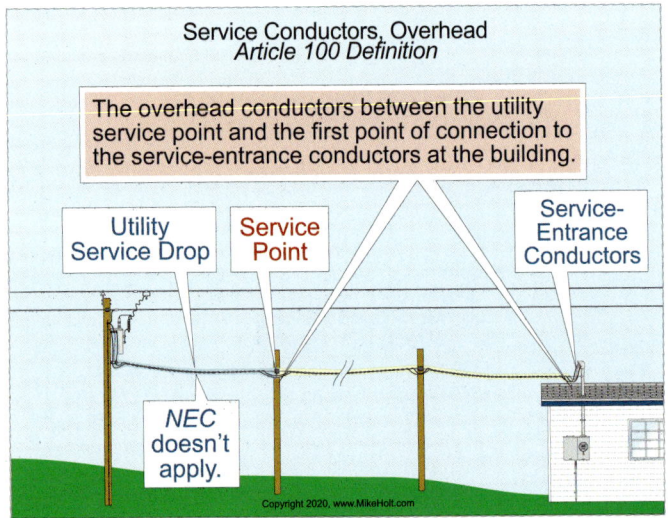
▶Figure 100–67

Author's Comment:

▸ The service point is typically determined by the serving electric utility. If the utility determines the service point is at the load side of their transformer, the overhead service conductors run to the service-entrance conductors. ▶Figure 100–68

Service Conductors, Underground (Underground Service Conductors). Underground conductors between the service point and the first point of connection to the service-entrance conductors in a terminal box, meter, or other enclosure; inside or outside the building wall. ▶Figure 100–69

Definitions | 100

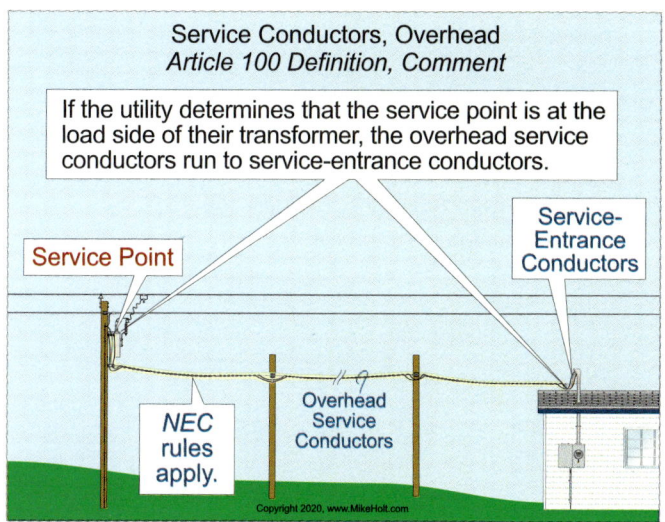
▶Figure 100–68

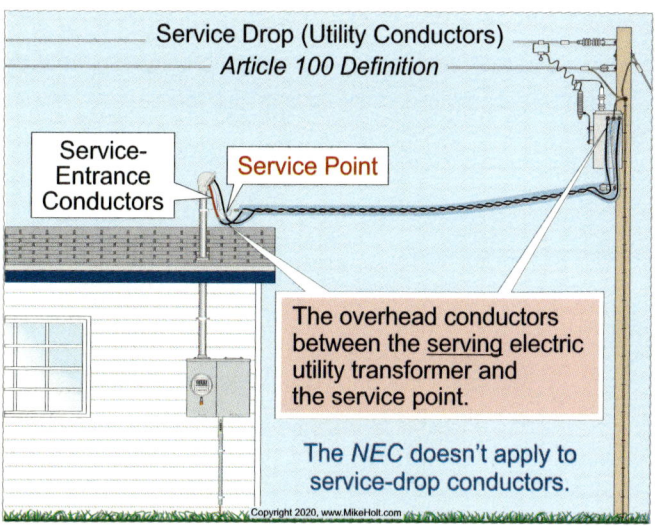
▶Figure 100–70

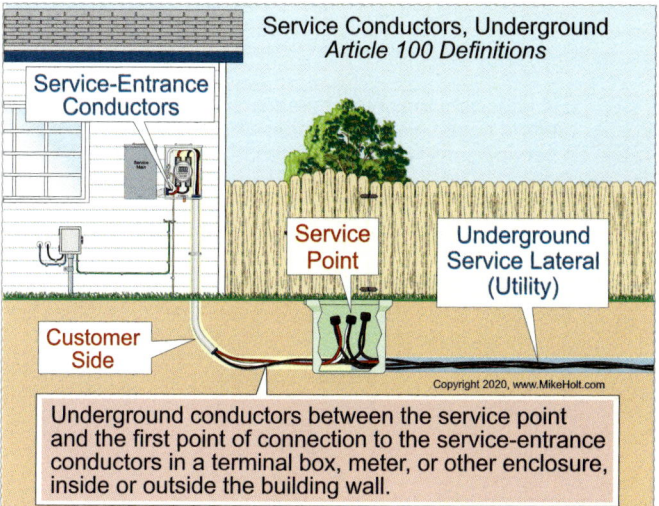
▶Figure 100–69

Author's Comment:

▸ Service conductors fall within the requirements of Article 230 since they are not under the exclusive control of the serving electric utility.

Note: Where there is no terminal box, meter, or other enclosure the point of connection is the point of entrance of the service conductors into the building.

Service Drop. Utility-owned overhead conductors between the serving electric utility and the service point. ▶Figure 100–70

Author's Comment:

▸ The NEC does not apply to service drops.

Service-Entrance Conductors, Overhead (Overhead Service-Entrance Conductors). The conductors between the terminals of the service disconnect and service drop or overhead service conductors. ▶Figure 100–71

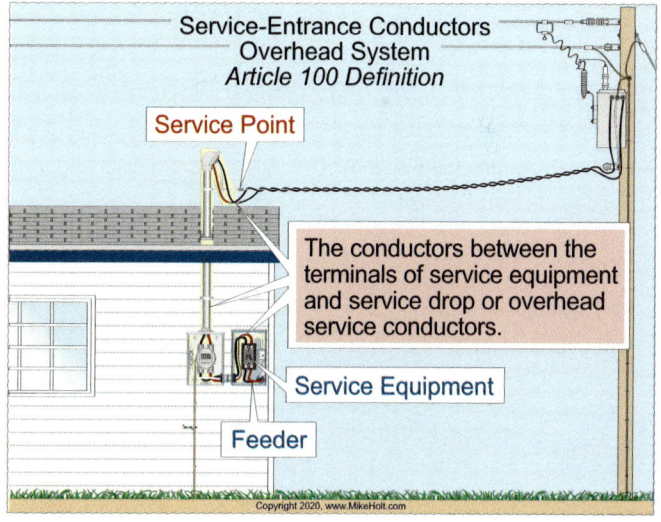
▶Figure 100–71

Author's Comment:

▸ Overhead service-entrance conductors are covered by the requirements of Article 230 since they are not under the exclusive control of the serving electric utility.

100 | Definitions

Service-Entrance Conductors, Underground (Underground Service-Entrance Conductors). The conductors between the terminals of the service disconnect and underground service point. ▶Figure 100–72

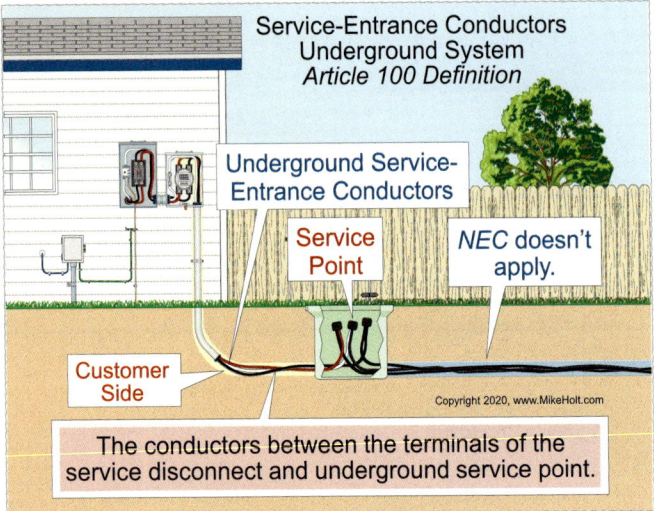

▶Figure 100–72

Author's Comment:

▸ Underground service-entrance conductors fall within the requirements of Article 230 since they are not under the exclusive control of the serving electric utility.

Service Equipment (Service Disconnect). Disconnects such as circuit breakers or switches connected to the serving electric utility, intended to control and disconnect the power from the serving electric utility. ▶Figure 100–73

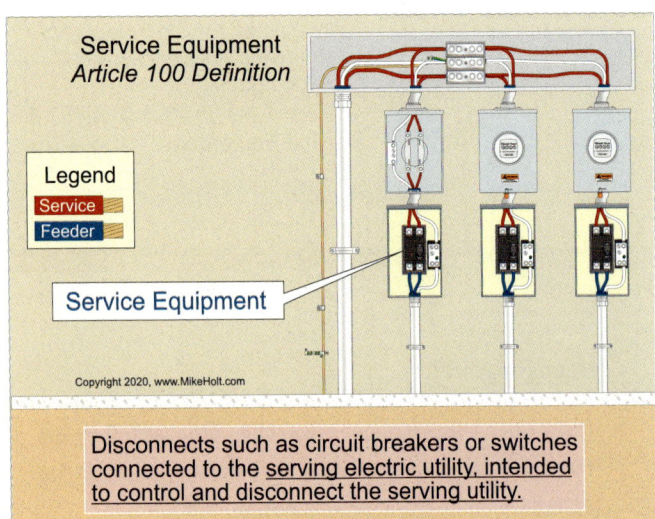

▶Figure 100–73

Author's Comment:

▸ It's important to know where a service begins and where it ends in order to properly apply the *Code* requirements. Sometimes the service ends before the metering equipment. ▶Figure 100–74 and ▶Figure 100–75

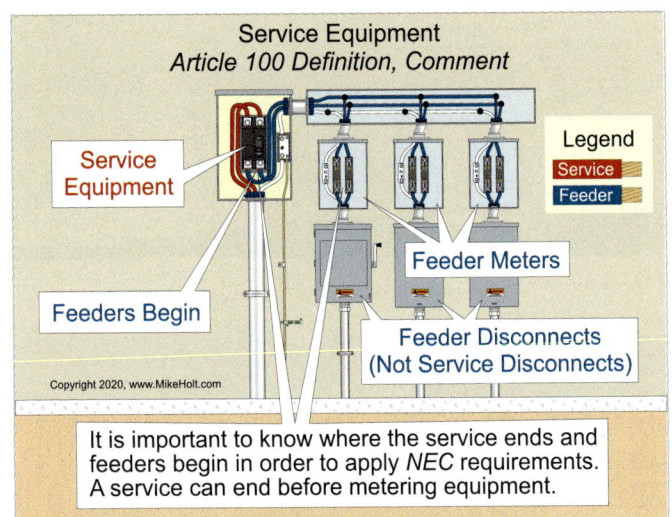

▶Figure 100–74

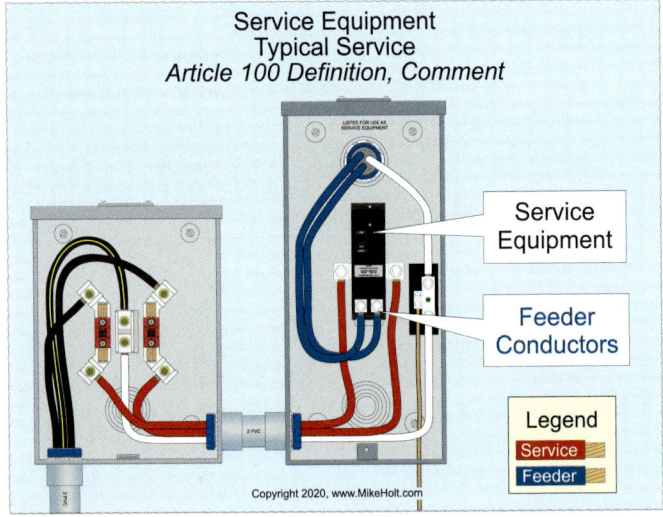

▶Figure 100–75

Author's Comment:

▸ Service equipment is often referred to as the "service disconnect" or "service main."

▸ Meter socket enclosures are not considered service equipment [230.66].

Definitions | 100

Service Point. The point where the serving electric utility conductors connect to customer-owned wiring. ▶Figure 100–76

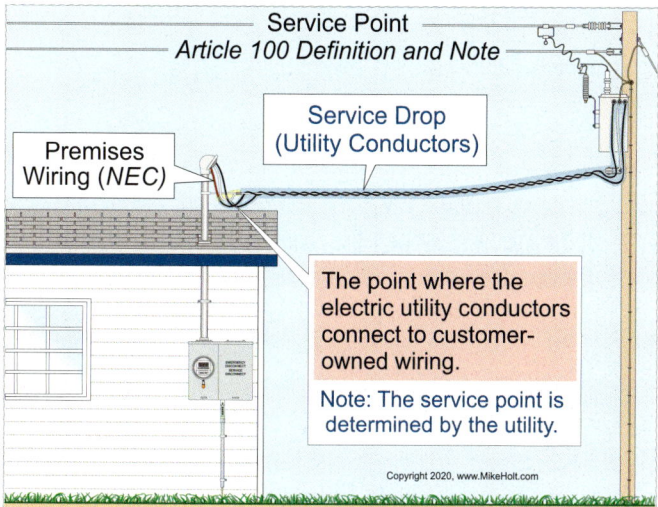
▶Figure 100–76

Author's Comment:

▸ The service point is typically determined by the serving electric utility and may vary with different utilities and different types of occupancies.

▸ For utility-owned transformers, the service point will be at the serving electric utility's transformer secondary terminals, at the service drop, or at the meter socket enclosure depending on where their conductors terminate. ▶Figure 100–77

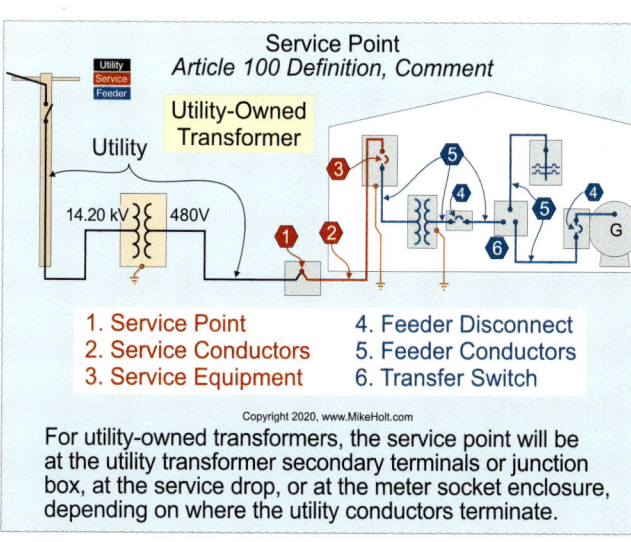
▶Figure 100–77

Author's Comment:

▸ For customer-owned transformers, the service point will be at the termination of the serving electric utility's conductors; often at the utility's pole. ▶Figure 100–78

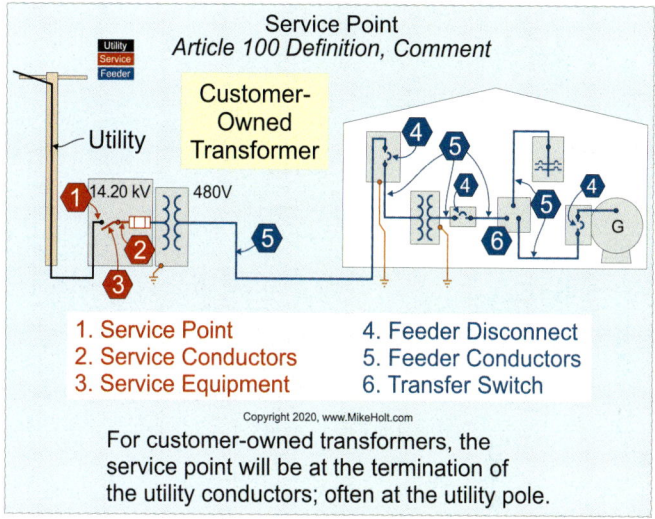
▶Figure 100–78

Ungrounded System. A power-supply system not connected to earth (ground). ▶Figure 100–79

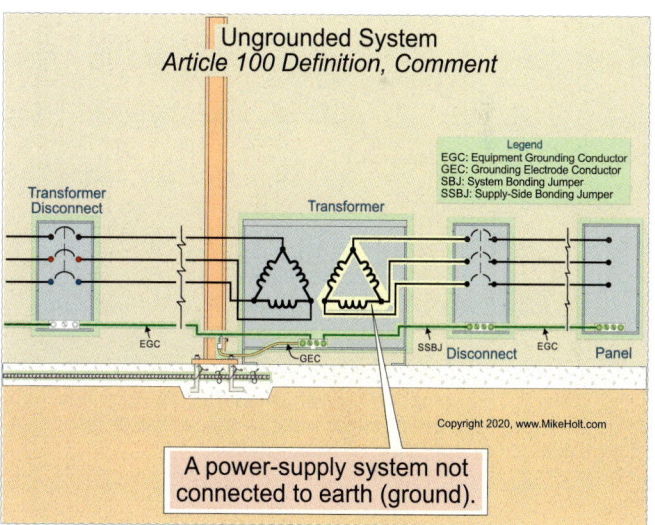
▶Figure 100–79

Author's Comment:

▸ An electrical system can be ungrounded, but the enclosure must still be connected to the Earth [250.4(B)].

100 | Definitions

Voltage of a Circuit. The greatest effective root-mean-square (RMS) difference of voltage between any two conductors of the circuit. ▶Figure 100-80

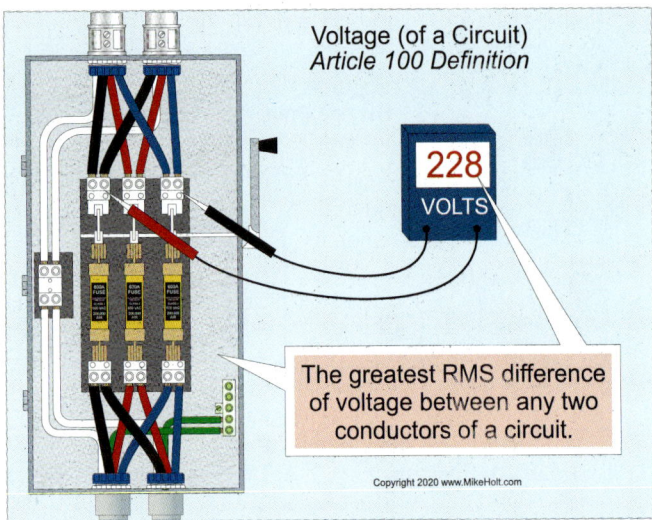

▶Figure 100-80

Voltage, Nominal (Nominal Voltage). A value assigned for conveniently designating voltage classes. Examples are 120/240V, 120/208V, or 277/480V [220.5(A)]. ▶Figure 100-81

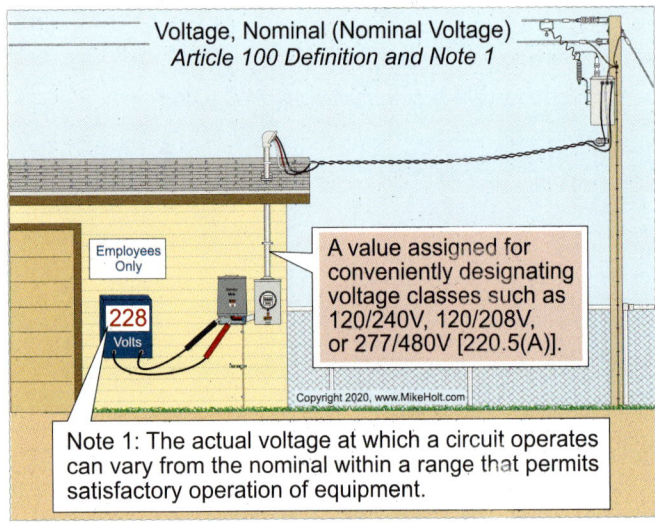

▶Figure 100-81

Note 1: The actual voltage at which a circuit operates can vary from the nominal within a range that permits satisfactory operation of equipment.

Author's Comment:

▸ Common voltage ratings of electrical equipment are 115V, 200V, 208V, 230V, and 460V. The electrical power supplied might be at the 240V, nominal, voltage but the voltage at the equipment will be less. Therefore, electrical equipment is rated at a value less than the nominal system voltage.

Voltage to Ground. For grounded systems, it is the voltage between a phase conductor and ground; typically the neutral. ▶Figure 100-82

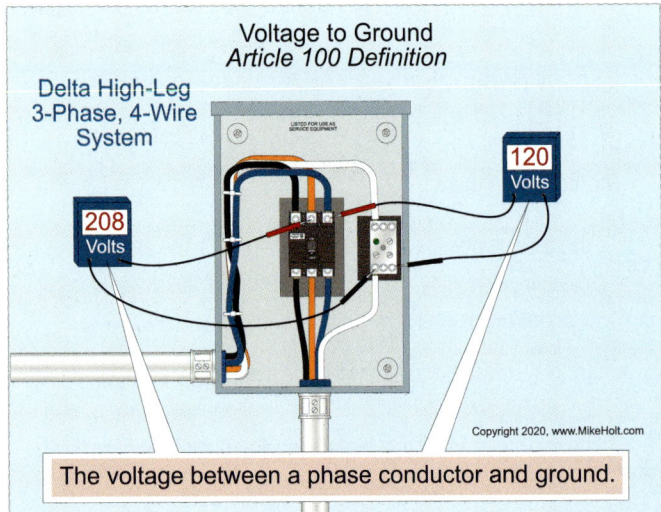

▶Figure 100-82

ARTICLE 110 — REQUIREMENTS FOR ELECTRICAL INSTALLATIONS

Introduction to Article 110—Requirements for Electrical Installations

Article 110 sets the stage for how the rest of the *NEC* is implemented. It is critical for you to completely understand all aspects of this article since it is the foundation for much of the *Code*. As you read and master Article 110, you are building your foundation for correctly applying the *NEC*. While the purpose of the *National Electrical Code* is to provide a safe installation, this article is perhaps focused a little more on providing an installation that is safe for the installer and maintenance electrician, so time spent here is a good investment.

110.1 Scope

Article 110 covers the general requirements for the examination and approval, installation and use, and access to spaces about electrical equipment. ▶Figure 110–1

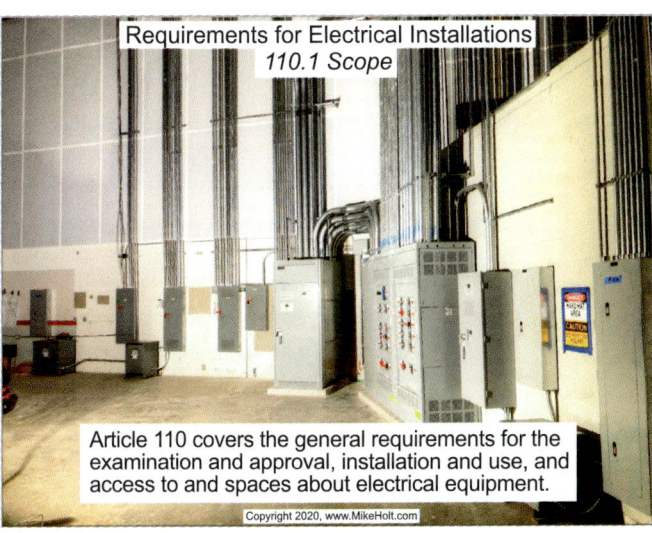

▶Figure 110–1

Note: See Annex J for information regarding ADA accessibility design.

Author's Comment:

▸ Requirements for people with disabilities include things like mounting heights for switches and receptacles, and requirements for the distance that objects (such as wall sconces) protrude from a wall.

110.2 Approval of Conductors and Equipment

The authority having jurisdiction must approve all electrical conductors and equipment. ▶Figure 110–2

▶Figure 110–2

110.3 | Requirements for Electrical Installations

Author's Comment:

▸ For a better understanding of product approval, review 90.4, 90.7, 110.3, and the definitions for "Approved," "Identified," "Labeled," and "Listed" in Article 100.

110.3 Examination, Identification, Installation, Use, and Product Listing (Certification) of Equipment

(A) Guidelines for Approval. The authority having jurisdiction must approve equipment. In doing so, consideration must be given to the following:

(1) Suitability for installation and use in accordance with the *NEC*

Note 1: Equipment may be new, reconditioned, refurbished, or remanufactured.

Note 2: Suitability of equipment use may be identified by a description marked on, or provided with, a product to identify the suitability of the product for a specific purpose, environment, or application. Special conditions of use or other limitations may be marked on the equipment, in the product instructions, or included in the appropriate listing and labeling information. Suitability of equipment may be evidenced by listing or labeling.

(2) Mechanical strength and durability

(3) Wire-bending and connection space

(4) Electrical insulation

(5) Heating effects under all conditions of use

(6) Arcing effects

(7) Classification by type, size, voltage, current capacity, and specific use

(8) Other factors contributing to the practical safeguarding of persons using or in contact with the equipment

(B) Installation and Use. Equipment that is listed, labeled, or both must be installed and used in accordance with any instructions included in the listing or labeling. ▸Figure 110–3

(C) Product Listing. Product testing, evaluation, and listing must be performed by a recognized qualified testing laboratory in accordance with standards that achieve effective safety to comply with the *NEC*.

Note: OSHA recognizes qualified electrical testing laboratories that provide product certification that meets their electrical standards.

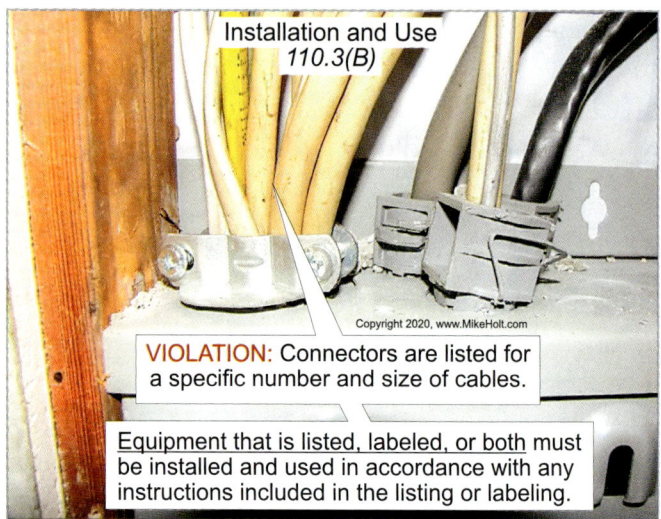

▸Figure 110–3

110.5 Conductor Material

Conductors must be copper, aluminum, or copper-clad aluminum unless otherwise provided in this *Code*; and when the conductor material is not specified in a rule, the sizes given in the *NEC* are based on a copper conductor. ▸Figure 110–4

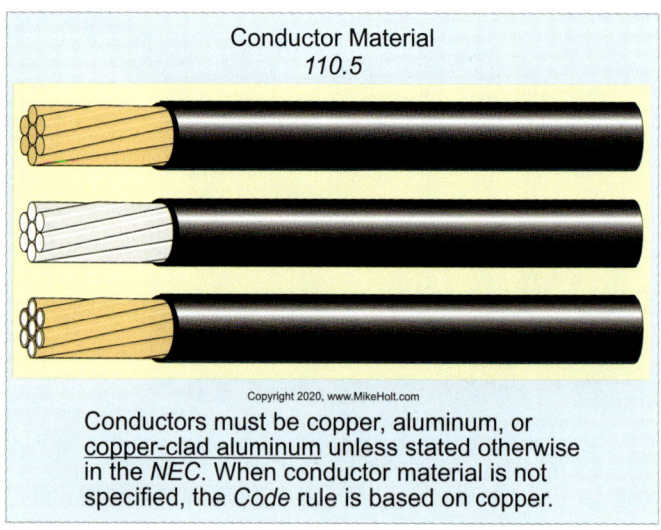

▸Figure 110–4

110.6 Conductor Sizes

Conductor sizes are expressed in American Wire Gage (AWG) or circular mils (cmil). ▸Figure 110–5

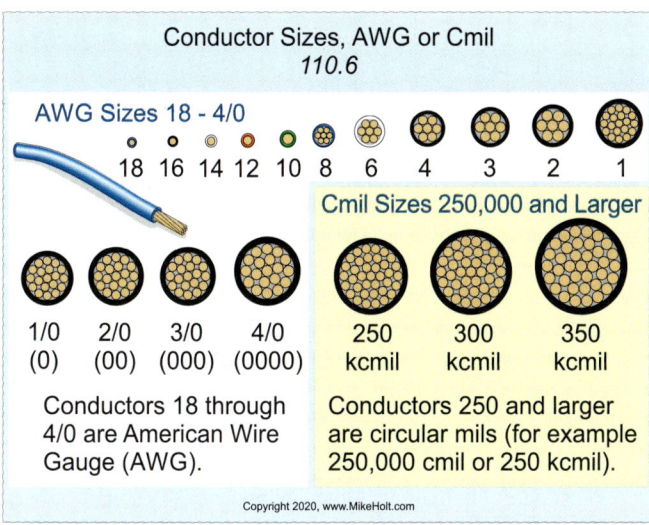
▶Figure 110-5

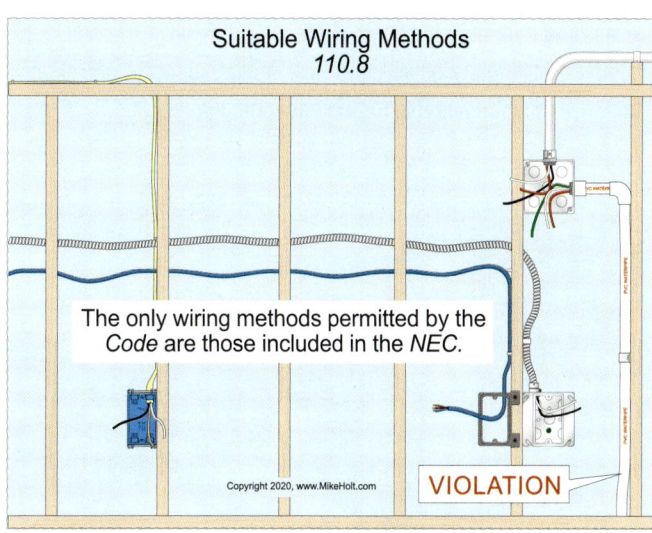
▶Figure 110-7

110.7 Wiring Integrity

Electrical installations must be free from short circuits, ground faults, or any connections to conductive metal parts unless required or permitted by the *Code*. ▶Figure 110-6

Author's Comment:

▶ See Chapter 3 for power and lighting wiring methods; Chapter 7 for signaling, remote-control, and power-limited circuit wiring methods; and Chapter 8 for communications circuits wiring methods.

110.11 Deteriorating Agents

Electrical equipment and conductors must be suitable for the environment and the conditions for which they will be used. Consideration must also be given to the presence of corrosive gases, fumes, vapors, liquids, or other substances that can have a deteriorating effect on conductors and equipment. ▶Figure 110-8

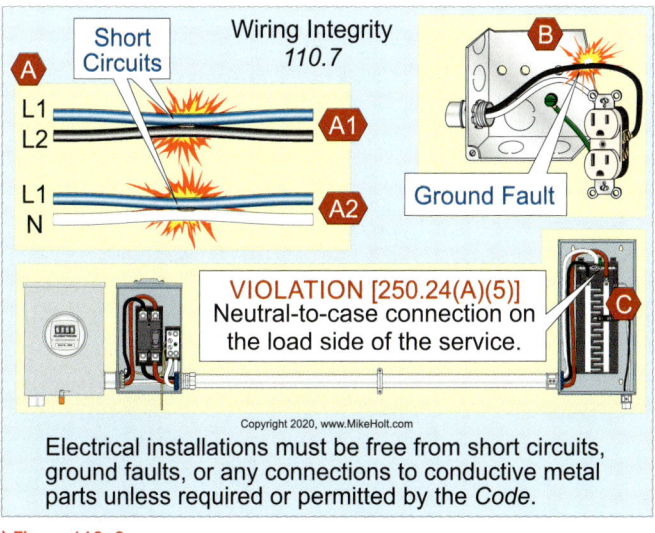
▶Figure 110-6

110.8 Suitable Wiring Methods

The only wiring methods permitted by the *NEC* are those included in the *Code*. ▶Figure 110-7

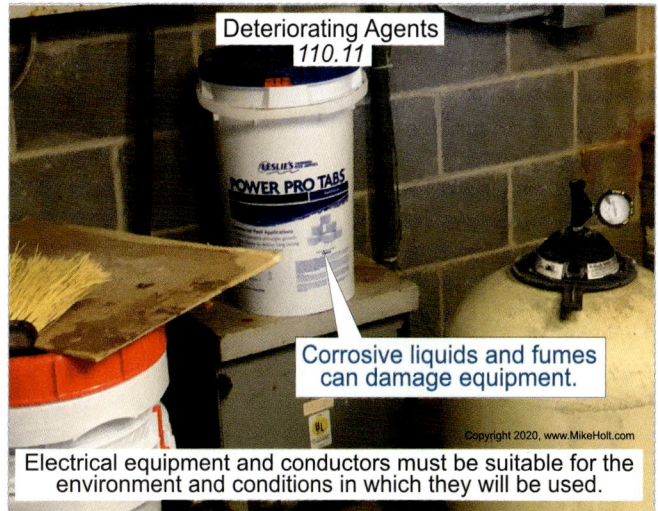
▶Figure 110-8

110.14 | Requirements for Electrical Installations

Note 1: Raceways, cable trays, cablebus, cable armor, boxes, cable sheathing, cabinets, elbows, couplings, fittings, supports, and support hardware must be suitable for the environment; see 300.6. ▶Figure 110-9

▶Figure 110-9

▶Figure 110-10

Note 2: Some cleaning and lubricating compounds contain chemicals that can cause plastic to deteriorate.

Equipment identified for indoor use must be protected against damage from the weather during construction.

Note 3: See Table 110.28 for NEMA enclosure-type designations.

Note 4: For minimum flood provisions, see the *International Building Code* (IBC) and the *International Residential Code* (IRC).

110.14 Conductor Termination and Splicing

Conductor terminal and splicing devices must be identified for the conductor material and must be properly installed and used in accordance with the manufacturer's instructions [110.3(B)]. ▶Figure 110-10

Author's Comment:

▸ Conductor terminals suitable for aluminum wire only will be marked "AL." Those acceptable for copper wire only will be marked "CU." Terminals suitable for both copper and aluminum will be marked "CU-AL" or "AL-CU." For 6 AWG and smaller, the markings can be printed on the container or on an information sheet inside the container. A "7" or "75" indicates a 75°C rated terminal, and a "9" or "90" indicates a 90°C rated terminal. If a terminal bears no marking, it can be used only with copper conductors. ▶Figure 110-11

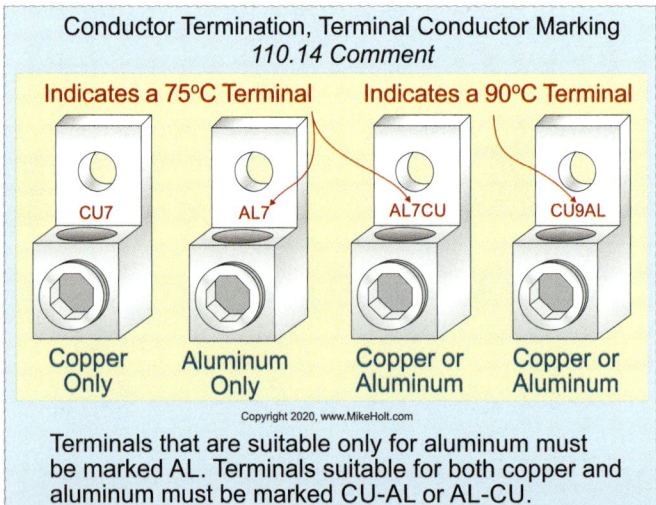
▶Figure 110-11

Connectors and terminals for conductors more finely stranded than Class B and Class C must be identified for the use of finely stranded conductors. ▶Figure 110-12

86 | *Mike Holt's Illustrated Guide to Understanding 2020 NEC Requirements for Bonding and Grounding*

Requirements for Electrical Installations | 110.14

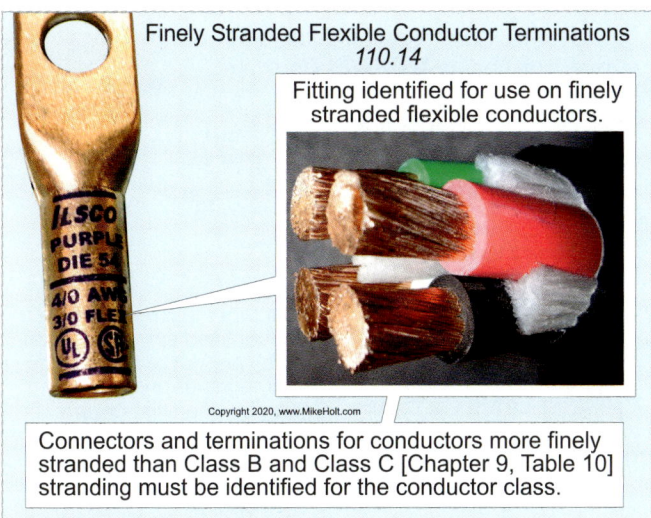
▶Figure 110–12

(A) Conductor Terminations. Conductor terminals must ensure a good connection without damaging the conductors.

Terminals are listed for one conductor unless marked otherwise. Terminals for more than one conductor must be identified for this purpose, either within the equipment instructions or on the terminal itself. ▶Figure 110–13

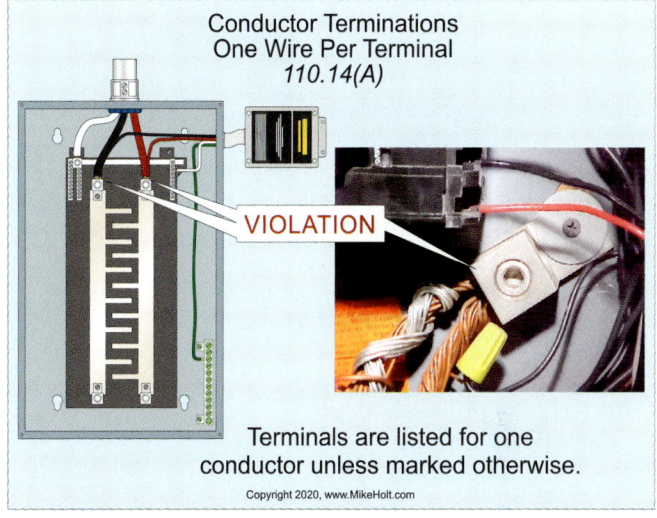
▶Figure 110–13

Author's Comment:

▸ According to Article 100, "Identified" means that it is recognized as suitable for a specific purpose, function, or environment by listing, labeling, or other means approved by the authority having jurisdiction.

▸ Conductor terminations must comply with the manufacturer's instructions as required by 110.3(B). For example, if the instructions for the device say, "Suitable for 18-12 AWG Stranded," then only stranded conductors can be used with the terminating device. If they say, "Suitable for 18-12 AWG Solid," then only solid conductors are permitted, and if the instructions say, "Suitable for 18-12 AWG," then either solid or stranded conductors can be used with the terminating device.

Copper and Aluminum Mixed. Copper and aluminum conductors (dissimilar metals) are not permitted to contact each other in a device unless the device is listed and identified for this purpose.

Author's Comment:

▸ Few terminations are listed for mixing aluminum and copper conductors, but if they are, that will be marked on the product package or terminal device. The reason copper and aluminum should not be in contact with each other is because corrosion develops between the two different metals due to galvanic action, resulting in increased contact resistance at the splicing device. This increased resistance can cause the splice to overheat and result in a fire.

Author's Comment:

▸ Split-bolt connectors are commonly listed for only two conductors, although some are listed for three. However, it is a common industry practice to terminate as many conductors as possible within a split-bolt connector, even though this violates the *NEC*. ▶Figure 110–14

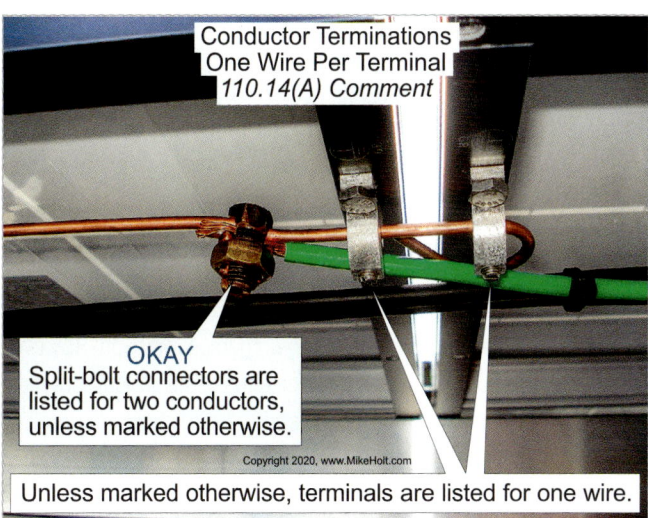
▶Figure 110–14

Mike Holt Enterprises • www.MikeHolt.com • 888.NEC.CODE (632.2633) | 87

(B) Conductor Splices. Conductors must be spliced by a splicing device that is identified for the purpose. ▶Figure 110–15

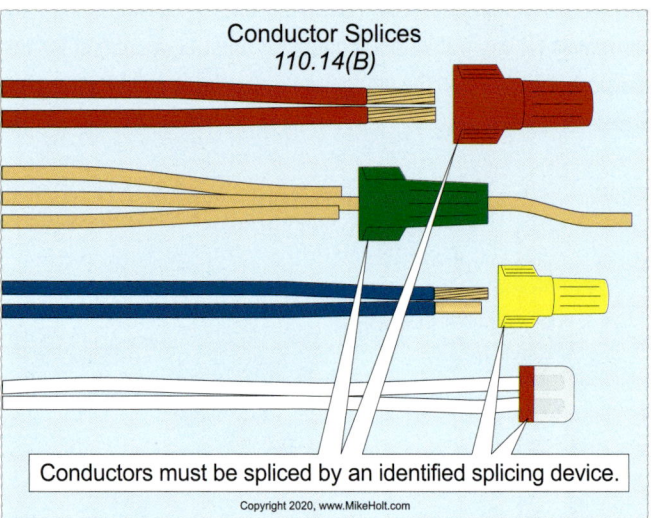

▶Figure 110–15

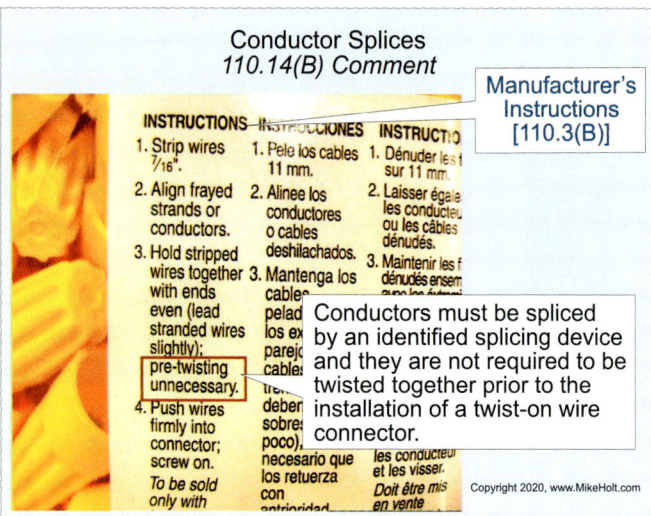

▶Figure 110–16

Author's Comment:

▸ Pre-twisting conductors before applying twist-on wire connectors has been a very common practice in the field for years. The question, and subsequent debate, has always been, "Is pre-twisting required?" Well, the *NEC* does not require pre-twisting of conductors. In fact, Ideal® made a statement about their Wing-Nut® twist-on connectors which said, "Pre-twisting is acceptable, but not required." So just follow the manufacturer's instructions and you will always know! 110.3(B).

▸ Reusing twist-on connectors seems to be another point of contention in the field. Should they be reused? Some say that they just never seem quite the same once they're used, while others say they reuse them all the time. Fortunately, we can once again defer to the manufacturer. Ideal® and 3M® both indicate in their information that it's perfectly fine to reuse their twist-on connectors. It seems that in both cases, pre-twisting or reusing wire connectors just might come down to a matter of personal preference. ▶Figure 110–16

Unused circuit conductors are not required to be removed. However, to prevent an electrical hazard, the free ends of the conductors must be insulated to prevent the exposed end(s) from touching energized parts. This requirement can be met by using an insulated twist-on or push-on wire connector. ▶Figure 110–17

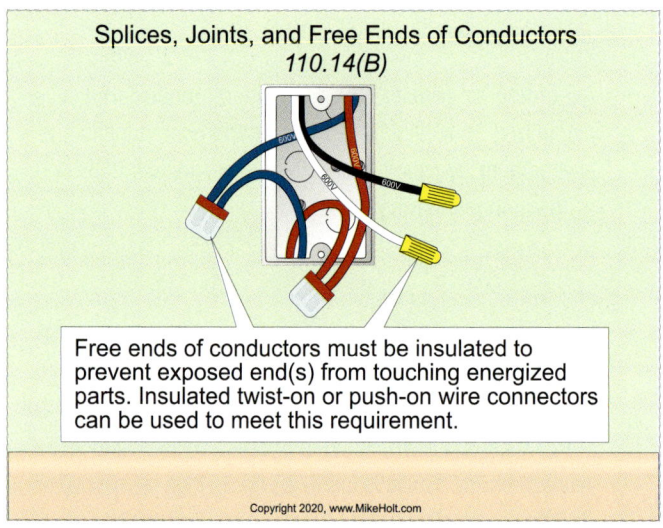

▶Figure 110–17

Author's Comment:

▸ According to Article 100, "Energized" means electrically connected to a source of voltage.

Underground Splices, Single Conductors. Single direct burial types UF or USE conductors can be spliced underground with a device that is listed for direct burial [300.5(E) and 300.15(G)]. ▶Figure 110–18

Underground Splices, Multiconductor Cable. Multiconductor UF or USE cable can have the individual conductors spliced underground with a listed splice kit that encapsulates the conductors and cable jacket.

Requirements for Electrical Installations | 110.14

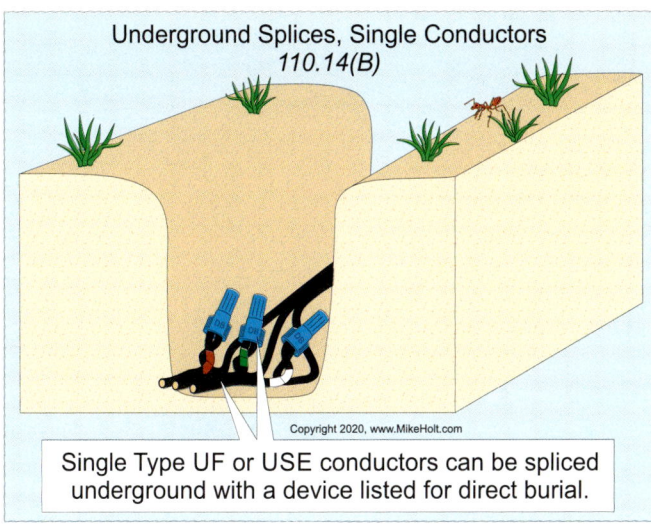
▶Figure 110-18

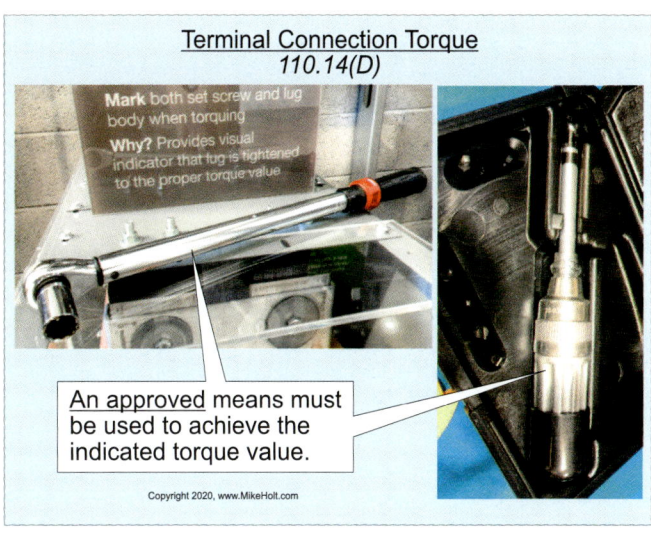
▶Figure 110-20

Author's Comment:

▶ Electrical connection failures are the cause of many equipment and building fires. Improper terminations, poor workmanship, not following the manufacturer's instructions, and improper torqueing can all cause poor electrical connections. Improper electrical terminations can damage and melt conductor insulation resulting in short circuits and ground faults.

(D) Terminal Connection Torque. Tightening torque values for terminal connections must be as indicated on equipment or installation instructions. An approved means (a torque tool) must be used to achieve the indicated torque value. ▶Figure 110-19 and ▶Figure 110-20

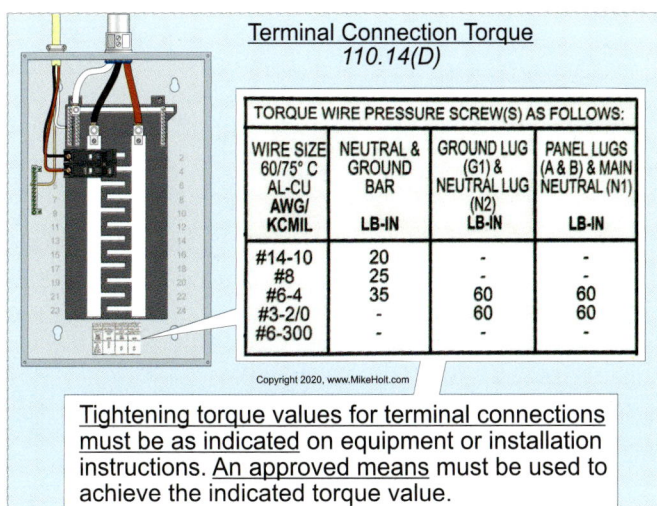
▶Figure 110-19

Author's Comment:

▶ Conductors must terminate in devices that have been properly tightened in accordance with the manufacturer's torque specifications included with equipment instructions. Failure to torque terminals properly can result in excessive heating of terminals or splicing devices due to a loose connection. A loose connection can also lead to arcing which increases the heating effect and may also lead to a short circuit or ground fault. Any of these can result in a fire or other failure, including an arc flash event. Improper torqueing is also a violation of 110.3(B), which requires all equipment to be installed in accordance with listing or labeling instructions.

Note 1: Examples of approved means of achieving the indicated torque values include the use of torque tools or devices such as shear bolts or breakaway-style devices with visual indicators that demonstrate the proper torque has been applied.

Note 2: The equipment manufacturer can be contacted if numeric torque values are not indicated on the equipment, or if the installation instructions are not available. Annex I of UL Standard 486A-486B, *Standard for Safety-Wire Connectors*, provides torque values in the absence of manufacturer's recommendations.

Note 3: Additional information for torqueing threaded connections and terminations can be found in Section 8.11 of NFPA 70B, *Recommended Practice for Electrical Equipment Maintenance.*

Notes

CHAPTER 1

PRACTICE QUESTIONS

Please use the 2020 *Code* book to answer the following questions.

CHAPTER 1—GENERAL RULES

Article 100—Definitions

1. Article 100 contains definitions essential to the application of the *Code*. Definitions are also found in _____.

   (a) the index
   (b) the annex
   (c) XXX.2 of other articles
   (d) article scope(s)

2. Equipment that is capable of being reached for operation, renewal, and inspection defines _____.

   (a) accessible (as applied to equipment)
   (b) accessible (as applied to wiring methods)
   (c) accessible, readily
   (d) all of these

3. "_____" means acceptable to the authority having jurisdiction.

   (a) Identified
   (b) Listed
   (c) Approved
   (d) Labeled

4. A device that, when inserted in a receptacle, establishes a connection between the conductors of the attached flexible cord and the conductors connected permanently to the receptacle is called a(n) "_____."

   (a) attachment plug
   (b) plug cap
   (c) plug
   (d) any of these

5. A device that, by insertion into a locking support and mounting receptacle, establishes a connection between the conductors of the attached utilization equipment and the branch-circuit conductors connected to the locking support and mounting receptacle is otherwise known as a(an) _____.

   (a) Cord Cap Attachment
   (b) Attachment Fitting
   (c) End Cap Fitting
   (d) Attachment Plug

6. A reliable conductor that ensures electrical conductivity between metal parts of the electrical installation that are required to be electrically connected is called a(n) "_____."

   (a) grounding electrode
   (b) auxiliary ground
   (c) bonding conductor or jumper
   (d) tap conductor

7. A conductor installed on the supply side of a service or within a service equipment enclosure, or for a separately derived system, to ensure the required electrical conductivity between metal parts required to be electrically connected is known as the "_____."

   (a) supply-side bonding jumper
   (b) ungrounded conductor
   (c) electrical supply source
   (d) grounding electrode conductor

Chapter 1 | Practice Questions

8. The connection between the grounded circuit conductor and the supply-side bonding jumper or equipment grounding conductor, or both, at a _____ is called a "system bonding jumper."

   (a) service disconnect
   (b) separately derived system
   (c) motor control center
   (d) separate building or structure disconnect

9. The NEC defines a(n) "_____" as a structure that stands alone or that is separated from adjoining structures by fire walls.

   (a) unit
   (b) apartment
   (c) building
   (d) utility

10. An enclosure designed for either surface mounting or flush mounting provided with a frame in which a door(s) can be hung is called a(n) "_____."

    (a) enclosure
    (b) outlet box
    (c) cutout box
    (d) cabinet

11. Coaxial cable is a cylindrical assembly composed of a conductor centered inside a metallic tube or shield, separated by a(n) _____ material and usually covered by an insulating jacket.

    (a) insulating
    (b) conductive
    (c) isolating
    (d) dielectric

12. Communications equipment is the electronic equipment that performs the telecommunications operations equipment includes equipment and conductors used for the transmission of _____.

    (a) audio
    (b) video
    (c) data
    (d) any of these

13. A(n) "_____" is a device, or group of devices, by which the conductors of a circuit can be disconnected from their source of supply.

    (a) feeder
    (b) enclosure
    (c) disconnecting means
    (d) conductor interrupter

14. An effective ground-fault current path is an intentionally constructed, low-impedance electrically conductive path designed and intended to carry current during a ground-fault condition from the point of a ground fault on a wiring system to _____.

    (a) ground
    (b) earth
    (c) the electrical supply source
    (d) the grounding electrode

15. As used in the NEC, equipment includes _____.

    (a) fittings
    (b) appliances
    (c) machinery
    (d) all of these

16. Accessible conductive parts bonded together to reduce voltage gradients in a designated area is known as a _____.

    (a) Solidly Grounded System
    (b) Equipotential Plane
    (c) Isolated Grounding System
    (d) Effective Ground-Fault Current Path

17. The NEC defines a "_____" as all circuit conductors between the service equipment, the source of a separately derived system, or other power supply source, and the final branch-circuit overcurrent device.

    (a) service
    (b) feeder
    (c) branch circuit
    (d) all of these

18. A fitting is defined as an accessory such as a locknut, bushing, or other part of a wiring system that is intended primarily to perform a(an) _____ rather than an electrical function.

    (a) mechanical
    (b) supplemental
    (c) auxiliary
    (d) physical

19. A(n) _____ is an unintentional, electrically conductive connection between an ungrounded conductor of an electrical circuit, and the normally noncurrent-carrying conductors, metallic enclosures, metallic raceways, metallic equipment, or earth.

    (a) grounded conductor
    (b) ground fault
    (c) equipment ground
    (d) bonding jumper

20. A system or circuit conductor that is intentionally grounded is called a(n) "_____."

    (a) grounding conductor
    (b) unidentified conductor
    (c) grounded conductor
    (d) grounding electrode conductor

21. A Class A GFCI trips when the ground-fault current is _____ or higher.

    (a) 4 mA
    (b) 5 mA
    (c) 6 mA
    (d) 7 mA

22. Connected (connecting) to ground or to a conductive body that extends the ground connection is called "_____."

    (a) equipment grounding
    (b) bonded
    (c) grounded
    (d) all of these

23. Connected to ground without the insertion of any resistor or impedance device is referred to as "_____."

    (a) grounded
    (b) solidly grounded
    (c) effectively grounded
    (d) a grounding conductor

24. A conductor used to connect the system grounded conductor, or the equipment to a grounding electrode or to a point on the grounding electrode system, is called the "_____ conductor."

    (a) main grounding
    (b) common main
    (c) equipment grounding
    (d) grounding electrode

25. A handhole enclosure is an enclosure for use in underground systems, provided with an open or closed bottom, and sized to allow personnel to _____.

    (a) enter and exit freely
    (b) reach into but not enter
    (c) have full working space
    (d) visually examine the interior

26. Recognized as suitable for the specific purpose, function, use, environment, and application is the definition of "_____."

    (a) labeled
    (b) identified (as applied to equipment)
    (c) listed
    (d) approved

27. A device that provides a means to connect intersystem bonding conductors for _____ systems to the grounding electrode system is an "intersystem bonding termination."

    (a) limited-energy
    (b) low-voltage
    (c) communications
    (d) power and lighting

28. The term "Luminaire" means a single individual lampholder by itself.

    (a) True
    (b) False

29. The common point on a wye-connection in a polyphase system is a "neutral point."

    (a) True
    (b) False

30. "Outline lighting" is an arrangement of _____ to outline or call attention to the shape of a building.

    (a) incandescent lamps
    (b) electric-discharge lighting
    (c) electrically powered light sources
    (d) any of these

31. Any current in excess of the rated current of equipment or the ampacity of a conductor is called "_____."

    (a) trip current
    (b) fault current
    (c) overcurrent
    (d) a short circuit

Chapter 1 | Practice Questions

32. A panel, including buses and automatic overcurrent devices, designed to be placed in a cabinet or cutout box and accessible only from the front is known as a "_____."
    (a) switchboard
    (b) disconnect
    (c) panelboard
    (d) switch

33. A "raceway" is an enclosed channel designed expressly for the holding of wires, cables, or busbars, with additional functions as permitted in the *Code*.
    (a) True
    (b) False

34. A contact device installed at an outlet for the connection of an attachment plug, or for the direct connection of electrical utilization equipment designed to mate with the corresponding contact device, is known as a(n) "_____."
    (a) attachment point
    (b) tap
    (c) receptacle
    (d) wall plug

35. A duplex receptacle is an example of a multiple receptacle that has two receptacles on the same _____.
    (a) yoke or strap
    (b) strap
    (c) device
    (d) cover plate

36. A(n) "_____ system" is an electrical source, other than a service, having no direct connection(s) to circuit conductors of any other electrical source other than those established by grounding and bonding connections.
    (a) separately derived
    (b) classified
    (c) direct
    (d) emergency

37. "Overhead service conductors" are the conductors between the _____ and the first point of connection to the service-entrance conductors at the building or other structure.
    (a) service disconnect
    (b) service point
    (c) grounding electrode
    (d) equipment grounding conductor

38. "Underground service conductors" are the underground conductors between the service point and the first point of connection to the service-entrance conductors in a terminal box, meter, or other enclosure, _____ the building wall.
    (a) inside or outside
    (b) concealed within
    (c) above
    (d) below

39. A "service drop" is defined as the overhead conductors between the utility electric supply system and the _____.
    (a) service equipment
    (b) service point
    (c) grounding electrode
    (d) equipment grounding conductor

40. "Overhead system service-entrance conductors" are the service conductors between the terminals of the _____ and a point where they are joined by a tap or splice to the service drop or overhead service conductors.
    (a) service equipment
    (b) service point
    (c) grounding electrode
    (d) equipment grounding conductor

41. "Underground system service-entrance conductors" are the service conductors between the terminals of the _____ and the point of connection to the service lateral or underground service conductors.
    (a) service equipment
    (b) service point
    (c) grounding electrode
    (d) equipment grounding conductor

42. "Service Equipment" includes the necessary equipment connected to the utility electric system and intended to constitute the _____ of the utility electric system.
    (a) main control
    (b) disconnect
    (c) Main control and disconnect
    (d) main control or disconnect

43. "Ungrounded" means not connected to ground or to a conductive body that extends the ground connection.
    (a) True
    (b) False

44. The "voltage of a circuit" is defined by the *Code* as the _____ root-mean-square (effective) difference of potential between any two conductors of the circuit concerned.

    (a) lowest
    (b) greatest
    (c) average
    (d) nominal

45. A nominal value assigned to a circuit or system for the purpose of conveniently designating its voltage class, such as 120/240V, is called "_____ voltage."

    (a) root-mean-square
    (b) circuit
    (c) nominal
    (d) source

Article 110—Requirements for Electrical Installations

46. In judging equipment for approval, considerations such as _____ shall be evaluated.

    (a) mechanical strength
    (b) wire-bending space
    (c) arcing effects
    (d) all of these

47. Product testing, evaluation, and listing (product certification) shall be performed by _____.

    (a) recognized qualified electrical testing laboratories
    (b) the manufacturer
    (c) qualified person
    (d) electrical engineer

48. Conductor sizes are expressed in American Wire Gage (AWG) or in _____.

    (a) inches
    (b) circular mils
    (c) square inches
    (d) cubic inches

49. Only wiring methods recognized as _____ are included in this *Code*.

    (a) expensive
    (b) efficient
    (c) suitable
    (d) cost effective

50. Unless identified for use in the operating environment, no conductors or equipment shall be _____ having a deteriorating effect on the conductors or equipment.

    (a) located in damp or wet locations
    (b) exposed to fumes, vapors, liquids, or gases
    (c) exposed to excessive temperatures
    (d) all of these

51. Some cleaning and lubricating compounds can cause severe deterioration of many plastic materials used for insulating and structural applications in equipment.

    (a) True
    (b) False

52. Unused openings other than those intended for the operation of equipment, intended for mounting purposes, or permitted as part of the design for listed equipment shall be _____.

    (a) filled with cable clamps or connectors only
    (b) taped over with electrical tape
    (c) repaired only by welding or brazing in a metal slug
    (d) closed to afford protection substantially equivalent to the wall of the equipment

53. Conductor terminal and splicing devices shall be _____ for the conductor material and they shall be properly installed and used.

    (a) listed
    (b) approved
    (c) identified
    (d) all of these

54. Connectors and terminals for conductors more finely stranded than Class B and Class C, as shown in Table 10 of Chapter 9, shall be _____ for the specific conductor class or classes.

    (a) listed
    (b) approved
    (c) identified
    (d) all of these

55. All _____ shall be covered with shall be covered with an insulation equivalent to that of the conductors or with an identified insulating device.

    (a) splices
    (b) joints
    (c) free ends of conductors
    (d) All of these

Chapter 1 | Practice Questions

56. Tightening torque values for terminal connections shall be as indicated on equipment or in installation instructions provide by the manufacturer. An approved means shall be used to _____ the indicated torque value.

    (a) maximize
    (b) adjust
    (c) optimize
    (d) achieve

57. Examples of approved means of achieving terminal connection torque values include torque tools or an experienced qualified person that can demonstrate that the proper torque has been applied.

    (a) True
    (b) False

CHAPTER 2

WIRING AND PROTECTION

Introduction to Chapter 2—Wiring and Protection

Chapter 2 provides the general rules for wiring and sizing services, feeders, and branch circuits; and for the overcurrent protection of conductors as well as the proper grounding and bonding of electrical circuits and systems. The rules in this chapter apply to all electrical installations covered by the *NEC*—except as modified in Chapters 5, 6, and 7 [90.3].

Communications Systems [Chapter 8] (twisted-pair conductors, antennas, and coaxial cable) are not subject to the general requirements of Chapters 1 through 4, or the special requirements of Chapters 5 through 7, unless there is a specific reference in Chapter 8 to a rule in Chapters 1 through 7 [90.3]'.

Author's Comment:

- In this textbook we will only cover the Article 250 requirements for grounding and bonding, a summary of follows.

▶ **Article 250—Grounding and Bonding.** Article 250 covers the grounding requirements for providing a path to the Earth to reduce overvoltage from lightning strikes, and the bonding requirements for the low-impedance fault current path necessary to facilitate the operation of overcurrent protective devices in the event of a ground fault.

Notes

ARTICLE 250

GROUNDING AND BONDING

Introduction to Article 250—Grounding and Bonding

No other article can match this one for misapplication, violation, and misinterpretation. The terminology used in Article 250 has been a source of much confusion but has been improved during the last few *NEC* revisions. It is very important for you to understand the difference between grounding and bonding in order to correctly apply the provisions of this article. Pay careful attention to the definitions of important terms located in Article 100 that apply to grounding and bonding. Article 250 covers the grounding requirements for providing a path to the Earth to reduce overvoltage from lightning strikes, and the bonding requirements that establish a low-impedance fault current path back to the source of the electrical supply to facilitate the operation of overcurrent protective devices in the event of a ground fault.

This article is arranged in a logical manner as illustrated in Figure 250.1 in the *NEC*. It may be a good idea for you to just read through the entire article first to get a big picture overview. Then, study Article 250 closely so you understand the details and remember to check Article 100 for the definitions of terms that may be new to you. The illustrations that accompany the text in this textbook will help you better understand the key points.

Part I. General

250.1 Scope

Article 250 covers the general requirements for the grounding and bonding of electrical installations. ▶Figure 250–1

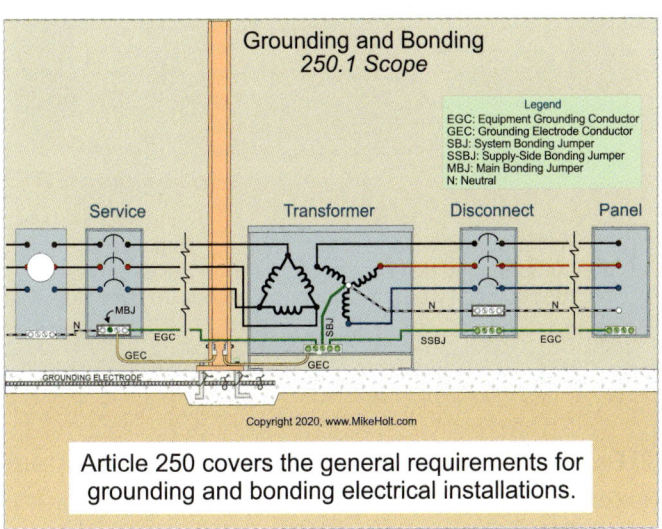

▶Figure 250–1

Author's Comment:

▸ There are two completely different concepts being covered in this article; "Grounding" which is the connection to the Earth, and "Bonding" which is mechanically connecting electrically conductive components together to ensure electrical conductivity between metal parts [Article 100]. While these two systems overlap each other, that portion of the electrical system that needs to be able to carry fault current to the source must be heartier and capable of handling excessive amounts of current. This is called the "Effective Ground-Fault Current Path." The effective ground-fault current path needs a low-impedance fault current path to the source so fault current can rise as quickly as possible to operate the overcurrent protective device as soon as possible. Since fault current can be thousands of amperes, the effective ground-fault current path must be designed to safely handle those high current levels. ▶Figure 250–2

250.4 | Grounding and Bonding

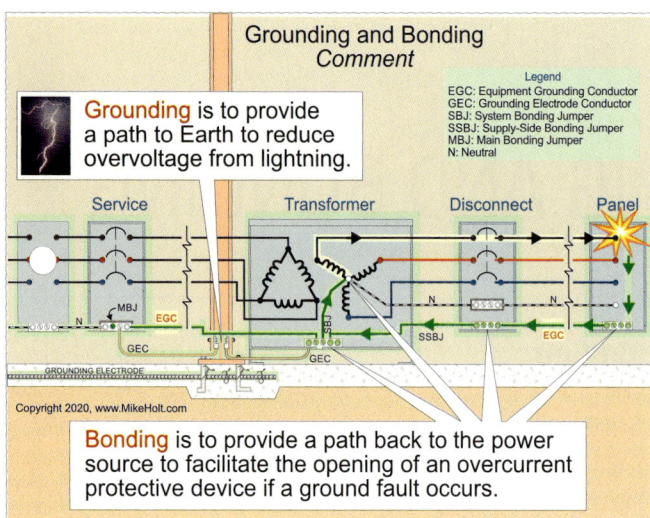

▶Figure 250–2

250.4 Performance Requirements for Grounding and Bonding

 Scan this QR code for a video of Mike explaining this topic; it's a sample from the videos that accompany this textbook. www.MikeHolt.com/20BGvideos

(A) Solidly Grounded Systems.

(1) Electrical System Grounding. Electrical power systems, such as the secondary winding of a transformer, are required to be connected to the Earth (grounded) in order to limit the voltage induced on the conductors by lightning strikes, line surges, or unintentional contact by higher-voltage lines, and to stabilize the secondary conductor's voltage to ground during normal operation. ▶Figure 250–3

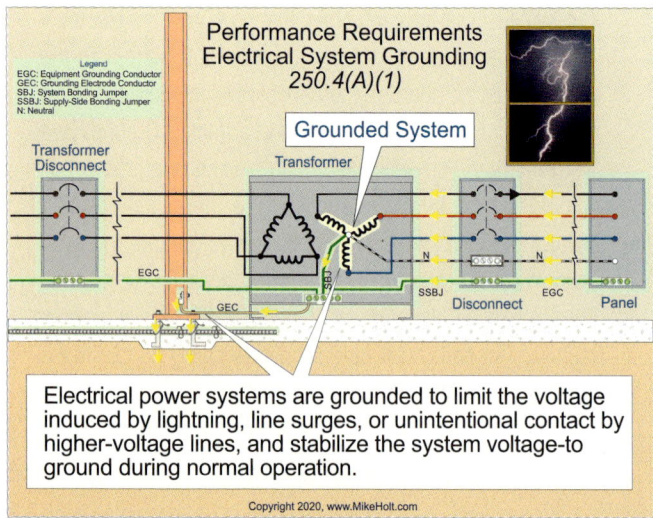

▶Figure 250–3

Author's Comment:

▸ System grounding helps reduce fires in buildings as well as voltage stress on electrical insulation, thereby ensuring longer insulation life for motors, transformers, and other system components. ▶Figure 250–4

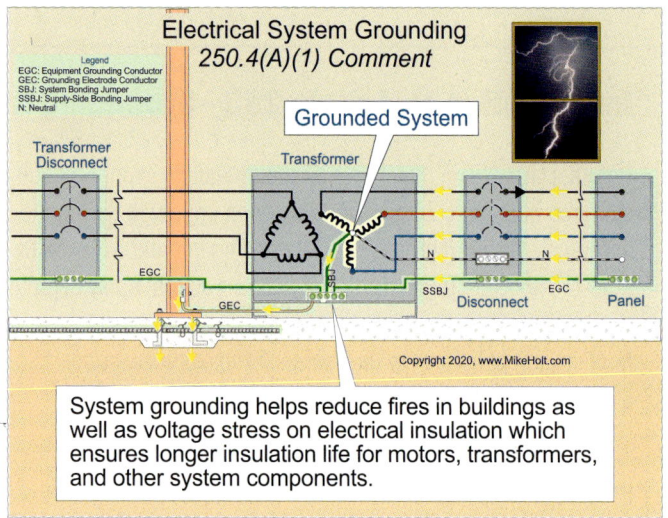

▶Figure 250–4

Note 1: To limit imposed voltage, the grounding electrode conductors should not be any longer than necessary and unnecessary bends and loops should be avoided. ▶Figure 250–5

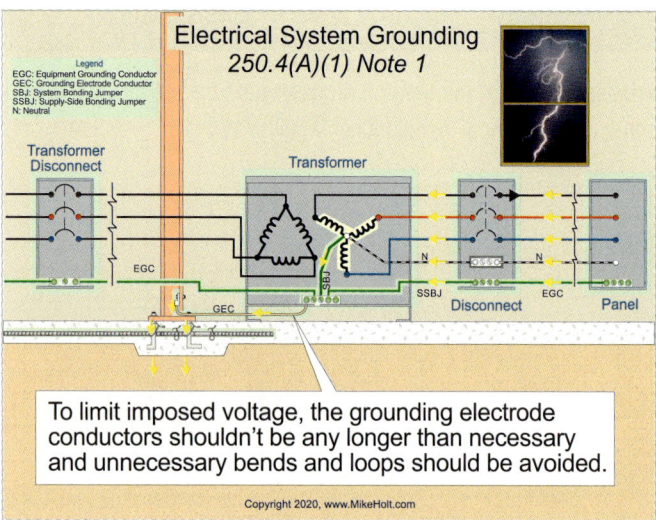

▶Figure 250–5

(2) Equipment Grounding. Metal parts of electrical equipment must be connected to other and to the Earth to reduce the voltage to ground on the metal parts from indirect lightning strikes. ▶Figure 250–6

Grounding and Bonding | 250.4

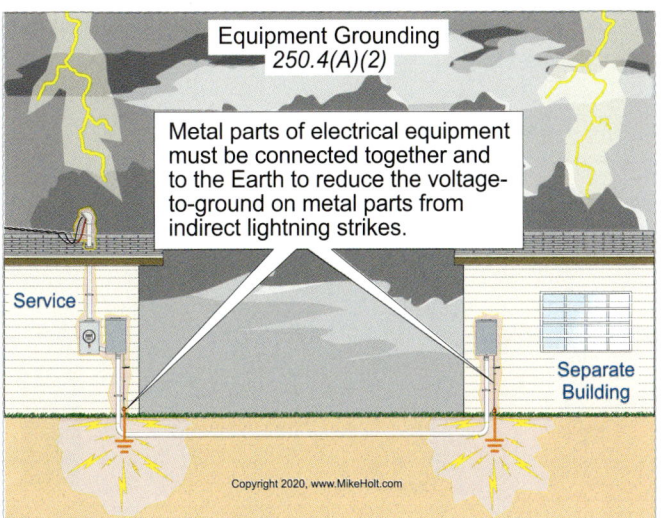
▶Figure 250-6

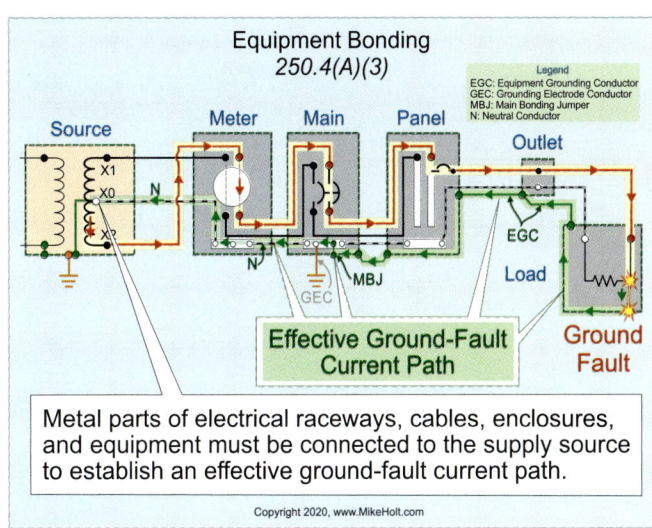
▶Figure 250-8

Danger

Failure to ground metal parts to earth can result in millions of volts of induced voltage on the metal parts of an electrical system generated by an indirect lightning strike. This energy seeks a path to the Earth within the building—possibly resulting in a fire and/or electric shock from a side flash. ▶Figure 250-7

Author's Comment:

▸ According to Article 100, an "Effective Ground-Fault Current Path" is an intentionally constructed low-impedance conductive path designed to carry fault current from the point of a ground fault to the source for the purpose of opening the circuit overcurrent protective device. ▶Figure 250-9

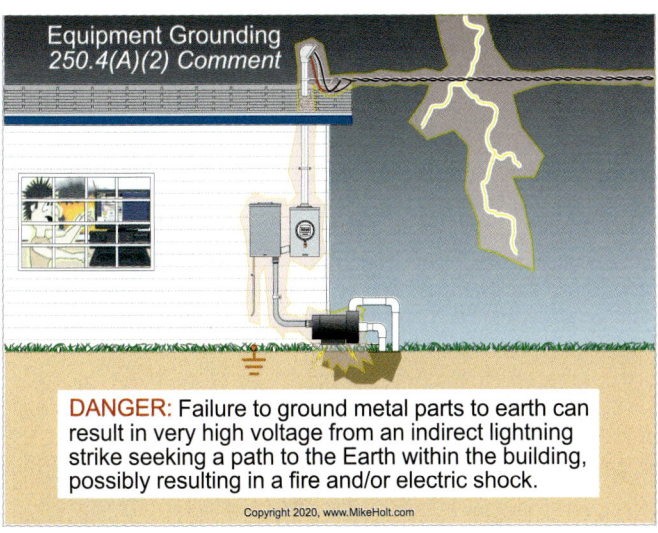
▶Figure 250-7

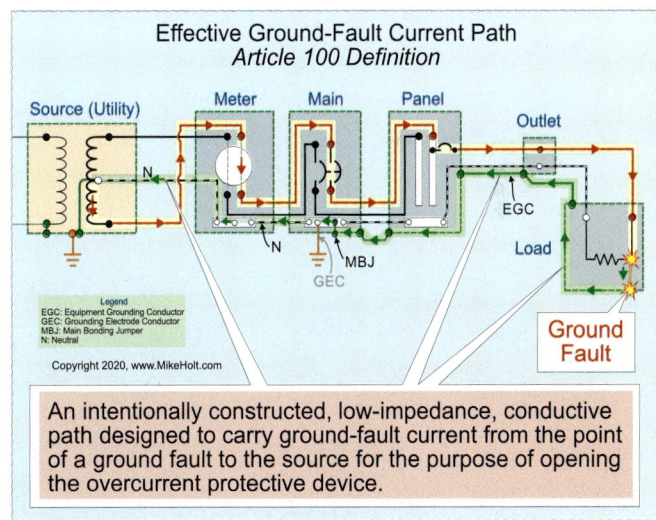
▶Figure 250-9

(3) Equipment Bonding. Metal parts of electrical raceways, cables, enclosures, and equipment must be connected together and to the supply system in a manner that establishes an effective ground-fault current path. See 250.4(A)(5). ▶Figure 250-8

Author's Comment:

▸ To quickly remove dangerous voltage on metal parts from a ground fault, the effective ground-fault current path must have sufficiently low impedance to the source so fault current will quickly rise to a level that will open the circuit overcurrent device. ▶Figure 250-10

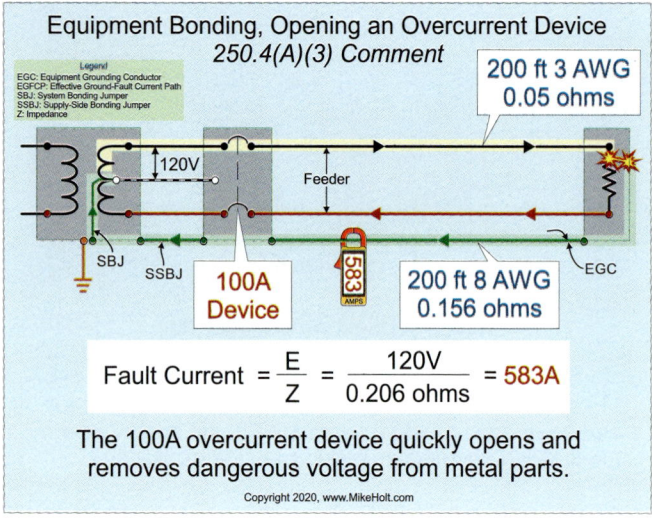

▶Figure 250-10

Author's Comment:

▸ The time it takes for an overcurrent device to open is dependent on the magnitude of the fault current. A higher fault current value will result in a shorter clearing time for the overcurrent protective device. For example, a 20A overcurrent device with an overload of 40A (two times the 20A rating) takes 25 to 150 seconds to open. The same device at 100A (five times the 20A rating) trips in 5 to 20 seconds. ▶Figure 250-11

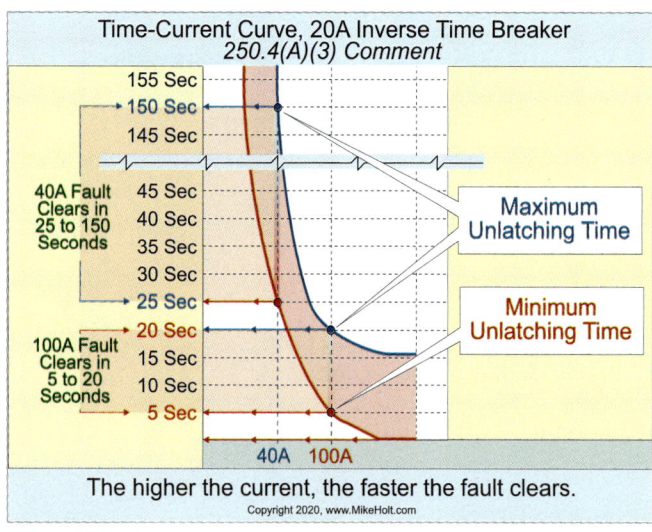

▶Figure 250-11

(4) Bonding Conductive Materials. Electrically conductive materials that are likely to become energized, such as metal water piping systems, metal sprinkler piping, metal gas piping, and other metal-piping systems, and exposed structural steel members must be connected (bonded) to the supply source via an effective ground-fault current path. ▶Figure 250-12

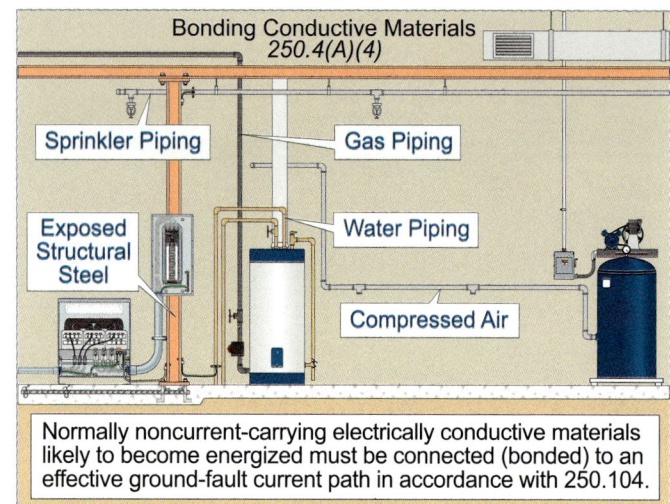

▶Figure 250-12

Author's Comment:

▸ According to the NFPA style manual, "Likely to Become Energized" means that an electrical conductor is present in some capacity.

(5) Effective Ground-Fault Current Path. Metal parts of electrical raceways, cables, enclosures, or equipment must be bonded together and to the supply source in a manner that creates a low-impedance path for ground-fault current facilitating the opening of the circuit overcurrent protective device. ▶Figure 250-13 and ▶Figure 250-14

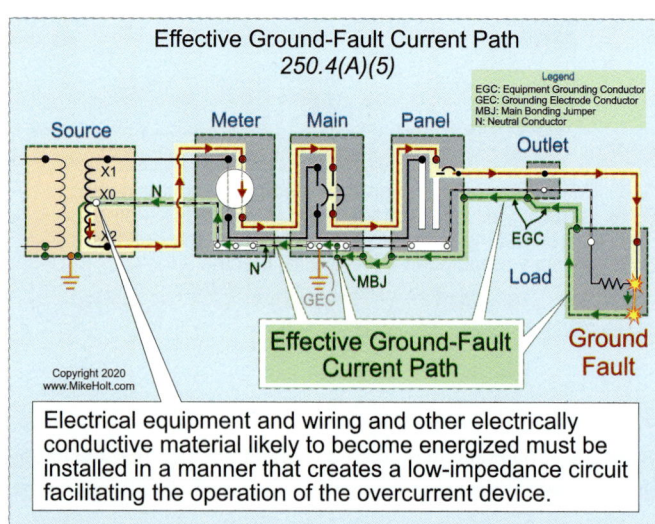

▶Figure 250-13

Grounding and Bonding | 250.4

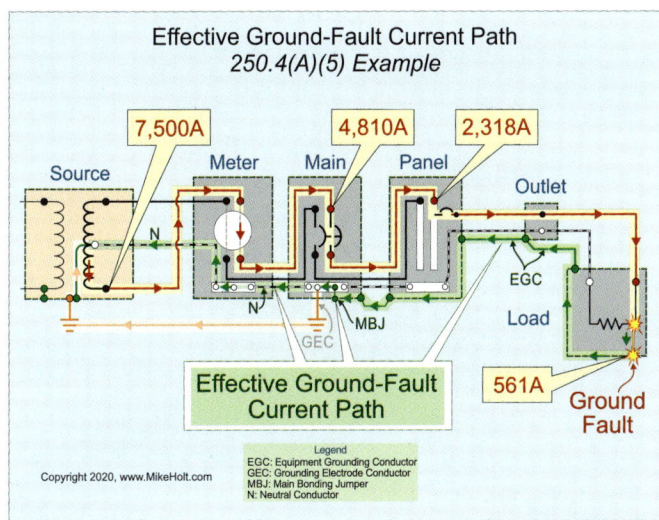
▶Figure 250-14

The effective ground-fault current path must be capable of safely carrying the maximum ground-fault current likely to be imposed on it from any point on the wiring system where a ground fault may occur to the electrical supply source.

The Earth is not permitted to serve as the required effective ground-fault current path, therefore an equipment grounding conductor of a type recognized in 250.118 is required to be installed with all circuits. ▶Figure 250-15

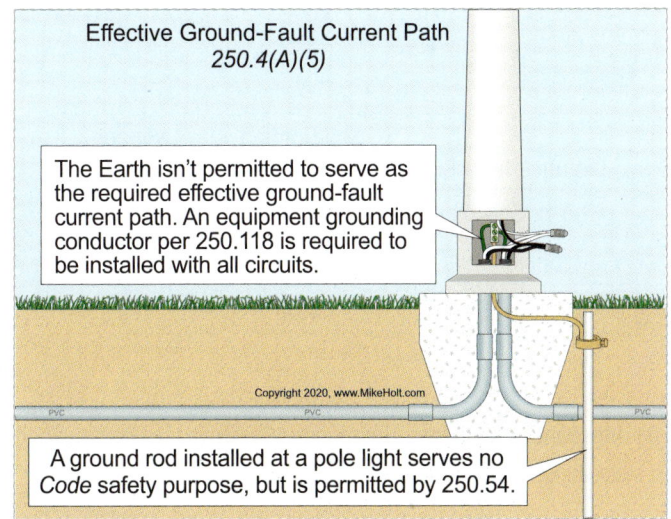
▶Figure 250-15

Danger

Earth grounding does not remove dangerous touch voltage. Because the contact resistance of a grounding electrode (like a ground rod) to the Earth is so high, very little fault current returns to the power supply. As a result, the circuit overcurrent protective device will not open, and all metal parts associated with the electrical installation, metal piping, and structural building steel will become and remain energized. ▶Figure 250-16

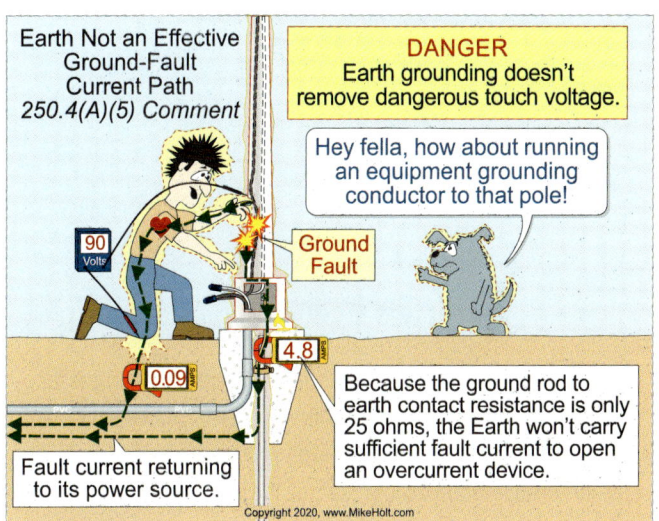
▶Figure 250-16

▶ **Example**

Question: What will the maximum fault current be when there is a 120V ground fault to the metal parts of a light pole that is grounded to a 25-ohm ground rod, but not bonded to an effective ground-fault current path? ▶Figure 250-17

(a) 3.70A (b) 4.80A (c) 5.20A (d) 6.40A

Solution:

I = Volts/Resistance

I = 120V/25 ohms

I = 4.80A

Answer: (b) 4.80A

250.4 | Grounding and Bonding

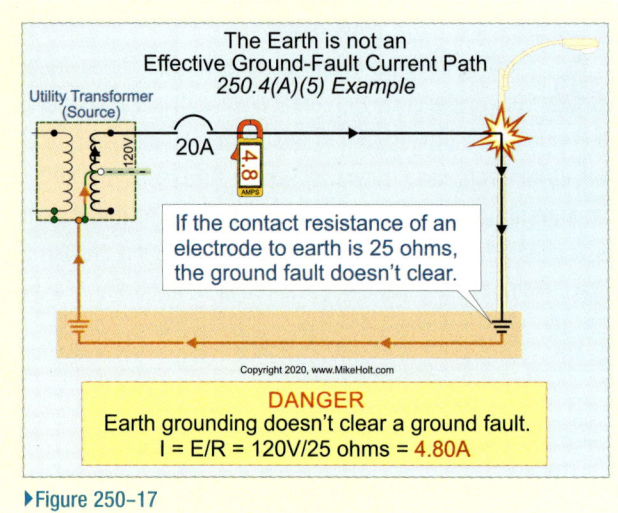
▶Figure 250–17

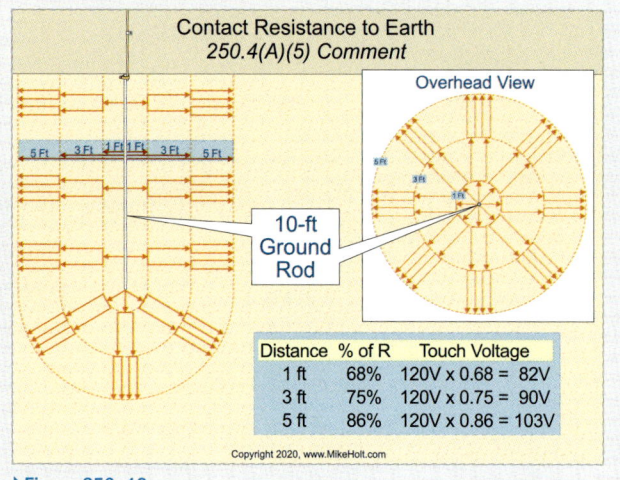
▶Figure 250–18

Earth Shells

According to ANSI/IEEE 142, *Recommended Practice for Grounding of Industrial and Commercial Power Systems* (Green Book) [4.1.1], the resistance of the soil outward from a 10-ft ground rod is equal to the sum of the series resistances of the Earth shells. The shell nearest the ground rod has the highest resistance and each successive shell has progressively larger areas and progressively lower resistances. Do not be concerned if you do not understand this statement; just review the table below.

Distance from Rod	Soil Contact Resistance
1 ft (Shell 1)	68% of total contact resistance
3 ft (Shells 1 and 2)	75% of total contact resistance
5 ft (Shells 1, 2, and 3)	86% of total contact resistance

Contact Resistance. The Earth is an excellent conductor due to an almost limitless number of parallel paths over which electrons can flow. However, the problem lies in the contact resistance between the grounding electrode and the Earth. The surface area of the electrode contacting the Earth is minimal compared to the Earth itself.

Since voltage is directly proportional to resistance, the voltage gradient of the Earth around an energized rod (assuming a 120V ground fault) will be as follows: ▶Figure 250–18 and ▶Figure 250–19

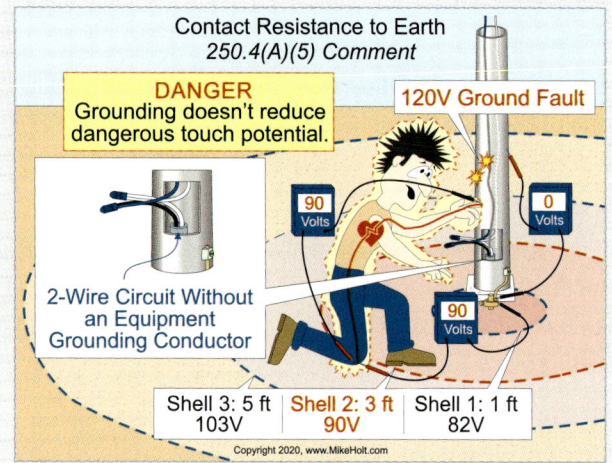
▶Figure 250–19

Distance from Rod	Soil Contact Resistance	Voltage Gradient
1 ft (Shell 1)	68%	82V
3 ft (Shells 1 and 2)	75%	90V
5 ft (Shells 1, 2, and 3)	86%	103V

(B) Ungrounded Systems. Ungrounded Systems must be grounded in accordance with 250.4(B)(1) through 250.4(B)(4).

Author's Comment:

▸ According to Article 100, an ungrounded system is "a power-supply system not connected to earth (ground)," as demonstrated in the secondary winding of a transformer where there is no connection between the system winding and earth (ground) or to a conductive body that extends the Earth (ground) connection. ▶Figure 250–20

Grounding and Bonding | 250.4

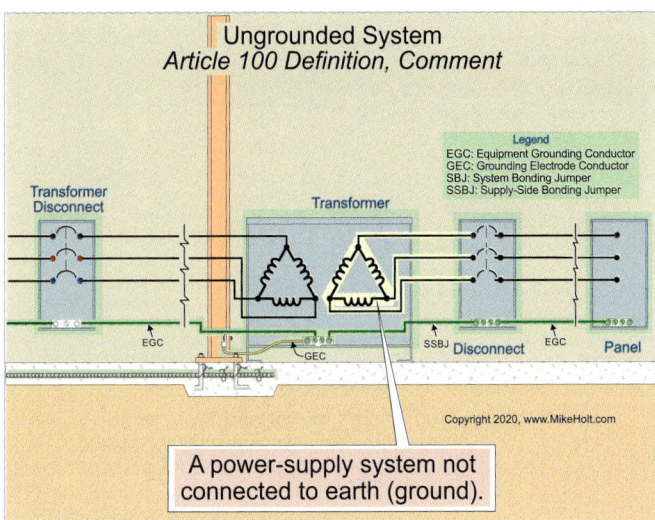
▶Figure 250–20

(1) Equipment Grounding. Metal parts of electrical equipment must be connected to each other and connected to the Earth to reduce the voltage to ground on the metal parts from indirect lightning strikes. ▶Figure 250–21

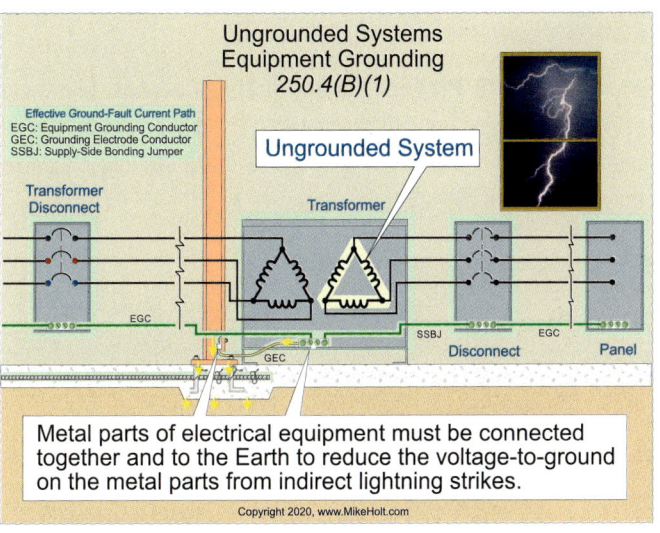
▶Figure 250–21

Danger

⚠ Failure to ground metal parts to earth can result in millions of volts of induced voltage on the metal parts of an electrical system from an indirect lightning strike. This energy seeks a path to the Earth within the building—possibly resulting in a fire and/or electric shock from a side flash.

(2) Equipment Bonding. Metal parts of electrical raceways, cables, enclosures, and equipment must be connected together and to the supply source in a manner that establishes an effective ground-fault current path. ▶Figure 250–22

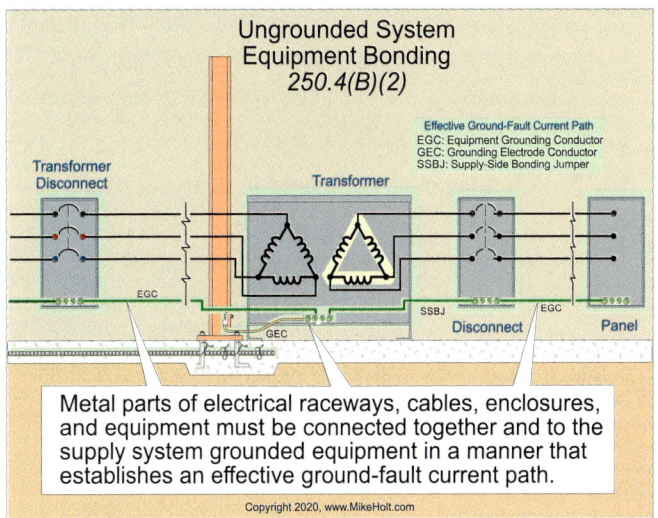
▶Figure 250–22

The effective ground-fault current path must be capable of safely carrying the maximum fault current likely to be imposed on it from any point on the wiring system should a ground fault occur at the electrical supply source.

Author's Comment:

▶ According to Article 100, an "Effective Ground-Fault Current Path" is an intentionally constructed low-impedance conductive path designed to carry fault current from the point of a ground fault to the source for the purpose of opening the circuit overcurrent protective device. ▶Figure 250–23

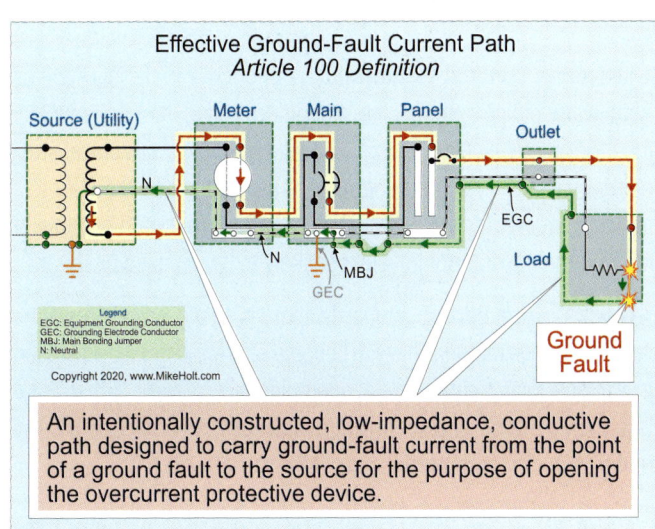
▶Figure 250–23

Mike Holt Enterprises • www.MikeHolt.com • 888.NEC.CODE (632.2633) | 105

250.6 | Grounding and Bonding

Author's Comment:

- To quickly remove dangerous voltage on metal parts from a ground fault, the effective ground-fault current path must have sufficiently low impedance to the source so fault current will quickly rise to a level that will open the circuit overcurrent protective device [250.4(A)(3)].

- The time it takes for an overcurrent protective device to open is dependent on the magnitude of the fault current. A higher fault current value will result in a shorter clearing time for the overcurrent device. For example, a 20A overcurrent protective device with an overload of 40A (two times the 20A rating) takes 25 to 150 seconds to open. The same device at 100A (five times the 20A rating) trips in 5 to 20 seconds. ▶Figure 250-24

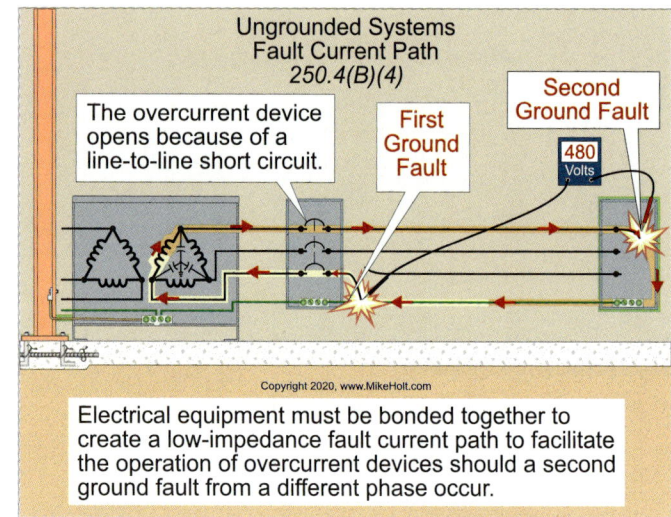

▶Figure 250-25

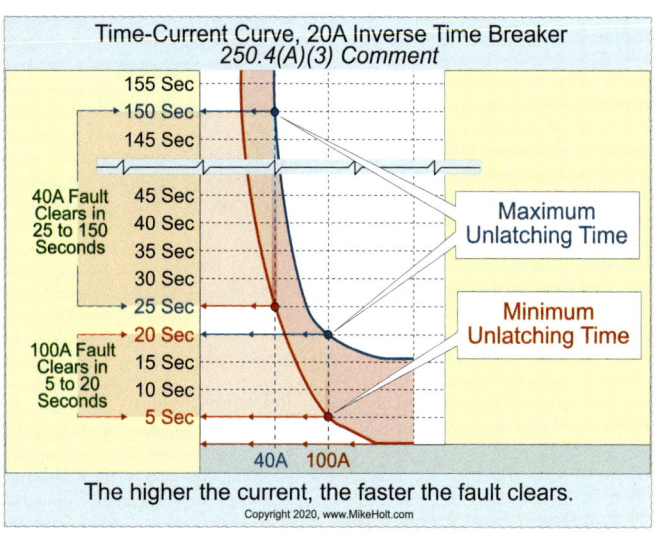

▶Figure 250-24

(3) Bonding Conductive Materials. Conductive materials such as metal water piping systems, metal sprinkler piping, metal gas piping, and other metal-piping systems, as well as exposed structural steel members likely to become energized must be bonded together in a manner that creates a low-impedance fault current path capable of carrying the maximum fault current likely to be imposed on it.

(4) Fault Current Path. Electrical equipment, wiring, and other electrically conductive material likely to become energized must be installed in a manner that creates a low-impedance fault current path to facilitate the operation of overcurrent devices should a second ground fault from a different phase occur. ▶Figure 250-25

250.6 Objectionable Current

 Scan this QR code for a video of Mike explaining this topic; it's a sample from the videos that accompany this textbook. www.MikeHolt.com/20BGvideos

(A) Arranged to Prevent Objectionable Current. Electrical systems and equipment must be installed in a manner that prevents neutral or circuit current from flowing on metal parts (objectionable current). ▶Figure 250-26

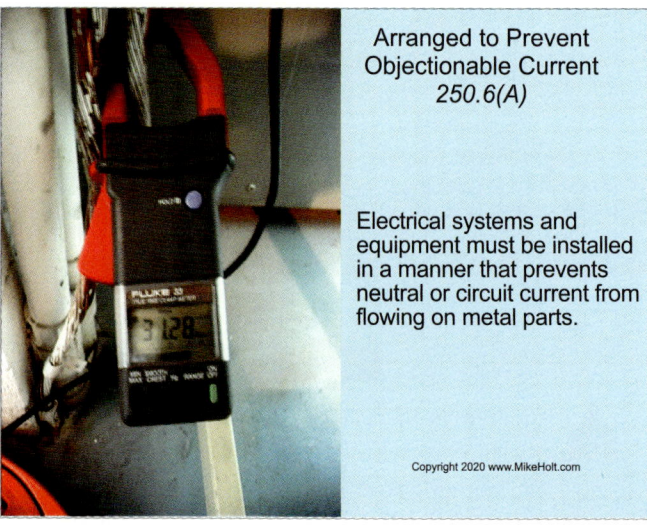

▶Figure 250-26

Objectionable Current

Objectionable neutral current occurs because of improper neutral-to-case connections or wiring errors that violate 250.142(B).

Panelboards. Objectionable neutral current will flow on metal parts and the equipment grounding conductor when the neutral conductor is connected to the metal case of a panelboard on the load side of the service disconnect. ▶Figure 250-27

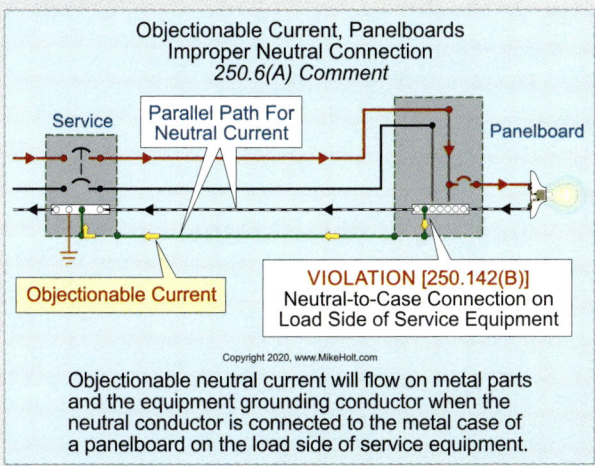

▶Figure 250-27

Transformers. Objectionable neutral current will flow on metal parts if the neutral conductor is connected to the circuit equipment grounding conductor at both the transformer and any other location on the load side of the system bonding jumper. ▶Figure 250-28

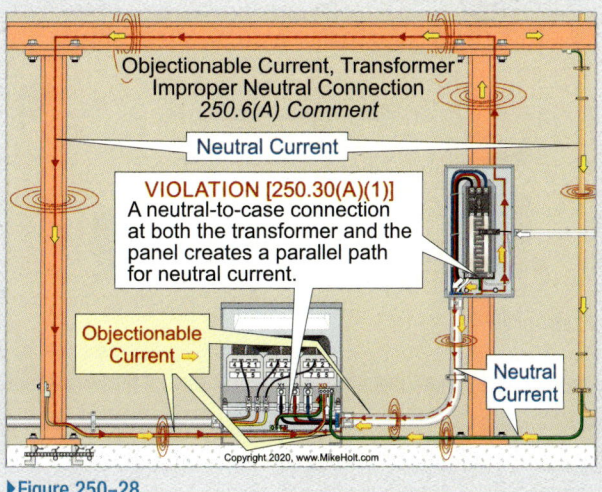

▶Figure 250-28

Generator. Objectionable neutral current will flow on metal parts and the equipment grounding conductor if a generator is connected to a transfer switch with a solidly connected neutral, and a neutral-to-case connection is made at the generator. ▶Figure 250-29

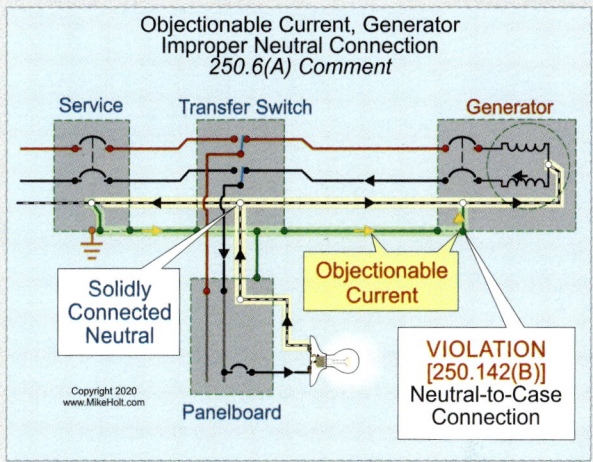

▶Figure 250-29

Disconnects. Objectionable neutral current will flow on metal parts and the equipment grounding conductor if the neutral conductor is connected to the metal case of a disconnect that is not part of the service disconnect. ▶Figure 250-30

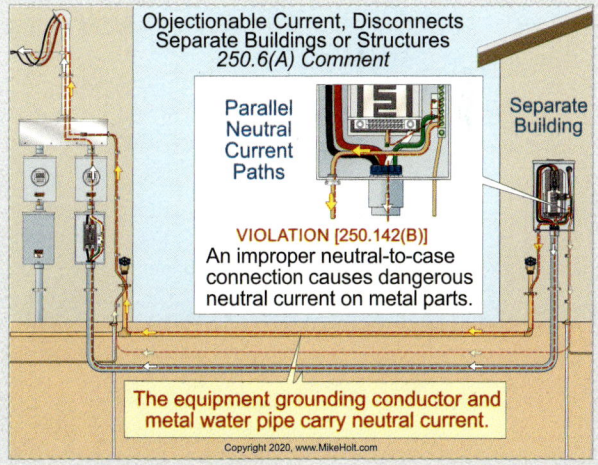

▶Figure 250-30

Wiring Errors. Objectionable neutral current will flow on metal parts and equipment grounding conductors if the neutral conductor from one system is used as the neutral conductor for a different system. ▶Figure 250-31

250.6 | Grounding and Bonding

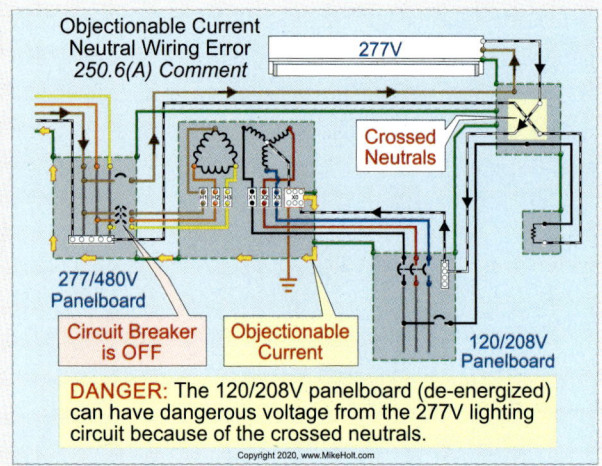

▶Figure 250–31

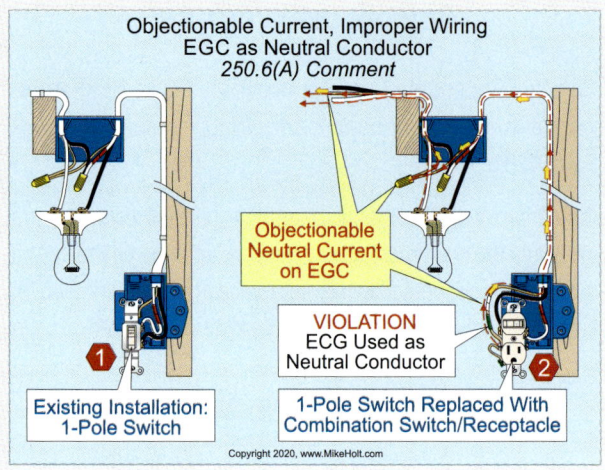

▶Figure 250–33

Improper Wiring. Objectionable neutral current will flow on the equipment grounding conductor if the circuit equipment grounding conductor is used as a neutral conductor, such as where:

▶ A 230V time-clock motor is replaced with a 115V time-clock motor, and the circuit equipment grounding conductor is used for neutral return current.

▶ A 115V water filter is wired to a 240V well-pump motor circuit, and the circuit equipment grounding conductor is used for neutral return current. ▶Figure 250–32

▶ The circuit equipment grounding conductor is used for neutral return current. ▶Figure 250–33

Dangers of Objectionable Current

Objectionable neutral current on metal parts can cause electric shock, fires, and the improper operation of electronic equipment and overcurrent protective devices such as GFPEs, GFCIs, and AFCIs.

Shock Hazard. When objectionable neutral current flows on metal parts or the equipment grounding conductor, electric shock and even death can occur from the elevated voltage. ▶Figure 250–34 and ▶Figure 250–35

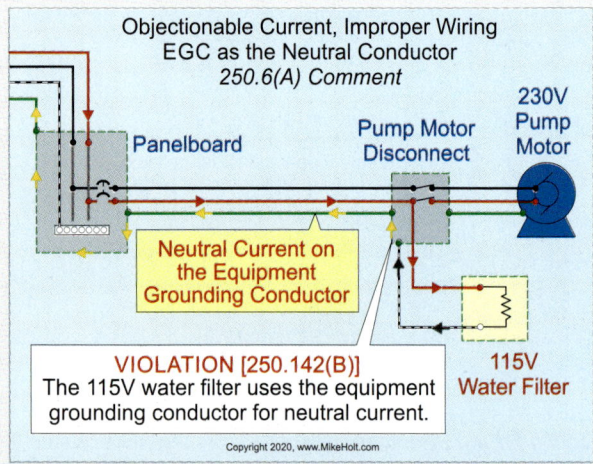

▶Figure 250–32

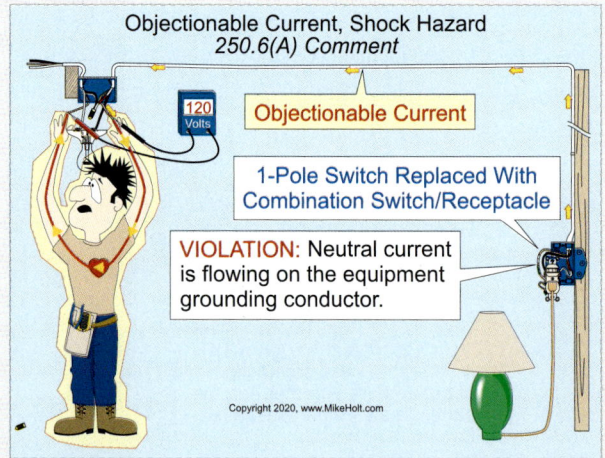

▶Figure 250–34

Fire Hazard. When objectionable neutral current flows on metal parts, a fire can ignite adjacent combustible material. Heat is generated whenever current flows, particularly over high-resistance parts. In addition, arcing at loose connections is especially dangerous in areas containing easily ignitible and explosive gases, vapors, or dust. ▶Figure 250–36

Grounding and Bonding | 250.6

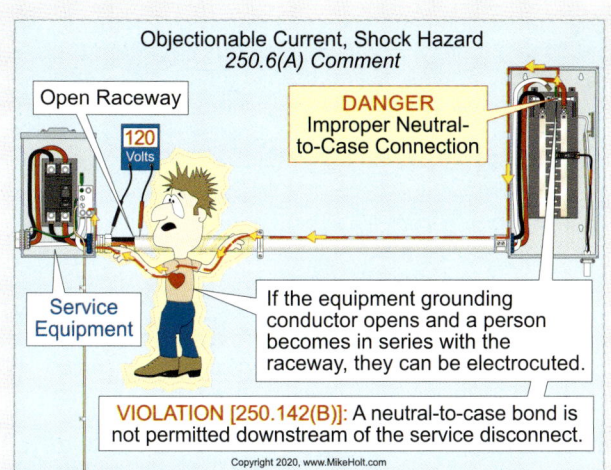
▶Figure 250–35

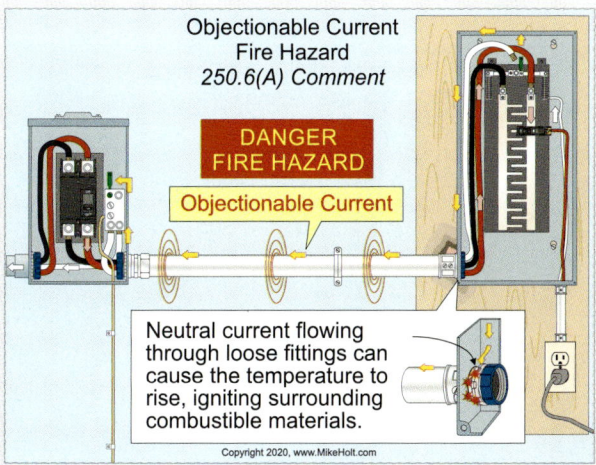
▶Figure 250–36

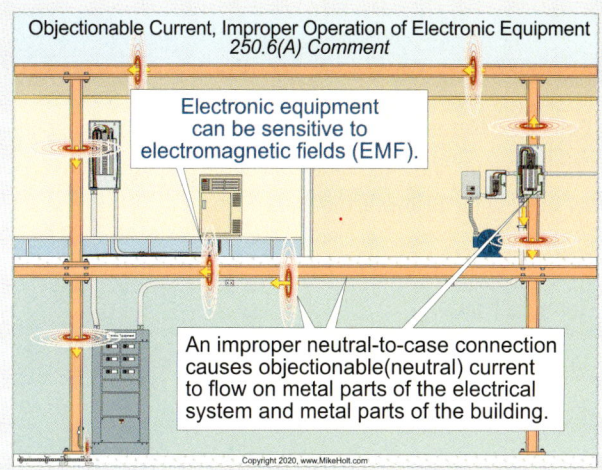
▶Figure 250–37

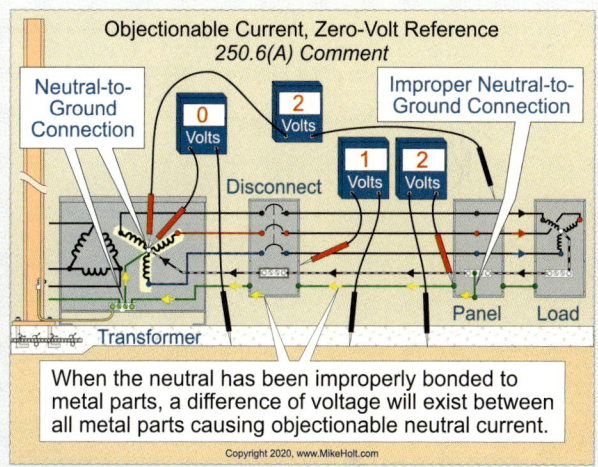
▶Figure 250–38

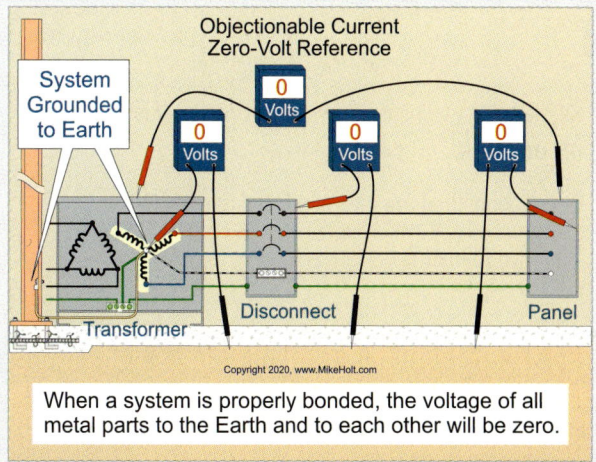
▶Figure 250–39

Improper Operation of Electronic Equipment. Objectionable neutral current flowing on metal parts of electrical equipment and building parts can create electromagnetic fields which negatively affect the performance of electronic devices; particularly medical equipment. ▶Figure 250–37

When objectionable neutral current travels on metal parts and equipment grounding conductors because the neutral has been improperly bonded to metal parts, a difference of voltage will exist between all metal parts. This situation can cause some electronic equipment to operate improperly. ▶Figure 250–38 and ▶Figure 250–39

Operation of Overcurrent Protective Devices. When objectionable neutral current travels on metal parts, electronic overcurrent protective devices equipped with ground-fault protection can trip because some neutral current flows on the circuit equipment grounding conductor instead of on the neutral conductor.

250.8 Connection of Grounding and Bonding Connectors

(A) Permitted Methods. Equipment grounding conductors, grounding electrode conductors, and bonding jumpers must be connected by one or more of the following methods:

(1) Listed pressure connectors

(2) Terminal bars

(3) Pressure connectors listed for grounding and bonding

(4) Exothermic welding

(5) Machine screws that engage at least two threads or are secured with a nut ▶Figure 250–40

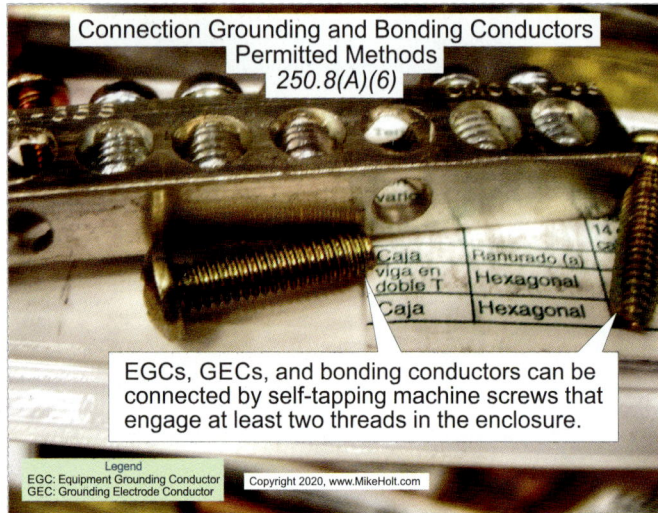

▶Figure 250–41

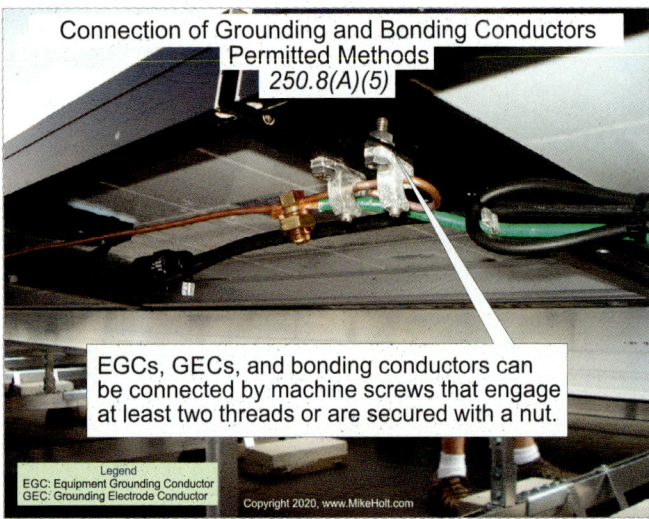

▶Figure 250–40

(6) Self-tapping machine screws that engage at least two threads in the enclosure ▶Figure 250–41

(7) Connections that are part of a listed assembly

(8) Other listed means

250.10 Protection of Ground Clamps and Fittings

Ground clamps and fittings subject to physical damage must be protected. ▶Figure 250–42

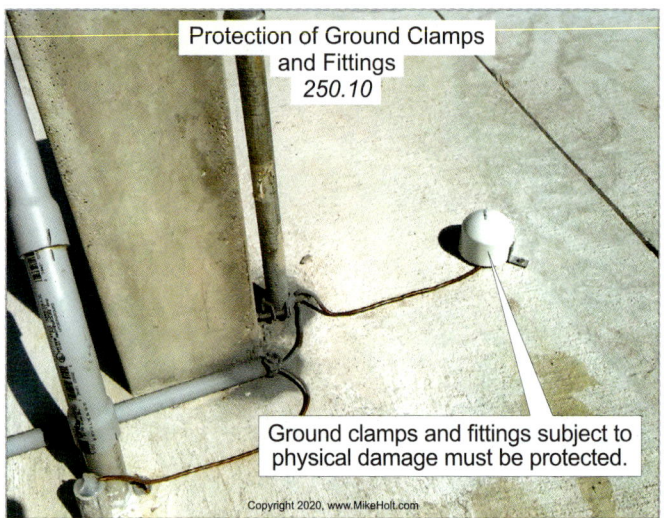

▶Figure 250–42

250.12 Clean Surfaces

Nonconductive coatings (such as paint) <u>on equipment to be grounded or bonded</u> must be removed to ensure good electrical continuity, or the termination fittings must be designed so to make such removal unnecessary [250.53(A) and 250.96(A)].

Author's Comment:

▸ Fittings such as locknuts are designed to cut through the nonconductive coating and establish the intended electrical continuity when they are properly tightened.

▸ Tarnish on copper water pipe need not be removed before making a termination.

Part II. System Grounding and Bonding

250.20 Systems Required to be Grounded

(A) Alternating-Current Systems Below 50V. The secondary of a transformer operating below 50V is not required to be grounded or bonded in accordance with 250.30 unless the transformer's primary supply is from: ▶Figure 250-43

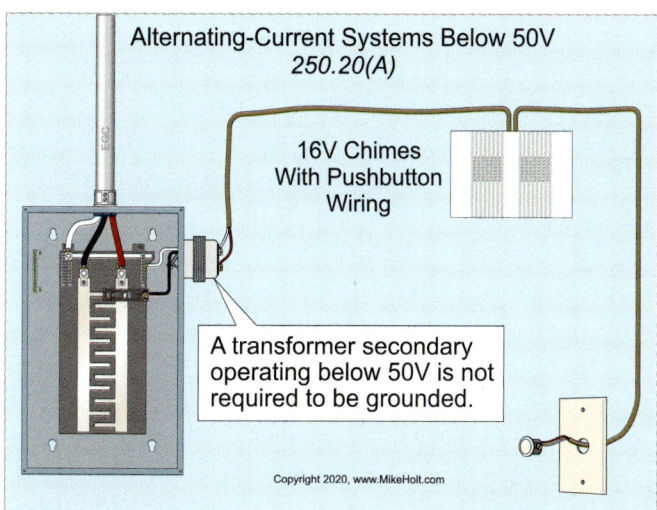

▶Figure 250-43

(1) A 277V or 480V system

(2) An ungrounded system

(B) Alternating-Current Systems 50V to 1,000V. The following systems must be grounded (connected to a grounding electrode) where the neutral conductor is used as a circuit conductor:

(1) Single-phase systems. ▶Figure 250-44

(2) Three-phase, wye-connected systems. ▶Figure 250-45

(3) Three-phase, high-leg delta-connected systems. ▶Figure 250-46

Note: According to Annex O of NFPA 70E, *Standard for Electrical Safety in the Workplace,* high-impedance grounding is an effective tool for reducing arc flash hazards.

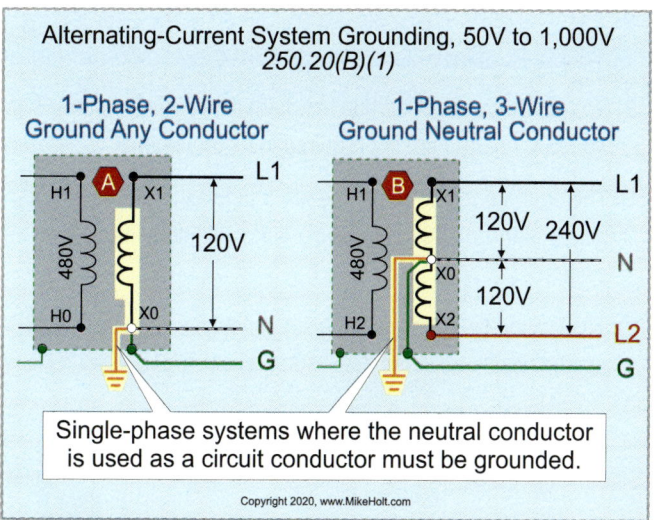

▶Figure 250-44

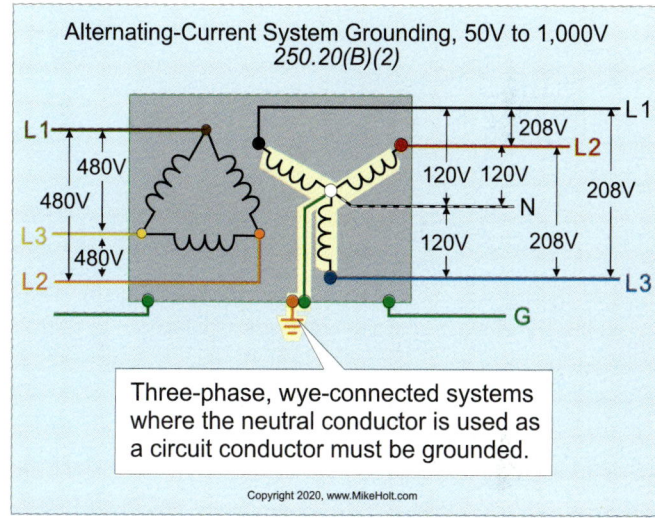

▶Figure 250-45

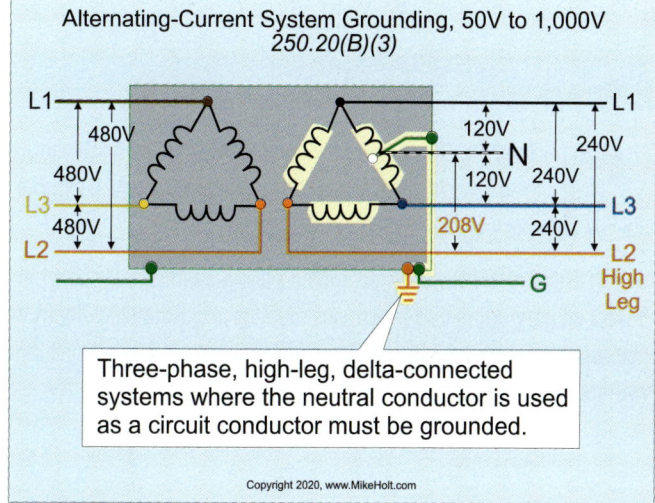

▶Figure 250-46

250.21 Ungrounded Systems

(B) Ground Detectors. Ungrounded alternating-current systems from 50V to 1,000V or less are not required to be grounded if:

(1) The ungrounded systems operating between 120V and 1,000V as permitted in 250.21(A) have ground detectors installed on the system.

(2) The ground detection sensing equipment is connected as close as practicable to where the system receives its supply. ▶Figure 250-47

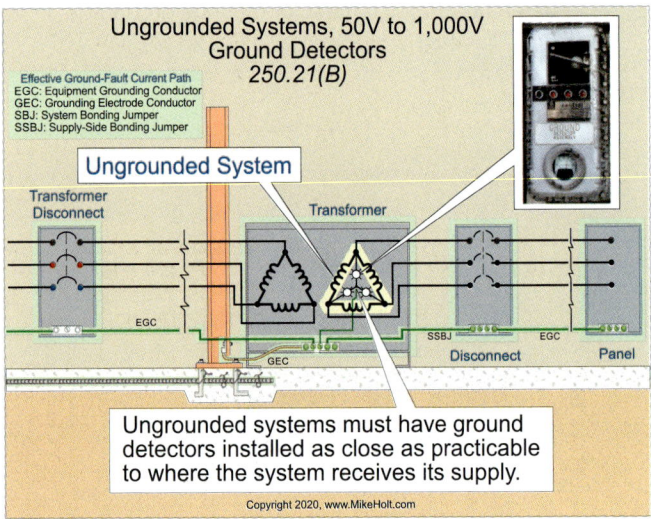

▶Figure 250-47

(C) Marking. Ungrounded systems must be legibly marked "**CAUTION UNGROUNDED SYSTEM OPERATING—___ VOLTS BETWEEN CONDUCTORS**" with sufficient durability to withstand the environment involved at the source or first disconnect of the system. ▶Figure 250-48

250.24 Grounding

 Scan this QR code for a video of Mike explaining this topic; it's a sample from the videos that accompany this textbook. www.MikeHolt.com/20BGvideos

(A) Grounded System. A premises wiring system supplied by a grounded alternating-current service must have a grounding electrode conductor connected to the service neutral conductor in accordance with the following:

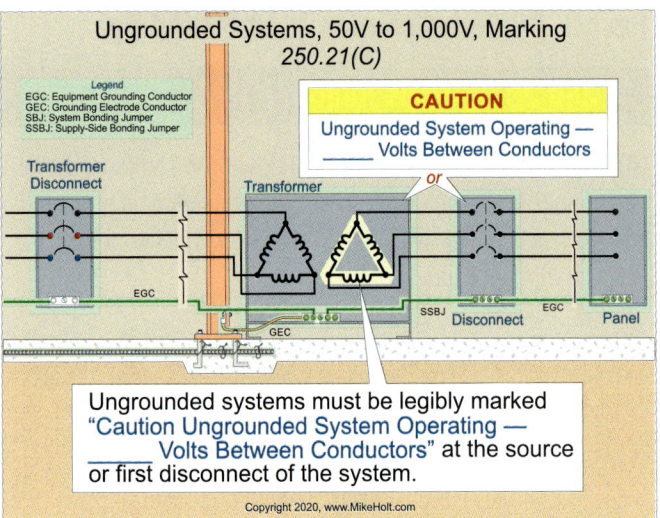

▶Figure 250-48

(1) General. The grounding electrode conductor connection to the neutral conductor at service equipment must be made at any accessible point from the load end of the overhead service conductors, service drop, underground service conductors, or service lateral, including the terminal or bus to which the service neutral conductor is connected at the service disconnecting means. ▶Figure 250-49

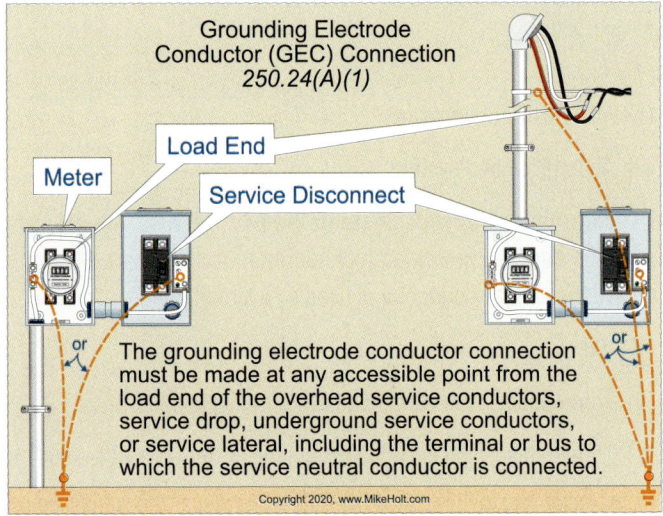

▶Figure 250-49

Author's Comment:

▸ Some inspectors require the grounding electrode conductor connection to the service neutral conductor to be made at the meter socket enclosure, while others insist the connection be made only within the service disconnect. Grounding at either location complies with this rule but be sure you know the local utility company's policy on connections inside the meter socket as many do not permit access to it once it is sealed.

(4) Main Bonding Jumper as Wire or Busbar. Where the main bonding jumper specified in 250.28 is a wire or busbar and is installed from the service neutral conductor terminal bar or bus to the equipment grounding terminal bar or bus in the service equipment, the grounding electrode conductor is permitted to be connected to the equipment grounding terminal, bar, or bus to which the main bonding jumper is connected. ▶Figure 250-50

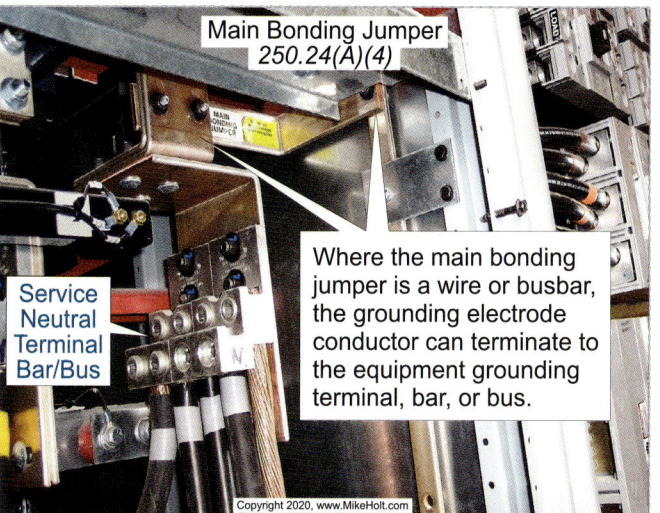

▶Figure 250-50

(5) Load-Side Grounding Connections. A neutral conductor is not permitted to be connected to metal parts of equipment, the equipment grounding conductor(s), or the ground on the load side of the service disconnecting means except as otherwise permitted in 250.142. ▶Figure 250-51

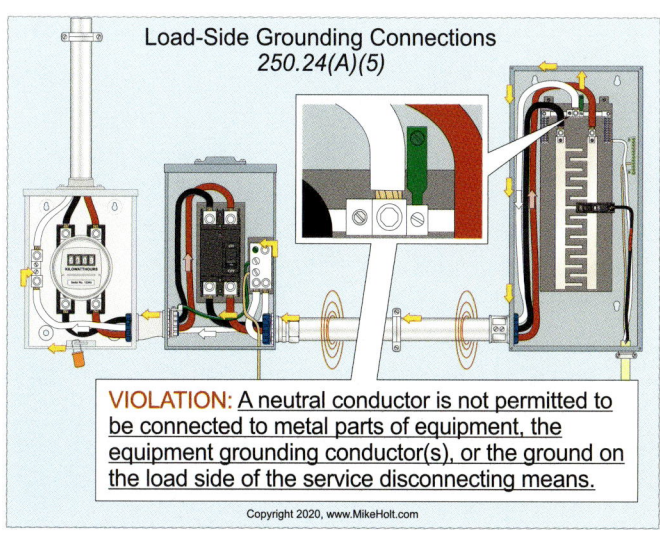

▶Figure 250-51

Author's Comment:

▸ If a neutral-to-case connection is made on the load side of the service disconnect, objectionable neutral current will flow on conductive metal parts of electrical equipment [250.6(A)]. Objectionable neutral current on metal parts of electrical equipment can be extremely dangerous. It does not take much current to cause electric shock or death (from ventricular fibrillation), as well as a fire. ▶Figure 250-52

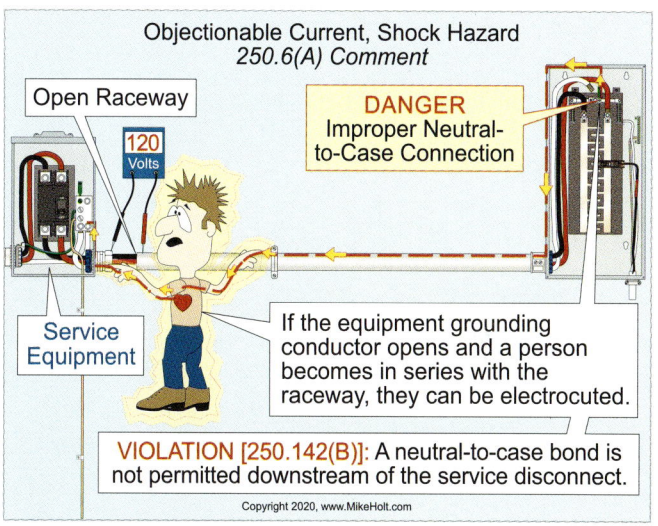

▶Figure 250-52

Note: See 250.30 for separately derived systems, 250.32 for connections at separate buildings, and 250.142 for where the neutral conductor is permitted to be connected to the equipment grounding conductor.

(B) Main Bonding Jumper. An unspliced main bonding jumper is required to connect the equipment grounding conductor(s) and the service-disconnect enclosure to the neutral conductor within the enclosure for each service disconnect in accordance with 250.28. ▶Figure 250-53

(C) Neutral Conductor Brought to Service Equipment. A neutral conductor(s) must be routed with the phase conductors to each service disconnecting means and be connected to each disconnecting mean's neutral conductor(s) terminal or bus. A main bonding jumper must connect the neutral conductor(s) to each service disconnecting means enclosure. ▶Figure 250-54 and ▶Figure 250-55

 Scan this QR code for a video of Mike explaining this topic; it's a sample from the videos that accompany this textbook. www.MikeHolt.com/20BGvideos

250.24 | Grounding and Bonding

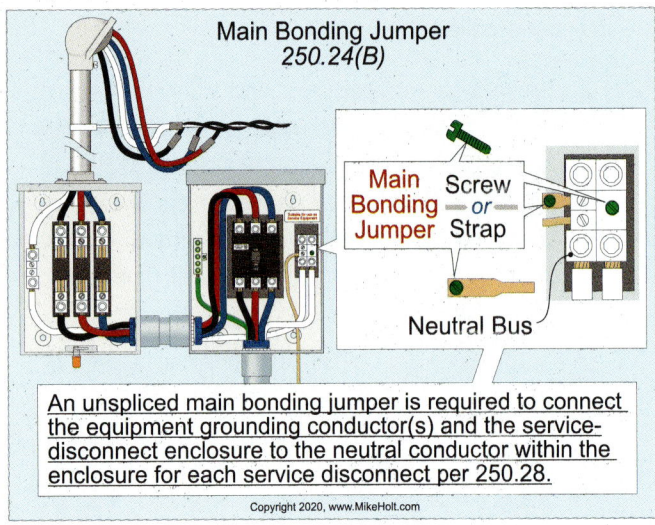

▶Figure 250–53

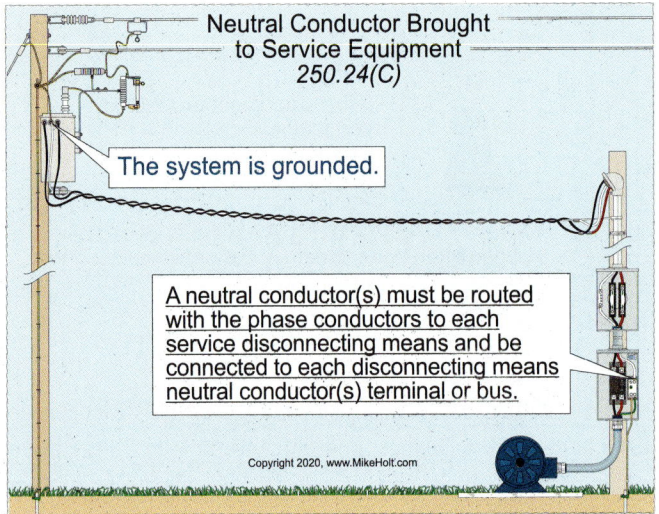

▶Figure 250–54

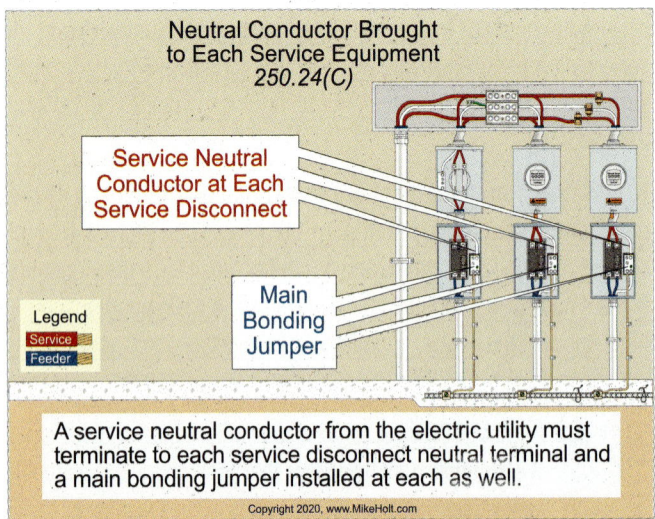

▶Figure 250–55

Author's Comment:

▸ The service neutral conductor provides the effective ground-fault current path to the power supply to ensure dangerous voltage from a ground fault will be quickly removed by the opening of the circuit overcurrent protective device [250.4(A)(3) and 250.4(A)(5)]. ▶Figure 250–56

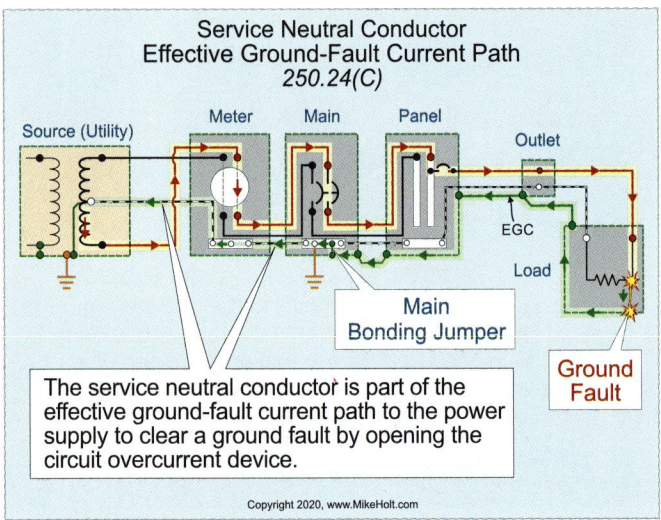

▶Figure 250–56

Author's Comment:

▸ The main bonding jumper is a vital component of bonding. It facilitates the operation of overcurrent protective devices and is a critical part of the grounding system since it bonds the neutral conductor, service enclosure, and the equipment grounding conductor to the grounding electrode system via the grounding electrode conductor.

▸ If the neutral conductor is opened, dangerous voltage will be present on metal parts under normal conditions, providing the potential for electric shock. If the Earth's ground resistance is 25 ohms and the load's resistance is 25 ohms, the voltage drop across each of these resistances will be half of the voltage source. Since the neutral is connected to the service disconnect, all metal parts will be elevated 60V above the Earth's voltage for a 120/240V system. ▶Figure 250–57

Grounding and Bonding | 250.24

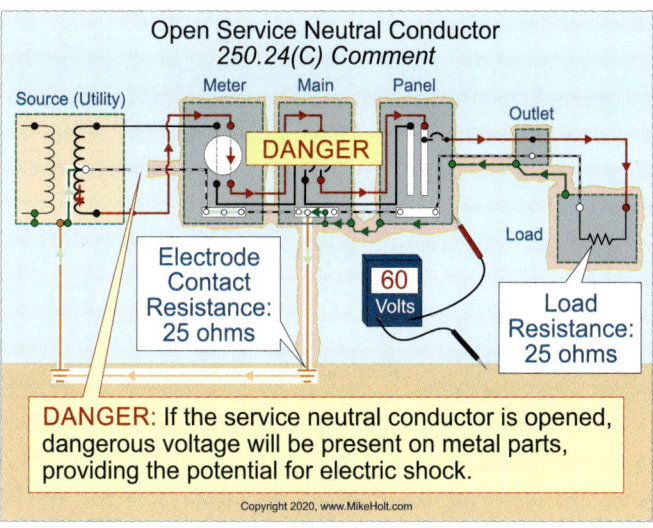
▶Figure 250-57

> **Danger**
>
> Dangerous voltage from a ground fault will not be removed from metal parts, metal piping, and structural steel if the service-disconnect enclosure is not connected to the service neutral conductor. This is because the contact resistance of a grounding electrode to the Earth is so great that insufficient ground-fault current returns to the power supply if that is the only ground-fault current return path available to open the circuit overcurrent device. ▶Figure 250-58

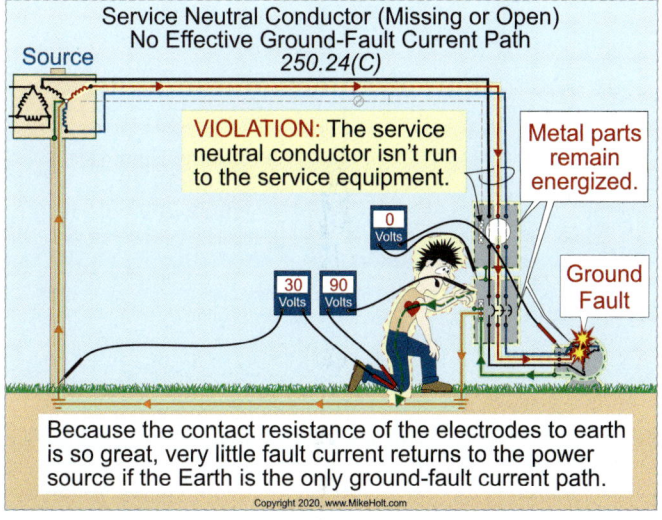
▶Figure 250-58

The neutral conductor(s) must be sized in accordance with the following:

(1) Sizing for a Single Raceway or Cable. The neutral conductor is not permitted to be smaller than specified in Table 250.102(C)(1).
▶Figure 250-59

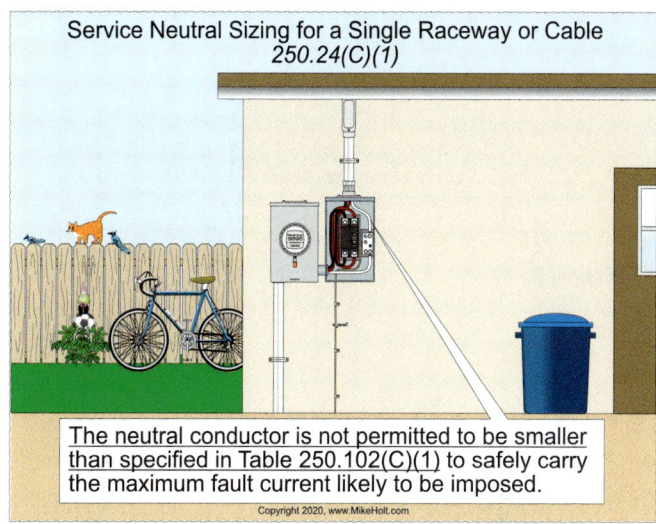
▶Figure 250-59

Author's Comment:

▸ In addition, the neutral conductors must have the capacity to carry the maximum unbalanced neutral current in accordance with 220.61.

▶ **Example**

Question: What is the minimum size service neutral conductor required when the service phase conductors are 350 kcmil and the maximum unbalanced load is 100A? ▶Figure 250-60

(a) 3 AWG (b) 2 AWG (c) 1 AWG (d) 1/0 AWG

Solution:

The unbalanced load of 100A requires a 3 AWG service neutral conductor, which is rated 100A at 75°C in accordance with Table 310.16 [110.14(C)(1)(a)(3) and 220.61], but the neutral conductor cannot be smaller than 2 AWG to carry fault current based on the 350 kcmil phase conductors. Therefore, 2 AWG is the minimum size service neutral conductor required [Table 250.102(C)(1)].

• • •

250.25 | Grounding and Bonding

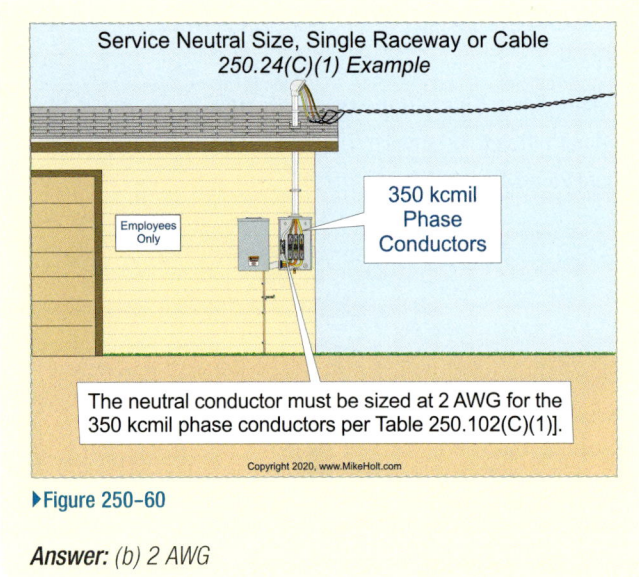

▶Figure 250-60

Answer: (b) 2 AWG

(2) Parallel Conductors in Two or More Raceways or Cables. If service-entrance conductors are installed in parallel in two or more raceways or cables, the neutral conductor must be installed in parallel with the phase conductors. The service neutral conductor is sized based on the circular mil area of the phase conductors in each raceway or cable of the parallel set in accordance with Table 250.102(C)(1) but cannot be smaller than 1/0 AWG. ▶Figure 250-61

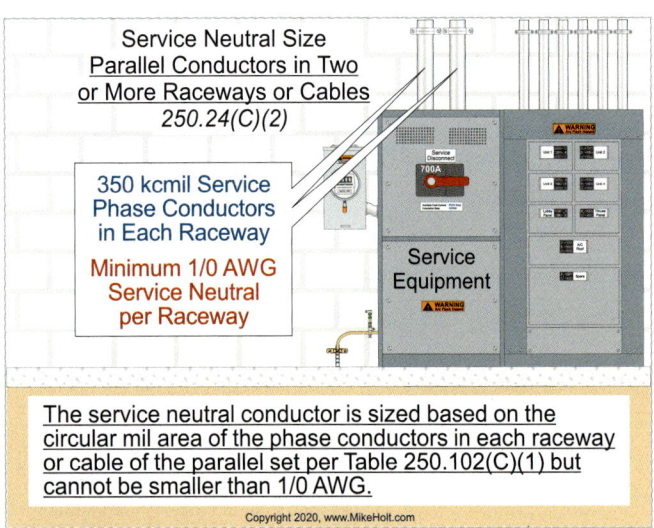

▶Figure 250-61

Note: See 310.10(G) for neutral conductors connected in parallel.

(3) Delta-Connected Service. The grounded conductor of a three-phase, 3-wire delta service must have an ampacity not less than that of the phase conductors.

(D) Grounding Electrode Conductor. A grounding electrode conductor must connect the equipment grounding conductors, the service-equipment enclosures, and the service neutral conductor to the grounding electrode system. This grounding electrode conductor is sized in accordance with 250.66. ▶Figure 250-62 and ▶Figure 250-63

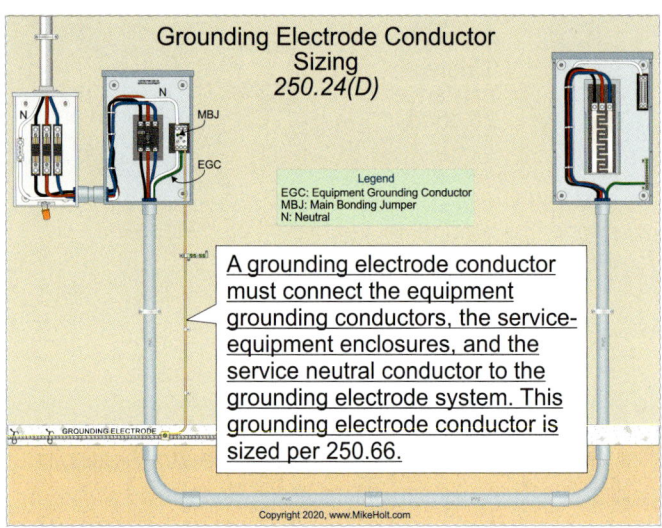

▶Figure 250-62

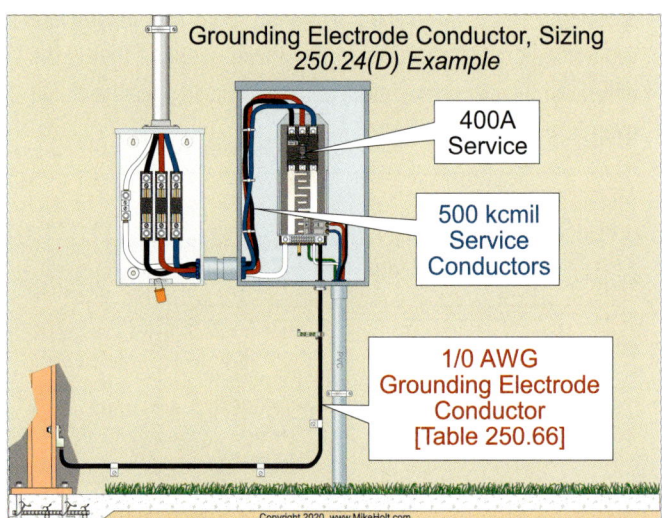

▶Figure 250-63

250.25 Grounding for Supply Side of the Service Disconnect

Electrical systems on the supply side of the service disconnect installed in accordance with 230.82 must be grounded and bonded in accordance with 250.24. ▶Figure 250-64

Grounding and Bonding | 250.28

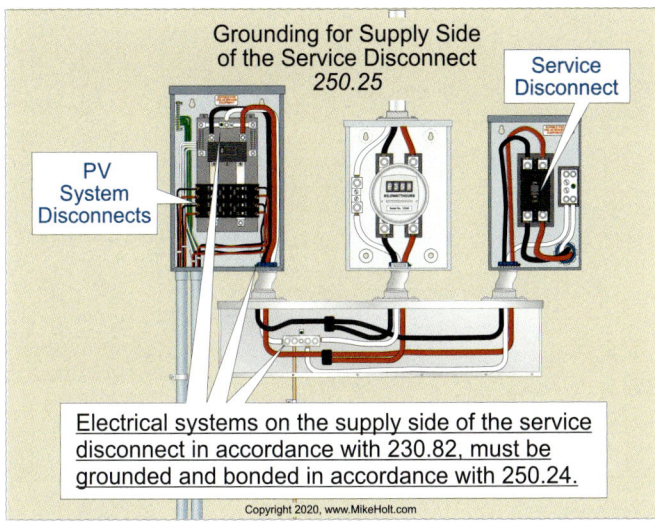
▶Figure 250–64

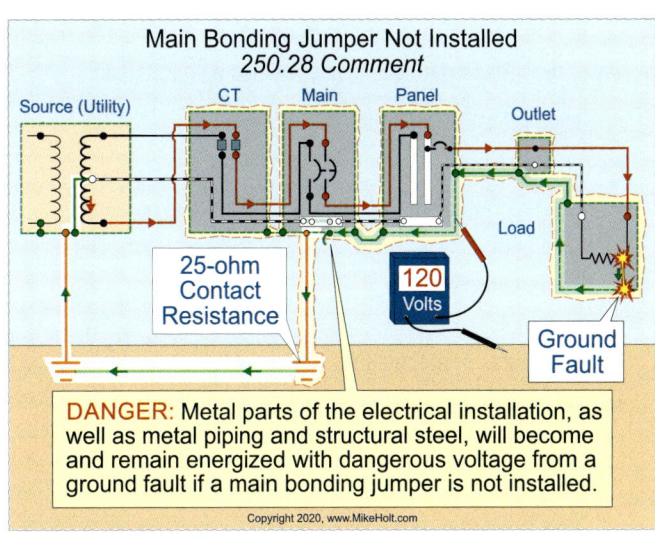
▶Figure 250–65

250.28 Main Bonding Jumper and System Bonding Jumper

Author's Comment:

▸ The primary purpose of the main and system bonding jumpers is to create a path for fault current to flow from a fault to the power supply to facilitate the opening of the circuit overcurrent protective device.

Danger

⚠ Metal parts of the electrical installation, as well as metal piping and structural steel, will become and remain energized with dangerous voltage from a ground fault if a main bonding jumper or system bonding jumper is not installed. A missing main or system bonding jumper causes an opening in the effective ground-fault current path back to the source and creates a condition where overcurrent devices will not open during a ground-fault condition. ▶Figure 250–65 and ▶Figure 250–66

Main and system bonding jumpers must be installed as follows:

(A) Material. The bonding jumper can be a wire, bus, or screw and can be made of copper, copper-clad aluminum, or aluminum. ▶Figure 250–67

(B) Construction. If the bonding jumper is a screw, it must be identified with a green finish visible when the screw is installed.

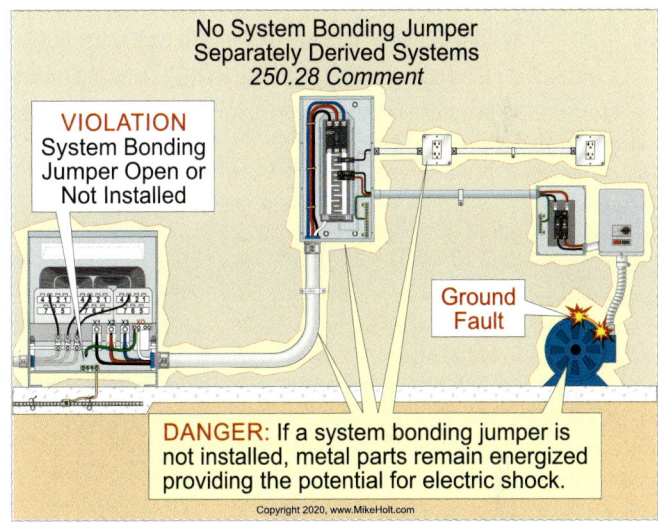
▶Figure 250–66

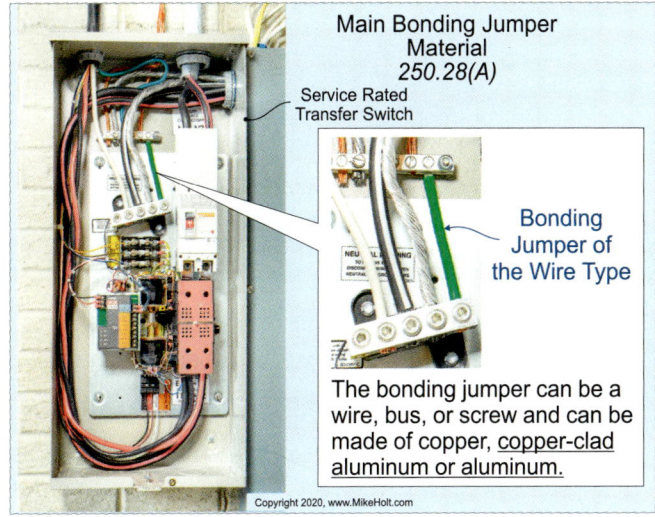
▶Figure 250–67

(C) Attachment. Main and system bonding jumpers must terminate by any of the following means in accordance with 250.8(A):

- Listed pressure connectors
- Terminal bars
- Pressure connectors listed as grounding and bonding equipment
- Exothermic welding
- Machine screw-type fasteners that engage not less than two threads or are secured with a nut
- Thread-forming machine screws that engage not less than two threads in the enclosure
- Connections that are part of a listed assembly
- Other listed means

(D) Size.

(1) Main and system bonding jumpers of the wire type must not be sized smaller than specified in Table 250.102(C)(1), based on the size/area of the phase conductor. ▸Figure 250-68 and ▸Figure 250-69

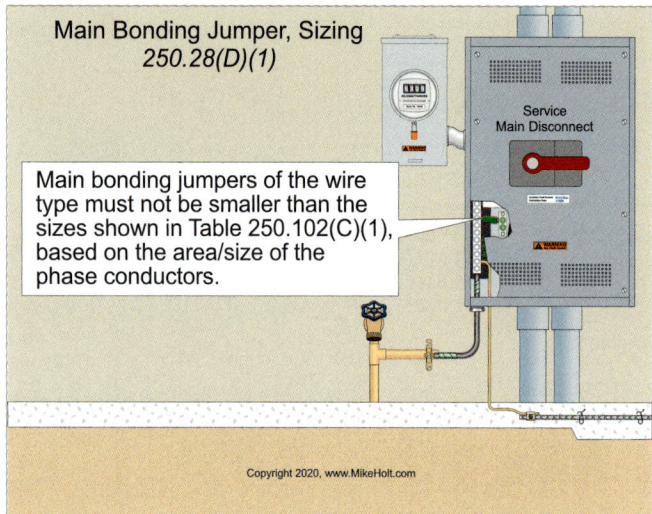

▸Figure 250-68

250.30 Separately Derived Systems

 Scan this QR code for a video of Mike explaining this topic; it's a sample from the videos that accompany this textbook. www.MikeHolt.com/20BGvideos

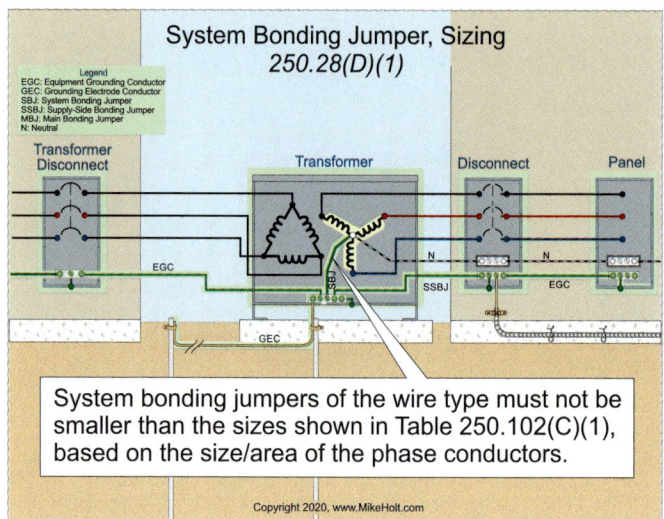

▸Figure 250-69

In addition to complying with 250.30(A) for grounded systems, or as provided in 250.30(B) for ungrounded systems, separately derived systems must comply with 250.20, 250.21, 250.22, or 250.26, as applicable.

Note 1: An alternate alternating-current power source, such as an on-site generator, is not a separately derived system if the neutral conductor is solidly interconnected to a service-supplied system neutral conductor. An example of such a situation is where alternate source transfer equipment does not include a switching action in the neutral conductor and allows it to remain solidly connected to the service-supplied neutral conductor when the alternate source is operational and supplying the load served. ▸Figure 250-70 and ▸Figure 250-71

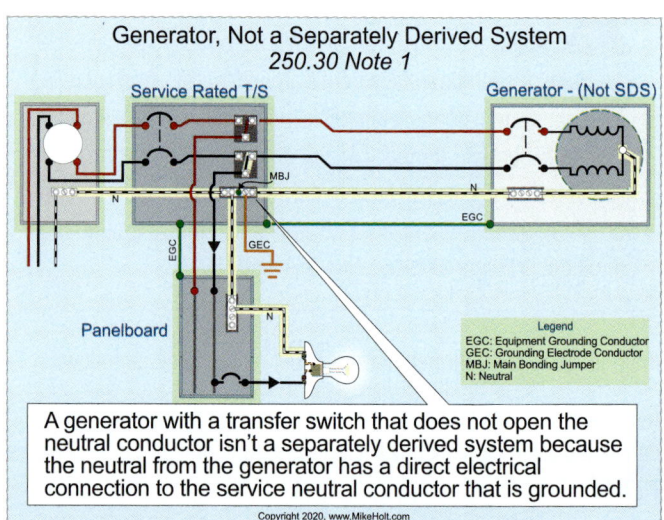

▸Figure 250-70

Grounding and Bonding | 250.30

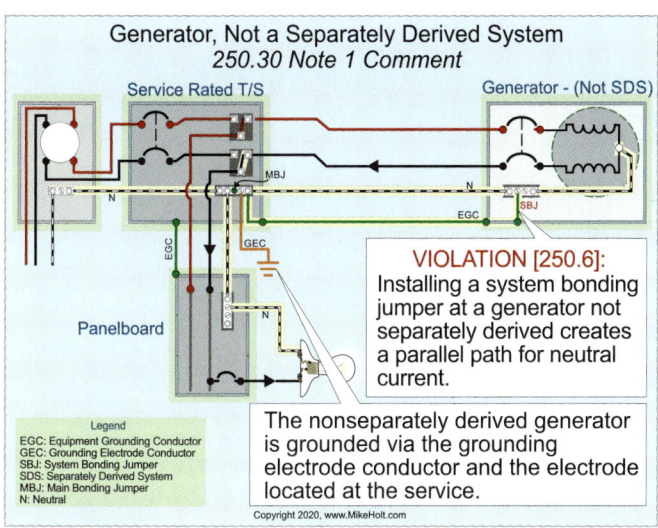
▶Figure 250–71

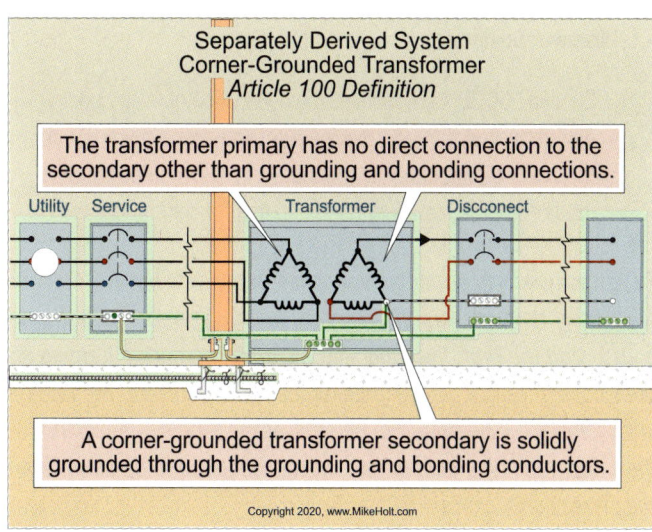
▶Figure 250–73

Author's Comment:

▸ According to Article 100, a "Separately Derived System" is a wiring system whose power is derived from a source, other than the serving electric utility, and where there is no direct electrical connection to the supply conductors of another system other than through grounding and bonding connections. ▶Figure 250–72

(A) Grounded Systems. Separately derived systems must be grounded and bonded in accordance with (A)(1) through (A)(8). A neutral-to-case connection is not permitted to be made on the load side of the system bonding jumper.

(1) System Bonding Jumper. A system bonding jumper must be installed at the same location where the grounding electrode conductor terminates to the neutral terminal of the separately derived system; either at the separately derived system or the secondary separately derived system disconnect, but not at both. ▶Figure 250–74

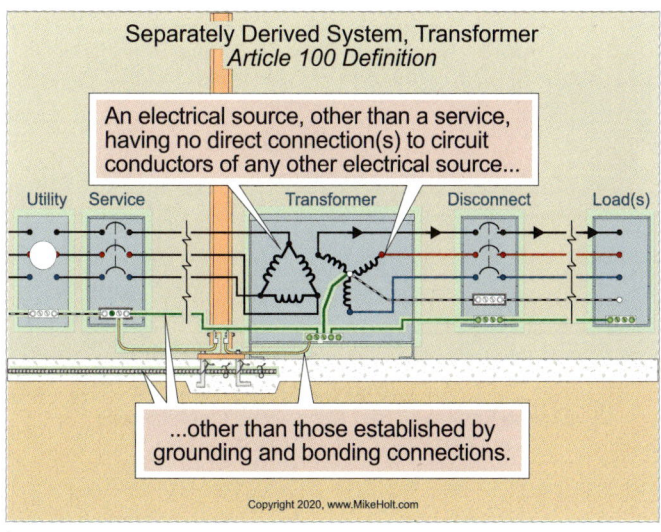
▶Figure 250–72

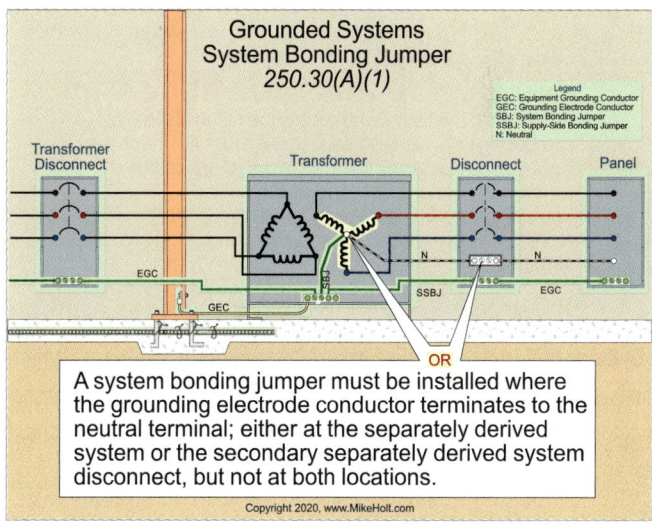
▶Figure 250–74

Author's Comment:

▸ Transformers are separately derived because the primary conductors have no direct electrical connection from the circuit conductors of one system to the circuit conductors of another. ▶Figure 250–73

250.30 | Grounding and Bonding

> **Author's Comment:**
>
> ▸ Section 250.30(A)(5) requires the connection of the grounding electrode conductor to be made at the same point where the neutral conductor is connected to the system bonding jumper in order to avoid parallel paths for neutral current.

Ex 2: If a building or structure is supplied by a feeder from an outdoor separately derived system, a system bonding jumper at both the source and the first disconnecting means is permitted if doing so does not establish a parallel path for the neutral current. The neutral conductor is not permitted to be smaller than the size specified for the system bonding jumper and it is not required to be larger than the phase conductor(s).

(a) System Bonding Jumper at Source. Where the system bonding jumper is installed at the separately derived system, it must connect the neutral conductor to the metal enclosure of the separately derived system. ▸Figure 250–75

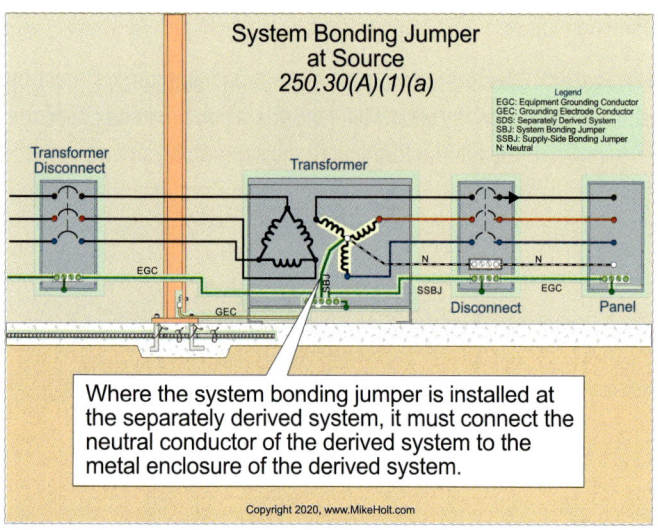
▸Figure 250–75

(b) System Bonding Jumper at First Disconnecting Means. Where the system bonding jumper is installed at the secondary system disconnect, it must connect the neutral conductor to the metal disconnect enclosure. ▸Figure 250–76

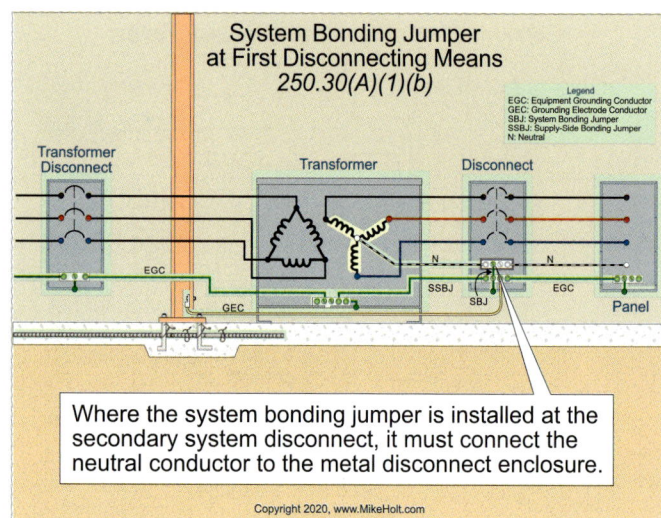
▸Figure 250–76

> **Danger**
>
> ⚠ During a ground fault, metal parts of electrical equipment, as well as metal piping and structural steel, will become and remain energized providing the potential for electric shock and fire if the system bonding jumper is not installed. ▸Figure 250–77

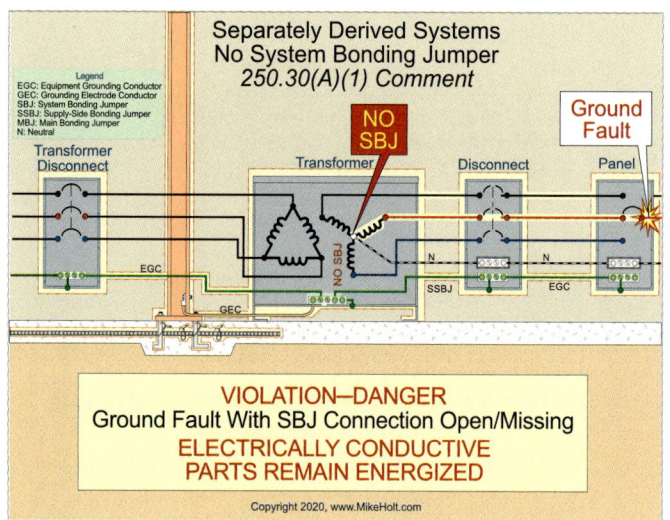
▸Figure 250–77

Grounding and Bonding | 250.30

Caution

⚠ Dangerous objectionable neutral current will flow on conductive metal parts of electrical equipment as well as metal piping and structural steel, in violation of 250.6(A), if more than one system bonding jumper is installed, or if it is not located where the grounding electrode conductor terminates to the neutral conductor. ▶Figure 250–78

▶ **Example**

Question: What size supply-side bonding jumper is required for flexible metal conduit containing 300 kcmil secondary conductors? ▶Figure 250–79

(a) 4 AWG   (b) 2 AWG   (c) 1/0 AWG   (d) 3/0 AWG

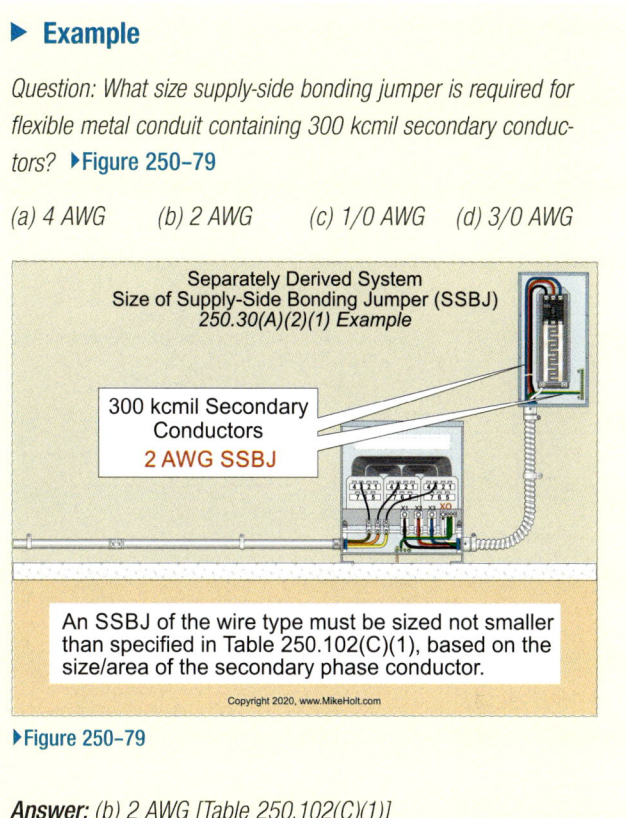

▶Figure 250–79

Answer: (b) 2 AWG [Table 250.102(C)(1)]

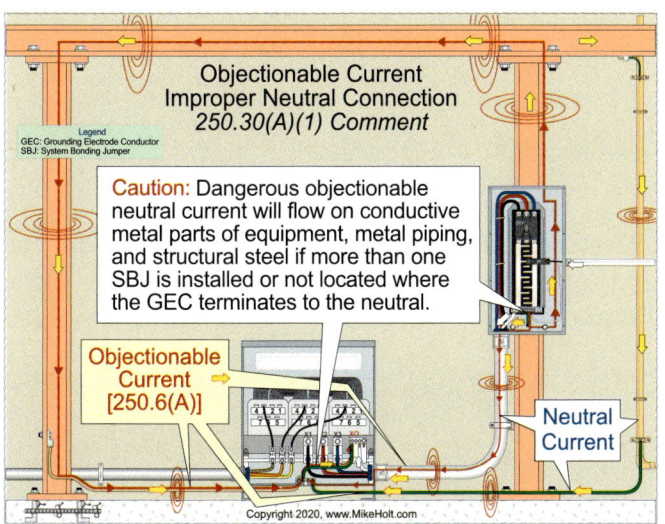

▶Figure 250–78

(2) Supply-Side Bonding Jumper to Disconnect. A supply-side bonding jumper must be installed at the first disconnecting means enclosure and it is not required to be larger than the derived phase conductors. The supply-side bonding jumper can be of a nonflexible metal raceway type or of the wire type.

Author's Comment:

▸ The supply-side bonding jumper can be RMC, IMC, or EMT run between the separately derived system enclosure and the secondary system disconnect enclosure. A nonmetallic or flexible raceway must have a supply-side bonding jumper of the wire type.

(1) A supply-side bonding jumper of the wire type must be sized in accordance with 250.102(C) based on the size/area of the secondary phase conductor in the raceway or cable.

(3) Neutral Conductor Size. The neutral conductor between the separately derived system and the secondary system disconnect is not required to be larger than the derived phase conductors. If the system bonding jumper is installed at the secondary system disconnect instead of at the separately derived system, the following apply:

(a) Sizing for Single Raceway. A secondary neutral conductor must be run from the separately derived system to the secondary system disconnect and the secondary neutral conductor must be sized not smaller than specified in Table 250.102(C)(1), based on the size/area of the secondary phase conductor.

▶ Example

Question: What size neutral conductor is required for a 75 kVA transformer with 250 kcmil secondary conductors? ▶Figure 250-80

(a) 2 AWG   (b) 1/0 AWG   (c) 4/0 AWG   (d) 250 kcmil

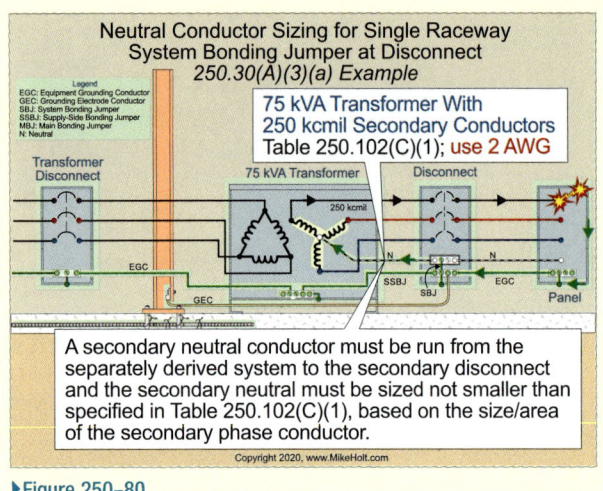

▶Figure 250-80

Answer: (a) 2 AWG [Table 250.102(C)(1)]

(b) Parallel Conductors in Two or More Raceways. A neutral conductor sized in accordance with 250.102(C)(1), but not smaller than 1/0 AWG must be installed in each raceway. ▶Figure 250-81

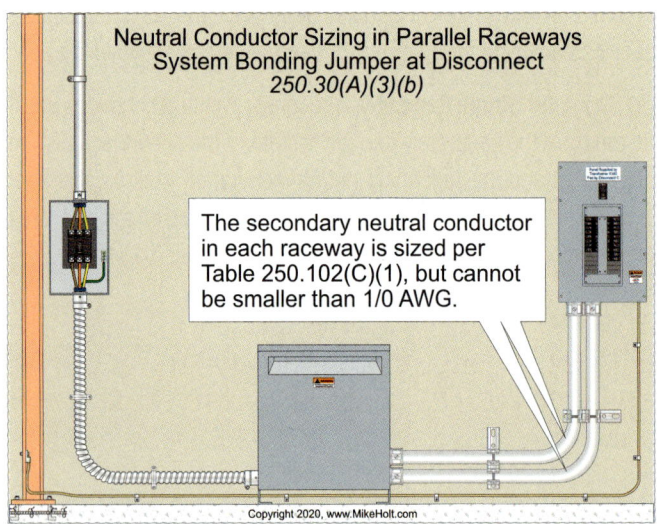

▶Figure 250-81

▶ Example

Question: What size neutral conductor is required for a 112.50 kVA transformer with two sets of 3/0 AWG secondary conductors?

(a) 4 AWG in each raceway   (b) 2 AWG in each raceway
(c) 1/0 AWG in each raceway   (d) 3/0 AWG in each raceway

Solution:

Table 250.102(C)(1) requires a minimum of a 4 AWG conductor based on the 3/0 AWG phase conductors but 1/0 AWG is the minimum neutral conductor size permitted if the conductors are run in parallel [310.10(G)(1)].

Answer: (c) 1/0 AWG in each raceway

(4) Grounding Electrode. Separately derived systems located indoors must be grounded to the building grounding electrode system. ▶Figure 250-82

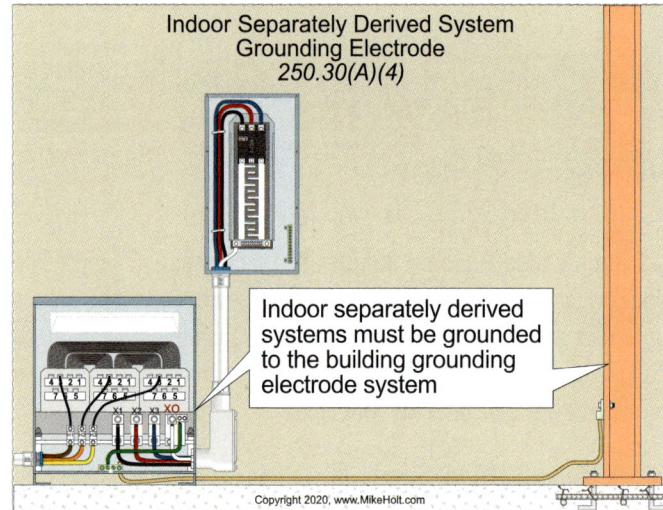

▶Figure 250-82

Separately derived systems located outdoors must be grounded in accordance with 250.30(C).

Author's Comment:

▸ The metal structural frame of a building is itself not a grounding electrode, but when it is properly connected to the grounding electrodes [250.68(C)(2)] it can be used as a grounding electrode conductor.

Note 1: Interior metal water piping in the area served by separately derived systems must be bonded to the separately derived system in accordance with 250.104(D).

(5) Grounding Electrode Conductor, Single Separately Derived System. The grounding electrode conductor for a separately derived system must be sized in accordance with 250.66, based on the area of the largest secondary phase conductor. It must also terminate to the building grounding electrode in accordance with 250.30(A)(4), or to the building structural steel as permitted in 250.68(C).

The grounding electrode conductor is required to terminate to the neutral conductor at the same point on the separately derived system where the system bonding jumper is connected. ▶Figure 250-83

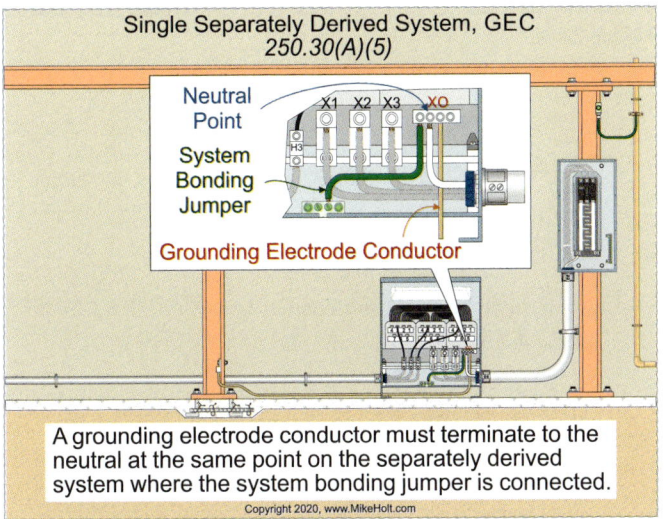
▶Figure 250-83

Author's Comment:

▸ System grounding is intended to reduce overvoltage caused by induction from multiple indirect lightning strikes or intermittent ground faults. System grounding helps reduce fires in buildings as well as voltage stress on electrical insulation and therefore ensures longer insulation life for motors, separately derived systems, and other system components. ▶Figure 250-84

▸ To prevent objectionable neutral current from flowing onto metal parts [250.6], the grounding electrode conductor must originate at the same point on the separately derived system as where the system bonding jumper is connected [250.30(A)(1)].

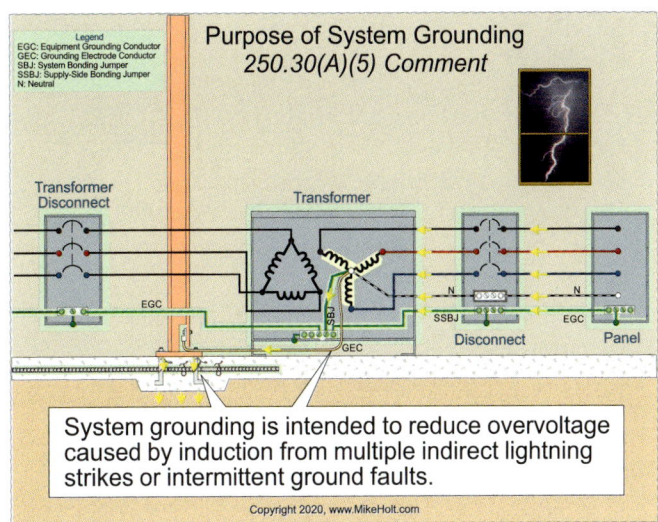
▶Figure 250-84

Ex 1: If the system bonding jumper is a wire or busbar [250.30(A)(1)], the grounding electrode conductor can terminate at the equipment grounding terminal, bar, or bus. ▶Figure 250-85

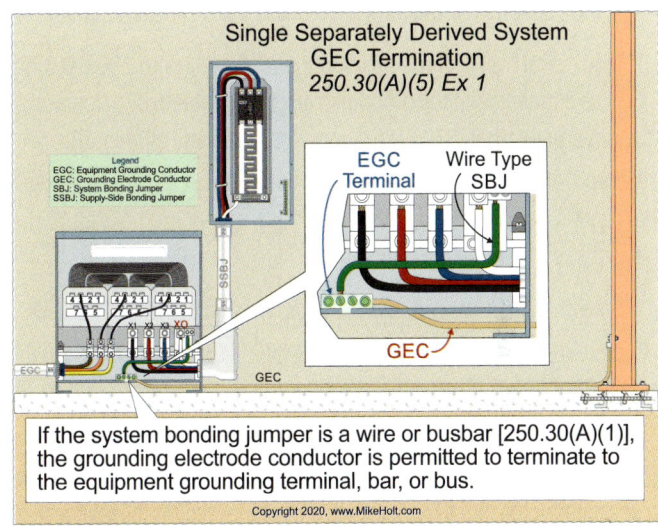
▶Figure 250-85

(6) Common Grounding Electrode Conductor, Multiple Separately Derived Systems. Where there are multiple separately derived systems, a grounding electrode conductor tap from each of them to a common grounding electrode conductor is permitted. This connection must be made at the same point on the separately derived system secondary as where the system bonding jumper is connected [250.30(A)(1)]. ▶Figure 250-86

(a) Common Grounding Electrode Conductor. The common grounding electrode conductor can be any of the following:

250.30 | Grounding and Bonding

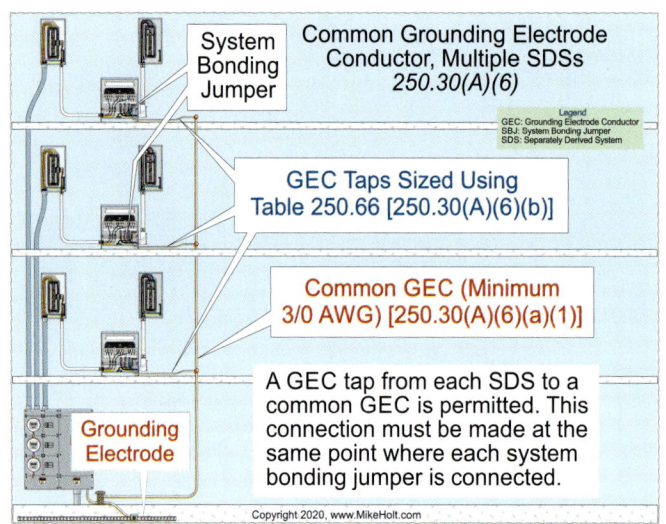
▶Figure 250–86

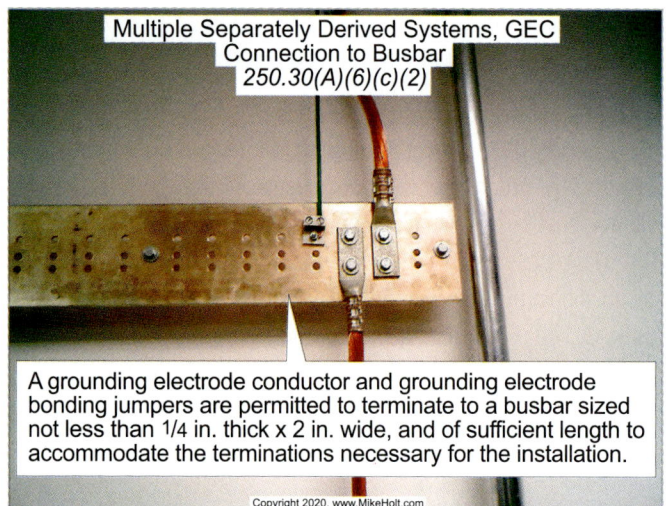
▶Figure 250–87

(1) An unspliced conductor not smaller than 3/0 AWG copper or 250 kcmil aluminum.

(2) Interior metal water pipe located not more than 5 ft from the point of entrance to the building [250.68(C)(1)].

(3) The metal frame of the building that complies with 250.68(C)(2) or is connected to the grounding electrode system by a conductor not smaller than 3/0 AWG copper or 250 kcmil aluminum.

(b) Tap Conductor Size. Grounding electrode conductor taps must be sized in accordance with Table 250.66, based on the area of the largest secondary phase conductor.

Ex: If the only electrodes present are of the types specified in 250.66(A), (B), or (C), the size of the common grounding electrode conductor is not required to be larger than the largest conductor required by 250.66(A), (B), or (C) for the type of electrode that is present.

(c) Connections. Tap connections to the common grounding electrode conductor must be made at an accessible location by any of the following methods:

(1) A connector listed as grounding and bonding equipment.

(2) Listed connections to aluminum or copper busbars not less than ¼ in. thick × 2 in. wide, and of sufficient length to accommodate the terminations necessary for the installation. ▶Figure 250–87

3) Exothermic welding.

(7) Installation. The grounding electrode conductor must comply with 250.64(A), (B), (C), and (E).

Author's Comment:

▸ According to 250.64, the grounding electrode conductor must be copper where within 18 in. of the surface of the Earth [250.64(A)], and:

▸ Be securely fastened to the surface on which it is carried [250.64(B)],

▸ Be adequately protected if exposed to physical damage [250.64(B)], and

▸ Metal enclosures enclosing a grounding electrode conductor must be made electrically continuous from the point of attachment to cabinets or equipment to the grounding electrode conductor [250.64(E)].

(8) Structural Steel and Metal Piping. To ensure dangerous voltage on metal parts from a ground fault is removed quickly, structural steel and metal piping in the area served by a separately derived system must be bonded to the secondary neutral conductor in accordance with 250.104(D).

Author's Comment:

▸ If the structural steel of a building is connected to the Earth in accordance with 250.68(C)(2), it is part of the grounding electrode system, and an indoor separately derived system is required to be connected to the building steel [250.30(A)(4)]. If the structural steel of a building is not in compliance with 250.68(C)(2), it must be bonded to the neutral conductor of the separately derived system via a bonding jumper in accordance with 250.104(D).

(C) Outdoor Source. Separately derived systems located outside the building must have the grounding electrode connection made at the separately derived system location. ▶Figure 250-88

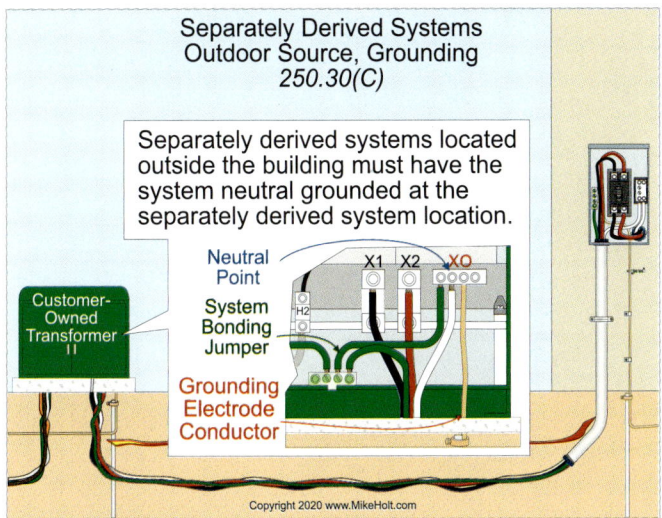

▶Figure 250-88

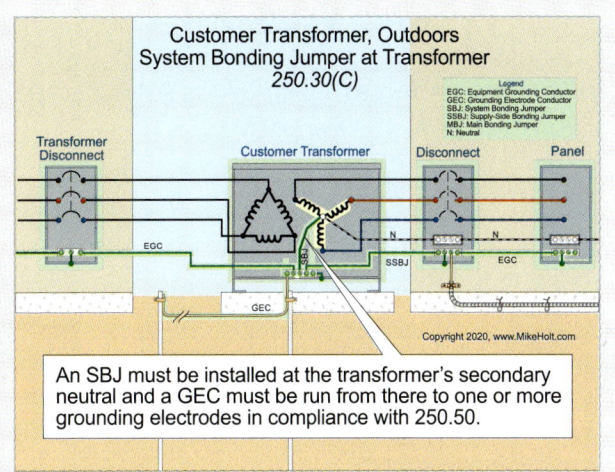

▶Figure 250-89

Author's Comment:

▸ A grounding electrode connection is required at the building disconnect supplied by the outdoor separately derived system [250.32(B)(2)].

Special Section 250.30
Separately Derived Systems
Outdoor Installations

Customer Transformer Outdoors. ▶Figure 250-89

System Bonding Jumper. Where a separately derived system is installed outdoors, a system bonding jumper sized in accordance with Table 250.102(C)(1), if of the wire type, must be installed at the separately derived system's secondary neutral [250.30(A)(1)]. ▶Figure 250-90

Grounding Electrode Conductor. A grounding electrode conductor sized in accordance with 250.66, based on the area of the largest secondary phase conductor [250.30(A)(5)], must be run from the separately derived system's neutral terminal to one or more grounding electrodes in compliance with 250.50 and in accordance with 250.30(C) [250.30(A)(4)].

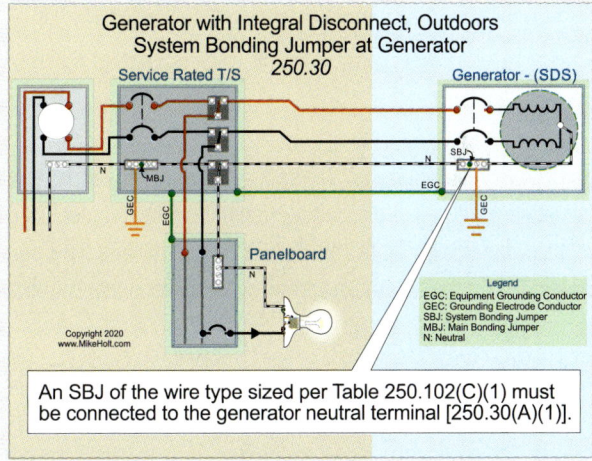

▶Figure 250-90

Where the system bonding jumper is a wire or busbar, the grounding electrode conductor can originate at the generator's equipment grounding terminal, bar, or bus [250.30(A)(5) Ex 1].

Supply-Side Bonding Jumper. A supply-side bonding jumper must be run from the separately derived system equipment's grounding conductor terminal to the secondary system disconnect enclosure's equipment grounding conductor terminal.

Where the supply-side bonding jumper is of the wire type it must be sized in accordance with Table 250.102(C)(1), based on the size/area of the secondary phase conductor [250.30(A)(2)].

Indoor Installations

Indoor Separately Derived System, System Bonding Jumper at Separately Derived System. ▶Figure 250-91

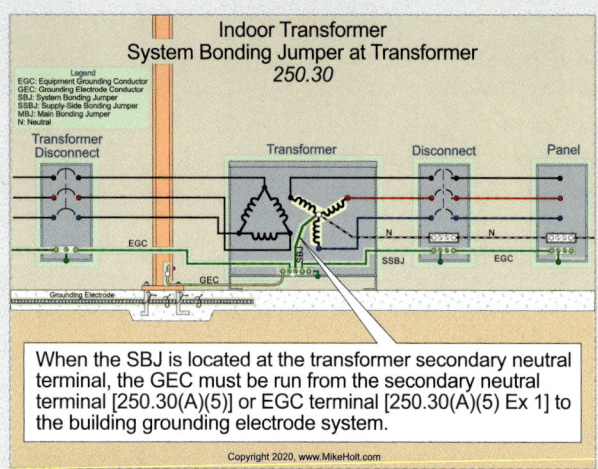

▶Figure 250-91

System Bonding Jumper. Where a separately derived system is installed indoors, the required system bonding jumper sized in accordance with Table 250.102(C)(1), if of the wire type, can be installed at the separately derived system's secondary neutral terminal [250.30(A)(1)(a)].

Grounding Electrode Conductor. A grounding electrode conductor sized in accordance with 250.66, based on the size/area of the secondary phase conductor, must be run from the separately derived system's neutral terminal to the building's grounding electrode system [250.30(A)(4)].

Where the system bonding jumper is a wire or busbar, the grounding electrode conductor can originate at the generator's equipment grounding terminal, bar, or bus [250.30(A)(5) Ex 1].

Supply-Side Bonding Jumper. A supply-side bonding jumper sized in accordance with Table 250.102(C)(1), if of the wire type, must be run from the separately derived system's equipment grounding conductor terminal to the secondary system disconnect enclosure's equipment grounding conductor terminal [250.30(A)(2)].

▶ **Example**

Question: What size supply-side bonding jumper is required between a 75 kVA transformer, with 250 kcmil secondary conductors in a single raceway, and the first disconnect? ▶Figure 250-92

(a) 4 AWG (b) 3 AWG (c) 2 AWG (d) 1 AWG

Answer: (c) 2 AWG; based on the 250 kcmil conductors [Table 250.102(C)(1)].

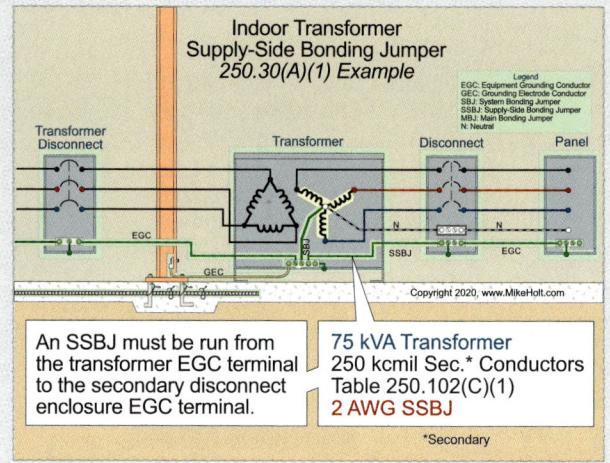

▶Figure 250-92

Separately Derived System Indoors, System Bonding Jumper at Secondary System Disconnect. ▶Figure 250-93

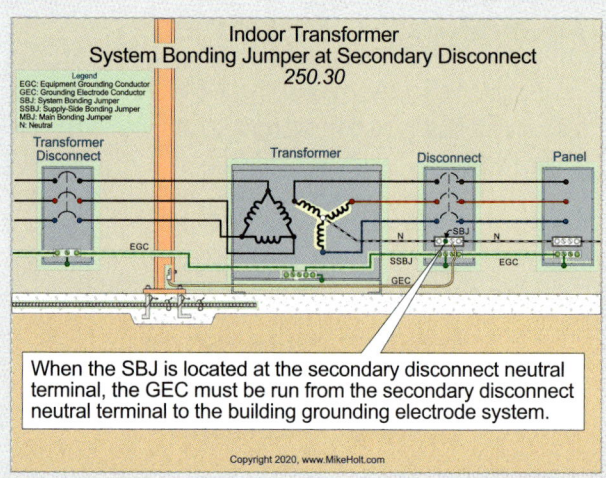

▶Figure 250-93

System Bonding Jumper. Where a separately derived system is installed indoors, the required system bonding jumper, sized in accordance with Table 250.102(C)(1), can be installed at the separately derived system's secondary system disconnect [250.30(A)(1)(b)].

Grounding Electrode Conductor. A grounding electrode conductor, sized in accordance with 250.66 based on the area of the largest secondary phase conductor, must be run from the separately derived system's neutral terminal to the building's grounding electrode system [250.30(A)(4)].

Where the system bonding jumper is a wire or busbar, the grounding electrode conductor can originate at the generator's equipment grounding terminal, bar, or bus [250.30(A)(5) Ex].

Supply-Side Bonding Jumper. A supply-side bonding jumper sized in accordance with Table 250.102(C)(1), if of the wire type, must be run from the separately derived system's equipment grounding conductor terminal to the secondary system's disconnect enclosure equipment grounding conductor terminal [250.30(A)(2)].

Sizing the Supply-Side Bonding Jumper for Parallel Raceways

Method 1. The supply-side bonding jumper can be run in each raceway and sized using Table 250.102(C)(1), based on the size/area of the phase conductors in each raceway [250.102(C)(2)].

Method 2. A single supply-side bonding jumper can be run for multiple raceways using Table 250.102(C)(1), based on the equivalent area of the phase conductors [250.102(C)(2)].

▶ **Example**

Question: What size single supply-side bonding jumper is required between a 112.60 kVA transformer, paralleled in two raceways with 3/0 AWG secondary conductors in each raceway, and the first disconnect?

(a) 4 AWG   (b) 3 AWG   (c) 2 AWG   (d) 1 AWG

Solution:

Determine the equivalent area for two 3/0 AWG conductors [250.102(2) and Chapter 9, Table 8].

3/0 AWG = 167,800 circular mills

2 conductors × 167,800 cmil = 335,600 cmil [Table 250.102(C)(1)]

One 2 AWG supply-side bonding jumper (minimum) is needed to bond both raceways. The 1/0 AWG minimum conductor size for parallel conductors does not apply to supply-side bonding jumpers or equipment grounding conductors.

Answer: (c) 2 AWG

Author's Comment:

▶ A supply-side bonding jumper can also be run with each parallel raceway based on the size of the phase conductor in each raceway [250.102(C)(2)]. If the phase conductors in each raceway are 3/0 AWG, then a 4 AWG conductor must be installed in each raceway [250.102(C)(1)].

Neutral Conductor. When the system bonding jumper is installed at a secondary system disconnect, a secondary neutral conductor in each raceway, sized no smaller than specified in Table 250.102(C)(1), must be run from the separately derived system's secondary to the secondary system's disconnect enclosure.

▶ **Example**

Question: What size neutral conductor is required for a 112.50 kVA transformer paralleled in two raceways with 3/0 AWG secondary conductors in each raceway?

(a) 3 AWG   (b) 2 AWG   (c) 1 AWG   (d) 1/0 AWG

Solution:

Table 250.102(C)(1) requires a minimum of a 2 AWG neutral conductor based on the equivalent size of two 3/0 AWG conductors (167,800 cmil × 2 conductors = 335,600 cmil), but the minimum size neutral conductor in parallel is 1/0 AWG [310.10(G)(1)].

Answer: (d) 1/0 AWG

Author's Comment:

▶ Be sure the 1/0 AWG conductor is large enough to handle the maximum unbalanced load [220.61].

▶ When a system bonding jumper is installed at the secondary system's disconnect, the secondary neutral conductor will serve as part of the effective ground-fault current path.

250.32 Buildings Supplied by a Feeder

(A) Grounding Electrode. A building supplied by a feeder must have a grounding electrode system and a grounding electrode conductor installed in accordance with Part III of Article 250. ▶Figure 250–94

Ex: A grounding electrode is not required for a building if it is supplied by a single branch circuit or multiwire branch circuit. ▶Figure 250–95

250.32 | Grounding and Bonding

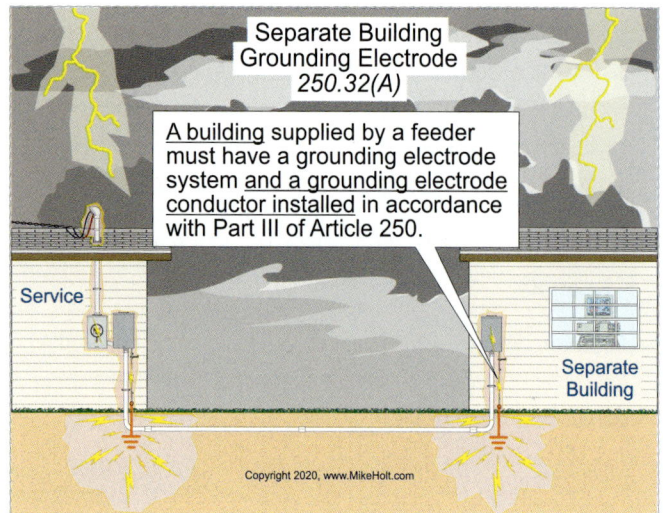
▶Figure 250–94

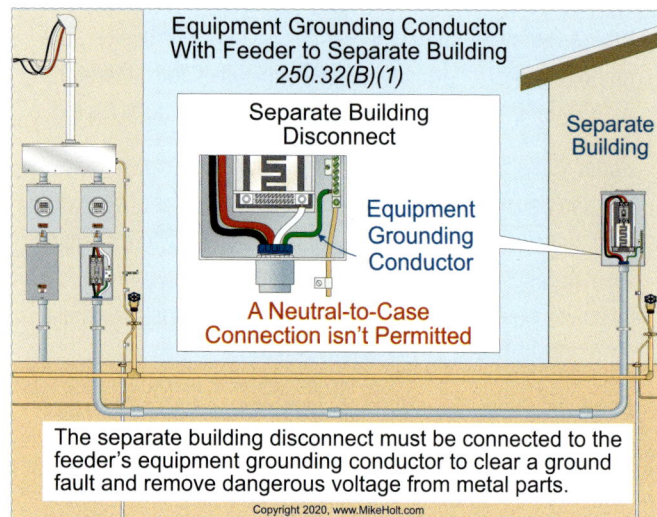
▶Figure 250–96

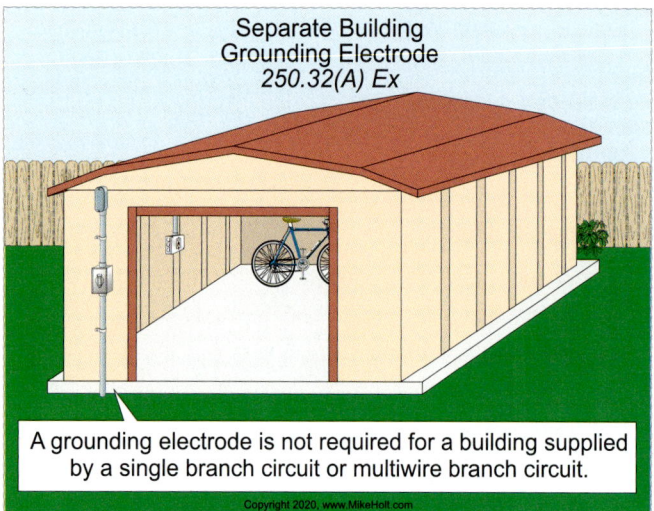
▶Figure 250–95

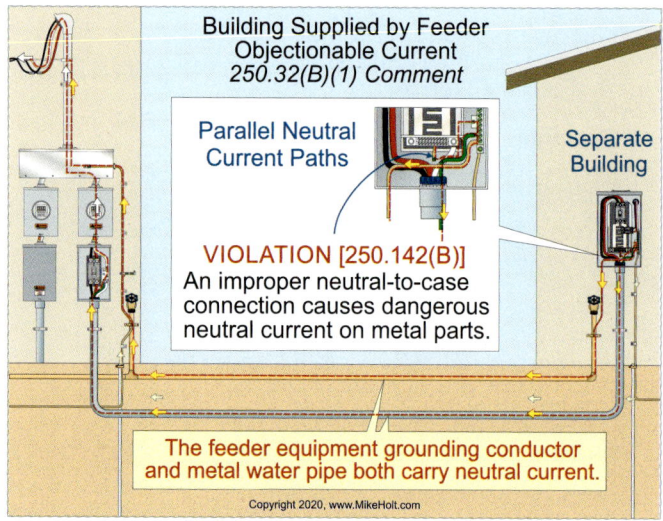
▶Figure 250–97

(B) Grounded Systems (Equipment Grounding Conductor).

(1) To clear a ground fault and remove dangerous voltage from metal parts due to a ground fault, the metal parts of the building disconnect must be connected to the feeder equipment grounding conductor of a type described in 250.118. ▶Figure 250–96

Where the supply circuit equipment grounding conductor is of the wire type, it must be sized in accordance with 250.122, based on the rating of the overcurrent protective device.

> **Caution**
> ⚡ To prevent dangerous objectionable neutral current from flowing on metal parts [250.6(A)], the supply circuit neutral conductor is not permitted to be connected to the remote building disconnect [250.142(B)]. ▶Figure 250–97

Ex 1: The neutral conductor can serve as the ground-fault return path for the building disconnect for existing installations where there are no continuous metallic paths between buildings and structures, ground-fault protection of equipment is not installed on the supply side of the circuit, and the neutral conductor is sized no smaller than the larger of:

(1) The maximum unbalanced neutral load in accordance with 220.61.

(2) The minimum equipment grounding conductor size in accordance with 250.122.

(2) Supplied by Separately Derived System.

(a) With Overcurrent Protection. If overcurrent protection is provided at the separately derived system, the installation must contain an equipment grounding conductor in accordance with 250.32(B)(1).

(b) Without Overcurrent Protection. If overcurrent protection is not provided at the separately derived system, the installation must comply with 250.30(A). ▶Figure 250–98

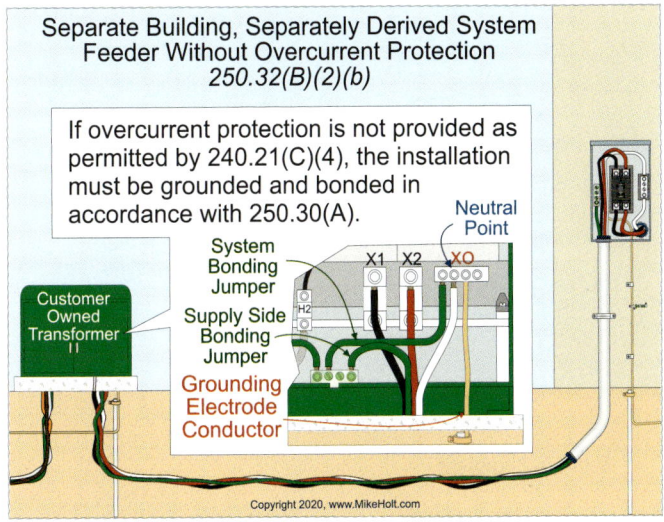

▶Figure 250–98

(E) Grounding Electrode Conductor Size. The grounding electrode conductor must terminate to the equipment grounding terminal of the disconnect (not the neutral terminal) and must be sized in accordance with 250.66 based, on the area of the largest phase conductor.

▶ **Example**

Question: What size grounding electrode conductor is required for a building disconnect supplied with a 3/0 AWG feeder with a concrete-encased electrode? ▶Figure 250–99

(a) 4 AWG   (b) 2 AWG   (c) 1 AWG   (d) 1/0 AWG

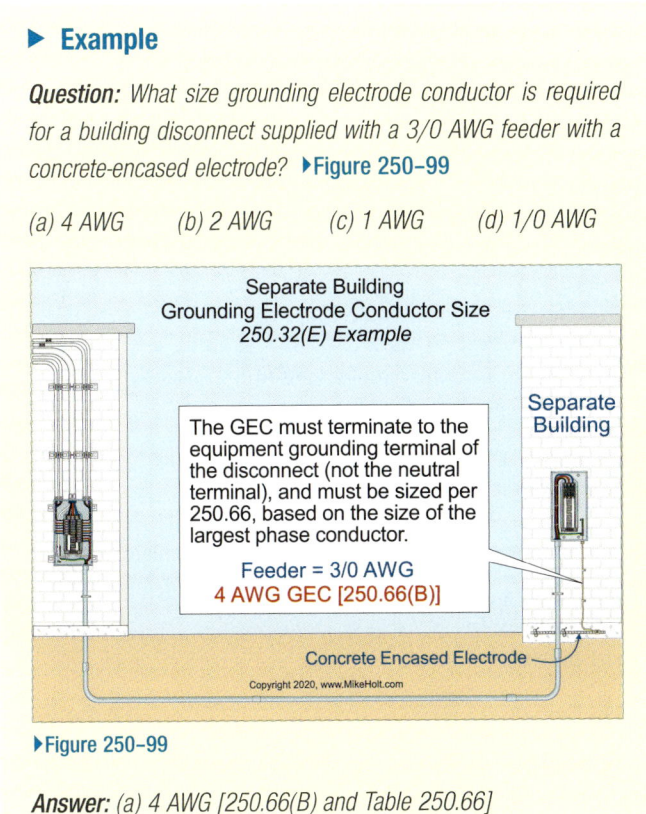

▶Figure 250–99

Answer: (a) 4 AWG [250.66(B) and Table 250.66]

Author's Comment:

▸ If the grounding electrode conductor is connected to a rod(s), the portion of the conductor that connects only to the rod(s) is not required to be larger than 6 AWG copper [250.66(A)]. If the grounding electrode conductor is connected to a concrete-encased electrode(s), the portion of the conductor that connects only to the concrete-encased electrode(s) is not required to be larger than 4 AWG copper [250.66(B)].

250.34 Generators—Portable and Vehicle- or Trailer-Mounted

(A) Portable Generators. A portable generator is not required to be connected to a grounding electrode (grounded) where all the following conditions are met:

(1) The generator only supplies equipment and/or receptacles mounted on the generator. ▶Figure 250–100

▶Figure 250–100

(2) The normally noncurrent-carrying metal parts of equipment and the equipment grounding conductor terminals of the receptacles are connected to the generator frame.

(B) Vehicle- or Trailer-Mounted Generators. A vehicle- or trailer-mounted generator is not required to be connected to a grounding electrode where all the following conditions are met:

(1) The generator frame is bonded to the vehicle or trailer frame,

(2) The generator only supplies equipment or receptacles mounted on the vehicle, trailer, or generator, and ▶Figure 250–101

250.36 | Grounding and Bonding

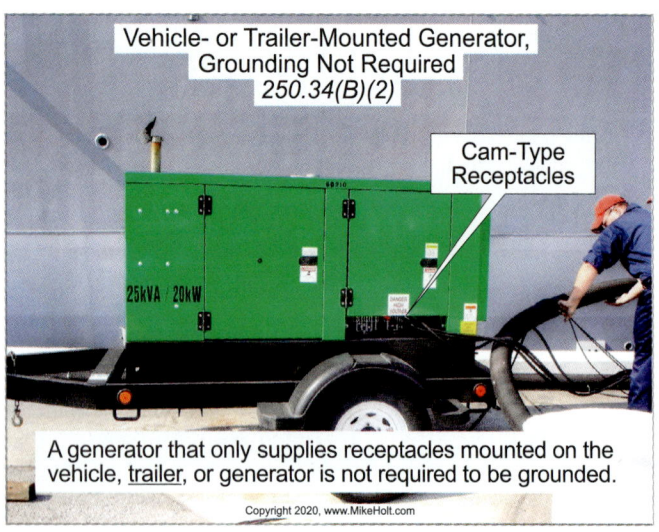
▶Figure 250–101

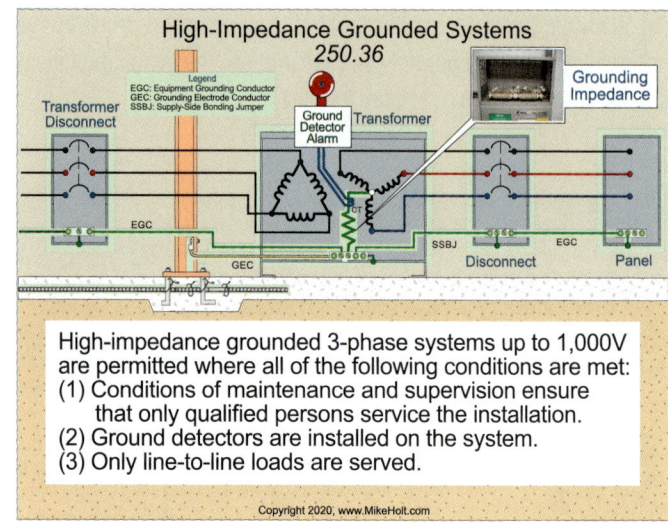
▶Figure 250–102

(3) The normally noncurrent-carrying metal parts of equipment and the equipment grounding conductor terminals of the receptacles are connected to the generator frame.

(C) Neutral Conductor Bonding. The generator manufacturer is required to bond the neutral conductor to the generator frame under all of the following conditions:

(1) The generator is a component of a separately derived system.

(2) A grounding-type receptacle(s) is mounted on the generator or is supplied by the generator.

(3) A receptacle on the generator is supplied by the generator with GFCI protection.

250.36 High-Impedance Grounded Systems

 Scan this QR code for a video of Mike explaining this topic; it's a sample from the videos that accompany this textbook. www.MikeHolt.com/20BGvideos

High-impedance grounded three-phase systems up to 1,000V are permitted where all the following conditions are met: ▶Figure 250–102

(1) Conditions of maintenance and supervision ensure that only qualified persons service the installation.

(2) Ground detectors are installed on the system.

(3) Only line-to-line loads are served.

Author's Comment:

▸ High-impedance grounded systems are generally referred to as "High-Resistance Grounded Systems" in the industry. They are generally used where sudden interruption of power will create increased hazards and where a reduction of incident energy is needed for worker safety.

(A) Grounding Impedance Location. To limit fault current to a very low value, high-impedance grounded systems must have a resistor installed between the neutral point of the separately derived system and the equipment grounding conductor. ▶Figure 250–103

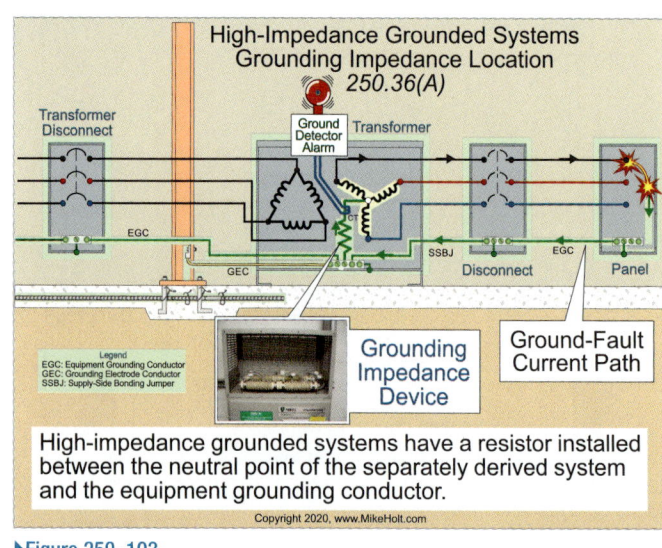
▶Figure 250–103

Note: According to Annex O of NFPA 70E, *Standard for Electrical Safety in the Workplace,* high-impedance grounding is an effective tool for reducing arc flash hazards.

Part III. Grounding Electrode System and Grounding Electrode Conductor

250.50 Grounding Electrode System

A grounding electrode system is comprised of bonding together the grounding electrodes described in 250.52(A)(1) through (A)(7) that are present at a building or structure. ▶Figure 250–104

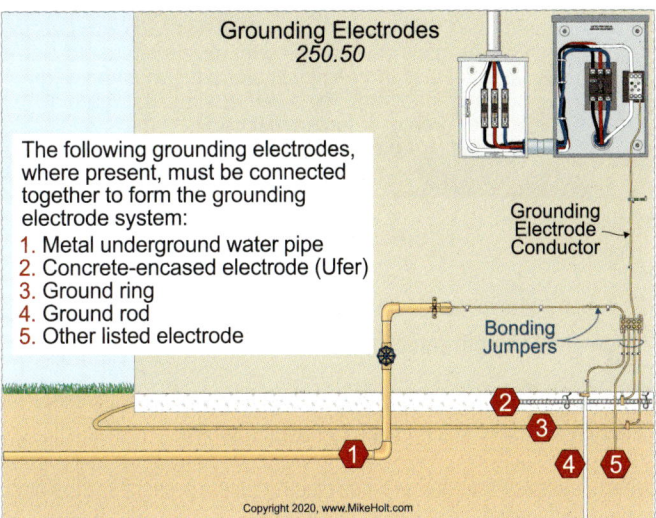
▶Figure 250–104

Ex: Concrete-encased electrodes are not required for existing buildings where the conductive steel reinforcing bars are not accessible without chipping up the concrete. ▶Figure 250–105

▶Figure 250–105

250.52 Grounding Electrode Types

(A) Electrodes.

(1) Underground Metal Water Pipe Electrode. Underground metal water pipe in direct contact with the Earth for 10 ft or more can serve as a grounding electrode. ▶Figure 250–106

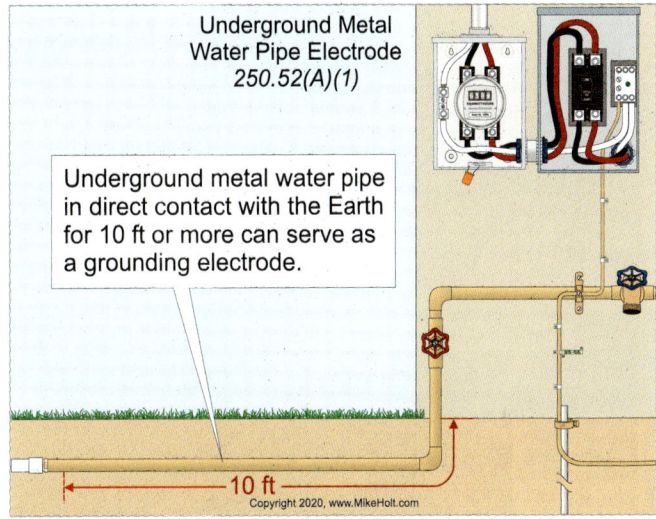
▶Figure 250–106

Author's Comment:

▸ Controversy about using metal underground water piping as a grounding electrode has existed since the early 1900s. The water industry believes that neutral current flowing on water piping corrodes the metal. For more information, contact the American Water Works Association about their report, *Effects of Electrical Grounding on Pipe Integrity and Shock Hazard*, Catalog No. 90702, 1.800.926.7337. ▶Figure 250–107

(2) Metal In-Ground Support Structure(s). Metal in-ground support structure(s) in direct contact with the Earth vertically for 10 ft or more can serve as a grounding electrode. ▶Figure 250–108

Note: Metal in-ground support structures include (but are not limited to) pilings, casings, and other structural metal.

(3) Concrete-Encased Electrode. Concrete-encased electrodes meeting the requirements of this subsection can serve as grounding electrodes. ▶Figure 250–109

(1) One or more electrically conductive steel reinforcing bars (rebar) of not less than ½ in. in diameter that are mechanically connected by steel tie wires to create a 20 ft or greater in length of steel can serve as a grounding electrode. ▶Figure 250–110

250.52 | Grounding and Bonding

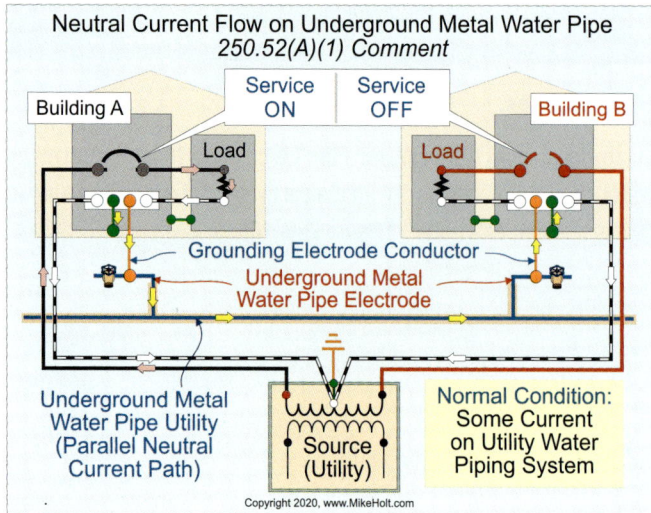
▶Figure 250–107

▶Figure 250–110

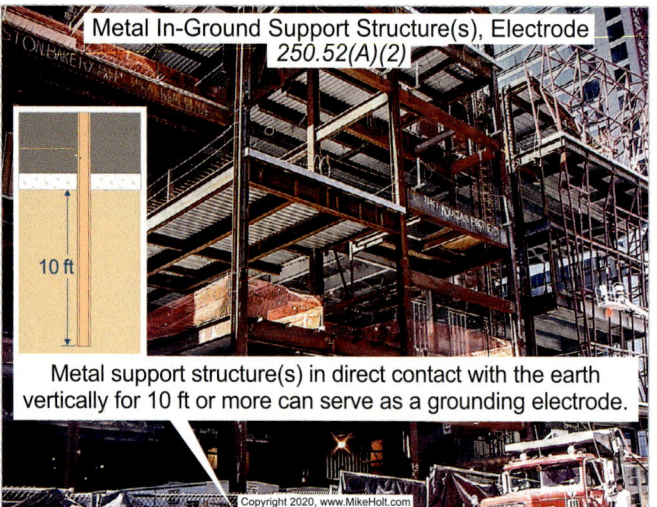
▶Figure 250–108

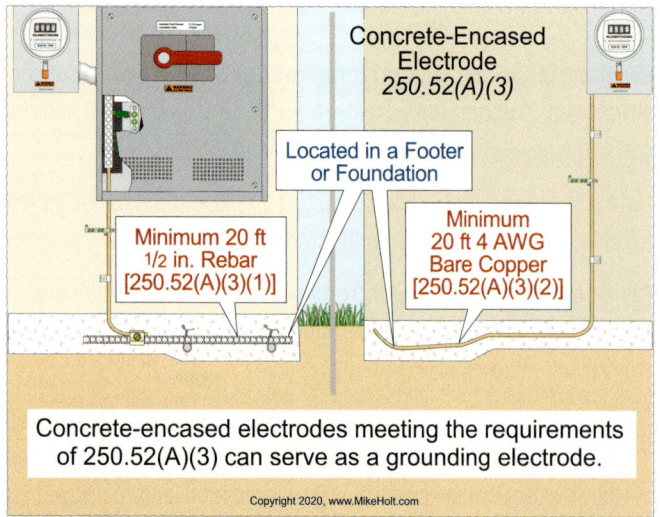
▶Figure 250–109

(2) A bare copper conductor not smaller than 4 AWG and 20 ft or greater in length can serve as a grounding electrode.

The rebar or bare copper conductor must be encased by at least 2 in. of concrete that is in direct contact with the Earth.

Where multiple concrete-encased electrodes are present at a building, only one is required to serve as a grounding electrode. ▶Figure 250–111

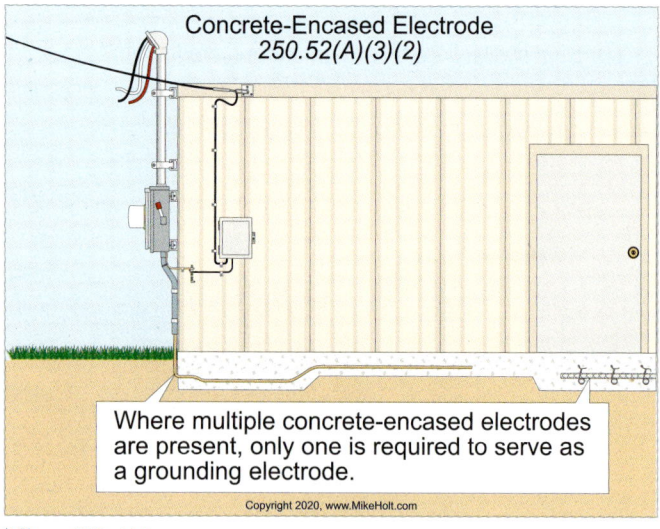
▶Figure 250–111

Note: Rebar in concrete that is not in direct contact with the Earth because of insulation, vapor barriers, or similar items is not considered to be a concrete-encased electrode. ▶Figure 250–112

Grounding and Bonding | 250.52

▶Figure 250-112

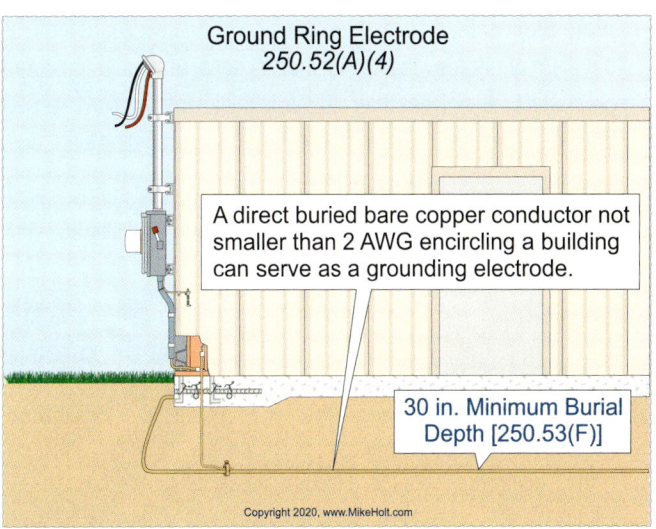
▶Figure 250-113

Author's Comment:

▶ A grounding electrode conductor to a concrete-encased grounding electrode is not required to be larger than 4 AWG copper [250.66(B)].

▶ A concrete-encased grounding electrode is also called a "Ufer Ground," named after a consultant working for the U.S. Army during World War II. The technique Herbert G. Ufer came up with was necessary because the site needing grounding had no underground water table and little rainfall. The desert site was a series of bomb storage vaults near of Flagstaff, Arizona. This type of grounding electrode generally offers the lowest ground resistance for the cost. In fact, Mr. Ufer's method is so effective that no other ground rods are necessary!

(4) Ground Ring. A direct buried bare copper conductor not smaller than 2 AWG encircling a building can serve as a grounding electrode. ▶Figure 250-113

Author's Comment:

▶ A ground ring encircling a building must not be installed less than 30 in. below the surface of the Earth [250.53(F)].

(5) Ground Rod. Ground rods must have at least 8 ft in length in contact with the Earth [250.53(G)].

(b) Ground rods must have a diameter of at least ⅝ in., unless listed. ▶Figure 250-114

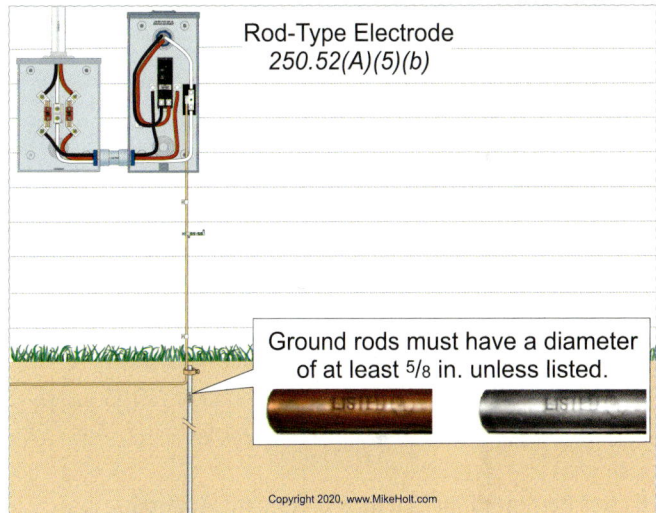
▶Figure 250-114

Author's Comment:

▶ The grounding electrode conductor, if it is the sole connection to the rod(s), is not required to be larger than 6 AWG copper [250.66(A)].

▶ The diameter of a ground rod has an insignificant effect on the contact resistance of a rod(s) to the Earth. However, larger diameter rods (¾ in. and 1 in.) are sometimes installed where mechanical strength is desired, or to compensate for the loss of the electrode's metal due to corrosion.

(6) Listed Electrode. Other listed grounding electrodes can serve as a grounding electrode.

250.53 | Grounding and Bonding

(7) Plate Electrode. A bare or electrically conductive coated iron or a steel plate of not less than ¼ in. in thickness, or a solid uncoated copper metal plate not less than 0.06 in. in thickness, with an exposed surface area of not less than 2 sq ft can serve as a grounding electrode.

(8) Metal Underground Systems. Metal underground systems, piping, and well casings can serve as a grounding electrode. ▶Figure 250-115

▶Figure 250-115

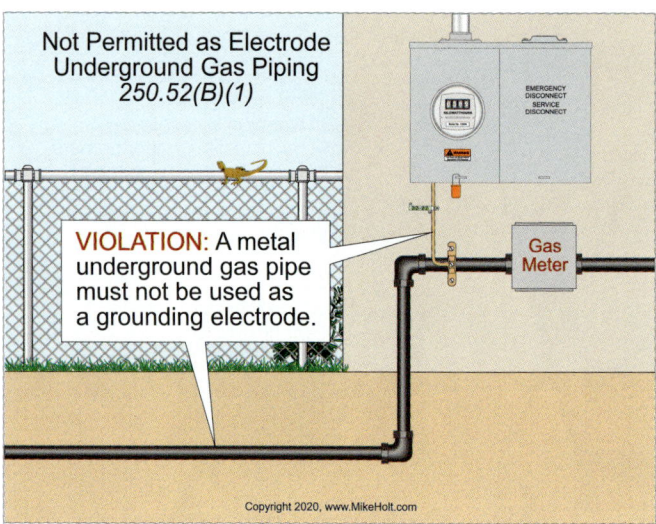

▶Figure 250-116

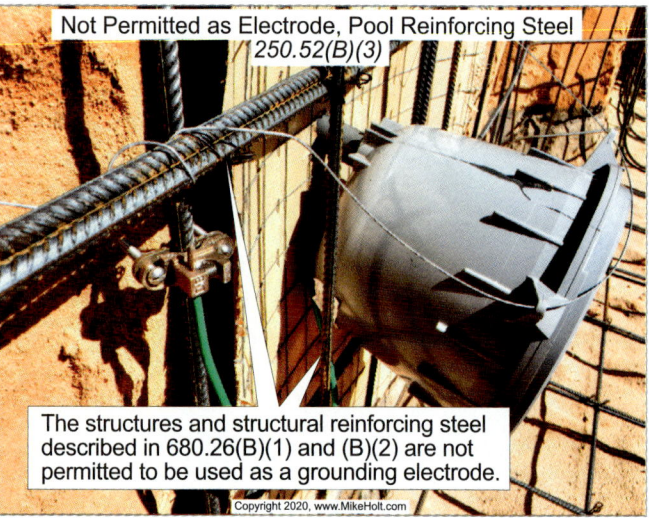

▶Figure 250-117

Author's Comment:

▸ The grounding electrode conductor to the metal underground system must be sized in accordance with Table 250.66, based on the area of the largest phase conductor.

(B) Not Permitted for Use as a Grounding Electrode.

(1) Underground metal gas piping systems are not permitted to be used as a grounding electrode. ▶Figure 250-116

(2) Aluminum is not permitted to be used as a grounding electrode.

(3) The structures and structural reinforcing steel described in 680.26(B)(1) and (B)(2) are not permitted to be used as a grounding electrode. ▶Figure 250-117

250.53 Grounding Electrode Installation Requirements

(A) Ground Rods.

(1) Below Permanent Moisture Level. If practicable, rod, pipe, and plate electrodes must be embedded below the permanent moisture level and must be free from nonconductive coatings such as paint or enamel.

(2) Supplemental Electrode. A single ground rod must be supplemented by an additional electrode. The supplemental electrode must be bonded to: ▶Figure 250-118

Grounding and Bonding | 250.53

 Scan this QR code for a video of Mike explaining this topic; it's a sample from the videos that accompany this textbook. www.MikeHolt.com/20BGvideos

(3) Supplemental Ground Rod, Spacing. The supplemental electrode must be installed not less than 6 ft from the ground rod. ▶Figure 250-120

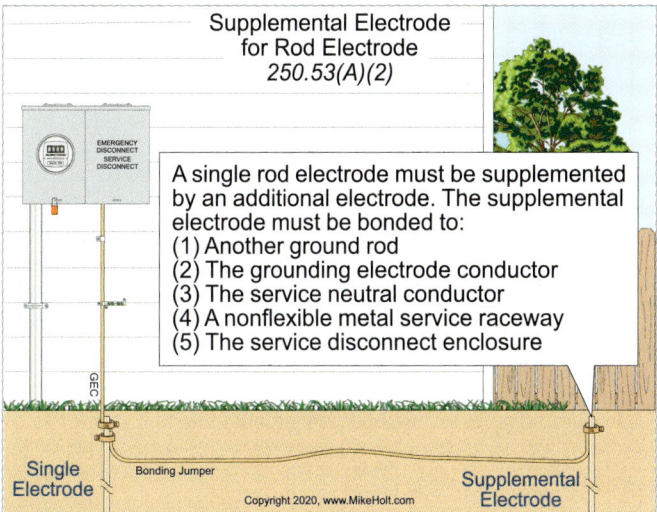

▶Figure 250-118

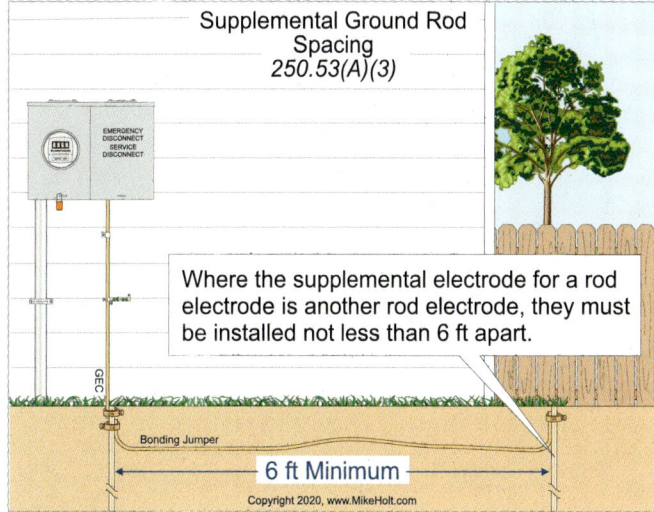

▶Figure 250-120

(1) Another ground rod

(2) The grounding electrode conductor

(3) The service neutral conductor

(4) A nonflexible metal service raceway

(5) The service-disconnect enclosure

Ex: A single ground rod electrode having a contact resistance to the Earth of 25 ohms or less is not required to have a supplemental electrode. ▶Figure 250-119

(4) Rod and Pipe Electrodes. The electrode must be installed such that at least 8 ft of length is in contact with the soil. It must be driven to a depth of not less than 8 ft except where rock bottom is encountered, the electrode must be driven at an oblique angle not to exceed 45 degrees from the vertical or, where rock bottom is encountered at an angle up to 45 degrees, the electrode is permitted to be buried in a trench that is at least 30 in. deep. ▶Figure 250-121

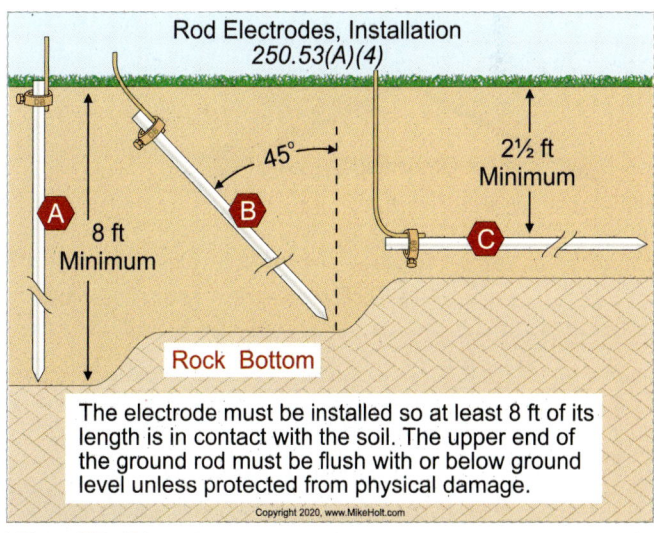

▶Figure 250-121

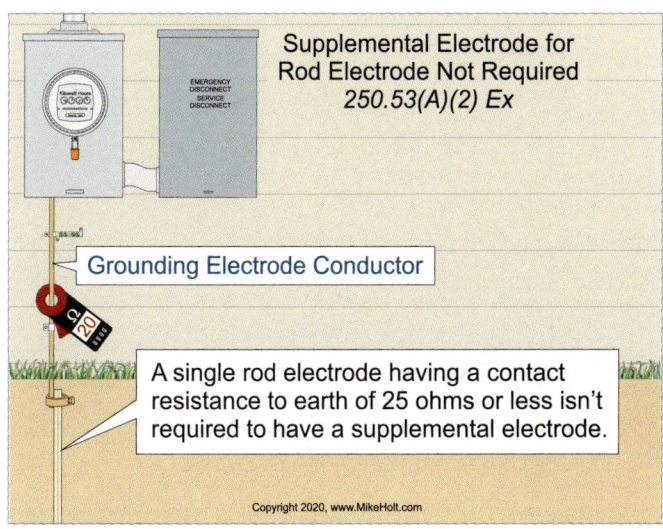

▶Figure 250-119

The upper end of the ground rod must be flush with or below ground level unless the grounding electrode conductor attachment is protected against physical damage as specified in 250.10. ▶Figure 250-122

Mike Holt Enterprises • www.MikeHolt.com • 888.NEC.CODE (632.2633) | 135

250.53 | Grounding and Bonding

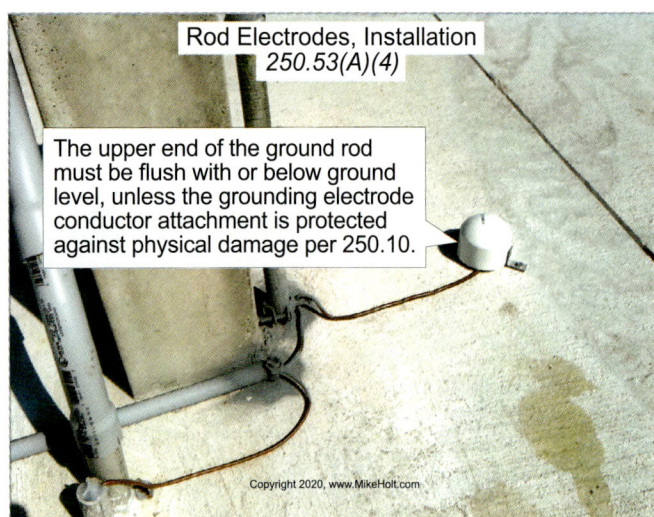

▶Figure 250–122

Author's Comment:

▸ When the grounding electrode attachment fitting is located underground (below ground level), it must be listed for direct soil burial [250.68(A) Ex 1 and 250.70].

(B) Electrode Spacing. Electrodes for premises systems must be located no closer than 6 ft from lightning protection system grounding electrodes.

Two or more grounding electrodes that are bonded together are considered a single grounding electrode system. ▶Figure 250–123

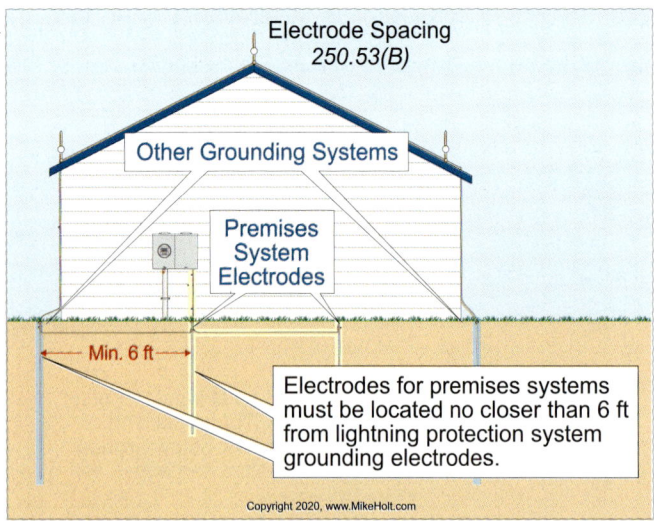

▶Figure 250–123

(C) Grounding Electrode Bonding Jumper. Grounding electrode bonding jumpers must be copper when within 18 in. of the Earth [250.64(A)]. Exposed grounding electrode bonding jumpers must be securely fastened to the surface and protected from physical damage [250.64(B)]. The bonding jumper to each electrode must be sized in accordance with 250.66, based on the area of the largest phase conductor. ▶Figure 250–124

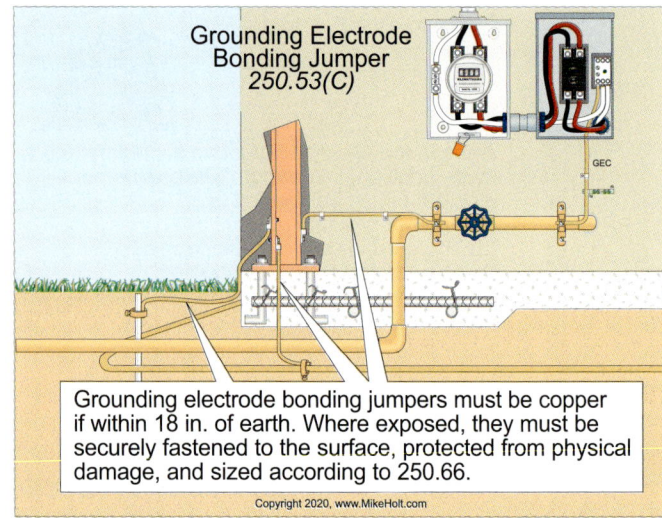

▶Figure 250–124

Author's Comment:

▸ Grounding electrode bonding jumpers must terminate by any of the following means in accordance with 250.8(A):

  ▸ Listed pressure connectors
  ▸ Terminal bars
  ▸ Pressure connectors listed as grounding and bonding equipment
  ▸ Exothermic welding
  ▸ Machine screw-type fasteners that engage not less than two threads or are secured with a nut
  ▸ Thread-forming machine screws that engage not less than two threads in the enclosure
  ▸ Connections that are part of a listed assembly
  ▸ Other listed means

When the grounding electrode conductor termination is encased in concrete or buried, the termination fittings must be listed for this purpose [250.70].

Rebar is not permitted to be used to interconnect the electrodes of grounding electrode systems.

(D) Underground Metal Water Pipe Electrode.

(1) Continuity. Continuity of the grounding path or the bonding connection to interior piping must not rely on water meters or filtering devices and similar equipment. ▶Figure 250–125

Grounding and Bonding | 250.53

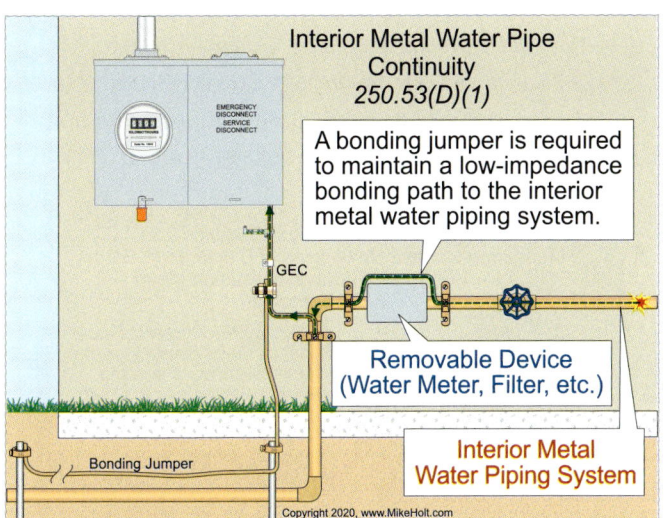
▶Figure 250–125

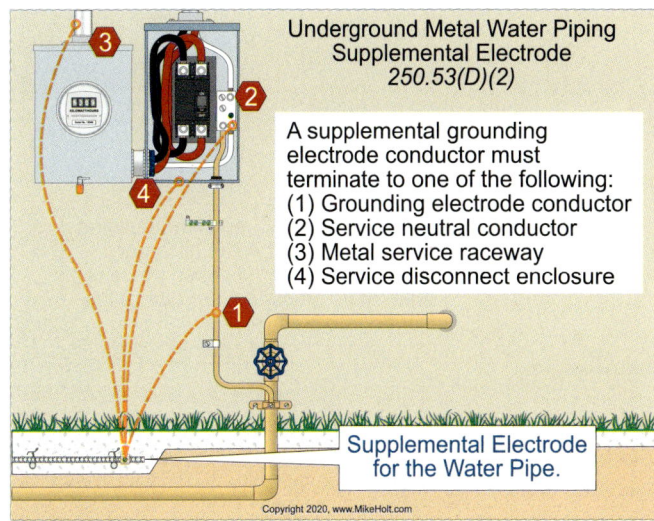
▶Figure 250–127

(2) Water Pipe Supplemental Electrode. When an underground metal water pipe grounding electrode is present, it must be supplemented by any of the following electrodes:

- Metal frame of the building electrode [250.52(A)(2)]
- Concrete-encased electrode [250.52(A)(3)] ▶Figure 250–126
- Rod electrode [250.52(A)(5)]
- Other type of listed electrode [250.52(A)(6)]
- Metal underground piping electrode [250.52(A)(8)]

(1) Grounding electrode conductor

(2) Service neutral conductor

(3) Metal service raceway

(4) Service-disconnect enclosure

Author's Comment:

- Because a metal underground waterpipe electrode could be replaced by a plastic water pipe, the supplemental electrode must be installed as if it is the only electrode for the system.

Ex: The supplemental electrode can be bonded to interior metal water piping located not more than 5 ft from the point of entrance to the building [250.68(C)(1)].

(E) Supplemental Rod Electrode. The grounding electrode conductor to a ground rod that serves as a supplemental electrode is not required to be larger than 6 AWG copper.

(F) Ground Ring. A ground ring encircling a building must be a bare 2 AWG or larger copper conductor installed not less than 30 in. below the surface of the Earth [250.52(A)(4)]. ▶Figure 250–128

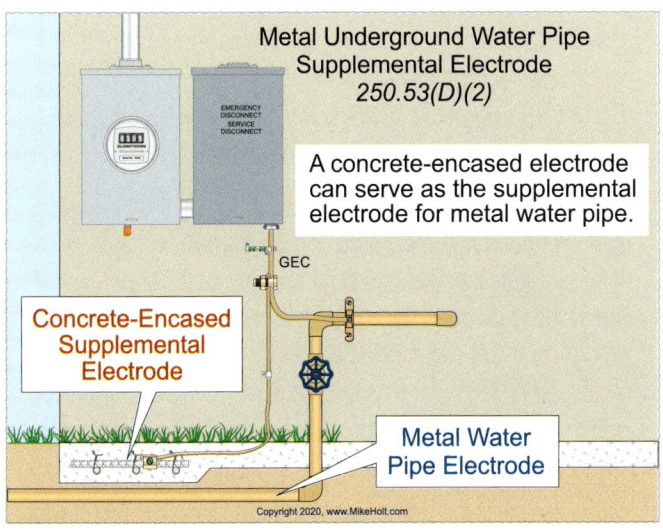
▶Figure 250–126

The grounding electrode conductor for the supplemental electrode must terminate to any of the following: ▶Figure 250–127

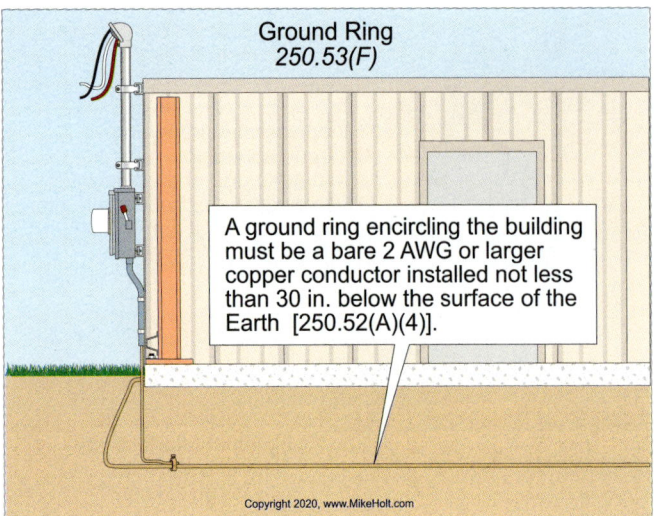
▶Figure 250–128

Measuring the Contact Resistance of Electrodes to Earth

A ground resistance clamp meter or a three-point fall-of-potential ground resistance meter can be used to measure the contact resistance of a grounding electrode to the Earth.

Ground Clamp Meter. The ground resistance clamp meter measures the contact resistance of the grounding electrode system to the Earth by injecting a high-frequency signal via the service neutral conductor to the serving electric utility's grounding system, and then measuring the strength of the return signal through the Earth to the grounding electrode being measured. ▶Figure 250–129

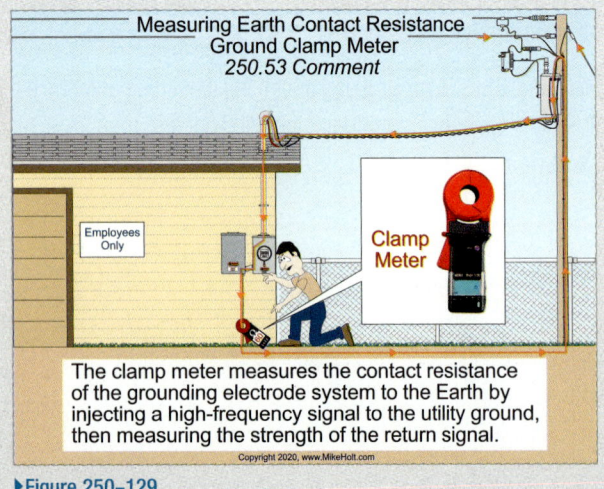
▶Figure 250–129

Fall-of-Potential Ground Resistance Meter. The three-point fall-of-potential ground resistance meter determines the contact resistance of a single grounding electrode to the Earth by using Ohm's Law where **Resistance = Voltage/Current**. ▶Figure 250–130

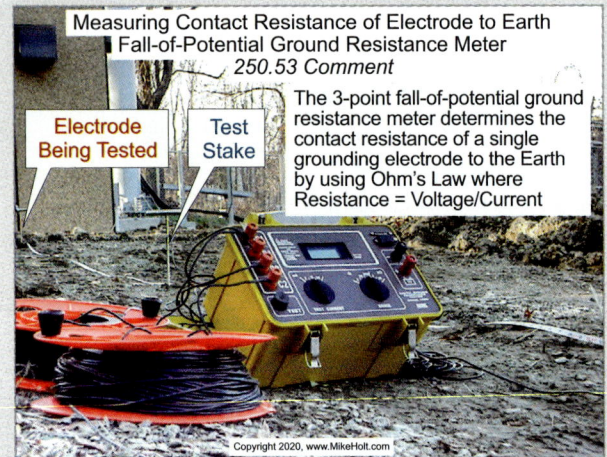
▶Figure 250–130

This meter divides the voltage difference between the electrode to be measured and a driven voltage test stake (P) by the current flowing between the electrode to be measured and a driven current test stake (C). The test stakes are typically made of ¼ in. diameter steel rods, 24 in. long, driven two-thirds of their length into the Earth.

The distance and alignment between the voltage and current test stakes, and the electrode, is extremely important to the validity of the Earth contact resistance measurements. For an 8-ft rod, the accepted practice is to space the current test stake (C) 80 ft from the electrode to be measured.

The voltage test stake (P) is positioned in a straight line between the electrode to be measured and the current test stake (C). The voltage test stake should be approximately 62 percent of the distance of where the current test stake is located from the electrode. If the current test stake (C) for an 8-ft ground rod is located 80 ft from the grounding electrode, the voltage test stake (P) will be about 50 ft from the electrode to be measured.

Grounding and Bonding | 250.54

▶ **Example**

Question: *If the voltage between the ground rod and the voltage test stake (P) is 3V, and the current between the ground rod and the current test stake (C) is 0.20A, what will be the Earth contact resistance of the electrode to the Earth?* ▶Figure 250–131

(a) 3 ohms   (b) 5 ohms   (c) 10 ohms   (d) 15 ohms

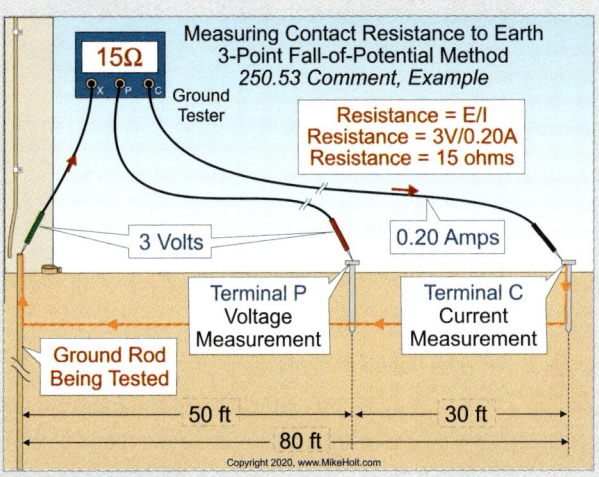

▶Figure 250–131

Solution:

Resistance = Voltage/Current

Voltage = 3V
Current = 0.20A

Resistance = 3V/0.20A
Resistance = 15 ohms

The Earth contact resistance of the electrode to the Earth will be 15 ohms.

Answer: (d) 15 ohms

Author's Comment:

▸ The three-point fall-of-potential meter should only be used to measure the contact resistance of one electrode to the Earth at a time, and that electrode must be independent and not connected to any part of the electrical system. The contact resistance of two electrodes bonded together cannot measured until they have been separated. The contact resistance of two separate electrodes to the Earth can be thought of as two resistors in parallel if they are outside each other's sphere of influence.

Soil Resistivity

The contact resistance of an electrode to the Earth is impacted by soil resistivity, which varies throughout the world. Soil resistivity is influenced by electrolytes, which consist of moisture, minerals, and dissolved salts. Because soil resistivity changes with moisture content, the contact resistance of a grounding system to the Earth varies with the seasons.

250.54 Auxiliary Grounding Electrodes

 Scan this QR code for a video of Mike explaining this topic; it's a sample from the videos that accompany this textbook. www.MikeHolt.com/20BGvideos

Grounding electrodes that are not required by the *NEC* are called "auxiliary electrodes" and can be connected to the equipment grounding conductors. Since they serve no purpose related to the electrical safety addressed by the *Code*, they have no *NEC* requirements. ▶Figure 250–132

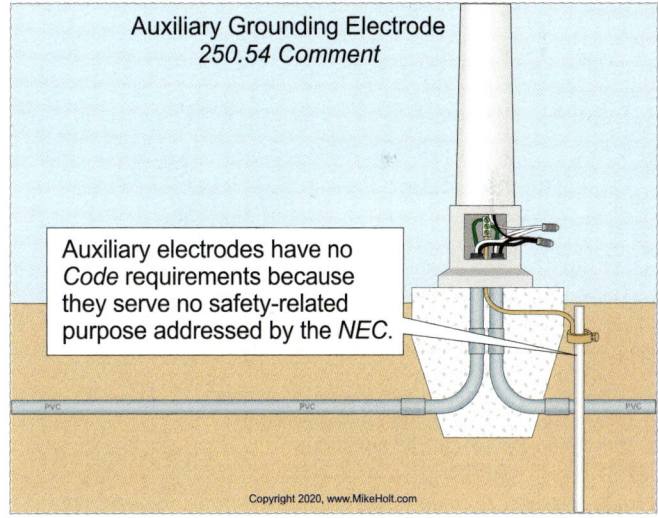

▶Figure 250–132

If an auxiliary electrode is installed, it is not required to be bonded to the building grounding electrode system, to have the grounding conductor sized to 250.66, nor must it comply with the 25-ohm single ground rod requirement of 250.53(A)(2) Ex.

250.58 | Grounding and Bonding

> **Caution:** An auxiliary electrode may cause equipment failures by providing a path for lightning to travel through electronic equipment. ▶Figure 250–133 and ▶Figure 250–134

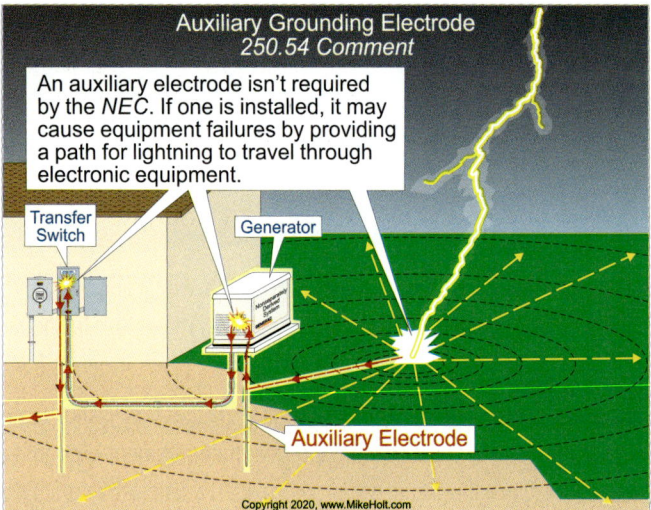

▶Figure 250–133

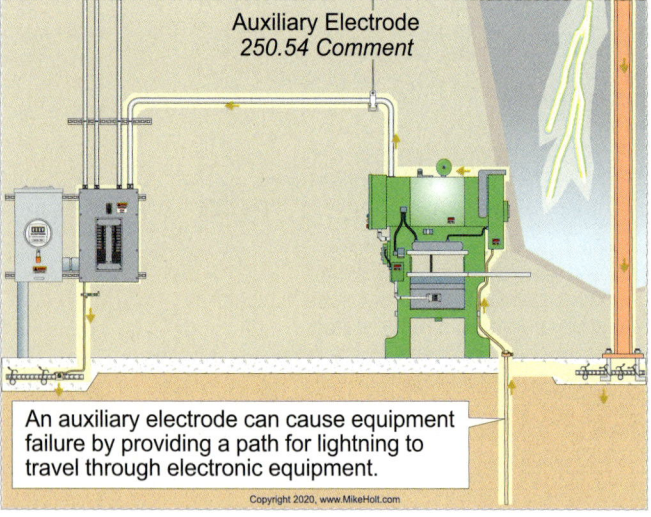

▶Figure 250–134

The Earth is not to be considered the effective ground-fault current path specified in 250.4(A)(5). ▶Figure 250–135

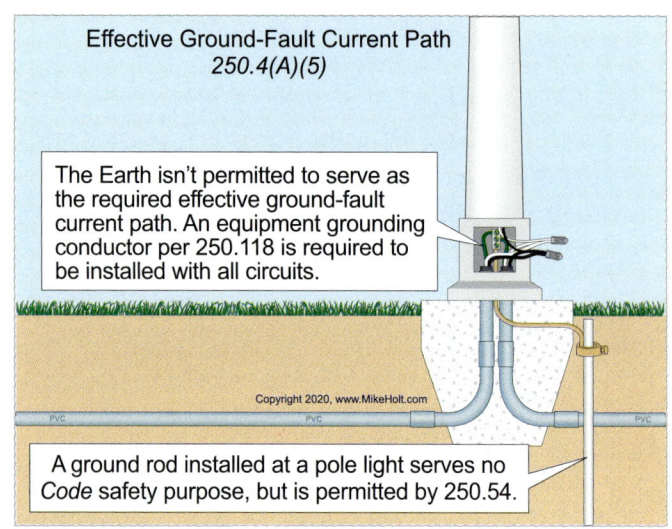

▶Figure 250–135

> **Danger:** Because the contact resistance of an electrode to the Earth is so great, very little fault current returns to the power supply if the Earth is the only fault current return path. As a result, the circuit overcurrent protective device will not open and clear the ground fault, and all metal parts associated with the electrical installation, metal piping, and structural building steel will become and remain energized. ▶Figure 250–136

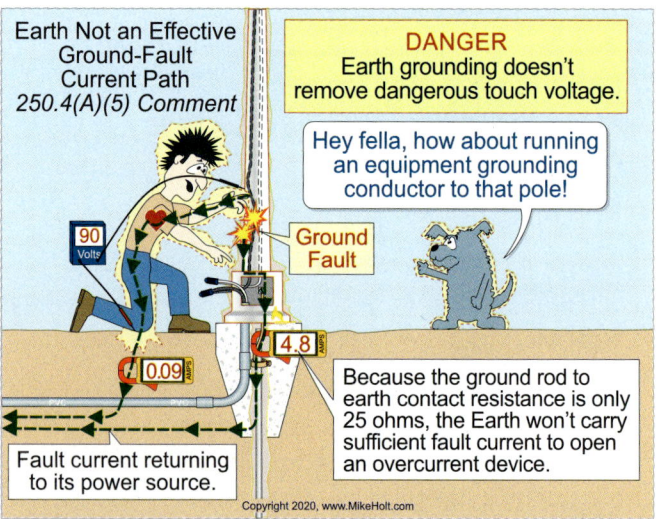

▶Figure 250–136

250.58 Common Grounding Electrode

Where more than one alternating-current system is connected to a grounding electrode at a building, the same grounding electrode must be used for all systems. ▶Figure 250–137

Grounding and Bonding | 250.64

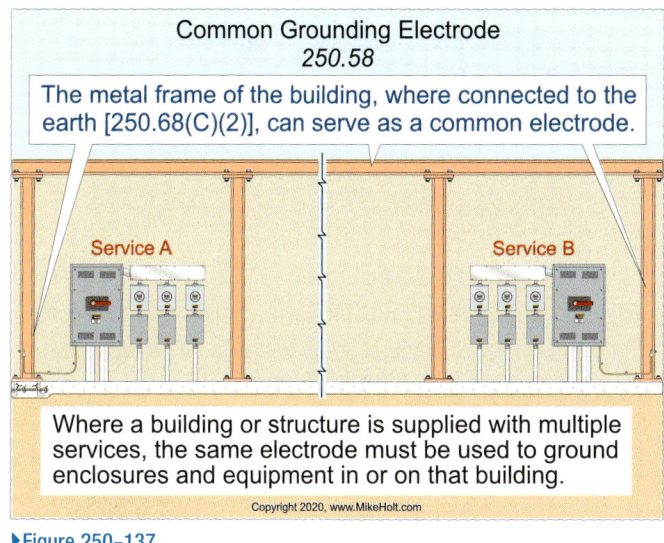
▶Figure 250-137

Caution

⚡ Potentially dangerous objectionable neutral current flows on the metal parts of an electrical system when multiple service disconnects are connected to the same electrode. This is because neutral current from each service can return to the utility via the common grounding electrode and its conductors and is especially a problem if a service neutral conductor is opened. ▶Figure 250-138

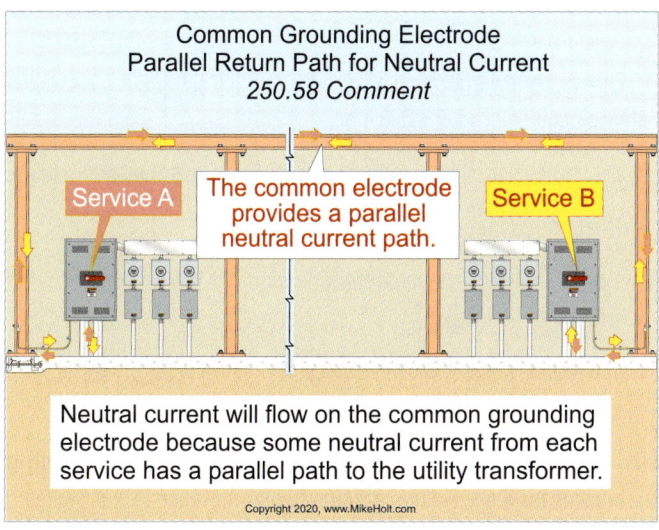
▶Figure 250-138

Two or more grounding electrodes that are bonded together are considered as a single grounding electrode system.

250.62 Grounding Electrode Conductor

Grounding electrode conductors of the wire type must be copper if within 18 in. of the Earth [250.64(A)]. ▶Figure 250-139

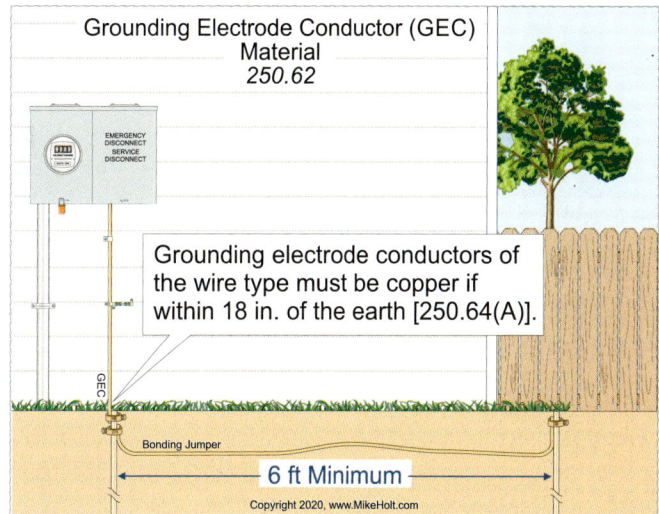
▶Figure 250-139

250.64 Grounding Electrode Conductor Installation

Grounding electrode conductors must be installed as specified in (A) through (F).

(A) Aluminum Conductors. Bare, covered, or insulated aluminum grounding electrode conductors must comply with the following:

(1) Bare or covered conductors without an extruded polymeric covering are not permitted to be installed where subject to corrosive conditions or to be installed in direct contact with concrete.

(2) Terminations made within listed enclosures identified for outdoor use are permitted within 18 in. of the Earth. If open-bottom enclosures are installed on a concrete pad, the concrete is not considered earth.

(3) Aluminum conductors external to buildings or equipment enclosures are not permitted to be terminated within 18 in. of the Earth.

(B) Conductor Protection. Where exposed, a grounding electrode conductor must be securely fastened to the surface on which it is carried.

(1) Not Exposed to Physical Damage. Grounding electrode conductors 6 AWG and larger can be installed exposed along the surface of the building if securely fastened and not exposed to physical damage. ▶Figure 250-140

250.64 | Grounding and Bonding

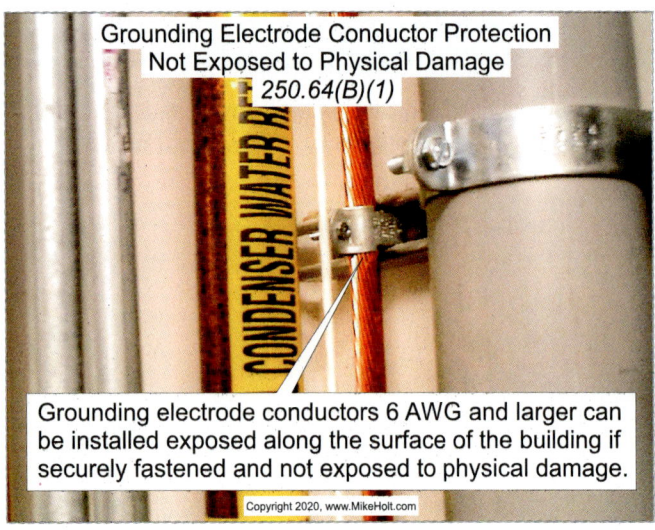
▶Figure 250-140

(2) Exposed to Physical Damage. Grounding electrode conductors subject to physical damage must be protected in rigid metal conduit (RMC), intermediate metal conduit (IMC), Schedule 80 rigid polyvinyl chloride conduit (PVC), reinforced thermosetting resin conduit Type XW (RTRC-XW), electrical metallic tubing (EMT), or cable armor. ▶Figure 250-141

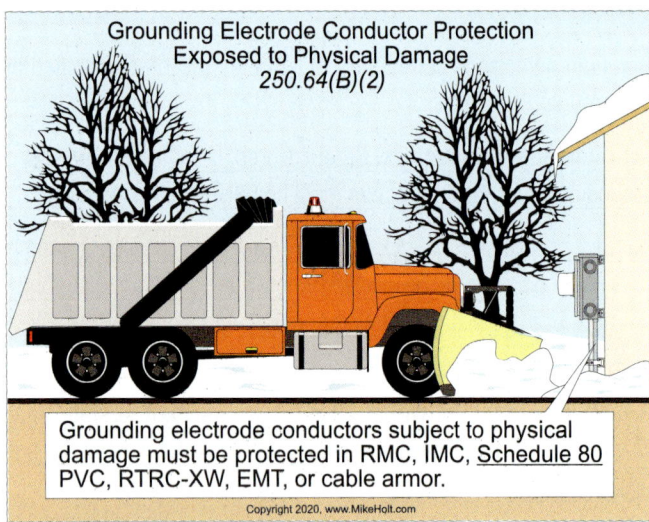
▶Figure 250-141

(3) Smaller Than 6 AWG. Grounding electrode conductors smaller than 6 AWG must be protected in RMC, IMC, Schedule 80 PVC, RTRC-XW, EMT, or cable armor.

Author's Comment:

▸ While Table 250.66 permits the use of 8 AWG copper as the grounding electrode conductor for the phase conductor typically used for a 100A service, use of a GEC smaller than 6 AWG is not common.

(4) In Contact with the Earth. Grounding electrode conductors and bonding jumpers in contact with the Earth are not required to comply with the cover requirements of 300.5 but must be protected where subject to physical damage. ▶Figure 250-142

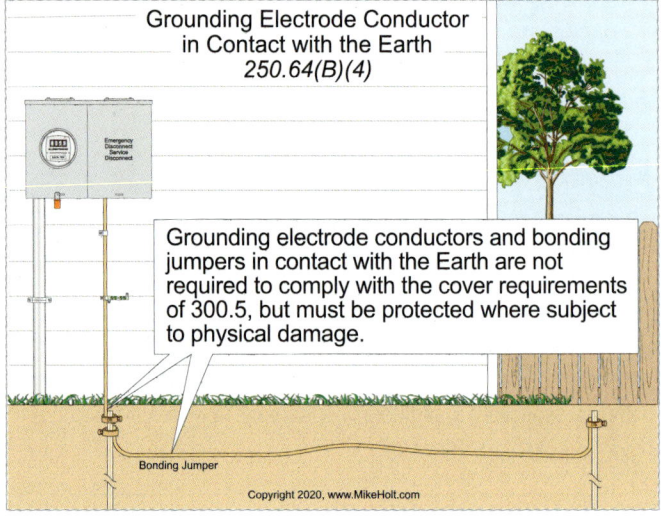
▶Figure 250-142

(C) Continuous. Grounding electrode conductor(s) must be installed without a splice or joint except by:

(1) Irreversible compression-type connectors or exothermic welding.

(2) Busbars connected together.

(3) Bolted, riveted, or welded connections of the structural metal frames of buildings.

(4) Threaded, welded, brazed, soldered, or bolted-flange connections of metal water piping.

(D) Grounding Electrode Conductor for Multiple Building Disconnects. If a building contains two or more service or building disconnects in separate enclosures, the grounding electrode connections must be made by any of the following methods:

(1) Common Grounding Electrode Conductor and Taps. The unspliced common grounding electrode conductor must be sized in accordance with 250.66, based on the sum of the circular mil area of the largest phase conductor supplying the equipment. ▶Figure 250-143

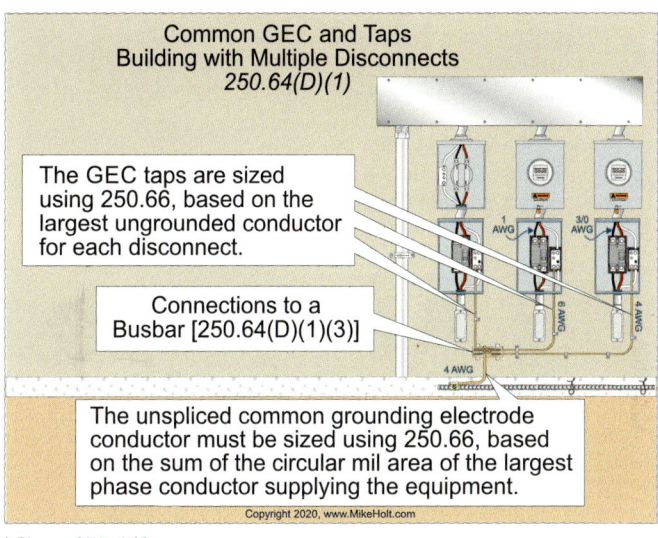

▶Figure 250-143

A grounding electrode conductor tap must extend from each disconnect and must be sized no smaller than specified in Table 250.66, based on the area of the largest phase conductor.

The grounding electrode conductor tap must be connected to the common grounding electrode conductor by any of the following methods:

(1) Exothermic welding.

(2) Connectors listed as grounding and bonding equipment.

(3) Connections to a busbar of sufficient length and not less than ¼ in. thick × 2 in. wide that is securely fastened and installed in an accessible location. ▶Figure 250-144

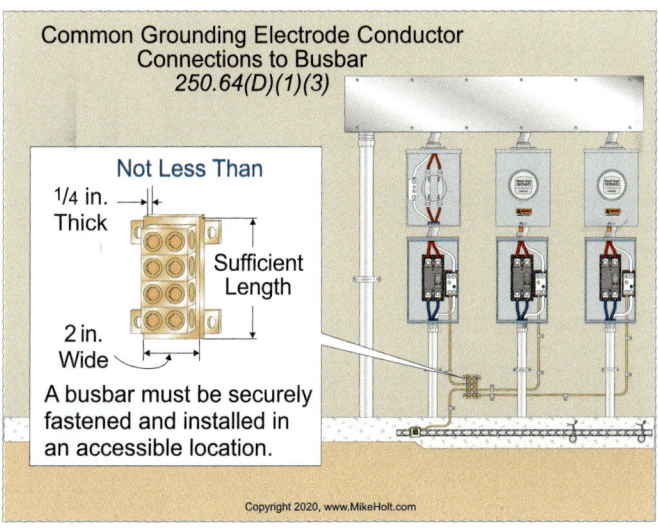

▶Figure 250-144

(2) Individual Grounding Electrode Conductors. An individual grounding electrode conductor from each disconnect sized in accordance with 250.66, based on the phase conductor(s) supplying the individual disconnect, must connect the grounding electrode system to one of the following:

(1) The service neutral conductor ▶Figure 250-145

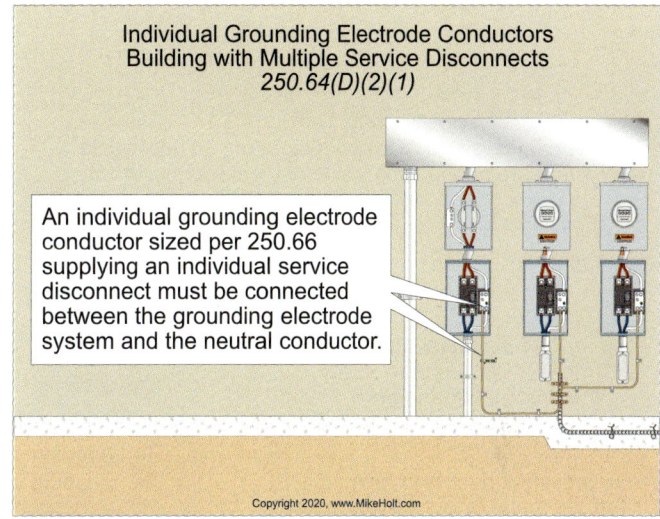

▶Figure 250-145

(2) The equipment grounding conductor of the feeder circuit

(3) The service supply-side bonding jumper

(3) Supply Side of Disconnects. A grounding electrode conductor from an accessible enclosure on the supply side of the disconnects, sized in accordance with 250.66 and based on the phase conductor(s) supplying the disconnect, must connect the grounding electrode system to one of the following:

(1) The service neutral conductor ▶Figure 250-146

(2) The equipment grounding conductor of the feeder circuit

(3) The service supply-side bonding jumper

(E) Ferrous Raceways Containing Grounding Electrode Conductors.

(1) General. To prevent inductive choking of grounding electrode conductors, ferrous metal raceways, enclosures, and cable armor containing grounding electrode conductors must have each end of the raceway or enclosure bonded to the grounding electrode conductor. ▶Figure 250-147

250.64 | Grounding and Bonding

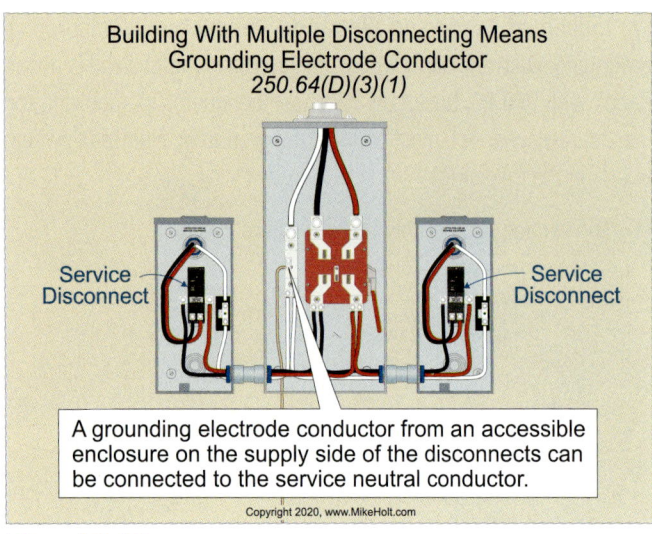
▶Figure 250-146

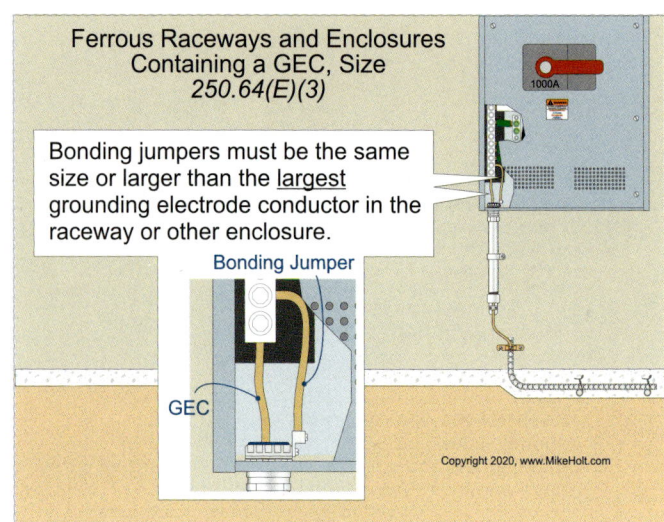
▶Figure 250-148

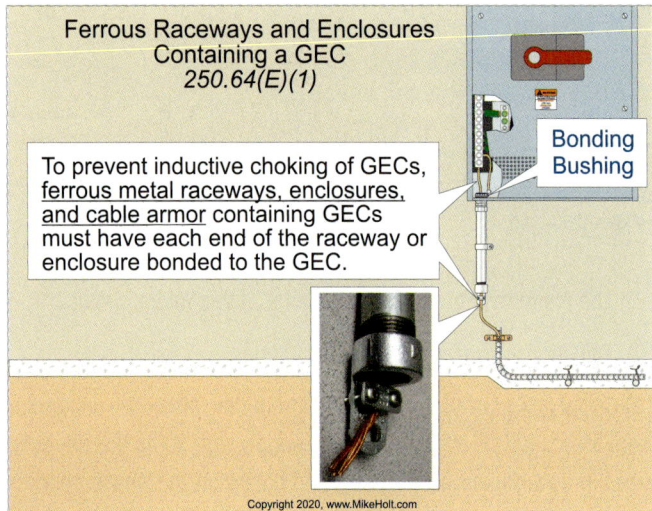
▶Figure 250-147

(2) Methods. Raceway bonding must be in accordance with 250.92(B)(2) through (B)(4).

(3) Size. Bonding jumpers must be the same size or larger than the largest grounding electrode conductor in the raceway or other enclosure. ▶Figure 250-148

Author's Comment:

▸ Nonferrous metal raceways, such as aluminum rigid metal conduit, enclosing the grounding electrode conductor are not required to meet the "bonding each end of the raceway to the grounding electrode conductor" provisions of this section.

Author's Comment:

▸ To save of time and effort, install the grounding electrode conductor in a nonmetallic raceway suitable for the application [352.10(F)]. ▶Figure 250-149

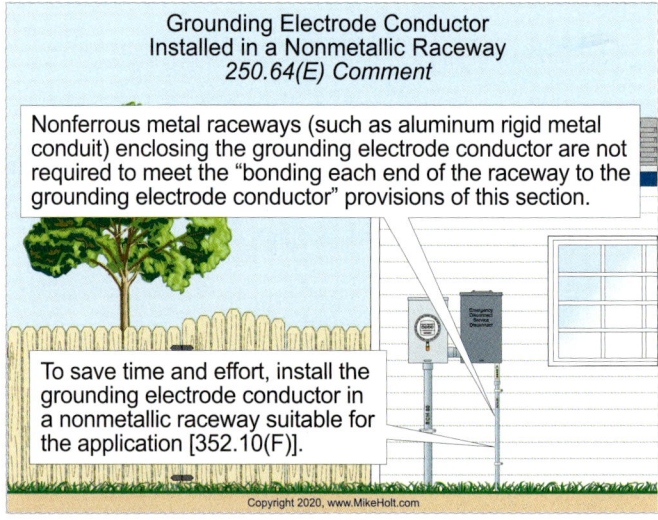
▶Figure 250-149

(F) Termination to Grounding Electrode.

(1) Single Grounding Electrode Conductor. A single grounding electrode conductor can terminate to any grounding electrode of the grounding electrode system. ▶Figure 250-150

Grounding and Bonding | **250.66**

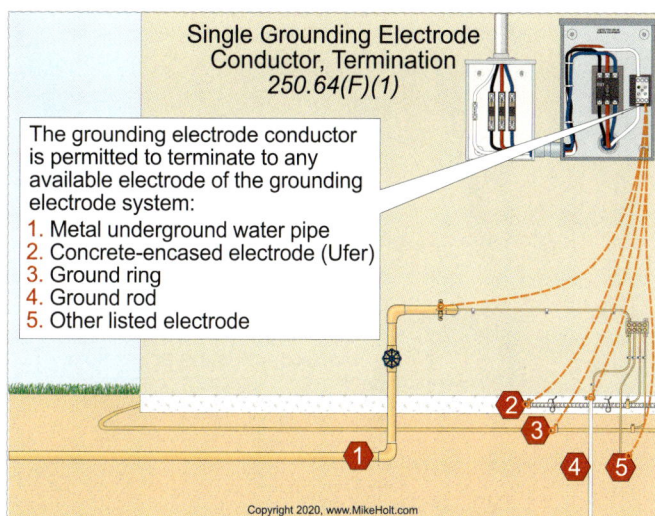

▶Figure 250-150

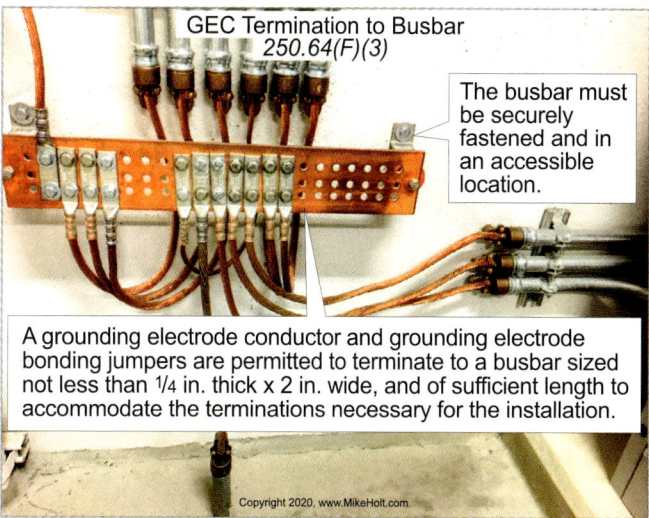

▶Figure 250-152

(2) Multiple Grounding Electrode Conductors. Where multiple grounding electrode conductors are installed [250.64(D)(2)], each one can terminate to any grounding electrode of the grounding electrode system. ▶Figure 250-151

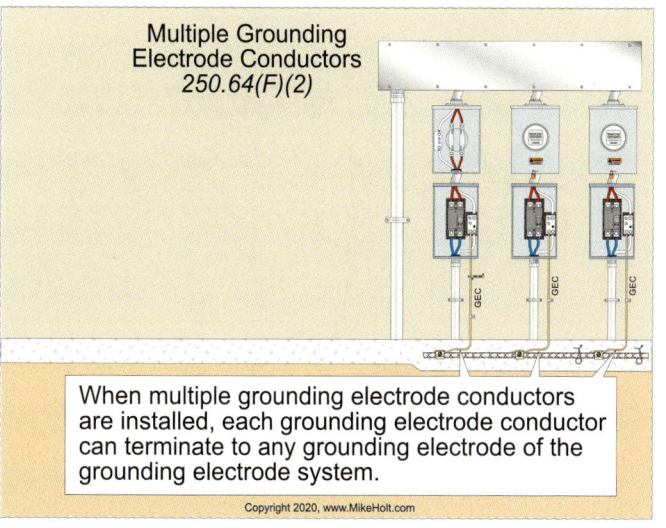

▶Figure 250-151

(3) Termination to Busbar. Grounding electrode conductors and grounding electrode bonding jumpers are permitted to terminate to a busbar not less than ¼ in. thick × 2 in. wide, and of sufficient length to accommodate the terminations necessary for the installation. The busbar must be securely fastened and installed in an accessible location. ▶Figure 250-152

250.66 Sizing Grounding Electrode Conductor

Except as permitted in (A) through (C), grounding electrode conductors must be sized in accordance with Table 250.66, based on the area of the largest phase conductor.

(A) Ground Rods. If a grounding electrode conductor or bonding jumper only connects to a ground rod [250.52(A)(5)], the grounding electrode conductor is not required to be larger than 6 AWG copper. ▶Figure 250-153

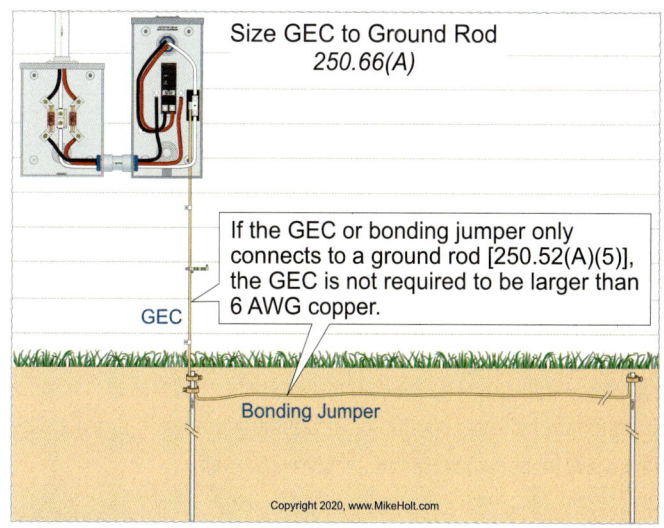

▶Figure 250-153

(B) Concrete-Encased Grounding Electrodes. If a grounding electrode conductor or bonding jumper only connects to a concrete-encased electrode [250.52(A)(3)], the grounding electrode conductor is not required to be larger than 4 AWG copper. ▶Figure 250-154

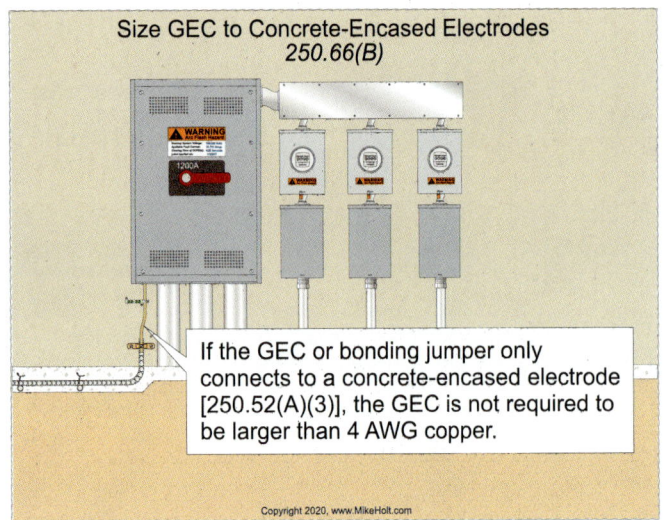
▶Figure 250–154

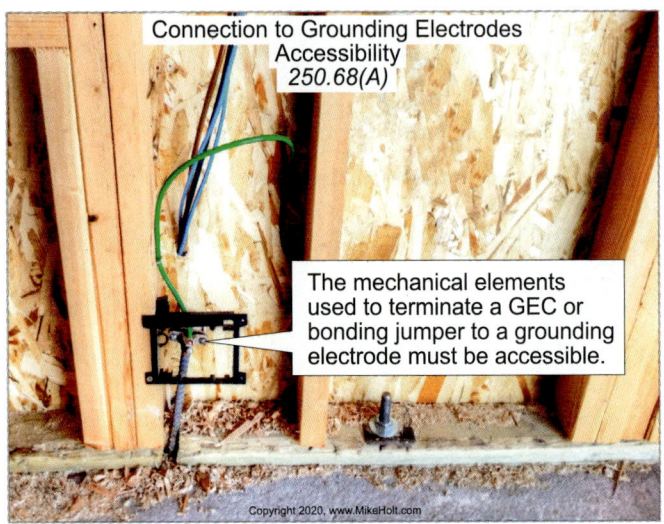
▶Figure 250–155

Table 250.66 Grounding Electrode Conductor	
AWG or Area of Parallel Copper Conductors	Copper Grounding Electrode Conductor
2 AWG or Smaller	8 AWG
1 or 1/0 AWG	6 AWG
2/0 or 3/0 AWG	4 AWG
Over 3/0 through 350 kcmil	2 AWG
Over 350 through 600 kcmil	1/0 AWG
Over 600 through 1,100 kcmil	2/0 AWG
Over 1,100 kcmil	3/0 AWG

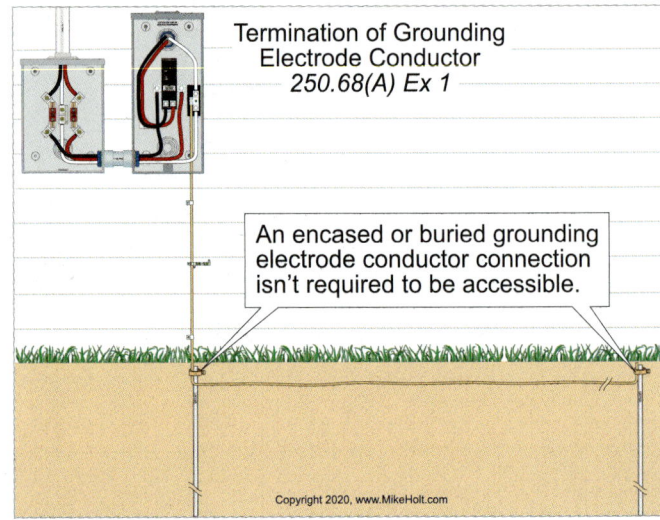
▶Figure 250–156

250.68 Grounding Electrode Conductor and Bonding Jumper Connection to Grounding Electrodes

(A) Accessibility. The mechanical elements used to terminate a grounding electrode conductor or bonding jumper to a grounding electrode must be accessible. ▶Figure 250–155

Ex 1: The termination is not required to be accessible if the termination to the electrode is encased in concrete or buried in the Earth. ▶Figure 250–156

Author's Comment:

▸ If the grounding electrode attachment fitting is encased in concrete or buried in the Earth, it must be listed for direct soil burial or concrete encasement [250.70].

Ex 2: Exothermic or irreversible compression connections, together with the mechanical means used to attach to fireproofed structural metal, are not required to be accessible.

(B) Integrity of Underground Metal Water Pipe Electrode. A bonding jumper must be installed around insulated joints and equipment likely to be disconnected for repairs or replacement for an underground metal water piping system used as a grounding electrode. The bonding jumper must be of sufficient length to allow the removal of such equipment while retaining the integrity of the grounding path. ▶Figure 250–157

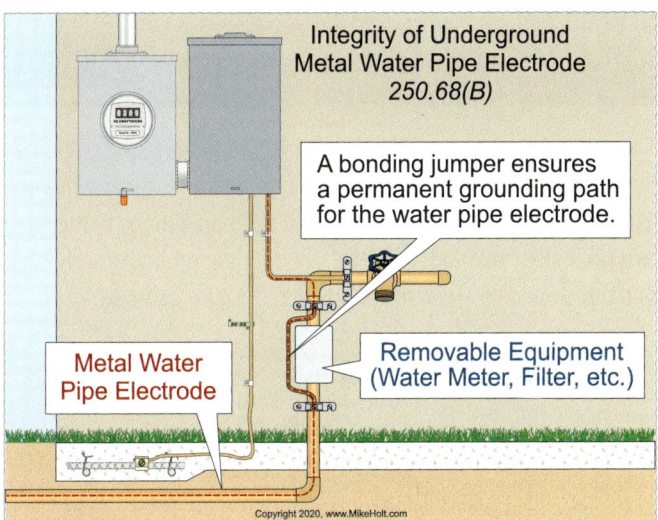

▶Figure 250–157

(C) Grounding Electrode Conductor Connections. Grounding electrode conductors and bonding jumpers are permitted to terminate at the following locations and be used to extend the connection to an electrode(s):

(1) Interior metal water piping that is electrically continuous with a metal underground water pipe electrode and is located not more than 5 ft from the point of entrance to the building, can be used to extend the connection to electrodes. Interior metal water piping located more than 5 ft from the point of entrance to the building is not permitted to be used as a conductor to interconnect electrodes of the grounding electrode system. ▶Figure 250–158

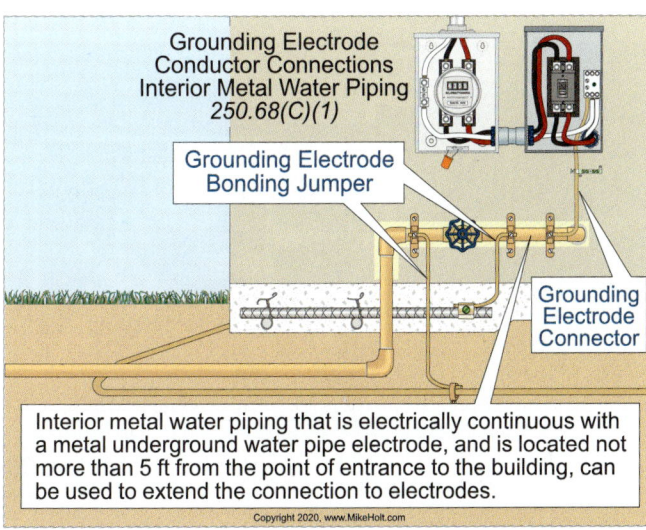

▶Figure 250–158

(2) The metal structural frame of a building can be used as a conductor to interconnect electrodes that are part of the grounding electrode system, or as a grounding electrode conductor where the hold-down bolts secure the structural steel column to a concrete-encased electrode [250.52(A)(3)]. The hold-down bolts must be connected to the concrete-encased electrode by welding, exothermic welding, the usual steel tie wires, or other approved means. ▶Figure 250–159 and ▶Figure 250–160

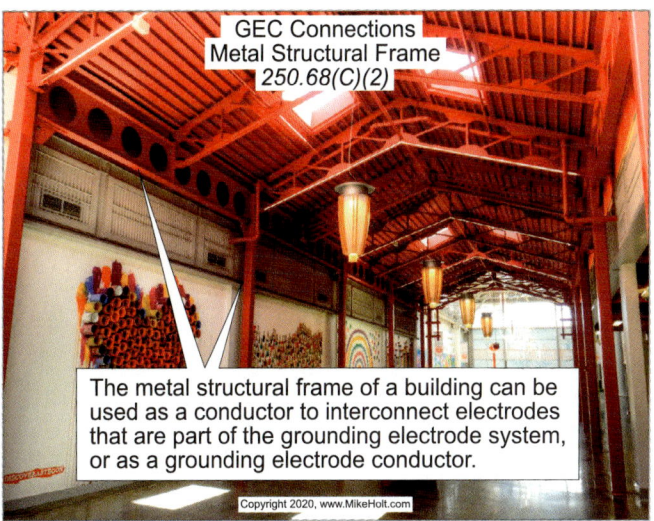

▶Figure 250–159

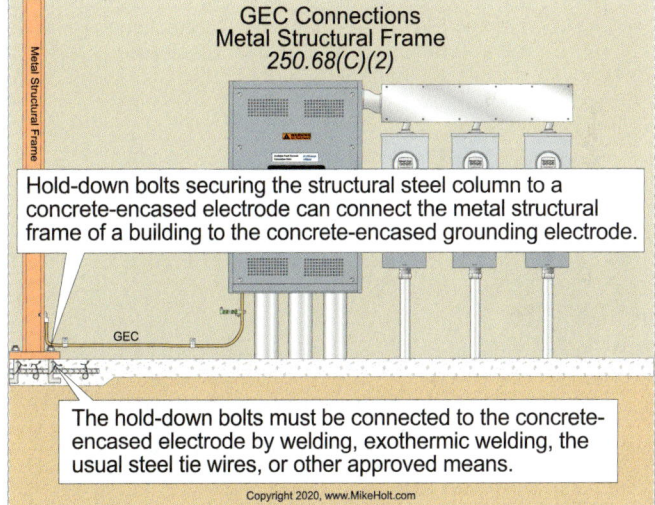

▶Figure 250–160

(3) A rebar-type concrete-encased electrode [250.52(A)(3)] with rebar extended to an accessible location above the concrete foundation or footing is permitted under the following conditions:

250.70 | Grounding and Bonding

(a) The additional rebar section must be continuous with the grounding electrode rebar or must be connected to the grounding electrode rebar and connected together by the usual steel tie wires, exothermic welding, welding, or other effective means. ▶Figure 250–161

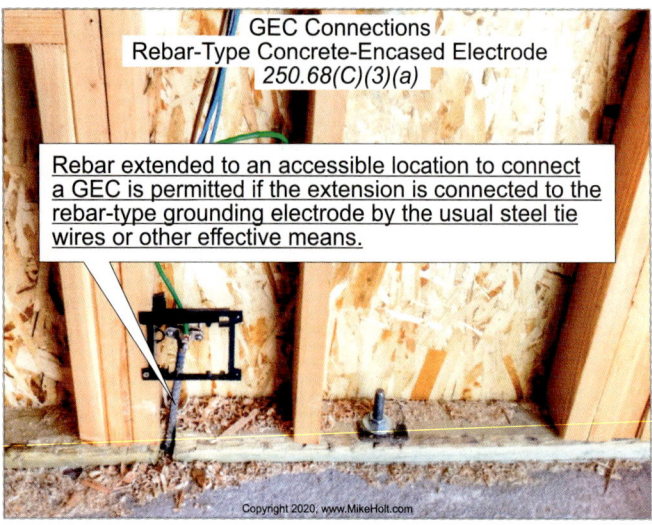

▶Figure 250–161

(b) The rebar extension is not permitted to be in contact with the Earth. ▶Figure 250–162

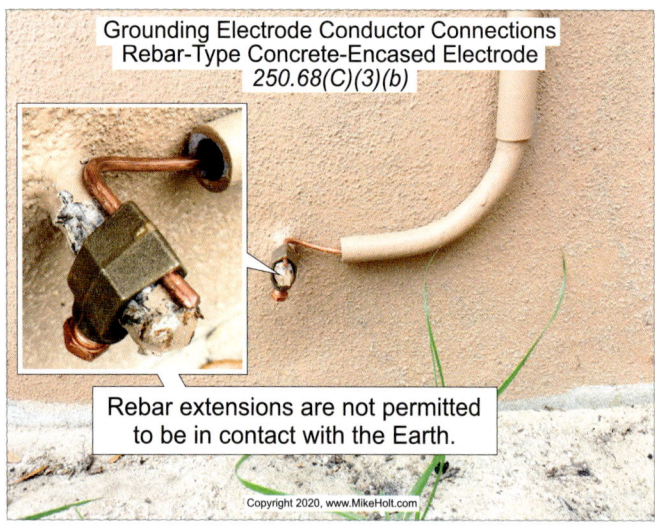

▶Figure 250–162

(c) The rebar extension is not permitted to be used as a conductor to interconnect the electrodes of grounding electrode systems.

250.70 Grounding Electrode Conductor Termination Fittings

The grounding electrode conductor must terminate to the grounding electrode by exothermic welding, listed lugs, listed pressure connectors, listed clamps, or other listed means. In addition, fittings terminating to a grounding electrode must be listed for the grounding electrode and the grounding electrode conductor. ▶Figure 250–163

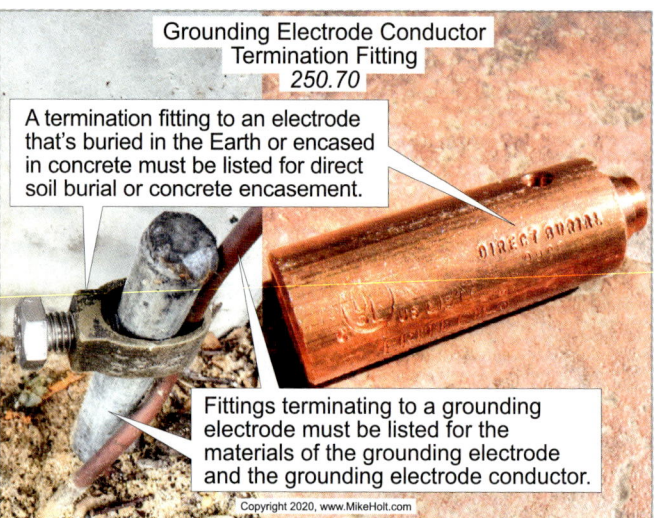

▶Figure 250–163

When the termination to a grounding electrode is buried in the Earth or encased in concrete, the termination fitting must be listed for direct soil burial or concrete encasement. ▶Figure 250–164

▶Figure 250–164

No more than one conductor can terminate on a single clamp or fitting unless the clamp or fitting is listed for multiple connections. ▶Figure 250-165

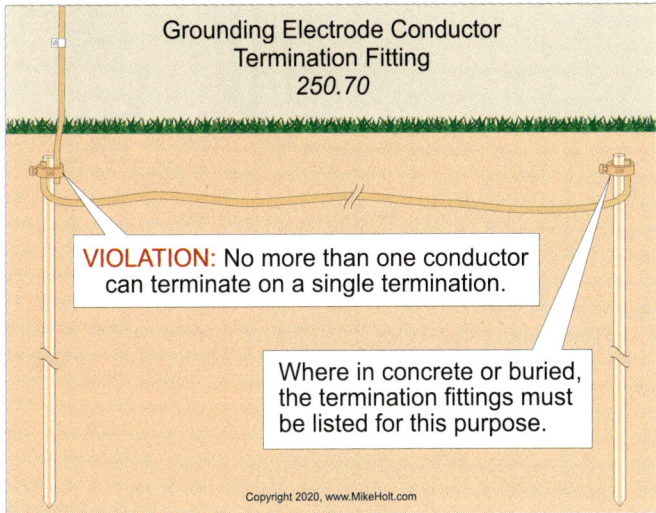

▶Figure 250-165

Part IV. Enclosure, Raceway, and Service Cable Connections

250.80 Service Raceways and Enclosures

Metal enclosures and raceways containing service conductors must be bonded to the service neutral conductor if the electrical system is grounded.

250.86 Other Enclosures

Metal raceways and enclosures containing conductors operating at 50V or more [250.20(A)] must be connected to the circuit equipment grounding conductor. ▶Figure 250-166

Author's Comment:

▸ Circuits described in 250.112(I) operating at less than 50V are not required to be grounded [250.20(A)].

Ex 2: Short sections of metal raceways used for the support or physical protection of cables are not required to be connected to the circuit equipment grounding conductor. ▶Figure 250-167

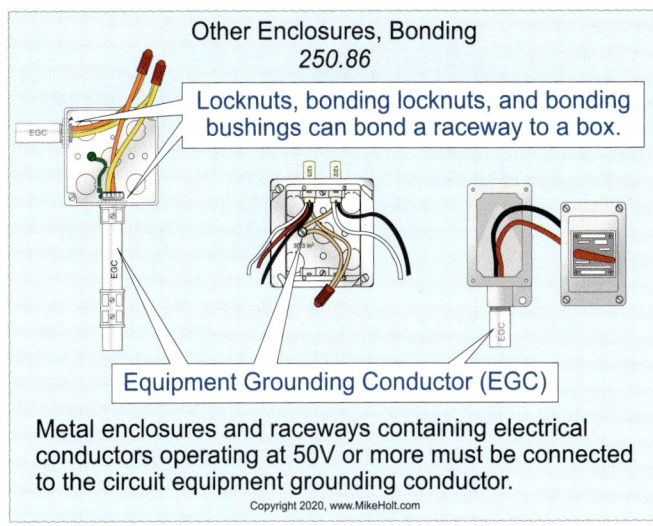

▶Figure 250-166

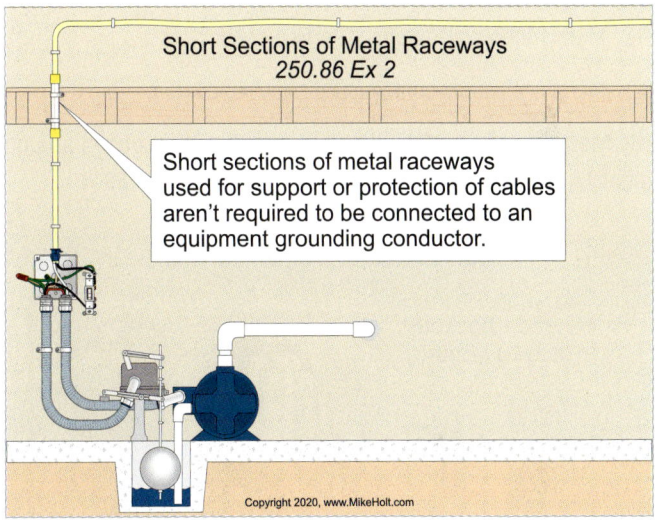

▶Figure 250-167

Part V. Bonding for Fault Current

250.90 General

Bonding must be provided where necessary to ensure electrical continuity and the capacity to conduct safely any fault current likely to be imposed

250.92 Bonding Equipment Containing Service Conductors

(A) Metal Raceways and Enclosures. The metal parts of equipment indicated below must be bonded together in accordance with 250.92(B). ▶Figure 250-168

250.92 | Grounding and Bonding

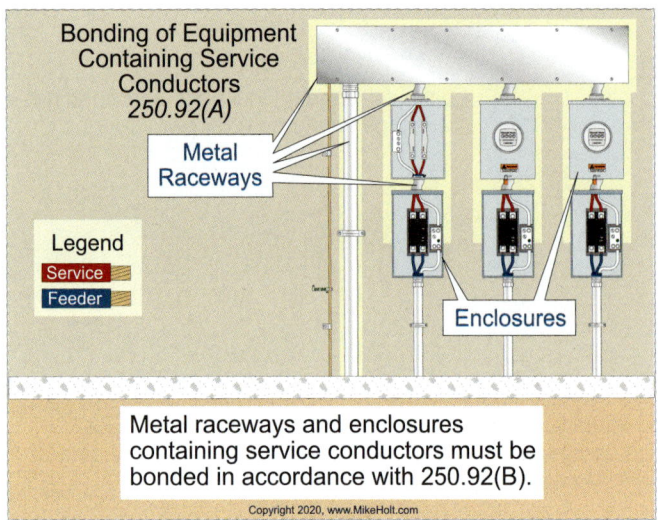
▶Figure 250–168

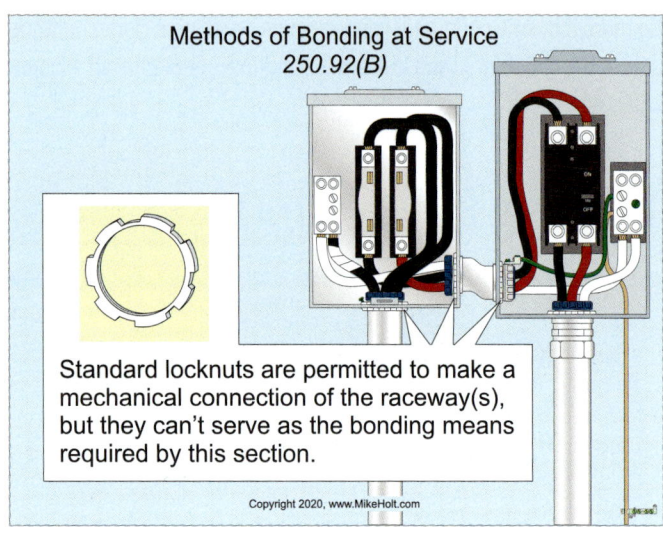
▶Figure 250–170

(1) Metal raceways containing service conductors.

(2) Metal enclosures containing service conductors.

(B) Methods of Bonding. Bonding jumpers are required around reducing washers or ringed knockouts. ▶Figure 250–169

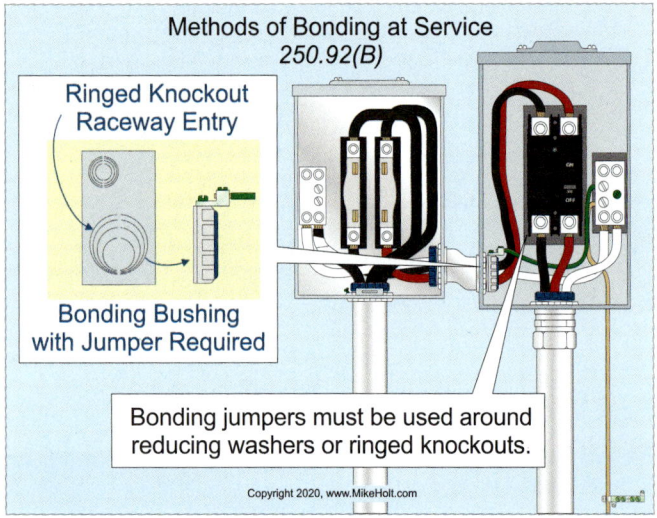
▶Figure 250–169

Standard locknuts are permitted to make a mechanical connection to the raceway(s), but they cannot serve as the bonding means required by this section. ▶Figure 250–170

Bonding must be ensured by one of the following methods:

(1) Bonding metal parts to the service neutral conductor. ▶Figure 250–171

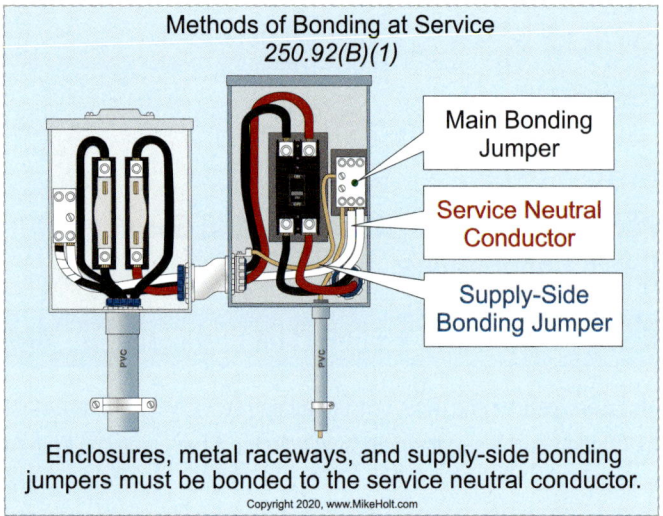
▶Figure 250–171

Author's Comment:

▸ A main bonding jumper is required to bond the service disconnect to the service neutral conductor [250.24(B) and 250.28].

▸ At the service disconnect, the service neutral conductor provides the effective ground-fault current path to the power supply [250.24(C)]; therefore, a supply-side bonding jumper is not required to be installed in PVC conduit containing service-entrance conductors [250.142(A)(1) and 352.60 Ex 2]. ▶Figure 250–172

(2) Terminating metal raceways to threaded couplings or listed threaded hubs. ▶Figure 250–173

Grounding and Bonding | 250.92

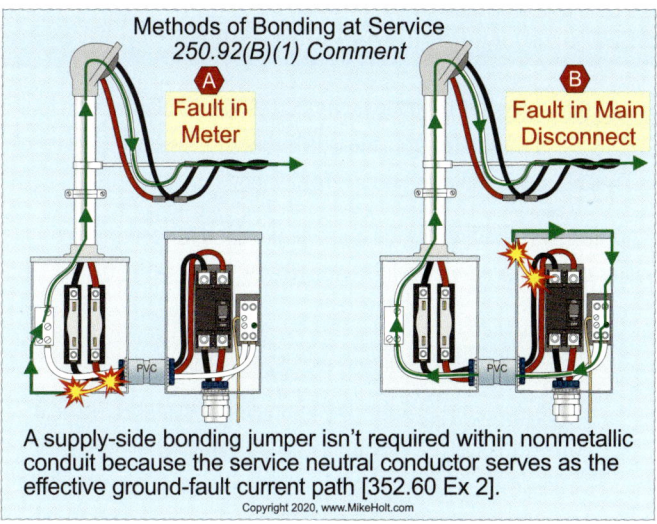
▶Figure 250-172

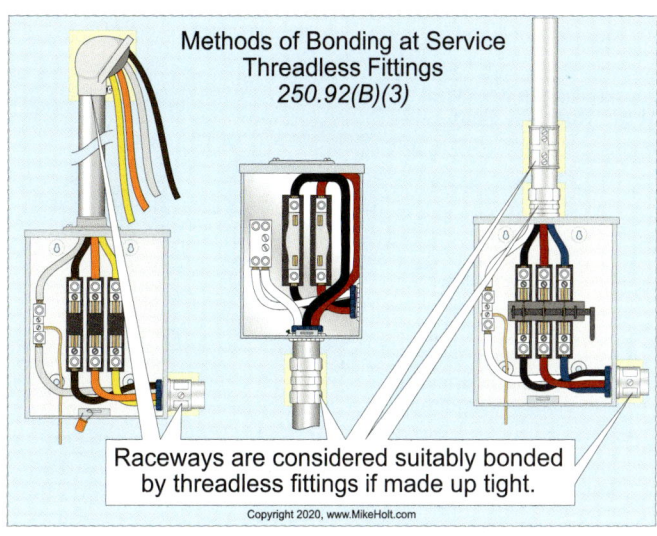
▶Figure 250-174

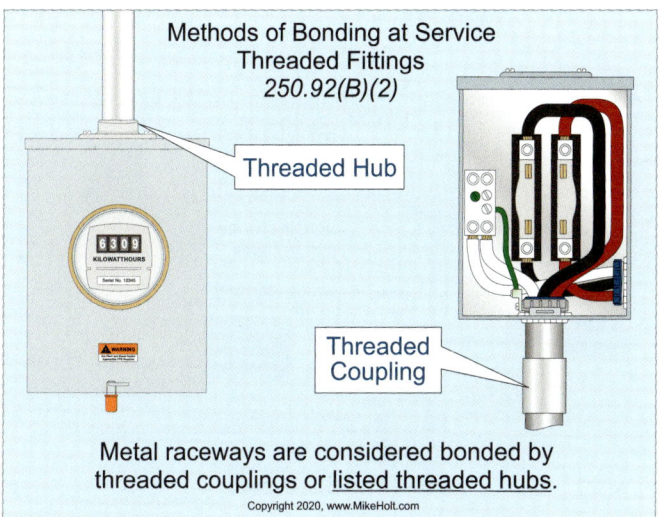
▶Figure 250-173

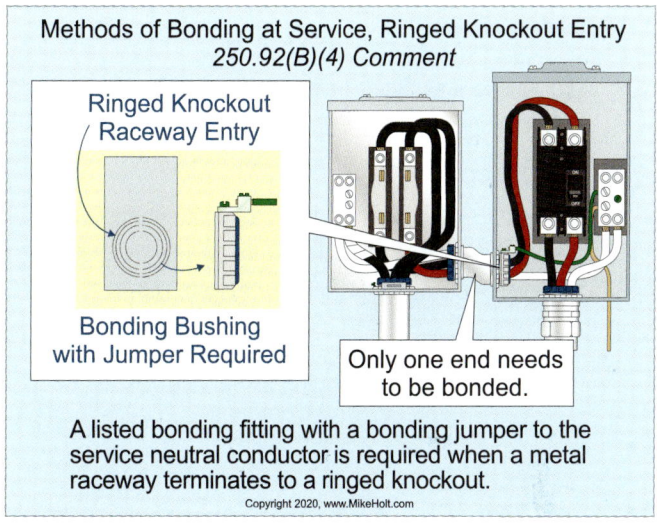
▶Figure 250-175

(3) Terminating metal raceways to threadless fittings. ▶Figure 250-174

(4) Using listed devices, such as bonding-type locknuts, bushings, wedges, or bushings with bonding jumpers to the service neutral conductor.

Author's Comment:

▸ A listed bonding wedge or bushing with a bonding jumper to the service neutral conductor is required when a metal raceway containing service conductors terminates to a ringed knockout. ▶Figure 250-175

Author's Comment:

▸ A supply-side bonding jumper of the wire type used for this purpose must be sized in accordance with Table 250.102(C)(1), based on the size/area of the service phase conductors within the raceway [250.102(C)].

▸ A bonding-type locknut, bonding wedge, or bonding bushing with a bonding jumper can be used for a metal raceway that terminates to an enclosure without a ringed knockout. ▶Figure 250-176

250.94 | Grounding and Bonding

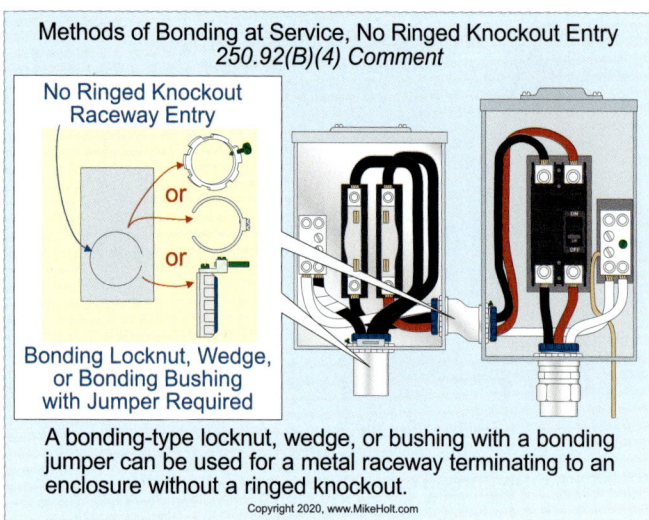

▶Figure 250-176

Author's Comment:

▸ A bonding locknut differs from a standard locknut in that it contains a bonding screw with a sharp point that drives into the metal enclosure to ensure a solid connection.

▸ Bonding one end of a service raceway to the service neutral provides the necessary low-impedance fault current path to the source required by this section. ▶Figure 250-177

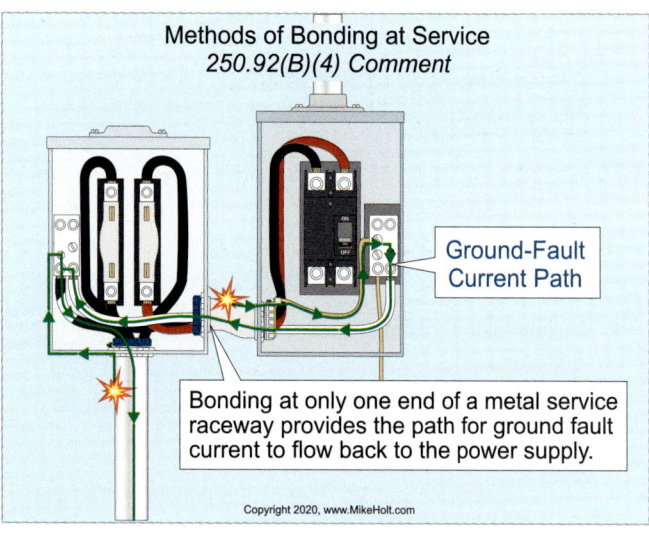

▶Figure 250-177

250.94 Bonding Communications Systems

 Scan this QR code for a video of Mike explaining this topic; it's a sample from the videos that accompany this textbook. www.MikeHolt.com/20BGvideos

A bonding termination device must be provided for communications systems in accordance with (A) and (B).

Author's Comment:

▸ These systems include communication systems (Article 805), radio and TV equipment (Article 810), and CATV (Article 820). Bonding communications systems together is intended to minimize damage from induced voltage differences between the systems that can be caused by lightning strikes. ▶Figure 250-178

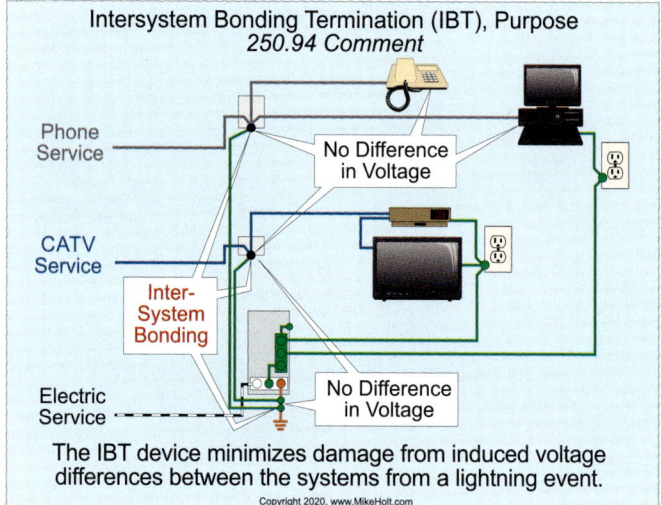

▶Figure 250-178

(A) Intersystem Bonding Termination Device. An intersystem bonding termination device must meet all of the following requirements:

(1) Be accessible. ▶Figure 250-179

(2) Have a capacity for at least three intersystem bonding conductors.

(3) Be installed so it does not interfere with the opening of any enclosure.

(4) Be securely mounted and electrically connected to the service disconnect, meter enclosure, or grounding electrode conductor. ▶Figure 250-180

(5) Be securely mounted and electrically connected to the building's disconnect or grounding electrode conductor.

Grounding and Bonding | 250.96

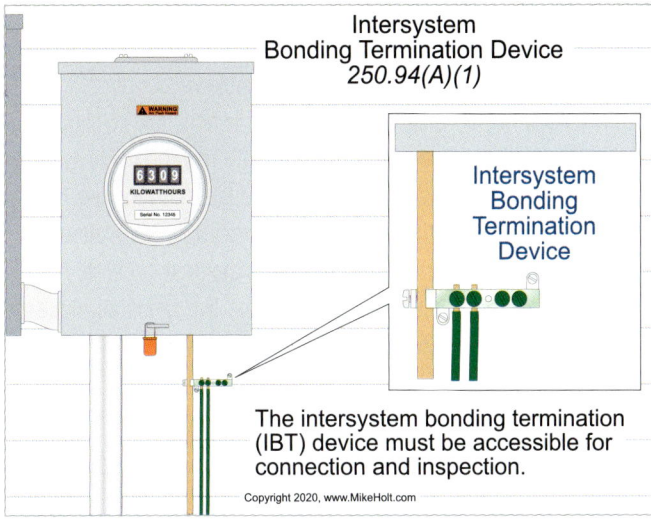
▶Figure 250-179

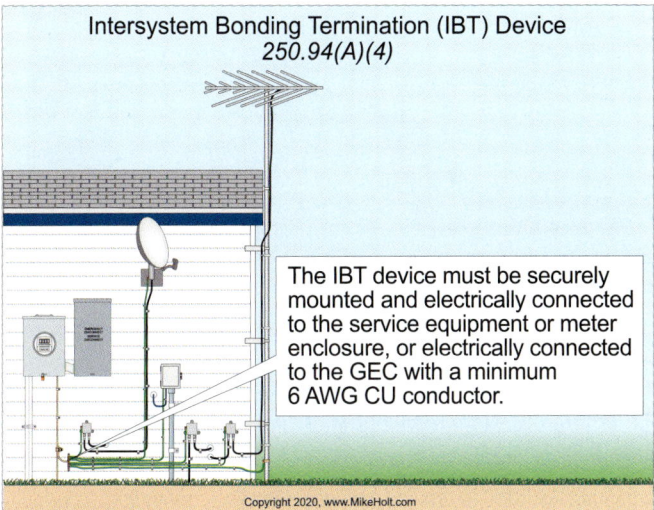
▶Figure 250-180

(6) Be listed as grounding and bonding equipment.

Author's Comment:

▸ According to Article 100, an "Intersystem Bonding Termination" is a device that provides a means to connect communications systems' (twisted wire, antennas, and coaxial cable) bonding conductors to the building grounding electrode system.

Ex: An intersystem bonding termination device is not required where communications systems are not likely to be used.

Note 2: Communications systems (twisted wire, antennas, and coaxial cable) must be bonded to the intersystem bonding termination in accordance with the following requirements: ▶Figure 250-181

▸ Antennas/Satellite Dishes [810.15 and 810.21]
▸ CATV [820.100]

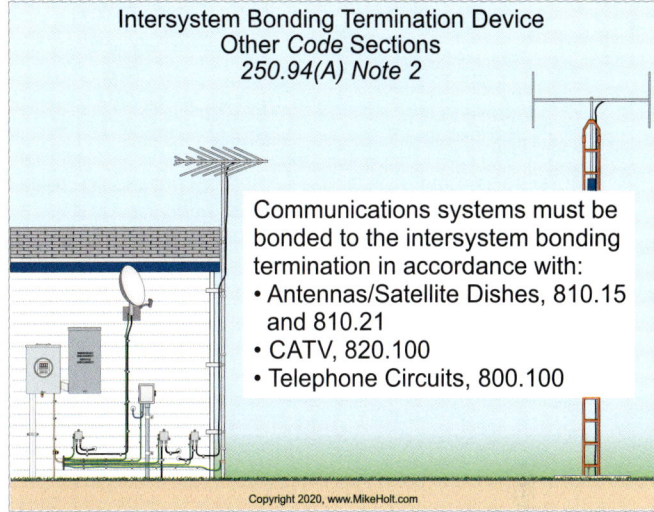
▶Figure 250-181

250.96 Bonding Other Enclosures

 Scan this QR code for a video of Mike explaining this topic; it's a sample from the videos that accompany this textbook. www.MikeHolt.com/20BGvideos

(A) Effective Ground-Fault Current Path. Metal parts intended to serve as equipment grounding conductors including raceways, cables, equipment, and enclosures must be bonded together to ensure they have the capacity to safely conduct any fault current likely to be imposed on them [110.10, 250.4(A)(5) and Table 250.122 Note].
▶Figure 250-182

Nonconductive coatings such as paint, lacquer, and enamel on equipment must be removed to ensure an effective ground-fault current path, or the termination fittings must be designed so such removal is unnecessary [250.12].

Author's Comment:

▸ The practice of driving a locknut tight with a screwdriver and pliers is considered sufficient in removing paint and other nonconductive finishes to ensure an effective ground-fault current path.

250.97 | Grounding and Bonding

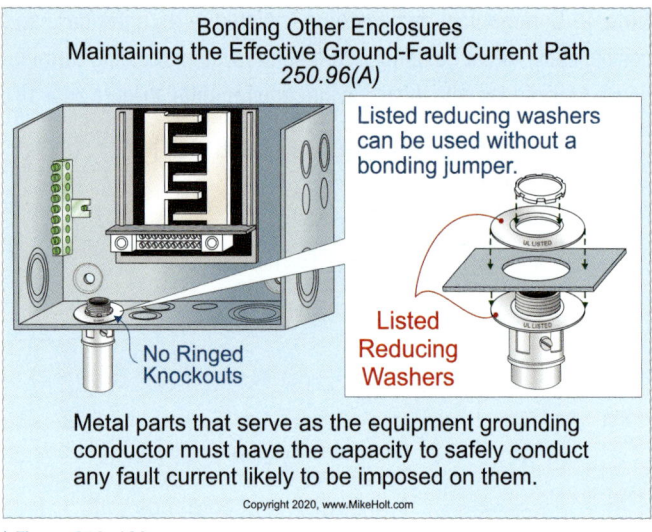
▶Figure 250–182

Author's Comment:

▸ Bonding jumpers for raceways and cables containing 277V or 480V circuits are required at ringed knockout terminations to ensure the ground-fault current path has the capacity to safely conduct the maximum ground-fault current likely to be imposed [110.10, 250.4(A)(5) and 250.96(A)]. Ringed knockouts are not listed to withstand the heat generated by a 277V ground fault, which generates five times as much heat as does a 120V ground fault. ▶Figure 250–184

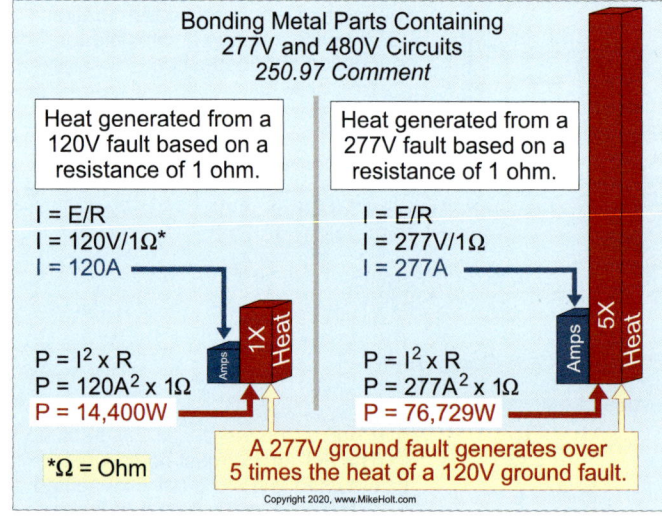
▶Figure 250–184

250.97 Bonding Metal Parts Containing 277V and 480V Circuits

 Scan this QR code for a video of Mike explaining this topic; it's a sample from the videos that accompany this textbook. www.MikeHolt.com/20BGvideos

Metal raceways or cables containing 277V or 480V circuits terminating at ringed knockouts must be bonded to the metal enclosure with a bonding jumper sized in accordance with 250.122 [250.102(D)]. ▶Figure 250–183

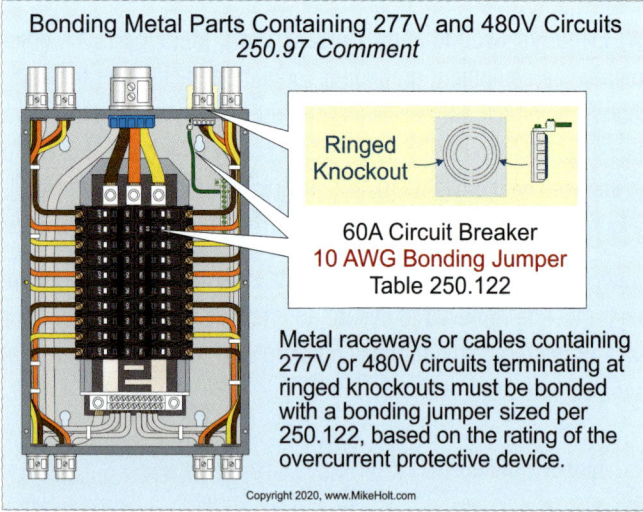
▶Figure 250–183

Ex: Where oversized, concentric, or eccentric knockouts are not encountered, or where a box or enclosure with concentric or eccentric knockouts is listed to provide a reliable bonding connection, a bonding jumper is not required if the following methods are used: ▶Figure 250–185

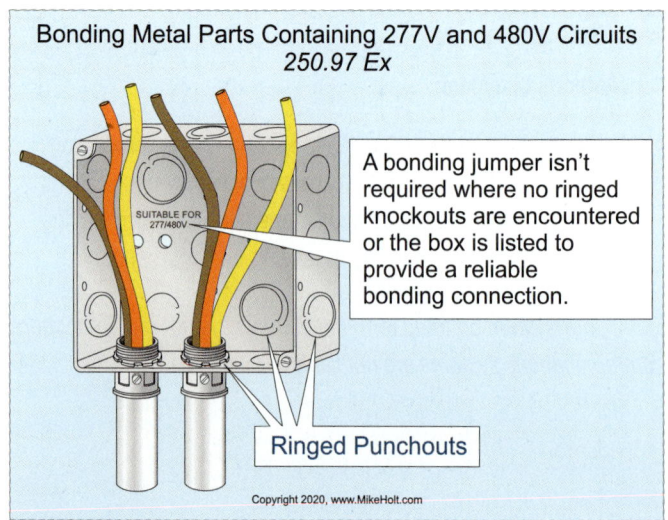
▶Figure 250–185

Grounding and Bonding | 250.102

(1) Metal connectors for metal-sheathed cables

(2) Two locknuts, on rigid metal conduit or intermediate metal conduit, one inside and one outside of boxes and cabinets

(3) Electrical metallic tubing connectors, flexible metal conduit connectors, and cable connectors with one locknut on the inside of boxes and cabinets

(4) Listed fittings

▸ Thread-forming machine screws that engage not less than two threads in the enclosure

▸ Connections that are part of a listed assembly

▸ Other listed means

(C) Supply-Side Bonding Jumper Sizing.

 Scan this QR code for a video of Mike explaining this topic; it's a sample from the videos that accompany this textbook. www.MikeHolt.com/20BGvideos

(1) Single Raceway or Cable Installations. Supply-side bonding jumpers must be sized in accordance with Table 250.102(C)(1), based on the size/area of the phase conductor within the raceway or cable. ▸Figure 250–187

250.98 Bonding Loosely Jointed Metal Raceways

Expansion, expansion-deflection, or deflection fittings and telescoping sections of metal raceways must be made electrically continuous using equipment bonding jumpers. ▸Figure 250–186

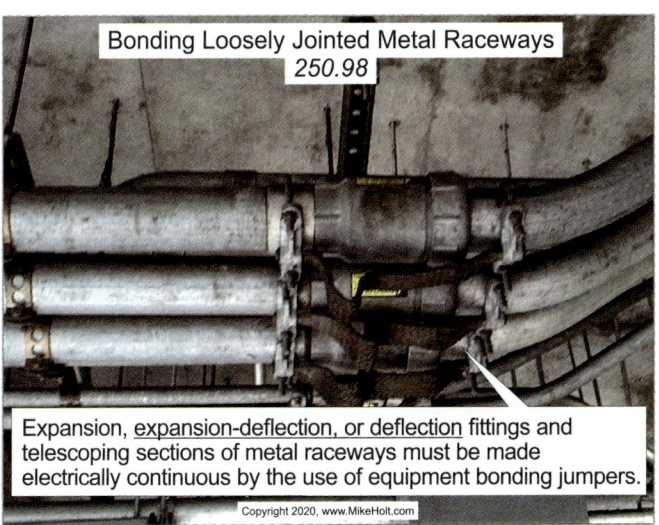

▸Figure 250–186

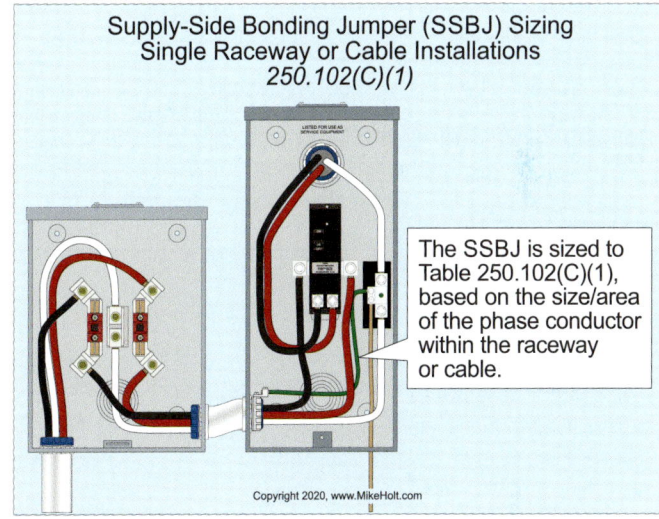

▸Figure 250–187

(2) Parallel Conductor Installations. If the phase supply conductors are paralleled in two or more raceways or cables, the supply-side bonding jumper for each is sized in accordance with Table 250.102(C)(1), based on the size/area of the phase conductors in each raceway or cable.

250.102 Neutral Conductor, Bonding Conductors, and Bonding Jumpers

(B) Termination. Equipment bonding jumpers must terminate by any of the following means in accordance with 250.8(A):

▸ Listed pressure connectors

▸ Terminal bars

▸ Pressure connectors listed as grounding and bonding equipment

▸ Exothermic welding

▸ Machine screw-type fasteners that engage not less than two threads or are secured with a nut

250.102 | Grounding and Bonding

Table 250.102(C)(1) Neutral Conductor, Main Bonding Jumper, System Bonding Jumper, and Supply-Side Bonding Jumper

Size of Largest Phase Conductor Per Raceway or Equivalent Area for Parallel Conductors		Size of Bonding Jumper or Neutral Conductor	
Copper	Aluminum or Copper-Clad Aluminum	Copper	Aluminum
2 or smaller	1/0 or smaller	8 CU	6 AL
1 or 1/0	2/0 or 3/0	6 CU	4 AL
2/0 or 3/0	Over 3/0 250 kcmil	4 CU	2 AL
Over 3/0–350 kcmil	Over 250–500 kcmil	2 CU	1/0 AL
Over 350–600 kcmil	Over 500–900 kcmil	1/0 CU	3/0 AL
Over 600–1,100 kcmil	Over 900–1,750 kcmil	2/0 CU	4/0 AL
Over 1,100 kcmil	Over 1,750 kcmil	See Notes 1 and 2.	

▶ **Example**

Question: What size supply-side bonding jumper is required for each of three metal raceways, each of which contain 400 kcmil service conductors? ▶Figure 250–188

(a) 4 AWG   (b) 2 AWG   (c) 1 AWG   (d) 1/0 AWG

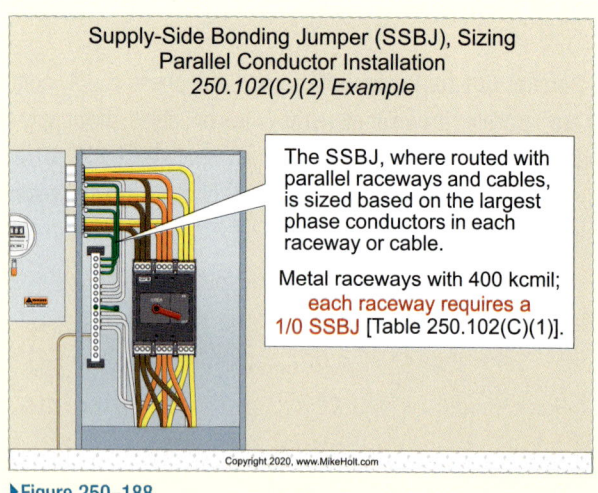
▶Figure 250–188

Solution:

A 1/0 AWG supply-side bonding jumper is required for each raceway. [250.102(C)(2) and Table 250.102(C)(1)]. A single supply-side bonding jumper is permitted for multiple raceways based on the equivalent area of the supply-side phase conductors.

Answer: (c) 1 AWG

▶ **Example**

Question: What size single supply-side bonding jumper is required for all three metal raceways, each of which contain 400 kcmil service conductors? ▶Figure 250–189

(a) 1/0 AWG   (b) 2/0 AWG   (c) 3/0 AWG   (d) 4/0 AWG

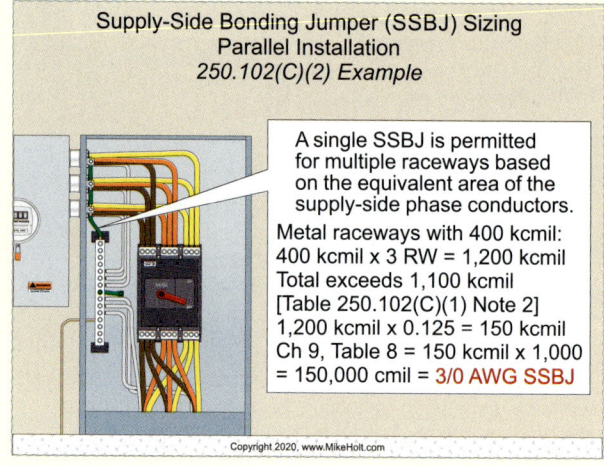
▶Figure 250–189

Solution:

A singe 3/0 AWG supply-side bonding jumper is required if using one conductor for all three raceways.

400 kcmil × 3 Raceways = 1,200 kcmil which exceeds 1,100 kcmil [Table 250.102(C)(1) Note 2]

Conductor kcmil at 12½ % = 1,200 kcmil × 0.125

Convert kcmil to cmil = 150 kcmil × 1,000

Total bonding jumper cmil = 150,000 cmil

Use a 3/0 AWG supply-side bonding jumper [Chapter 9, Table 8].

Answer: (c) 3/0 AWG

Note 1: The term "supply conductors" includes phase conductors that do not have overcurrent protection on their supply side and terminate at the service disconnect or the first disconnect of a separately derived system.

Note 2: See Chapter 9, Table 8 for the circular mil area of conductors 18 AWG through 4/0 AWG.

(D) Load-Side Bonding Jumper Sizing. Bonding jumpers on the load side of feeder and branch-circuit overcurrent devices are sized in accordance with 250.122.

▶ **Example**

Question: What size equipment bonding jumper is required for each metal raceway where the circuit conductors are protected by a 1,200A overcurrent protective device? ▶Figure 250–190

(a) 1/0 AWG   (b) 2/0 AWG   (c) 3/0 AWG   (d) 4/0 AWG

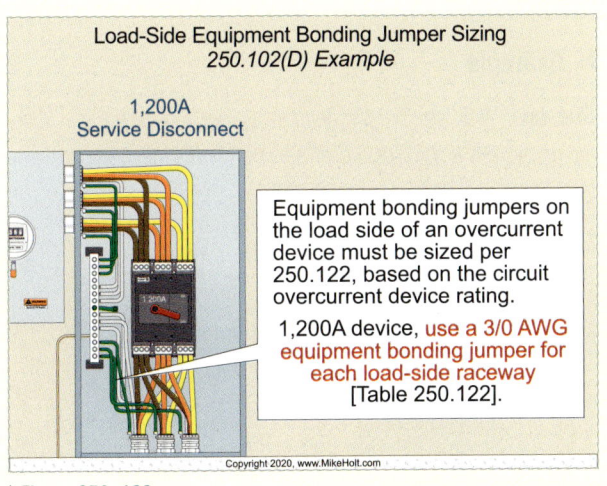
▶Figure 250–190

Answer: (c) 3/0 AWG [Table 250.122]

If a single bonding jumper is used to bond two or more metal raceways, it must be sized in accordance with 250.122, based on the rating of the largest circuit overcurrent protective device. ▶Figure 250–191

(E) Installation of Bonding Jumpers. Bonding jumpers can be installed inside or outside of a raceway or an enclosure.

(2) Outside a Raceway. Bonding jumpers installed outside a raceway must be routed with the raceway and the conductor cannot exceed 6 ft in length. ▶Figure 250–192

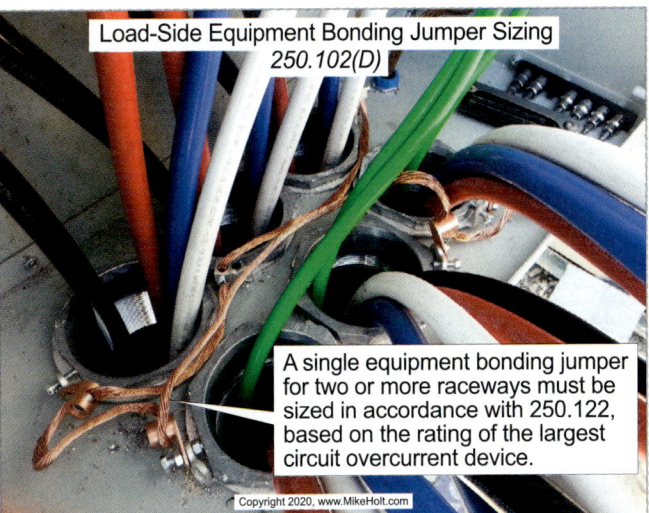
▶Figure 250–191

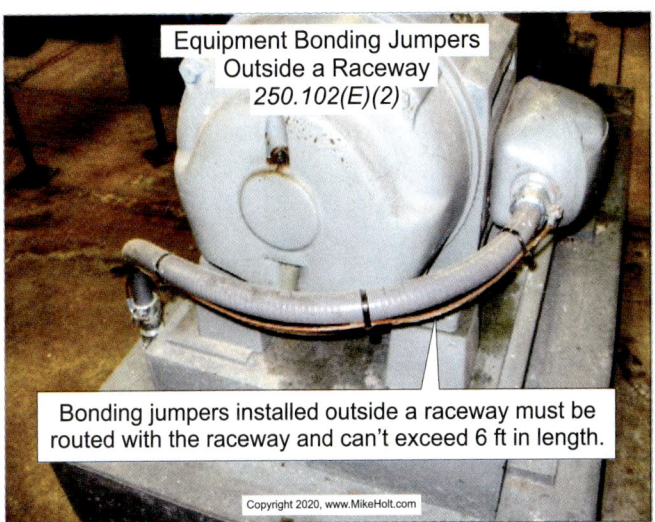
▶Figure 250–192

250.104 Bonding of Piping Systems and Exposed Structural Metal

(A) Metal Water Piping System. Electrically continuous metal water piping systems, including sprinkler piping, must be bonded in accordance with 250.104(A)(1), (A)(2), or (A)(3).

(1) Buildings Supplied by a Service. Electrically continuous metal water piping must be bonded to any one of the following: ▶Figure 250–193

(1) Service-disconnect enclosure,

(2) Service neutral conductor,

250.104 | Grounding and Bonding

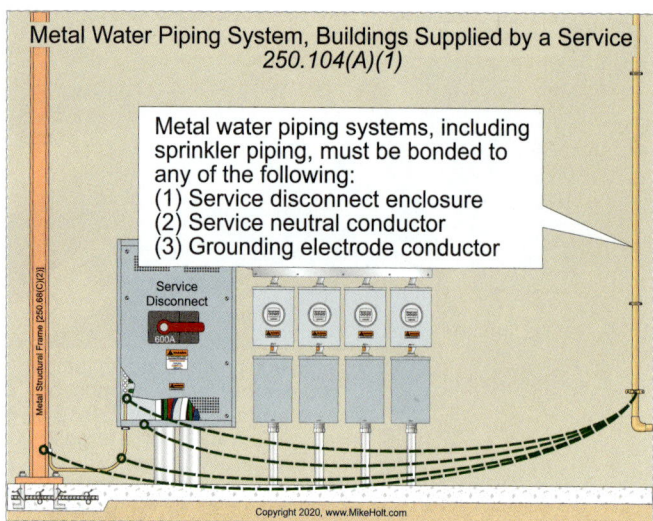
▶Figure 250–193

The metal piping system bonding jumper must be copper where within 18 in. of the surface of earth [250.64(A)], must be adequately protected if exposed to physical damage [250.64(B)], and points of attachment must be accessible.

A ferrous metal raceway containing a grounding electrode conductor must be made electrically continuous by bonding each end of the raceway to the grounding electrode conductor [250.64(E)].

Metal water piping system bonding jumpers must be sized in accordance with Table 250.102(C)(1), based on the size/area of the service phase conductors and not required to be larger than 3/0 copper or 250 kcmil aluminum or copper-clad aluminum, except as permitted in 250.104(A)(2) and (A)(3).

(3) Grounding electrode conductor if of sufficient size, or

(4) One of the grounding electrodes of the grounding electrode system if the grounding electrode conductor or bonding jumper to the electrode is of sufficient size.

Author's Comment:

▶ The intent of this rule is to remove dangerous voltage from a ground fault on metal parts from a ground fault to electrically conductive metal water piping systems and metal sprinkler piping. ▶Figure 250–194

▶ **Example**

Question: What size bonding jumper is required for a metal water piping system if the 300 kcmil service conductors are paralleled in two raceways? ▶Figure 250–195

(a) 1/0 AWG   (b) 2/0 AWG   (c) 3/0 AWG   (d) 4/0 AWG

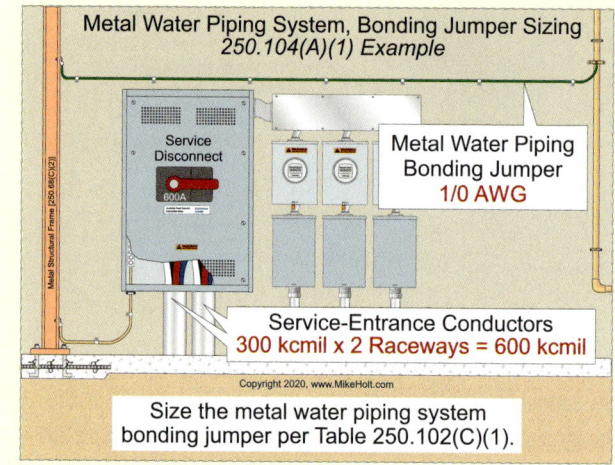
▶Figure 250–195

Solution:

A 1/0 AWG bonding jumper is required based on 600 kcmil conductors (300 kcmil × 2 raceways) [250.102(C)(1)].

Answer: (a) 1/0 AWG

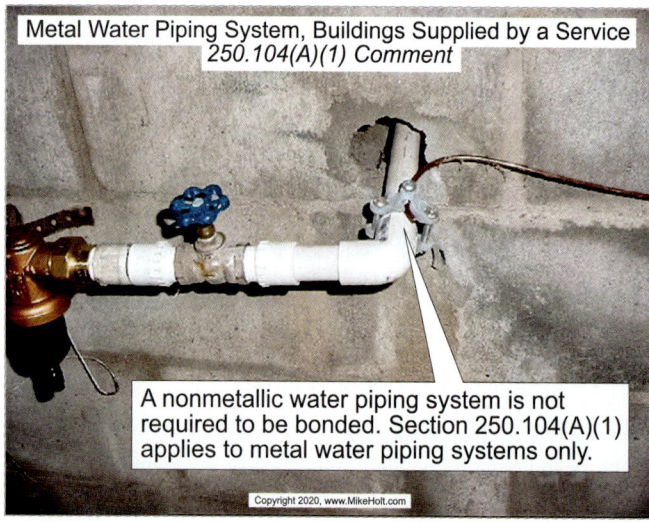
▶Figure 250–194

Author's Comment:

▶ If hot and cold metal water pipes are electrically connected, only one bonding jumper is required; either to the cold or hot water pipe.

158 | Mike Holt's Illustrated Guide to Understanding 2020 NEC Requirements for Bonding and Grounding

Grounding and Bonding | 250.104

▸ Bonding is not required for isolated sections of metal water piping connected to a nonmetallic water piping system. In fact, these isolated sections of metal piping should not be bonded because they could become a shock hazard under certain conditions. ▸Figure 250-196

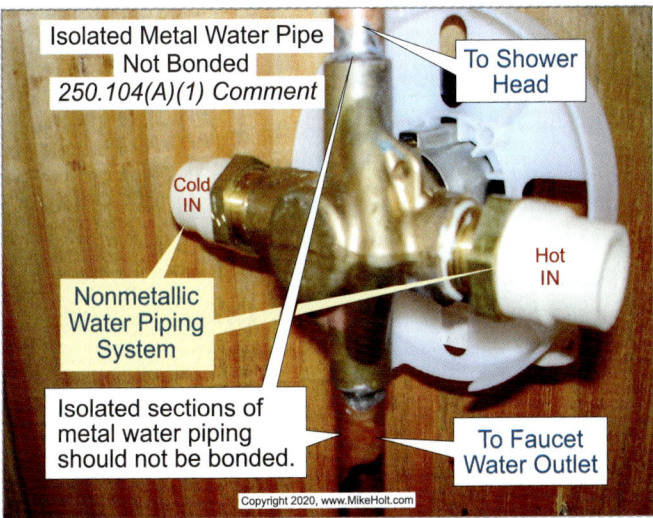
▸Figure 250-196

(2) Bonding Multiple Occupancy Buildings. When an electrically continuous metal water piping system in an individual occupancy is metallically isolated from other occupancies in a building, the metal water piping system for that occupancy can be bonded to the equipment grounding terminal of the occupancy's switchgear, switchboard, or panelboard. The bonding jumper must be sized based on the rating of the circuit overcurrent protective device in accordance with 250.122 [250.102(D)]. ▸Figure 250-197

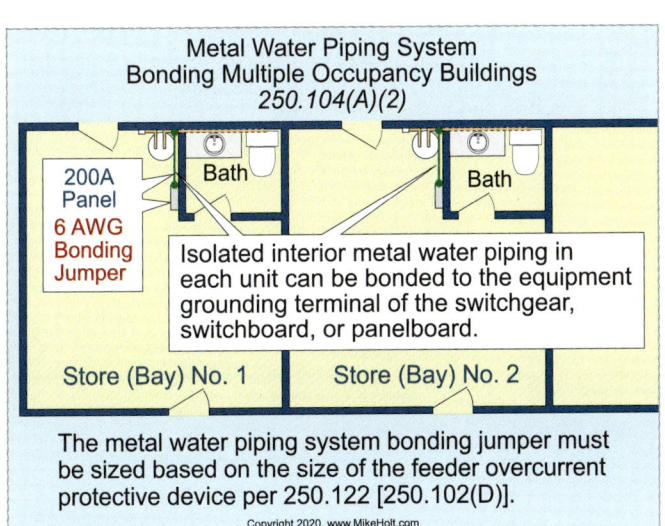
▸Figure 250-197

(3) Buildings Supplied by a Feeder. The metal water piping system of a building supplied by a feeder must be bonded to one of the following:

(1) The equipment grounding terminal of the building's disconnect enclosure,

(2) The feeder equipment grounding conductor, or

(3) One of the building's grounding electrodes of the grounding electrode system if the grounding electrode or bonding jumper to the electrode is of sufficient size.

The bonding jumper is sized in accordance with 250.102(D) and is not required to be larger than the largest feeder phase or branch-circuit conductor supplying the building.

(B) Bonding Other Metal-Piping Systems. Metal-piping systems in or attached to a building must be bonded. The piping is considered bonded when it is connected to an appliance that is connected to the circuit equipment grounding conductor. ▸Figure 250-198

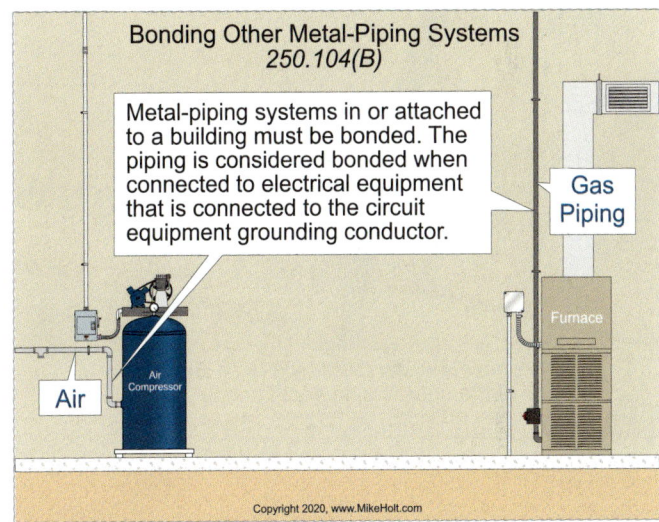
▸Figure 250-198

Note 1: Bonding piping and metal air ducts within the premises will provide additional safety, but this is not required by the *NEC*. ▸Figure 250-199

Note 2: Additional information for gas piping systems can be found in NFPA 54, *National Fuel Gas Code,* and NFPA 780, *Standard for the Installation of Lightning Protection Systems.* ▸Figure 250-200

(C) Bonding Exposed Structural Metal. Exposed structural metal that is interconnected to form a metal building frame must be bonded to any of the following: ▸Figure 250-201

250.104 | Grounding and Bonding

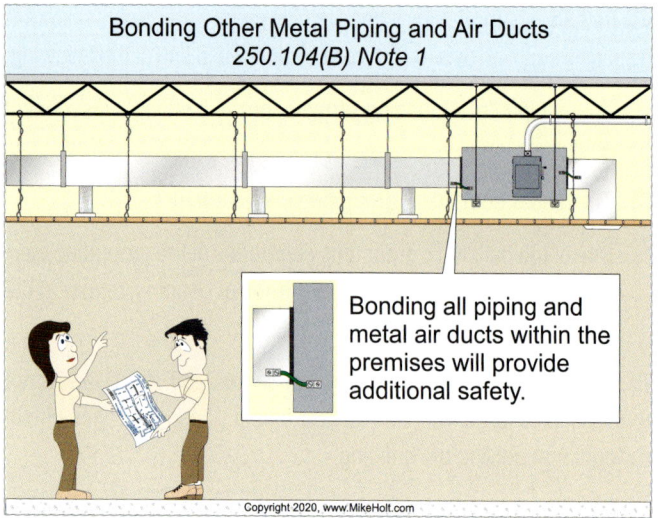
▶Figure 250–199

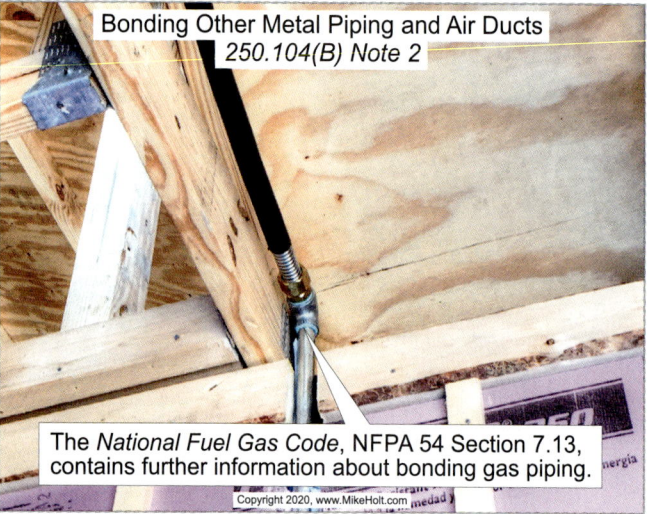
▶Figure 250–200

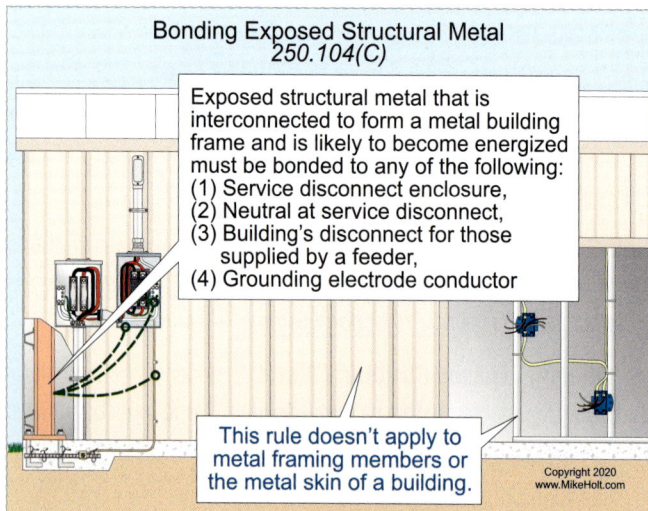
▶Figure 250–201

(1) The service-disconnect enclosure,

(2) The neutral at the service disconnect,

(3) The building's disconnect enclosure for those supplied by a feeder,

(4) The grounding electrode conductor where of sufficient size, or

(5) One of the grounding electrodes of the grounding electrode system if the grounding electrode conductor or bonding jumper to the electrode is of sufficient size.

The structural metal bonding conductor must be sized in accordance with Table 250.102(C)(1), based on the size/area of the supply phase conductors and is not required to be larger than 3/0 copper or 250 kcmil aluminum or copper-clad aluminum. The bonding jumper must be copper where within 18 in. of the surface of the Earth [250.64(A)], be securely fastened to the surface on which it is carried [250.64(B)] and be adequately protected if exposed to physical damage [250.64(B)]. In addition, all points of attachment must be accessible, except as permitted in 250.68(A) Ex 1 and 2.

(D) Transformers. Metal water piping systems and structural metal that is interconnected to form a building frame must be bonded to the transformer secondary winding in accordance with 250.104(D)(1) through (D)(3).

(1) Bonding Metal Water Pipe. Metal water piping systems located in the area served by a transformer must be bonded to the secondary neutral conductor where the grounding electrode conductor is connected at the transformer. ▶Figure 250–202

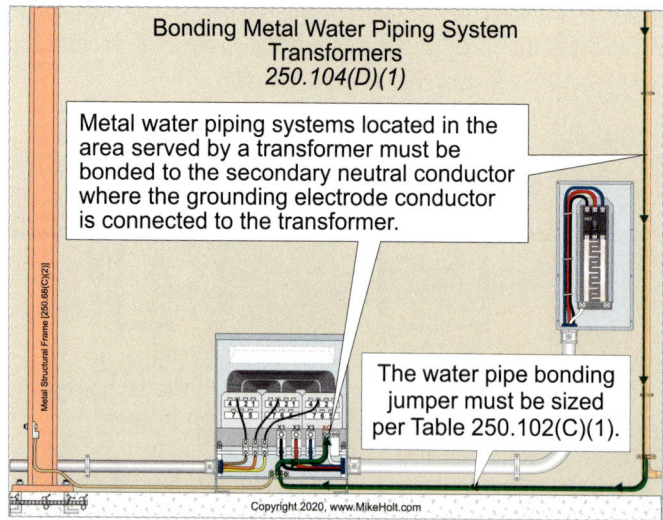
▶Figure 250–202

The bonding jumper must be sized in accordance with Table 250.102(C)(1), based on the size/area of the secondary phase conductors and is not be required to be larger than 3/0 copper or 250 kcmil aluminum or copper-clad aluminum.

Ex 2: The metal water piping system can be bonded to the metal structural building frame if it serves as the grounding electrode [250.52(A)(1)] for the transformer. ▶Figure 250–203

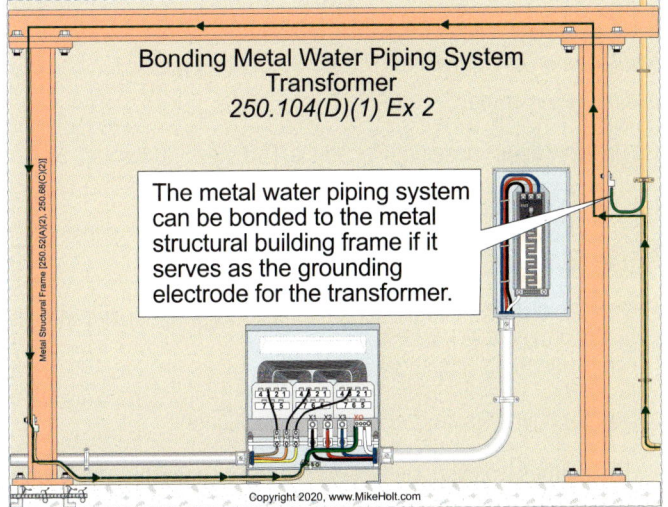
▶Figure 250–203

(2) Bonding Exposed Structural Metal. Exposed structural metal that is interconnected to form the building frame located in the area served by a transformer must be bonded to the secondary neutral conductor where the grounding electrode conductor is connected at the transformer.

The bonding jumper must be sized in accordance with Table 250.102(C)(1), based on the size/area of the secondary phase conductors and is not be required to be larger than 3/0 copper or 250 kcmil aluminum or copper-clad aluminum.

Ex 1: Bonding to the transformer is not required if the metal structural frame serves as the grounding electrode [250.52(A)(2)] for the transformer. ▶Figure 250–204

250.106 Lightning Protection Systems

When a lightning protection system is installed in accordance with NFPA 780, *Standard for the Installation of Lightning Protection Systems,* the lightning protection electrode system must be bonded to the building grounding electrode system. ▶Figure 250–205

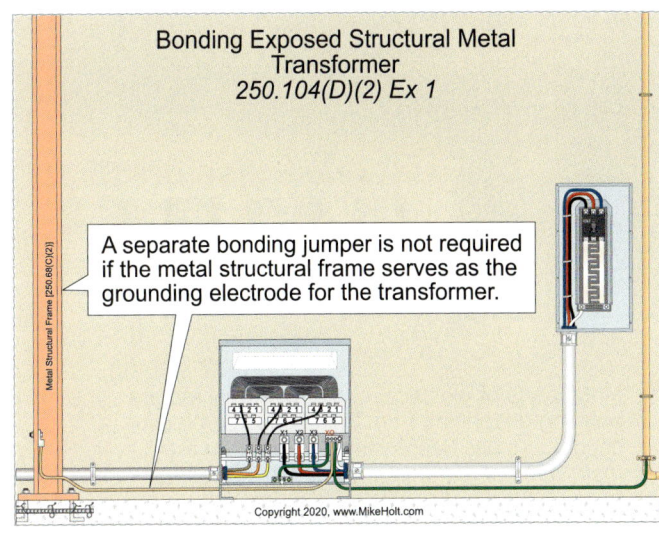
▶Figure 250–204

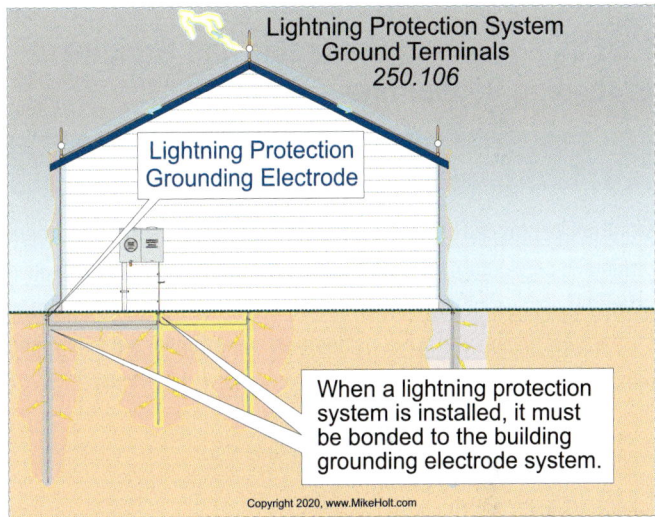
▶Figure 250–205

Note 1: See NFPA 780, *Standard for the Installation of Lightning Protection Systems,* which contains detailed information on grounding, bonding, and side-flash distances from lightning protection systems.

Note 2: To minimize the likelihood of arcing between metal parts due to induced voltage, metal raceways, enclosures, and other metal parts of electrical equipment may require bonding or spacing from the lightning protection conductors in accordance with NFPA 780, *Standard for the Installation of Lightning Protection Systems.* ▶Figure 250–206

250.109 | Grounding and Bonding

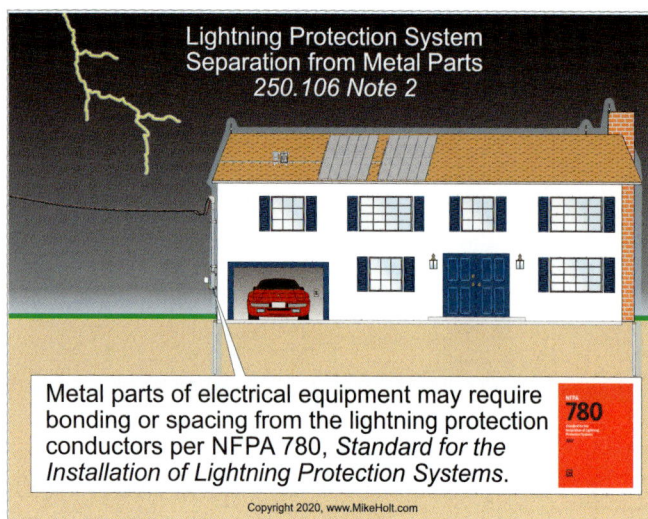

▶Figure 250–206

Part VI. Equipment Grounding and Equipment Grounding Conductors

250.109 Metal Enclosures

Metal enclosures can be used to connect bonding jumpers or equipment grounding conductors (or both) together to become part of an effective ground-fault current path. Metal covers and metal fittings attached to these metal enclosures are considered as being connected to bonding jumpers or equipment grounding conductors, or both. ▶Figure 250–207

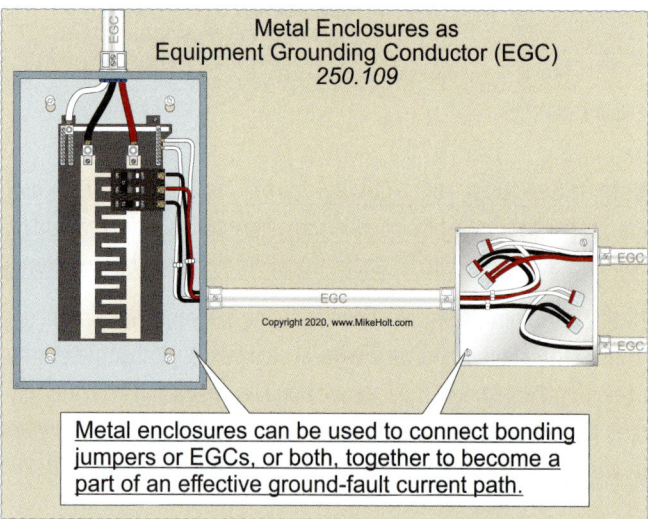

▶Figure 250–207

250.114 Equipment Connected by Cord and Plug

Exposed, normally noncurrent-carrying metal parts of cord-and-plug-connected equipment must be connected to the equipment grounding conductor of the circuit suppling the equipment under any of the following conditions:

Ex: Listed tools, listed appliances, and listed equipment covered in 250.114(2) through (4) are not required to be connected to an equipment grounding conductor where protected by a system of double insulation or its equivalent. Double insulated equipment must be distinctively marked.

(1) In hazardous (classified) locations. [Articles 500 through 517].

(2) Where operated at over 150V to ground.

Ex 1 to (2): Motors that are guarded.

Ex 2 to (2): Metal frames of exempted electrically heated appliances.

(3) In residential occupancies:

   a. Refrigerators, freezers, and air conditioners.

   b. Clothes-washing, clothes-drying, and dish-washing machines; ranges; kitchen waste disposers; IT equipment; sump pumps; and electrical aquarium equipment.

Author's Comment:

▶ Electric ranges and clothes dryers are shipped from the factory with a bonding strap that bonds the metal frame of the appliance to the neutral termination of the cord connection terminal block. This bonding strap may or may not have to be removed! The *Code* requires an insulated neutral for these appliances using a 4-wire branch circuit and the bonding strap should be removed, but that was not always the case. If an existing 3-wire branch circuit is to supply a replacement appliance, the factory-installed bonding strap must remain in place [250.140 Ex]. ▶Figure 250–208

   c. Hand-held, stationary or fixed, and light industrial motor-operated tools.

   d. Motor-operated hedge clippers, lawn mowers, snow-blowers, and wet scrubbers.

   e. Portable handlamps and portable luminaires.

(4) In other than residential occupancies:

   a. Refrigerators, freezers, and air conditioners.

Grounding and Bonding | 250.118

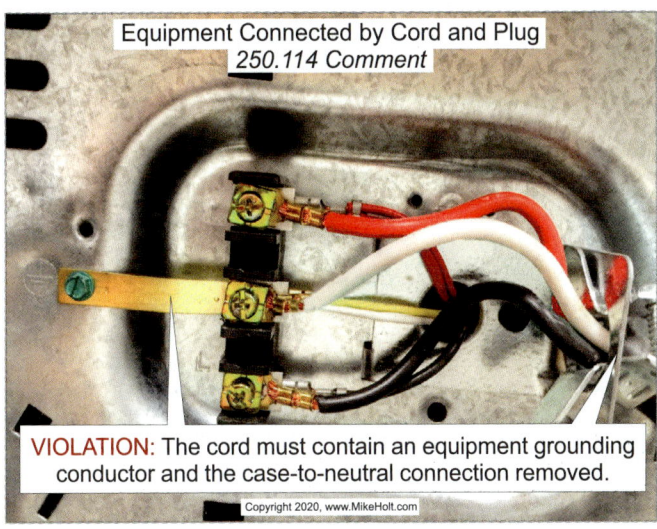
▶Figure 250–208

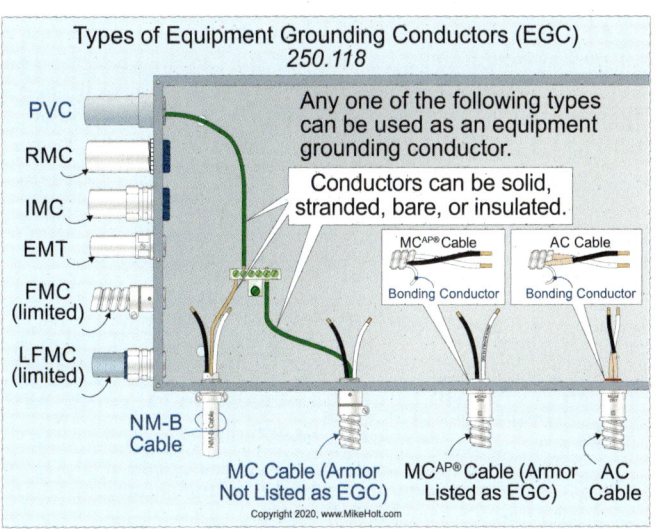
▶Figure 250–209

b. Clothes-washing, clothes-drying, and dish-washing machines; IT equipment; sump pumps; and electrical aquarium equipment.

c. Hand-held, stationary or fixed, and light industrial motor-operated tools.

d. Motor-operated hedge clippers, lawn mowers, snow-blowers, and wet scrubbers.

e. Portable handlamps and portable luminaires.

f. Appliances used in damp or wet locations or by persons standing on the ground, standing on metal floors, or working inside of metal tanks or boilers.

g. Tools likely to be used in wet or conductive locations

Ex: Tools and portable handlamps and portable luminaires likely to be used in wet or conductive locations are not required to be connected to an equipment grounding conductor where supplied through an isolating transformer with an ungrounded secondary not over 50V.

250.118 Types of Equipment Grounding Conductors

The equipment grounding conductor can be any one of the following types: ▶Figure 250–209

Note: The equipment grounding conductor is intended to serve as part of the effective ground-fault current path [Article 100]. ▶Figure 250–210

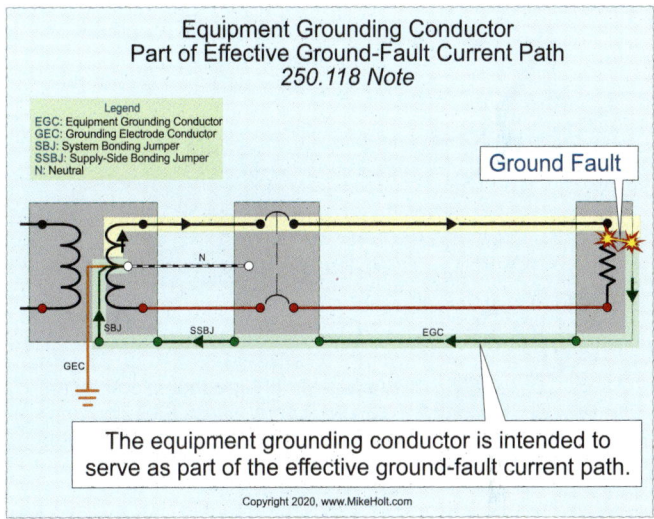
▶Figure 250–210

Author's Comment:

▸ The effective ground-fault current path [Article 100] is an intentionally constructed low-impedance conductive path designed to carry fault current from the point of a ground fault on a wiring system to the electrical supply source. Its purpose is to quickly remove dangerous voltage from a ground fault by opening the circuit overcurrent protective device. ▶Figure 250–211

(1) A bare or insulated copper, aluminum, or copper-clad aluminum conductor sized in accordance with 250.122. ▶Figure 250–212

(2) Rigid metal conduit.

250.118 | Grounding and Bonding

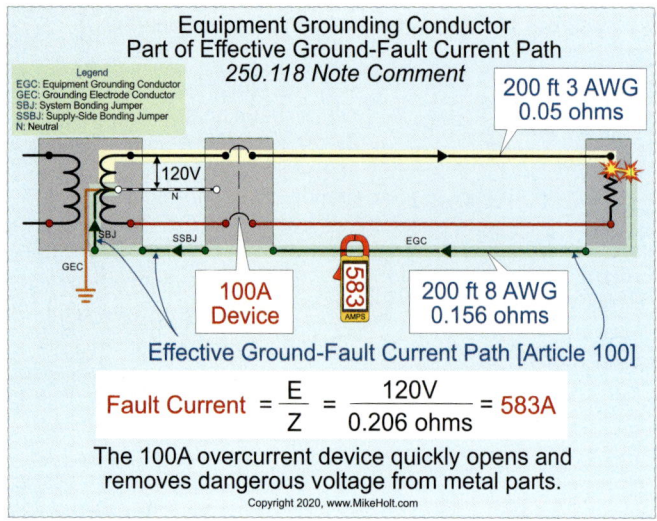
▶Figure 250–211

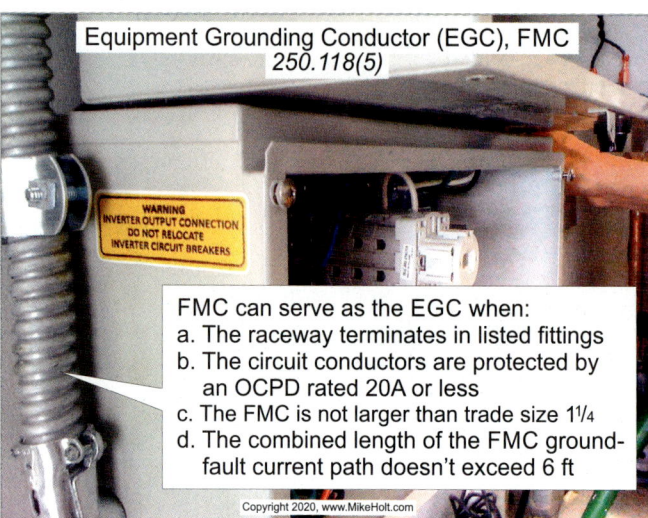
▶Figure 250–213

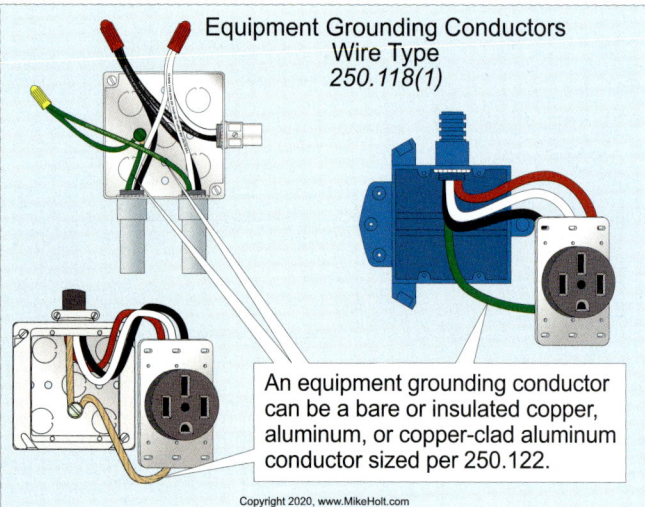
▶Figure 250–212

(3) Intermediate metal conduit.

(4) Electrical metallic tubing.

(5) Listed flexible metal conduit where: ▶Figure 250–213

　a. The raceway terminates in listed fittings.

　b. The circuit conductors are protected by an overcurrent device rated 20A or less.

　c. The size of the flexible metal conduit does not exceed 1¼.

　d. The combined length of the flexible conduit in the same effective ground-fault current path does not exceed 6 ft.

e. If flexibility is required to minimize the transmission of vibration from equipment or to provide flexibility for equipment that requires movement after installation, an equipment grounding conductor of the wire type must be installed with the circuit conductors in accordance with 250.102(E). ▶Figure 250–214

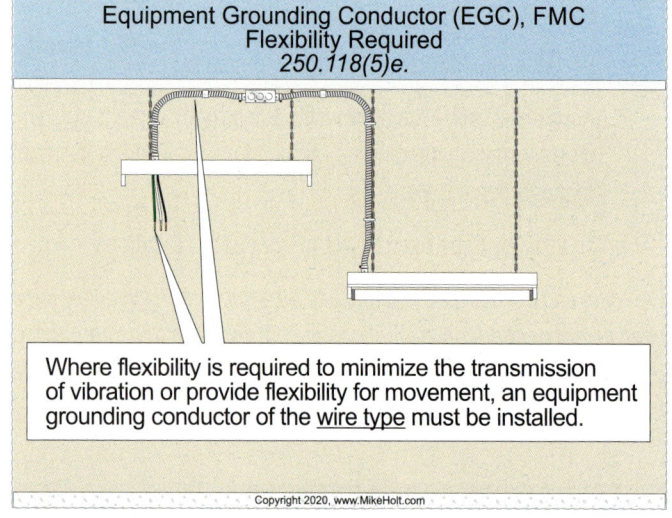
▶Figure 250–214

(6) Listed liquidtight flexible metal conduit where: ▶Figure 250–215

　a. The raceway terminates in listed fittings.

　b. For ⅜ in. through ½ in., the circuit conductors are protected by overcurrent protective devices rated 20A or less.

Grounding and Bonding | 250.118

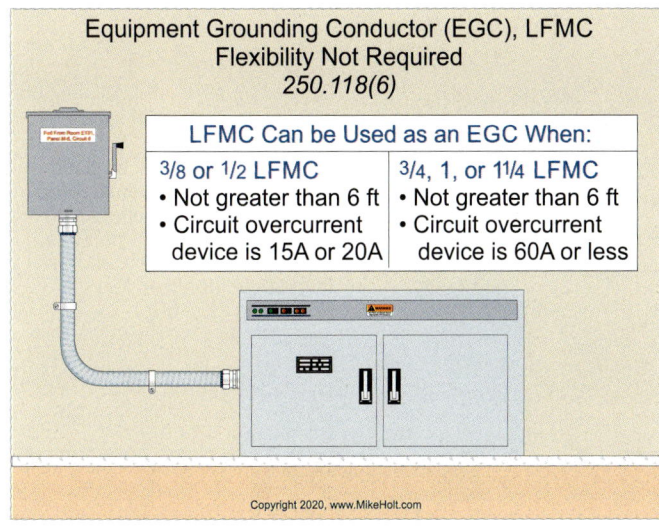
▶Figure 250-215

Author's Comment:

▸ The internal aluminum bonding strip is not an equipment grounding conductor, but it allows the interlocked armor of Type AC cable to serve as an equipment grounding conductor because it reduces the impedance of the armored spirals to ensure a ground fault will be cleared. It is the aluminum bonding strip in combination with the cable armor that creates the circuit equipment grounding conductor. Once the bonding strip exits the cable it can be cut off because it no longer serves any purpose.

(10) Type MC cable:

a. That contains an insulated or uninsulated equipment grounding conductor. ▶Figure 250-217

c. For ¾ in. through 1¼ in., the circuit conductors are protected by overcurrent protective devices rated 60A or less.

d. The combined length of the flexible metal conduit in the same effective ground-fault current path does not exceed 6 ft.

e. If flexibility is required to minimize the transmission of vibration from equipment or to provide flexibility for equipment that requires movement after installation, an equipment grounding conductor of the wire type must be installed with the circuit conductors in accordance with 250.102(E).

(8) The sheath of Type AC cable. ▶Figure 250-216

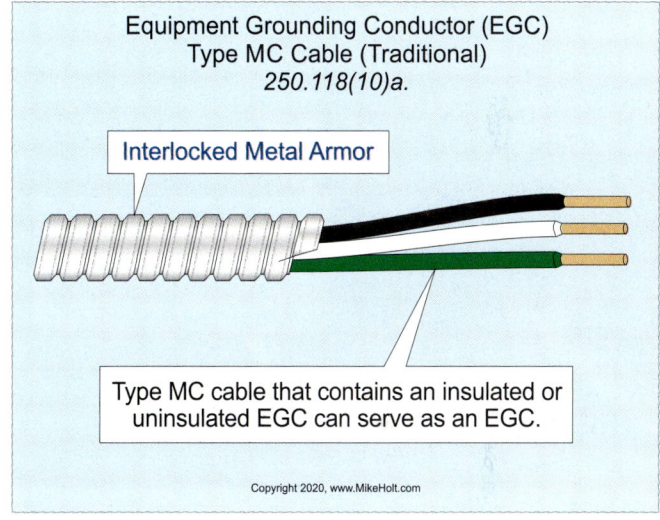
▶Figure 250-217

b. Where the metallic sheath and uninsulated equipment grounding/bonding conductor is listed and identified as an equipment grounding conductor. ▶Figure 250-218

Author's Comment:

▸ Once the bare aluminum grounding/bonding conductor of Type MC cable exits the cable it can be cut off because it no longer serves any purpose. The effective ground-fault current path must be maintained by the use of fittings specifically listed for Type MC$^{AP®}$ cable [330.40]. See 300.12, 300.15, and 330.100. ▶Figure 250-219

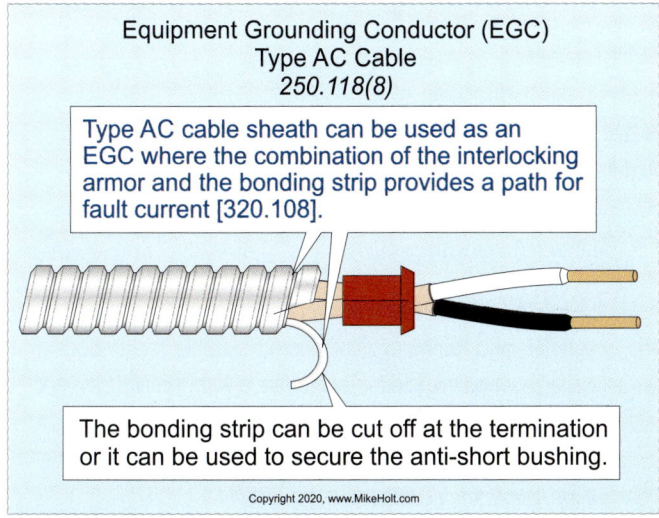
▶Figure 250-216

(9) The sheath of Type MI cable.

250.118 | Grounding and Bonding

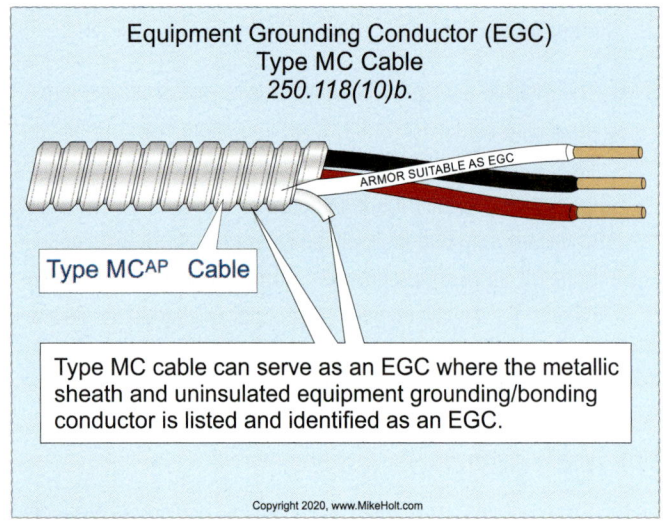
▶Figure 250–218

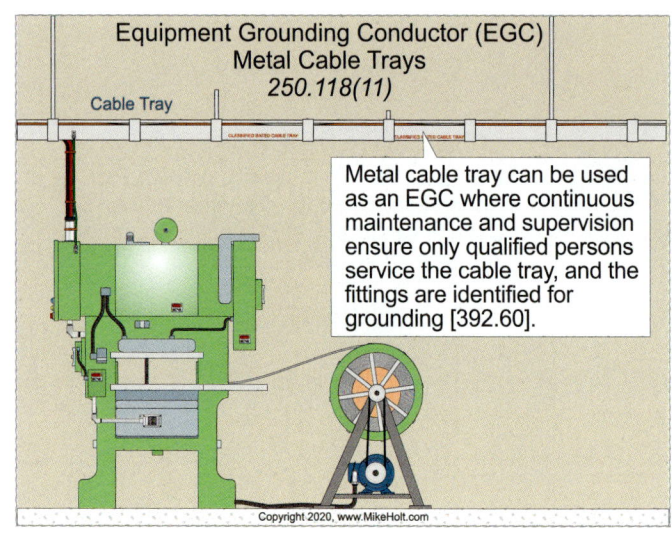
▶Figure 250–220

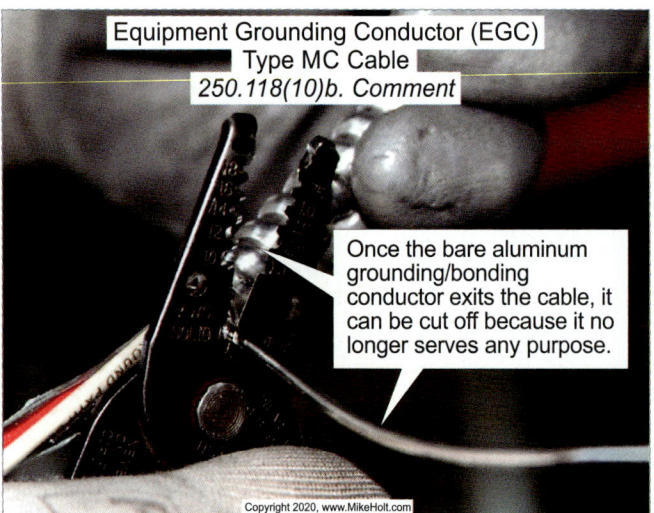
▶Figure 250–219

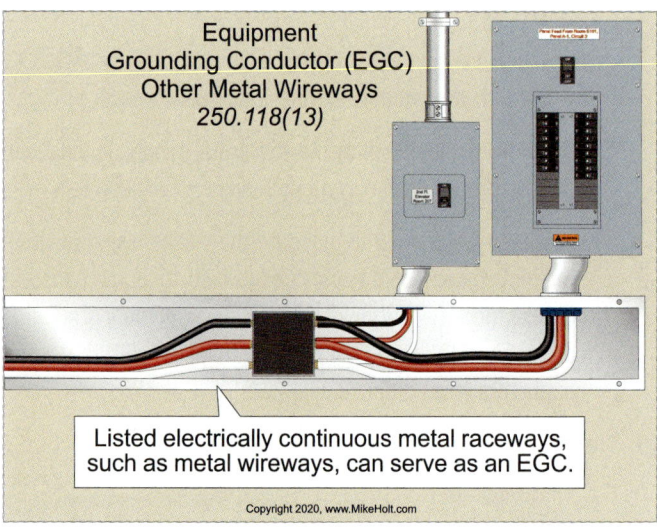
▶Figure 250–221

    c. When the metallic sheath of smooth or corrugated tube-type MC cable is listed and identified as an equipment grounding conductor it can serve as an equipment grounding conductor.

(11) Metal cable trays if continuous maintenance and supervision ensure only qualified persons will service the cable tray; the cable tray and fittings are identified for grounding; and the cable tray, fittings [392.10], and raceways are bonded together using bolted mechanical connectors or bonding jumpers sized and installed in accordance with 250.102 [392.60]. ▶Figure 250–220

(13) Other listed electrically continuous metal raceways such as metal wireways [Article 376] or strut-type channel raceways [384.60]. ▶Figure 250–221

(14) Surface metal raceways listed for grounding [Article 386].

Note: For a definition of effective ground-fault current path, see Article 100.

Author's Comment:

▶ Listed offset nipples and metal fittings for metal cable, conduit, and tubing are considered suitable for grounding circuits where installed in accordance with the *NEC*, except as noted for flexible metal conduit fittings and liquid-tight flexible metal conduit fittings. See UL Product Spec™ *Guide, Information for "Conduit Fittings" (DWTT)*.

250.119 Identification of Equipment Grounding Conductors

 Scan this QR code for a video of Mike explaining this topic; it's a sample from the videos that accompany this textbook. www.MikeHolt.com/20BGvideos

Unless required to be insulated in this *Code*, equipment grounding conductors can be bare or covered.

Insulated equipment grounding conductors 6 AWG and smaller must have a continuous outer finish that is either green or green with one or more yellow stripes. ▶Figure 250-222

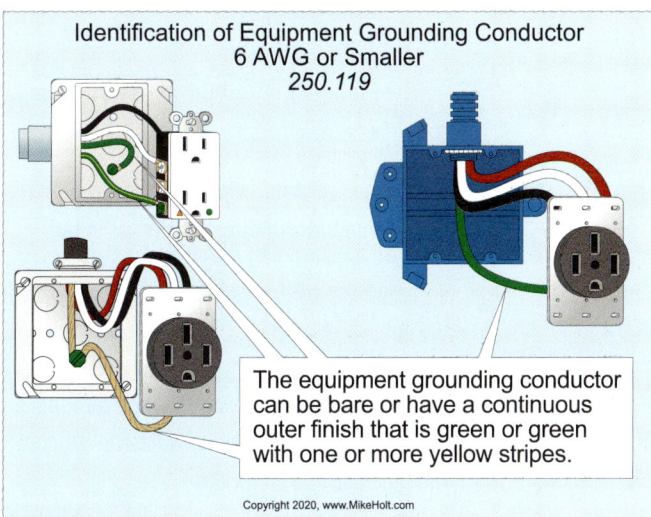

▶Figure 250-222

Conductors with insulation that is green, or green with one or more yellow stripes, are not permitted to be used for a phase or neutral conductor.

Author's Comment:

▸ The *NEC* neither requires nor prohibits the use of the color green for the identification of grounding electrode conductors. ▶Figure 250-223

(A) Conductors 4 AWG and Larger.

(1) Identified Where Accessible. Insulated equipment grounding conductors 4 AWG and larger can be reidentified at the time of installation where the conductor is accessible. ▶Figure 250-224

(2) Identification Methods. Identification must encircle the conductor and be accomplished by: ▶Figure 250-225

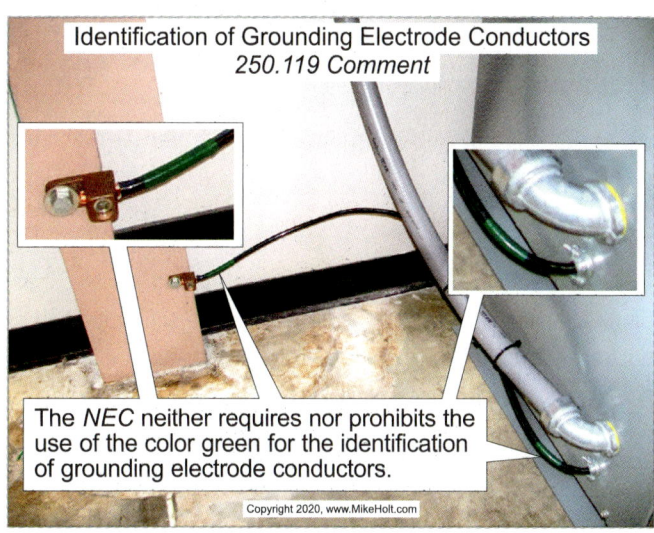

▶Figure 250-223

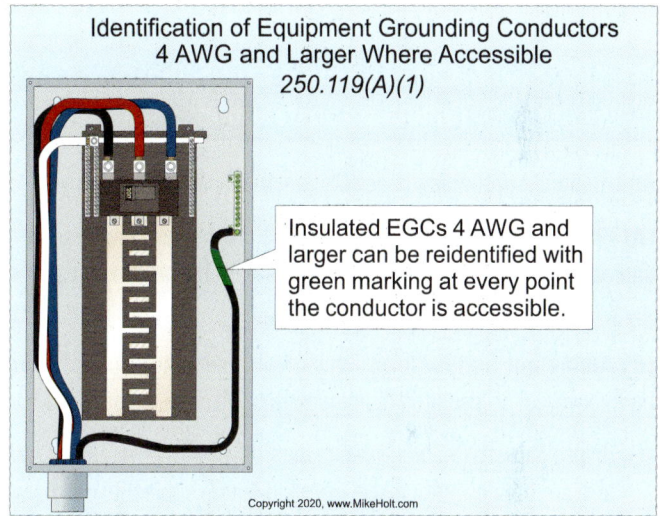

▶Figure 250-224

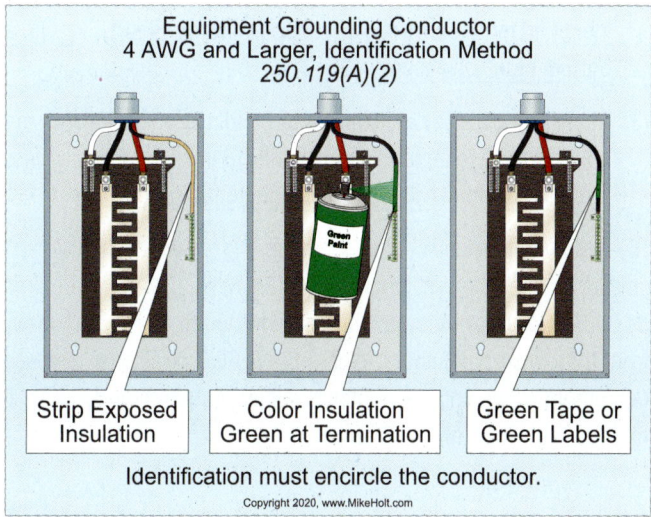

▶Figure 250-225

250.120 | Grounding and Bonding

a. Removing the conductor insulation

b. Coloring the insulation green at termination

c. Marking the insulation at termination with green tape or green adhesive labels

(B) Multiconductor Cable.

One or more insulated conductors in a multiconductor cable, at the time of installation, are permitted to be permanently identified as equipment grounding conductors at each end and at every point where the conductors are accessible by one of the following means:

(1) Stripping the insulation from the entire exposed length.

(2) Coloring the exposed insulation green.

(3) Marking the exposed insulation with green tape or green adhesive labels. Identification must encircle the conductor.

250.120 Equipment Grounding Conductor Installation

An equipment grounding conductor must be installed as follows:

(A) Fittings Made Tight. For raceways, cable trays, cable armor, cablebus framework, or cable sheaths, the fittings and terminations must be made tight using suitable tools.

(B) Aluminum Conductors. Equipment grounding conductors of bare, covered, or insulated aluminum must be installed as follows:

(1) Unless part of a Chapter 3 wiring method, bare or covered conductors are not permitted to be installed where subject to corrosive conditions or in direct contact with concrete, masonry, or the Earth.

(2) Terminations made within outdoor enclosures that are listed and identified for the environment are permitted within 18 in. of the bottom of the enclosure.

(3) Aluminum conductors external to buildings or enclosures are not permitted to be terminated within 18 in. of the Earth, unless terminated within a listed wire connector system.

(C) Exposed. Exposed equipment grounding conductors 8 AWG and smaller for direct-current circuits [250.134(B) Ex.2], such as required by 690.45 for solar PV systems, are permitted to be run separately from the circuit conductors. Where the 8 AWG or smaller exposed equipment grounding conductor is subject to physical damage, it must be installed within a raceway or cable.

250.121 Restricted Use of Equipment Grounding Conductors

(A) Grounding Electrode Conductor. An equipment grounding conductor is not permitted to be used as a grounding electrode conductor. ▶Figure 250–226

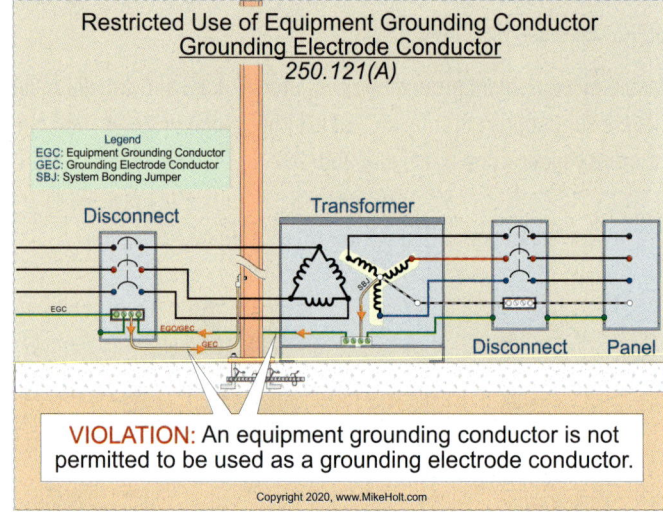

▶Figure 250–226

Ex: An equipment grounding conductor meeting the requirements for an equipment grounding conductor and grounding electrode conductor can be used as a grounding electrode conductor.

(B) Metal Frame of Building. The structural metal frame of a building must not be used as an equipment grounding conductor.

Author's Comment:

▸ Here is a perfect example of why it is so important for you have a complete understanding of the terminology used throughout the *Code*. While the structural metal frame of a building is not permitted to be used as an "equipment grounding conductor," the metal structure of a building is permitted to be used as a "grounding electrode conductor." Knowing the difference, is what makes the difference!

250.122 Sizing Equipment Grounding Conductors

 Scan this QR code for a video of Mike explaining this topic; it's a sample from the videos that accompany this textbook. www.MikeHolt.com/20BGvideos

Grounding and Bonding | 250.122

(A) General. Equipment grounding conductors must be sized not smaller than shown in Table 250.122; however, the equipment grounding conductor is not required to be larger than the phase conductors. ▶Figure 250–227

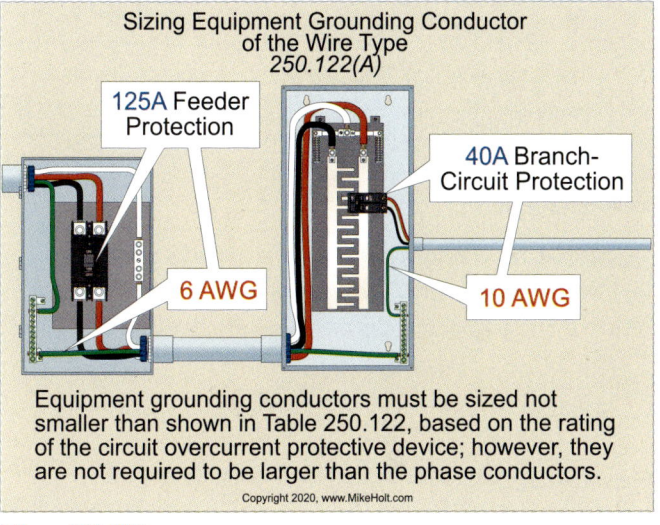

▶Figure 250–227

(B) Increased in Size. If phase conductors are increased in size for any reason other than as required in 310.15(B) or 310.15(C), wire-type equipment grounding conductors, if installed, must be increased in size proportionately to the increase in the circular mil area of the phase conductors. ▶Figure 250–228

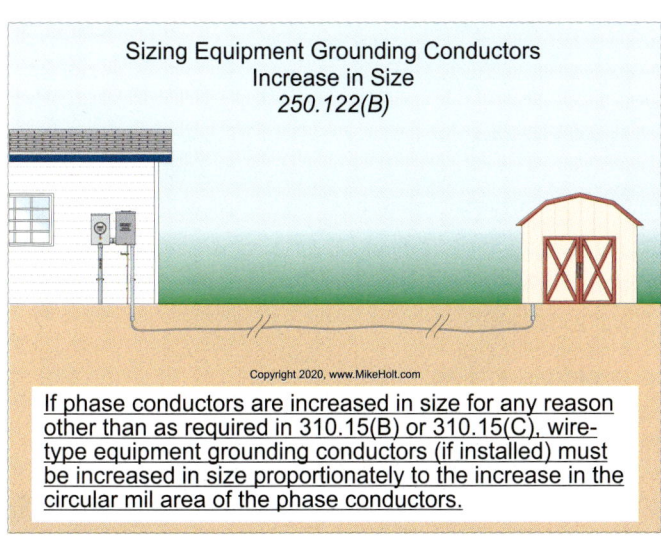

▶Figure 250–228

Ex: Equipment grounding conductors can be sized by a qualified person to provide an effective ground-fault current path in accordance with 250.4(A)(5) or (B)(4).

Author's Comment:

▸ Phase conductors are sometimes increased in size to accommodate conductor voltage drop, short-circuit rating, or simply for future capacity.

Table 250.122 Sizing Equipment Grounding Conductor	
Overcurrent Protective Device Rating	Copper Conductor
15A	14 AWG
20A	12 AWG
25A–60A	10 AWG
70A–100A	8 AWG
110A–200A	6 AWG
225A–300A	4 AWG
350A–400A	3 AWG
450A–500A	2 AWG
600A	1 AWG
700A–800A	1/0 AWG
1,000A	2/0 AWG
1,200A	3/0 AWG

Note: Where necessary to comply with 250.4(A)(5) or (B)(4), the equipment grounding conductor might be required to be sized larger than given in this table.

▶ **Example**

Question: *If the phase conductors for a 40A circuit (with 75°C terminals) are increased in size from 8 AWG to 6 AWG due to voltage drop, the circuit equipment grounding conductor must be increased in size from 10 AWG to _____.* ▶Figure 250–229

(a) 8 AWG   (b) 6 AWG   (c) 4 AWG   (d) 3 AWG

Solution:

The circular mil area of 6 AWG is 59 percent more than 8 AWG (26,240 cmil/16,510 cmil) [Chapter 9, Table 8]. According to Table 250.122, the circuit equipment grounding conductor for a 40A overcurrent protective device will be 10 AWG (10,380 cmil), but the circuit equipment grounding conductor for this circuit must be increased in size by a multiplier of 159 percent.

Conductor Size = 10,380 cmil × 159%
Conductor Size = 16,504 cmil

The circuit equipment grounding conductor must be increased to 8 AWG [Chapter 9, Table 8].

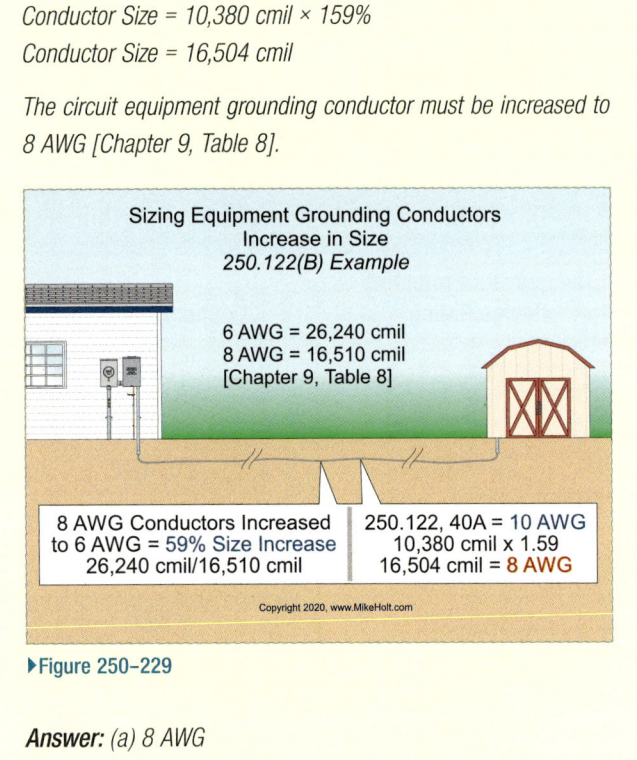
▶Figure 250–229

Answer: (a) 8 AWG

(C) Multiple Circuits. A single equipment grounding conductor sized in accordance with Table 250.122 when multiple circuits are installed in the same raceway, cable, trench, or cable tray. ▶Figure 250–230

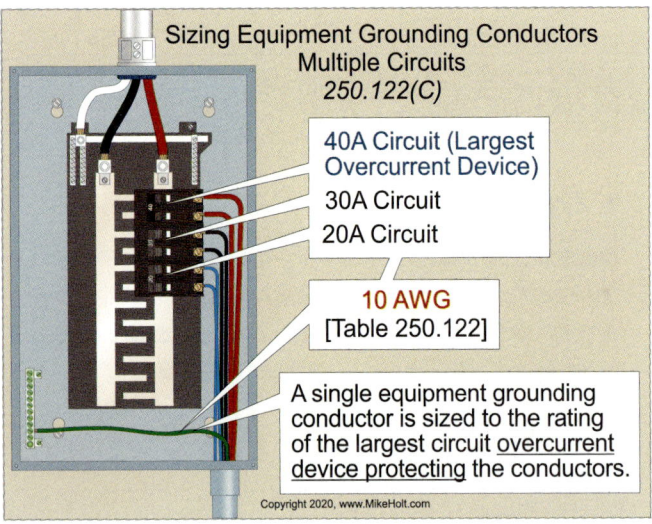
▶Figure 250–230

(D) Motor Branch Circuits. Equipment grounding conductors for motor circuits must be sized in accordance with 250.122(D)(1) or (D)(2).

(1) General. The equipment grounding conductor must not be smaller than determined by 250.122(A), based on the rating of the motor circuit branch-circuit short-circuit and ground-fault protective device sized in accordance with 430.52(C)(1) Ex 1.

> **Author's Comment:**
>
> ▸ The equipment grounding conductor is not required to be larger than the motor circuit conductors. See 250.122(A).
>
> ▶ **Example**
>
> **Question:** What size equipment grounding conductor of the wire type is required for a 14 AWG motor branch circuit [430.22], protected with a 2-pole, 40A circuit breaker in accordance with 430.22 and 430.52(C)(1)? ▶Figure 250–231
>
> (a) 14 AWG   (b) 12 AWG   (c) 10 AWG   (d) 8 AWG
>
>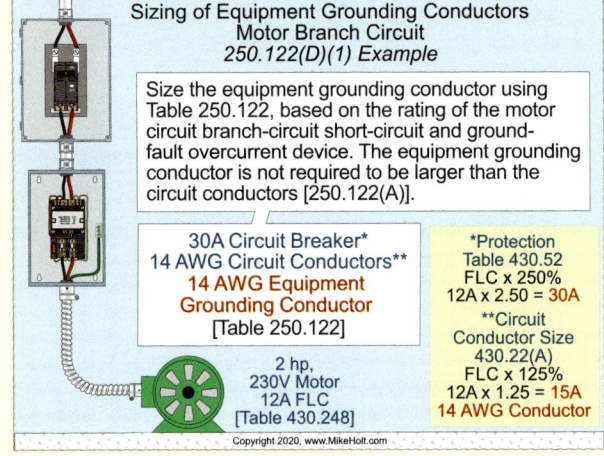
> ▶Figure 250–231
>
> **Solution:**
>
> The equipment grounding conductor is not required to be larger than the 14 AWG motor branch-circuit conductors [250.122(D)(1) and 250.122(A)].
>
> **Answer:** (a) 14 AWG

(F) Parallel Conductors. Where circuit conductors are installed in parallel in accordance with 310.10(G), an equipment grounding conductor of the wire type must be installed in accordance with the following:

 Scan this QR code for a video of Mike explaining this topic; it's a sample from the videos that accompany this textbook. www.MikeHolt.com/20BGvideos

(1) Nonmetallic Raceways or Cable Trays

(a) Parallel Conductors in a Single Nonmetallic Raceway or Cable Tray. If parallel circuit conductors are installed in a single nonmetallic raceway or cable tray, a single wire-type equipment grounding conductor, sized in accordance with Table 250.122 based on the rating of the circuit overcurrent protective device, must be installed with the parallel circuit conductors. ▶Figure 250–232

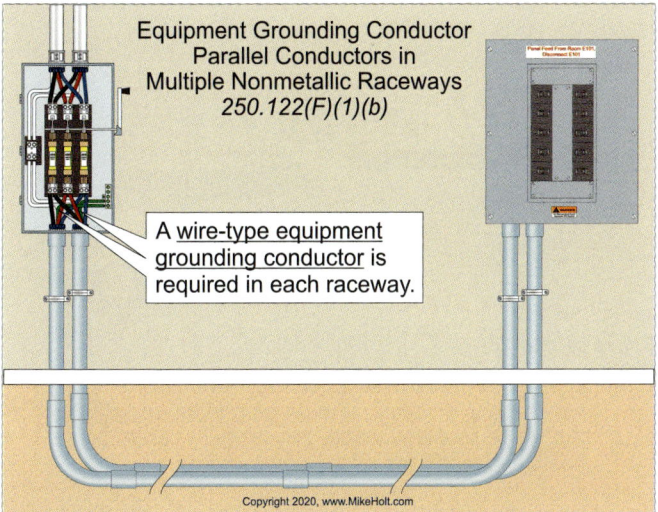

▶Figure 250–232

(b) Parallel Conductors in Multiple Nonmetallic Raceways. If parallel circuit conductors are installed in multiple nonmetallic raceways, a wire-type equipment grounding conductor is required in each raceway.

The equipment grounding conductors in each raceway must be sized in accordance with Table 250.122. ▶Figure 250–233

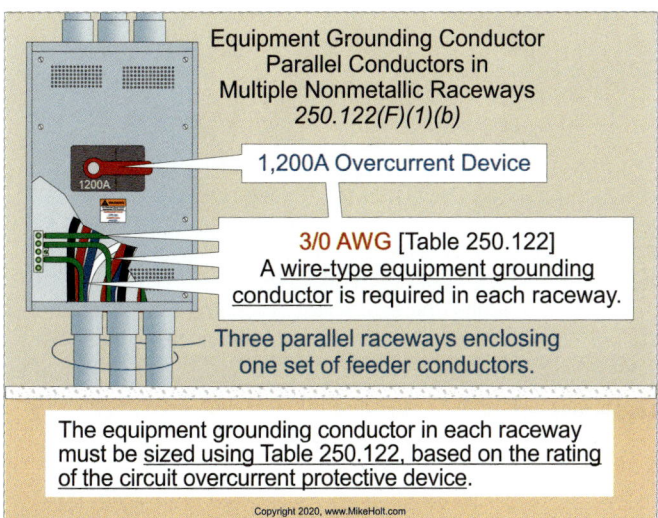

▶Figure 250–233

▶ **Example**

Question: What size copper equipment grounding conductor of the wire type is required for a 4,000A feeder containing thirteen parallel sets of 500 kcmil conductors per phase in PVC conduit?

(a) 250 kcmil   (b) 300 kcmil   (c) 400 kcmil   (d) 500 kcmil

Solution:

According to Table 250.122, the equipment grounding conductor in each raceway must not be smaller than 500 kcmil.

Answer: (d) 500 kcmil

(c) Wire-Type Equipment Grounding Conductors in Cable Trays. Wire-type equipment grounding conductors installed in cable trays must meet the minimum requirements of 392.10(B)(1)(c).

(d) Metal Raceways or Cable Trays. Metal raceways can serve as the required equipment grounding conductor in accordance with 250.118 and cable trays complying with 392.60(B) can serve as the required equipment grounding conductor.

(2) Parallel Multiconductor Cables.

(a) Except as provided in 250.122(F)(2)(c) for raceway or cable tray installations, the equipment grounding conductor in each multiconductor cable must be sized in accordance with 250.122, based on the overcurrent protective device for the feeder or branch circuit. ▶Figure 250–234

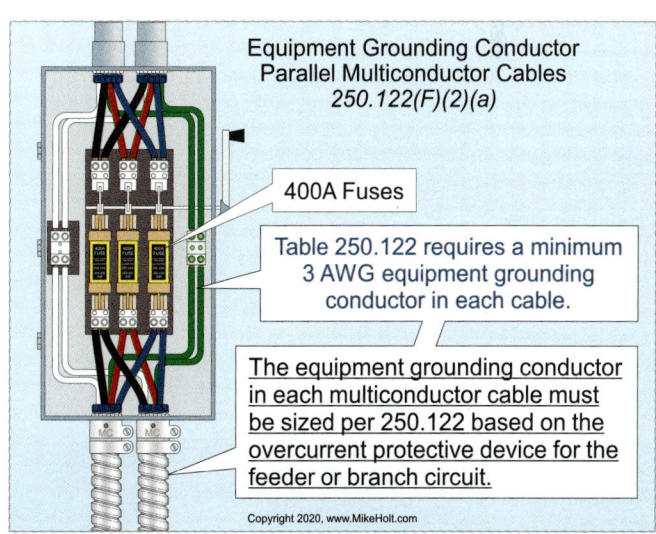

▶Figure 250–234

(b) If circuit conductors of multiconductor cables are connected in parallel, the equipment grounding conductor(s) in each cable must be connected in parallel.

250.134 | Grounding and Bonding

(c) If multiconductor cables are paralleled in the same raceway or cable tray, a single equipment grounding conductor sized in accordance with 250.122 is permitted in combination with the equipment grounding conductors provided within the multiconductor cables and all equipment grounding conductors must be connected together.

(d) Equipment grounding conductors installed in cable trays must meet the requirements of 392.10(B)(1)(c).

Cable trays complying with 392.60(B) and metal raceways in accordance with 250.118 can be used as the required equipment grounding conductor.

(G) Feeder Tap Conductors. Equipment grounding conductors for feeder taps are not permitted to be smaller than shown in Table 250.122, based on the ampere rating of the overcurrent device ahead of the feeder on the supply side of the tap. The feeder equipment grounding conductor for the feeder tap is not be required to be larger than the tap conductors. ▶Figure 250-235

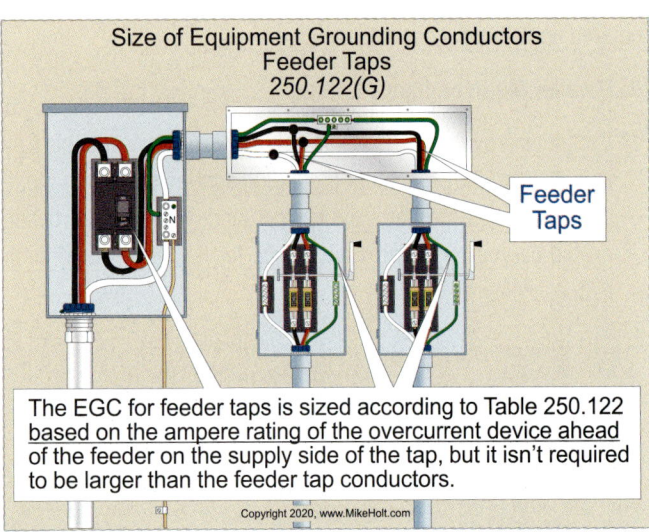

▶Figure 250-235

Part VII. Methods of Equipment Grounding Conductor Connections

250.134 Equipment Connected by Permanent Wiring Methods

Except as permitted for services or separately derived systems [250.142(A)], metal parts of equipment, raceways, and enclosures must be connected to an equipment grounding conductor by any of the following methods:

(1) Equipment Grounding Conductor. By connecting to one of the equipment grounding conductor types identified in 250.118(2) through (14).

(2) With Circuit Conductors. Where an equipment grounding conductor of the wire type is installed, it must be contained within the same raceway, cable tray, trench, cable, or flexible cord as the circuit conductors. ▶Figure 250-236

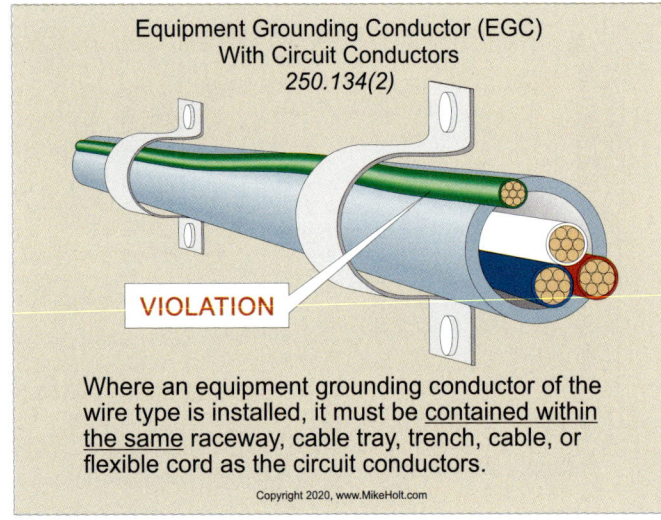

▶Figure 250-236

Ex 2: For direct-current circuits, the equipment grounding conductor is permitted to be run separately from the circuit conductors. ▶Figure 250-237

▶Figure 250-237

250.136 Equipment Secured to Grounded Metal Supports

Metal equipment and enclosures secured to and in electrical contact with a metal rack or structure are considered connected to an equipment grounding conductor if the metal rack or structure is connected to an equipment grounding conductor in accordance with 250.134. ▶Figure 250-238

▶Figure 250-238

250.138 Cord-and-Plug-Connected

(A) Equipment Grounding Conductor. Metal parts of cord-and-plug-connected equipment must be connected to an equipment grounding conductor that terminates to a grounding-type attachment plug. ▶Figure 250-239

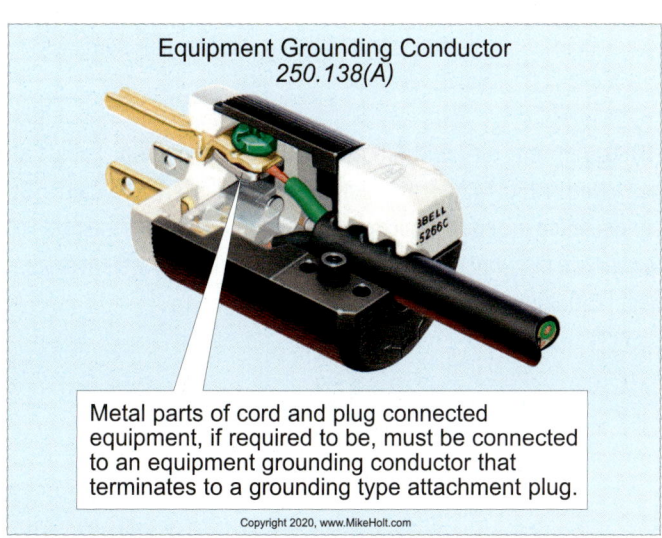
▶Figure 250-239

250.140 Frames of Ranges, Ovens, and Clothes Dryers

The frames of electric ranges, wall-mounted ovens, counter-mounted cooking units, clothes dryers, and outlet boxes that are part of the circuit for these appliances must be connected to the circuit equipment grounding conductor in accordance with 250.134. ▶Figure 250-240

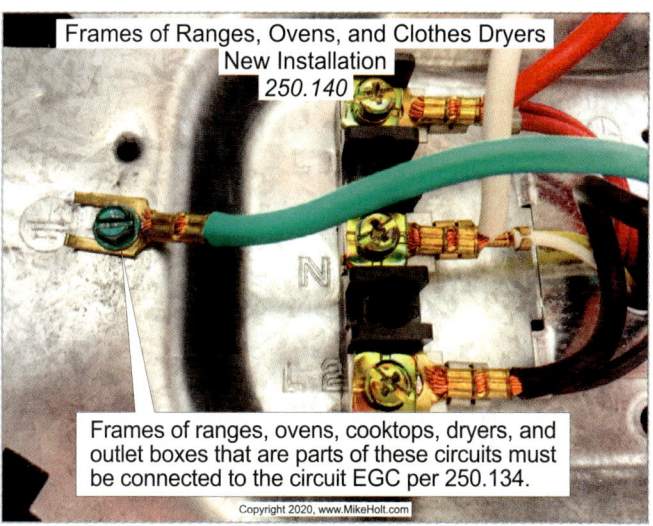
▶Figure 250-240

Caution

⚡ Ranges, dryers, and ovens may have their metal cases connected to the neutral conductor at the factory. This neutral-to-case connection must be removed when these appliances are installed in new construction, and a 4-wire flexible cord and receptacle must be used [250.142(B)]. ▶Figure 250-241

Ex: For existing installations, if an equipment grounding conductor is not present in the outlet box, the frames of electric ranges, wall-mounted ovens, counter-mounted cooking units, clothes dryers, and outlet boxes that are part of the circuit for these appliances may be connected to the circuit's neutral conductor. ▶Figure 250-242

250.142 | Grounding and Bonding

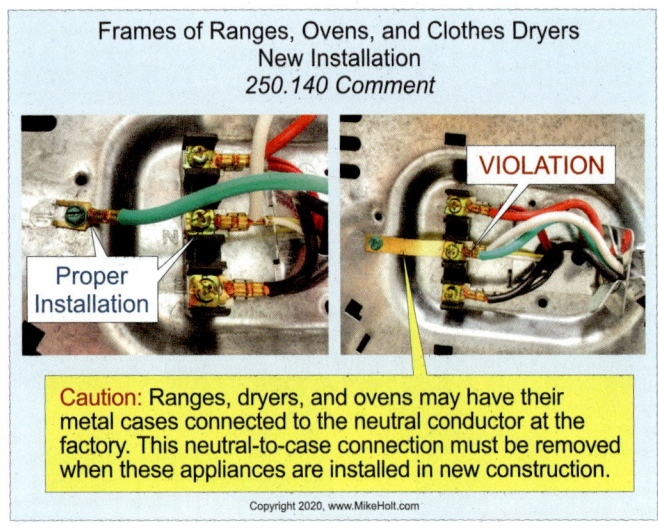
▶Figure 250–241

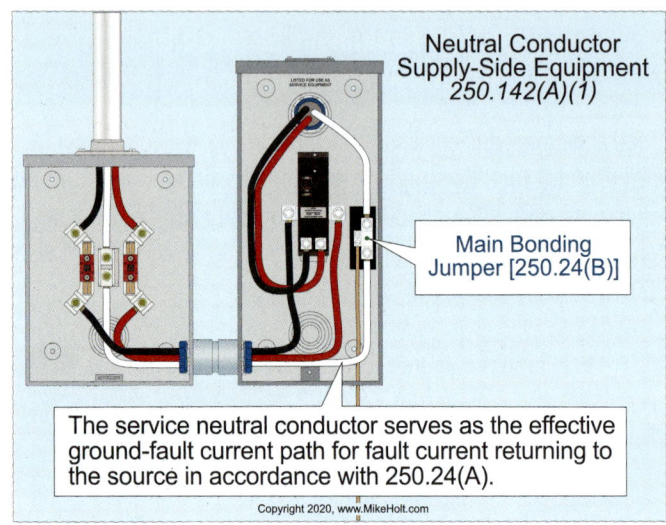
▶Figure 250–243

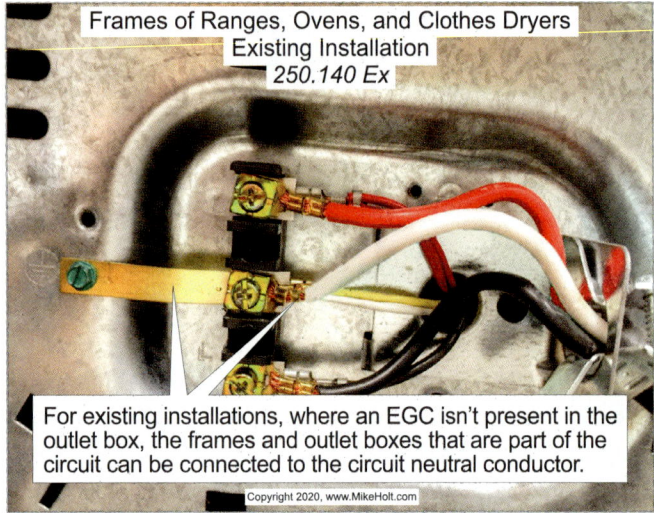
▶Figure 250–242

250.142 Neutral Conductor for Effective Ground-Fault Current Path

(A) Services and Separately Derived Systems. The neutral conductor is permitted to be connected to metal parts of equipment, raceways, and enclosures for the purpose of serving as the effective ground-fault current path for fault current returning to the source at any of the following locations:

(1) Services. On the supply side of service disconnect in accordance with 250.24(A). ▶Figure 250–243

Author's Comment:

▸ The neutral-to-case connection between the service neutral conductor and the service-disconnect enclosure is accomplished by the required installation of the main bonding jumper in accordance with 250.24(B).

(2) On the supply side or within the enclosure of the main disconnecting means for separate buildings as provided in 250.32(B)(1) Ex 1.

(3) Separately Derived Systems. On the supply side or within the separately derived system disconnect in accordance with 250.30(A)(1).

Author's Comment:

▸ The neutral-to-case connection between the separately derived system's secondary neutral conductor and the equipment grounding conductor is accomplished by the required installation of the system bonding jumper in accordance with 250.30(A)(1).

(B) Equipment on Load Side of Service Disconnect. Except as permitted in 250.142(A), the neutral conductor is not permitted to be connected to the equipment grounding conductor on the load side of the service disconnect [250.24] or separately derived system disconnect [250.30(A)]. ▶Figure 250–244

Grounding and Bonding | 250.146

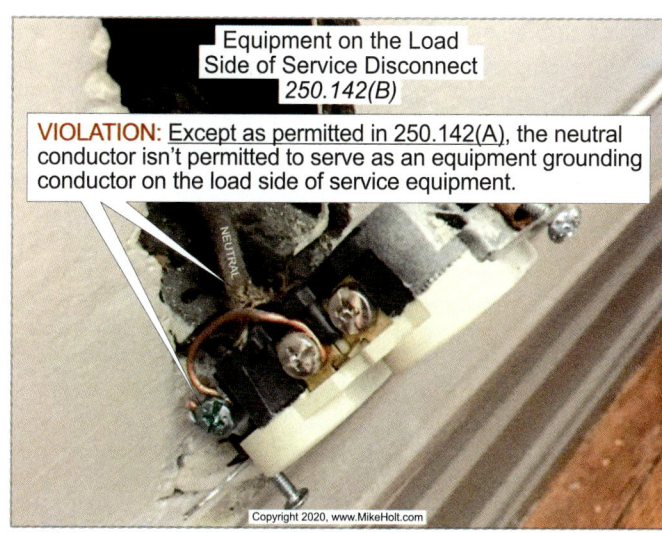
▶Figure 250–244

Ex 1: In existing installations, the frames of ranges, wall-mounted ovens, counter-mounted cooking units, and clothes dryers can be connected to the neutral conductor in accordance with 250.140 Ex.

Ex 2: The neutral conductor can be connected to meter socket enclosures on the load side of the service disconnect if: ▶Figure 250–245

(1) Ground-fault protection of equipment is not provided on service disconnect,

(2) Meter socket enclosures are immediately adjacent to the service disconnect, and

(3) The neutral conductor is sized in accordance with 250.122.

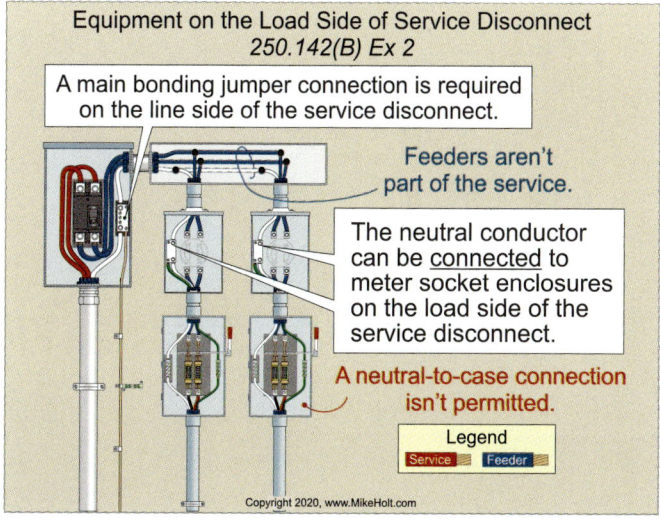
▶Figure 250–245

250.146 Connecting Receptacle Grounding Terminal to an Equipment Grounding Conductor

An equipment bonding conductor is required to connect the grounding contacts of a receptacle to a metal box connected to an equipment grounding conductor, except as permitted in (A) through (D). ▶Figure 250–246

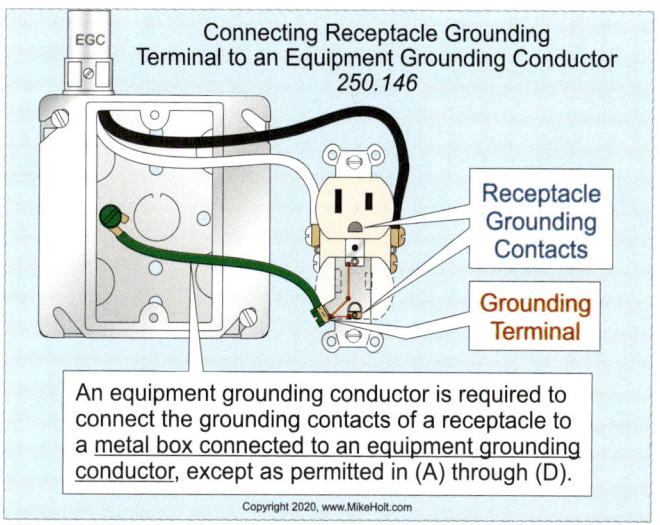
▶Figure 250–246

Author's Comment:

▸ The *NEC* does not restrict the position of the receptacle grounding terminal; it can be up, down, or sideways. *Code* proposals to specify the mounting position of receptacles have always been rejected. ▶Figure 250–247

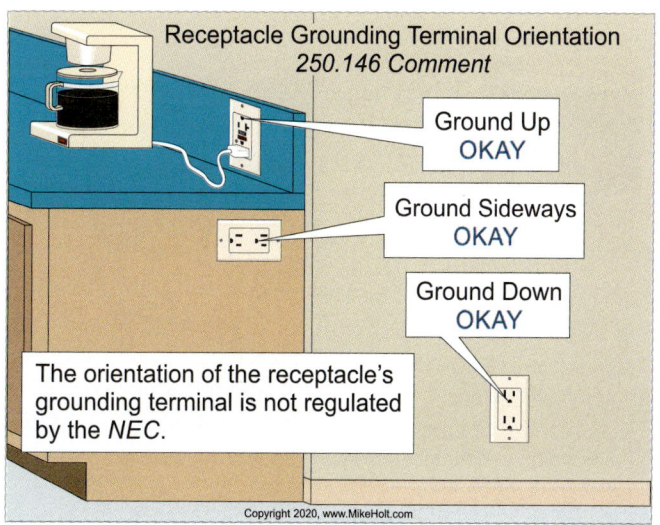
▶Figure 250–247

250.146 | Grounding and Bonding

(A) Surface-Mounted Box. A receptacle having direct metal-to-metal contact between the receptacle strap or yoke and a surface metal box is considered to be connected to the required effective ground-fault current path. To ensure sufficient metal-to-metal contact, at least one of the insulating retaining washers on the yoke screw must be removed. ▶Figure 250-248

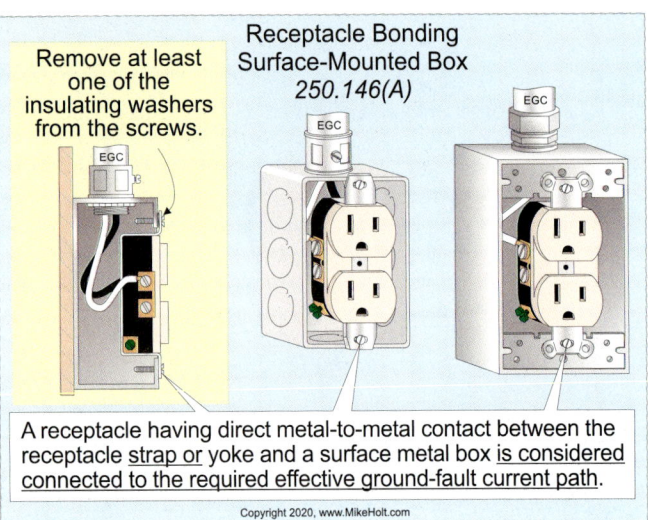

▶Figure 250-248

A receptacle installed on a cover is considered to be connected to the required effective ground-fault current path under both of the following conditions:

(1) The receptacle is attached to the metal cover with at least two fasteners that have a thread locking, or screw or nut locking means.

(2) The cover mounting holes are located on a flat non-raised portion of the cover. ▶Figure 250-249

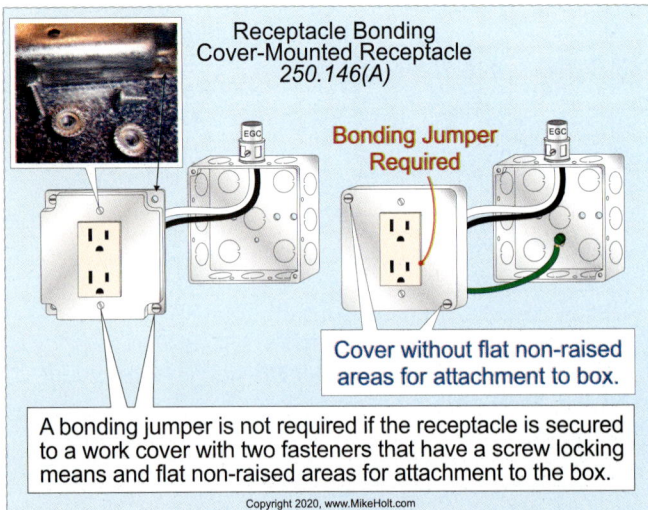

▶Figure 250-249

(B) Self-Grounding Receptacles. Receptacle yokes listed as self-grounding establish the equipment bonding between the receptacle yoke and a metal box. ▶Figure 250-250

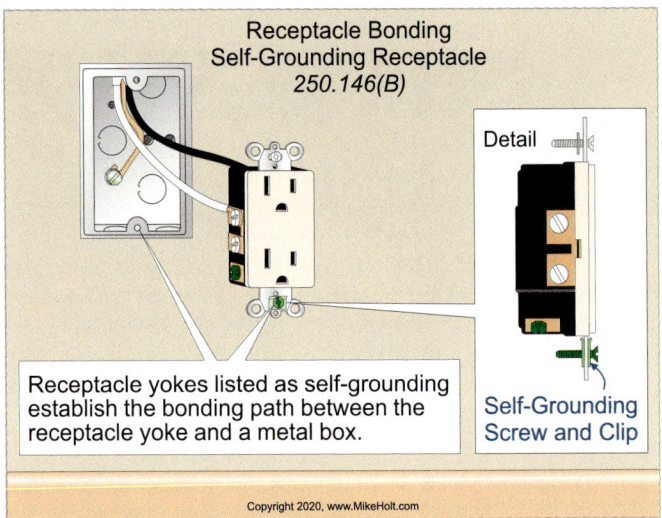

▶Figure 250-250

(C) Floor Boxes. Listed metal floor boxes must establish the bonding path between the receptacle yoke and a metal box.

(D) Isolated Ground Receptacles. The grounding terminal of an isolated ground receptacle must be connected to an insulated equipment grounding conductor. ▶Figure 250-251

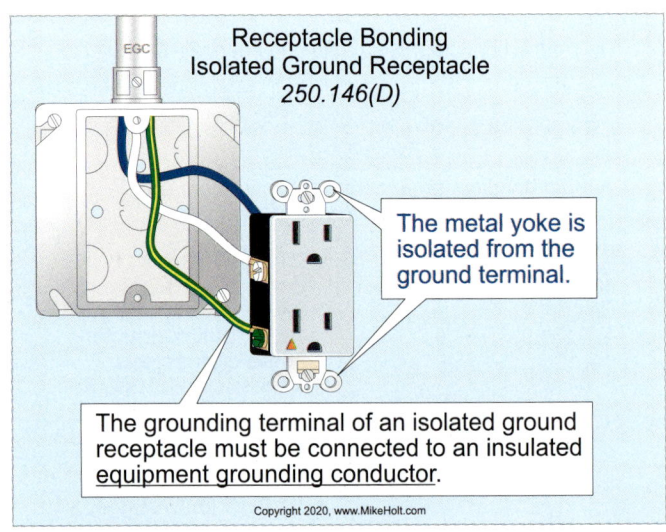

▶Figure 250-251

Note: Use of an isolated equipment grounding conductor does not relieve the requirement for connecting the raceway system and outlet box to an equipment grounding conductor. ▶Figure 250-252

Grounding and Bonding | 250.146

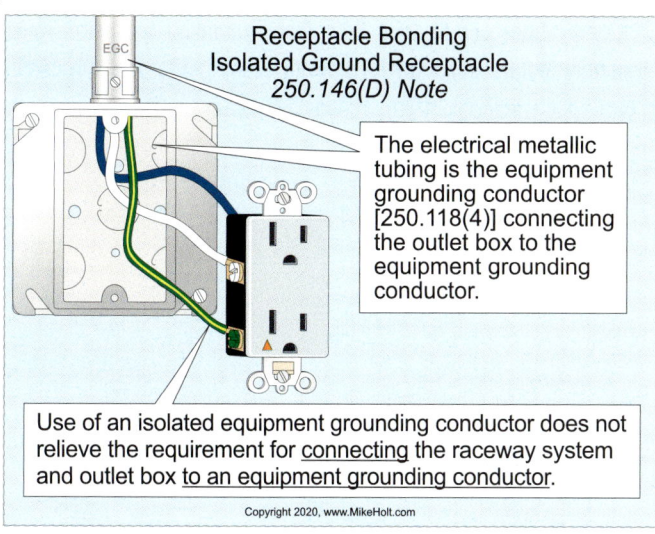
▸Figure 250–252

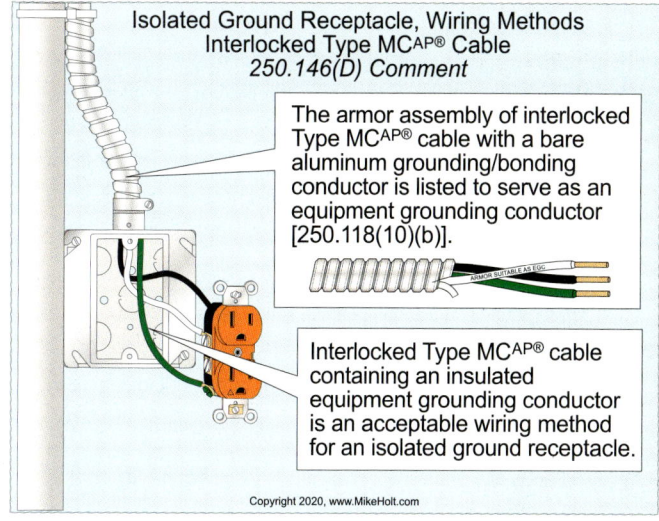
▸Figure 250–254

Author's Comment:

▸ Type AC cable containing an insulated equipment grounding conductor can be used to supply isolated ground receptacles because the metal armor of the cable is listed as an equipment grounding conductor [250.118(8)]. ▸Figure 250–253

▸ Interlocked Type MC$^{AP®}$ cable with a 10 AWG bare aluminum grounding/bonding conductor can be used to supply isolated ground receptacles because the combination of the metal armor and the 10 AWG bare aluminum conductor is listed as an equipment grounding conductor [250.118(10)(b)]. An interlocked Type MC$^{AP®}$ cable is an acceptable wiring method to use for an isolated ground receptacle. ▸Figure 250–254

Caution

Type MC Cable. The metal armor sheath of traditional interlocked Type MC cable containing an insulated equipment grounding conductor is not listed as an equipment grounding conductor. Therefore, this wiring method with a single equipment grounding conductor cannot supply an isolated ground receptacle. Type MC cable with two insulated equipment grounding conductors is acceptable, since one bonds to the metal box and the other one connects to the isolated ground receptacle. ▸Figure 250–255

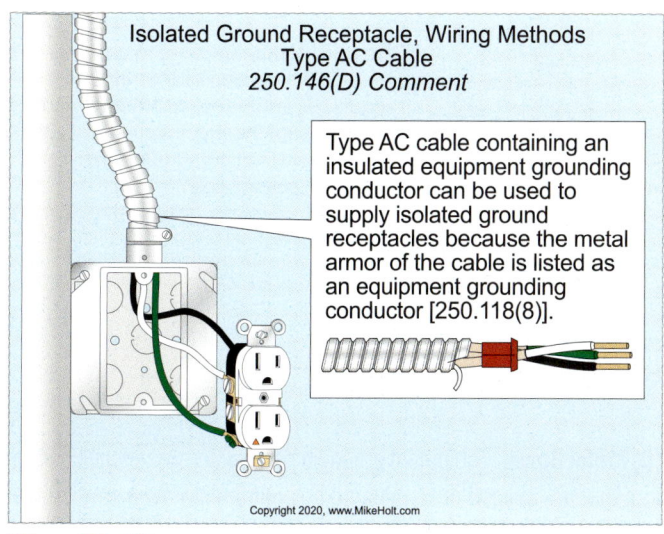
▸Figure 250–253

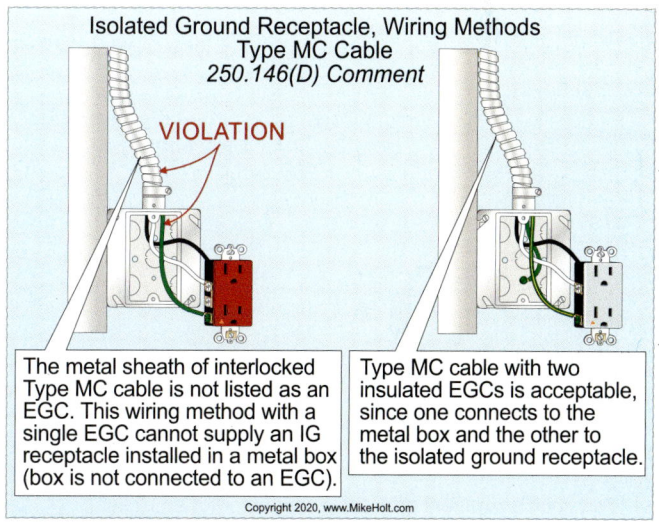
▸Figure 250–255

Mike Holt Enterprises • www.MikeHolt.com • 888.NEC.CODE (632.2633) | 177

250.148 | Grounding and Bonding

Author's Comment:

▸ When should an isolated ground receptacle be installed and how should the isolated ground system be designed? These questions are design issues and are not answered based on the NEC alone [90.1(A)]. In most cases, using isolated ground receptacles is a waste of money. For example, IEEE 1100, *Powering and Grounding Electronic Equipment (Emerald Book)* states, "The results from the use of the isolated ground method range from no observable effects, the desired effects, or worse noise conditions than when standard equipment bonding configurations are used to serve electronic load equipment [8.5.3.2]."

▸ In reality, few electrical installations truly require an isolated ground system. For those systems that can benefit from one, engineering opinions differ as to what is a proper design. Making matters worse—of those properly designed, few are correctly installed and even fewer are properly maintained.

250.148 Continuity and Attachment of Equipment Grounding Conductors in Boxes

Equipment grounding conductors associated with circuit conductors that are spliced or terminated on equipment within a box must be connected in, or to, the box in accordance with 250.8 and 250.148(A) through (D).

Ex: The circuit equipment grounding conductor for an isolated ground receptacle [250.146(D)] is not required to be connected to the other equipment grounding conductors or to the metal box. ▸Figure 250–256

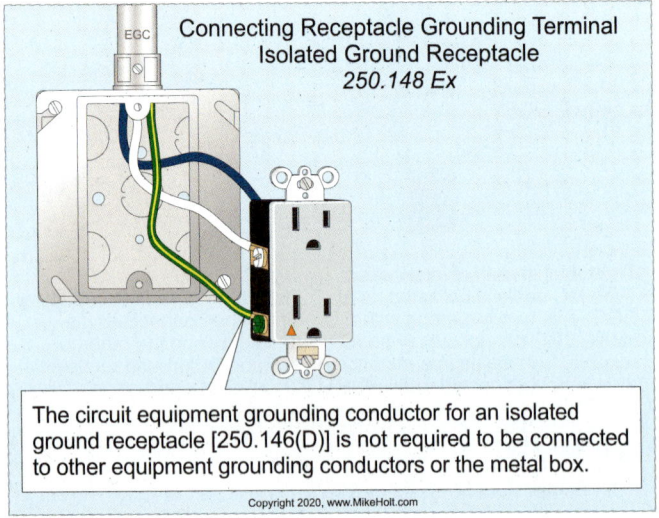

▸Figure 250–256

(A) Connections and Splices. Equipment grounding conductors must be connected and spliced with a device identified for the purpose in accordance with 110.14(B). ▸Figure 250–257

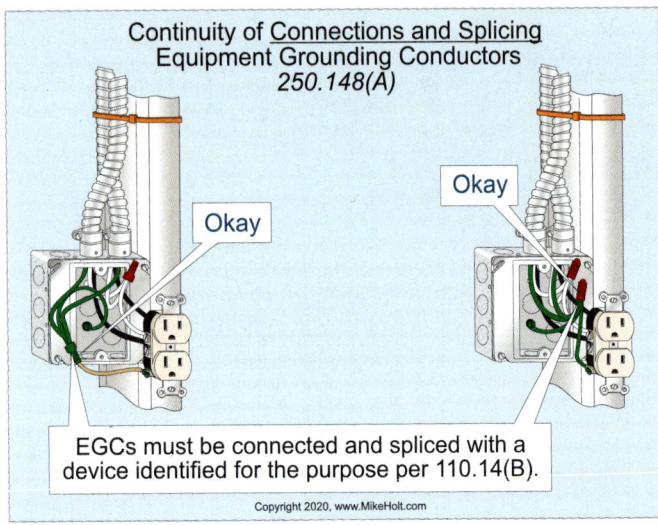

▸Figure 250–257

(B) Continuity of Equipment Grounding Conductors. Equipment grounding conductors must terminate in such a manner that the disconnection or removal of a receptacle, luminaire, or other device will not interrupt the electrical continuity of the equipment grounding conductor(s) providing an effective ground-fault current path. ▸Figure 250–258

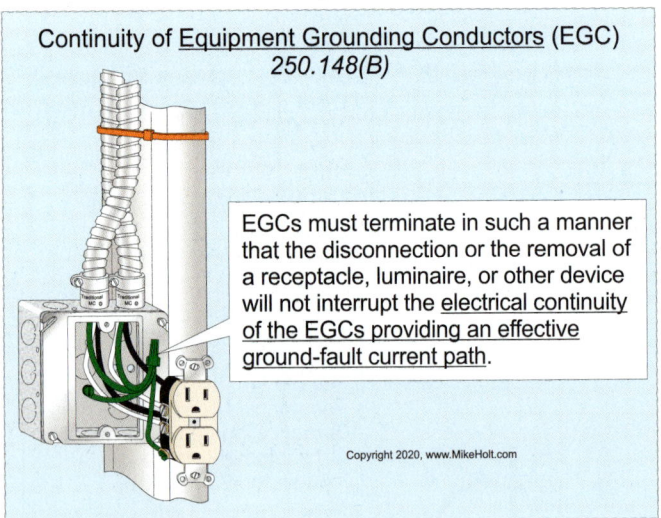

▸Figure 250–258

(C) Metal Boxes. Equipment grounding conductors for circuit conductors that are spliced or terminated on equipment within a metal box must be spliced together [250.148] and have a connection to the metal box in accordance with 250.8. ▸Figure 250–259

Grounding and Bonding | 250.148

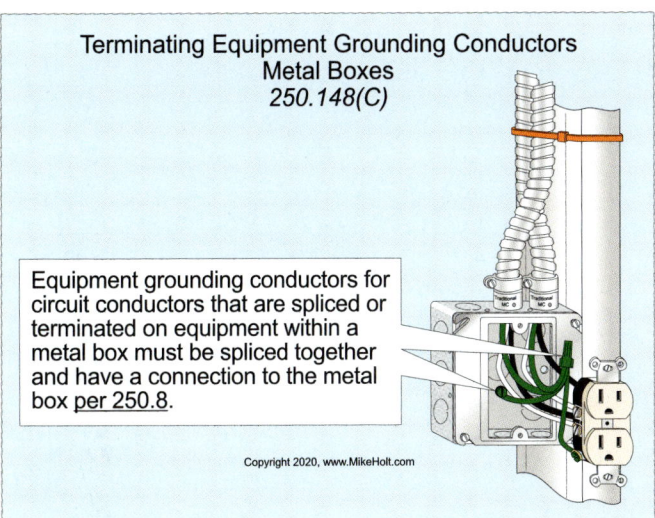
▶Figure 250-259

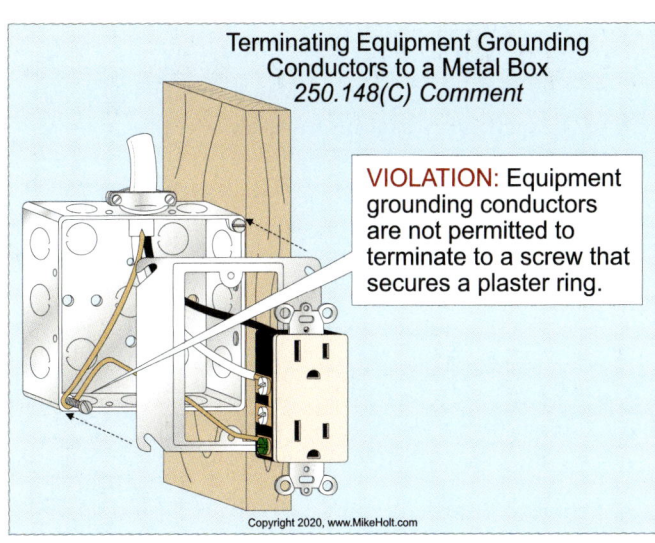
▶Figure 250-260

Author's Comment:

▸ Equipment grounding conductors are not permitted to terminate to a screw that secures a plaster ring. ▶Figure 250-260

(D) Nonmetallic Boxes. Equipment grounding conductors in a nonmetallic outlet box must be arranged such that a connection can be made to any fitting or device in that box requiring connection to an equipment grounding conductor.

Notes

CHAPTER 2

PRACTICE QUESTIONS

Please use the 2020 *Code* book to answer the following questions.

CHAPTER 2—WIRING AND PROTECTION

Article 250—Grounding and Bonding

Part I. General

1. Grounded electrical systems shall be connected to earth in a manner that will _____.

    (a) limit voltages due to lightning, line surges, or unintentional contact with higher-voltage lines
    (b) stabilize the voltage-to-ground during normal operation
    (c) facilitate overcurrent device operation in case of ground faults
    (d) limit voltages due to lightning, line surges, or unintentional contact with higher-voltage lines and stabilize the voltage-to-ground during normal operation

2. For grounded systems, normally noncurrent-carrying conductive materials enclosing electrical conductors or equipment shall be connected to earth so as to limit the voltage-to-ground on these materials.

    (a) True
    (b) False

3. In grounded systems, normally noncurrent-carrying electrically conductive materials that are likely to become energized shall be connected _____ in a manner that establishes an effective ground-fault current path.

    (a) together
    (b) to the electrical supply source
    (c) to the closest grounded conductor
    (d) together and to the electrical supply source

4. For grounded systems, electrical equipment and other electrically conductive material likely to become energized shall be installed in a manner that creates a _____ from any point on the wiring system where a ground fault may occur to the electrical supply source.

    (a) circuit facilitating the operation of the overcurrent device
    (b) low-impedance circuit
    (c) circuit capable of safely carrying the ground-fault current likely to be imposed on it
    (d) all of these

5. For ungrounded systems, noncurrent-carrying conductive materials enclosing electrical conductors or equipment, or forming part of such equipment, shall be connected together and to the supply system grounded equipment in a manner that creates a low-impedance path for ground-fault current that is capable of carrying _____.

    (a) the maximum branch-circuit current
    (b) at least twice the maximum ground-fault current
    (c) the maximum fault current likely to be imposed on it
    (d) the equivalent of the main service rating

6. Electrically conductive materials that are likely to _____ in ungrounded systems shall be connected together and to the supply system grounded equipment in a manner that creates a low-impedance path for ground-fault current that is capable of carrying the maximum fault current likely to be imposed on it.

    (a) become energized
    (b) require service
    (c) be removed
    (d) be coated with paint or nonconductive materials

Chapter 2 | Practice Questions

7. The grounding of electrical systems, circuit conductors, surge arresters, surge-protective devices, and conductive normally noncurrent-carrying metal parts of equipment shall be installed and arranged in a manner that will prevent objectionable current.

    (a) True
    (b) False

8. Equipment grounding conductors, grounding electrode conductors, and bonding jumpers shall be connected by _____.

    (a) listed pressure connectors
    (b) terminal bars
    (c) exothermic welding
    (d) any of these

9. Ground clamps and fittings that are exposed to physical damage shall be enclosed in _____ or equivalent protective covering.

    (a) metal or wood
    (b) wood or rubber
    (c) concrete
    (d) metal or plastic

10. _____ on equipment to be grounded shall be removed from contact surfaces to ensure good electrical continuity.

    (a) Paint
    (b) Lacquer
    (c) Enamel
    (d) any of these

Part II. System Grounding

11. Ungrounded alternating-current systems from 50V to 1,000V or less that are not required to be grounded in accordance with 250.20(b) shall have _____.

    (a) ground detectors installed for ac systems operating at not less than 120V and at 1,000V or less
    (b) the ground detection sensing equipment connected as close as practicable to where the system receives its supply
    (c) ground detectors installed for ac systems operating at not less than 120V and at 1,000V or less and the ground detection sensing equipment connected as close as practicable to where the system receives its supply
    (d) ground-fault protection for equipment

12. Ungrounded alternating-current systems from 50V to less than 1,000V shall be legibly marked "Caution: Ungrounded System—Operating _____ Volts Between Conductors" at _____ of the system, with sufficient durability to withstand the environment involved.

    (a) the source
    (b) the first disconnecting means
    (c) every junction box
    (d) the source or the first disconnecting means

13. Where an alternating-current system operating at 1,000V or less is grounded at any point, the _____ conductor(s) shall be routed with the ungrounded conductors to each service disconnecting means and shall be connected to each disconnecting means grounded conductor(s) terminal or bus.

    (a) ungrounded
    (b) grounded
    (c) grounding
    (d) paralleled

14. The grounded conductor brought to service equipment shall be routed with the phase conductors and shall not be smaller than specified in Table _____ when the service-entrance conductors are 1,100 kcmil copper and smaller.

    (a) 250.102(C)(1)
    (b) 250.122
    (c) 310.16
    (d) 430.52

15. A grounding electrode conductor, sized in accordance with 250.66, shall be used to connect the equipment grounding conductors, the service-equipment enclosures, and, where the system is grounded, the grounded service conductor to the grounding electrode(s).

    (a) True
    (b) False

16. A main bonding jumper shall be a _____ or similar suitable conductor.

    (a) wire
    (b) bus
    (c) screw
    (d) any of these

17. Main bonding jumpers and system bonding jumpers shall not be smaller than specified in _____.

    (a) Table 250.102(C)(1)
    (b) Table 250.122
    (c) Table 310.16
    (d) Chapter 9, Table 8

18. Where the supply conductors are larger than 1,100 kcmil copper or 1,750 kcmil aluminum, the main bonding jumper shall have an area that is _____ the area of the largest phase conductor when of the same material.

    (a) at least equal to
    (b) at least 50 percent of
    (c) not less than 12½ percent of
    (d) not more than 12½ percent of

19. A grounded conductor shall not be connected to normally noncurrent-carrying metal parts of equipment on the _____ side of the system bonding jumper of a separately derived system except as otherwise permitted in Article 250.

    (a) supply
    (b) grounded
    (c) high-voltage
    (d) load

20. An unspliced _____ that is sized based on the derived phase conductors shall be used to connect the grounded conductor and the supply-side bonding jumper, or the equipment grounding conductor, or both, at a separately derived system.

    (a) system bonding jumper
    (b) equipment grounding conductor
    (c) grounded conductor
    (d) grounding electrode conductor

21. If a building or structure is supplied by a feeder from an outdoor separately derived system, a system bonding jumper at both the source and the first disconnecting means shall be permitted if doing so does not establish a(an) _____ path for the grounded conductor.

    (a) series
    (b) parallel
    (c) conductive
    (d) effective

22. If the source of a separately derived system and the first disconnecting means are located in separate enclosures, a supply-side bonding jumper of the wire type shall comply with 250.102(C), based on _____.

    (a) the size of the primary conductors
    (b) the size of the secondary overcurrent protection
    (c) the size of the derived ungrounded conductors
    (d) one third the size of the primary grounded conductor

23. For a single separately derived system, the grounding electrode conductor connects the grounded conductor of the derived system to the grounding electrode at the same point on the separately derived system where the _____ is connected.

    (a) metering equipment
    (b) transfer switch
    (c) system bonding jumper
    (d) largest circuit breaker

24. Grounding electrode conductor taps from a separately derived system to a common grounding electrode conductor are permitted when a building or structure has multiple separately derived systems, provided that the taps terminate at the same point as the system bonding jumper.

    (a) True
    (b) False

25. The common grounding electrode conductor installed for multiple separately derived systems shall be permitted to be a _____ pipe that complies with 250.68(C)(1).

    (a) metal gas
    (b) metal water
    (c) PVC water
    (d) any of these

26. The common grounding electrode conductor installed for multiple separately derived systems shall be permitted to be the metal structural frame of the building or structure that complies with 250.68(C)(2) or is connected to the grounding electrode system by a conductor not smaller than _____ or 250 kcmil aluminum.

    (a) 6 AWG copper
    (b) 1/0 AWG copper
    (c) 3/0 AWG copper or 250 kcmil aluminum
    (d) 4/0 AWG aluminum

Chapter 2 | Practice Questions

27. In an area served by a separately derived system, the _____ shall be connected to the grounded conductor of the separately derived system.

    (a) structural steel
    (b) metal piping
    (c) metal building skin
    (d) structural steel and metal piping

28. A grounding electrode shall be required if a building or structure is supplied by a feeder.

    (a) True
    (b) False

29. A grounding electrode at a separate building or structure shall be required where one multiwire branch circuit serves the building or structure.

    (a) True
    (b) False

30. For a separate building or structure supplied by a feeder or branch circuit, the grounded conductor can serve as the ground-fault return path for the building/structure disconnecting means for existing installations made in compliance with previous editions of the *Code* as long as the installation continues to meet the condition(s) that _____.

    (a) there are no continuous metallic paths between buildings and structures
    (b) ground-fault protection of equipment is not installed on the supply side of the feeder
    (c) the neutral conductor is sized no smaller than the larger required by 220.61 or 250.122
    (d) all of these

31. For a separate building or structure supplied by a separately derived system when overcurrent protection is provided where the conductors originate, the supply conductors shall contain _____.

    (a) an equipment grounding conductor
    (b) copper conductors only
    (c) GFI protection for the feeder
    (d) all of these

32. The frame of a portable generator shall not be required to be connected to a(n) _____ if the generator only supplies equipment mounted on the generator, cord-and-plug-connected equipment using receptacles mounted on the generator, or both.

    (a) grounding electrode
    (b) grounded conductor
    (c) ungrounded conductor
    (d) equipment grounding conductor

33. The frame of a vehicle-mounted generator shall not be required to be connected to a(n) _____ if the generator only supplies equipment mounted on the vehicle or cord-and-plug-connected equipment, using receptacles mounted on the vehicle.

    (a) grounding electrode
    (b) grounded conductor
    (c) ungrounded conductor
    (d) equipment grounding conductor

Part III. Grounding Electrode System and Grounding Electrode Conductor

34. Concrete-encased electrodes of _____ shall not be required to be part of the grounding electrode system where the steel reinforcing bars or rods aren't accessible for use without disturbing the concrete.

    (a) hazardous (classified) locations
    (b) health care facilities
    (c) existing buildings or structures
    (d) agricultural buildings with equipotential planes

35. One or more metal in-ground support structure(s) in direct contact with the earth vertically for _____ ft or more, with or without concrete encasement is permitted to be a grounding electrode in accordance with 250.52.

    (a) 4
    (b) 6
    (c) 8
    (d) 10

36. A bare 4 AWG copper conductor installed horizontally near the bottom or vertically, and within that portion of a concrete foundation or footing that is in direct contact with the earth, can be used as a grounding electrode when the conductor is at least _____ ft in length.

    (a) 10
    (b) 15
    (c) 20
    (d) 25

37. An electrode encased by at least 2 in. of concrete, located horizontally near the bottom or vertically and within that portion of a concrete foundation or footing that is in direct contact with the earth, shall be permitted as a grounding electrode when it consists of _____.

    (a) bare copper conductor not smaller than 8 AWG
    (b) bare copper conductor not smaller than 6 AWG
    (c) bare copper conductor not smaller than 4 AWG
    (d) bare copper conductor not smaller than 1/0 AWG

38. Reinforcing bars for use as a concrete-encased electrode can be bonded together by the usual steel tie wires or other effective means.

    (a) True
    (b) False

39. A ground ring encircling the building or structure can be used as a grounding electrode when the _____.

    (a) ring is in direct contact with the earth
    (b) ring consists of at least 20 ft of bare copper conductor
    (c) bare copper conductor is not smaller than 2 AWG
    (d) all of these

40. Grounding electrodes of the rod type less than _____ in. in diameter shall be listed.

    (a) ½
    (b) ⅝
    (c) ¾
    (d) 1

41. Grounding electrodes of bare or electrically conductive coated iron or steel plates shall be at least _____ in. thick.

    (a) ⅛
    (b) ¼
    (c) ½
    (d) ¾

42. Local metal underground systems or structures such as underground tanks are permitted to serve as grounding electrodes.

    (a) True
    (b) False

43. Swimming pool structures and structural _____ [680.26(B)(1) and (B)(2)] shall not be used as a grounding electrode.

    (a) reinforcing steel
    (b) equipotential planes
    (c) pool shells
    (d) pool pump houses

44. Where the resistance-to-ground of 25 ohms or less is not achieved for a single rod electrode, _____.

    (a) other means besides electrodes shall be used in order to provide grounding
    (b) the single rod electrode shall be supplemented by one additional electrode
    (c) additional electrodes must be added until 25 ohms is achieved
    (d) any of these

45. Two or more grounding electrodes bonded together are considered a single grounding electrode system.

    (a) True
    (b) False

46. Where a metal underground water pipe is used as a grounding electrode, the continuity of the grounding path or the bonding connection to interior piping shall not rely on _____ and similar equipment.

    (a) bonding jumpers
    (b) water meters or filtering devices
    (c) grounding clamps
    (d) all of these

47. When installing auxiliary electrodes, the earth shall not be used as an effective ground-fault current path.

    (a) True
    (b) False

48. Bare aluminum or copper-clad aluminum grounding electrode conductors shall not be used where in direct contact with _____ or where subject to corrosive conditions.

    (a) masonry or the earth
    (b) bare copper conductors
    (c) wooden framing members
    (d) all of these

49. Aluminum or copper-clad aluminum conductors external to buildings or equipment enclosures shall not be terminated within _____ of the earth.

    (a) 12 in.
    (b) 16 in.
    (c) 18 in.
    (d) 24 in.

50. Grounding electrode conductors _____ AWG and larger that are not exposed to physical damage can be run along the surface of the building construction without metal covering or protection.

    (a) 10
    (b) 8
    (c) 6
    (d) 4

51. A(n) _____ AWG or larger copper or aluminum grounding electrode conductor exposed to physical damage shall be protected in rigid metal conduit, IMC, PVC conduit, reinforced thermosetting resin conduit Type XW (RTRC-XW), EMT, or cable armor.

    (a) 10
    (b) 8
    (c) 6
    (d) 4

52. Grounding electrode conductors smaller than _____ AWG shall be protected in rigid metal conduit, IMC, PVC conduit, electrical metallic tubing, or cable armor.

    (a) 10
    (b) 8
    (c) 6
    (d) 4

53. Grounding electrode conductors and grounding electrode bonding jumpers in contact with _____ shall not be required to comply with 300.5 but shall be buried or otherwise protected if subject to physical damage.

    (a) water
    (b) the earth
    (c) metal
    (d) all of these

54. Where a building or structure contains more than one service disconnect in separate enclosures, grounding electrode conductor connections shall be permitted to be _____.

    (a) multiple individual grounding electrode conductors
    (b) one grounding electrode conductor at a common location
    (c) a common grounding electrode conductor and taps
    (d) any of these

55. Ferrous metal raceways and enclosures for grounding electrode conductors shall be electrically continuous from the point of attachment to cabinets or equipment to the grounding electrode.

    (a) True
    (b) False

56. Ferrous metal raceways and enclosures for grounding electrode conductors shall be bonded at each end of the raceway or enclosure to the grounding electrode or grounding electrode conductor to create a(n) _____ parallel path.

    (a) mechanically
    (b) electrically
    (c) physically
    (d) effective

57. A grounding electrode conductor shall be permitted to be run to any convenient grounding electrode available in the grounding electrode system where the other electrode(s), if any, is connected by bonding jumpers that are installed in accordance with 250.53(C).

    (a) True
    (b) False

58. Bonding jumper(s) from grounding electrode(s) shall be permitted to be connected to an aluminum or copper busbar not less than _____ and of sufficient length to accommodate the number of terminations necessary for the installation in accordance with 250.64(F).

    (a) ⅛ in. thick x 1 in. wide
    (b) ⅛ in. thick x 2 in. wide
    (c) ¼ in. thick x 1 in. wide
    (d) ¼ in. thick x 2 in. wide

59. What size copper grounding electrode conductor is required for a service that has three sets of 600 kcmil copper conductors per phase?

    (a) 1 AWG
    (b) 1/0 AWG
    (c) 2/0 AWG
    (d) 3/0 AWG

60. In an ac system, if the size of the grounding electrode conductor or bonding jumper connected to a concrete-encased electrode does not extend on to other types of electrodes that require a larger size of conductor, the grounding electrode conductor shall not be required to be larger than _____ AWG copper.

    (a) 10
    (b) 8
    (c) 6
    (d) 4

61. Mechanical elements used to terminate a grounding electrode conductor to a grounding electrode shall be accessible.

    (a) True
    (b) False

62. When an underground metal water piping system is used as a grounding electrode, bonding shall be provided around insulated joints and around any equipment that is likely to be disconnected for repairs or replacement.

    (a) True
    (b) False

63. Interior metal water piping that is electrically continuous with a metal underground water pipe electrode and is located not more than _____ ft from the point of entrance to the building shall be permitted to extend the connection to an electrode(s).

    (a) 2
    (b) 4
    (c) 5
    (d) 6

64. The metal structural frame of a building shall be permitted to be used as a conductor to interconnect electrodes that are part of the grounding electrode system, or as a grounding electrode conductor. Hold-down bolts securing the structural steel column that are connected to a concrete-encased electrode that complies with 250.52(A)(3) and is located in the support footing or foundation shall be permitted to connect the metal structural frame of a building or structure to the concrete-encased grounding electrode.

    (a) True
    (b) False

65. A rebar-type concrete-encased electrode installed in accordance with 250.52(A)(3) with an additional rebar section extended from its location within the concrete to an accessible location that is not subject to _____ shall be permitted for connection of grounding electrode conductors and bonding jumpers.

    (a) physical damage
    (b) moisture
    (c) corrosion
    (d) any of these

66. A rebar-type concrete-encased electrode installed in accordance with 250.52(A)(3) with an additional rebar section extended from its location within the concrete foundation or footing to an accessible location that is not subject to corrosion is permitted for connection of grounding electrode conductors and bonding jumpers providing _____.

    (a) the rebar is continuous or effectively connected to the grounding electrode rebar
    (b) the rebar extension is not in direct contact with the earth without corrosion protection
    (c) the rebar is not used as a conductor to interconnect the grounding electrode system
    (d) all of these

Chapter 2 | Practice Questions

Part IV. Enclosure, Raceway, and Service Cable Connections

67. Metal enclosures and raceways for other than service conductors shall be connected to the neutral conductor.

    (a) True
    (b) False

Part V. Bonding for Fault Current

68. Bonding shall be provided where necessary to ensure _____ and the capacity to conduct safely any fault current likely to be imposed.

    (a) electrical continuity
    (b) fiduciary responsibility
    (c) listing requirements are met
    (d) sufficient electrical demand

69. Service metal raceways and metal-clad cables are considered effectively bonded when using threadless couplings and connectors that are _____.

    (a) nonmetallic
    (b) made up tight
    (c) sealed
    (d) classified

70. A means external to enclosures for connecting intersystem _____ conductors shall be provided at the service equipment or metering equipment enclosure and disconnecting means of buildings or structures supplied by a feeder.

    (a) bonding
    (b) ungrounded
    (c) secondary
    (d) bonding and ungrounded

71. The intersystem bonding termination shall _____.

    (a) be accessible for connection and inspection
    (b) consist of a set of terminals with the capacity for connection of not less than three intersystem bonding conductors
    (c) not interfere with opening the enclosure for a service, building/structure disconnecting means, or metering equipment
    (d) all of these

72. The intersystem bonding termination shall _____.

    (a) be securely mounted and electrically connected to service equipment, the meter enclosure, or exposed nonflexible metallic service raceway, or be mounted at one of these enclosures and be connected to the enclosure or grounding electrode conductor with a minimum 6 AWG copper conductor
    (b) be securely mounted to the building/structure disconnecting means, or be mounted at the disconnecting means and be connected to the metallic enclosure or grounding electrode conductor with a minimum 6 AWG copper conductor
    (c) have terminals that are listed as grounding and bonding equipment
    (d) all of these

73. Supply-side bonding jumpers shall be no smaller than the sizes specified in _____.

    (a) Table 250.102(C)(1)
    (b) Table 250.122
    (c) Table 310.16
    (d) Table 250.66

74. Where ungrounded supply conductors are paralleled in two or more raceways or cables, the bonding jumper for each raceway or cable shall be based on the size of the _____ in each raceway or cable.

    (a) overcurrent protection for conductors
    (b) grounded conductors
    (c) ungrounded supply conductors
    (d) sum of all conductors

75. An equipment bonding jumper can be installed on the outside of a raceway, providing the length of the equipment bonding jumper is not more than _____ in. and the equipment bonding jumper is routed with the raceway.

    (a) 12
    (b) 24
    (c) 36
    (d) 72

76. The bonding jumper used to bond the metal water piping system shall be sized in accordance with _____ except as permitted in 250.104(A)(2) and 250.104(A)(3).

    (a) Table 250.102(C)(1)
    (b) Table 250.122
    (c) Table 310.16
    (d) Table 310.15(6)

77. Metal water piping system(s) shall be bonded to the _____, or to one or more grounding electrodes used, if the grounding electrode conductor or bonding jumper to the grounding electrode is of sufficient size.

    (a) grounded conductor at the service
    (b) service equipment enclosure
    (c) grounding electrode conductor if of sufficient size
    (d) any of these

78. Bonding jumper(s) for the bonding of metal water piping systems shall be sized in accordance with Table 250.102(C)(1) and are not be required to be larger than _____ copper or 250 kcmil aluminum or copper-clad aluminum

    (a) 1/0 AWG
    (b) 2/0 AWG
    (c) 3/0 AWG
    (d) 4/0 AWG

79. Where isolated metal water piping systems are installed in a multiple-occupancy building, the water pipes can be bonded with bonding jumpers sized in accordance with 250.104(D).

    (a) True
    (b) False

80. The metal water piping system(s) installed in or attached to a building or structure [250.104(A)(3)] shall be bonded to _____.

    (a) the building or structure disconnecting means enclosure where located at the building or structure
    (b) the equipment grounding conductor run with the supply conductors
    (c) one or more grounding electrodes used
    (d) any of these

81. A building or structure shall have the interior metal water piping system bonded with a bonding jumper sized in accordance with _____.

    (a) Table 250.66
    (b) Table 250.102(D)
    (c) Table 250.122
    (d) Table 310.16

82. Metal piping, including gas piping shall be considered bonded by the equipment grounding conductor for the circuit that is likely to energize the piping system.

    (a) True
    (b) False

83. Exposed structural metal interconnected to form a metal building frame that is not intentionally grounded or bonded and is likely to become energized, shall be bonded to the _____.

    (a) service equipment enclosure or building disconnecting means
    (b) grounded conductor at the service
    (c) grounding electrode conductor where of sufficient size
    (d) any of these

84. Metal water piping systems and structural metal that is interconnected to form a building frame shall be bonded to separately derived systems in accordance with 250.104(D)(1) through 250.104(D)(3).

    (a) True
    (b) False

85. The grounded conductor of each separately derived system shall be bonded to the nearest available point of the metal water piping system(s) in the area served by each separately derived system and each bonding jumper shall be sized in accordance with Table 250.102(C)(1) based on the largest ungrounded conductor of the separately derived system.

    (a) True
    (b) False

86. A separate water piping bonding jumper shall be required if the metal frame of a building or structure is used as the grounding electrode for a separately derived system and is bonded to the metal water piping in the area served by the separately derived system.

    (a) True
    (b) False

Chapter 2 | Practice Questions

87. If exposed structural metal that is interconnected to form the building frame exists in the area served by the separately derived system, it shall be bonded to the grounded conductor of each separately derived system and each bonding jumper shall be sized in accordance with Table 250.102(C)(1) based on the largest ungrounded conductor of the service.

    (a) True
    (b) False

88. Lightning protection system ground terminals _____ bonded to the building or structure grounding electrode system.

    (a) shall be
    (b) shall not be
    (c) shall be permitted to be
    (d) must be effectively

Part VI. Equipment Grounding and Equipment Grounding Conductors

89. Listed FMC can be used as the equipment grounding conductor if the conduit does not exceed trade size _____.

    (a) 1¼
    (b) 1½
    (c) 2
    (d) 2¼

90. Type MC cable provides an effective ground-fault current path and is recognized by the *NEC* as an equipment grounding conductor when _____.

    (a) it contains an insulated or uninsulated equipment grounding conductor in compliance with 250.118(1)
    (b) the cable assembly contains a bare copper conductor
    (c) only when it is hospital grade Type MC cable
    (d) it is terminated with bonding bushings

91. An equipment grounding conductor shall be identified by _____.

    (a) a continuous outer finish that is green
    (b) being bare
    (c) a continuous outer finish that is green with one or more yellow stripes
    (d) any of these

92. An equipment grounding conductor is not permitted to be used as a grounding electrode conductor under any circumstance(s).

    (a) True
    (b) False

93. The structural metal frame of a building may be used as an equipment grounding conductor provided that _____.

    (a) the connection is by exothermic weld
    (b) the connection is by irreversible pressure connector
    (c) the metal frame of a building is not permitted to be used as an equipment grounding conductor
    (d) it is approved by the authority having jurisdiction

94. When a single equipment grounding conductor is used for multiple circuits in the same raceway, cable, or cable tray, the single equipment grounding conductor shall be sized according to the _____.

    (a) combined rating of all the overcurrent devices
    (b) largest overcurrent device protecting the circuit conductors
    (c) combined rating of all the loads
    (d) any of these

95. If conductors are installed in parallel in the same raceway or cable tray, a single wire-type conductor shall be permitted as the equipment grounding conductor and sized in accordance with 250.122, based on the _____.

    (a) feeder
    (b) branch circuit
    (c) overcurrent protective device
    (d) service conductors

96. If multiconductor cables are installed in parallel in the same raceway, auxiliary gutter, or cable tray, _____ equipment grounding conductor(s) that is(are) sized in accordance with 250.122 shall be permitted in combination with the equipment grounding conductors provided within the multiconductor cables and shall all be connected together.

    (a) one
    (b) two
    (c) three
    (d) four

97. Equipment grounding conductors for feeder taps are not required to be larger than the tap conductors.

    (a) True
    (b) False

Part VII. Methods of Equipment Grounding Conductor Connections

98. Electrical equipment secured to and in _____ contact with a metal rack or structure provided for its support shall be permitted to be considered as being connected to an equipment grounding conductor if the metal rack or structure is connected to an equipment grounding conductor by one of the means indicated in 250.134.

    (a) electrical
    (b) direct
    (c) metal to metal
    (d) mechanical

99. Metal parts of cord-and-plug-connected equipment, if grounded, shall be connected to an equipment grounding conductor that terminates to a grounding-type attachment plug.

    (a) True
    (b) False

100. Frames of electric ranges, wall-mounted ovens, counter-mounted cooking units, _____, shall be connected to the equipment grounding conductor.

    (a) washing machines
    (b) dishwashers
    (c) microwaves
    (d) clothes dryers

101. A grounded circuit conductor is permitted to ground noncurrent-carrying metal parts of equipment, raceways, and other enclosures on the supply side or within the enclosure of the ac service disconnecting means.

    (a) True
    (b) False

102. Where the box is mounted on the surface, direct metal-to-metal contact between the device yoke and the box shall be permitted to ground the receptacle to the box if at least _____ of the insulating washers of the receptacle is (are) removed.

    (a) one
    (b) two
    (c) three
    (d) four

103. Receptacle yokes designed and _____ as self-grounding can, in conjunction with the supporting screws, establish the equipment bonding between the device yoke and a flush-type box.

    (a) approved
    (b) advertised
    (c) listed
    (d) installed

104. A connection between equipment grounding conductors and a metal floor box shall be by _____.

    (a) a grounding screw used for no other purpose
    (b) equipment listed for grounding
    (c) a listed grounding device
    (d) any of these

Notes

CHAPTER 3

WIRING METHODS AND MATERIALS

Introduction to Chapter 3—Wiring Methods and Materials

Chapter 3 focuses on wiring methods and materials, and provides some very specific installation requirements for conductors, cables, boxes, raceways, and fittings. It includes detailed information about the installations and restrictions involved with wiring methods.

Not fully understanding the information in this chapter may be the reason many people incorrectly apply its rules. Pay careful attention to each and every detail to be sure your installations comply with these requirements.

Disregarding the rules for the wiring methods found in Chapter 3 can result in problems with power quality and can lead to fire, shock, and overall poor installations.

The type of wiring method you will use depends on several factors; job specifications, *Code* requirements, the environment, need, the type of building construction, and cost effectiveness just to name a few.

This chapter 3 begins with rules common to most wiring methods [Article 300]. It then covers conductors [Article 310], boxes [Article 312], and enclosures [Article 314]. The following articles become more specific and deal more in-depth with individual wiring methods such as specific types of cables [Articles 320 through 340] and various raceways [Articles 342 through 390]. The chapter winds up with Article 392, a support system.

Notice as you read through the various wiring methods that the *Code* attempts to use similar section numbering for similar topics from one article to the next, using the same digits after the decimal point in the section number for the same topic. This makes it easier to locate the specific requirements of a particular article. For example, the rules for securing and supporting can be found in the section that ends with ".30" of each article.

Wiring Method Articles

▸ **Article 300—General Requirements for Wiring Methods and Materials.** Article 300 contains the general requirements for all wiring methods included in the *NEC*, except signaling and communications systems, which are covered in Chapters 7 and 8.

▸ **Article 310—Conductors for General Wiring.** This article contains the general requirements for conductors, such as insulation markings, ampacity ratings, and conductor use. There is also a section that addresses single-family dwelling service and feeder conductors exclusively. Article 310 does not apply to conductors that are part of flexible cords, fixture wires, or conductors that are an integral part of equipment [90.6 and 300.1(B)].

▸ **Article 314—Outlet, Device, Pull, and Junction Boxes; Conduit Bodies; Fittings; and Handhole Enclosures.** Installation requirements for outlet boxes, pull and junction boxes, as well as conduit bodies and handhole enclosures are contained in this article.

Chapter 3 | Wiring Methods and Materials

Cable Articles

Articles 320 through 340 address specific types of cables. If you take the time to become familiar with the various types of cables, you will be able to:

▸ Understand what is available for doing the work.

▸ Recognize cable types that have special *NEC* requirements.

▸ Avoid buying cable you cannot install due to *Code* requirements you cannot meet with that wiring method.

Here is a brief overview of those included in this textbook:

▸ **Article 320—Armored Cable (Type AC).** Armored cable is an assembly of insulated conductors, 14 AWG through 1 AWG, individually wrapped with wax paper. The conductors are contained within a flexible metal (steel or aluminum) spiral sheath that interlocks at the edges. Armored cable looks like flexible metal conduit. Many electricians call this metal cable "BX®."

▸ **Article 330—Metal-Clad Cable (Type MC).** Metal-clad cable encloses insulated conductors in a metal sheath of either corrugated or smooth copper or aluminum tubing, or spiral interlocked steel or aluminum. The physical characteristics of Type MC cable make it a versatile wiring method permitted in almost any location and for almost any application. The most commonly used Type MC cable is the interlocking kind, which looks similar to armored cable or flexible metal conduit.

▸ **Article 334—Nonmetallic-Sheathed Cable (Type NM).** Nonmetallic-sheathed cable is commonly referred to by its trade name "Romex®." It encloses two, three, or four insulated conductors, 14 AWG through 2 AWG, within a nonmetallic outer jacket. Because this cable is manufactured in this manner, it contains a separate (usually bare) equipment grounding conductor. Nonmetallic-sheathed cable is most commonly used for residential wiring applications but may sometimes be permitted for use in commercial occupancies.

Raceway Articles

Articles 342 through 390 address specific types of raceways; refer to Article 100 for the definition of a raceway. If you take the time to become familiar with the various types of raceways, you will be able to:

▸ Understand what is available for doing the work.

▸ Recognize raceway types that have special *Code* requirements.

Here is a brief overview of each those included in this textbook:

▸ **Article 348—Flexible Metal Conduit (Type FMC).** Flexible metal conduit is a raceway of circular cross section made of a helically wound, interlocked metal strip of either steel or aluminum. It is commonly called "Greenfield" (after its inventor) or "Flex."

▸ **Article 350—Liquidtight Flexible Metal Conduit (Type LFMC).** Liquidtight flexible metal conduit is a raceway of circular cross section with an outer liquidtight, nonmetallic, sunlight-resistant jacket over an inner flexible metal core, with associated couplings, connectors, and fittings. It is listed for the installation of electrical conductors. Liquidtight flexible metal conduit is commonly called "Sealtite®" or simply "liquidtight." Liquidtight flexible metal conduit is similar in construction to flexible metal conduit, but it has an outer thermoplastic covering.

▸ **Article 352—Rigid Polyvinyl Chloride Conduit (Type PVC).** Rigid polyvinyl chloride conduit is a nonmetallic raceway of circular cross section with integral or associated couplings, connectors, and fittings. It is listed for the installation of electrical conductors.

▸ **Article 356—Liquidtight Flexible Nonmetallic Conduit (Type LFNC).** Liquidtight flexible nonmetallic conduit (most commonly referred to as "Carflex®") is a raceway of circular cross section with an outer liquidtight, nonmetallic, sunlight-resistant jacket over an inner flexible core with associated couplings, connectors, and fittings.

- **Article 358—Electrical Metallic Tubing (EMT).** Electrical metallic tubing is a nonthreaded thinwall raceway of circular cross section designed for the physical protection and routing of conductors and cables. Compared to rigid metal conduit and intermediate metal conduit, electrical metallic tubing is relatively easy to bend, cut, and ream. EMT is not threaded, so all connectors and couplings are of the threadless type. It is available in a range of colors, such as red and blue.

- **Article 362—Electrical Nonmetallic Tubing (ENT).** Electrical nonmetallic tubing is a pliable, corrugated, circular raceway made of PVC. ENT resembles flexible tubing and is often referred to as "Smurf Pipe" or "Smurf Tube," because it was only available in blue when it first came out and the nickname is a reference to the children's cartoon characters "The Smurfs." It is now available in additional colors such as red and yellow.

- **Article 386—Surface Metal Raceways.** A surface metal raceway is a metal raceway intended to be mounted to the surface of a structure, with associated accessories, in which conductors are placed after the raceway has been installed as a complete system.

Cable Tray

- **Article 392—Cable Trays.** A cable tray system is a unit or assembly of units or sections with associated fittings that form a structural system used to securely fasten or support cables and raceways. A cable tray is not a raceway; it is a support system for raceways, cables, and enclosures.

Notes

ARTICLE 300 — GENERAL REQUIREMENTS FOR WIRING METHODS AND MATERIALS

Introduction to Article 300—General Requirements for Wiring Methods and Materials

Article 300 contains the general requirements for all wiring methods included in the *NEC*. However, it does not apply to twisted-pair cable and coaxial cable (which are covered in Chapters 7 and 8), unless Article 300 is specifically referenced.

This article is primarily concerned with how to install, route, splice, protect, and secure conductors and raceways. How well you understand and apply the requirements of Article 300 will usually be evident in the finished work. Many of its requirements will affect the appearance, longevity, and even the safety of the installation. Imagine your surprise if you are shoveling some soil onto a plant in the garden and your shovel hits an electrical service cable! After studying and learning the rules in this article, you will immediately realize that the burial depth requirements of 300.5 were possibly overlooked or ignored. Even worse, they might not even have been known at the time of installation.

A good understanding of this article will start you on the path to correctly and safely installing the wiring methods included in Chapter 3. Be sure to carefully consider the accompanying illustrations and refer to the definitions in Article 100 as needed.

300.1 Scope

(A) All Wiring Installations. Article 300 contains the general requirements for wiring methods and materials for power and lighting. ▶Figure 300–1

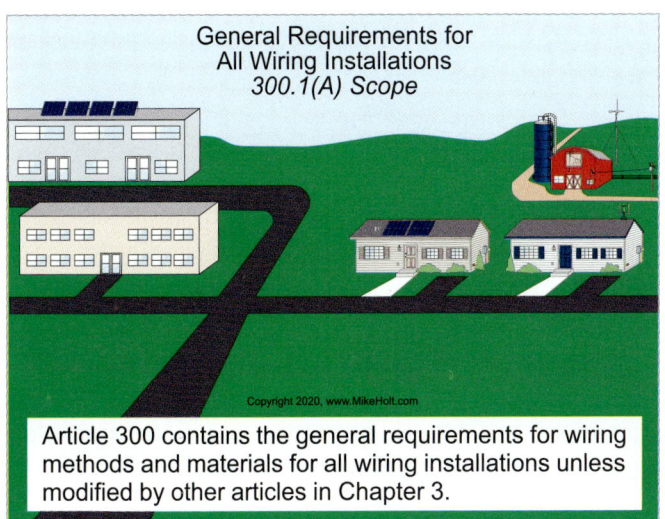

▶Figure 300–1

Author's Comment:

▸ The requirements contained in Article 300 do not apply to the wiring methods for Class 2 and 3 circuits, fire alarm circuits, and communications systems (twisted-pair conductors and coaxial cable). However, the chapters that contain the rules for such wiring methods (Chapters 7 and 8) may refer to Article 300 and those specific references will then apply.

(B) Integral Parts of Equipment. The requirements contained in Article 300 do not apply to the integral parts of electrical equipment. ▶Figure 300–2

Author's Comment:

▸ Integral wiring of equipment is covered by various product standards and not the *NEC*. It is the intent of this *Code* that factory-installed internal wiring of equipment processed by a qualified testing laboratory does not need to be inspected [90.7].

(C) Trade Sizes. Designators for raceway trade sizes are given in Table 300.1(C).

300.3 | General Requirements for Wiring Methods and Materials

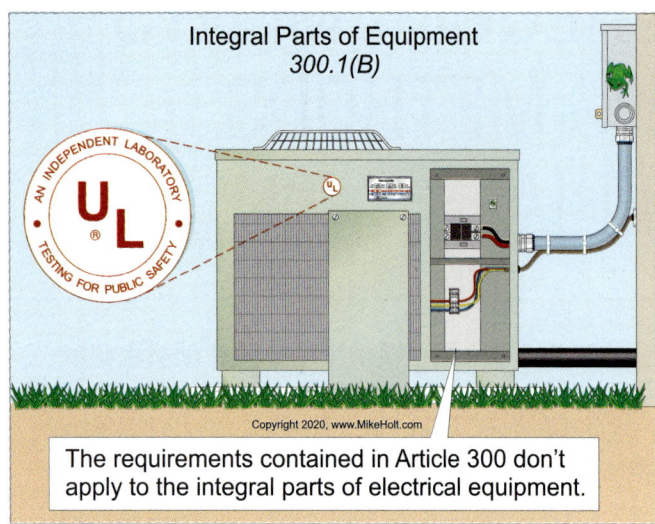

▶Figure 300–2

Author's Comment:

▸ Industry practice is to describe raceways using inch sizes, such as ½ in., 2 in., and so on; however, the proper reference is to use "Trade Size ½," or "Trade Size 2." In this textbook we use the proper reference and identify raceway sizes using the phrase "Trade Size."

300.3 Conductors

(A) Single Conductors. Conductors must be installed in a Chapter 3 wiring method such as in a raceway, cable, or enclosure. ▶Figure 300–3

▶Figure 300–3

(B) Circuit Conductors Grouped Together. All conductors of a circuit, including the neutral and equipment grounding conductors, must be installed together in the same raceway, cable, trench, cord, or cable tray; except as permitted by (1) through (4).

Author's Comment:

▸ Keeping all circuit conductors together helps minimize induction since the individual electromagnetic fields will cancel each other out and help maintain the low-impedance ground-fault current path. See 300.5(I). ▶Figure 300–4

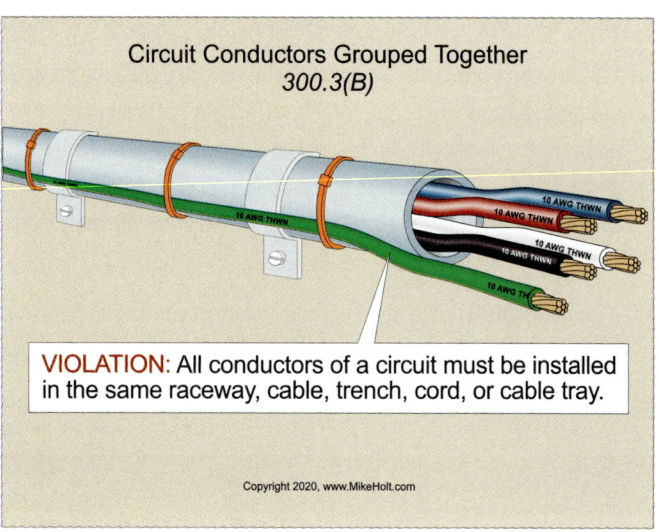

▶Figure 300–4

(1) Paralleled Installations. Conductors installed in parallel in accordance with 310.10(G) must have all circuit conductor sets grouped together within the same raceway, cable tray, trench, or cable. ▶Figure 300–5

Author's Comment:

▸ Grouping in sets when paralleling circuits helps minimize the inductive heating of ferrous metal raceways and enclosures for alternating-current circuits. See 250.102(E), 300.3(B), 300.5(I), 300.20(A), 376.20, 378.20, and 392.8(D) for similar requirements. ▶Figure 300–6

Connections, taps, or extensions made from paralleled conductors must connect to all conductors of the paralleled set.

General Requirements for Wiring Methods and Materials | 300.3

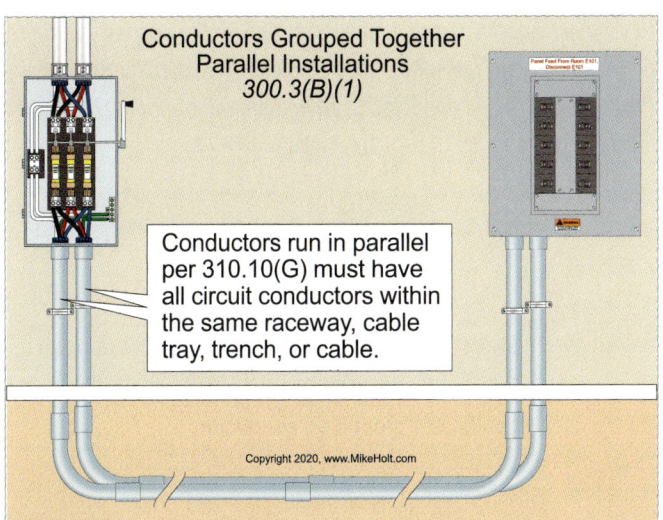

▶Figure 300–5

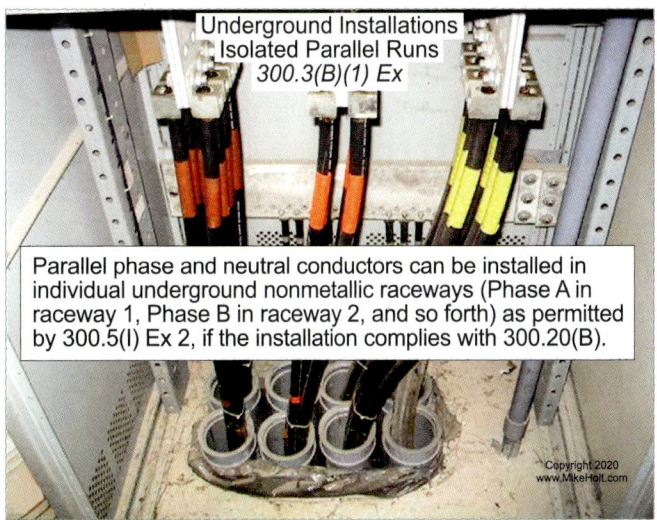

▶Figure 300–7

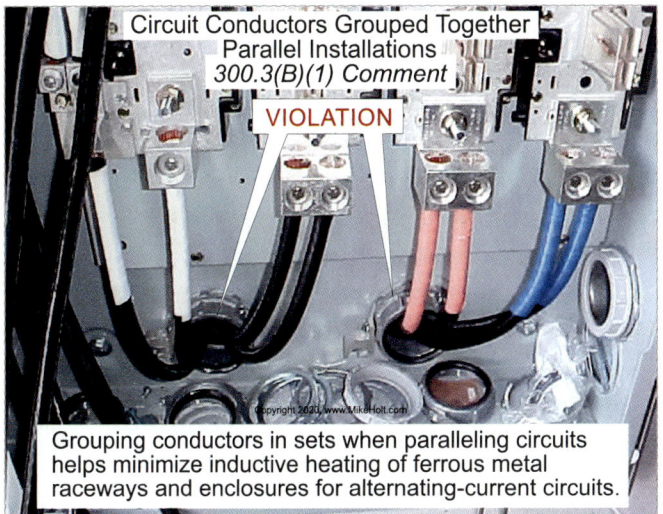

▶Figure 300–6

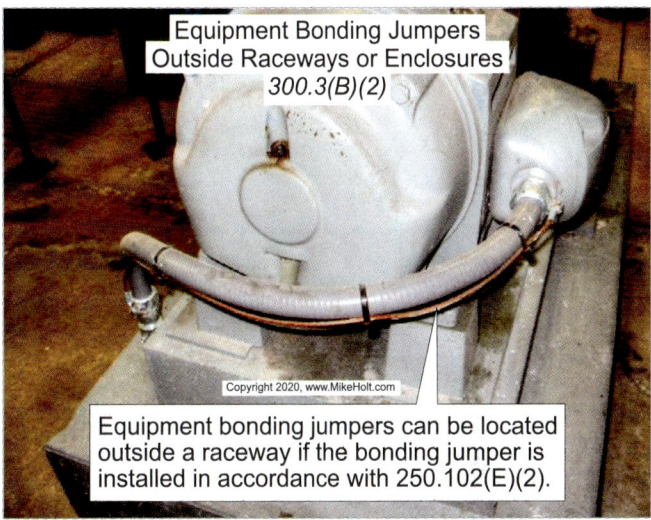

▶Figure 300–8

Ex: Parallel phase and neutral conductors can be installed in individual underground nonmetallic raceways (Phase A in raceway 1, Phase B in raceway 2, and so forth) as permitted by 300.5(I) Ex 2 if the installation complies with 300.20(B). ▶Figure 300–7

(2) Outside a Raceway or an Enclosure. Equipment bonding jumpers can be located outside of a raceway if the bonding jumper is installed in accordance with 250.102(E)(2). ▶Figure 300–8

For direct-current circuits, the equipment grounding conductor can be run separately from the circuit conductors in accordance with 250.134(B) Ex 2. ▶Figure 300–9

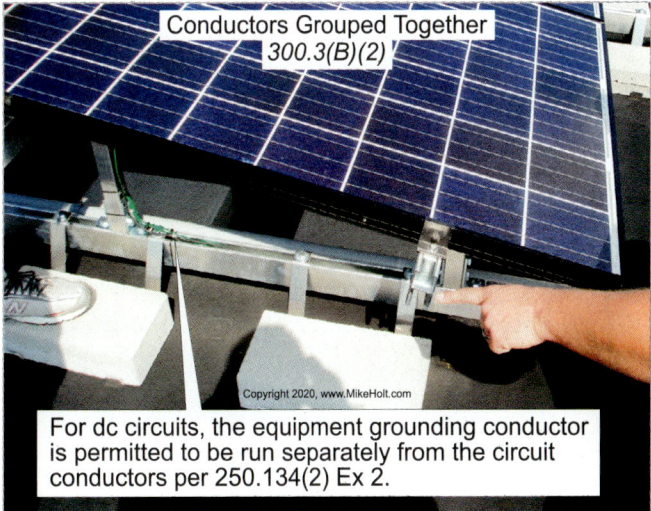

▶Figure 300–9

300.10 | General Requirements for Wiring Methods and Materials

300.10 Electrical Continuity

Metal raceways, cable armor, and other metal enclosures must be metallically joined into a continuous electrical conductor to provide effective electrical continuity [110.10 and 250.4(A)]. ▶Figure 300–10

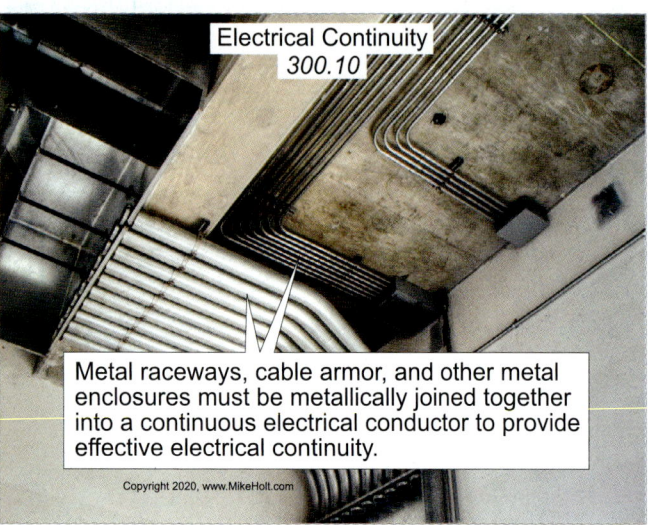

▶Figure 300–10

Author's Comment:

▸ The purpose of effective electrical continuity is to establish the effective ground-fault current path necessary to facilitate the operation of the circuit overcurrent protective device in the event of a ground fault [250.4(A)(3)]. ▶Figure 300–11

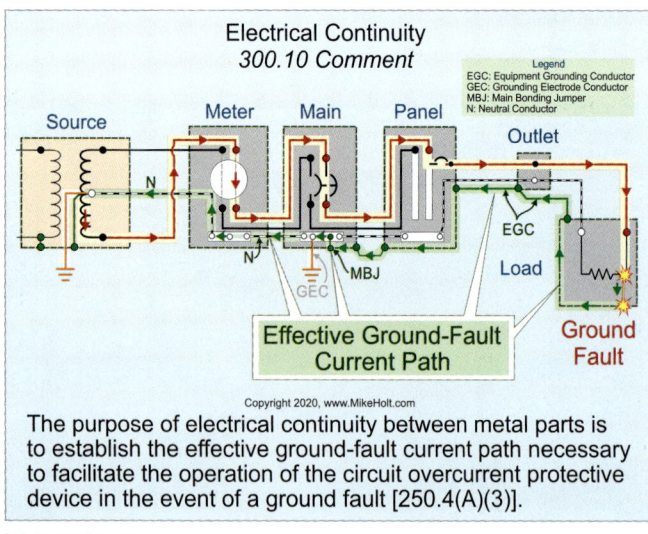

▶Figure 300–11

Ex 1: Short lengths of metal raceways used for the support or protection of cables are not required to be electrically continuous, nor are they required to be connected to an equipment grounding conductor [250.86 Ex 2 and 300.12 Ex 1]. ▶Figure 300–12

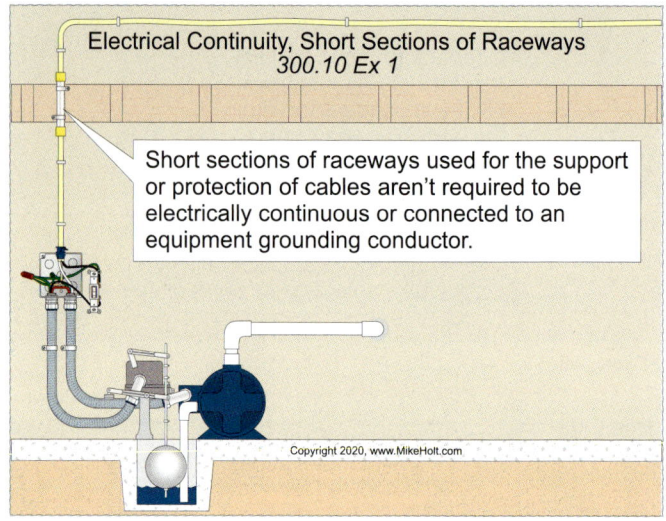

▶Figure 300–12

300.20 Induced Alternating Currents in Ferrous Metal Parts

(A) Conductors Grouped Together. To minimize the induction heating of ferrous metal raceways and enclosures, and to maintain an effective ground-fault current path, all conductors of a circuit (including any neutral and equipment grounding conductors) must be installed in the same raceway, cable, trench, cord, or cable tray. See 250.102(E), 300.3(B), 300.5(I), and 392.8(D). ▶Figure 300–13 and ▶Figure 300–14

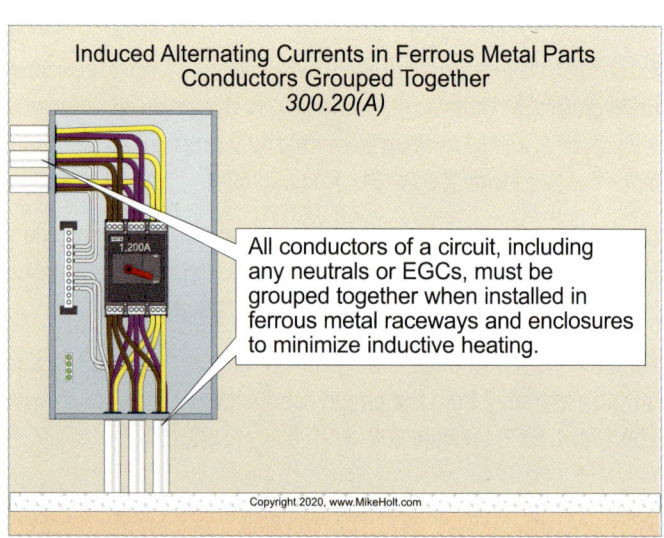

▶Figure 300–13

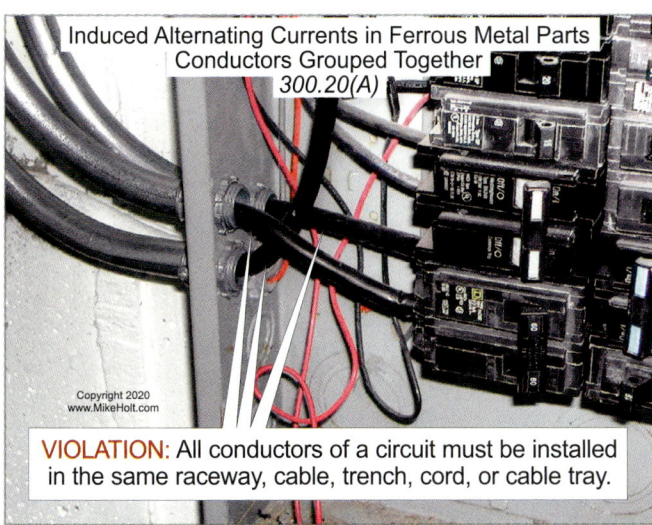

▶Figure 300-14

Notes

ARTICLE 314

OUTLET, DEVICE, PULL, AND JUNCTION BOXES; CONDUIT BODIES; AND HANDHOLE ENCLOSURES

Introduction to Article 314—Outlet, Device, Pull, and Junction Boxes; Conduit Bodies; and Handhole Enclosures

Article 314 contains the installation requirements for outlet boxes, pull and junction boxes, conduit bodies, and handhole enclosures.

Article 314 will help you understand these rules so your installation will be compliant with the *NEC*. As always, the illustrations will help you visualize the finished installation.

314.1 Scope

Article 314 contains the installation requirements for outlet boxes, pull and junction boxes, conduit bodies, and handhole enclosures. ▶Figure 314-1

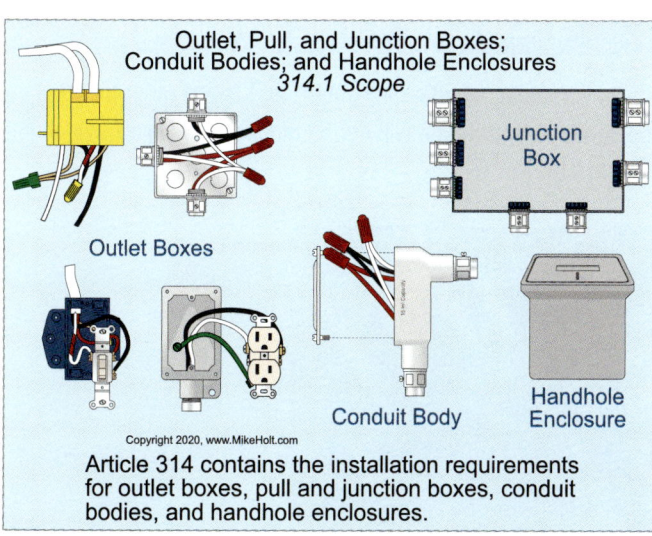

▶Figure 314-1

314.3 Nonmetallic Boxes

Nonmetallic boxes can only be used with nonmetallic cables and raceways.

Ex 1: Metal raceways and cables can be used with nonmetallic boxes if the raceways and cables are bonded together in the nonmetallic box. ▶Figure 314-2

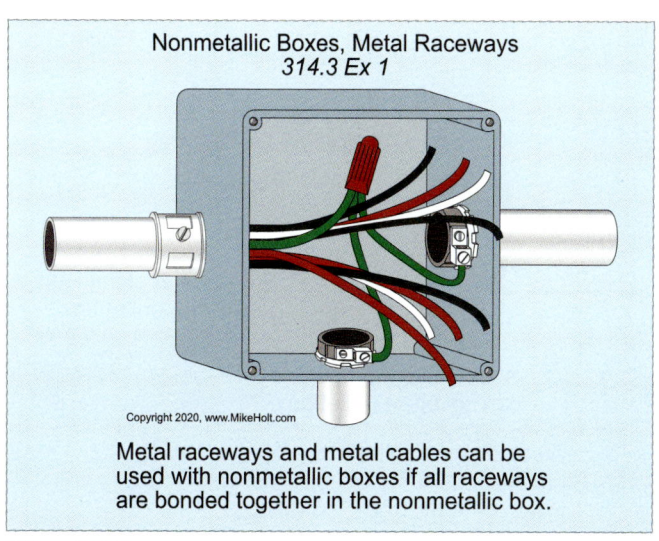

▶Figure 314-2

314.4 Metal Boxes

Metal boxes must be connected to an equipment grounding conductor in accordance with 250.148. ▶Figure 314-3

Mike Holt Enterprises • www.MikeHolt.com • 888.NEC.CODE (632.2633) | 203

314.25 | Outlet, Device, Pull, and Junction Boxes; Conduit Bodies; and Handhole Enclosures

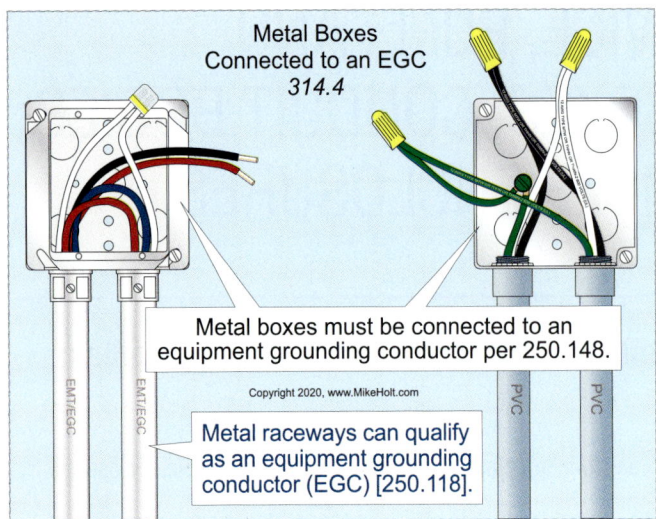

▶Figure 314-3

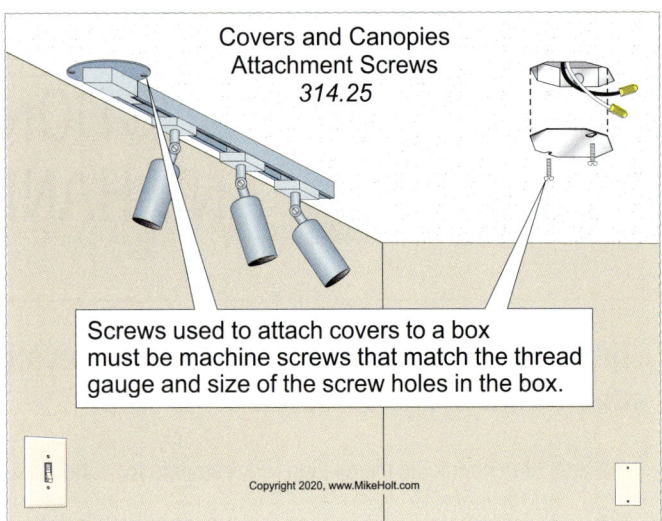

▶Figure 314-5

Part II. Installation

314.25 Covers and Canopies

When the installation is complete, each outlet box must be provided with a cover, faceplate, fixture canopy, or similar device. ▶Figure 314-4

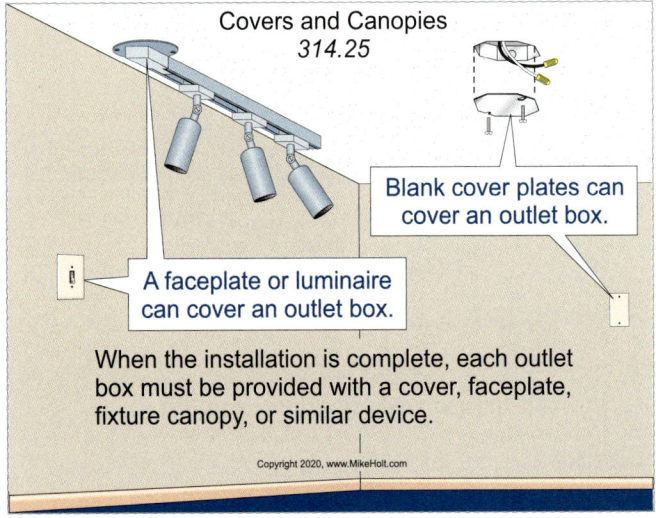

▶Figure 314-4

Screws used for attaching covers to the box must be machine screws that match the thread gage and size of the screw holes in the box. ▶Figure 314-5

(A) Metal Covers. Metal covers are only permitted if they can be connected to the circuit equipment grounding conductor [250.109].

Author's Comment:

▶ Metal switch cover plates are connected to the circuit equipment grounding conductor in accordance with 404.9(B) and metal receptacle cover plates are connected to the circuit equipment grounding conductor in accordance with 406.6(B).

314.28 Sizing Pull and Junction Boxes

Boxes containing conductors 4 AWG and larger must be sized so the conductor insulation will not be damaged. ▶Figure 314-6 and ▶Figure 314-7

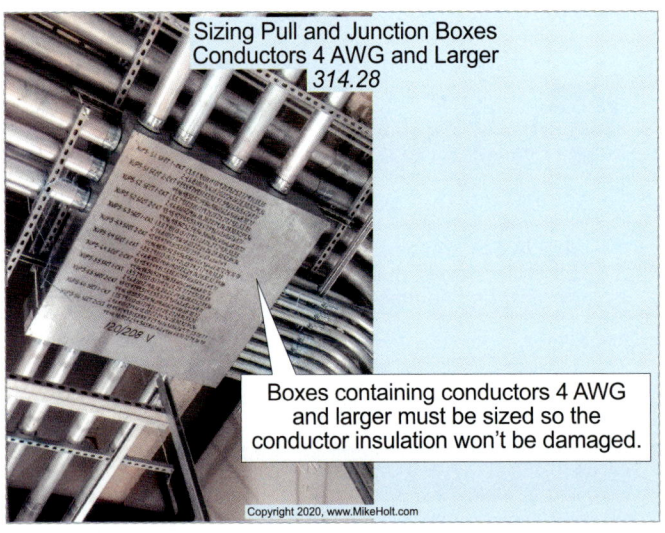

▶Figure 314-6

Outlet, Device, Pull, and Junction Boxes; Conduit Bodies; and Handhole Enclosures | 314.30

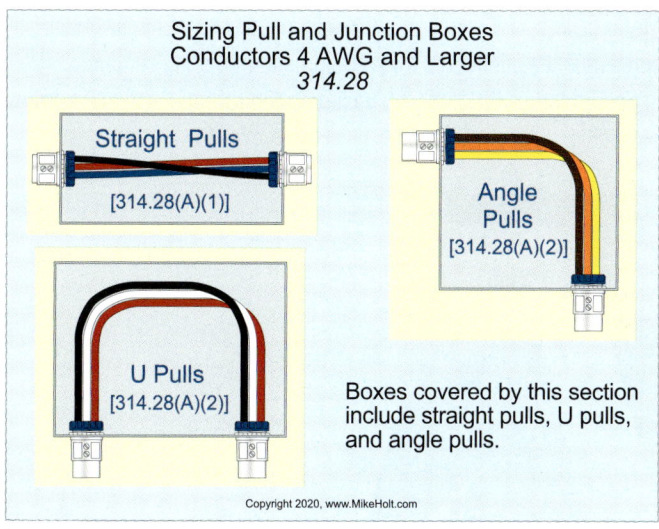

▶Figure 314–7

Author's Comment:

▸ The requirements for sizing boxes containing conductors 6 AWG and smaller are contained in 314.16.

▸ If conductors 4 AWG and larger enter a box or other enclosure, a fitting that provides a smooth, rounded, insulating surface (such as a bushing or adapter) is required to protect them from abrasion during and after installation [300.4(G)].

(C) Covers. Metal covers must be connected to an equipment grounding conductor of a type recognized in 250.118, in accordance with 250.110 [250.4(A)(3)]. ▶Figure 314–8

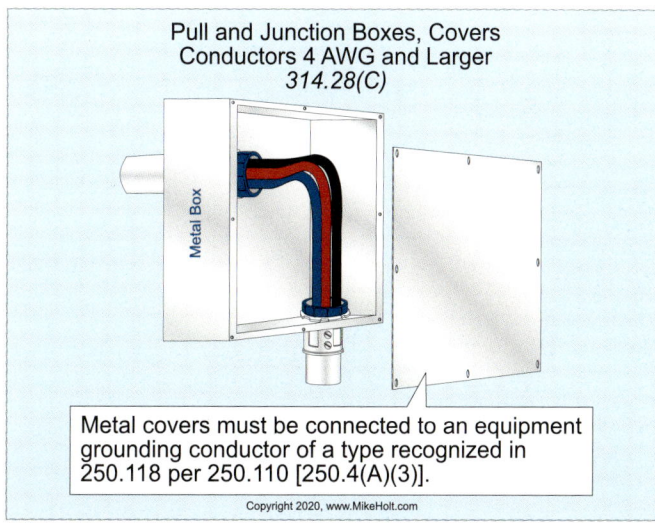

▶Figure 314–8

314.30 Handhole Enclosures

Handhole enclosures must be identified for underground use and be designed and installed to withstand all loads likely to be imposed on them. ▶Figure 314–9

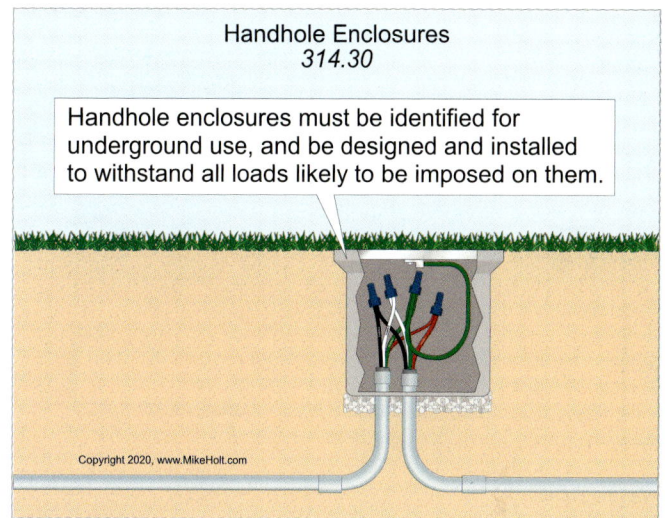

▶Figure 314–9

(B) Wiring Entries. Underground raceways and cables entering a handhole are not required to be mechanically connected to the handhole. ▶Figure 314–10

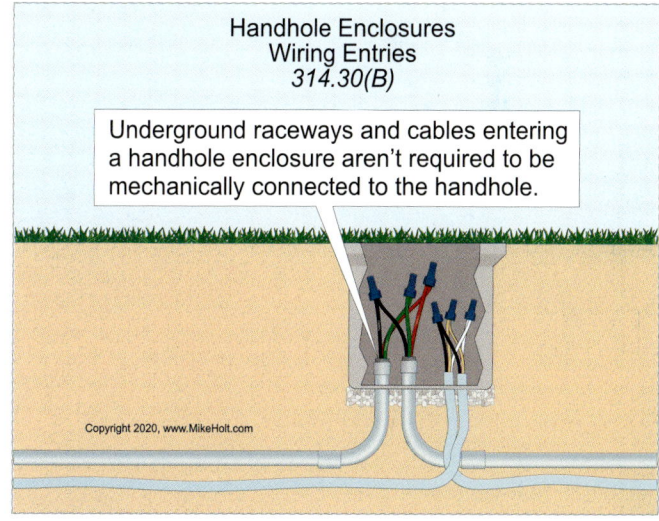

▶Figure 314–10

(C) Enclosure Wiring. Splices or terminations within a handhole must be listed for wet locations [110.14(B)].

314.30 | Outlet, Device, Pull, and Junction Boxes; Conduit Bodies; and Handhole Enclosures

(D) Covers. Handhole covers must have an identifying mark or logo that prominently identifies the function of the handhole, such as "electric." Handhole covers must require the use of tools to open, or they must weigh over 100 lb. ▶Figure 314–11

Metal covers and exposed conductive surfaces of handhole enclosures must be connected to an equipment grounding conductor sized in accordance with 250.122, based on the rating of the overcurrent protective device [250.102(D)]. ▶Figure 314–12

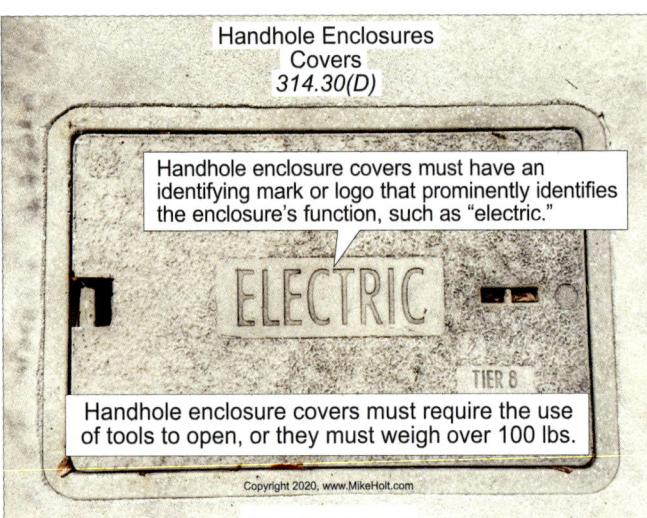
▶Figure 314–11

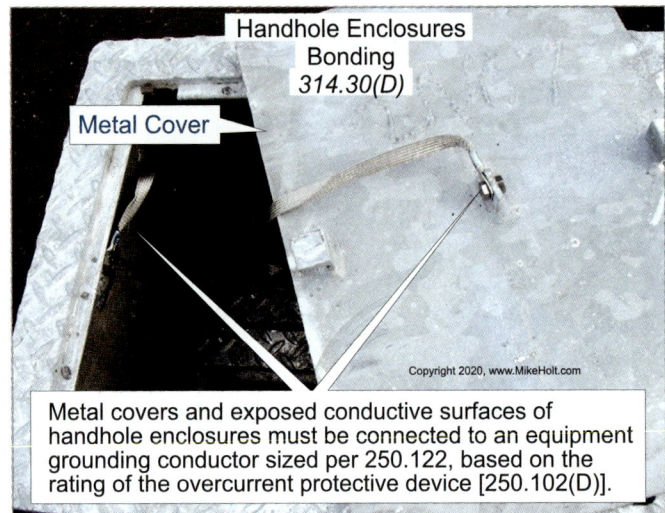
▶Figure 314–12

ARTICLE 320 — ARMORED CABLE (TYPE AC)

Introduction to Article 320—Armored Cable (Type AC)

Armored cable (Type AC) is an assembly of insulated conductors, 14 AWG through 1 AWG, individually wrapped in wax paper (jute) and contained within a flexible spiral metal sheath. To the casual observer the outside appearance of armored cable is like flexible metal conduit and metal-clad cable (Type MC). Type AC cable has been referred to as "BX®" cable over the years.

320.1 Scope

This article covers the use, installation, and construction specifications of armored cable, Type AC. ▶Figure 320–1

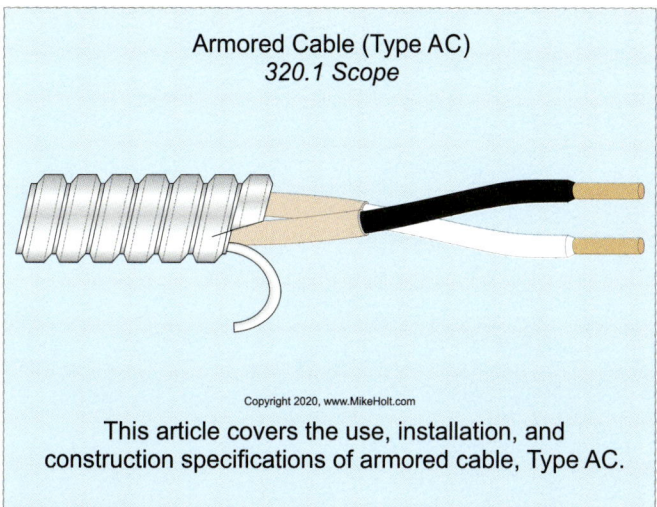

This article covers the use, installation, and construction specifications of armored cable, Type AC.

▶Figure 320–1

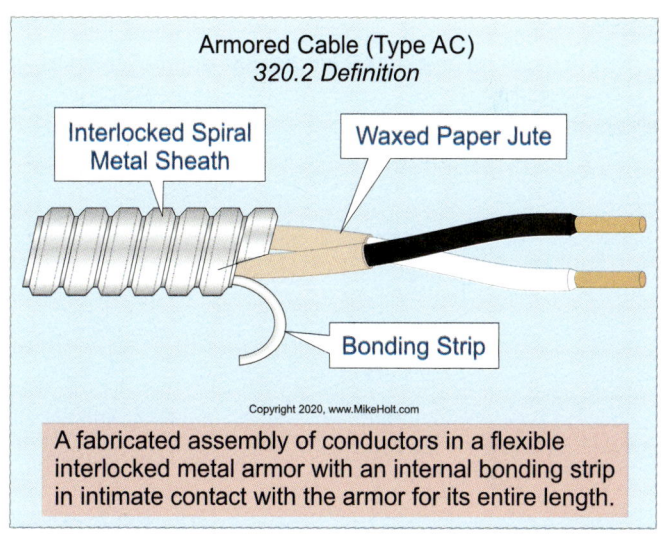

A fabricated assembly of conductors in a flexible interlocked metal armor with an internal bonding strip in intimate contact with the armor for its entire length.

▶Figure 320–2

Author's Comment:

▸ Type AC cable conductors are contained within a flexible metal sheath that interlocks at the edges with an internal aluminum bonding strip, giving the cable an outside appearance of flexible metal conduit. The advantages of any flexible cable, as compared to raceway wiring methods, are that there are no limit to the number of bends between terminations and the cable can be quickly installed.

320.2 Definition

Armored Cable (Type AC). A fabricated assembly of conductors in a flexible interlocked metal armor with an internal bonding strip in intimate contact with the armor for its entire length. ▶Figure 320–2

320.108 Equipment Grounding Conductor

Type AC cable provides an adequate path for fault current and can serve as an equipment grounding conductor [250.118(8)]. ▶Figure 320-3

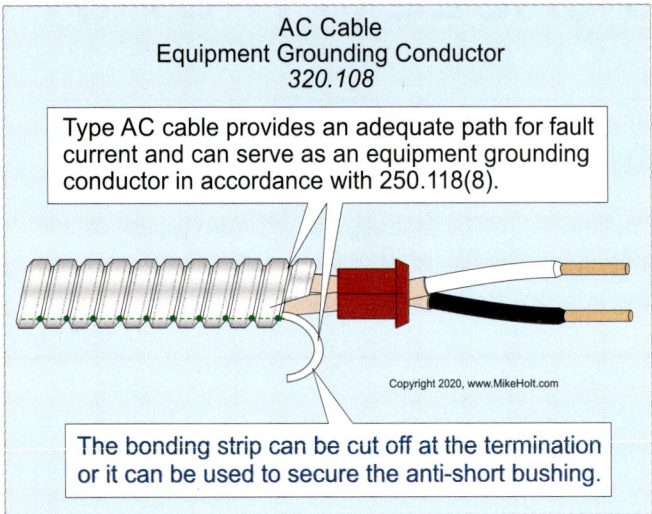

▶Figure 320-3

Author's Comment:

▶ The internal aluminum bonding strip is not an equipment grounding conductor, but it allows the interlocked armor to serve as one because it reduces the impedance of the armored spirals to ensure a ground fault will be cleared. It is the combination of the aluminum bonding strip and the cable armor that creates the equipment grounding conductor. Once the bonding strip exits the cable, it can be cut off because it no longer serves any purpose. The effective ground-fault current path must be maintained by using fittings specifically listed for Type AC cable [320.40]. See 300.12, 300.15, and 300.10.

ARTICLE 330

METAL-CLAD CABLE (TYPE MC)

Introduction to Article 330—Metal-Clad Cable (Type MC)

Metal-clad cable (Type MC) is probably the most often used metal-protected wiring method. Type MC cable encloses insulated conductors in a metal sheath of either corrugated or smooth copper or aluminum tubing, or in spiral interlocked steel or aluminum. The physical characteristics of Type MC cable make it a versatile wiring method that can be used in almost any location, and for almost any application. The most commonly used Type MC cable is the interlocking kind, which looks like armored cable or flexible metal conduit. Traditional interlocked Type MC cable is not permitted to serve as an equipment grounding conductor; therefore, this cable must contain an equipment grounding conductor in accordance with 250.118(1). Another type of Type MC cable is called interlocked Type MC^AP® cable. It contains a bare aluminum grounding/bonding conductor running just below the metal armor, which allows the sheath to serve as an equipment grounding conductor [250.118(10)(b)].

330.1 Scope

Article 330 covers the use, installation, and construction specifications of metal-clad cable, Type MC. ▶Figure 330–1

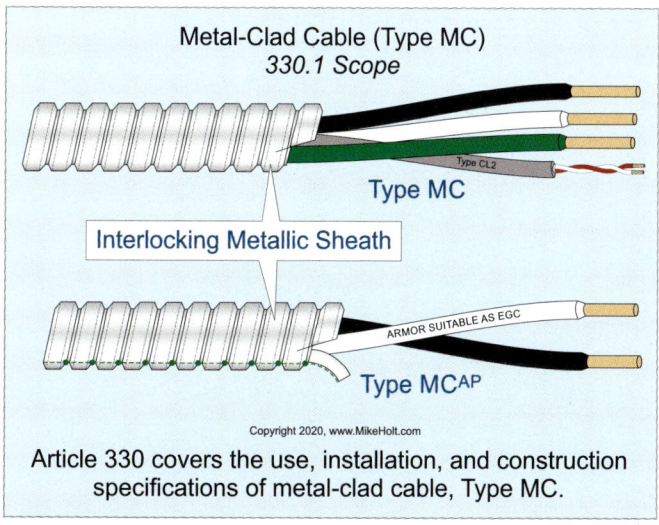

▶Figure 330–1

330.2 Definition

Metal-Clad Cable (Type MC). A factory assembly of insulated circuit conductors, with or without optical fiber members, enclosed in an armor of interlocking metal tape; or a smooth or corrugated metallic sheath. ▶Figure 330–2

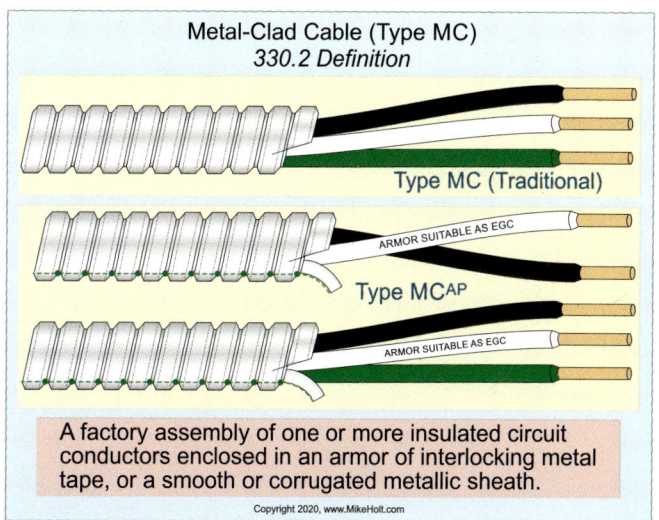

▶Figure 330–2

330.108 | Metal-Clad Cable (Type MC)

330.108 Equipment Grounding Conductor

If Type MC cable is to serve as an equipment grounding conductor, it must comply with 250.118(10)a and 250.122.

> **Author's Comment:**

- The outer sheath of:
  - Traditional interlocked Type MC cable is not permitted to serve as an equipment grounding conductor; therefore, this cable must contain an equipment grounding conductor in accordance with 250.118(10)a [250.118(1)]. ▶Figure 330-3
  - Interlocked Type MC$^{AP®}$ cable combines the metallic sheath with an uninsulated aluminum grounding/bonding conductor and is listed and identified as an equipment grounding conductor [250.118(10)b]. ▶Figure 330-4

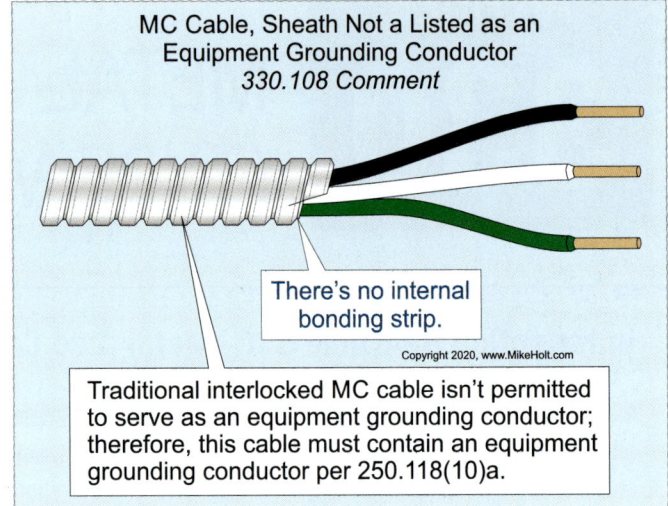

▶Figure 330-3

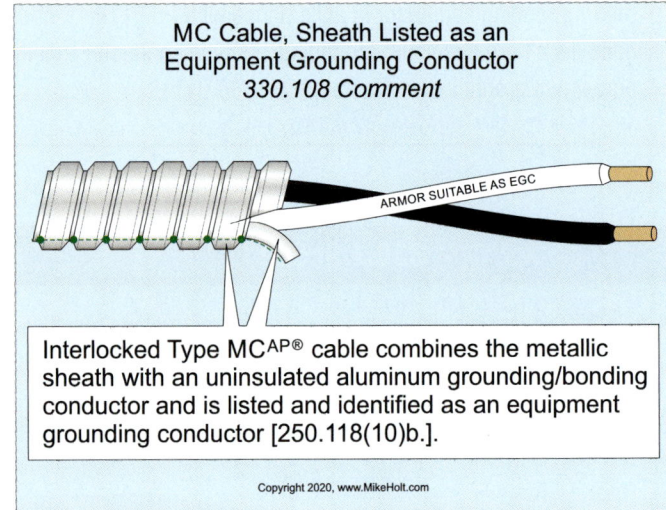

▶Figure 330-4

ARTICLE 334 — NONMETALLIC-SHEATHED CABLE (TYPE NM)

Introduction to Article 334—Nonmetallic-Sheathed Cable (Type NM)

Nonmetallic-sheathed cable (Type NM) provides very limited physical protection for the conductors inside, so the installation restrictions are stringent. Its low cost and relative ease of installation make it a common wiring method for residential and commercial branch circuits.

334.1 Scope

Article 334 covers the use, installation, and construction specifications of nonmetallic-sheathed cable, Type NM. ▶Figure 334–1

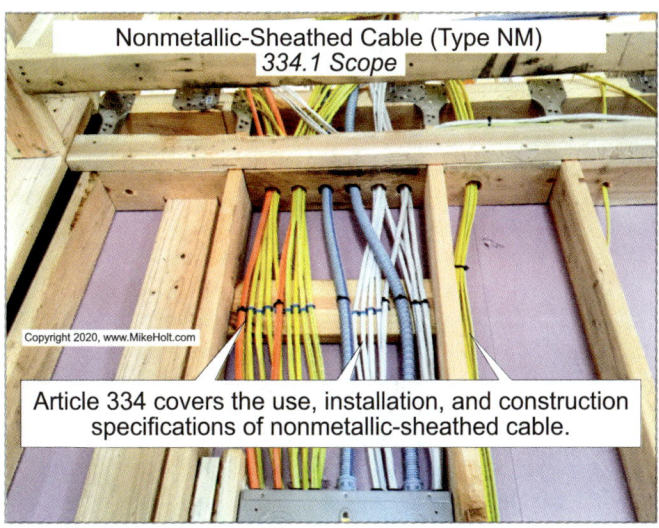

▶Figure 334–1

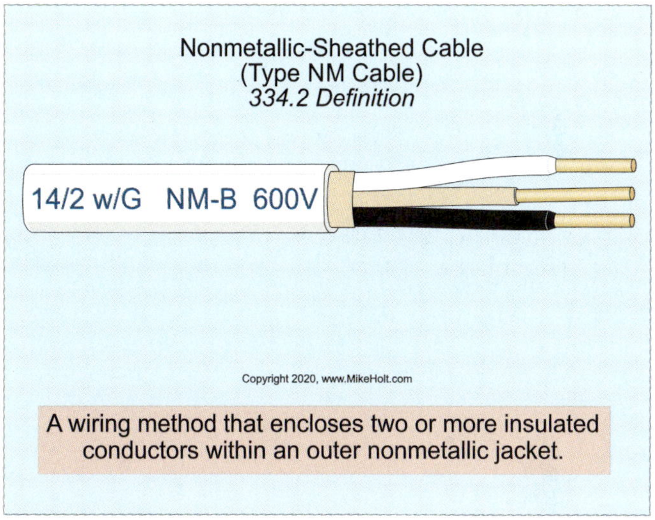

▶Figure 334–2

Author's Comment:

▸ It is the generally accepted practice in the electrical industry to call Type NM cable "Romex®," a registered trademark of the Southwire Company.

334.2 Definition

Nonmetal-Sheathed Cable (Type NM). A wiring method that encloses two or more insulated conductors within a nonmetallic jacket. ▶Figure 334–2

334.108 Equipment Grounding Conductor

Type NM cable must have an insulated, covered, or bare equipment grounding conductor. ▶Figure 334–3

334.108 | Nonmetallic-Sheathed Cable (Type NM)

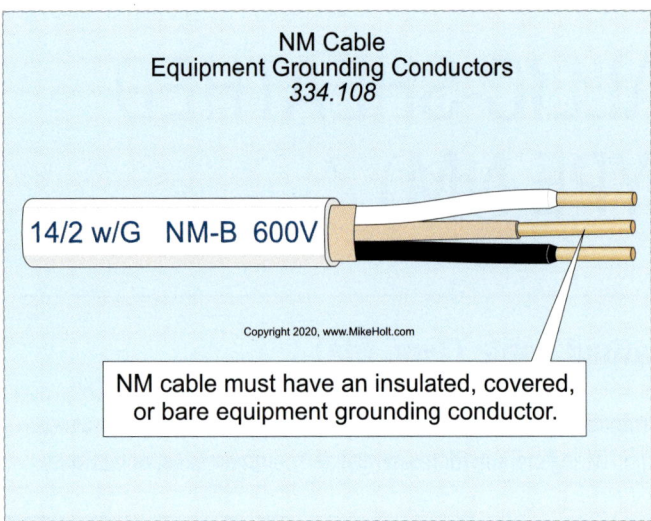
▶Figure 334-3

ARTICLE 348 — FLEXIBLE METAL CONDUIT (TYPE FMC)

Introduction to Article 348—Flexible Metal Conduit (Type FMC)

Flexible metal conduit (Type FMC), commonly called "Greenfield" (after its inventor) or "flex," is an interlocked metal strip type of raceway made of either steel or aluminum. It is primarily used where flexibility is necessary or where equipment moves, shakes, or vibrates.

348.1 Scope

Article 348 covers the use, installation, and construction specifications for flexible metal conduit (FMC) and associated fittings. ▶Figure 348–1

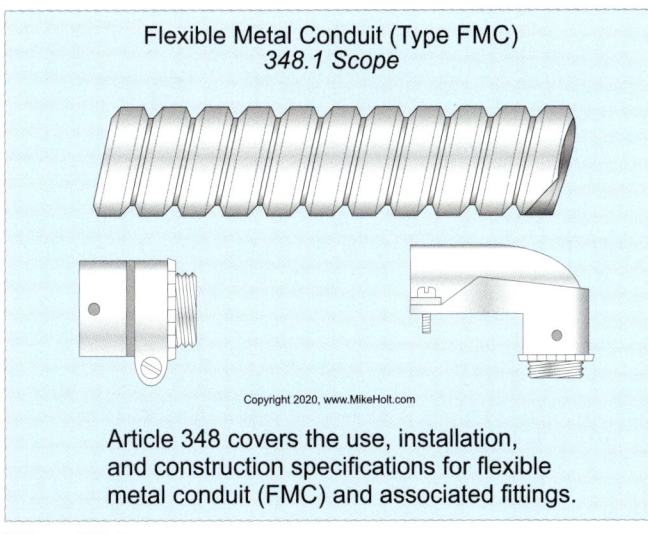

▶Figure 348–1

348.2 Definition

Flexible Metal Conduit (Type FMC). A raceway of circular cross section made of a helically wound, formed, interlocked metal strip, listed for the installation of electrical conductors. ▶Figure 348–2

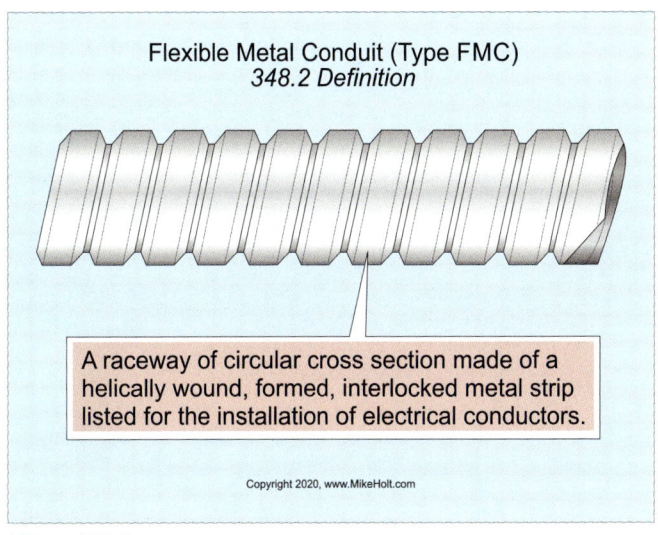

▶Figure 348–2

348.60 Equipment Grounding and Bonding Conductors

If flexibility is necessary to minimize the transmission of vibration from equipment, or to provide flexibility for equipment that requires movement after installation, an equipment grounding conductor of the wire type must be installed with the circuit conductors in accordance with 250.118(5). ▶Figure 348–3

If flexibility is not necessary after installation, and vibration is not a concern, the metal armor of FMC can serve as an equipment grounding conductor if the circuit conductors contained in the raceway are protected by an overcurrent protective device rated 20A or less, and the combined length of the raceway in the same ground-fault return path does not exceed 6 ft [250.118(5)]. ▶Figure 348–4

348.60 | Flexible Metal Conduit (Type FMC)

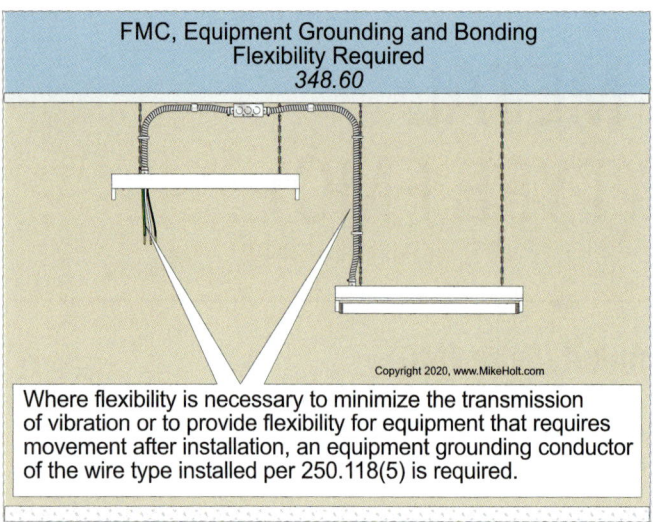
▶Figure 348-3

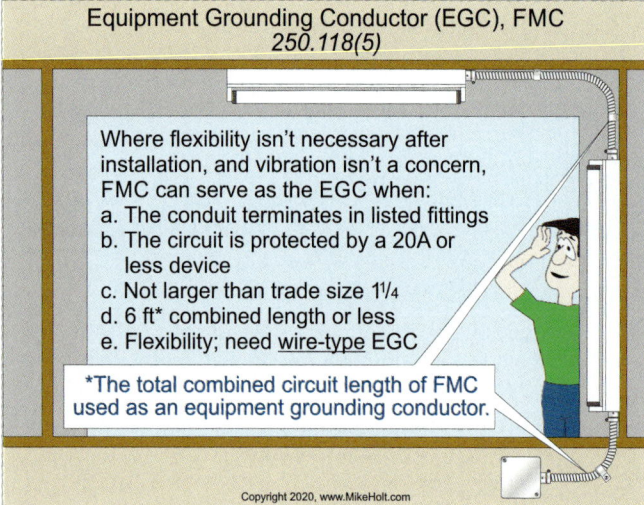
▶Figure 348-4

The equipment bonding jumper can be installed inside or outside the flexible metal conduit. Where installed outside the FMC, the length of the equipment bonding jumper is not permitted to exceed 6 ft and it must be routed with the flexible metal conduit in accordance with 250.102(E)(2).

ARTICLE 350 — LIQUIDTIGHT FLEXIBLE METAL CONDUIT (TYPE LFMC)

Introduction to Article 350—Liquidtight Flexible Metal Conduit (Type LFMC)

Liquidtight flexible metal conduit (Type LFMC), with its associated connectors and fittings, is a flexible raceway commonly used for connections to equipment that vibrates or must be occasionally moved. Liquidtight flexible metal conduit is commonly called "Sealtight®" or "liquidtight." It is similar in construction to flexible metal conduit but has an outer liquidtight thermoplastic covering. LFMC has the same primary purpose as flexible metal conduit, but also provides protection from liquids and some corrosive effects.

350.1 Scope

Article 350 covers the use, installation, and construction specifications of liquidtight flexible metal conduit (Type LFMC) and associated fittings. ▶Figure 350-1

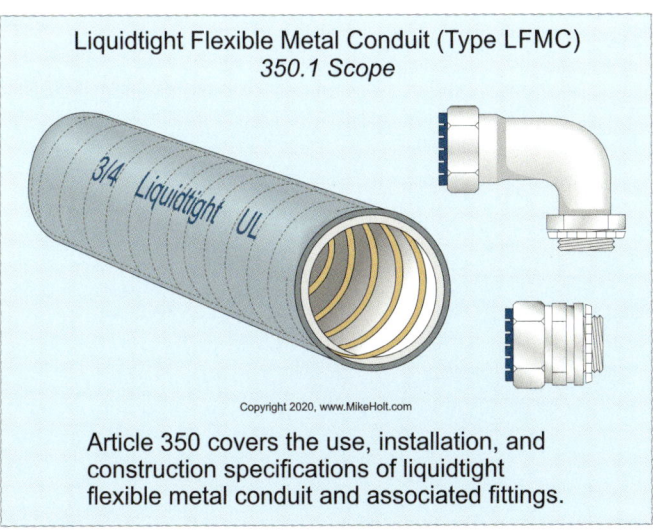

▶Figure 350-1

350.2 Definition

Liquidtight Flexible Metal Conduit (Type LFMC). A raceway of circular cross section, having an outer liquidtight, nonmetallic, sunlight-resistant jacket over an inner flexible metal core, with associated connectors and fittings, listed for the installation of electrical conductors. ▶Figure 350-2

▶Figure 350-2

350.60 Equipment Grounding and Bonding Conductors

If flexibility is necessary to minimize the transmission of vibration from equipment, or to provide flexibility for equipment that requires movement after installation, an equipment grounding conductor of the wire type must be installed with the circuit conductors in accordance with 250.118(6). ▶Figure 350-3

350.60 | Liquidtight Flexible Metal Conduit (Type LFMC)

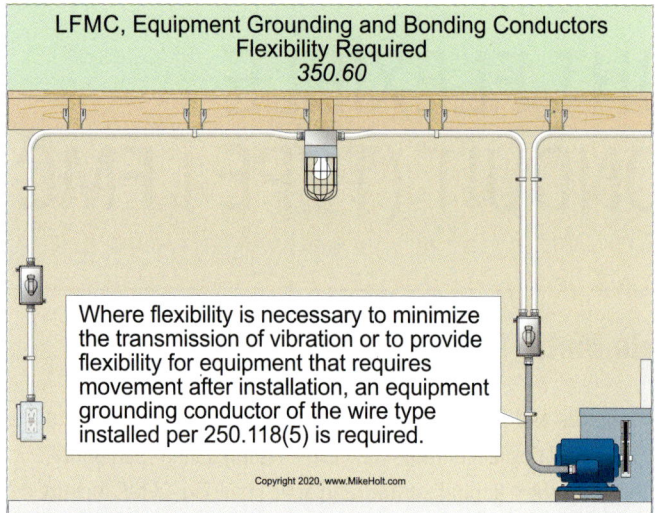
▶Figure 350–3

The equipment bonding jumper can be installed inside or outside the liquidtight flexible metal conduit. Where the bonding jumper is installed outside the LFMC, the length of the equipment bonding jumper cannot exceed 6 ft, and it must be routed with the liquidtight flexible metal conduit in accordance with 250.102(E)(2). ▶Figure 350–5

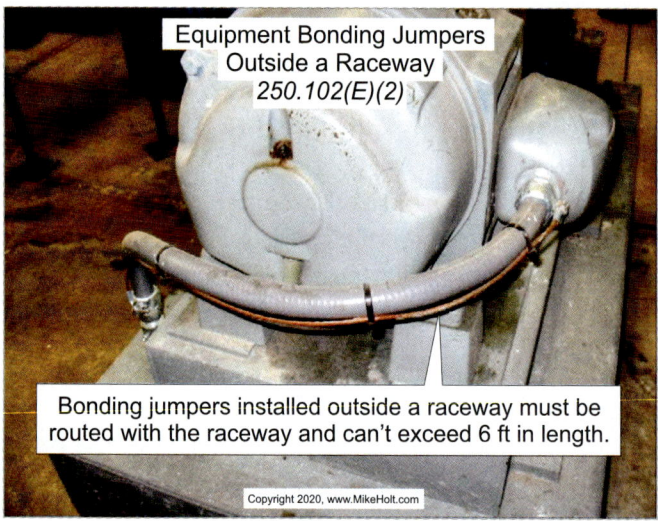
▶Figure 350–5

If flexibility is not necessary after installation, and vibration is not a concern, the metal armor of liquidtight flexible metal conduit can serve as an equipment grounding conductor if the circuit conductors contained in the raceway are protected by an overcurrent protective device rated 20A or less, and the combined length of the raceway in the same ground-fault return path does not exceed 6 ft in accordance with 250.118(6). ▶Figure 350–4

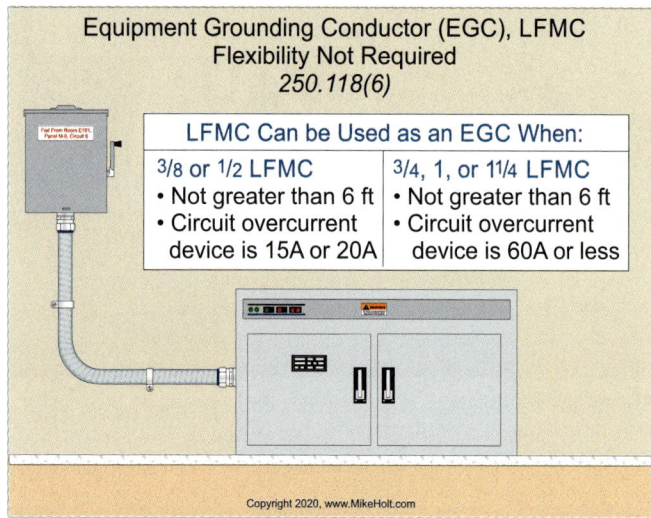
▶Figure 350–4

ARTICLE 352 — RIGID POLYVINYL CHLORIDE CONDUIT (TYPE PVC)

Introduction to Article 352—Rigid Polyvinyl Chloride Conduit (Type PVC)

Rigid polyvinyl chloride conduit (Type PVC) is a rigid nonmetallic conduit that provides many of the advantages of rigid metal conduit, while allowing installation in wet or corrosive areas. It is an inexpensive raceway and easily installed, lightweight, easily cut and glued together, and relatively strong. However, rigid polyvinyl chloride (PVC) is brittle when cold and will sag when hot. This type of conduit is commonly used as an underground raceway because of its low cost, ease of installation, and resistance to corrosion and decay.

352.1 Scope

Article 352 covers the use, installation, and construction specifications of polyvinyl chloride conduit (Type PVC) and associated fittings. ▶Figure 352–1

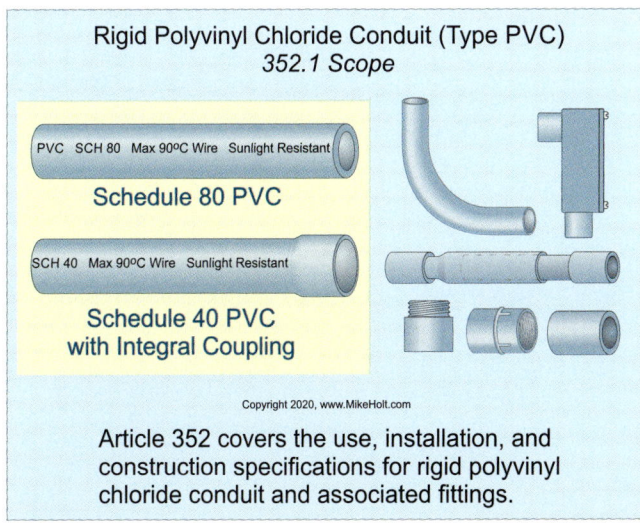
▶Figure 352–1

352.2 Definition

Rigid Polyvinyl Chloride Conduit (Type PVC). A rigid nonmetallic raceway of circular cross section with integral or associated couplings, listed for the installation of electrical conductors. ▶Figure 352–2

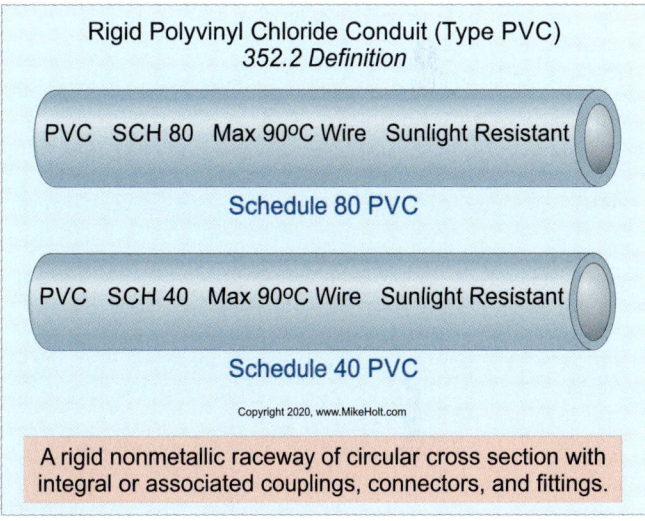
▶Figure 352–2

352.60 Equipment Grounding Conductor

If equipment is required to be connected to an equipment grounding conductor, a separate one of the wire type must be installed inside the raceway [300.2(B)]. ▶Figure 352–3

Ex 2: An equipment grounding conductor is not required in PVC conduit if the neutral conductor is used for equipment grounding at the service disconnect in accordance with 250.142(A) [250.24(C)]. ▶Figure 352–4

352.60 | Rigid Polyvinyl Chloride Conduit (Type PVC)

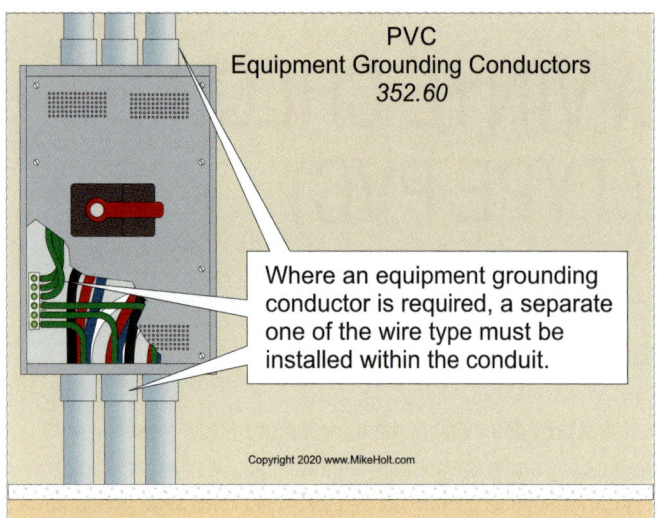
▶Figure 352-3

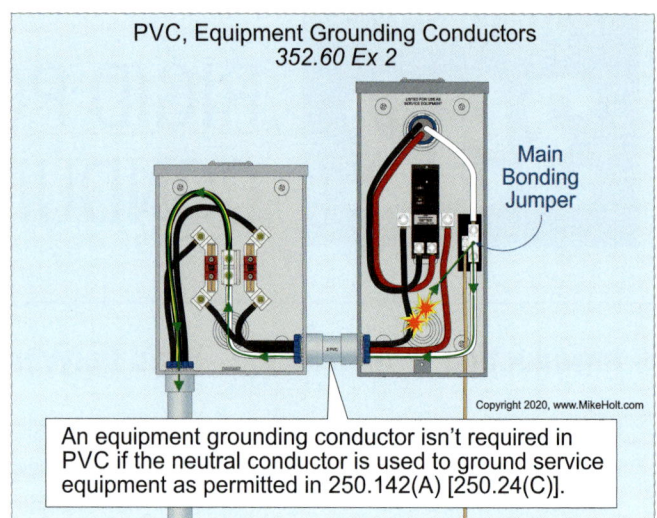
▶Figure 352-4

ARTICLE 356 — LIQUIDTIGHT FLEXIBLE NONMETALLIC CONDUIT (TYPE LFNC)

Introduction to Article 356—Liquidtight Flexible Nonmetallic Conduit (Type LFNC)

Liquidtight flexible nonmetallic conduit (Type LFNC) is a listed raceway of circular cross section with an outer liquidtight, nonmetallic, sunlight-resistant jacket over an inner flexible core with associated couplings, connectors, and fittings. It is commonly referred to as "Carflex®."

356.1 Scope

Article 356 covers the use, installation, and construction specifications of liquidtight flexible nonmetallic conduit (Type LFNC) and associated fittings. ▶Figure 356–1

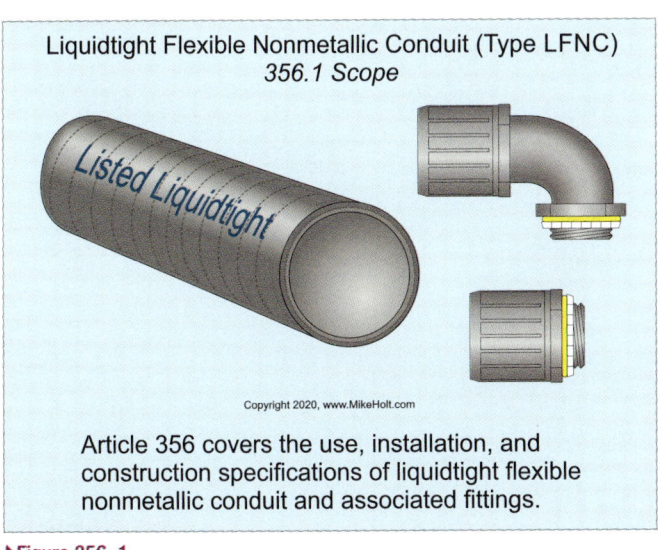

▶Figure 356–1

356.2 Definition

Liquidtight Flexible Nonmetallic Conduit (Type LFNC). A raceway of circular cross section, with an outer liquidtight, nonmetallic, sunlight-resistant jacket over a flexible inner core, with associated couplings, connectors, and fittings, listed for the installation of electrical conductors. ▶Figure 356–2

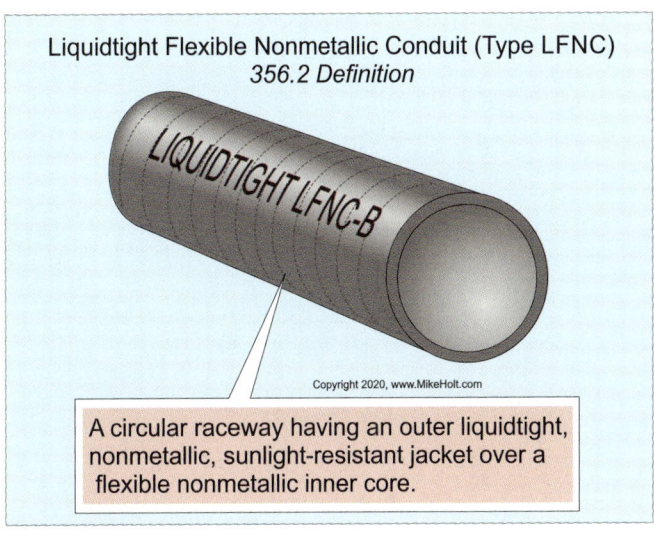

▶Figure 356–2

356.60 Equipment Grounding Conductor

If equipment grounding is required, a separate equipment grounding conductor of the wire type must be installed inside the conduit [250.134(B)].

Author's Comment:

▸ An equipment grounding conductor is not required to be installed in a nonmetallic raceway supplying nonmetallic equipment because there is nothing in the nonmetallic box that requires a connection to an equipment grounding conductor. ▶Figure 356–3

356.60 | Liquidtight Flexible Nonmetallic Conduit (Type LFNC)

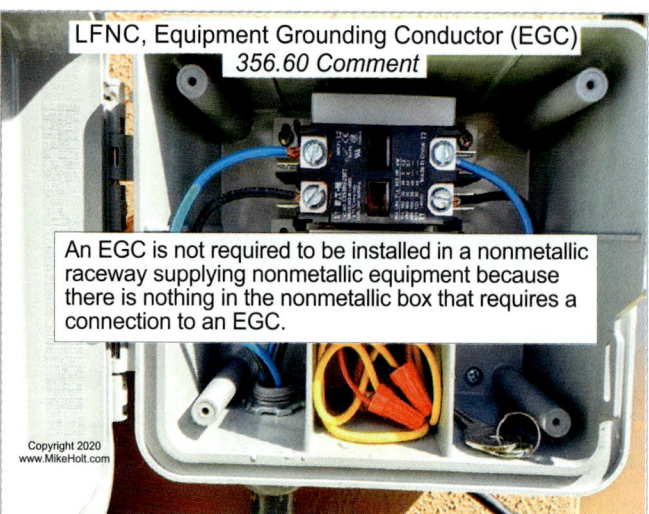

Figure 356-3

ARTICLE 358 — ELECTRICAL METALLIC TUBING (TYPE EMT)

Introduction to Article 358—Electrical Metallic Tubing (Type EMT)

Electrical metallic tubing (Type EMT) is perhaps the most commonly used raceway in commercial and industrial installations. It is a lightweight raceway that is relatively easy to bend, cut, and ream. Because EMT is not threaded, all connectors and couplings are of the threadless type (either set-screw or compression) and provide for quick, easy, and inexpensive installations as compared to other metallic raceway systems; all of which make it very popular. Electrical metallic tubing is manufactured in both galvanized steel and aluminum; the steel type is used most often.

358.1 Scope

Article 358 covers the use, installation, and construction specifications of electrical metallic tubing (Type EMT) and associated fittings. ▶Figure 358–1

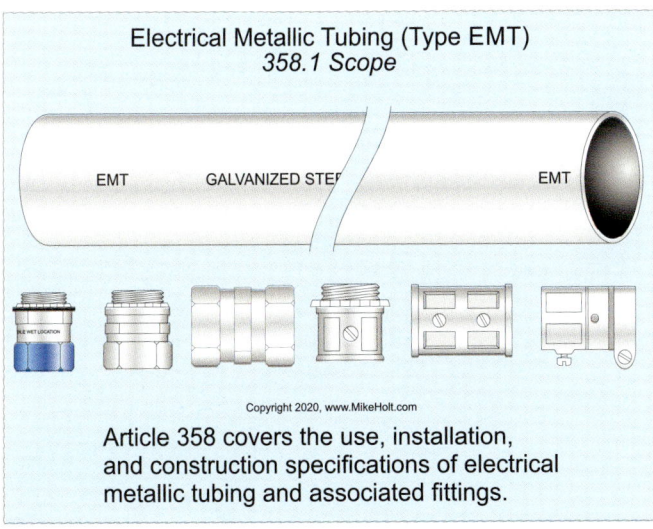

▶Figure 358–1

358.2 Definition

Electrical Metallic Tubing (Type EMT). An unthreaded thinwall circular metallic raceway used for the installation of electrical conductors. When joined together with listed fittings and enclosures as a complete system, it is a reliable wiring method providing both physical protection for conductors as well an effective ground-fault current path. ▶Figure 358–2

▶Figure 358–2

358.42 Couplings and Connectors

Couplings and connectors must be made up tight to maintain an effective ground-fault current path to safely conduct fault current in accordance with 250.4(A)(5), 250.96(A), and 300.10.

If buried in masonry or concrete, threadless EMT fittings must be of the concrete-tight type. If installed in wet locations, they must be listed for use in wet locations and prevent moisture or water from entering or accumulating inside the enclosure in accordance with 314.15. ▶Figure 358–3

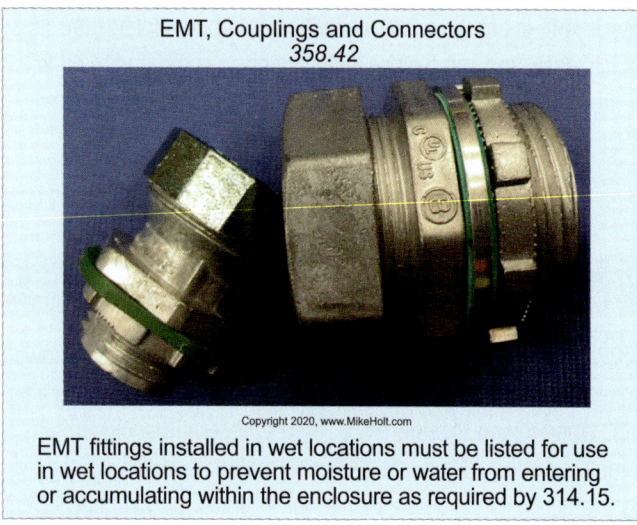

EMT fittings installed in wet locations must be listed for use in wet locations to prevent moisture or water from entering or accumulating within the enclosure as required by 314.15.

▶Figure 358–3

358.60 Equipment Grounding Conductor

EMT can serve as an equipment grounding conductor [250.118(4)].
▶Figure 358–4

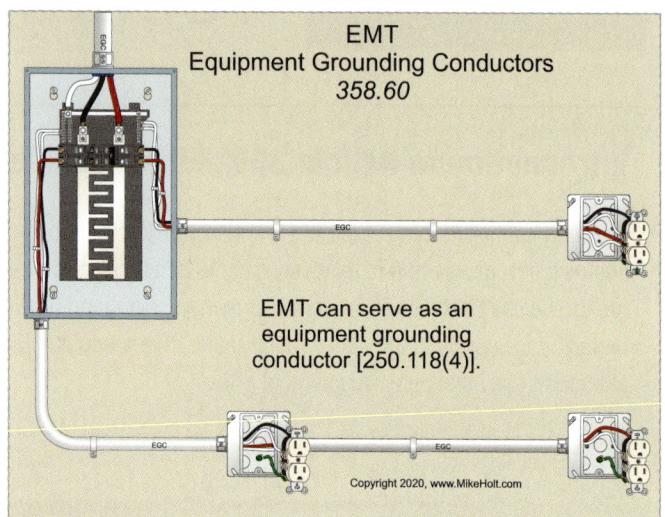

▶Figure 358–4

ARTICLE 362 — ELECTRICAL NONMETALLIC TUBING (TYPE ENT)

Introduction to Article 362—Electrical Nonmetallic Tubing (Type ENT)

Electrical nonmetallic tubing is a pliable, corrugated, circular raceway. It resembles the flexible tubing you might see used at swimming pools and is often referred to as "Smurf Pipe" or "Smurf Tube" (as a reference to the children's cartoon characters "The Smurfs") because it was only available in blue when it first came out. It can now be purchased in additional colors such as red and yellow.

362.1 Scope

Article 362 covers the use, installation, and construction specifications of electrical nonmetallic tubing (Type ENT) and associated fittings. ▶Figure 362–1

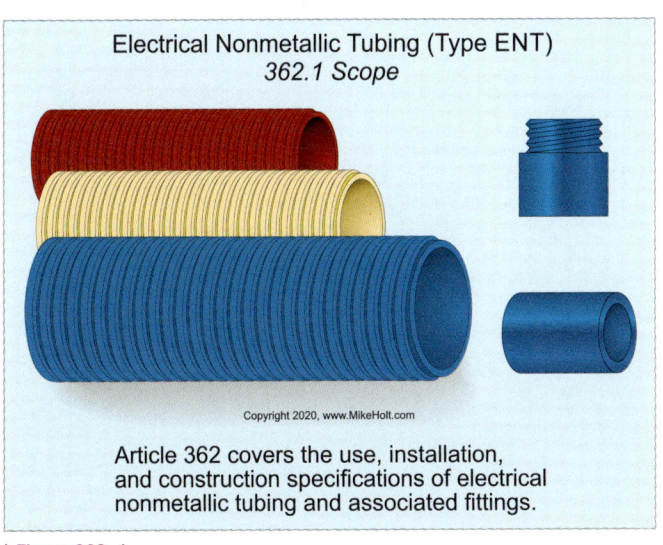

▶Figure 362–1

362.2 Definition

Electrical Nonmetallic Tubing (Type ENT). A pliable corrugated raceway of circular cross section, with integral or associated couplings, connectors, and fittings that are listed for the installation of electrical conductors. It is composed of a material that is resistant to moisture and chemical atmospheres and is flame retardant. ▶Figure 362–2

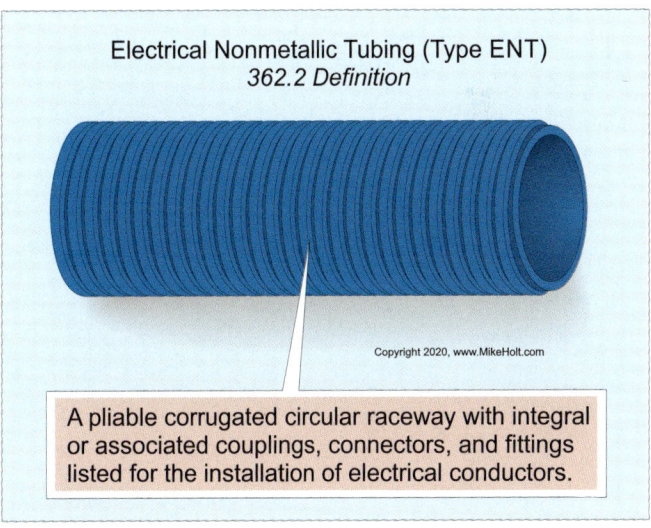

▶Figure 362–2

Electrical nonmetallic tubing can be bent by hand with reasonable force but without other assistance.

362.60 Equipment Grounding Conductor

If equipment grounding is required, a separate equipment grounding conductor of the wire type must be installed inside the raceway. ▶Figure 362–3

362.60 | Electrical Nonmetallic Tubing (Type ENT)

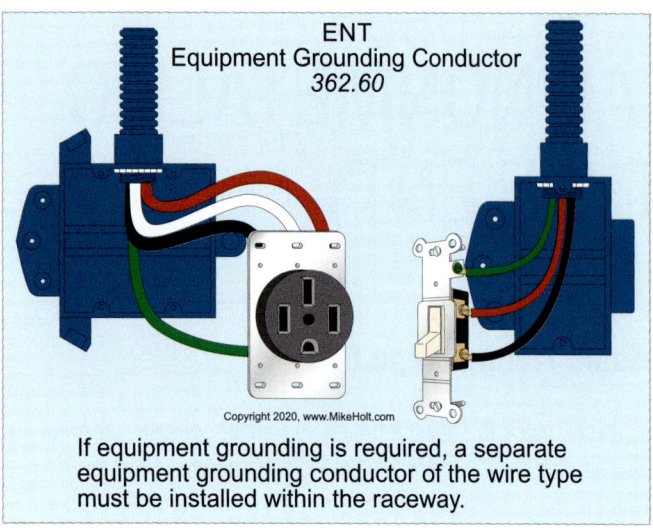

Figure 362-3

ARTICLE 386 SURFACE METAL RACEWAYS

Introduction to Article 386—Surface Metal Raceways

Using a surface metal raceway is a common method of adding a raceway when exposed traditional raceway systems are not acceptable, and concealing the raceway is not economically feasible. They come in several colors and are available with colored or real wood inserts designed to make them look like molding rather than raceways. A surface metal raceway is commonly known as "Wiremold®" in the field.

386.1 Scope

This article covers the use, installation, and construction specifications of surface metal raceways and associated fittings. ▶Figure 386–1

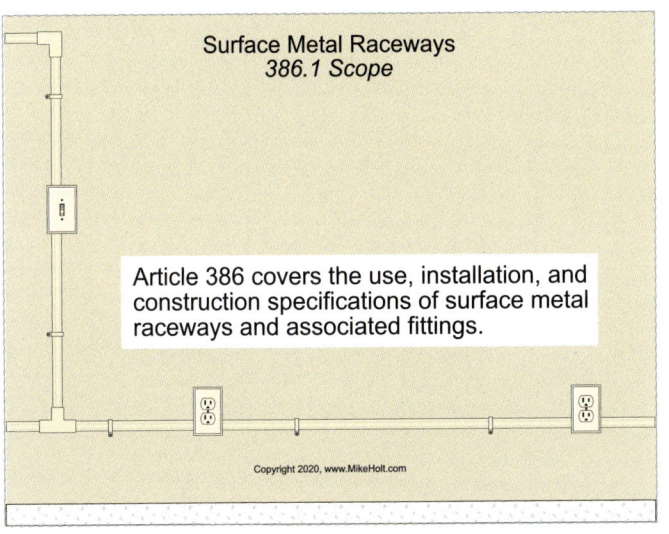

▶Figure 386–1

386.2 Definition

Surface Metal Raceway. A metal raceway with associated fittings in which conductors are placed after the raceway has been installed as a complete system [300.18(A)]. ▶Figure 386–2

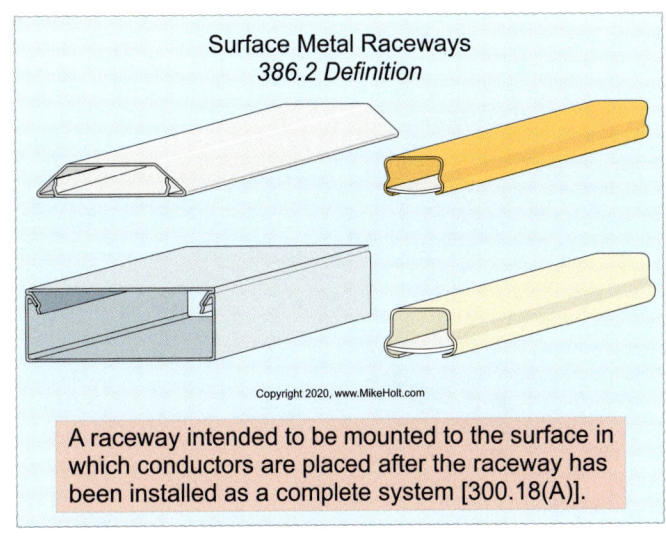

▶Figure 386–2

Author's Comment:

▸ Surface metal raceways are available in different shapes and sizes and can be mounted on walls, ceilings, or floors. Some of them have two or more separate compartments, which permit the separation of power and lighting conductors from low-voltage or limited-energy conductors or cables (control, signaling, and communications cables and conductors) [386.70].

386.60 Equipment Grounding Conductor

Surface metal raceway fittings must be mechanically and electrically joined together in a manner that does not subject the conductors to abrasion. Surface metal raceways that allow a transition to another wiring method, such as knockouts for connecting raceways, must have a means for the termination of an equipment grounding conductor.

A surface metal raceway is suitable as an equipment grounding conductor in accordance with 250.118(14). ▶Figure 386-3

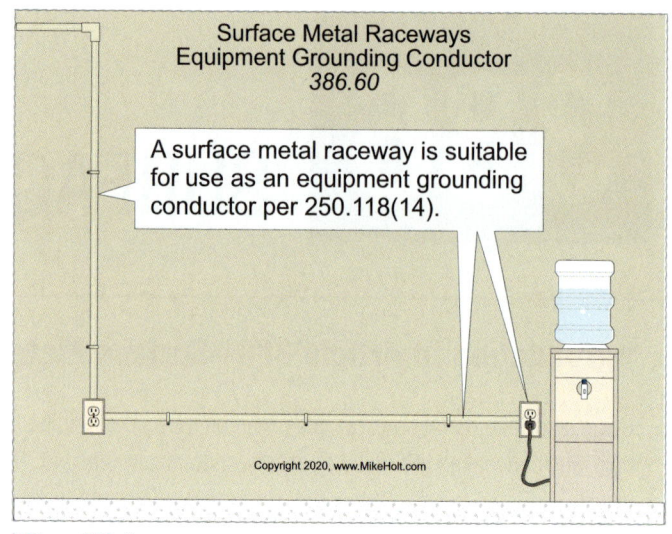

▶Figure 386-3

ARTICLE 392 CABLE TRAYS

Introduction to Article 392—Cable Trays

A cable tray system is a unit or an assembly of units or sections with associated fittings that forms a structural system used to securely fasten or support cables and raceways.

Cable tray systems include ladder, ventilated trough, ventilated channel, solid bottom, and other similar structures. They are manufactured in many forms—from a simple hanger or wire mesh to a substantial, rigid, steel support system. Cable trays are designed and manufactured to support specific wiring methods, as identified in 392.10(A).

392.1 Scope

Article 392 covers cable tray systems, including ladder, ventilated trough, ventilated channel, solid bottom, and other similar structures. ▶Figure 392–1

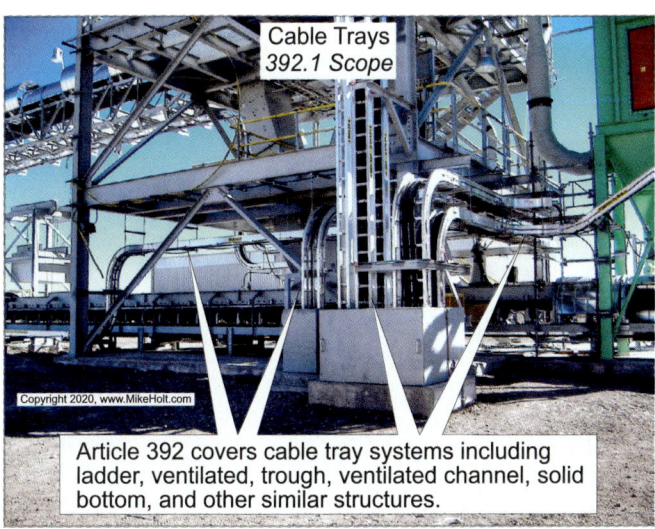

▶Figure 392–1

392.2 Definition

Cable Tray System. A unit or assembly of units or sections with associated fittings forming a rigid structural system used to securely fasten or support cables and raceways. ▶Figure 392–2

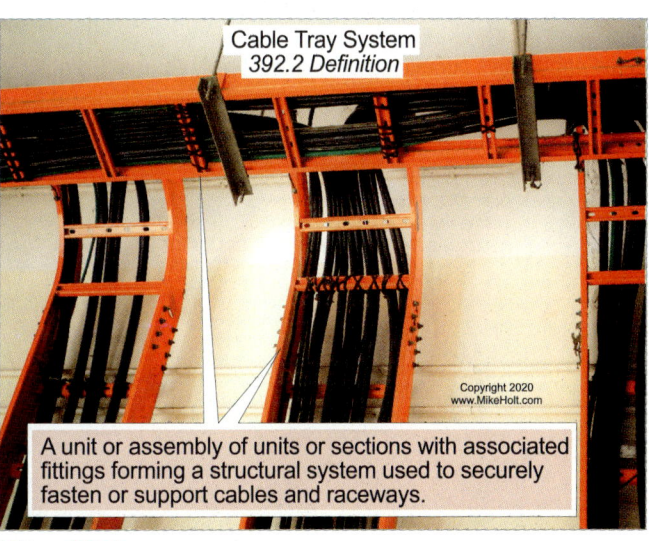

▶Figure 392–2

Author's Comment:

▶ A cable tray is not a raceway, it is a support system for cables and raceways.

392.60 Equipment Grounding Conductor

(A) Used as an Equipment Grounding Conductor. Metal cable trays can be used as equipment grounding conductors where continuous maintenance and supervision ensure that only qualified persons will service the cable tray system. ▶Figure 392–3

392.60 | Cable Trays

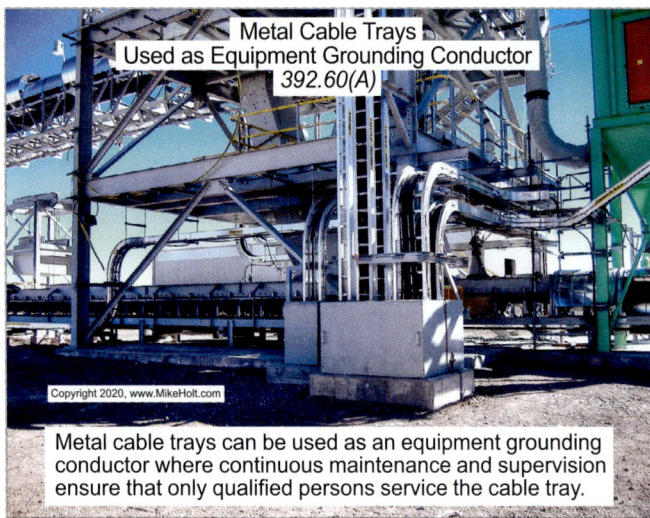

▶Figure 392–3

Metal cable trays containing single conductors must be bonded together to ensure they have the capacity to conduct safely any fault current likely to be imposed, in accordance with 250.96(A).

Metal cable trays containing communications, data, and signaling conductors and cables must be electrically continuous through approved connections or the use of a bonding jumper. ▶Figure 392–4

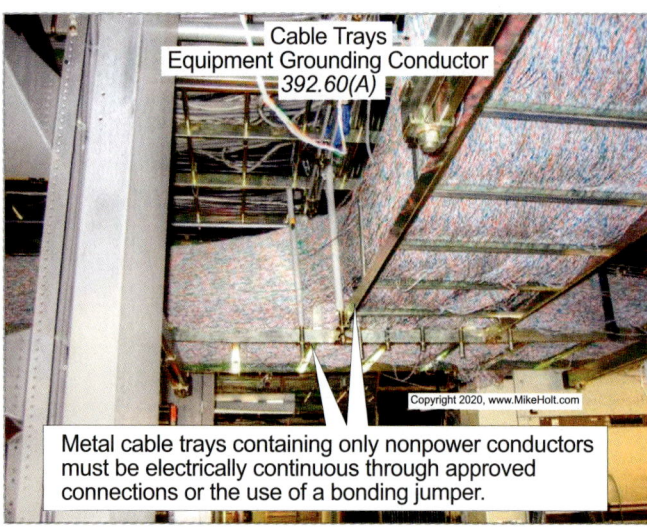

▶Figure 392–4

(B) Serve as an Equipment Grounding Conductor. Metal cable trays can serve as equipment grounding conductors where the following requirements have been met [392.10(C)]:

(1) Metal cable trays and fittings are identified as an equipment grounding conductor.

(4) Cable tray sections, fittings, and connected raceways are effectively bonded to each other to ensure electrical continuity and the capacity to conduct safely any fault current likely to be imposed on them [250.96(A)]. This is accomplished by using bolted mechanical connectors or bonding jumpers sized in accordance with 250.102. ▶Figure 392–5

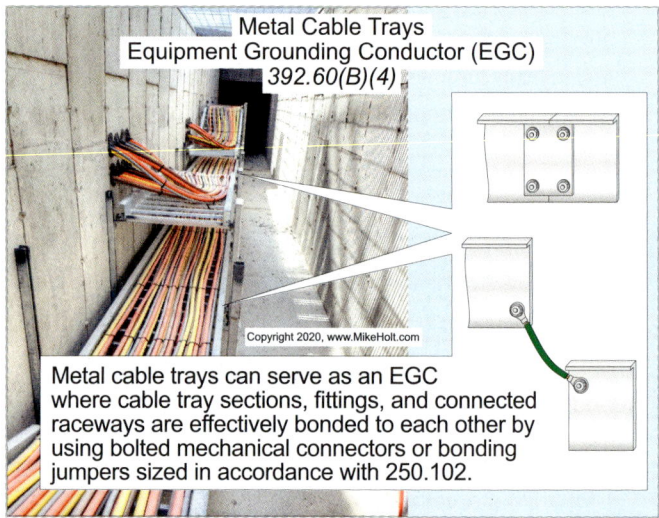

▶Figure 392–5

228 | *Mike Holt's Illustrated Guide to Understanding 2020 NEC Requirements for Bonding and Grounding*

408.40 | Switchboards and Panelboards

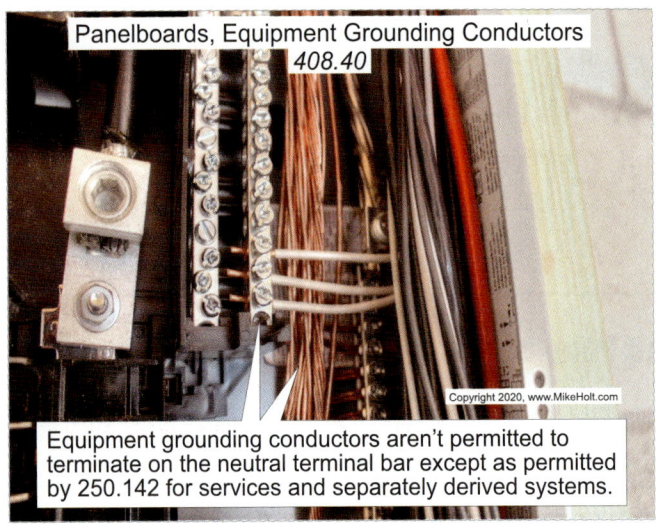

Figure 408–3

Caution: Many panelboards are rated for use as service disconnects, which means they are supplied with a main bonding jumper [250.28]. This screw or strap is not permitted to be installed except when the panelboard is used for a service disconnect [250.24(A)(5)] or a separately derived system [250.30(A)(1)].

CHAPTER 3

PRACTICE QUESTIONS

Please use the 2020 *Code* book to answer the following questions.

CHAPTER 3—WIRING METHODS AND MATERIALS

1. The provisions of Article 300 apply to the conductors that form an integral part of equipment or listed utilization equipment.

    (a) True
    (b) False

2. The requirement to run all paralleled circuit conductors within the same _____ applies separately to each portion of the paralleled installation.

    (a) raceway or auxiliary gutter
    (b) cable tray or trench
    (c) cable or cord
    (d) all of these

3. Metal raceways, cable armor, and other metal enclosures shall be _____ joined together into a continuous electric conductor so as to provide effective electrical continuity.

    (a) electrically
    (b) permanently
    (c) metallically
    (d) physically

4. Nonmetallic boxes can be used with _____.

    (a) nonmetallic sheaths
    (b) nonmetallic raceways
    (c) flexible cords
    (d) all of these

5. Screws used for the purpose of attaching covers or other equipment to the box shall be either machine screws matching the thread gauge and size that is integral to the box or be in accordance with the manufacturer's instructions.

    (a) True
    (b) False

6. All _____ shall be provided with covers compatible with the box or conduit body construction and suitable for the conditions of use.

    (a) pull boxes
    (b) junction boxes
    (c) conduit bodies
    (d) all of these

7. Handhole enclosures shall be designed and installed to withstand _____.

    (a) 600 lb
    (b) 3,000 lb
    (c) 6,000 lb
    (d) all loads likely to be imposed on them

8. Underground raceways and cable assemblies entering a handhole enclosure shall extend into the enclosure, but they are not required to be _____.

    (a) bonded
    (b) insulated
    (c) mechanically connected to the handhole enclosure
    (d) below minimum cover requirements after leaving the handhole

Chapter 3 | Practice Questions

9. Conductors, splices, or terminations in a handhole enclosure shall be listed as suitable for _____.

    (a) wet locations
    (b) damp locations
    (c) direct burial in the earth
    (d) exterior use

10. The _____ rating is permitted to be used for ampacity adjustment and correction calculations, provided the final calculated ampacity does not exceed that of a 60

    (a) 60
    (b) 75
    (c) 90
    (d) 104

11. _____ is a raceway of circular cross section made of a helically wound, formed, interlocked metal strip.

    (a) Type MC cable
    (b) Type AC cable
    (c) LFMC
    (d) FMC

12. EMT couplings and connectors shall be made up _____.

    (a) of metal
    (b) in accordance with industry standards
    (c) tight
    (d) to be readily accessible

13. A surface metal raceway is a metal raceway that is intended to be mounted to the surface of a structure, with associated couplings, connectors, boxes, and fittings for the installation of electrical conductors.

    (a) True
    (b) False

14. Metal cable trays containing only nonpower conductors (such as communications, data, and signaling conductors and cables) shall be electrically continuous through approved connections or the use of a(n) _____.

    (a) grounding electrode conductor
    (b) bonding jumper
    (c) equipment grounding conductor
    (d) grounded conductor

CHAPTER 4
EQUIPMENT FOR GENERAL USE

Introduction to Chapter 4—Equipment for General Use

With the first three chapters of the *NEC* behind you, this fourth one is necessary for building a solid foundation in general equipment installations. It helps you apply the first three chapters to installations involving general equipment. You need to understand the first four chapters of the *Code* to properly apply the requirements to Chapters 5, 6, and 7, and at times to Chapter 8.

Chapter 4 is arranged in the following manner:

▶ **Article 404—Switches.** The requirements of Article 404 apply to switches of all types. These include snap (toggle) switches, dimmer switches, fan switches, knife switches, circuit breakers, and automatic switches such as time clocks, timers, and switches and circuit breakers used for a disconnecting means.

▶ **Article 406—Receptacles and Attachment Plugs (Caps).** This article covers the rating, type, and installation of receptacles and attachment plugs (cord caps). It also covers flanged surface inlets.

▶ **Article 408—Switchboards and Panelboards.** Article 408 covers specific requirements for switchboards, panelboards, and distribution boards that supply lighting and power circuits.

> **Author's Comment:**
>
> ▶ See Article 100 for the definitions of "Panelboard" and "Switchboard."

▶ **Article 410—Luminaires, Lampholders, and Lamps.** This article contains the requirements for luminaires, lampholders, and lamps. Because of the many types and applications of luminaires, manufacturer's instructions are very important and helpful for proper installation. Underwriters Laboratories produces a pamphlet called the *Luminaire Marking Guide*, which provides information for properly installing common types of incandescent, fluorescent, and high-intensity discharge (HID) luminaires. Spaces dedicated to the cultivation and growth of agricultural products (such as "hot houses") that reproduce the natural effects of sunlight and seasonal temperatures may present unique conditions. Additional requirements are addressed in the Horticultural Part XVI.

▶ **Article 440—Air-Conditioning and Refrigeration Equipment.** Article 440 applies to electrically driven air-conditioning and refrigeration equipment with a motorized hermetic refrigerant compressor. The requirements in this article are in addition to, or amend, the requirements in Article 430 and others.

▶ **Article 450—Transformers.** This article covers the installation of transformers.

Notes

ARTICLE 404 SWITCHES

Introduction to Article 404—Switches

The requirements of Article 404 address switches of all types, including snap (toggle) switches, dimmer switches, fan switches, knife switches, circuit breakers, and automatic switches such as time clocks and timers.

404.1 Scope

The requirements of Article 404 apply to all types of switches, switching devices, and circuit breakers. ▶Figure 404–1

▶Figure 404–1

(1) Metal Boxes. The switch is mounted with metal screws to a metal box or a metal cover that is connected to an equipment grounding conductor in accordance with 250.148. ▶Figure 404–2 and ▶Figure 404–3

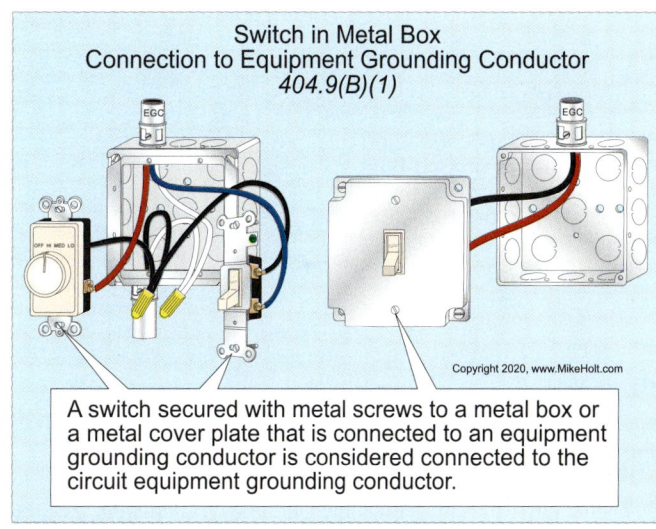

▶Figure 404–2

Author's Comment:

▸ Direct metal-to-metal contact between the device yoke of a switch and the box is not required. The switch is connected to the effective ground-fault current path when the yoke is mounted with metal screws to a metal box. ▶Figure 404–4

404.9 General-Use Snap Switches, Dimmers, and Control Switches

(B) Grounding. The metal mounting yokes for switches, dimmers, and control switches must be connected to an equipment grounding conductor and metal faceplates must be bonded to the equipment grounding conductor. Snap switches, dimmers, control switches, and metal faceplates are considered connected to an equipment grounding conductor using either of the following methods:

404.12 | Switches

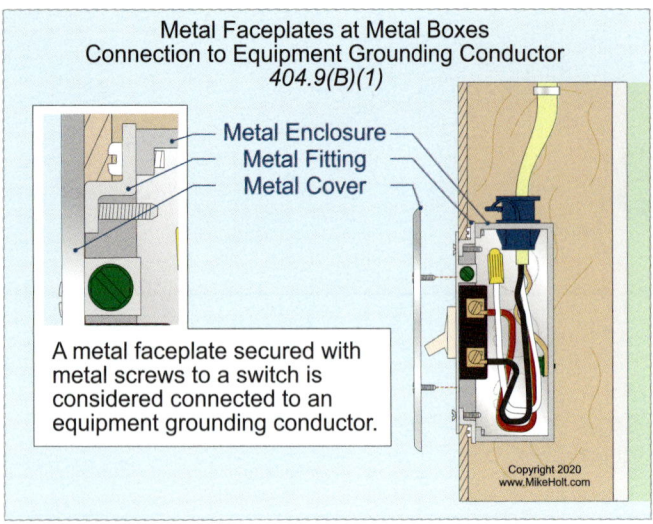
▶Figure 404–3

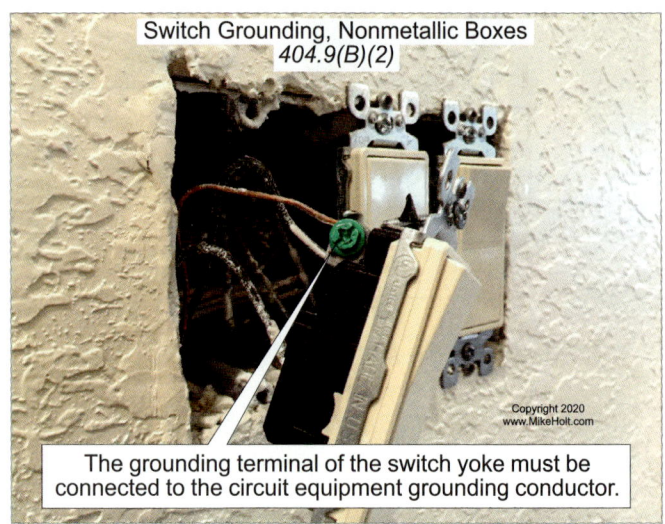
▶Figure 404–5

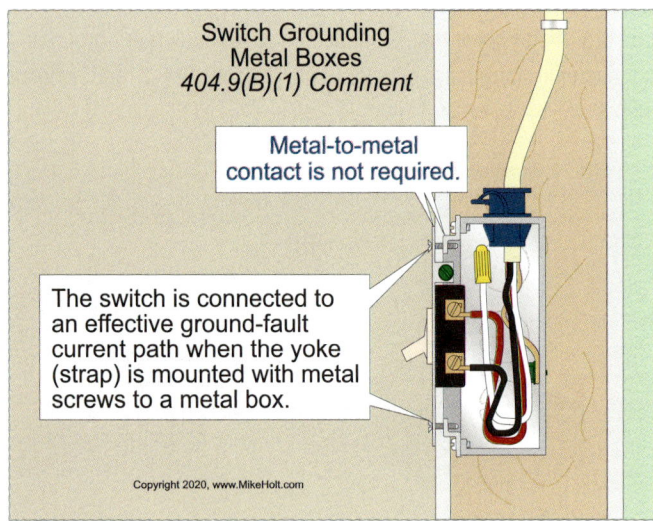
▶Figure 404–4

(2) Nonmetallic Boxes. The grounding terminal of the switch yoke must be connected to the circuit equipment grounding conductor. ▶Figure 404–5

Ex 1: Where no means exists within the box for bonding to an equipment grounding conductor, or if the wiring method at the existing switch does not contain an equipment grounding conductor, a switch without such a connection to the equipment grounding conductor is permitted for replacement purposes only. A switch installed under this exception must have a faceplate that is nonmetallic with nonmetallic screws, or the replacement switch must be GFCI protected.

Ex 2: Listed assemblies are not required to be bonded to an equipment grounding conductor if all of the following conditions are met:

(1) The device is provided with a nonmetallic faceplate and the device is designed such that no metallic faceplate replaces the one provided,

(2) The device does not have a mounting means to accept other configurations of faceplates,

(3) The device is equipped with a nonmetallic yoke, and

(4) Parts of the device that are accessible after the faceplate is installed are manufactured of nonmetallic material.

Ex 3: An equipment grounding conductor is not required for bonding a snap switch with an integral nonmetallic enclosure complying with 300.15(E).

404.12 Grounding of Enclosures

Metal enclosures for switches and circuit breakers must be connected to an equipment grounding conductor of a type recognized in 250.118 [250.4(A)(3)]. Where nonmetallic enclosures are used with metal raceways or metal-armored cables, they must comply with 314.3 Ex 1 or Ex 2.

ARTICLE 406 — RECEPTACLES AND ATTACHMENT PLUGS (CAPS)

Introduction to Article 406—Receptacles and Attachment Plugs (Caps)

This article covers the rating, type, and installation of receptacles and attachment plugs (cord caps). It also covers flanged surface inlets.

406.1 Scope

Article 406 covers the rating, type, and installation of receptacles and attachment plugs (cord caps). ▶Figure 406–1

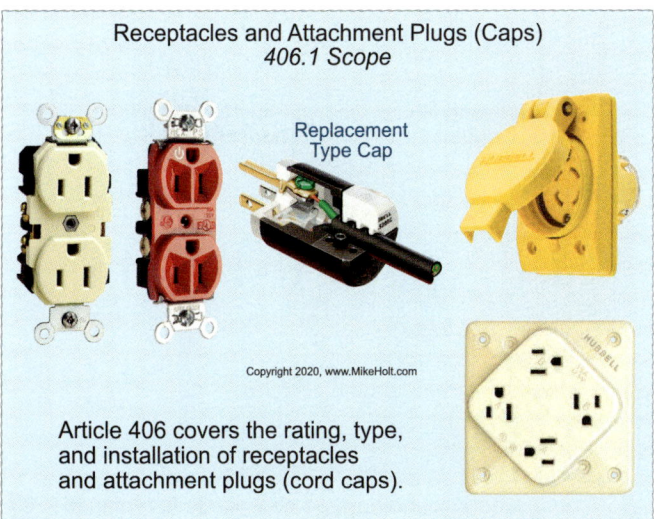

▶Figure 406–1

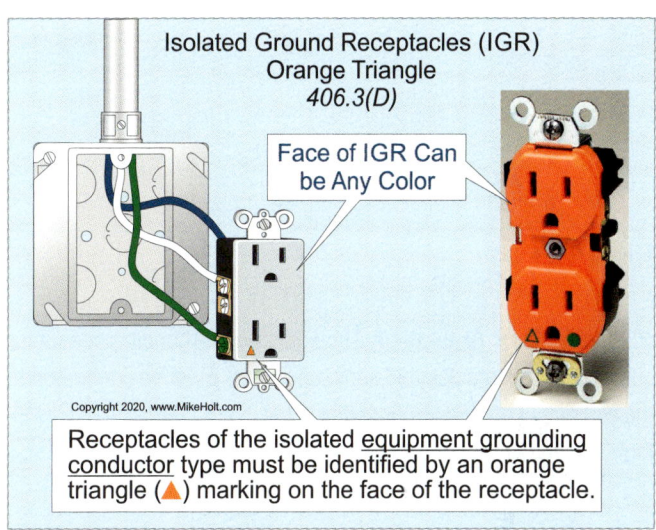

▶Figure 406–2

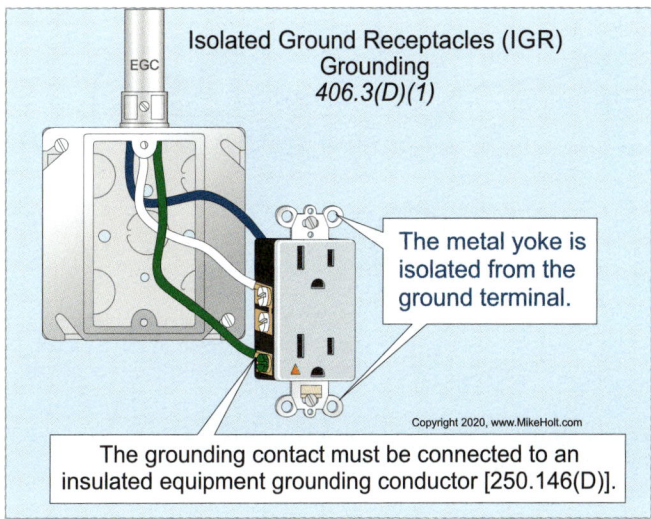

▶Figure 406–3

406.3 Receptacle Rating and Type

(D) Isolated Ground Receptacles. Receptacles of the isolated equipment grounding conductor type must be identified by an orange triangle marking on the face of the receptacle. ▶Figure 406–2

(1) Isolated ground receptacles must have the grounding contact of the receptacle connected to an insulated equipment grounding conductor installed with the circuit conductors, in accordance with 250.146(D). ▶Figure 406–3

406.4 | Receptacles and Attachment Plugs (Caps)

406.4 General Installation Requirements

(A) Grounding Type. Receptacles installed on 15A and 20A branch circuits must be of the grounding type, except as permitted for 2-wire receptacle replacements as permitted in 406.4(D)(2). ▶Figure 406-4

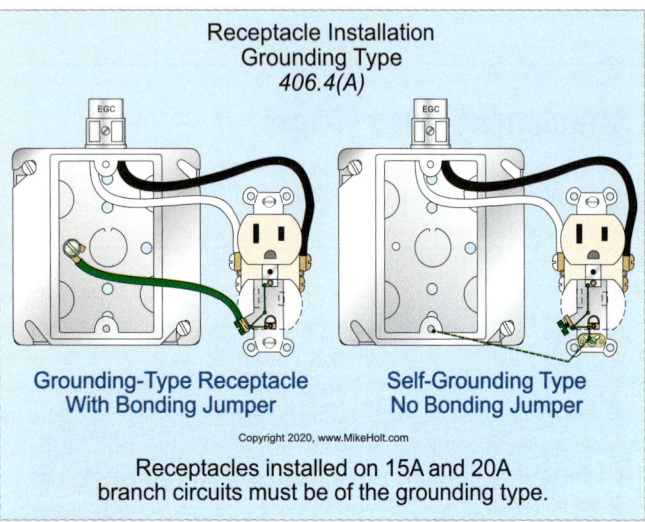

▶Figure 406-4

(C) Methods of Grounding. The equipment grounding conductor contacts of receptacles and cord connectors must be connected to the equipment grounding conductor of the circuit supplying the receptacle or cord connector. ▶Figure 406-5

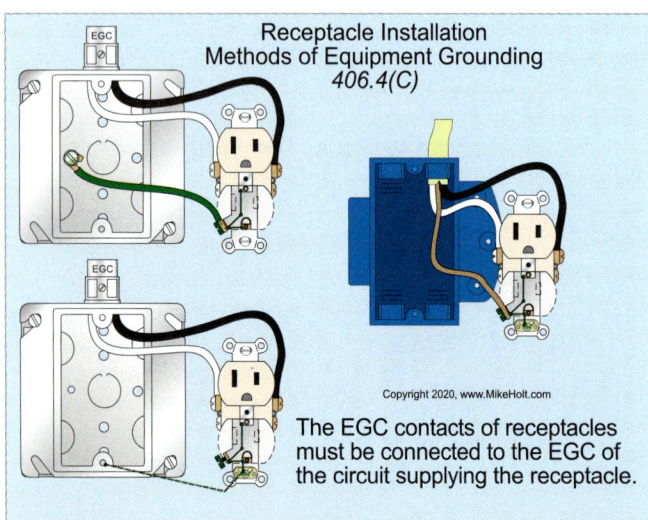

▶Figure 406-5

Note: For installation requirements for reducing electromagnetic interference, see 250.146(D).

The branch-circuit wiring method must include or provide an equipment grounding conductor to which the equipment grounding conductor contacts of the receptacle or cord connector are connected.

Note 1: See 250.118 for acceptable grounding means.

(D) Receptacle Replacement. If the receptacle to be replaced is in a location that requires AFCI- and/or GFCI-type receptacles, they must be installed at a readily accessible location.

(1) Equipment Grounding Conductor in Outlet Box. If an equipment grounding conductor exists in an outlet box, replacement receptacles must be of the grounding type and the receptacle's grounding terminal must be connected to the circuit equipment grounding conductor in accordance with 406.11.

(2) No Equipment Grounding Conductor in Box. If an equipment grounding conductor does not exist in the outlet box, replacement receptacles can be a:

(a) Nongrounding-type receptacle.

(b) GFCI-type receptacle if the receptacle or the cover plate is marked "No Equipment Ground." ▶Figure 406-6

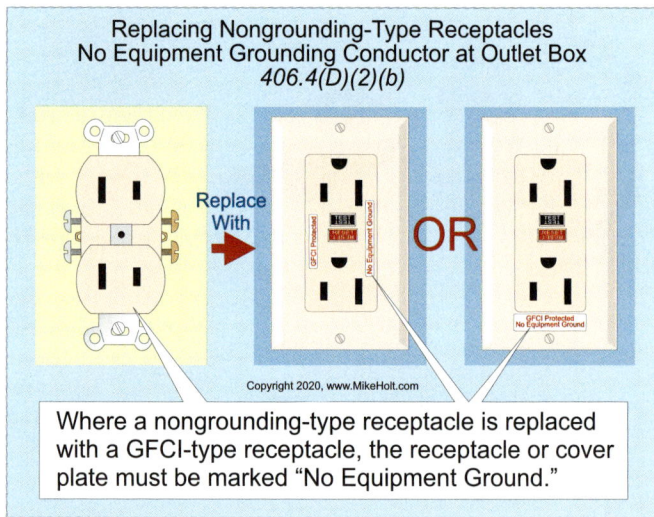

▶Figure 406-6

(c) GFCI-protected grounding-type receptacle if the receptacle or the cover plate is marked "GFCI Protected" and "No Equipment Ground." ▶Figure 406-7

Receptacles and Attachment Plugs (Caps) | **406.4**

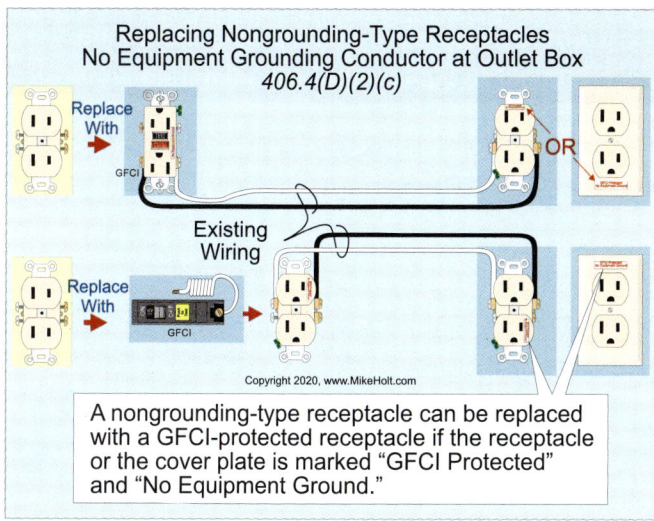
▶Figure 406–7

Caution

The permission to replace nongrounding-type receptacles with GFCI-protected grounding-type receptacles does not apply to new receptacle outlets that extend from an existing outlet box not connected to an equipment grounding conductor [250.130(C)]. ▶Figure 406–9

Author's Comment:

▸ GFCI protection functions properly on a 2-wire circuit without an equipment grounding conductor because the circuit's equipment grounding conductor serves no role in the operation of a GFCI device. See the Article 100 definition of "Ground-Fault Circuit Interrupter" in this textbook for more information. ▶Figure 406–8

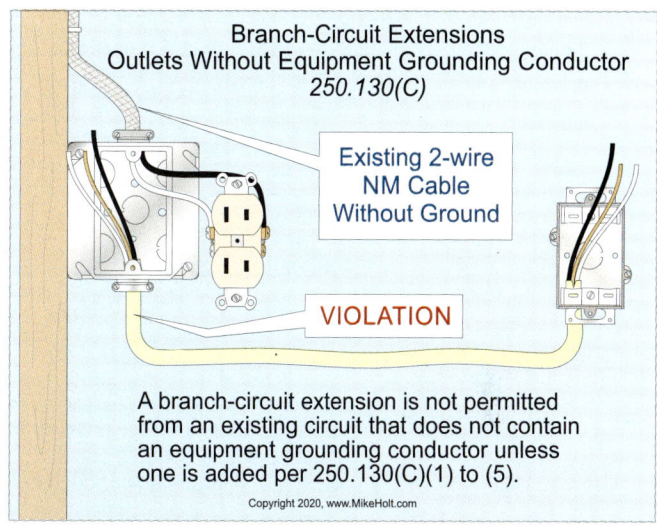
▶Figure 406–9

Note 1: Some equipment or appliance manufacturers require the branch circuit to the equipment or appliance to include an equipment grounding conductor.

Note 2: See 250.114 for a list of cord-and-plug-connected equipment or appliances that require an equipment grounding conductor.

(3) GFCI Protection Required. When existing receptacles are replaced in locations where GFCI protection is required, the replacement receptacles must be GFCI protected.

Ex: Where the outlet box size will not permit the installation of the GFCI receptacle, a GFCI-protected grounding-type receptacle marked "GFCI Protected" and "No Equipment Ground" in accordance with 406.4(D) is permitted.

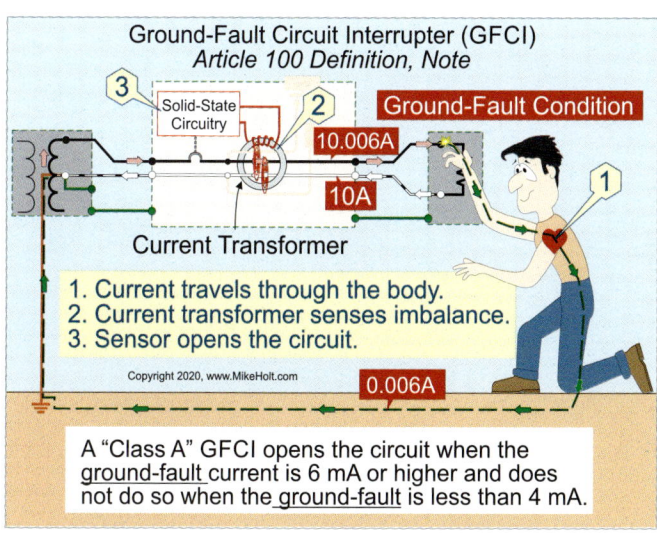
▶Figure 406–8

Author's Comment:

▸ See 210.8 for specific locations requiring GFCI-protection.

▸ Where an *NEC* rule requires GFCI protection, it can be provided by a GFCI circuit breaker, GFCI receptacle, or downstream of a feed-thru type GFCI receptacle.

406.6 Receptacle Faceplates

(B) Grounding. Metal faceplates for receptacles must be connected to the circuit equipment grounding conductor.

Author's Comment:

- The *Code* does not specify how this is accomplished, but 517.13(B) Ex 1 for health care facilities permits the metal mounting screw(s) securing the faceplate to a metal outlet box or wiring device to be suitable for this purpose. ▶Figure 406–10

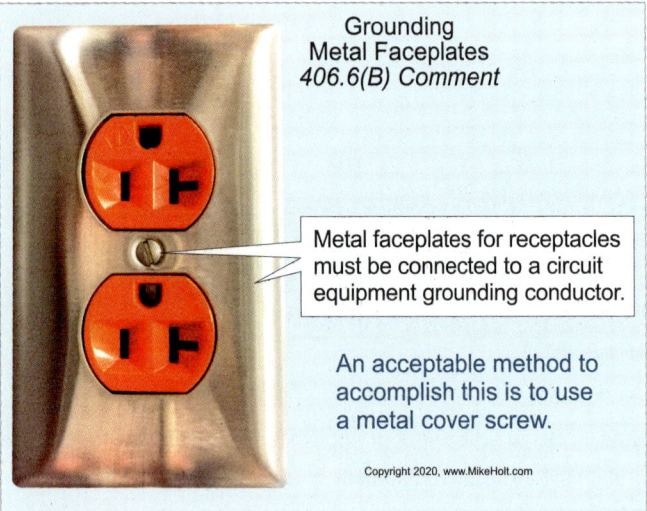

▶Figure 406–10

406.11 Connecting Receptacle Grounding Terminal to Equipment Grounding Conductor

The grounding terminal of receptacles must be connected to an equipment grounding conductor in accordance with 250.146.

ARTICLE 408 — SWITCHBOARDS AND PANELBOARDS

Introduction to Article 408—Switchboards and Panelboards

Article 408 covers the specific requirements for switchboards and panelboards that control power and lighting circuits. You must understand the detailed grounding and overcurrent protection requirements for panelboards.

408.1 Scope

Article 408 covers the requirements for switchboards and panelboards that control power and lighting circuits. ▶Figure 408–1

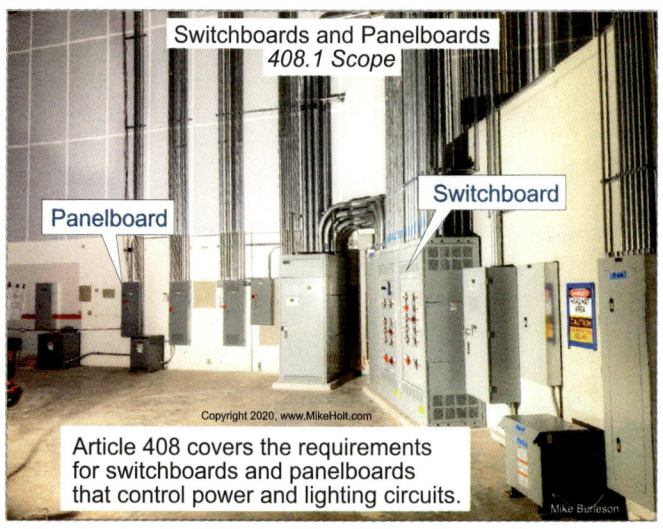

▶Figure 408–1

Author's Comment:

▶ See Article 100 for the definitions for "Switchboard" and "Panelboard."

408.40 Equipment Grounding Conductor

Metal cabinets containing panelboards must be connected to an equipment grounding conductor of a type recognized in 250.118 [215.6 and 250.4(A)(3)]. Where a panelboard cabinet contains equipment grounding conductors of the wire type, a terminal bar for them must be installed and bonded to the metal cabinet. ▶Figure 408–2

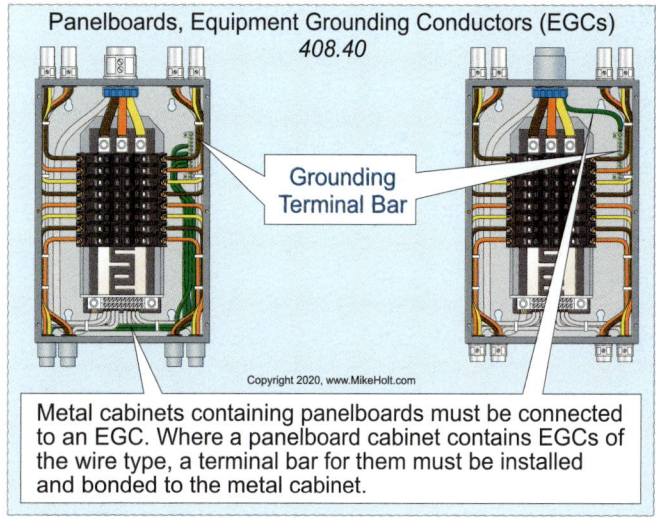

▶Figure 408–2

Equipment grounding conductors are not permitted to terminate on the neutral terminal bar except as permitted by 250.142(A) for services and separately derived systems. ▶Figure 408–3

408.40 | Switchboards and Panelboards

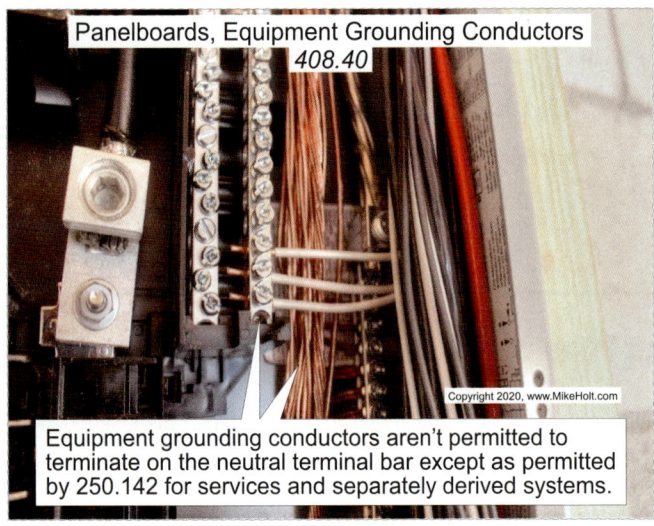

▶Figure 408-3

> **Caution:** Many panelboards are rated for use as service disconnects, which means they are supplied with a main bonding jumper [250.28]. This screw or strap is not permitted to be installed except when the panelboard is used for a service disconnect [250.24(A)(5)] or a separately derived system [250.30(A)(1)].

ARTICLE 410 — LUMINAIRES, LAMPHOLDERS, AND LAMPS

Introduction to Article 410—Luminaires, Lampholders, and Lamps

This article covers luminaires, lamps, decorative lighting products, and lighting for temporary seasonal and holiday use.

Part I. General

410.1 Scope

Article 410 covers luminaires, lampholders, lamps, decorative lighting products, lighting accessories for temporary seasonal and holiday use, portable flexible lighting products, and the wiring and equipment of such products and lighting installations. ▶Figure 410–1

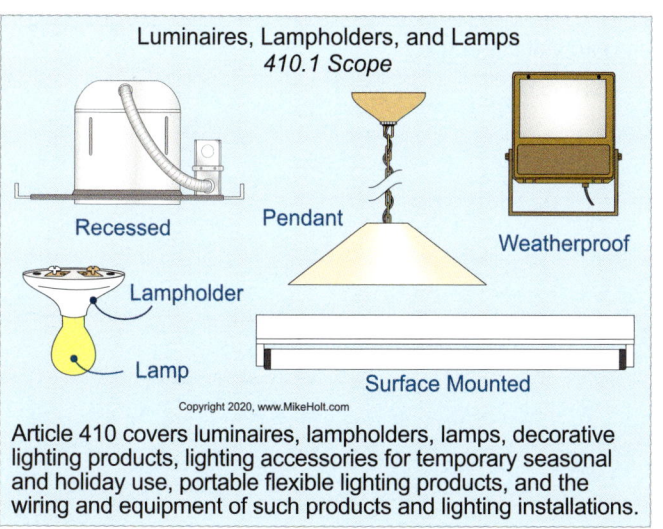

▶Figure 410–1

Author's Comment:

▶ Because of the many types and applications of luminaires, manufacturers' instructions are very important and helpful for proper installation. UL produces a pamphlet called the *Luminaire Marking Guide*, which provides information for properly installing common types of incandescent, fluorescent, and high-intensity discharge (HID) luminaires.

410.30 Supports

(B) Poles.

(5) Metal poles used for the support of luminaires must be connected to an equipment grounding conductor of a type recognized in 250.118 [250.4(A)(5)]. ▶Figure 410–2

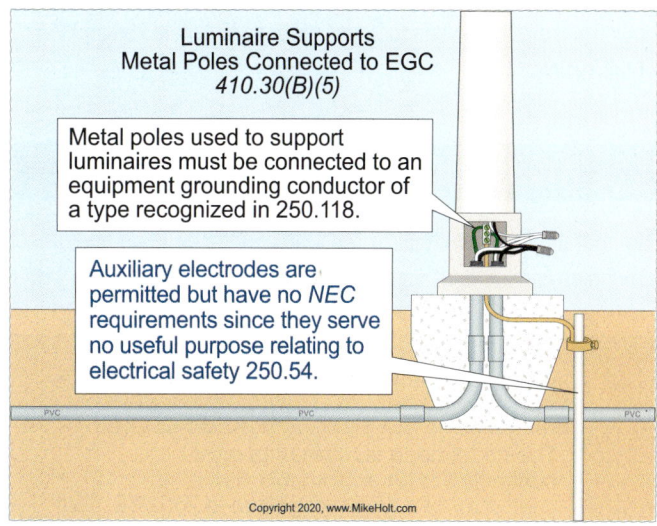

▶Figure 410–2

Danger

Because the contact resistance of an electrode to the Earth is so high, very little fault current returns to the power supply if the Earth is the only fault current return path. As a result, the circuit overcurrent protective device will not open and clear the ground fault, and the metal pole will become and remain energized by the circuit voltage. ▶Figure 410–3

410.40 | Luminaires, Lampholders, and Lamps

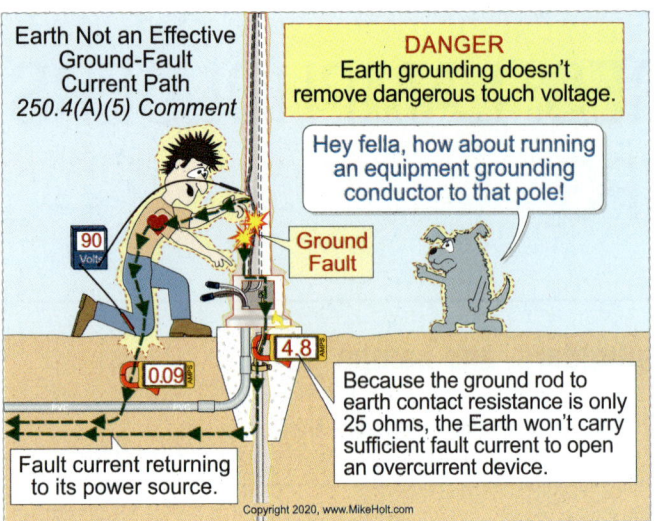

▶Figure 410-3

Ex 1: Replacement luminaires are permitted to connect an equipment grounding conductor in the same manner as replacement receptacles in compliance with 250.130(C). The luminaire must then comply with 410.42.

Ex 2: Where no equipment grounding conductor exists at the outlet, replacement luminaires that are GFCI protected or do not have exposed conductive parts are not required to be connected to an equipment grounding conductor.

410.46 Equipment Grounding Conductor Attachment

Luminaires with exposed metal parts must be provided with a means for connecting an equipment grounding conductor.

Part V. Grounding (Bonding)

Part XVI. Special Provisions for Horticultural Lighting Equipment

410.40 General

Luminaires and lighting equipment must be connected to the circuit equipment grounding conductor as required in Article 250 and Part V of this article.

410.182 Grounding

Lighting equipment identified for horticultural use must be connected to the circuit equipment grounding conductor as required in Article 250 and Part V of this article.

410.44 Equipment Grounding Conductor

The metal parts of luminaires must be connected to an equipment grounding conductor of a type recognized in 250.118. ▶Figure 410-4

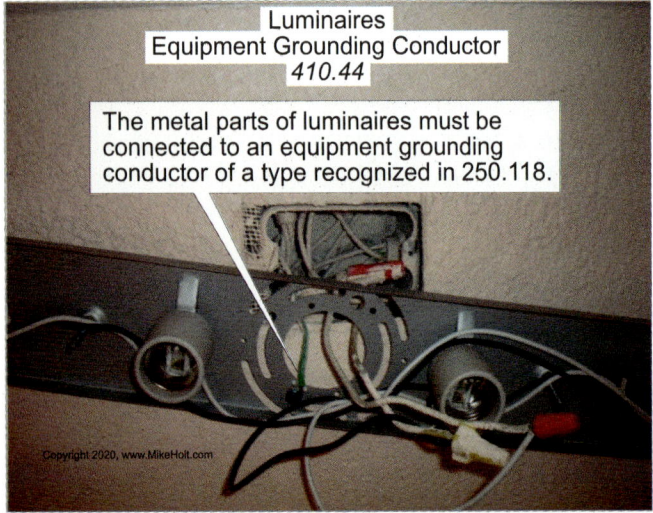

▶Figure 410-4

ARTICLE 440 AIR-CONDITIONING AND REFRIGERATION EQUIPMENT

Introduction to Article 440—Air-Conditioning and Refrigeration Equipment

This article applies to electrically driven air-conditioning and refrigeration equipment. Each equipment manufacturer has the motor for a given air-conditioning unit built to its own specifications. Cooling and other characteristics are different from those of nonhermetic motors.

440.1 Scope

Article 440 applies to electrically driven air-conditioning and refrigeration equipment. ▶Figure 440-1

▶Figure 440-1

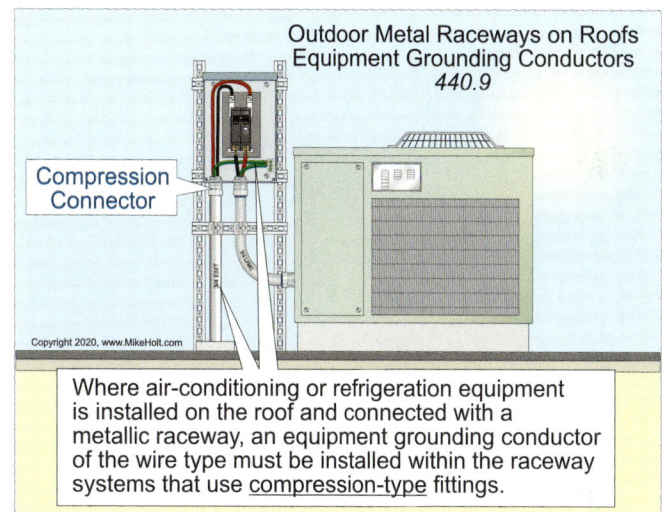

▶Figure 440-2

Author's Comment:

▸ When the wiring method for rooftop units is not a threaded type system, you cannot rely on the raceway to serve as the equipment grounding conductor as permitted by 250.118 and must install an appropriately sized wire-type equipment grounding conductor instead.

440.9 Grounding and Bonding

Where air-conditioning or refrigeration equipment is installed on a roof and connected with a metallic raceway, an equipment grounding conductor of the wire type must be installed within metallic raceway systems that use compression-type fittings. ▶Figure 440-2

Mike Holt Enterprises • www.MikeHolt.com • 888.NEC.CODE (632.2633) | 243

Notes

ARTICLE 450 TRANSFORMERS

Introduction to Article 450—Transformers

Essentially, this article covers transformers supplying power and lighting loads. So, for the purposes of Article 450 only, a transformer is an individual power transformer, single- or poly-phase, identified by a single nameplate—unless otherwise indicated.

450.1 Scope

Article 450 covers the installation requirements of all transformers. ▶Figure 450–1

▶Figure 450–1

Ex 4: Class 2 and 3 transformers that comply with Article 725.

Ex 5: Sign and outline transformers complying with Article 600.

Ex 6: Electric-discharge lighting transformers that comply with Article 410.

Ex 7: Transformers for power-limited fire alarm circuits complying with Article 760 Part III.

450.10 Grounding and Bonding

(A) Dry-Type Transformer Enclosures. A terminal bar for equipment grounding conductors, system bonding jumpers, supply-side bonding jumpers, and grounding electrode conductors must be installed and bonded inside the transformer enclosure. ▶Figure 450–2

▶Figure 450–2

Notes

CHAPTER 4

PRACTICE QUESTIONS

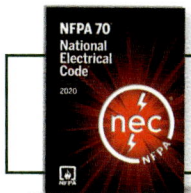

Please use the 2020 *Code* book to answer the following questions.

CHAPTER 4—EQUIPMENT FOR GENERAL USE

1. Snap switches, dimmers, and control switches are considered to be part of the effective ground-fault current path when _____.

    (a) the switch is connected to the intersystem bonding termination
    (b) the switch is mounted with metal screws to a metal box or a metal cover that is connected to an equipment grounding conductor
    (c) an equipment grounding conductor or equipment bonding jumper is connected to the equipment grounding termination of the snap switch
    (d) the switch is mounted with metal screws to a metal box or a metal cover that is connected to an equipment grounding conductor or an equipment grounding conductor or equipment bonding jumper is connected to the equipment grounding termination of the snap switch

2. Where no means exists within the enclosure for bonding a snap switch to an equipment grounding conductor, it shall be permitted for replacement purposes only where the wiring method does not include an equipment grounding conductor and the switch is _____.

    (a) located within 6 ft vertically from ground
    (b) GFCI protected
    (c) AFCI protected
    (d) located within 3 ft horizontally from ground

3. The metal mounting yoke of a replacement switch is not required to be connected to an equipment grounding conductor if the wiring at the existing switch does not contain an equipment grounding conductor, and the _____.

    (a) switch faceplate is metallic and installed with nonmetallic screws
    (b) circuit is GFCI protected
    (c) the switch is mounted to a nonmetallic box
    (d) circuit is AFCI protected

4. Snap switches in listed assemblies are not required to be connected to an equipment grounding conductor if _____.

    (a) the device is provided with a nonmetallic faceplate and the device is designed such that no metallic faceplate replaces the one provided
    (b) the device is equipped with a nonmetallic yoke
    (c) all parts of the device that are accessible after installation of the faceplate are manufactured of nonmetallic material
    (d) all of these

5. A snap switch with an integral nonmetallic enclosure complying with 300.15(E) is required to be connected to an equipment grounding conductor.

    (a) True
    (b) False

6. Metal enclosures for switches or circuit breakers shall be connected to the circuit _____ conductor.

    (a) grounded
    (b) grounding
    (c) equipment grounding
    (d) any of these

Chapter 4 | Practice Questions

7. Where nonmetallic enclosures for switches are used with metal raceways or metal armored cables, they shall _____.

   (a) provide an internal bonding means between all entries
   (b) have and integral bonding means if entries are threaded
   (c) have an external bonding jumper from raceway to raceway
   (d) provide an internal bonding means between all entries and have and integral bonding means if entries are threaded

8. Where a grounding means exists in the receptacle enclosure a(n) _____-type receptacle shall be used.

   (a) isolated ground
   (b) grounding
   (c) GFCI
   (d) dedicated

9. When replacing a non-grounding-type receptacle where attachment to an equipment grounding conductor does not exist in the receptacle enclosure, a _____ can be used as the replacement.

   (a) non-grounding-type receptacle
   (b) grounding receptacle
   (c) GFCI-type receptacle
   (d) non-grounding-type receptacle or GFCI-type receptacle

10. Where attachment to an equipment grounding conductor does not exist in the receptacle enclosure, a non-grounding-type receptacle shall be permitted to be replaced with a GFCI-type receptacle; however, some equipment or appliance manufacturers require that the _____ to the equipment or appliance includes an equipment grounding conductor.

    (a) feeder
    (b) branch circuit
    (c) small-appliance circuit
    (d) power cord

11. When replacing receptacles in locations that would require GFCI protection under the current *NEC*, _____ receptacles shall be installed.

    (a) dedicated
    (b) isolated ground
    (c) GFCI-protected
    (d) grounding

12. Metal faceplates for receptacles shall be grounded.

    (a) True
    (b) False

13. When separate equipment grounding conductors are provided in panelboards, a _____ shall be secured inside the cabinet.

    (a) grounded conductor
    (b) terminal lug
    (c) terminal bar
    (d) bonding jumper

14. Article 410 covers luminaires, portable luminaires, lampholders, pendants, incandescent filament lamps, arc lamps, electric-discharge lamps, and _____, and the wiring and equipment forming part of such products and lighting installations.

    (a) decorative lighting products
    (b) lighting accessories for temporary seasonal and holiday use
    (c) portable flexible lighting products
    (d) all of these

15. Metal raceways shall be bonded to the metal pole with a(n) _____.

    (a) grounding electrode
    (b) grounded conductor
    (c) equipment grounding conductor
    (d) any of these

16. Luminaires and lighting equipment shall be connected to a(an) _____.

    (a) grounding electrode conductor
    (b) grounded conductor
    (c) equipment grounding conductor
    (d) any of these

17. Luminaires and equipment shall be mechanically connected to an equipment grounding conductor as specified in 250.118 and shall be sized in accordance with _____.

    (a) Table 250.66
    (b) Table 250.102
    (c) Table 250.122
    (d) Table 310.16

18. Article 440 applies to electric motor-driven air-conditioning and refrigerating equipment that has a hermetic refrigerant motor-compressor.

    (a) True
    (b) False

19. Where air-conditioning and refrigeration equipment is installed outdoors on a roof, a(n) _____ conductor of the wire type shall be installed in outdoor portions of metallic raceway systems that use compression-type fittings.

    (a) equipment grounding
    (b) grounding
    (c) equipment bonding
    (d) bonding

20. The equipment grounding conductor terminal bar of a dry-type transformer shall be bonded to the enclosure in accordance with 250.12 and shall not be installed on or over any _____.

    (a) ungrounded conductor terminations
    (b) transformer coils or windings
    (c) vented portion of the enclosure
    (d) all of these

Notes

CHAPTER 5

SPECIAL OCCUPANCIES

Introduction to Chapter 5—Special Occupancies

Chapter 5, which covers special occupancies, is the first of four *NEC* chapters dealing with special topics.

What exactly is a "Special Occupancy"? It is a location where a facility, or its use, creates specific conditions requiring additional measures to ensure the "practical safeguarding of people and property" purpose of the *NEC* as put forth in Article 90.

Many people struggle to understand the rules for special occupancies (especially hazardous locations), mostly because of the narrowness of application. If you study the illustrations and explanations here, you will better understand them.

- **Article 501—Class I Hazardous (Classified) Locations.** A Class I hazardous (classified) location is an area where flammable or combustible liquid-produced vapors or flammable gases may present the hazard of a fire or explosion.

- **Article 502—Class II Hazardous (Classified) Locations.** A Class II hazardous (classified) location is an area where the possibility of fire or explosion may exist due to the presence of combustible dust.

- **Article 503—Class III Hazardous (Classified) Locations.** Class III hazardous (classified) locations are hazardous because fire or explosion risks may exist due to easily ignitible fibers/flyings. These include materials such as cotton and rayon, which are found in textile mills and clothing manufacturing plants. They can also include establishments and industries such as sawmills and woodworking plants.

- **Article 517—Health Care Facilities.** Article 517 applies to electrical wiring in human health care facilities such as hospitals, nursing homes, limited care facilities, clinics, medical and dental offices, and ambulatory care—whether permanent or movable. It does not apply to animal veterinary facilities.

- **Article 525—Carnivals, Circuses, Fairs, and Similar Events.** This article covers the installation of portable wiring and equipment for temporary carnivals, circuses, exhibitions, fairs, traveling attractions, and similar functions including wiring in or on structures.

- **Article 547—Agricultural Buildings.** Article 547 covers agricultural buildings or those parts of buildings or adjacent areas where excessive dust or dust with water may accumulate, or where a corrosive atmosphere exists.

- **Article 555—Marinas, Boatyards, Floating Buildings, and Commercial and Noncommercial Docking Facilities.** This article covers the installation of wiring and equipment in the areas comprised of fixed or floating piers, wharves, docks, and other areas in marinas, boatyards, boat basins, boathouses, and similar locations used (or intended to be used) for the repair, berthing, launching, storing, or fueling of small craft, and the mooring of floating buildings.

Notes

ARTICLE 501 — CLASS I HAZARDOUS (CLASSIFIED) LOCATIONS

Introduction to Article 501—Class I Hazardous (Classified) Locations

If enough flammable or combustible gases, vapors, or liquids are or may be present to produce an explosive or ignitable mixture, you have a Class I location. Examples of such locations include some fuel storage areas, certain solvent storage areas, grain processing facilities (where hexane is used), plastic extrusion areas where oil removal is part of the process, refineries, and paint storage areas. Article 501 contains Class I, Division 1 and Division 2 installation requirements, including wiring methods, seals, and specific equipment requirements.

Part I. General

501.1 Scope

Article 501 covers requirements for electrical equipment and wiring in Class I, Division 1 and Division 2 locations where flammable gases or flammable liquid-produced vapors may be present in the air and in quantities sufficient to produce explosive or ignitible mixtures [500.5(B)]. ▶Figure 501–1

▶Figure 501–1

501.30 Grounding and Bonding

Because of the explosive conditions associated with electrical installations in hazardous (classified) locations [500.5], electrical continuity of metal parts of equipment and raceways must be ensured regardless of the voltage of the circuit.

(A) Bonding. Locknuts are not suitable for bonding purposes in hazardous (classified) locations; therefore, bonding jumpers or other approved means of bonding must be used for all intervening raceways, fittings, boxes, enclosures, and so forth between Class I locations and service equipment or separately derived systems. ▶Figure 501–2

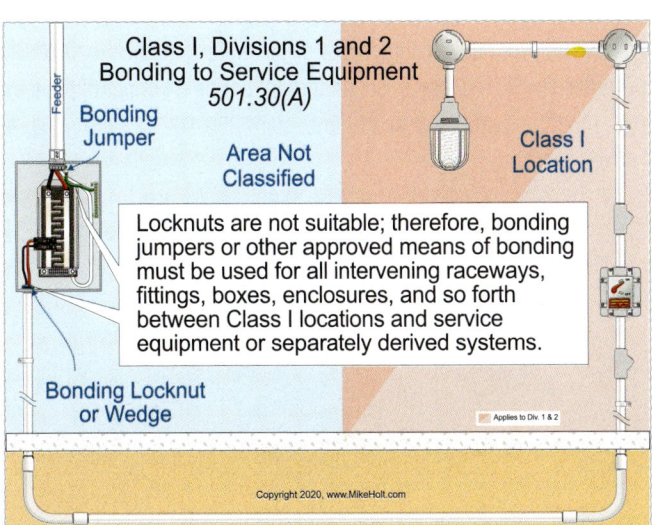

▶Figure 501–2

501.30 | Class I Hazardous (Classified) Locations

Author's Comment:

▸ Regardless of the circuit voltage, electrical continuity of the metal parts of equipment and raceways in hazardous (classified) locations must be ensured by the use bonding-type locknuts, wedges, or bushings with bonding jumpers [250.92(B)(4)]; whether or not equipment grounding conductors of the wire type are installed in the raceway [250.100]. Locknuts alone are not enough to serve this purpose.

▸ A separate equipment grounding conductor is not required if a metal raceway is used for equipment grounding. Threaded couplings and hubs made up wrenchtight provide a suitable low-impedance fault current path [250.100]. ▸Figure 501-3

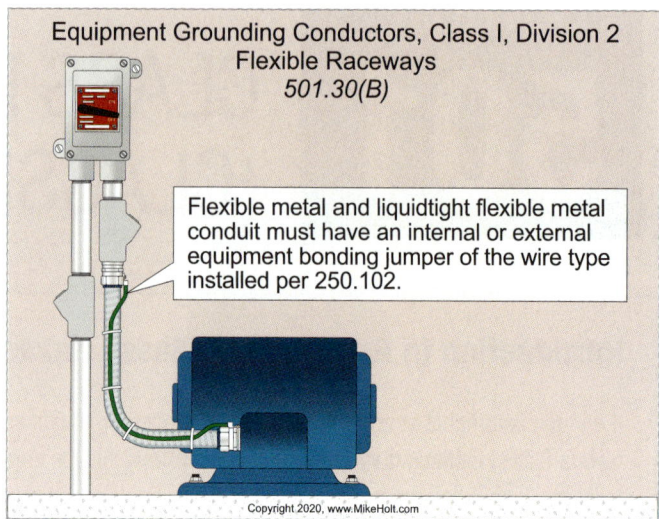

▸Figure 501-4

Author's Comment:

▸ Bonding jumpers are sized in accordance with Table 250.122, based on the rating of the overcurrent protective device [250.102(D)]. Where installed outside a raceway, the length of bonding jumpers are not permitted to exceed 6 ft and they must be routed with the raceway [250.102(E)(2)]. ▸Figure 501-5

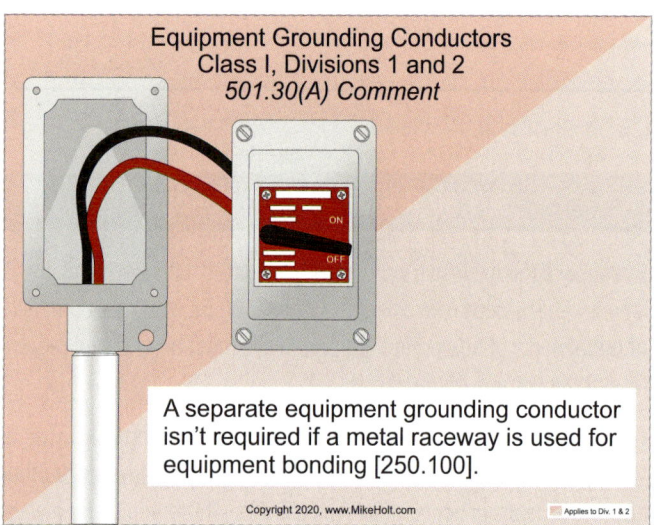

▸Figure 501-3

(B) Equipment Grounding Conductor, Flexible Raceway. Where flexible metal conduit or liquidtight flexible metal conduit is installed as permitted by 501.10(B)(2), an equipment bonding jumper of the wire type must be installed in accordance with 250.102. ▸Figure 501-4

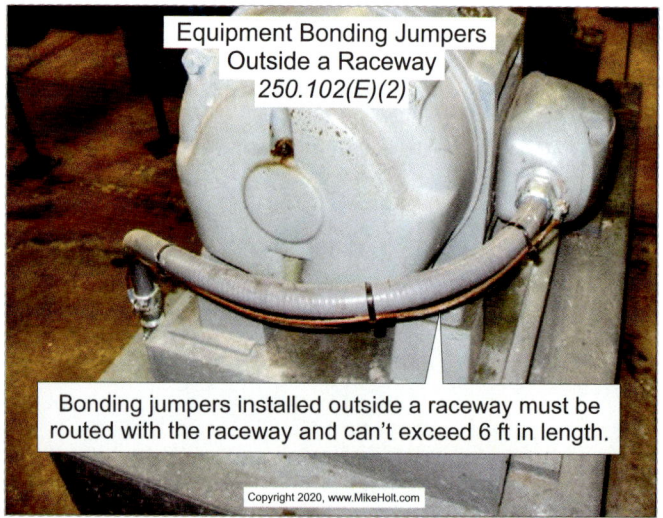

▸Figure 501-5

ARTICLE 502 — CLASS II HAZARDOUS (CLASSIFIED) LOCATIONS

Introduction to Article 502—Class II Hazardous (Classified) Locations

If an area has combustible dust present, it is considered a Class II location. Examples of such locations include flour mills, grain silos, coal bins, wood pulp storage areas, and munitions plants.

502.1 Scope

Article 502 covers the requirements for electrical equipment and wiring in Class II, Division 1 and 2 locations where fire or explosion hazards may exist due to the presence of combustible dust. ▶Figure 502–1

▶Figure 502–1

502.30 Grounding and Bonding

Because of the explosive conditions associated with electrical installations in hazardous (classified) locations [500.5], electrical continuity of the metal parts of equipment and raceways must be ensured regardless of the voltage of the circuit.

(A) Bonding. Locknuts are not suitable for bonding purposes in hazardous (classified) locations; therefore, bonding jumpers or other approved means of bonding must be used. Such means of bonding apply to all intervening raceways, fittings, boxes, enclosures, and so forth between Class II locations and service disconnects or the grounding point of a separately derived system. ▶Figure 502–2

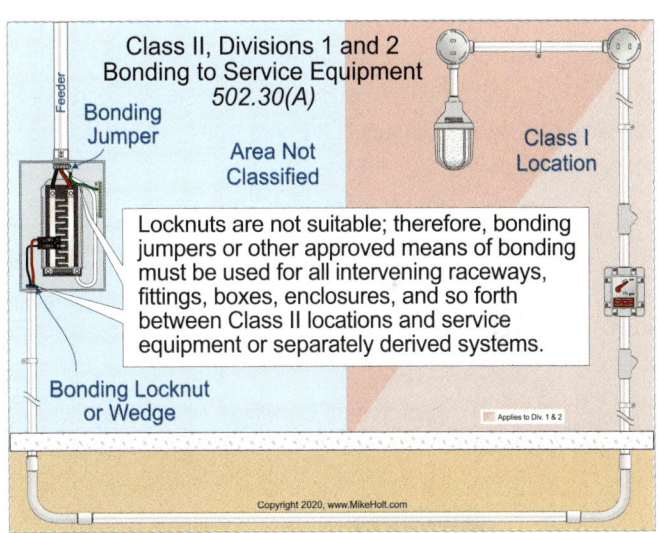

▶Figure 502–2

Author's Comment:

▶ A separate equipment grounding conductor is not required if a metal raceway is used for equipment grounding. Threaded couplings and hubs made up wrenchtight provide a suitable low-impedance ground-fault current path [250.100]. ▶Figure 502–3

502.30 | Class II Hazardous (Classified) Locations

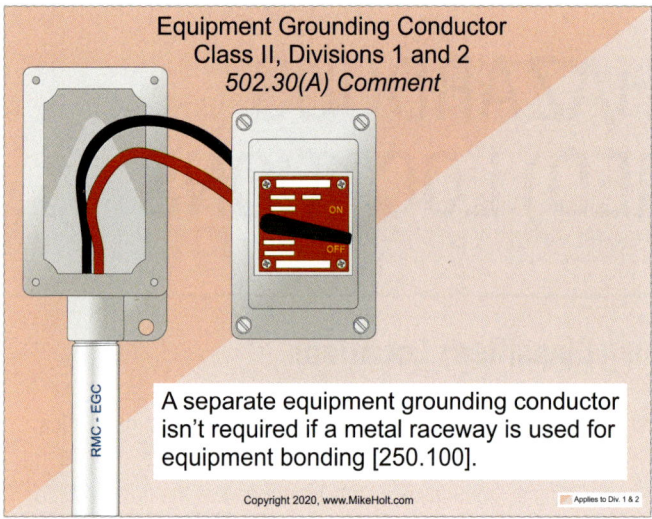
▶Figure 502-3

Author's Comment:

▸ The special bonding requirements for Class 2 locations are the same as those for 501.30(A) Class 1 Locations.

(B) Equipment Grounding Conductor, Type LFMC. Where liquidtight flexible metal conduit is installed as permitted by 501.10(A)(4), an equipment bonding jumper of the wire type must be installed in accordance with 250.102. ▶Figure 502-4

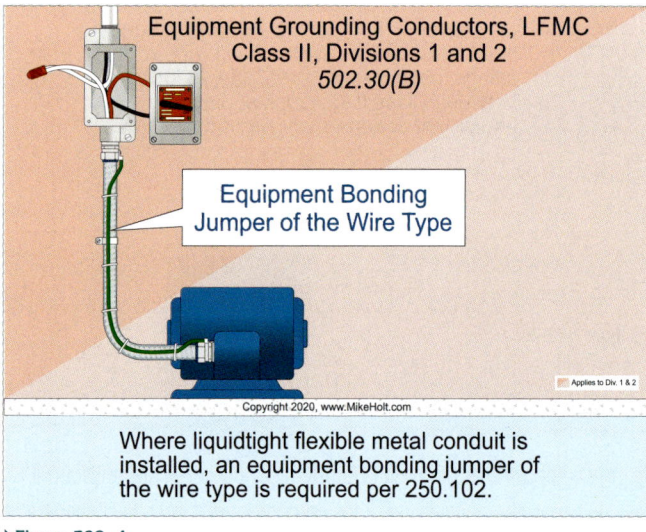
▶Figure 502-4

Author's Comment:

▸ Bonding jumpers must be sized in accordance with 250.122, based on the rating of the overcurrent protective device [250.102(D)]. Where a bonding jumper is installed outside a raceway, the length is not permitted to exceed 6 ft and it must be routed with the raceway [250.102(E)(2)]. ▶Figure 502-5

▶Figure 502-5

ARTICLE 503 — CLASS III HAZARDOUS (CLASSIFIED) LOCATIONS

Introduction to Article 503—Class III Hazardous (Classified) Locations

The Class III location scope can be a bit cumbersome, and some may have a hard time comprehending what it means. If there are easily ignitable fibers/flyings present, it might be a Class III location. Examples of such locations include sawmills, textile mills, and fiber processing plants. In many cases, the distinction between Class II and Class III locations is simply be the size of the combustible or ignitible particles in the area. The definition of "Combustible Dust" in Article 100 defines it based on the size of the particles, so the same material (such as sawdust) can be subject to Article 503 if the predominant material is "larger" than the definition.

Author's Comment:

▸ Article 100 defines "Combustible Dust" as dust particles that are 500 microns in size or smaller. That's approximately 2/100ths of an inch!

503.1 Scope

Article 503 covers the requirements for electrical equipment and wiring for all voltages in Class III, Division 1 and 2 locations. These are locations where fire or explosion hazards might exist because easily ignitable fibers or materials producing combustible flyings are handled, manufactured, or used but are not likely to be suspended in the air in large enough quantities to produce ignitible mixtures [500.5(D)]. ▸Figure 503–1

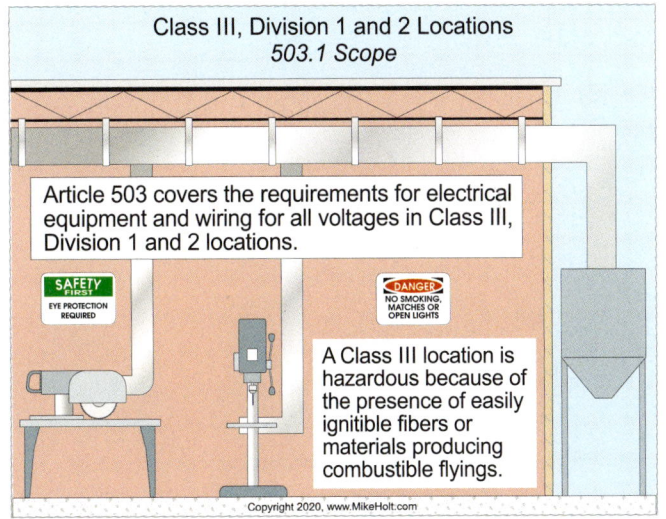

▸Figure 503–1

503.30 Grounding and Bonding

Because of the explosive conditions associated with electrical installations in hazardous (classified) locations [500.5], electrical continuity of the metal parts of equipment and raceways must be ensured regardless of the voltage of the circuit.

(A) Bonding. Locknuts are not suitable for bonding purposes in hazardous (classified) locations; therefore, bonding jumpers or other approved means of bonding must be used. Such means of bonding apply to all intervening raceways, fittings, boxes, and enclosures between Class III locations and service disconnects.

(B) Type of Equipment Bonding Conductor. Where liquidtight flexible metal conduit is located, an equipment bonding jumper of the wire type must be installed in accordance with 250.102. ▸Figure 503–2

503.30 | Class III Hazardous (Classified) Locations

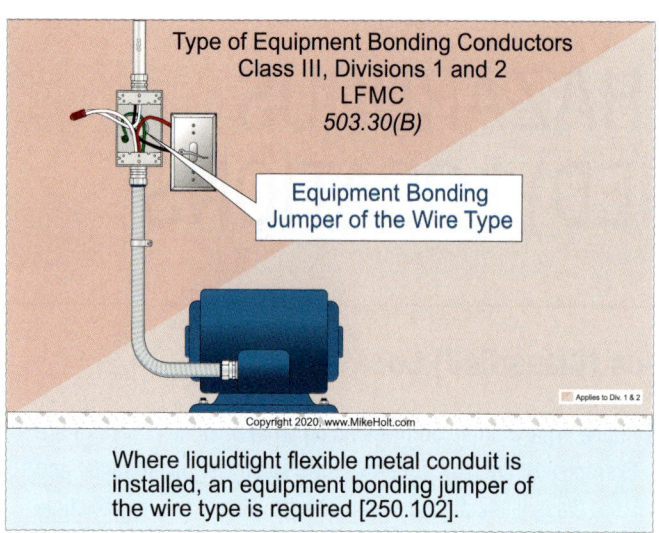

▶Figure 503–2

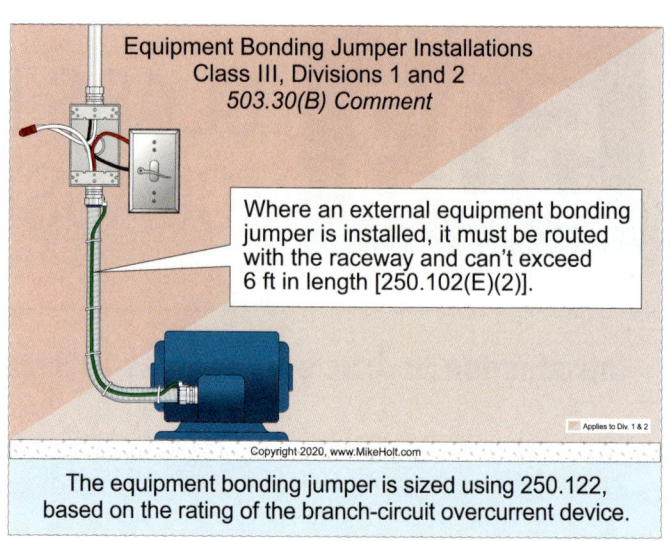

▶Figure 503–3

Author's Comment:

▸ Bonding jumpers must be sized in accordance with 250.122, based on the rating of the overcurrent protective device [250.102(D)]. Where bonding jumpers are installed outside a raceway, the length is not permitted to exceed 6 ft and they must be routed with the raceway [250.102(E)(2)]. ▶Figure 503–3

ARTICLE 517 — HEALTH CARE FACILITIES

Introduction to Article 517—Health Care Facilities

Health care facilities differ from other types of buildings in many important ways. Article 517 is primarily concerned with those parts of health care facilities where patients are examined and treated. Whether those facilities are permanent or movable, they still fall under the scope of this article. However, Article 517's wiring and protection requirements do not apply to business offices or waiting rooms and they do not apply to animal veterinary facilities.

This article contains many specialized definitions that only apply to health care facilities. While you do not need to be able to quote them, you should have a clear understanding of what the terms mean.

Be aware that the *NEC* is just one of the standards that applies to health care facilities; there may be additional requirements from other standards and special requirements for sophisticated equipment.

517.1 Scope

Article 517 applies to electrical wiring in health care facilities, such as hospitals, nursing homes, limited care and supervisory care facilities, clinics, medical and dental offices, and ambulatory care facilities that provide services to human beings. ▶Figure 517-1

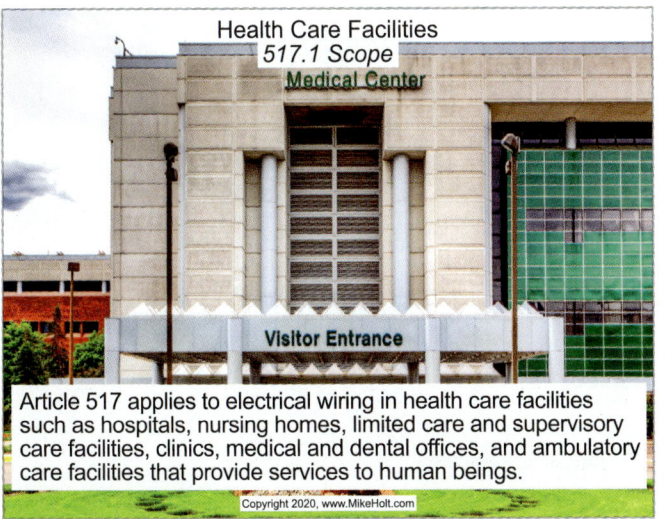

▶Figure 517-1

Author's Comment:

▸ This article does not apply to animal veterinary facilities.

▸ Areas of health care facilities not used for the treatment of patients, such as business offices and waiting rooms, are not required to comply with the provisions contained in Article 517.

517.2 Definitions

Patient Care Space. Any space of a health care facility where patients are intended to be examined or treated. ▶Figure 517-2

Note 2: Business offices, corridors, lounges, day rooms, dining rooms, or similar areas are not classified as patient care spaces.

Patient Care Vicinity. A space (within a location intended for the examination and treatment of patients) extending 6 ft beyond the normal location of the patient bed, chair, table, treadmill, or other device that supports the patient during examination and treatment and extending vertically to 7 ft 6 in. above the floor. ▶Figure 517-3

517.12 | Health Care Facilities

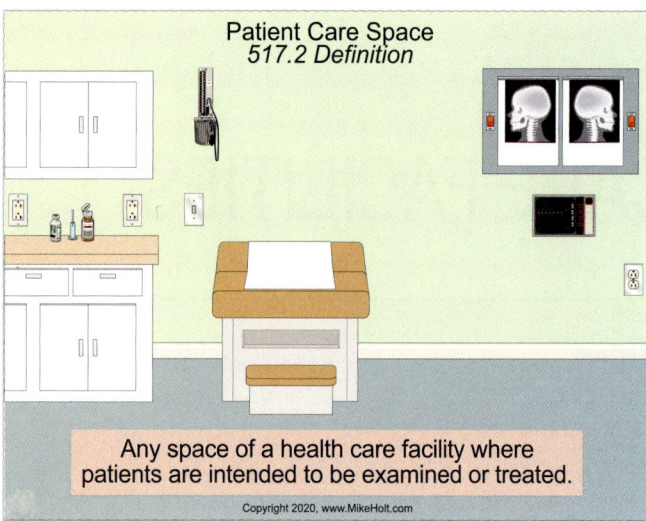

▶Figure 517–2

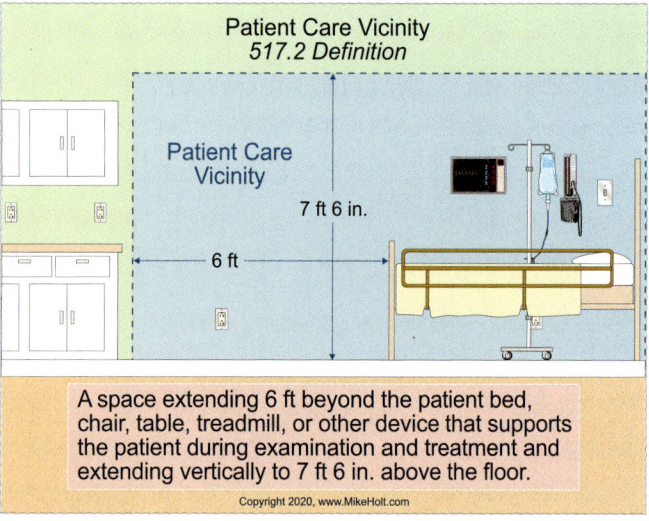

▶Figure 517–3

517.12 Wiring Methods

Wiring methods must comply with the Chapter 1 through 4 provisions, except as modified in this article.

517.13 Equipment Grounding Conductor for Receptacles and Fixed Electrical Equipment in Patient Care Spaces

Wiring in patient care spaces must comply with (A) and (B):

Author's Comment:

▸ Patient care spaces, as designated by the facility administrator, include patient rooms as well as examining rooms, therapy areas, treatment rooms, and some patient corridors. They do not include business offices, corridors, lounges, day rooms, dining rooms, or similar areas not classified as patient care spaces [517.2].

▸ Equipment grounding requirements in patient care spaces are based on the concept of two different types of equipment grounding conductors so if there is an installation error, the effective ground-fault current paths are not lost. One effective ground-fault current path is "mechanical" (the wiring method), and the other is of the "wire type." Section 517.13(A) requires the wiring method to be a metal raceway or metal cable that qualifies as an equipment grounding conductor in accordance with 250.118, and 517.13(B) requires an insulated copper equipment grounding conductor of the wire type in accordance with 250.118.

(A) Wiring Methods. Branch-circuit conductors serving patient care spaces must be in a metal raceway or metal cable having a metal sheath that qualifies as an equipment grounding conductor in accordance with 250.118. ▶Figure 517–4

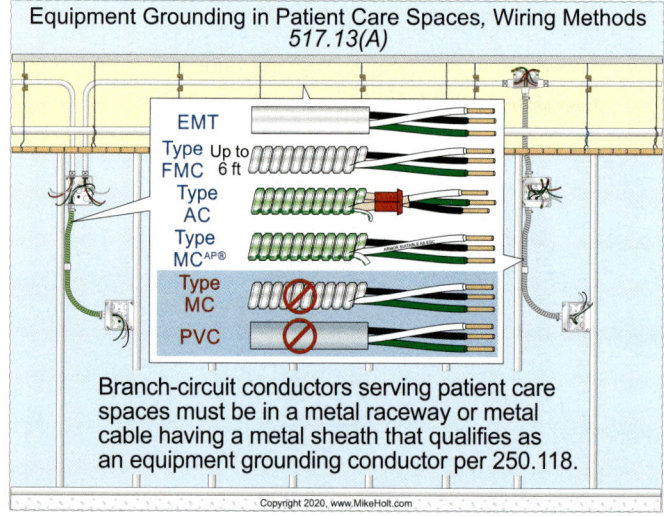

▶Figure 517–4

Author's Comment:

▸ The metal sheath of traditional Type MC interlocked cable does not qualify as an equipment grounding conductor [250.118(10)(a)]; therefore, this wiring method is not permitted to be used for circuits in patient care spaces. ▶Figure 517–5

Health Care Facilities | **517.13**

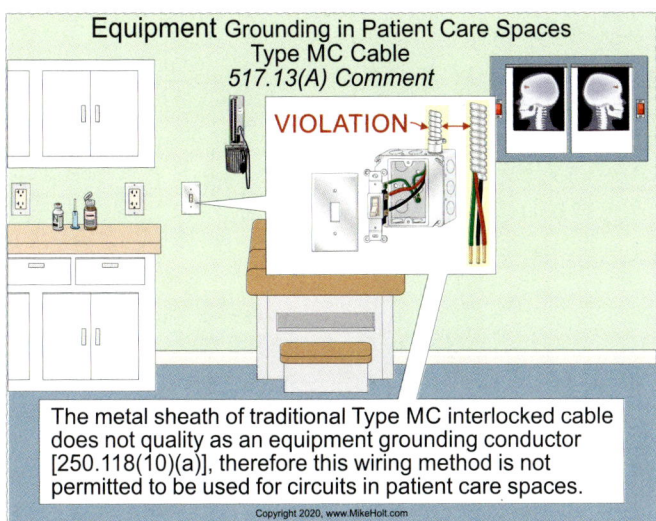
▶Figure 517–5

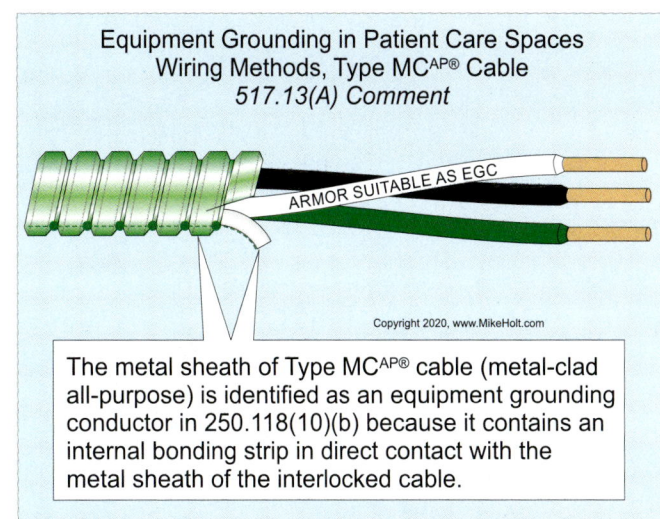
▶Figure 517–7

Author's Comment:

▸ The metal sheath of Type AC cable is identified as an equipment grounding conductor in 250.118(8) because it contains an internal bonding strip in direct contact with the metal sheath of the interlocked cable. ▶Figure 517–6

(B) Insulated Equipment Grounding Conductors.

(1) General. The following equipment must be directly connected to an insulated copper equipment grounding conductor that has green insulation along its entire length. Such conductors must be contained in a suitable wiring method as required in 517.13(A).

(1) The grounding contact of receptacles, other than isolated ground receptacles, must be directly connected to a green insulated copper equipment grounding conductor. ▶Figure 517–8

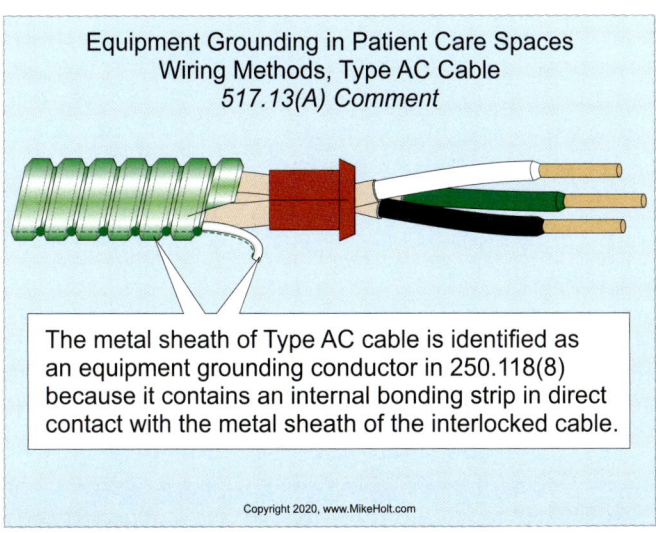
▶Figure 517–6

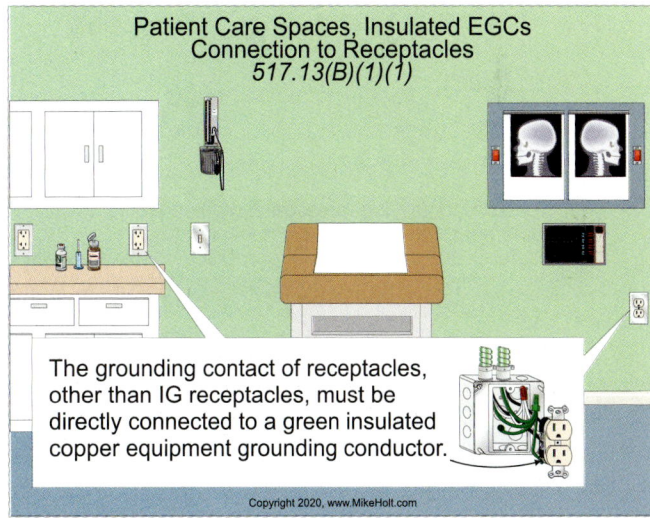
▶Figure 517–8

Author's Comment:

▸ The metal sheath of Type MC$^{AP®}$ cable (metal-clad all-purpose) is identified as an equipment grounding conductor in 250.118(10)(b) because it contains an internal bonding strip in direct contact with the metal sheath of the interlocked cable. ▶Figure 517–7

(2) Metal enclosures containing circuit conductors must be directly connected to a green insulated copper equipment grounding conductor. ▶Figure 517–9

517.16 | Health Care Facilities

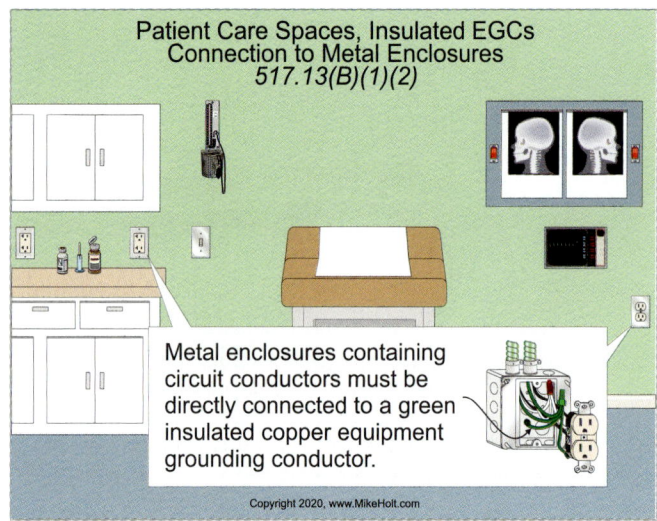
▶Figure 517–9

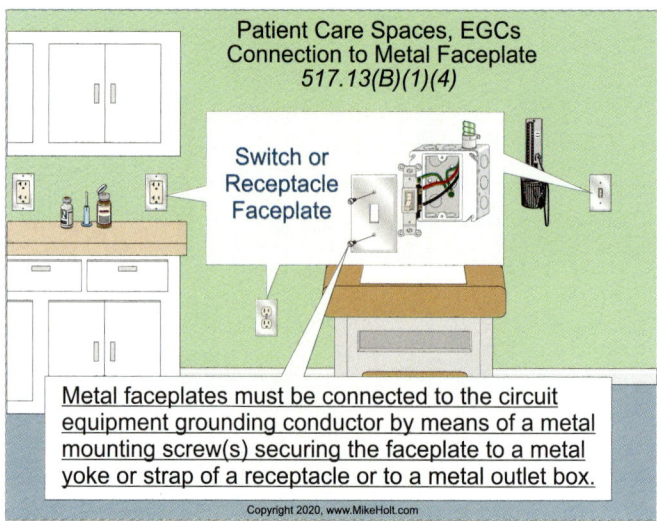
▶Figure 517–11

(3) Noncurrent-carrying metal parts of fixed electrical equipment must be directly connected to an insulated copper equipment grounding conductor. ▶Figure 517–10

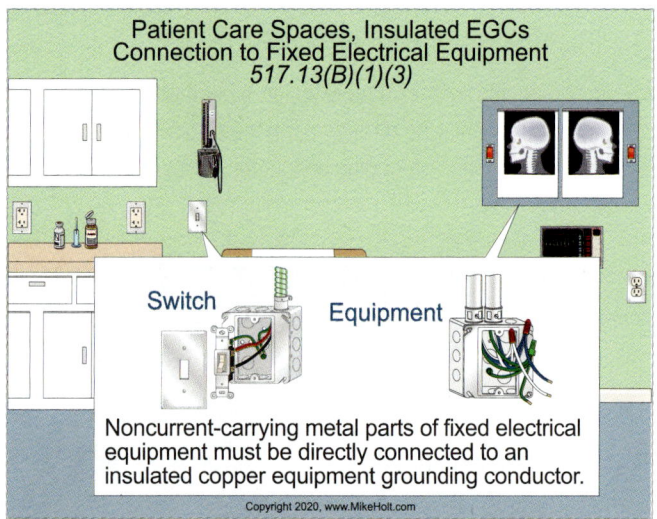
▶Figure 517–10

(4) Metal faceplates must be connected to the circuit equipment grounding conductor by means of a metal mounting screw(s) securing the faceplate to a metal yoke or strap of a receptacle, or to a metal outlet box. ▶Figure 517–11

Ex 2: Circuits for luminaires located more than 7½ ft above the floor and switches located outside the patient care vicinity must be installed in a 517.13(A) wiring method; an equipment grounding conductor of the wire type is not required within the wiring method. ▶Figure 517–12

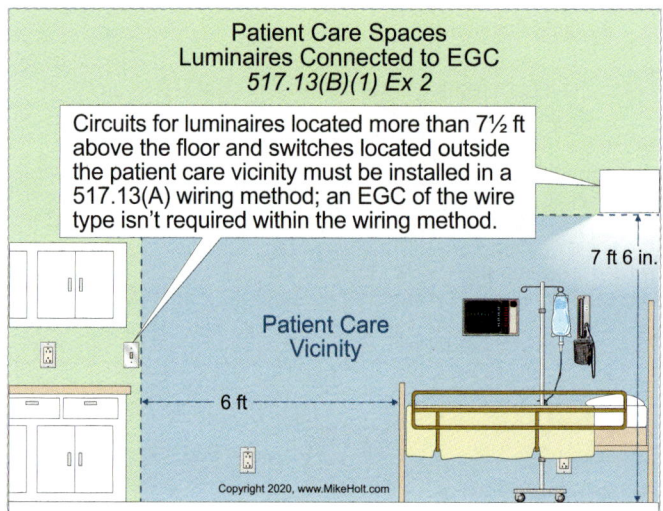
▶Figure 517–12

(2) Sizing. Equipment grounding conductors and equipment bonding jumpers must be sized in accordance with 250.122. ▶Figure 517–13

517.16 Isolated Ground Receptacles

An isolated ground receptacle, if used, must not defeat the purposes of the safety features of the grounding systems detailed in 517.13. ▶Figure 517–14

(A) Inside Patient Care Vicinity. An isolated ground receptacle must not be installed within a patient care vicinity. ▶Figure 517–15

Health Care Facilities | 517.16

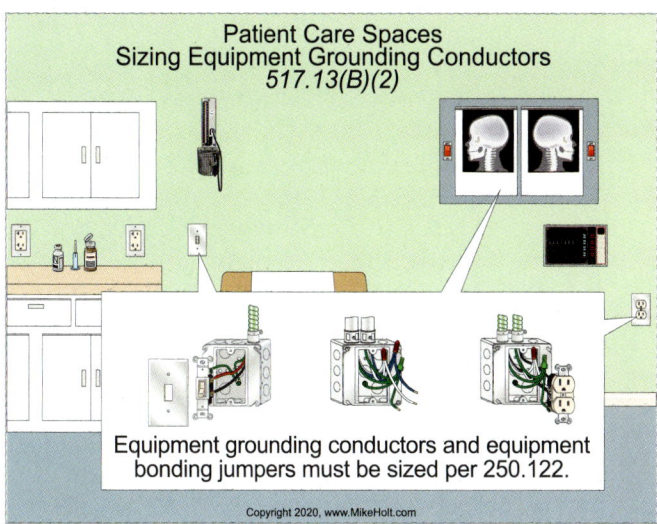
▶Figure 517-13

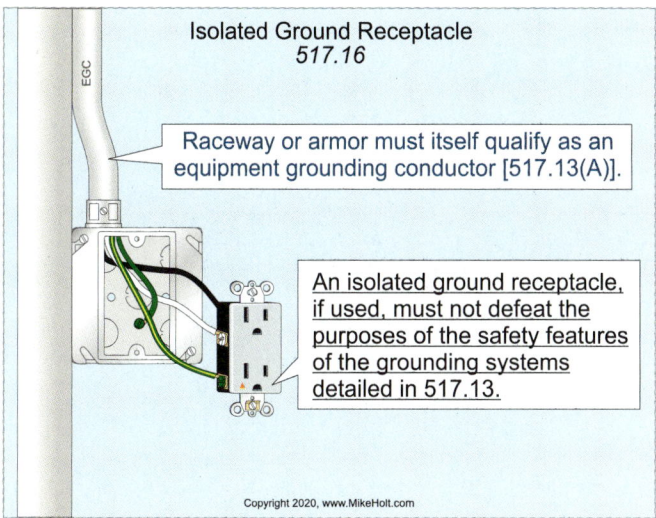
▶Figure 517-14

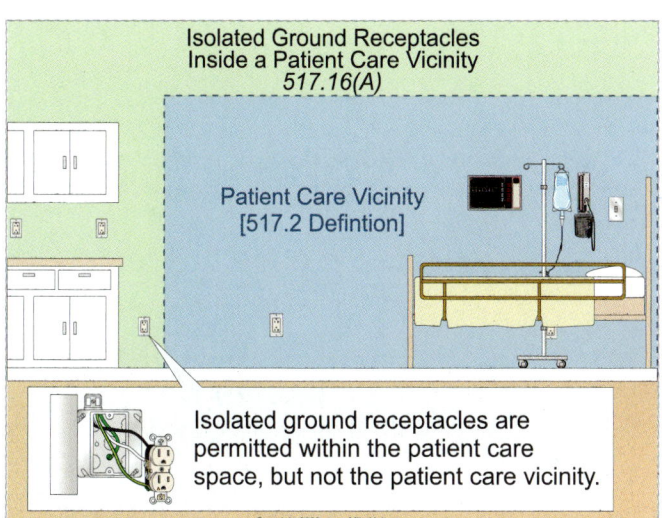
▶Figure 517-15

Author's Comment:

▸ A patient care vicinity is a space extending 6 ft beyond the normal location of the patient bed, chair, table, treadmill, or other device that supports the patient during examination and treatment and extends vertically to 7 ft 6 in. above the floor [517.2 Definition].

(B) Outside Patient Care Vicinity. Isolated ground receptacle(s) within the patient care space (as defined in 517.2), but outside the patient care vicinity must comply with the following:

(1) The equipment grounding terminal of isolated grounding receptacles must be connected to an insulated equipment grounding conductor in accordance with 250.146(D) and installed in a wiring method described in 517.13(A). The equipment grounding conductor connected to the equipment grounding terminals of the isolated grounding receptacle must have green insulation with one or more yellow stripes along its entire length. ▶Figure 517-16

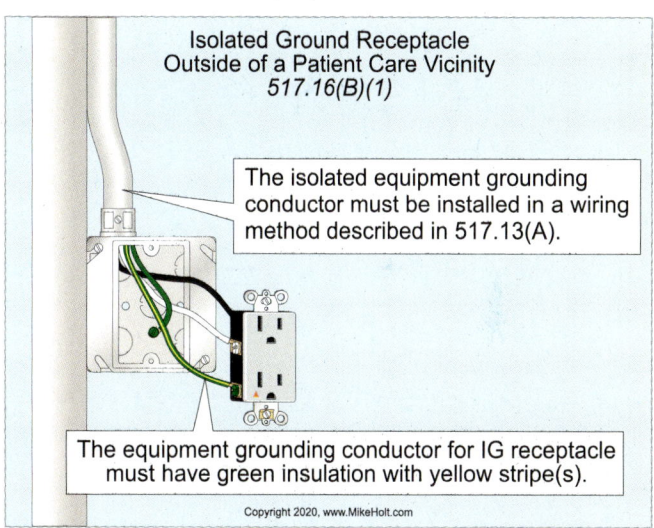
▶Figure 517-16

(2) The insulated equipment grounding conductor required by 517.13(B)(1) must be connected to the metal enclosure containing the receptacle as required by 517.13(B)(1)(2).

Note 2: Care should be taken in specifying a system containing isolated ground receptacles, because the impedance of the effective ground-fault current path is dependent on the equipment grounding conductor(s) and does not benefit from any conduit or building structure in parallel with the equipment grounding conductor.

Notes

ARTICLE 525 — CARNIVALS, CIRCUSES, FAIRS, AND SIMILAR EVENTS

Introduction to Article 525—Carnivals, Circuses, Fairs, and Similar Events

This article covers the installation of portable wiring and equipment for temporary carnivals, circuses, exhibitions, fairs, traveling attractions, and similar functions; including wiring in or on structures.

525.1 Scope

Article 525 covers the installation of portable wiring and equipment for carnivals, circuses, exhibitions, fairs, traveling attractions, and similar functions. ▶Figure 525–1

▶Figure 525–1

525.31 Equipment Grounding

Metal parts of electrical equipment must be connected to an equipment grounding conductor of a type recognized by 250.118.

525.32 Portable Equipment Grounding Conductor Continuity

The continuity of the circuit equipment grounding conductors for portable electrical equipment must be verified each time the equipment is connected.

Author's Comment:

▶ Verification of the circuit equipment grounding conductors is necessary to ensure electrical safety. This rule does not specify how they are verified, what circuits must be verified, how the verification is recorded, or who is required or qualified to perform the verification.

Notes

ARTICLE 547 — AGRICULTURAL BUILDINGS

Introduction to Article 547—Agricultural Buildings

Three factors (dust, moisture, and an overall corrosive environment) have a tremendous influence on the lifespan of agricultural equipment. Dust gets into mechanisms and causes premature wear. Adding electricity to the dust presents two additional dangers: fire and explosion. Dust from hay, grain, fertilizer, and litter materials (such as straw) are highly flammable. Another factor to consider in agricultural buildings is moisture, which causes corrosion. Water is present for many reasons, including during wash down. Excrement from farm animals may cause corrosive vapors that eat at mechanical equipment and wiring methods and can cause electrical equipment to fail. For these reasons, Article 547 includes requirements for dealing with dust, moisture, and corrosion.

This article also has other rules. For example, you must install equipotential planes in all concrete floor confinement areas of livestock buildings containing metallic equipment accessible to animals and likely to become energized. Livestock have a low tolerance to small voltage differences, which can cause loss of milk production and, at times, their fatality. As a result, the *NEC* contains specific requirements for an equipotential plane in buildings that house livestock.

547.1 Scope

Article 547 applies to agricultural buildings or to that part of a building (or adjacent areas of similar nature) as specified in (A) or (B). ▶Figure 547–1

Article 547 applies to agricultural buildings, or to that part of a building or adjacent areas of similar nature per (A) or (B).
(A) Buildings or areas where excessive dust and/or dust with water may accumulate.
(B) Buildings or areas where a corrosive atmosphere exists.

▶Figure 547–1

(A) Excessive Dust and Dust with Water. Buildings or areas where excessive dust and/or dust with water may accumulate such as areas of poultry, livestock, and fish confinement systems where litter or feed dust may accumulate.

(B) Corrosive Atmosphere. Buildings or areas where a corrosive atmosphere exists, and where the following conditions exist:

(1) Poultry and animal excrement.

(2) Corrosive particles that may combine with water.

(3) Areas made damp or wet by periodic washing.

547.2 Definitions

Equipotential Plane, (as applied to agricultural buildings). An area where conductive elements are embedded in or placed under concrete, bonded to all metal structures and nonelectrical equipment that <u>could</u> become energized, and connected to the electrical system to minimize voltage differences within the plane. ▶Figure 547–2

547.5 | Agricultural Buildings

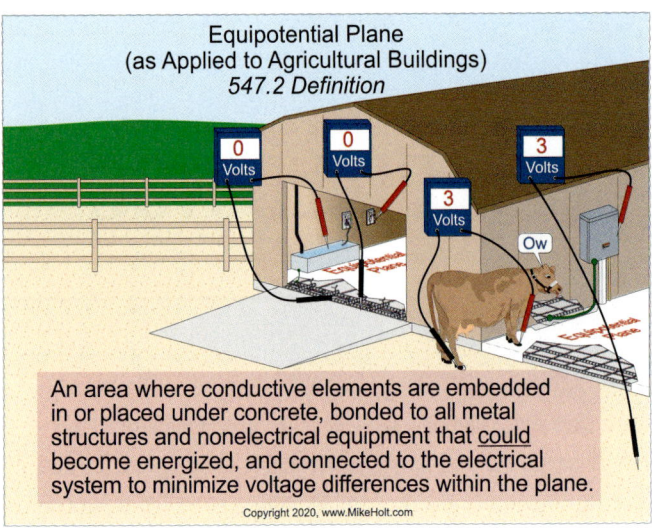
▶Figure 547-2

547.5 Wiring Methods

(A) Wiring Systems. Types UF, NMC, and SE cables with copper conductors, jacketed Type MC cable, PVC conduit, or liquidtight flexible nonmetallic conduit can be installed in agricultural building spaces.

(C) Equipment Enclosures, Boxes, Conduit Bodies, and Fittings.

(1) Excessive Dust. Equipment enclosures, boxes, conduit bodies, and fittings in areas of agricultural buildings where excessive dust may be present must be designed to minimize the entrance of dust. They must have no openings, such as holes for attachment screws, through which dust can enter the enclosure. ▶Figure 547-3

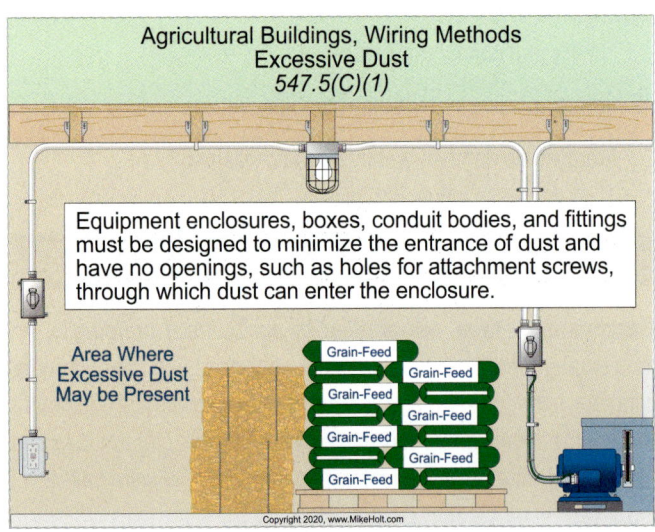
▶Figure 547-3

Author's Comment:

▸ Weatherproof boxes and covers can be used to meet this requirement.

(2) Damp or Wet Locations. In damp or wet locations of agricultural buildings, equipment enclosures, boxes, conduit bodies, and fittings must prevent moisture from entering or accumulating within. Boxes, conduit bodies, and fittings must be listed for use in wet locations and enclosures must be weatherproof.

(3) Corrosive Atmosphere. Where wet dust, excessive moisture, corrosive gases or vapors, or other corrosive conditions may be present in an agricultural building, equipment enclosures, boxes, conduit bodies, and fittings must have corrosion-resistant properties suitable for the conditions.

Note 1: See Table 110.28 for appropriate enclosures for the location.

(D) Flexible Connections. Where necessary for flexible connections, dusttight flexible connectors, liquidtight flexible metal conduit, liquidtight flexible nonmetallic conduit, or flexible cord listed for hard usage can be used.

(E) Physical Protection. Electrical wiring and equipment must be protected where subject to physical damage.

(F) Separate Equipment Grounding Conductor. Where the equipment grounding conductor is not part of a listed cable assembly, it must be insulated when installed underground. ▶Figure 547-4

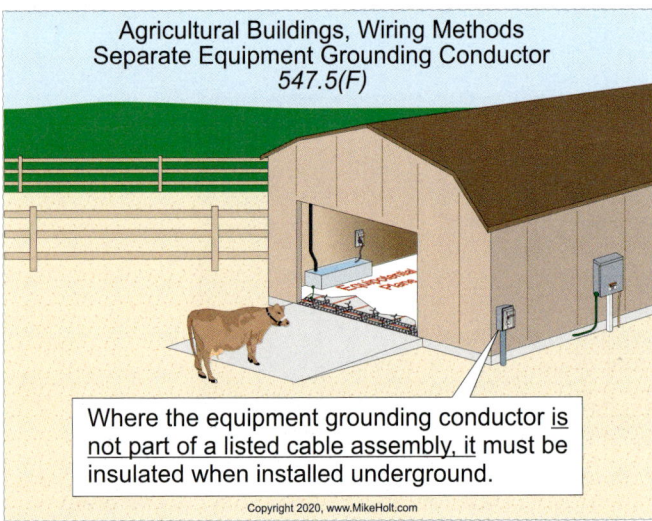
▶Figure 547-4

Agricultural Buildings | **547.10**

547.10 Equipotential Planes

(A) Where Required. Equipotential planes must be installed as follows:

(1) Indoor Concrete Confinement Areas. An equipotential plane must be installed in indoor livestock confinement areas where metallic equipment accessible to livestock, that may become energized, is located. ▶Figure 547-5

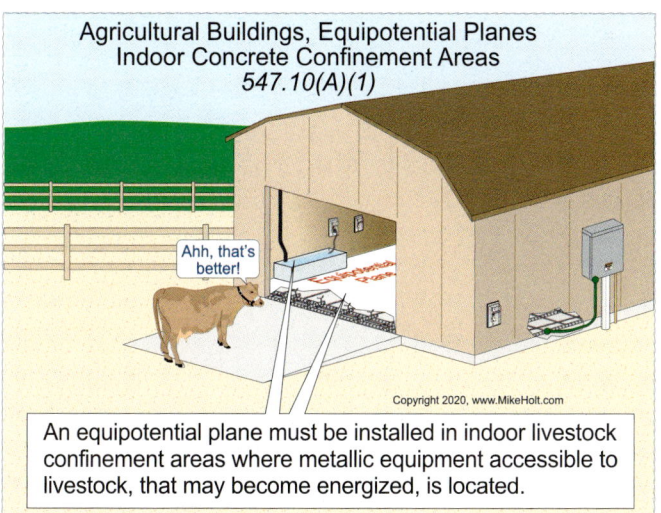

▶Figure 547-5

(2) Outdoor Concrete Confinement Areas. An equipotential plane must be installed in outdoor livestock confinement areas where metallic equipment accessible to livestock may become energized is located. ▶Figure 547-6

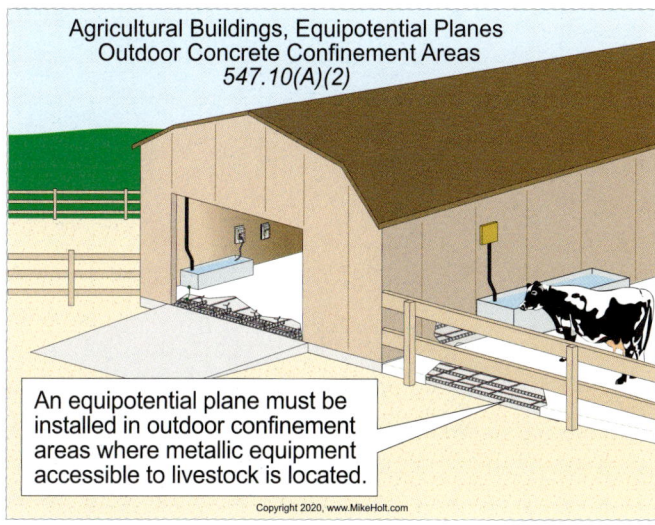

▶Figure 547-6

(B) Bonding. The equipotential plane must be connected to the building electrical grounding system with a bonding conductor not smaller than 8 AWG using pressure connectors or clamps approved by the authority having jurisdiction. ▶Figure 547-7

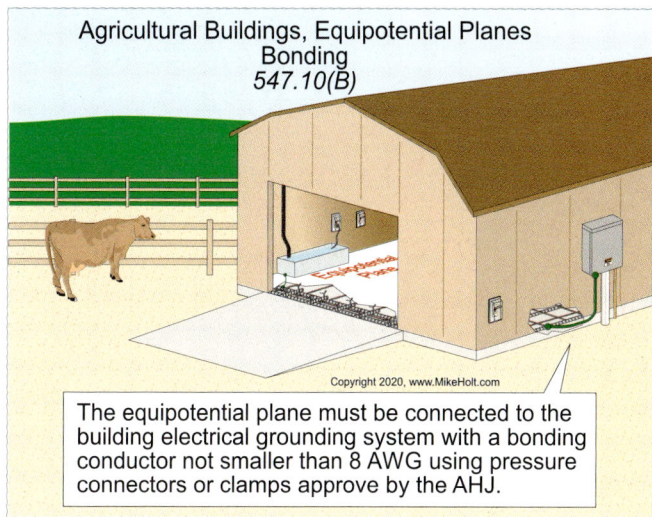

▶Figure 547-7

Note 1: ASABE Standard EP473.2, *Equipotential Planes in Animal Containment Areas,* provides the recommendation of a voltage gradient ramp at the entrances of agricultural buildings.

Note 2: See the American Society of Agricultural and Biological Engineers (ASABE) EP342.2, *Safety for Electrically Heated Livestock Waterers.*

Author's Comment:

▸ The bonding requirements contained in Article 547 are unique because of the sensitivity of livestock to small voltage differences, especially in wet or damp concrete animal confinement areas.

▸ In most instances the voltage difference between metal parts and the Earth will be too low to present a shock hazard to people. However, livestock might detect the voltage difference if they come into contact with the metal parts. Although voltage differences may not be life threatening to them, it is been reported that as little as 0.50V RMS can adversely affect milk production.

Notes

ARTICLE 555 — MARINAS, BOATYARDS, AND DOCKING FACILITIES

Introduction to Article 555—Marinas, Boatyards, and Docking Facilities

Water levels are not constant. Ocean tides rise and fall, while lakes and rivers vary in depth in response to rain and melting snow and ice. To provide power to a marina, boatyard, floating building, or docking facility, you must allow for these variations in water level between the point of use and the electric power source. Article 555 addresses this issue.

555.1 Scope

Article 555 covers the installation of wiring and equipment for fixed or floating piers, wharfs, docks, floating buildings, and other areas in marinas and boatyards. ▶Figure 555–1

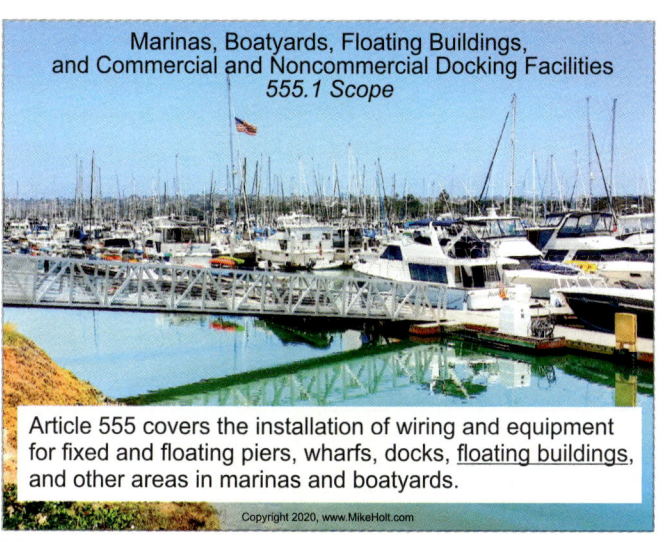

▶Figure 555–1

555.13 Bonding of Non-Current-Carrying Metal Parts

Metal parts in contact with the water, metal piping, and noncurrent-carrying metal parts likely to become energized must be connected to the grounding bus in the panelboard using a solid copper conductor; insulated, covered, or bare; not smaller than 8 AWG.

Connections to bonded parts must be made in accordance with 250.8.

555.37 Equipment Grounding Conductor

(A) Equipment to be Connected to the Equipment Grounding Conductor. The following items must be connected to an equipment grounding conductor run with the circuit conductors in the same raceway, cable, or trench:

(1) Metal boxes, metal cabinets, and all other metal enclosures.

(2) Metal frames of utilization equipment.

(3) Grounding terminals of grounding-type receptacles.

(B) Type of Equipment Grounding Conductor. The equipment grounding conductor must be an insulated conductor with a continuous outer finish that is either green or green with one or more yellow stripes.

(C) Size of Equipment Grounding Conductor. The insulated equipment grounding conductor must be sized in accordance with 250.122, but not smaller than 12 AWG.

(D) Branch-Circuit Equipment Grounding Conductor. The insulated equipment grounding conductor for branch circuits must terminate at a grounding terminal in a remote panelboard or the grounding terminal in the main service equipment.

(E) Feeder Equipment Grounding Conductor. Where a feeder supplies a remote panelboard, an insulated equipment grounding conductor must extend from a grounding terminal in the service equipment to a grounding terminal in the remote panelboard.

Notes

CHAPTER 5

PRACTICE QUESTIONS

Please use the 2020 *Code* book to answer the following questions.

CHAPTER 5—SPECIAL OCCUPANCIES

1. Article 501 covers the requirements for electrical and electronic equipment and wiring for all voltages in Class I locations where fire or explosion hazards may exist due to flammable _____.

    (a) gases
    (b) vapors
    (c) liquids
    (d) any of these

2. In Class I locations, the locknut-bushing and double-locknut types of contacts shall not be depended on for bonding purposes.

    (a) True
    (b) False

3. When FMC or LFMC is used as permitted in Class I, Division 2 locations, it shall include an equipment bonding jumper of the wire type in compliance with 250.102.

    (a) True
    (b) False

4. Article 502 covers the requirements for electrical and electronic equipment and wiring in Class II, Division 1 and 2 locations where fire or explosion hazards may exist due to _____.

    (a) gases or vapors
    (b) fibers/flyings
    (c) combustible dust
    (d) all of these

5. In Class II locations, a permitted method of bonding is the use of bonding jumpers with proper fittings.

    (a) True
    (b) False

6. Where LFMC is used in a Class II, Division 1 location as permitted in 502.10, it shall _____.

    (a) not be unsupported
    (b) not exceed 6 ft in length
    (c) include an equipment bonding jumper of the wire type
    (d) be listed for use in Class I locations

7. Article 503 covers the requirements for electrical and electronic equipment and wiring in Class III locations where fire or explosion hazards may exist due to ignitible _____.

    (a) gases or vapors
    (b) fibers/flyings
    (c) dust
    (d) all of these

8. In Class III locations, locknut-bushing and double-locknut types of fittings may be depended on for bonding purposes.

    (a) True
    (b) False

9. Where LFMC is used in a Class III location as permitted in 503.10, it shall _____.

    (a) not be unsupported
    (b) not exceed 6 ft in length
    (c) include an equipment bonding jumper of the wire type in accordance with 250.102
    (d) be listed for use in a Class I hazardous (classified) location

Chapter 5 | Practice Questions

10. Article 517 applies to electrical construction and installation criteria in health care facilities that provide services to _____.

    (a) human beings
    (b) animals
    (c) children only
    (d) intellectually challenged persons

11. In patient care spaces, luminaires more than _____ ft above the floor and switches located outside of the patient care vicinity shall be permitted to be connected to an equipment grounding return path complying with 517.13(a) or (B).

    (a) 7 ft
    (b) 7½ ft
    (c) 7¾ ft
    (d) 8 ft

12. Outside of patient care vicinities, the equipment grounding terminals of isolated ground receptacles installed in branch circuits for patient care _____ in accordance with 250.146(d) installed in a wiring method described in 517.13(A).

    (a) vicinities
    (b) spaces
    (c) bathrooms
    (d) vicinities or spaces

13. At circuses and carnivals, all equipment to be grounded shall be connected to a(n) _____ conductor of a type recognized by 250.118.

    (a) equipment grounding
    (b) grounded
    (c) grounding electrode
    (d) ungrounded

14. The continuity of the equipment grounding conductors at carnivals, circuses, fairs, and similar events shall be verified each time that portable electrical equipment is connected.

    (a) True
    (b) False

15. Agricultural buildings where excessive dust and dust with water may accumulate, including all areas of _____ confinement systems where litter dust or feed dust may accumulate shall comply with Article 547.

    (a) poultry
    (b) livestock
    (c) fish
    (d) all of these

16. An equipotential plane is an area where wire mesh or other conductive elements are embedded in or placed under concrete and bonded to _____.

    (a) all metal structures
    (b) fixed nonelectrical equipment that could become energized
    (c) the electrical grounding system
    (d) all of these

17. Enclosures and fittings installed in areas of agricultural buildings where excessive dust may be present shall be designed to minimize the entrance of dust and shall have no openings through which dust can enter the enclosure.

    (a) True
    (b) False

18. In damp or wet locations of agricultural buildings, equipment enclosures and fittings shall be located or equipped to prevent moisture from _____ within the enclosure, box, conduit body, or fitting.

    (a) entering and accumulating
    (b) draining from
    (c) creating a short-circuit
    (d) causing damage

19. Where _____ may be present in an agricultural building, enclosures and fittings shall have corrosion-resistance properties suitable for the conditions.

    (a) wet dust or excessive moisture
    (b) corrosive gases or vapors
    (c) other corrosive conditions
    (d) any of these

20. An equipotential plane shall be installed in all concrete floor confinement areas of livestock buildings, and all outdoor confinement areas with a concrete slab that contains metallic equipment accessible to livestock and that may become energized.

    (a) True
    (b) False

21. The equipotential plane in an agricultural building shall be connected to the electrical grounding system with a solid copper, insulated, covered, or bare conductor and not smaller than _____ AWG.

    (a) 10
    (b) 8
    (c) 6
    (d) 4

22. The equipment grounding conductor at a marina is required to be an insulated conductor for all circuits.

    (a) True
    (b) False

23. The equipotential bonding of all non-current carrying metal parts required in _____ shall be installed to reduce voltage gradients in the marina dock area.

    (a) Article 250
    (b) Article 690
    (c) Section 555.13
    (d) Section 555.50

Notes

CHAPTER 6

SPECIAL EQUIPMENT

Introduction to Chapter 6—Special Equipment

Chapter 6, which covers special equipment, is the second of the four *NEC* chapters dealing with special topics. Chapters 5 and 7 focus on special occupancies and special conditions respectively, while Chapter 8 covers communications systems. Remember, the first four chapters of the *Code* are sequential and form a foundation for each of the subsequent four.

What exactly is "Special Equipment"? It is equipment that, by the nature of its use, construction, or by its unique nature creates a need for additional measures to ensure the "safeguarding of people and property" mission of the *NEC* as stated in Article 90. The *Code* groups the articles in this chapter logically, as you might expect.

▶ **Article 600—Electric Signs and Outline Lighting.** This article covers the installation of conductors and equipment for electric signs and outline lighting as defined in Article 100. They include all products and installations that utilize neon tubing such as signs, decorative elements, skeleton tubing, or art forms.

▶ **Article 645—Information Technology Equipment.** This article applies to equipment, power-supply wiring, equipment interconnecting wiring, and grounding for information technology equipment and systems including terminal units in an information technology equipment room.

▶ **Article 680—Swimming Pools, Spas, Hot Tubs, Fountains, and Similar Installations.** Article 680 covers the installation of electric wiring and equipment that supplies swimming, wading, therapeutic and decorative pools, fountains and splash pads, hot tubs, spas, and hydromassage bathtubs whether permanently installed or storable.

▶ **Article 690—Solar Photovoltaic (PV) Systems.** This article focuses on reducing the electrical hazards that may arise from installing and operating solar PV systems, to the point where they can be considered safe for people and property. The requirements of the *NEC* Chapters 1 through 4 apply to these installations, except as specifically modified here.

Notes

ARTICLE 600 — ELECTRIC SIGNS AND OUTLINE LIGHTING

Introduction to Article 600—Electric Signs and Outline Lighting

One of the first things you will notice when entering a strip mall is that there is a sign for every store. Every commercial occupancy needs a form of identification, and the standard method is the electric sign, so 600.5 requires a sign outlet for the entrance of each tenant location. Article 600 requires a disconnect within sight of a sign unless it can be locked in the open position.

> **Author's Comment:**
> ▸ Article 100 defines an electric sign as any "fixed, stationary, or portable self-contained, electrically illuminated utilization equipment with words or symbols designed to convey information or attract attention."

Freestanding signs, such as those that might be erected in a parking lot, must be located at least 14 ft above vehicle areas unless they are protected from physical damage.

Neon art forms or decorative elements are subsets of electric signs and outline lighting. If installed and not attached to an enclosure or sign body, they are considered skeleton tubing for the purpose of applying the requirements of Article 600. However, if that neon tubing is attached to an enclosure or sign body, which may be a simple support frame, it is considered a sign or outline lighting subject to all the provisions that apply to signs and outline lighting, such as 600.3 which requires the product to be listed.

600.1 Scope

Article 600 covers the installation of conductors, equipment, and field wiring for electric signs, retrofit kits, and outline lighting. It also covers installations and equipment using neon tubing such as signs, decorative elements, skeleton tubing, or art forms. ▸Figure 600–1

Note: Sign and outline lighting systems can include cold cathode neon tubing, high-intensity discharge lamps (HID), fluorescent or incandescent lamps, light emitting diodes (LEDs), and electroluminescent and inductance lighting.

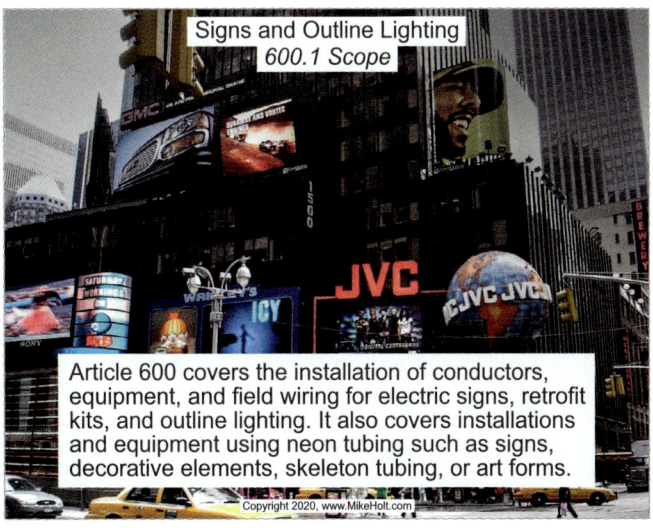

▸Figure 600–1

600.7 Grounding and Bonding

(A) Equipment Grounding Conductor and Grounding

(1) Equipment Grounding Conductor. Metal equipment of signs, outline lighting systems, and skeleton tubing must be connected to the circuit equipment grounding conductor of a type recognized in 250.118. ▶Figure 600–2

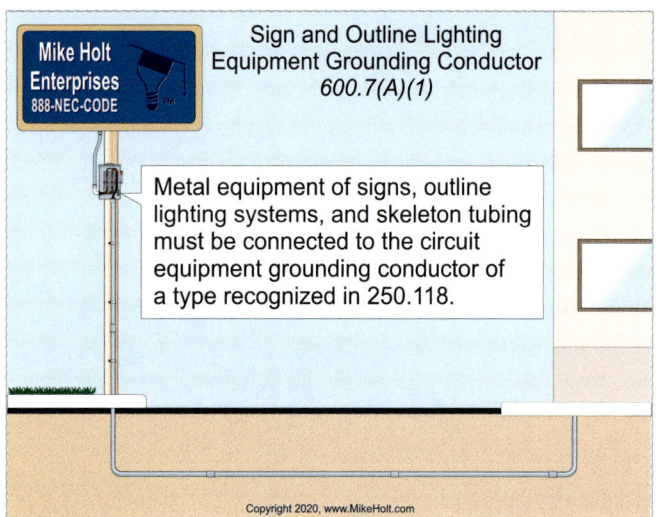

▶Figure 600–2

(2) Size of Equipment Grounding Conductor. If the equipment grounding conductor is of the wire type, it must be sized in accordance with 250.122.

(3) Connections. Equipment grounding conductor connections must be made in accordance with 250.130 in a method specified in 250.8.

Author's Comment:

▶ According to 250.8, equipment grounding conductors of the wire type must terminate in any of the following:

(1) Listed pressure connectors

(2) Terminal bars

(3) Pressure connectors listed for grounding and bonding

(4) Exothermic welding

(5) Machine screws that engage at least two threads or are secured with a nut

(6) Self-tapping machine screws that engage at least two threads

(7) Connections that are part of a listed assembly

(8) Other listed means

(4) Auxiliary Grounding Electrode. Auxiliary grounding electrodes are not required for signs and outline lighting, but if installed, they must comply with 250.54. ▶Figure 600–3

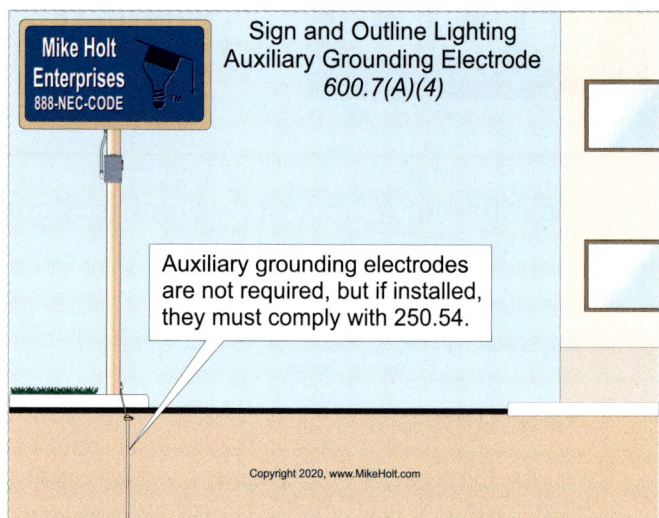

▶Figure 600–3

Author's Comment:

▶ According to 250.54, auxiliary electrodes need not be bonded to the building's grounding electrode system, the grounding conductor to the electrode need not be sized in accordance with 250.66, and the contact resistance of the electrode to the Earth is not required to comply with the 25-ohm requirement of 250.53(A)(2) Ex.

▶ The Earth must not be used as the effective ground-fault current path required by 250.4(A)(4) and 250.4(A)(5). This is because the contact resistance of a grounding electrode to the Earth is high, and very little ground-fault current returns to the electrical supply source via the Earth. The result is the circuit overcurrent protective device will not open and clear a ground fault; therefore, metal parts will remain energized with dangerous voltage. ▶Figure 600–4

(B) Bonding.

(1) Metal Parts. Metal parts of signs and outline lighting systems must be bonded to the transformer or power-supply equipment grounding conductor.

Ex: The metal parts of a section sign or outline lighting system supplied by a remote Class 2 power supply are not required to be connected to an equipment grounding conductor.

Electric Signs and Outline Lighting | 600.7

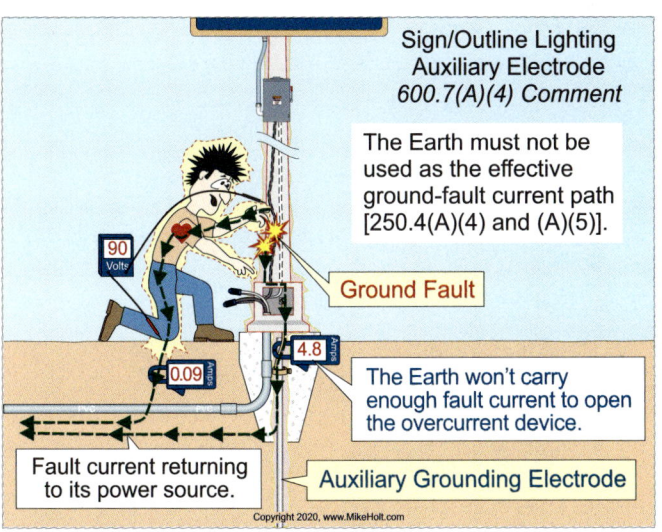

▶Figure 600-4

(4) Flexible Metal Conduit Length. Listed flexible metal conduit or listed liquidtight flexible metal conduit for secondary circuit conductors for neon tubing can be used as a bonding means if the total length of the conduit does not exceed 100 ft.

(7) Bonding Conductors.

(1) Bonding conductors must be copper and not smaller than 14 AWG.

(2) Bonding conductors installed outside a sign or raceway must be protected from physical damage.

(2) Bonding Connections. Bonding connections must be made in accordance with 250.8.

Author's Comment:

▶ According to 250.8, bonding conductors must terminate in any of the following methods:

(1) Listed pressure connectors

(2) Terminal bars

(3) Pressure connectors listed for grounding and bonding

(4) Exothermic welding

(5) Machine screws that engage at least two threads or are secured with a nut

(6) Self-tapping machine screws that engage at least two threads

(7) Connections that are part of a listed assembly

(8) Other listed means

Notes

ARTICLE 645 — INFORMATION TECHNOLOGY EQUIPMENT

Introduction to Article 645—Information Technology Equipment

One of the unique things about Article 645 is the requirement for a shutoff switch for information technology equipment rooms [645.10]. This requirement seems to be wrong on its face because it allows someone to shut power to the IT room off from a single point. So, despite having a UPS and taking every precaution against a power outage, the IT system is still vulnerable to a shutdown from a readily accessible switch.

645.1 Scope

Article 645 provides optional wiring methods and materials for information technology equipment (ITE) and systems in an information technology equipment room as an alternative to those required in other chapters of this *Code*. ▶Figure 645–1

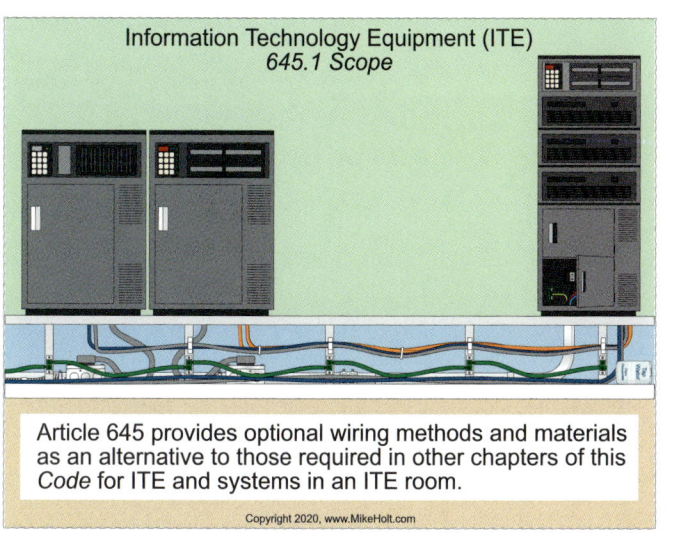

▶Figure 645–1

Note 1: An information technology equipment room is an enclosed area specifically designed to comply with the construction and fire protection provisions of NFPA 75, *Standard for the Fire Protection of Information Technology Equipment*.

645.15 Equipment Grounding and Bonding

Exposed metal parts of an information technology system must be connected to the circuit equipment grounding conductor or be double insulated. ▶Figure 645–2

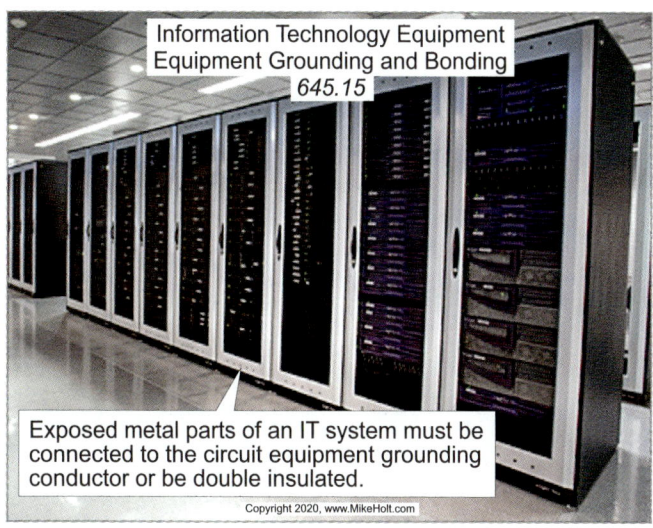

▶Figure 645–2

Where signal reference structures are installed, they must be bonded to the circuit equipment grounding conductor for the information technology equipment. ▶Figure 645–3

645.15 | Information Technology Equipment

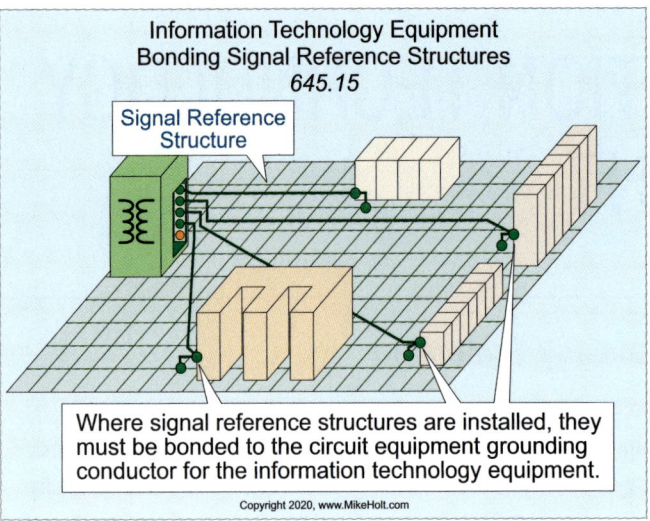

▶Figure 645-3

Note 2: If isolated ground receptacles are installed, they must be connected to an insulated equipment grounding conductor in accordance with 250.146(D) and 406.3(D).

ARTICLE 680 — SWIMMING POOLS, SPAS, HOT TUBS, FOUNTAINS, AND SIMILAR INSTALLATIONS

Introduction to Article 680—Swimming Pools, Spas, Hot Tubs, Fountains, and Similar Installations

The requirements contained in Article 680 apply to the installation of electrical wiring and equipment for swimming pools, spas, hot tubs, fountains and splash pads, and hydromassage bathtubs. The overriding concern of this article is to keep people and electricity separated. Article 680 is divided into seven parts that apply to certain types of installations, so be careful to determine which parts of this article apply to what and where. For instance, Part I and Part II apply to spas and hot tubs installed outdoors, except as modified in Part IV. In contrast, hydromassage bathtubs are only covered by Part VII. Read the details of this article carefully so you will be able to provide a safe installation.

- **Part I. General.**
- **Part II. Permanently Installed Pools.** Installations of permanently installed pools must comply with both Parts I and II of this article.
- **Part III. Storable Swimming Pools, Storable Spas, and Storable Hot Tubs.** Installations of storable pools, storable spas, and storable hot tubs must comply with Parts I and III of Article 680.
- **Part IV. Spas and Hot Tubs.** Spas and hot tubs must comply with Parts I and IV of this article; outdoor spas and hot tubs must also comply with Part II in accordance with 680.42.
- **Part V. Fountains.** Parts I and II apply to permanently installed fountains. If they have water in common with a pool, Part II also applies. Self-contained, portable fountains are covered by Article 422, Parts II and III.
- **Part VI. Pools and Tubs for Therapeutic Use.** Parts I and VI apply to pools and tubs for therapeutic use in health care facilities, gymnasiums, athletic training rooms, and similar installations. If they are portable appliances, then Article 422, Parts II and III apply.
- **Part VII. Hydromassage Bathtubs.** Only Part VII of this article applies to hydromassage bathtubs.

Part I. General Requirements for Pools, Spas, Hot Tubs, and Fountains

Author's Comment:

- The requirements contained in Part I of Article 680 apply to permanently installed pools [680.20], storable pools [680.30], spas and hot tubs [680.42 and 680.43], and fountains [680.50].

680.1 Scope

Article 680 applies to the installation of electric wiring and equipment for swimming pools, hot tubs, spas, fountains, and hydromassage bathtubs. ▶Figure 680–1

680.2 Definitions

The definitions in this section apply only within this article.

Corrosive Environment. Areas where pool sanitation chemicals are stored, handled, or dispensed; and confined areas under decks adjacent to such areas as well as areas with circulation pumps, automatic chlorinators, filters, open areas under decks adjacent to or abutting the pool structure, and similar locations. ▶Figure 680–2

Note: Sanitation chemicals and pool water pose a risk of corrosion (gradually damaging or destroying materials) due to the presence of oxidizers (for example; calcium hypochlorite, sodium hypochlorite, bromine, and chlorinated isocyanurates) and chlorinating agents that release chlorine when dissolved in water. More information about swimming pool chemicals can be found on or in the following:

680.2 | Swimming Pools, Spas, Hot Tubs, Fountains, and Similar Installations

▶Figure 680-1

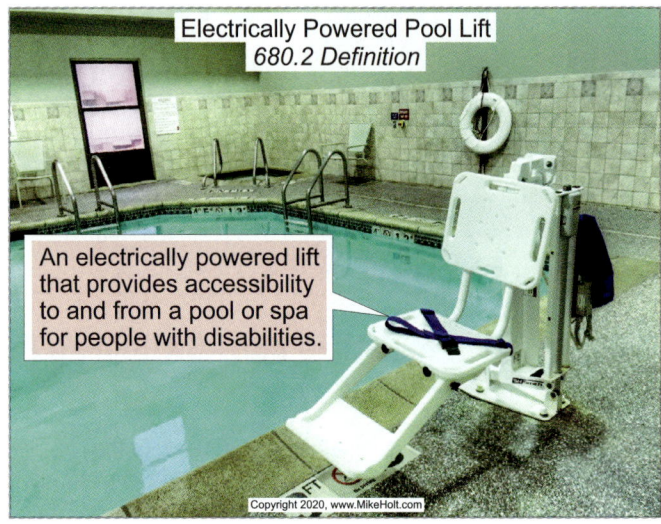

▶Figure 680-3

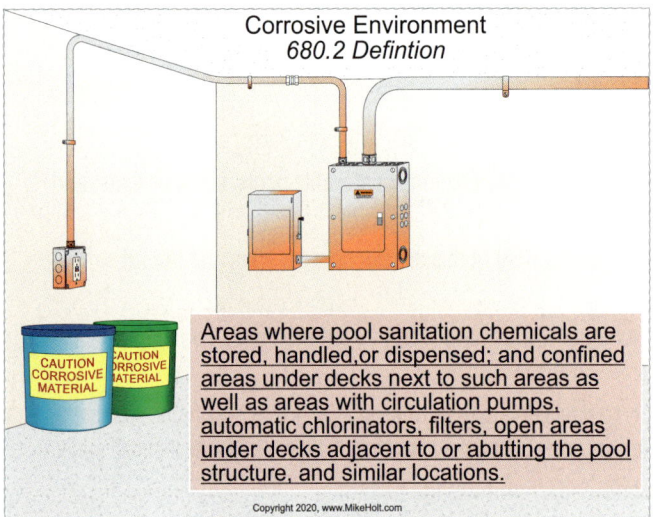

▶Figure 680-2

▶Figure 680-4

(1) Environmental Protection Agency website

(2) NFPA 400, *Hazardous Materials Code*

(3) Advisory: Swimming Pool Chemicals: Chlorine, OSWER 90-008.1, available from the *EPA National Service Center for Environmental Publications* (NSCEP)

Electrically Powered Pool Lift. An electrically powered lift that provides accessibility to and from a pool or spa for people with disabilities. ▶Figure 680-3

Forming Shell. A structure designed to support a wet-niche luminaire. ▶Figure 680-4

Fountain. An ornamental structure or recreational water feature from which one or more jets or streams of water are discharged into the air; including splash pads, ornamental pools, display pools, and reflection pools. This definition does not include drinking water fountains or water coolers. ▶Figure 680-5

Hydromassage Bathtub. A permanently installed bathtub with a recirculating piping system designed to accept, circulate, and discharge water after each use. ▶Figure 680-6

Immersion Pool. A pool for the ceremonial or ritual immersion of users which is designed and intended to have its contents drained or discharged. ▶Figure 680-7

Swimming Pools, Spas, Hot Tubs, Fountains, and Similar Installations | **680.2**

▶Figure 680–5

▶Figure 680–6

▶Figure 680–7

Low-Voltage Contact Limit. A voltage not exceeding the following values: ▶Figure 680–8

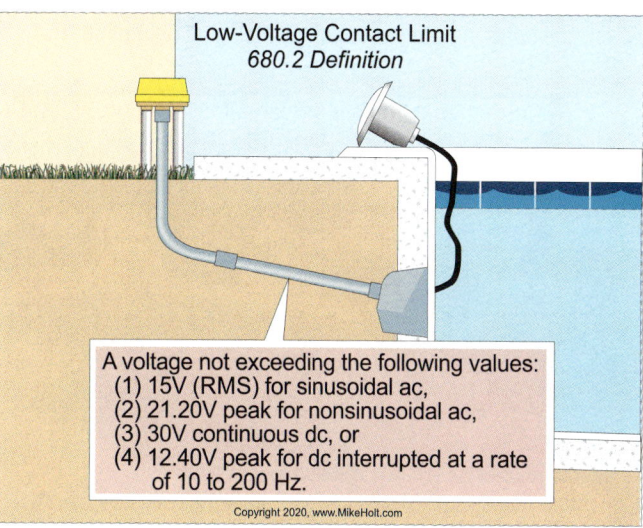
▶Figure 680–8

(1) 15V (RMS) for sinusoidal alternating current.

(2) 21.20V peak for nonsinusoidal alternating current.

(3) 30V for continuous direct current.

(4) 12.40V peak for direct current that is interrupted at a rate of 10 to 200 Hz.

Maximum Water Level. The highest level water reaches before it spills out. ▶Figure 680–9

▶Figure 680–9

680.2 | Swimming Pools, Spas, Hot Tubs, Fountains, and Similar Installations

Permanently Installed Swimming, Wading, Immersion, and Therapeutic Pools. Pools constructed in the ground or partially in the ground, pools capable of holding water of a depth greater than 42 in., and pools installed inside of a building. ▶Figure 680–10

▶Figure 680–10

Pool. Manufactured or field-constructed equipment designed to contain water on a permanent or semipermanent basis and used for swimming, wading, immersion, or other purposes.

> **Author's Comment:**
> ▸ The definition of a pool includes baptisteries (immersion pools), which must comply with the requirements of Article 680.

Spa or Hot Tub. A hydromassage pool or tub designed for recreational or therapeutic use typically not drained after each use. ▶Figure 680–11

Splash Pad. A fountain with a pool depth 1 in. or less intended for recreational use by pedestrians. This definition does not include showers intended for hygienic rinsing prior to use of a pool, spa, or other water feature. ▶Figure 680–12

Wet-Niche Luminaire. A luminaire intended to be installed in a forming shell where it will be completely surrounded by water. ▶Figure 680–13

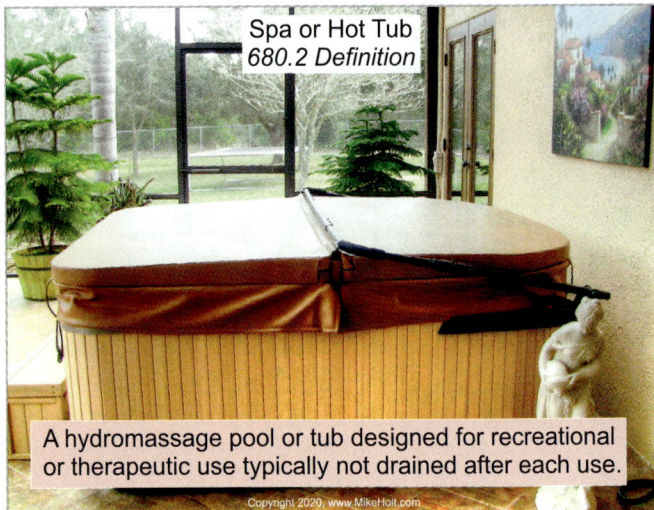

▶Figure 680–11

▶Figure 680–12

▶Figure 680–13

680.6 Bonding and Equipment Grounding

Electrical equipment must be bonded in accordance with Part V of Article 250 and must meet the requirements of Parts VI and VII of that article. Equipment must be connected by the wiring methods in Chapter 3 unless modified by this article. Equipment subject to these requirements include:

(1) Through-wall lighting assemblies and underwater luminaires except for listed low-voltage lighting.

(2) All electrical equipment within 5 ft of the inside wall of the specified body of water.

(3) All electrical equipment associated with the water recirculating system.

(4) Junction boxes.

(5) Transformer and power-supply enclosures.

(6) Ground-fault circuit interrupters.

(7) Sub-panels that supply associated equipment.

680.7 Bonding and Equipment Grounding Terminals

Terminals used for bonding and equipment grounding must be identified as suitable for use in wet and corrosive environments and be listed for direct burial use. ▶Figure 680–14

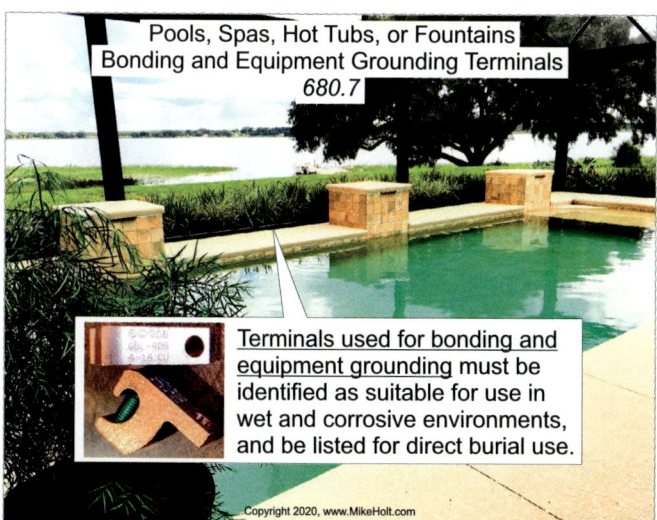

▶Figure 680–14

Part II. Permanently Installed Pools

680.21 Pool Motors

(A) Wiring Methods. The wiring to a pool-associated motor must comply with 680.21(A)(1) unless modified by (A)(2) or (A)(3).

(1) General. Branch-circuit wiring for pool-associated motors installed in corrosive locations must be rigid metal conduit, intermediate metal conduit, rigid polyvinyl chloride conduit, reinforced thermosetting resin conduit [680.14], or Type MC cable listed for the location. ▶Figure 680–15

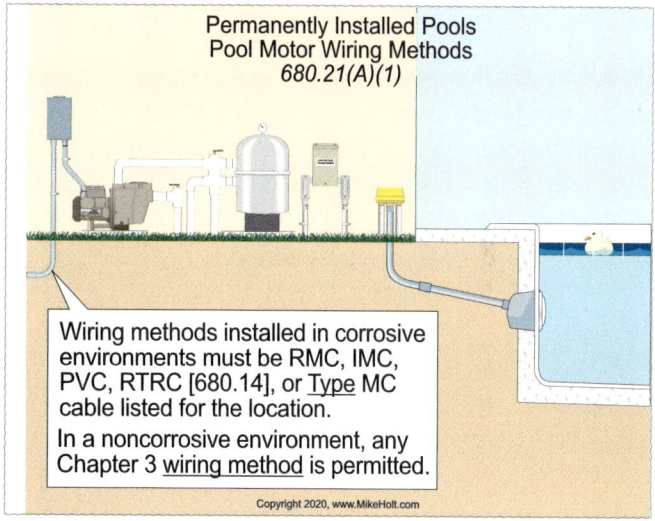

▶Figure 680–15

The wiring methods must contain an insulated copper equipment grounding conductor sized in accordance with 250.122, but in no case can it be sized smaller than 12 AWG. ▶Figure 680–16

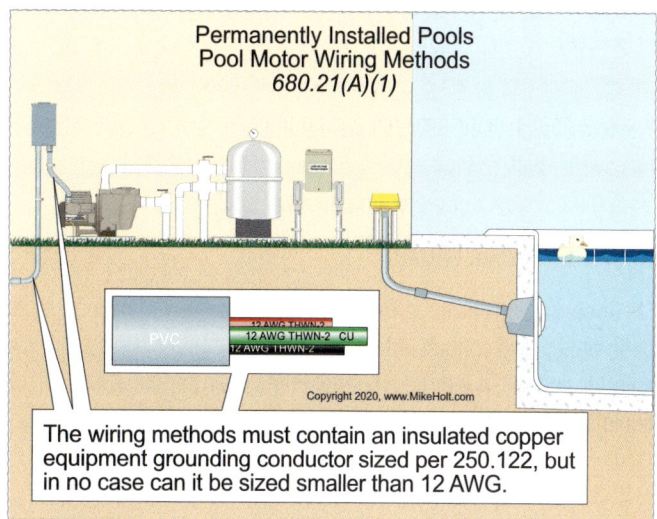

▶Figure 680–16

Where installed in noncorrosive environments, any Chapter 3 wiring method is permitted.

(2) Flexible Connections. Liquidtight flexible metal or liquidtight flexible nonmetallic conduit are permitted.

680.23 Underwater Pool Luminaires

(B) Wet-Niche Luminaires.

(2) Wiring to the Forming Shell.

(a) Metal Conduit. Metal conduit must be listed and identified as red brass or stainless steel.

(b) Nonmetallic Raceway. A nonmetallic raceway run to the forming shell of a wet-niche luminaire must contain an 8 AWG insulated (solid or stranded) copper conductor that terminates to the forming shell. ▶Figure 680-17 and ▶Figure 680-18

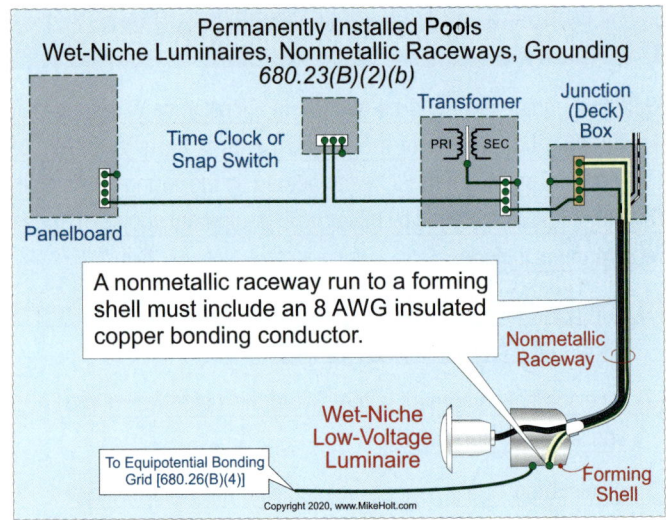
▶Figure 680-18

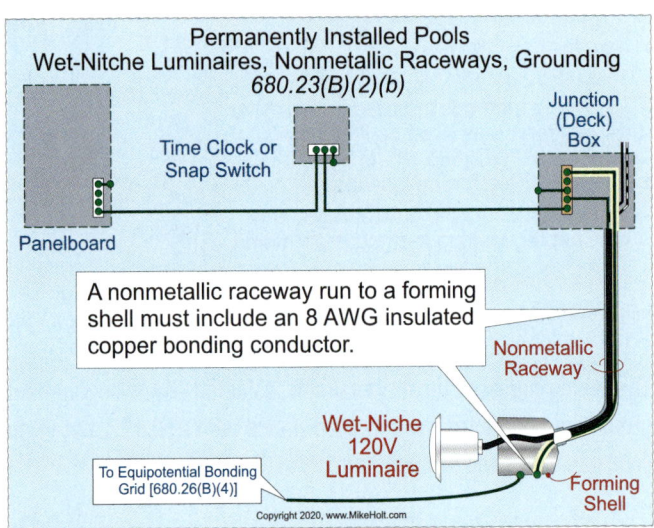
▶Figure 680-17

The termination of the 8 AWG bonding jumper in the forming shell must be covered with a listed potting compound to protect the connection from the possible deteriorating effects of pool water.

(F) Branch-Circuit Wiring.

(1) General. Branch-circuit wiring installed in corrosive locations, must be in rigid metal conduit, intermediate metal conduit, rigid polyvinyl chloride conduit, reinforced thermosetting resin conduit [680.14], or liquidtight flexible nonmetallic conduit. ▶Figure 680-19

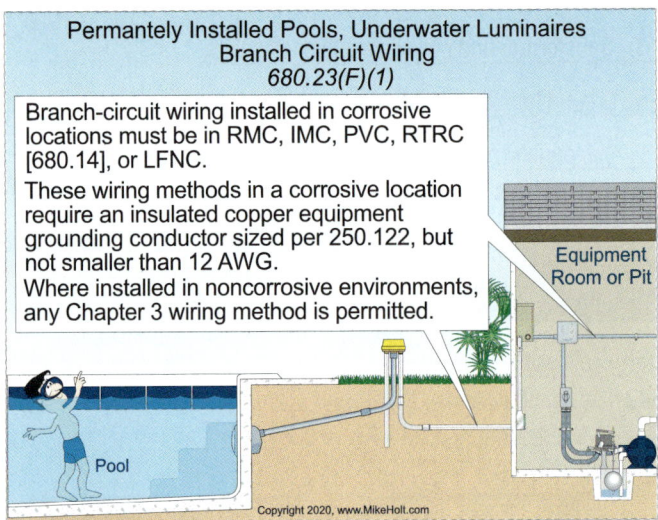
▶Figure 680-19

Wiring methods in corrosive environments must contain an insulated copper equipment grounding conductor sized in accordance with 250.122, but not smaller than 12 AWG.

Where installed in noncorrosive environments, any Chapter 3 wiring method is permitted.

(2) Branch-Circuit Equipment Grounding Conductor. Branch-circuit conductors for all through-wall underwater pool luminaires must have insulated copper equipment grounding conductors without joint or splice except as permitted in 680.23(F)(2)(a) and (b) sized in accordance with 250.122, but not smaller than 12 AWG. ▶Figure 680-20

Swimming Pools, Spas, Hot Tubs, Fountains, and Similar Installations | **680.25**

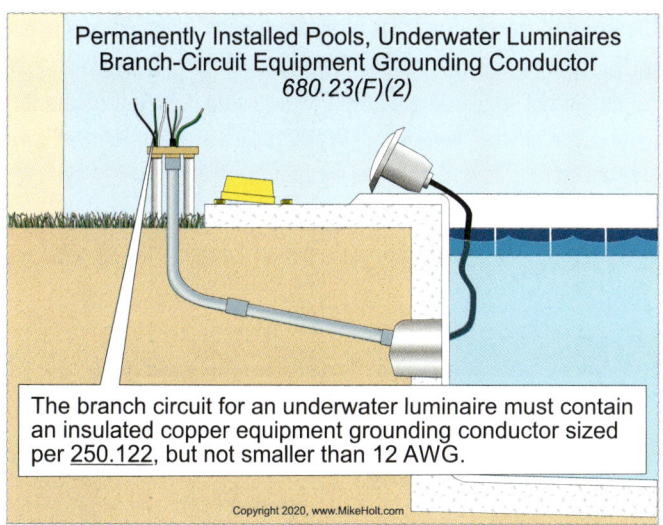
▶Figure 680–20

The circuit equipment grounding conductor for the underwater pool luminaire is not permitted to be spliced, except for the following applications:

(a) If more than one underwater pool luminaire is supplied by the same branch circuit, the circuit equipment grounding conductor can terminate at a listed pool junction box meeting the requirements of 680.24(A).

(b) The circuit equipment grounding conductor can terminate at the grounding terminal of a listed pool transformer meeting the requirements of 680.23(A)(2). ▶Figure 680–21

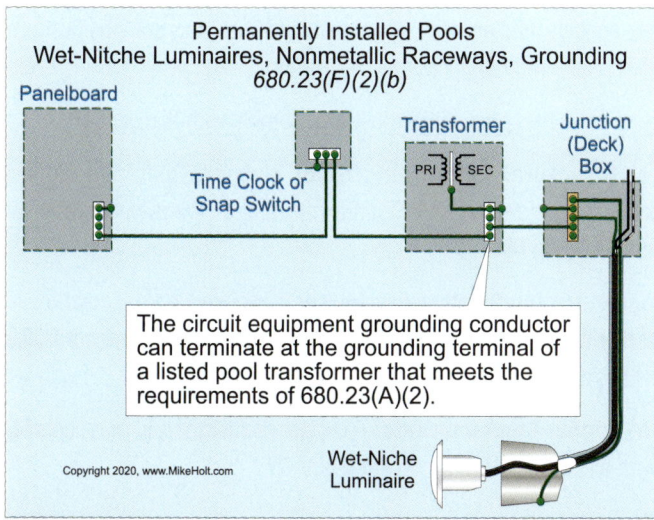
▶Figure 680–21

(3) Conductors. The branch-circuit conductors for the underwater pool luminaire on the load side of a GFCI or transformer used to comply with 680.23(A)(8) are not permitted to occupy raceways or enclosures with other conductors unless the other conductors are:

(1) GFCI protected or,

(2) Equipment grounding conductors and bonding jumpers as required by 680.23(B)(2)(b) or,

(3) Supply conductors to a feed-through-type GFCI.

680.24 Junction Box, Transformer, or GFCI Enclosure

(F) Grounding. The junction box [680.24(A)], transformer enclosure, or GFCI enclosure [680.24(B)] for an underground pool luminaire must be connected to the grounding terminals of the supply-circuit panelboard. ▶Figure 680–22

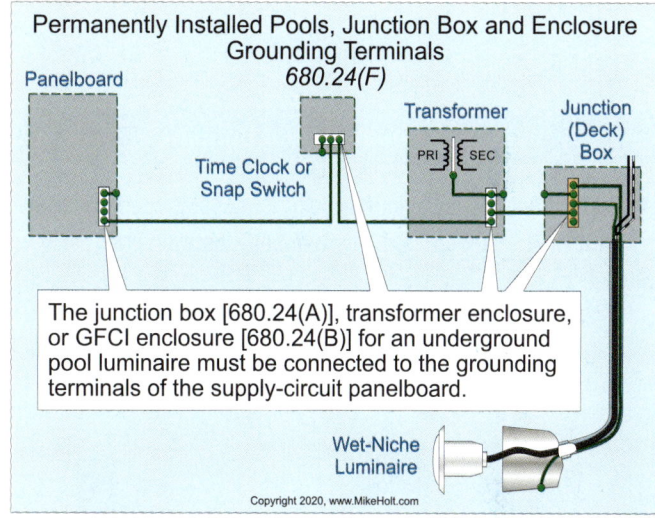
▶Figure 680–22

680.25 Feeders

(A) Wiring Methods. Where feeder wiring is installed in corrosive environments, the wiring methods must be rigid metal conduit, intermediate metal conduit, rigid polyvinyl chloride conduit, reinforced thermosetting resin conduit, or liquidtight flexible nonmetallic conduit.

The wiring methods in corrosive environments must have insulated copper equipment grounding conductors sized in accordance with Table 250.122, but not smaller than 12 AWG. ▶Figure 680–23

Where installed in noncorrosive environments, any Chapter 3 wiring method is permitted.

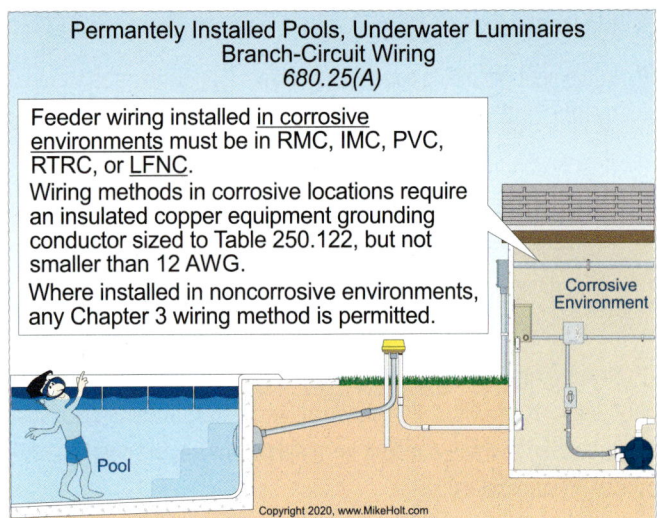

▶Figure 680–23

680.26 Equipotential Bonding

(A) Performance. Equipotential bonding is intended to reduce voltage gradients in the area around a permanently installed pool. ▶Figure 680–24

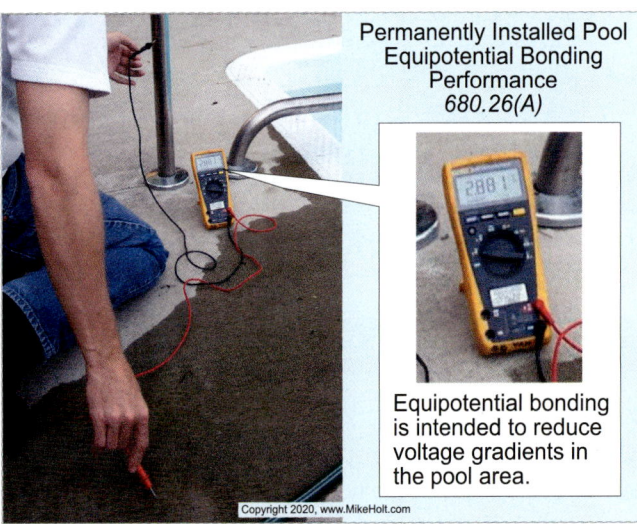

▶Figure 680–24

Author's Comment:

▸ Equipotential bonding is intended to eliminate voltage potential between the pool water, the pool shell, and the metallic parts in the area surrounding the pool.

(B) Bonded Parts. The parts of a permanently installed pool listed in (B)(1) through (B)(7) must be bonded together with a solid copper conductor not smaller than 8 AWG with a listed pressure connector, terminal bar, or other listed means in accordance with 250.8(A). ▶Figure 680–25

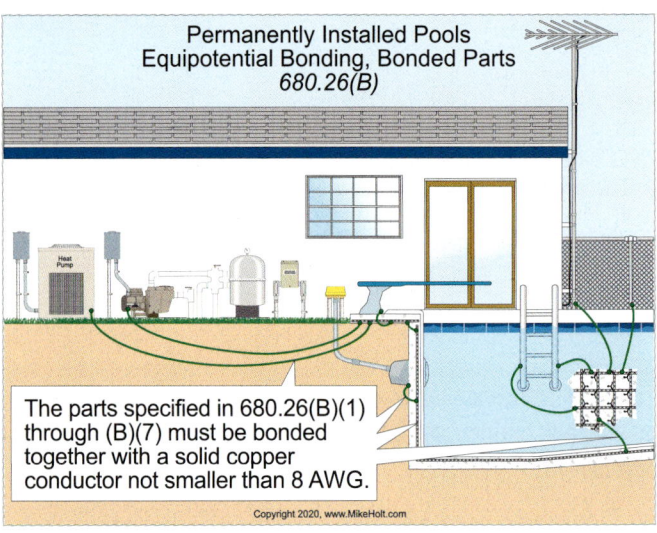

▶Figure 680–25

Equipotential bonding is not required to extend to (or be attached to) any panelboard, service disconnect, or grounding electrode.

(1) Conductive Pool Shells. Cast-in-place concrete, pneumatically applied or sprayed concrete, and concrete block with painted or plastered coatings are considered conductive materials due to water permeability and porosity. Vinyl liners and fiberglass composite shells are considered nonconductive materials.

Reconstructed pool shells must also comply with this section.

(a) Structural Reinforcing Steel. Unencapsulated structural reinforcing steel bonded together by steel tie wires or the equivalent. ▶Figure 680–26

Where structural reinforcing steel is encapsulated in a nonconductive compound, a copper conductor grid must be installed in accordance with 680.26(B)(1)(b).

(b) Copper Conductor Grid. A copper conductor grid must comply with all of the following: ▶Figure 680–27

(1) Be constructed of minimum 8 AWG bare solid copper conductors bonded to each other at all points of crossing in accordance with 250.8, or other approved means.

(2) Conform to the contour of the pool.

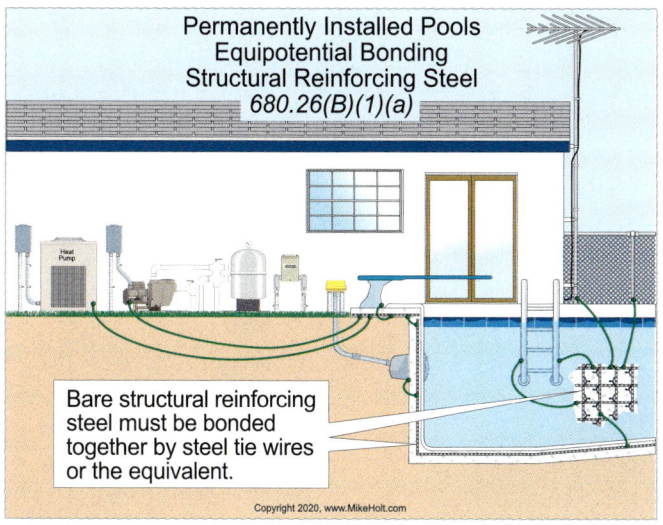
▶Figure 680-26

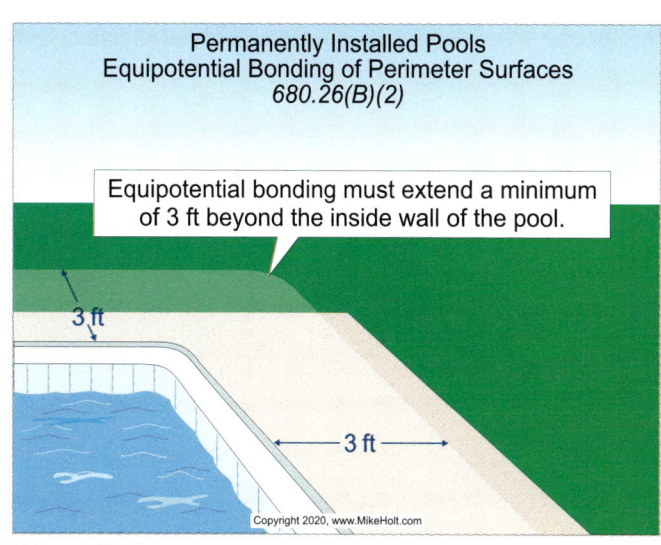
▶Figure 680-28

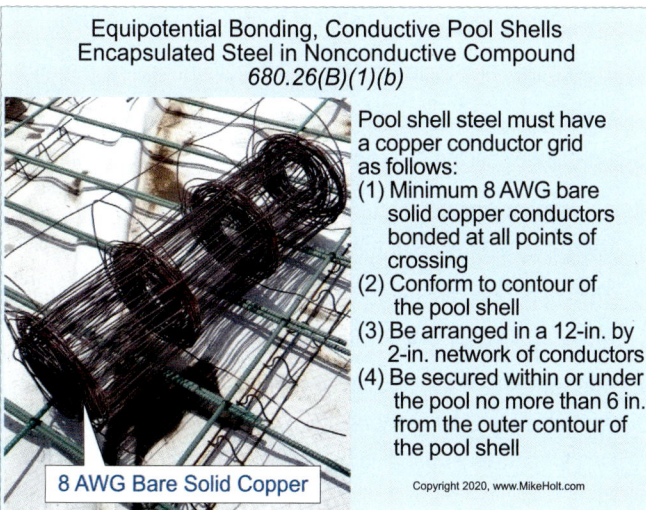
▶Figure 680-27

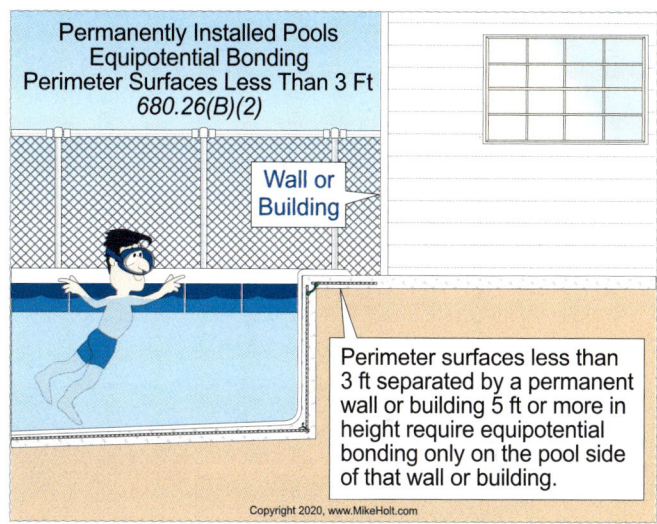
▶Figure 680-29

(3) Be arranged in a 12-in. by 12-in. network of conductors in a uniformly spaced perpendicular grid pattern with a tolerance of 4 in.

(4) Be secured within or under the pool no more than 6 in. from the outer contour of the pool shell.

(2) Perimeter Surfaces. Equipotential perimeter bonding must extend a minimum of 3 ft horizontally from the inside walls of a pool where not separated by a building or permanent wall 5 ft in height. ▶Figure 680-28 and ▶Figure 680-29

For conductive pool shells equipotential bonding for perimeter surfaces must be attached to the concrete pool reinforcing steel at a minimum of four points uniformly spaced around the perimeter of the pool and be one of the following: ▶Figure 680-30

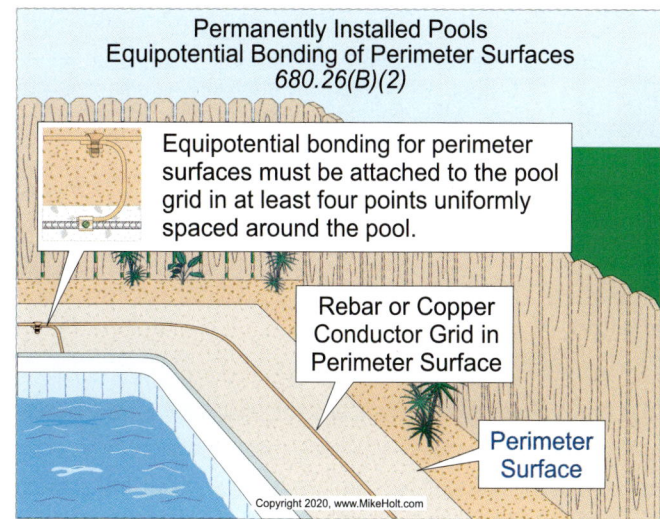
▶Figure 680-30

(a) Structural Reinforcing Steel. Unencapsulated structural reinforcing steel bonded together by steel tie wires or the equivalent in accordance with 680.26(B)(1)(a). ▶Figure 680–31

▶Figure 680–31

Author's Comment:

▸ The *NEC* does not provide any guidance on the installation requirements for structural reinforcing steel when used as a perimeter equipotential bonding method. ▶Figure 680–32

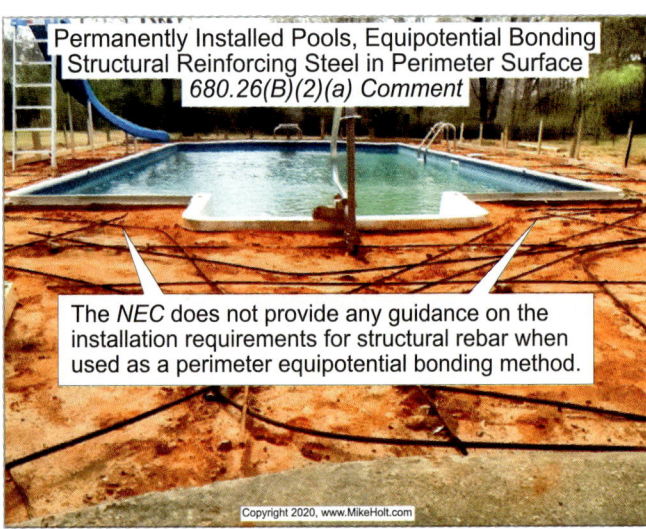

▶Figure 680–32

(b) Copper Ring. Where structural reinforcing steel is not available or is encapsulated in a nonconductive compound, a copper conductor can be used for equipotential perimeter bonding where the following requirements are met: ▶Figure 680–33

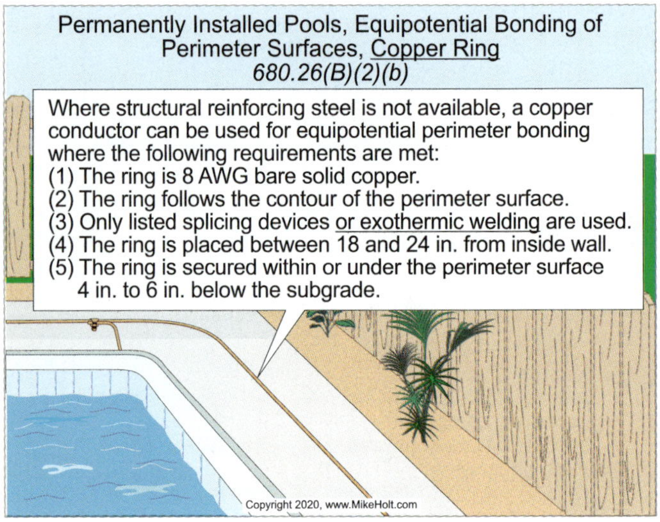

▶Figure 680–33

(1) The copper ring is constructed of 8 AWG bare solid copper.

(2) The copper ring conductor follows the contour of the perimeter surface.

(3) Only listed splicing devices or exothermic welding are used.

(4) The copper ring conductor is placed between 18 in. and 24 in. from the inside walls of the pool.

(5) The copper ring conductor is secured within or under the perimeter surface 4 in. to 6 in. below the subgrade.

(c) Copper Grid. Where structural reinforcing steel is not available or is encapsulated in a nonconductive compound, a copper grid can be used for perimeter bonding where all the following requirements are met:

(1) The copper grid is constructed of 8 AWG solid bare copper and arranged in a 12-in. by 12-in. network of conductors in a uniformly spaced perpendicular grid pattern with a tolerance of 4 in. in accordance with 680.26(B)(1)(b)(3).

(2) The copper grid follows the contour of the perimeter surface extending 3 ft horizontally beyond the inside walls of the pool.

(3) Only listed splicing devices or exothermic welding are used.

(4) The copper grid is secured within or under the deck or unpaved surfaces between 4 in. and 6 in. below the subgrade.

(3) Metallic Components. Metallic parts of the pool structure must be bonded together.

(5) Metal Fittings. Metal fittings sized over 4 in. in any direction and located within (or attached to) the pool structure, such as ladders and handrails, must be connected to the swimming pool equipotential bonding means. ▶Figure 680–34

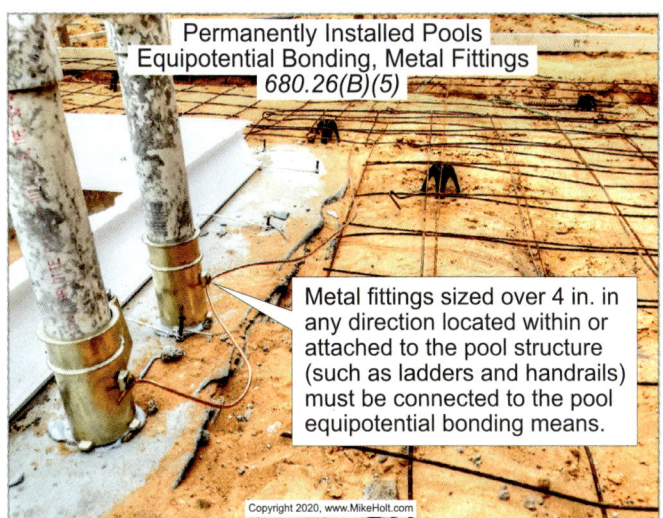

▶Figure 680-34

Metallic pool cover anchors 1 in. or less in any dimension and 2 in. or less in length are not required to be bonded to the equipotential bonding means.

(6) Electrical Equipment. Metal parts of electrical equipment associated with the pool water circulating system, such as water heaters, pump motors, and metal parts of pool covers must be connected to the swimming pool equipotential bonding means. ▶Figure 680-35

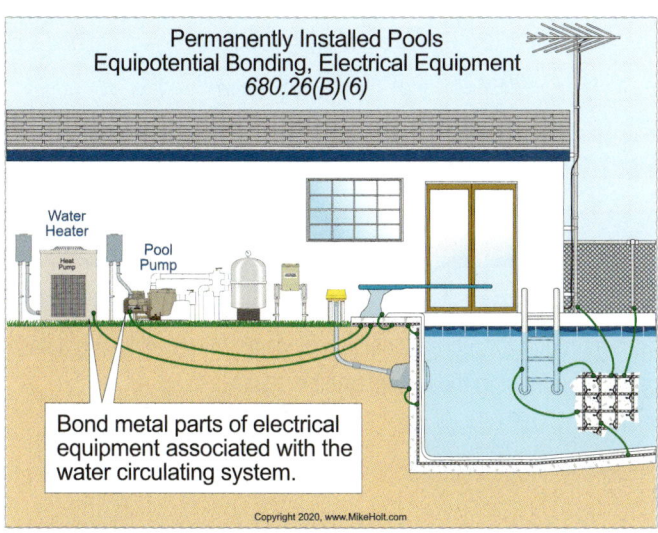

▶Figure 680-35

(a) Double-Insulated Water-Pump Motors. Where a double-insulated water-pump motor is installed, a solid 8 AWG copper conductor of sufficient length to make a bonding connection to a replacement motor from the swimming pool equipotential bonding means to an accessible point in the vicinity of the pool pump motor must be provided. Where there is no connection between the swimming pool equipotential bonding means and the equipment grounding system for the premises, this bonding conductor must be connected to the equipment grounding conductor of the motor circuit.

(7) Fixed Metal Parts. Fixed metal parts such as metal-sheathed cables and raceways, metal piping, metal awnings, metal fences, and metal door and window frames located within 5 ft horizontally [680.26(B)(7) Ex 2] and 12 ft vertically [680.26(B)(7) Ex 3] from the inside wall of the pool, must be connected to the swimming pool equipotential bonding means. ▶Figure 680-36

▶Figure 680-36

Ex 1: Those separated from the pool by a permanent barrier that prevents contact by a person are not be required to be bonded.

(C) Pool Water. If the pool water in a nonconductive pool structure does not have a direct electrical connection to one of the bonded parts described in 680.26(B), an approved corrosion-resistant conductive surface that is at least 9 sq in. in contact with the water must be bonded in accordance with 680.26(B). ▶Figure 680-37

Part IV. Spas, Hot Tubs, and Permanently Installed Immersion Pools

680.40 General

Electrical installations for spas and hot tubs must comply with Part I as well as Part IV of Article 680.

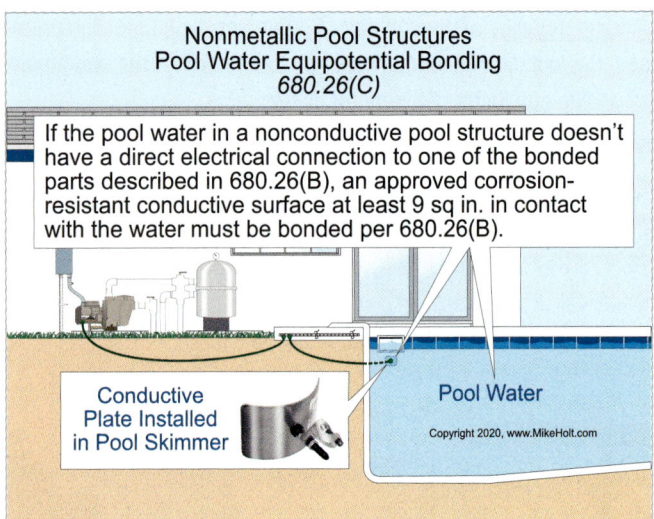
▶Figure 680–37

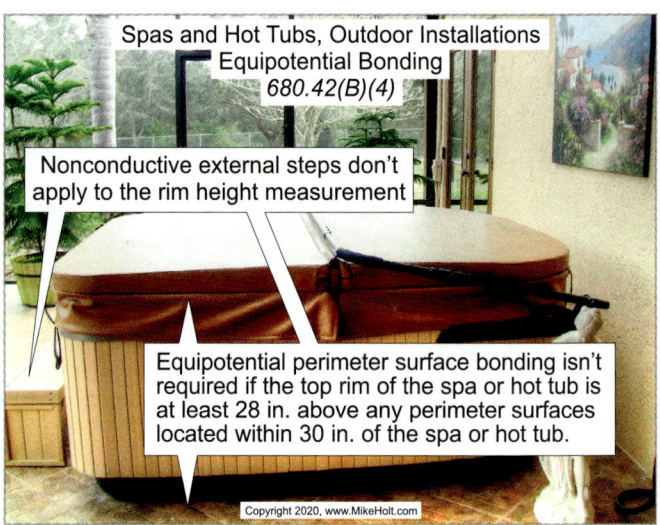
▶Figure 680–39

680.42 Outdoor Installations

(B) Equipotential Bonding. Equipotential bonding of perimeter surfaces for spas and hot tubs is not required if all the following conditions apply:

(1) The spa or hot tub is listed, labeled, and identified as a self-contained spa or hot tub for aboveground use. ▶Figure 680–38

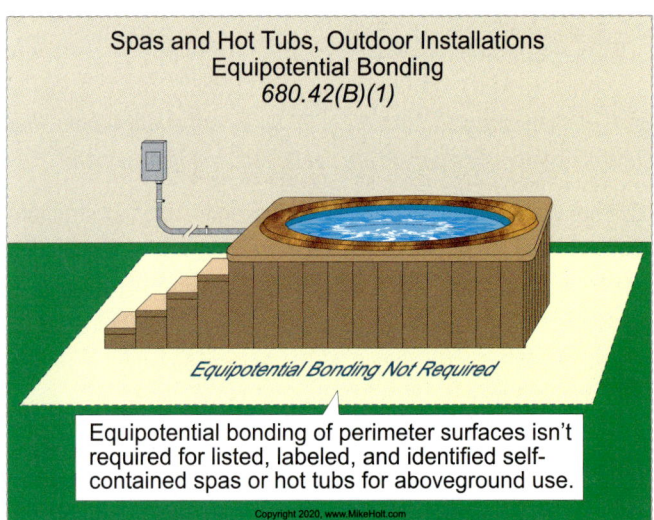
▶Figure 680–38

(2) The spa or hot tub is not identified as suitable only for indoor use.

(3) The spa or hot tub is located on or above grade.

(4) The top rim of the spa or hot tub is at least 28 in. above any perimeter surface located within 30 in. of the spa or hot tub. Nonconductive external steps do not apply to the rim height measurement. ▶Figure 680–39

680.43 Indoor Installations

Electrical installations for an indoor spa or hot tub must comply with Parts I and II of Article 680, except as modified by this section.

Indoor installations of spas or hot tubs can be connected by any of the wiring methods contained in Chapter 3.

Ex 2: The equipotential bonding requirements for perimeter surfaces contained in 680.26(B)(2) do not apply to a listed self-contained spa or hot tub installed above an indoor finished floor.

Part V. Fountains

680.50 General

The general installation requirements contained in Part I apply to fountains intended for recreational use by pedestrians, including splash pads, in addition to those contained in Part V.

Author's Comment:

▸ According to 680.2, a "Fountain" is defined as an ornamental structure or recreational water feature from which one or more jets or streams of water are discharged into the air including splash pads, ornamental pools, display pools, and reflection pools.

680.54 Connection to an Equipment Grounding Conductor

(A) Connection to Equipment Grounding Conductor. The following equipment must be connected to the circuit equipment grounding conductor:

(1) Other than listed low-voltage luminaires not requiring grounding, all electrical equipment located within the fountain or within 5 ft of the inside wall of the fountain.

(2) All electrical equipment associated with the recirculating system of the fountain.

(3) Panelboards that are not part of the service equipment and supply any electrical equipment associated with the fountain.

Note: See 250.122 for sizing these conductors.

(B) Bonding. The following parts must be bonded together and connected to an equipment grounding conductor on a branch circuit supplying the fountain:

(1) All metal piping systems associated with the fountain

(2) All metal fittings within or attached to the fountain

(3) Metal parts of electrical equipment associated with the fountain water-circulating system, including pump motors

(4) Metal raceways within 5 ft of the inside wall or perimeter of the fountain and not separated from it by a permanent barrier

(5) All metal surfaces within 5 ft of the inside wall or perimeter of the fountain and not separated from it by a permanent barrier

(6) Electrical devices and controls not associated with the fountain and located less than 5 ft from its inside wall or perimeter

680.55 Methods of Equipment Grounding

(A) Additional Requirements. The grounding requirements of 680.21(A), 680.23(B)(3), 680.23(F)(1) and (2), 680.24(F), and 680.25 apply to fountains.

(B) Supplied by Flexible Cord. Fountain equipment supplied by a flexible cord must have all exposed metal parts connected to an insulated copper equipment grounding conductor that is an integral part of the cord. ▶Figure 680-40

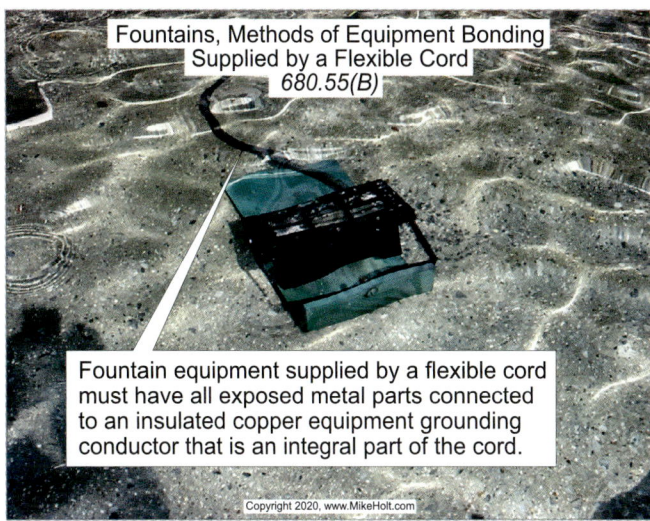

▶Figure 680-40

Part VII. Hydromassage Bathtubs

680.70 General

A hydromassage bathtub must only comply with the requirements of Part VII; it is not required to comply with the other parts of this article.

Author's Comment:

▶ According to 680.2, a "Hydromassage Bathtub" is defined as a permanently installed bathtub with a recirculating piping system designed to accept, circulate, and discharge water after each use.

680.74 Equipotential Bonding

(A) General. The following parts must be bonded together.

(1) Metal fittings within, or attached to, the hydromassage bathtub structure that are in contact with the circulating water.

(2) Metal parts of electrical equipment associated with the hydromassage bathtub water circulating system, including pump and blower motors.

(3) Metal-sheathed cables, metal raceways, and metal piping within 5 ft of the inside walls of the hydromassage bathtub and not separated from its area by a permanent barrier.

(4) Exposed metal surfaces within 5 ft of the inside walls of the hydromassage bathtub and not separated from it by a permanent barrier.

(5) Metal parts of electrical devices not associated with the hydromassage bathtub located within 5 ft from the hydromassage bathtub.

Ex 1: Small conductive surfaces not likely to become energized, such as air and water jets, supply valve assemblies, drain fittings not connected to metallic piping, towel bars, mirror frames, and similar nonelectrical equipment not connected to metal framing are not required to be bonded. ▶Figure 680–41

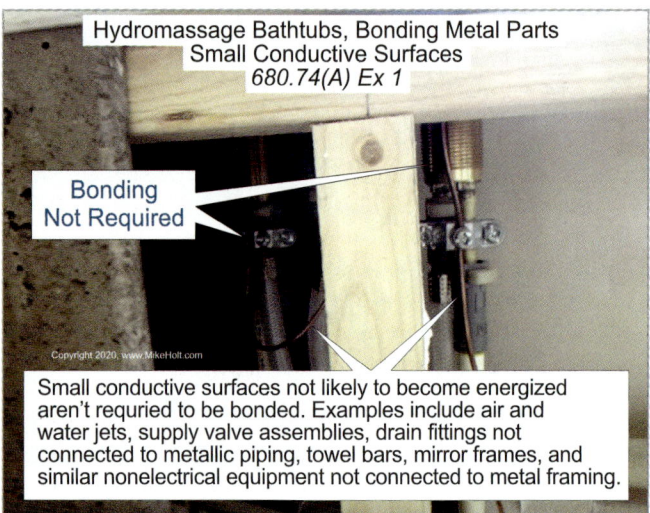

▶Figure 680–41

Ex 2: Double-insulated motors and blowers are not required to be bonded.

(B) Bonding Conductor. Metal parts required to be bonded by 680.74(A) must be bonded together using a solid copper conductor not smaller than 8 AWG. Bonding jumpers are not required to be extended or attached to any remote panelboard, service disconnect, or any electrode.

A bonding jumper long enough to terminate on a replacement nondouble-insulated pump or blower motor must be provided, and it must terminate to the equipment grounding conductor of the branch circuit of the motor when a double-insulated circulating pump or blower motor is used.

Part VIII. Electrically Powered Pool Lifts

680.80 General

Electrically powered pool lifts as defined in 680.2 must comply with Part VIII of this article. Part VIII is not subject to the requirements of other parts of this article except where the requirements are specifically referenced. ▶Figure 680–42

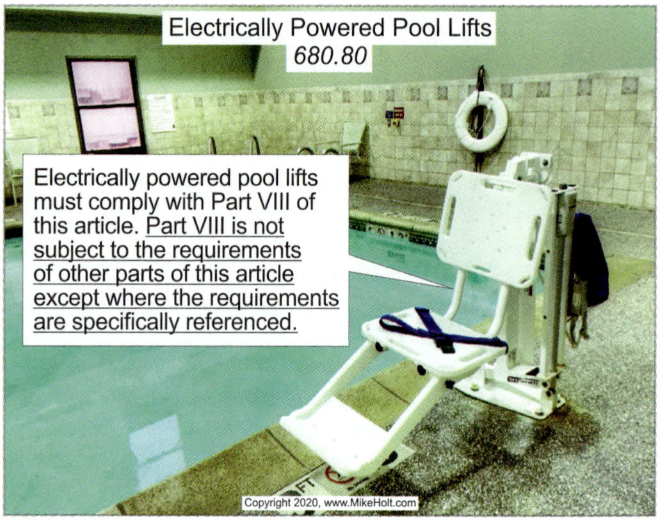

▶Figure 680–42

680.83 Bonding

Electrically powered pool lifts must be bonded in accordance with 680.26(B)(5) and (B)(7). ▶Figure 680–43

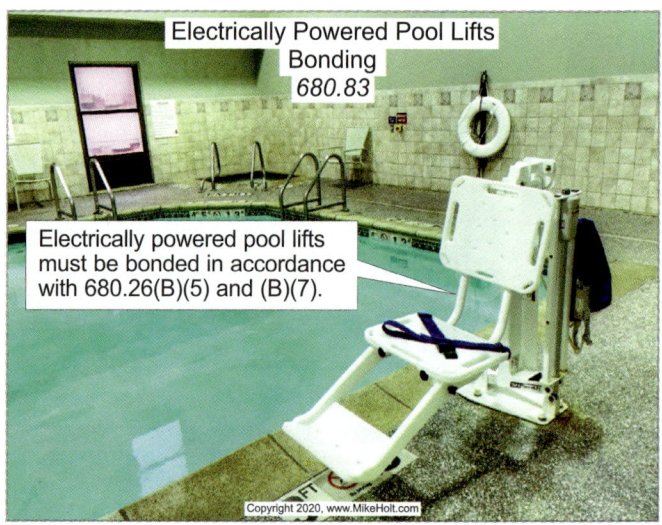

▶Figure 680–43

ARTICLE 690 — SOLAR PHOTOVOLTAIC (PV) SYSTEMS

Introduction to Article 690—Solar Photovoltaic (PV) Systems

You have seen (or maybe own) devices powered by photovoltaic cells such as night lights, car coolers, and toys. They generally consist of a small solar module powering a small device running on less than 10V direct current and drawing only a fraction of an ampere. A solar PV system that powers a building or interconnects with an electric utility to offset a building's energy consumption operates on the same principals but on a much larger scale.

Solar PV systems that provide electrical power to an electrical system are large, heavy, and complex. There are mechanical and site selection issues that require expert knowledge as well as complex structural and architectural concerns that must be addressed.

The purpose of the *NEC* is to safeguard persons and property from the hazards arising from the use of electricity [90.1(A)]. Article 690 keeps that theme by focusing on reducing electrical hazards that might arise from installing and operating a PV system—to a point where it can be considered safe for people and property.

This article consists of eight Parts and the general *Code* requirements of Chapters 1 through 4 apply to these installations, except as specifically modified by Article 690.

Part I. General

690.1 Scope

The requirements contained in Article 690 apply to solar photovoltaic systems. ▶Figure 690-1

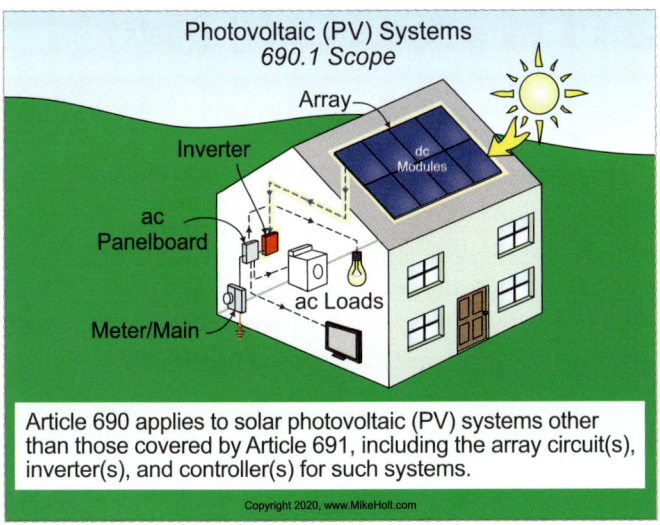

▶Figure 690-1

The systems covered by this article include those that are interactive (operate in parallel with the electric utility), stand-alone systems, or a combination of the two. PV systems can provide either alternating-current or direct-current power.

Energy storage systems are permitted to be connected to, but are not a part of, PV systems.

Note 1: See Informational Note Figure 690.1(a) that identifies PV system power source components and Informational Note Figure 690.1(b) showing five common configurations of PV systems that are covered in Article 690.

Note 2: Article 691 covers the installation of large-scale PV electric supply stations with a generating capacity of not less than 5,000 kW and not under the electric utility control. Facilities covered by that article have specific design and safety features unique to large-scale PV supply stations and are operated for the sole purpose of providing electric supply to a system operated by a regulated utility for the transfer of electric energy.

690.2 Definitions

The definitions in this section only apply within this article.

Array. An array is a mechanically and electrically integrated grouping of modules, inverter(s), dc-to-dc converter(s), and associated wiring on a support structure. ▶Figure 690–2

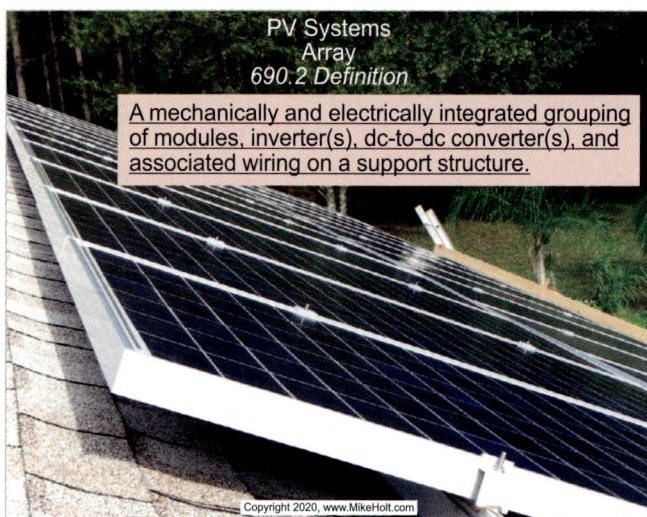
▶Figure 690–2

Grounded, Functionally. A functionally grounded PV system is one that has an electrical ground reference for operational purposes that is not solidly grounded. ▶Figure 690–3

▶Figure 690–3

Note: A functionally grounded PV system is connected to ground through an electronic means that is internal to an inverter. Purposes for functionally grounded systems include ground-fault detection and protection, as well as performance-related issues for some power sources.

Module. A PV module is a unit of environmentally protected solar cells and components designed to produce direct-current power. ▶Figure 690–4

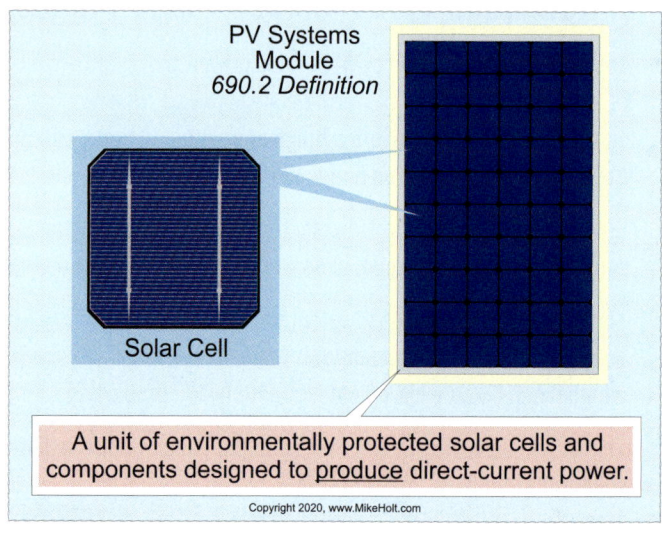
▶Figure 690–4

Author's Comment:

▶ PV modules use sunlight to generate direct-current (dc) electricity by using light (photons) to move electrons in a semi-conductor. This is known as the "photovoltaic effect."

Part IV. Wiring Methods and Materials

690.31 Wiring Methods

(D) PV System Direct-Current Circuits on or in Buildings. When the PV system direct-current circuit is located inside a building and it exceeds 30V or 8A, the PV system's direct-current circuit conductors must be installed in a metal raceway, Type MC cable where the armor sheath is listed as an equipment grounding conductor in accordance with 250.118(10), or a metal enclosure. ▶Figure 690–5

Solar Photovoltaic (PV) Systems | **690.43**

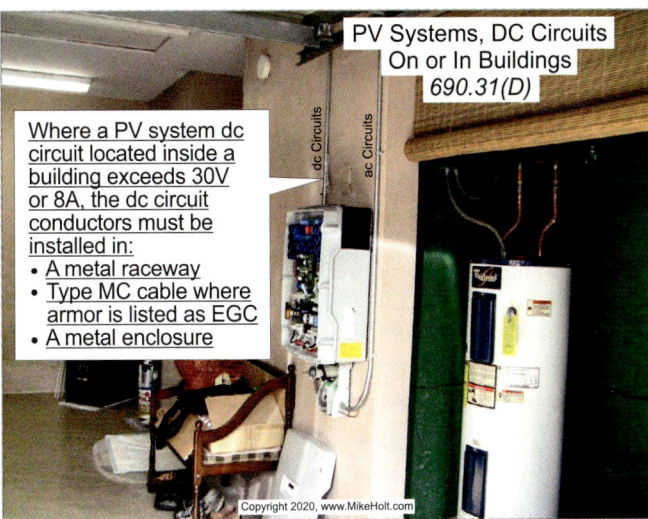

▶Figure 690-5

types identified in 250.118(2) through (14), or an equipment grounding conductor of the wire type contained within the same wiring method as the circuit conductors. However, the equipment grounding conductor for a direct-current circuit can be run separately from the circuit conductors when within the array [250.134 Ex 2, 690.31(C), and 690.46].

(A) Photovoltaic Module Mounting Systems and Devices. Devices listed, labeled, and identified for bonding PV modules can be used to secure and bond PV module frames to metal support structures, and to bond PV modules to adjacent PV modules. ▶Figure 690-7 and ▶Figure 690-8

Part V. Grounding and Bonding

690.43 Equipment Grounding and Bonding

Exposed metal parts of PV module frames, electrical equipment, and any enclosure containing PV system conductors must be connected to the PV system circuit equipment grounding conductor in accordance with 250.134 or 250.136. ▶Figure 690-6

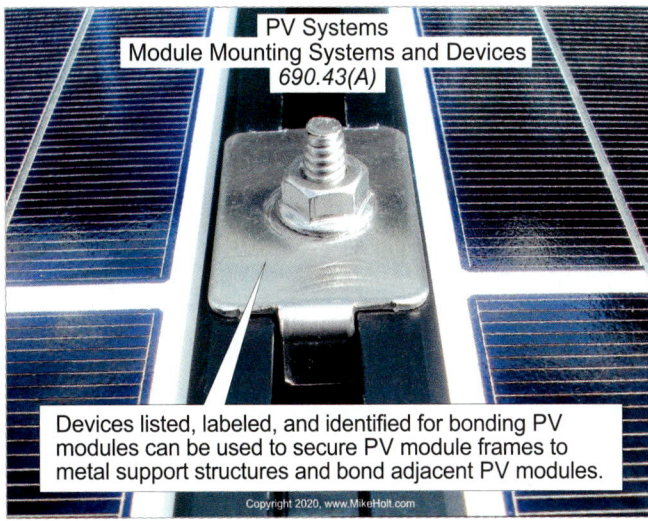

▶Figure 690-7

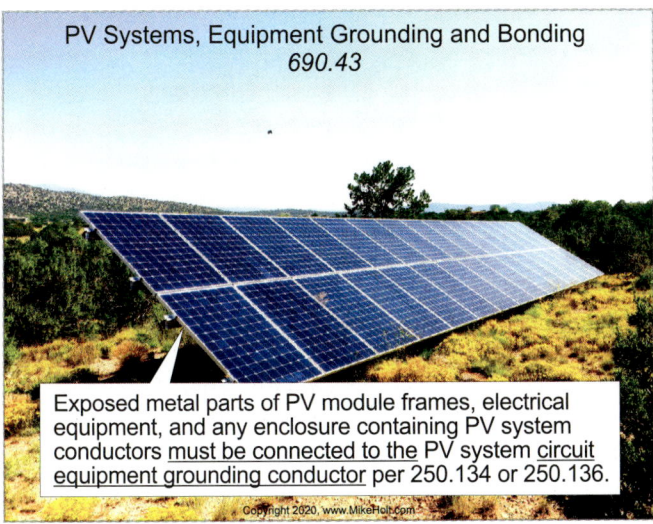

▶Figure 690-6

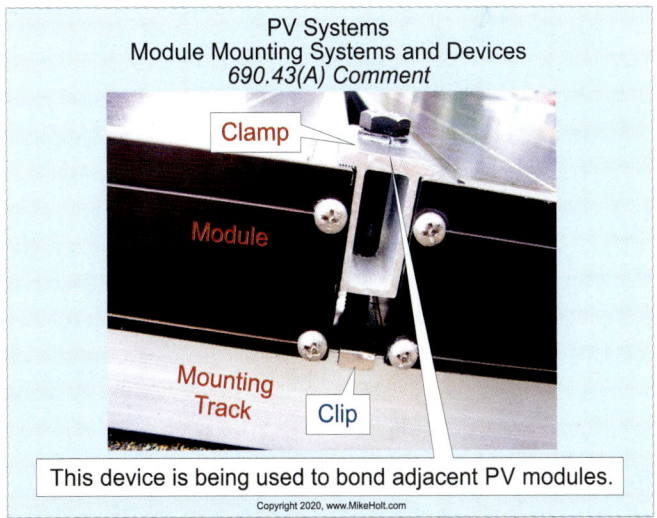

▶Figure 690-8

Author's Comment:

▸ According to 250.134, metal parts of equipment, raceways, and enclosures must be connected to an equipment grounding conductor using one of the equipment grounding conductor

(B) Equipment Secured to Grounded Metal Support Structure.
Metallic support structures listed, labeled, and identified for bonding and grounding metal parts of PV systems can be used to bond PV equipment to the metal support structure that has been connected to the PV circuit equipment grounding conductor.

Metallic support structures used as an equipment grounding conductor must have identified bonding jumpers between separate metallic sections, or the support structure must be identified for equipment bonding purposes and be connected to the PV circuit equipment grounding conductor as required by 690.43. ▶Figure 690–9

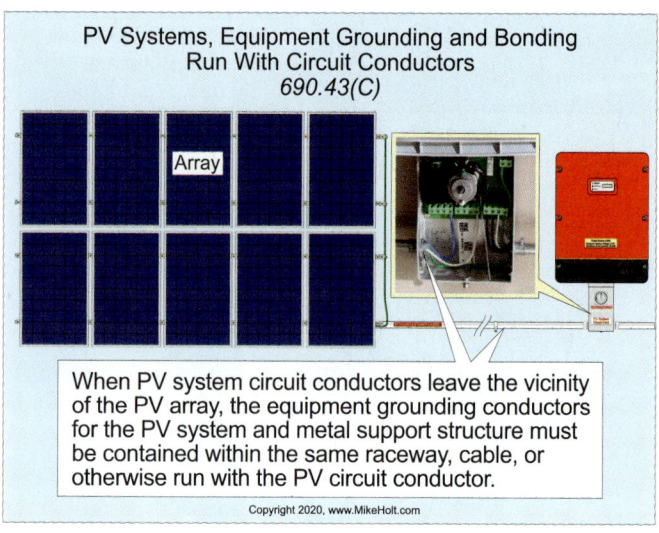

▶Figure 690–10

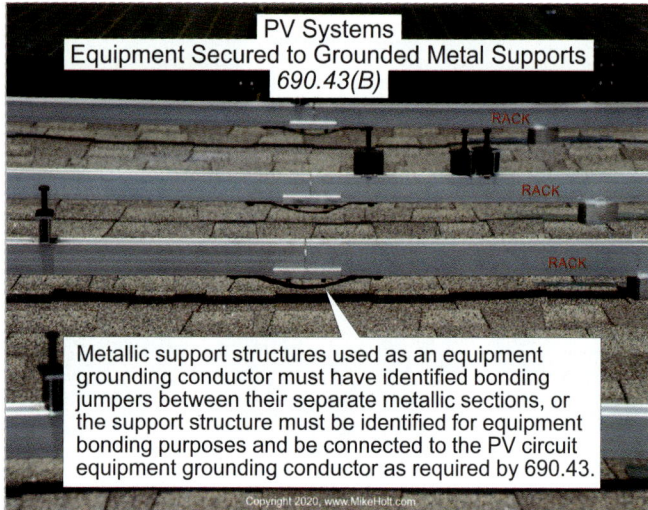

▶Figure 690–9

Author's Comment:

▸ Exposed equipment grounding conductors 8 AWG (solid or stranded) and smaller for direct-current circuits [250.134(B) Ex 2] are permitted to be run separately from the circuit conductors where not subject to physical damage [250.120(C)].

(C) With Circuit Conductors. When PV system circuit conductors leave the vicinity of the PV array, the equipment grounding conductors for the PV system and metal support structure must be contained within the same raceway, cable, or otherwise run with the PV circuit conductor. ▶Figure 690–10

(D) Bonding Over 250V. The bonding requirements contained in 250.97 apply only to solidly grounded PV system circuits operating over 250V to ground. ▶Figure 690–11

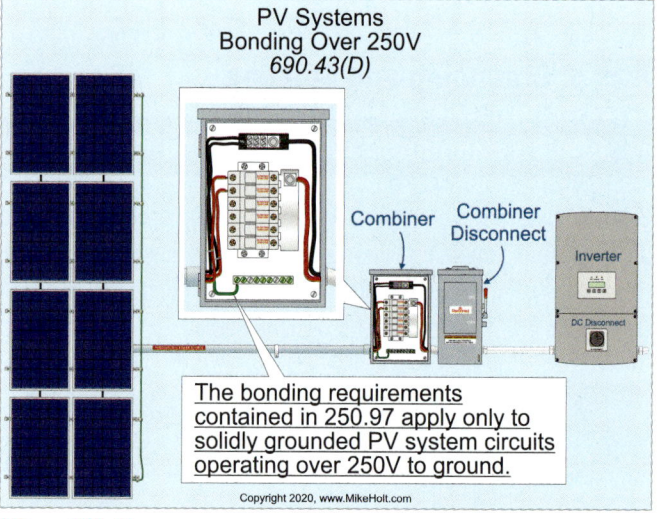

▶Figure 690–11

Author's Comment:

▸ Exposed equipment grounding conductors 8 AWG (solid or stranded) and smaller for direct-current circuits [250.134(B) Ex.2], such as required by 690.45 for solar PV systems are permitted to be run separately from the circuit conductors. Where the 8 AWG (solid or stranded) or smaller exposed equipment grounding conductor is subject to physical damage, it must be installed within a raceway or cable [250.120(C)].

690.45 Size of Equipment Grounding Conductors

Equipment grounding conductors for PV system circuits must be sized in accordance with 250.122, based on the circuit overcurrent protection ampere rating. ▶Figure 690-12

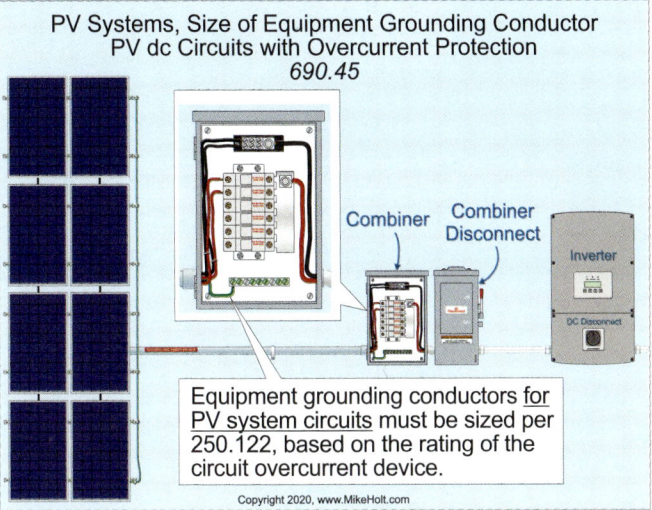
▶Figure 690-12

Where no overcurrent protective device is used in the PV system direct-current circuit, the equipment grounding conductor for the system's direct-current circuit must be sized in accordance with Table 250.122, based on an assumed overcurrent device for the circuit sized in accordance with 690.9(B).

Equipment grounding conductors are not required to be increased in size to address voltage-drop considerations. ▶Figure 690-13

▶Figure 690-13

690.47 Grounding Electrode System

(A) Building or Structure Supporting a PV System. A building or structure supporting a PV system must utilize a grounding electrode system installed in accordance with Part III of Article 250. ▶Figure 690-14

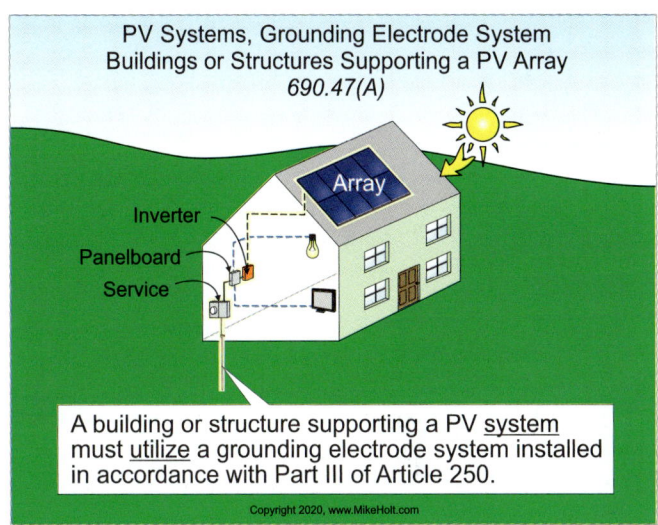
▶Figure 690-14

Author's Comment:

▶ Part III of Article 250 addresses grounding electrode systems, grounding electrode types, and grounding electrode installation requirements.

The PV array equipment grounding conductors must be connected to a grounding electrode system in accordance with Part VII of Article 250. This connection is required in addition to the equipment grounding conductor requirements contained in 690.43(C). The PV array equipment grounding conductors must be sized in accordance with 690.45.

For specific PV system grounding configurations as permitted in 690.41(A), one of the following must apply:

(1) PV Systems Not Solidly Grounded. For PV systems that are not solidly grounded systems, the PV output circuit equipment grounding conductor can be used to ground the PV system equipment grounding conductors to the grounding electrode if the PV output circuit equipment grounding conductor terminates to distribution equipment that is connected to a grounding electrode system. ▶Figure 690-15

The use of the PV output circuit equipment grounding conductor to serve as the required PV equipment grounding conductor connection to ground is the only connection to ground required for the PV system. ▶Figure 690-16

690.47 | Solar Photovoltaic (PV) Systems

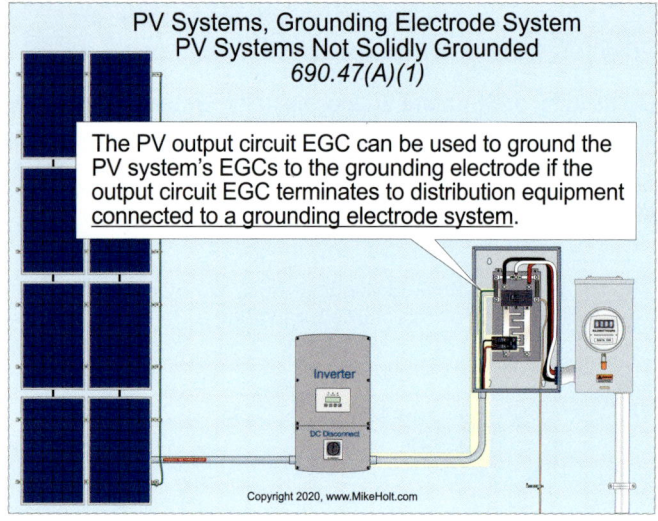
▶Figure 690-15

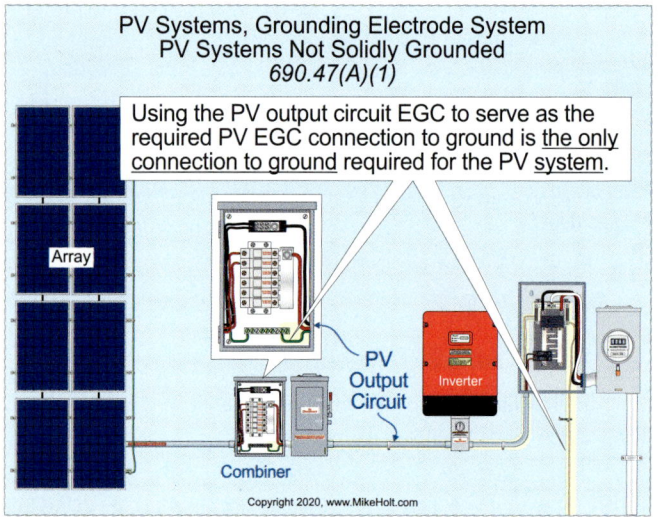
▶Figure 690-16

(2) PV Systems Solidly Grounded. For PV systems that are solidly grounded as permitted in 690.41(A)(5), the grounded electrode conductor must be sized in accordance with 250.166.

Note: Most PV systems are functionally grounded rather than solidly grounded. For functionally grounded PV systems with an interactive inverter output, the alternating-current equipment grounding conductor is connected to associated grounded ac distribution equipment. This connection is most often the connection to ground for ground-fault protection and equipment grounding of the PV array.

(B) Grounding Electrodes and Grounding Electrode Conductors.
Additional grounding electrodes are permitted (but not required) to be installed in accordance with 250.52 or 250.54, and they are permitted to be connected directly to the PV frames or support structure. The conductor used for this purpose must be sized in accordance with 250.66. ▶Figure 690-17

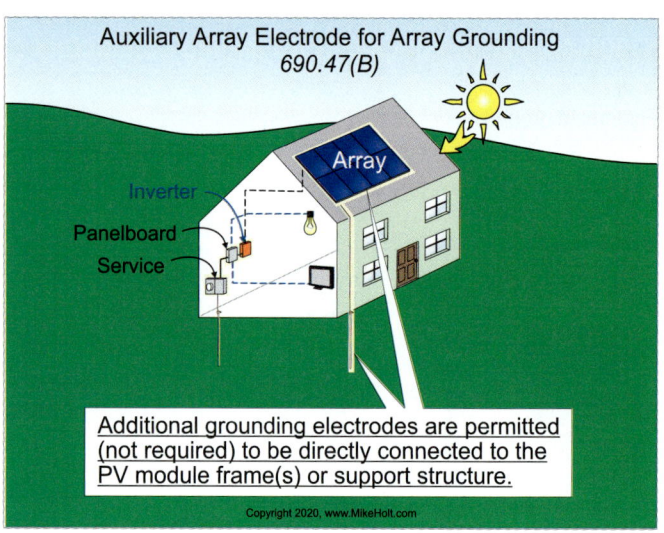
▶Figure 690-17

A support structure for a ground-mounted PV array can be considered a grounding electrode if it meets the requirements of 250.52. ▶Figure 690-18

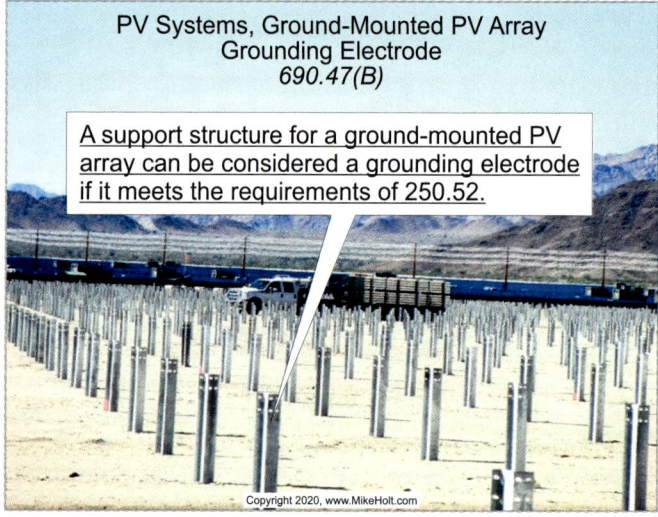
▶Figure 690-18

PV arrays mounted on buildings are permitted to use the metal structural frame of the building as an electrode if the requirements of 250.68(C)(2) are met.

CHAPTER 6

PRACTICE QUESTIONS

Please use the 2020 *Code* book to answer the following questions.

CHAPTER 6—SPECIAL EQUIPMENT

1. Metal equipment of signs, outline lighting, and skeleton tubing systems shall be grounded by connection to the _____ of the supply branch circuit(s) or feeder using the types of equipment grounding conductors specified in 250.118.

   (a) grounding electrode conductor
   (b) equipment grounding conductor
   (c) neutral conductor
   (d) ground rod

2. An electrically powered lift that provides accessibility to and from a pool or spa for people with disabilities is known as an "electrically powered _____ lift."

   (a) spa
   (b) disability
   (c) pool
   (d) tub

3. An ornamental structure or recreational water feature from which one or more jets or streams of water are discharged into the air, including splash pads, and _____ pools are defined as a fountain.

   (a) ornamental
   (b) wading
   (c) seasonal
   (d) permanently installed

4. For pools, fountains, and similar installations, the "low-voltage contact limit" is a voltage not exceeding _____.

   (a) 15V (RMS) for sinusoidal ac or 21.20V peak for nonsinusoidal ac
   (b) 30V for continuous dc
   (c) 12.40V peak for dc that is interrupted at a rate of 10 to 200 Hz
   (d) all of these

5. Permanently installed swimming pools include those constructed in the ground or partially in the ground, and all others capable of holding water in a depth greater than _____ in.

   (a) 36
   (b) 42
   (c) 48
   (d) 54

6. A spa or hot tub is a hydromassage pool or tub and is generally not designed to have the contents drained or discharged after each use.

   (a) True
   (b) False

7. A wet-niche luminaire is intended to be installed in a _____.

   (a) transformer
   (b) forming shell
   (c) hydromassage bathtub
   (d) all of these

Chapter 6 | Practice Questions

8. When installed for swimming pools, grounding and bonding terminals shall be _____ for use in wet and corrosive environments.

    (a) identified
    (b) labeled
    (c) listed
    (d) approved

9. Branch circuits installed in corrosive environments for pool-associated motors shall be installed in wiring methods including _____ conduit shall include an insulated copper equipment grounding conductor sized in accordance with Table 250.122, but not smaller than 12 AWG.

    (a) Type ENT
    (b) Type EMT
    (c) flexible metal
    (d) PVC or rigid metal

10. Wet-niche luminaires shall be connected to an equipment grounding conductor not smaller than _____ AWG.

    (a) 12 AWG
    (b) 10 AWG
    (c) 8 AWG
    (d) 6 AWG

11. The feeder to a swimming pool panelboard at a separate building or structure where installed in a corrosive environment can be supplied with any Chapter 3 wiring method provided the feeder has a separate insulated copper equipment grounding conductor.

    (a) True
    (b) False

12. An 8 AWG or larger solid copper equipotential bonding conductor shall be extended to service equipment to eliminate voltage gradients in the pool area.

    (a) True
    (b) False

13. A(n) _____ or larger pool bonding conductor for the perimeter surface(s) of a conductive pool shell, shall be connected to the equipotential bonding grid either by exothermic welding or by pressure connectors in accordance with 250.8.

    (a) 12 AWG
    (b) 10 AWG
    (c) 8 AWG
    (d) 6 AWG

14. For equipotential bonding, the perimeter surface to be bonded shall be considered to extend for _____ ft horizontally beyond the inside walls of the pool and shall include unpaved surfaces and other types of paving.

    (a) 3
    (b) 5
    (c) 10
    (d) 12

15. Which of the following shall be bonded?

    (a) Metal parts of electrical equipment associated with the pool water circulating system.
    (b) Pool structural metal.
    (c) Metal fittings within or attached to the pool.
    (d) all of these

16. Metallic pool cover anchors intended for insertion in a concrete or masonry deck surface, 1 in. or less in any dimension and 2 in. or less in length shall require bonding.

    (a) True
    (b) False

17. Where a double-insulated pool water pump motor is installed, a solid _____ AWG copper conductor of sufficient length to make a bonding connection to a replacement motor shall be extended from the swimming pool equipotential bonding means to an accessible point in the vicinity of the pool pump motor.

    (a) 12 AWG
    (b) 10 AWG
    (c) 8 AWG
    (d) 6 AWG

18. Metal piping systems associated with a fountain shall be bonded to the equipment grounding conductor of the _____.

    (a) branch circuit supplying the fountain
    (b) bonding grid
    (c) equipotential plane
    (d) grounding electrode system

19. Where installed for hydromassage bathtubs, _____ shall be bonded together.

    (a) all exposed metal surfaces that are within 5 ft of the inside walls of the tub and not separated from the tub area by a permanent barrier
    (b) double-insulated motors
    (c) small conductive surfaces such as towel bars and mirror frames.
    (d) internal metallic components

20. For hydromassage bathtubs, small conductive surfaces not likely to become energized, such as air and water jets, supply valve assemblies, and drain fittings not connected to metallic piping, and towel bars, mirror frames, and similar nonelectrical equipment not connected to _____ shall not be required to be bonded.

    (a) metal framing
    (b) nonmetallic framing
    (c) metal gas piping
    (d) any of these

21. Where installed for hydromassage bathtubs, double-insulated _____ shall not be bonded.

    (a) motors and blowers
    (b) cords
    (c) cables
    (d) fittings

22. The 8 AWG solid bonding jumper required for equipotential bonding in the area of hydromassage bathtubs shall not be required to be extended to any _____.

    (a) remote panelboard
    (b) service equipment
    (c) electrode
    (d) any of these

23. In accordance with Article 690, a functionally grounded system has an electrical ground reference for operational purposes that is not _____ grounded.

    (a) effectively
    (b) sufficiently
    (c) solidly
    (d) any of these

24. In PV systems, a(n) _____ is a complete, environmentally protected unit consisting of solar cells and other components, designed to produce direct-current power.

    (a) interface
    (b) battery
    (c) module
    (d) cell bank

25. Where inside buildings, PV system dc circuits that exceed 30 volts or 8 amperes shall be contained in _____.

    (a) metal raceways
    (b) Type MC cables
    (c) metal enclosures
    (d) metal raceways or metal enclosures

26. Exposed non

    (a) grounding jumper
    (b) bonding jumper
    (c) equipment grounding conductor
    (d) grounding jumper or bonding jumper

27. Devices and systems used for mounting PV modules that are also used for bonding module frames shall be _____ for bonding PV modules. Devices that mount adjacent PV modules shall be permitted for bonding adjacent PV modules.

    (a) listed
    (b) labeled
    (c) identified
    (d) all of these

28. Metallic support structures shall have _____ bonding jumpers connected between the separate metallic sections or shall be _____ for equipment bonding and shall be connected to the equipment grounding conductor.

    (a) listed
    (b) labeled
    (c) identified
    (d) all of these

Chapter 6 | Practice Questions

29. Where no overcurrent protection is provided for the PV circuit, an assumed overcurrent device rated in accordance with 690.9(b) shall be used to size the equipment grounding conductor in accordance with _____.

    (a) 250.66
    (b) 250.102(C)(1)
    (c) 250.122
    (d) Table 250.122

30. Other than those required by section 690.47(A), additional grounding electrodes and grounding electrode conductors shall be permitted. The conductors shall be sized in accordance with _____.

    (a) Table 250.66
    (b) Table 250.122
    (c) Table 310.16
    (d) Table 250.66 or Table 250.122

CHAPTER 8
COMMUNICATIONS SYSTEMS

Introduction to Chapter 8—Communications Systems

Chapter 8 of the *Code* covers the wiring requirements for communications systems such as telephones, radio and TV antennas, satellite dishes, closed-circuit television (CCTV), and coaxial cable systems. ▶Figure 1

Communications systems are not subject to the general requirements contained in Chapters 1 through 4 or the special requirements of Chapters 5 through 7, except where a Chapter 8 rule specifically refers to one in those chapters [90.3]. Also, installations of communications equipment under the exclusive control of communications utilities located outdoors, or in building spaces used exclusively for such installations, are exempt from the *NEC* [90.2(B)(4)].

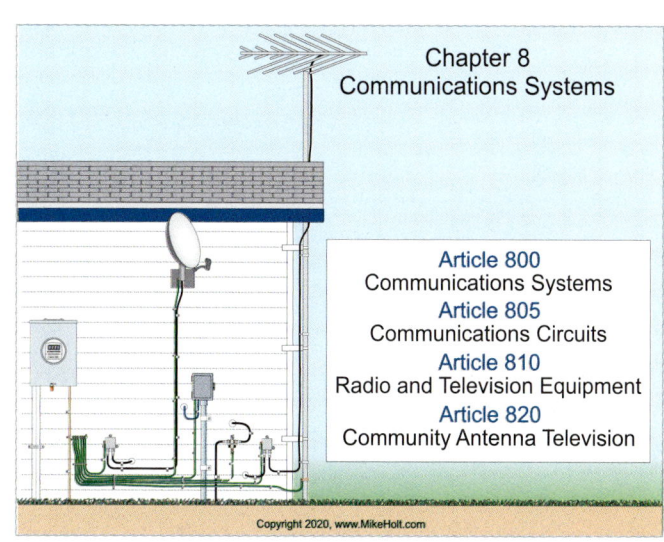
▶Figure 1

▶ **Article 800—General Requirements for Communications Systems.** This article covers general requirements for the installation of communications circuits, community antenna television and radio distribution systems, network-powered broadband communications systems, and premises-powered broadband communications systems, unless modified by Articles 805 or 820.

▶ **Article 810—Radio and Television Equipment.** This article covers antenna systems for radio and television receiving equipment, amateur radio transmitting and receiving equipment, and certain features of transmitter safety. It also includes antennas such as multi-element, vertical rod and dish, and the wiring and cabling connecting them to the equipment.

▶ **Article 820—Community Antenna Television (CATV) and Radio Distribution Systems (Coaxial Cable).** Article 820 addresses the installation of coaxial cables to distribute limited-energy high-frequency signals for television, cable TV, and closed-circuit television (CCTV), which is often used for security purposes.

Notes

ARTICLE 800 — GENERAL REQUIREMENTS FOR COMMUNICATIONS SYSTEMS

Introduction to Article 800—General Requirements for Communications Systems

This article contains the general rules for the installations of the systems covered by Articles 805 and 820 and these general rules along with the more specific ones in the respective articles apply. Note that the scope of this article does not include Article 810, Radio and Television Equipment which article remains stand-alone from the rest of the *Code*, including the Chapter 8 Articles. The specific rules in Articles 805, 820, 830, and 840 supplement or modify the requirements in Article 800. This is like the language in 90.3 that says the general rules in Chapters 1 through 4 may be modified by the specific rules in Chapters 5 through 7.

Part I. General

800.1 Scope

This article covers general requirements for communications systems. These general requirements apply to communications circuits, community antenna television and radio distribution systems, and network- and premises-powered broadband communications systems, unless modified by Articles 805 or 820. ▶Figure 800–1

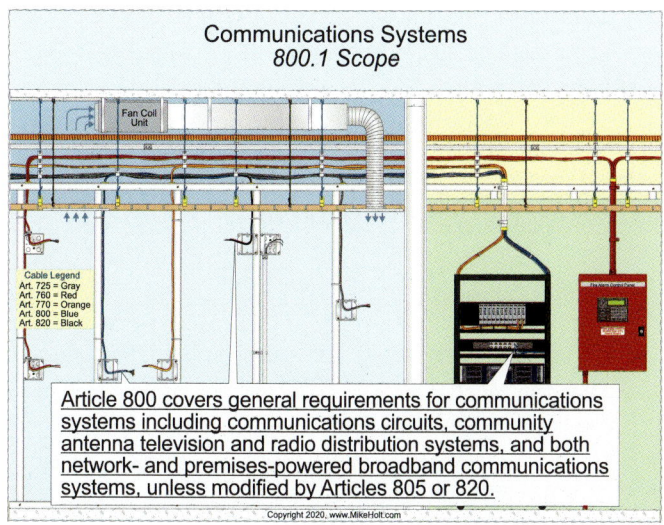

▶Figure 800–1

800.100 Cable and Primary Protector Bonding and Grounding

(A) Bonding Conductor or Grounding Electrode Conductor.

(1) Insulation. The conductor must be listed and can be insulated, covered, or bare.

(2) Material. The conductor must be copper or other corrosion-resistant conductive material and can be stranded or solid.

(3) Size. The conductor is not permitted to be smaller than 14 AWG with a current-carrying capacity of not less than the grounded metallic sheath member(s) or protected conductor(s) of the communications cable or coaxial cable. The bonding conductor or grounding electrode conductor is not required to be larger than 6 AWG. ▶Figure 800–2

(4) Length. The bonding conductor or grounding electrode conductor must be as short as practicable. For one- and two-family dwellings, the bonding conductor or grounding electrode conductor is not permitted to exceed 20 ft in length. ▶Figure 800–3

Note: Limiting the length of the bonding conductor or grounding electrode conductor helps limit induced voltage differences between the building's power and communications systems during lightning events.

800.100 | General Requirements for Communications Systems

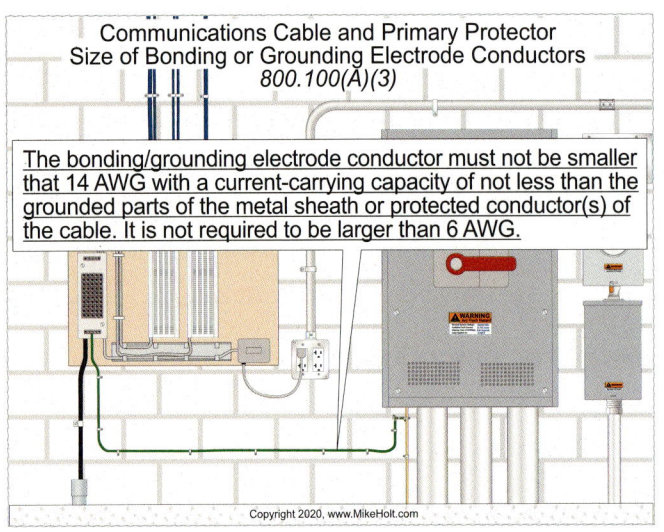
▶ Figure 800–2

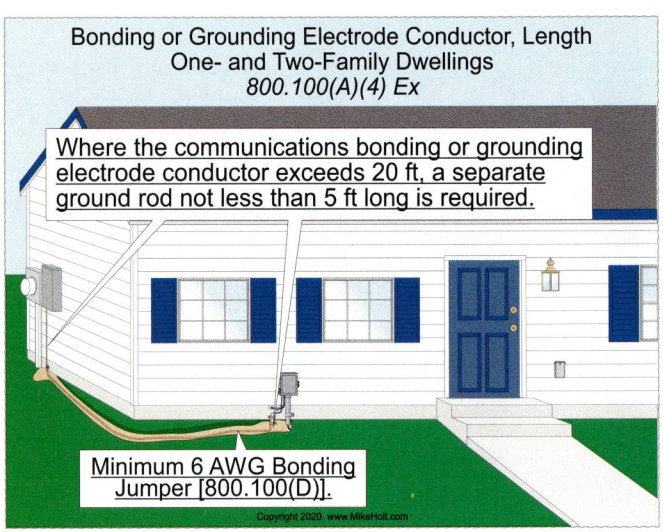
▶ Figure 800–4

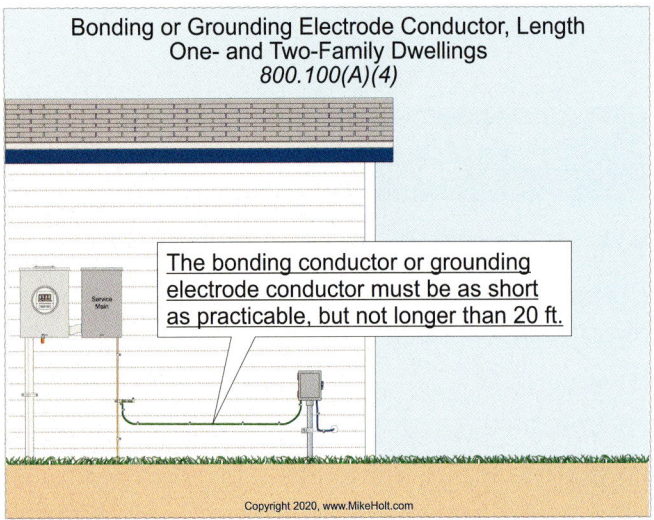
▶ Figure 800–3

Ex: If the bonding conductor or grounding electrode conductor is over 20 ft in length for one- and two-family dwellings, a separate ground rod not less than 5 ft long [800.100(B)(3)(2)] with fittings suitable for the application [800.100(C)] must be installed. The additional ground rod must be bonded to the power grounding electrode system with a minimum 6 AWG conductor [800.100(D)]. ▶ Figure 800–4

(5) Run in Straight Line. Run in as straight a line as practicable.

Author's Comment:

▸ Lightning does not like to travel around corners or through loops, which is why the grounding electrode conductor or bonding jumper must be run as straight as practicable.

(6) Physical Protection. The bonding conductor and grounding electrode conductor are not permitted to be subject to physical damage. If installed in a metal raceway, both ends of the raceway must be bonded to the contained conductor or connected to the same terminal or electrode to which the bonding conductor or grounding electrode conductor is connected.

Author's Comment:

▸ Installing the bonding conductor or grounding electrode conductor in PVC conduit is a better practice.

(B) Electrode. The bonding conductor or grounding electrode conductor must be connected in accordance with (B)(1), (B)(2), or (B)(3):

(1) Buildings with an Intersystem Bonding Termination. The bonding conductor must terminate to the intersystem bonding termination as required by 250.94. ▶ Figure 800–5

Author's Comment:

▸ According to the Article 100 definition, an "Intersystem Bonding Termination" is a device that provides a means to connect intersystem bonding conductors for communications systems to the grounding electrode system. ▶ Figure 800–6

Note: Figure 800.100(B)(1) in the *NEC* illustrates the connection of the bonding conductor in buildings or structures equipped with an intersystem bonding termination.

General Requirements for Communications Systems | 800.100

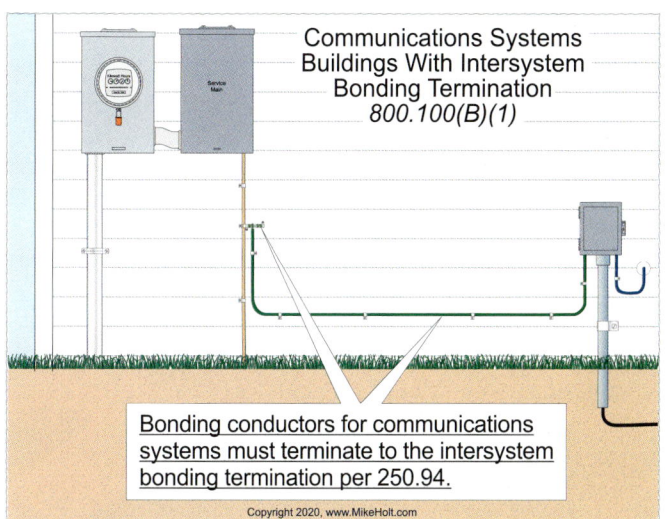
▶Figure 800-5

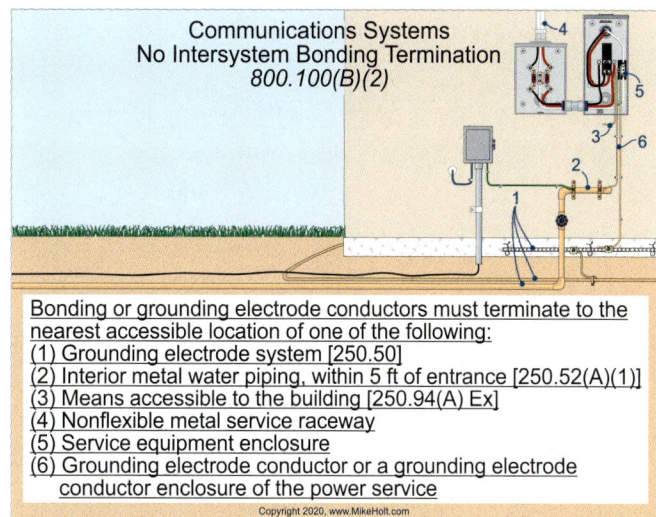
▶Figure 800-7

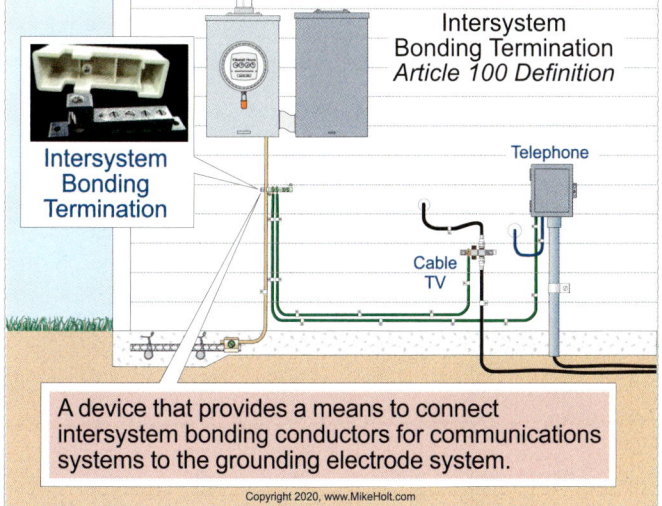
▶Figure 800-6

(2) Building Without Intersystem Bonding Termination. The bonding conductor or grounding electrode conductor must terminate to the nearest accessible location of one of the following: ▶Figure 800-7

(1) Building grounding electrode system [250.50].

(2) Interior metal water piping system, within 5 ft from its point of entrance [250.52(A)(1)].

(3) In accordance with 250.94(A) Ex.

(4) Nonflexible metal service raceway.

(5) Service-disconnect enclosure.

(6) Grounding electrode conductor or the grounding electrode conductor metal enclosure of the power service.

(7) Grounding electrode conductor or the grounding electrode of a remote building disconnect [250.32].

The intersystem bonding termination must be mounted on the fixed part of an enclosure so it will not interfere with the opening of an enclosure door. A bonding device is not permitted to be mounted on a door or cover, even if the door or cover is nonremovable.

For the purposes of this section, mobile home service equipment or the mobile home disconnecting means located within 30 ft of the exterior wall of the mobile home it serves, or at a mobile home disconnecting means connected to an electrode by a grounding electrode conductor in accordance with 250.32 and located within 30 ft of the exterior wall of the mobile home it serves, is considered to meet the requirements of this section.

Note: Informational Note Figure 800.100(B)(2) illustrates the connection of the bonding conductor in buildings or structures equipped with an intersystem bonding termination or a terminal block providing access to the building grounding means.

(3) In Buildings Without Intersystem Bonding Termination or Grounding Means. If the building has no intersystem bonding termination, as described in 800.100(B)(2), the grounding electrode conductor must be connected to one of the following: ▶Figure 800-8

(1) Any individual grounding electrodes described in 250.52(A)(1), (A)(2), (A)(3), or (A)(4).

(2) Any individual grounding electrode described in 250.52(A)(5), (A)(7), and (A)(8).

(3) For communications circuits within the scope of Article 805, to a ground rod not less than 5 ft in length located no less than 6 ft from electrodes of other systems.

800.180 | General Requirements for Communications Systems

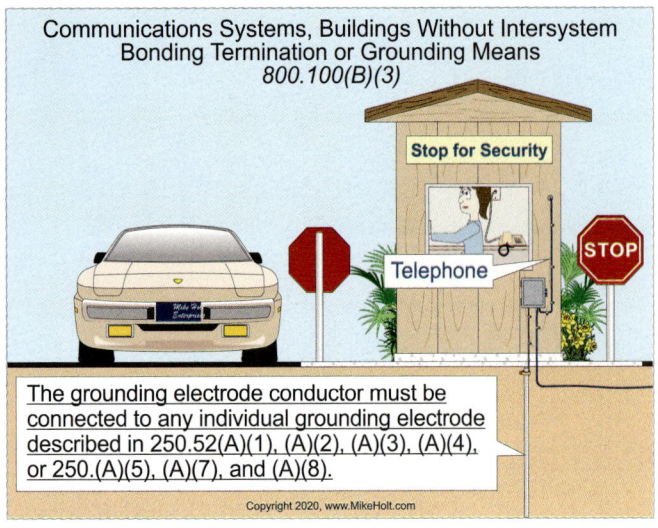
▶Figure 800-8

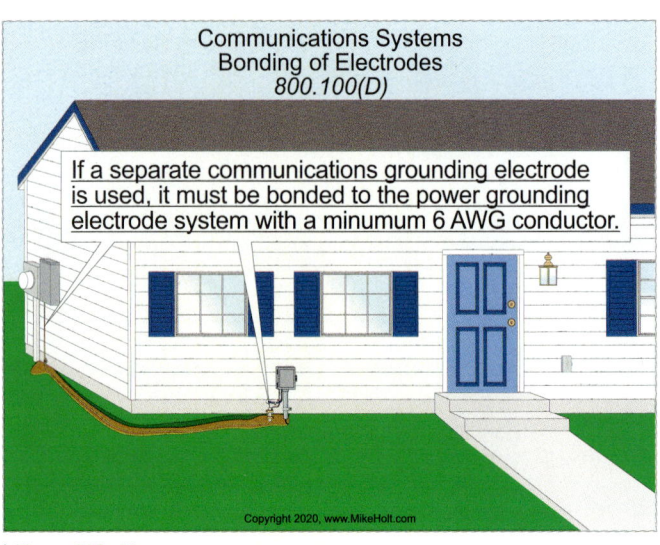
▶Figure 800-10

(C) Electrode Connection. Terminations at the grounding electrode must be by exothermic welding, listed lugs, listed pressure connectors, or listed clamps. Grounding fittings that are concrete-encased or buried in the Earth must be listed for direct burial [250.70]. ▶Figure 800-9

Note 2: Bonding separate electrodes together helps reduce induced voltage differences between the power and communications systems during lightning events. ▶Figure 800-11

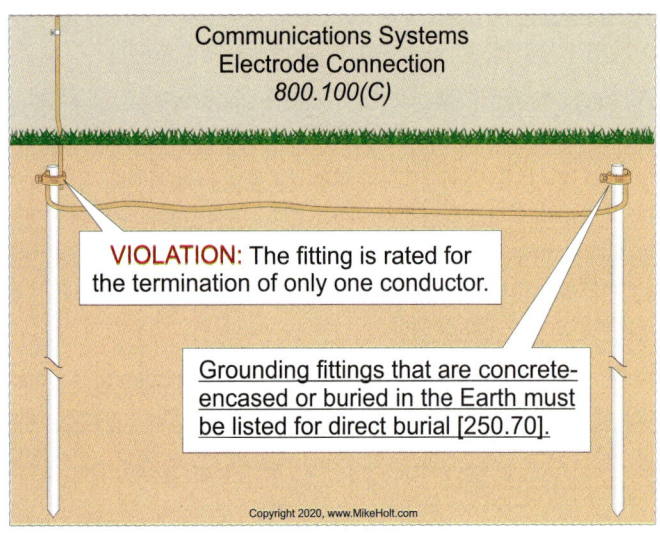
▶Figure 800-9

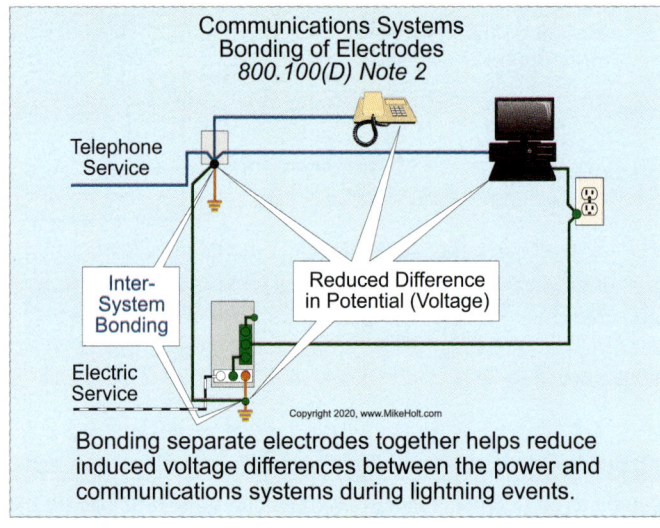
▶Figure 800-11

(D) Bonding of Electrodes. If a separate grounding electrode (such as a rod) is installed for a communications system, it must be bonded to the building's power grounding electrode system with a minimum 6 AWG conductor. ▶Figure 800-10

800.180 Grounding Devices

Where bonding or grounding is required, devices used to connect a shield, sheath, or noncurrent-carrying metallic members of a cable to a bonding conductor or grounding electrode conductor must be listed or be part of listed equipment.

ARTICLE 810
RADIO AND TELEVISION SATELLITE EQUIPMENT

Introduction to Article 810—Radio and Television Satellite Equipment

Unlike other articles in this chapter, Article 810 is not covered by the general rules in Article 800. As a result it stands completely alone in the *NEC* unless a rule in 810 references a specific rule elsewhere in the *Code*.

This article covers transmitter and receiver (antenna) equipment, and its associated wiring and cabling. Here are a few key points to remember about Article 810:

▸ Keep the bonding conductor or grounding electrode conductor as straight as practicable and protect it from physical damage.

▸ If the mast is not bonded properly, you risk flashovers and possible electrocution.

▸ Remember that the purpose of bonding is to prevent a difference of voltage between metallic objects and other conductive items, such as swimming pools.

Note: See Figure 800(a) and Figure 800(b) in the *NEC* for examples of bonding conductors and grounding electrode conductors.

810.1 Scope

Article 810 contains the installation requirements for wiring television and radio receiving equipment such as digital satellite receiving equipment for television signals, and amateur/citizen band radio equipment antennas. ▸Figure 810–1

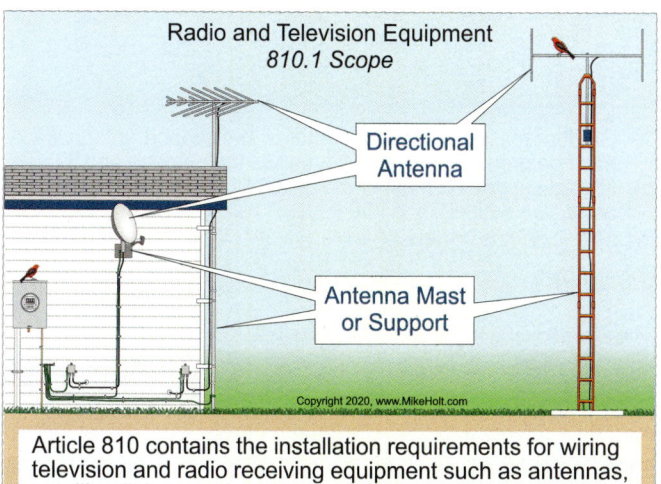

Article 810 contains the installation requirements for wiring television and radio receiving equipment such as antennas, satellite dishes, and amateur citizen band radio antennas.

▸Figure 810–1

Author's Comment:

▸ Article 810 covers:

  ▸ Antennas that receive local television signals.

  ▸ Satellite antennas, which are often referred to as satellite dishes.

  ▸ Roof-mounted antennas for AM/FM/XM radio reception.

  ▸ Amateur radio transmitting and receiving equipment, including HAM radio equipment (a noncommercial [amateur] communications system). ▸Figure 810–2

810.4 Community Television Antenna

The antenna for community television systems must be installed in accordance with this article, but the coaxial cable beyond the point of entrance must be installed in accordance with Article 820. ▸Figure 810–3

810.6 | Radio and Television Satellite Equipment

▶Figure 810-2

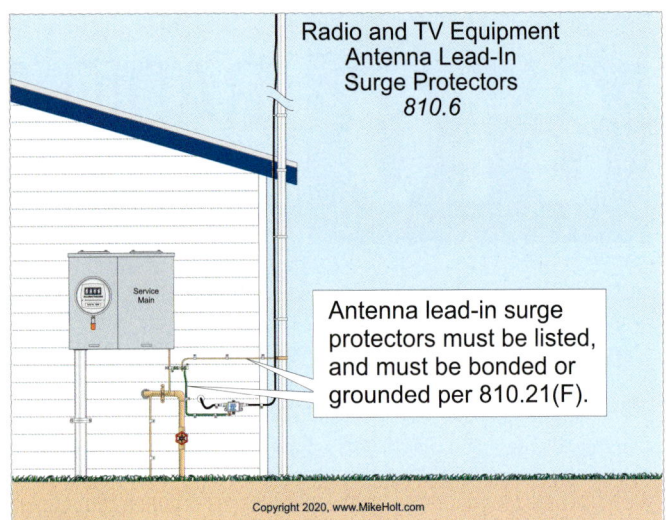
▶Figure 810-4

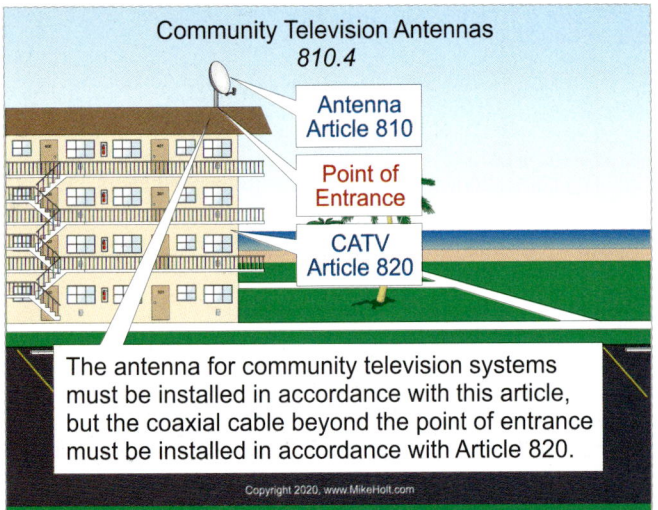
▶Figure 810-3

Author's Comment:

▸ A community TV antenna is used for multiple-occupancy facilities such as apartments, condominiums, motels, and hotels.

810.6 Antenna Lead-In Protectors

Antenna lead-in surge protectors must be listed and bonded or grounded in accordance with 810.21(F). ▶Figure 810-4

810.7 Grounding Devices

Fittings used to connect bonding jumpers or grounding electrode conductors to equipment must be listed.

810.15 Metal Antenna Supports—Grounding

Outdoor masts and metal structures that support antennas must be grounded in accordance with 810.21, unless the antenna and its related supporting mast or structure are within a zone of protection defined by a 150-ft radius rolling sphere. ▶Figure 810-5

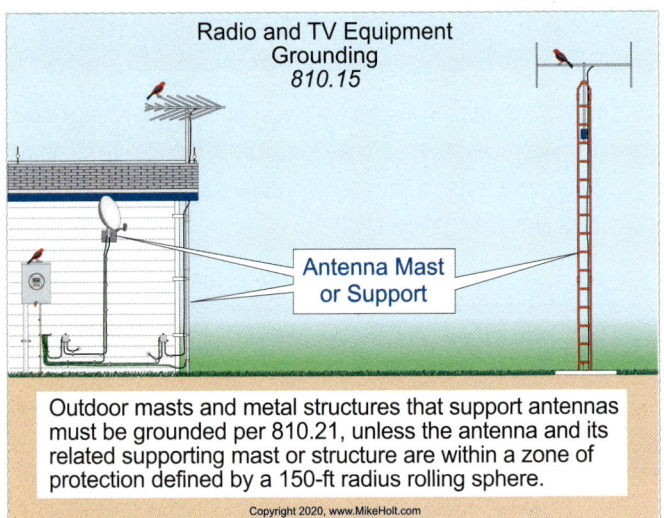
▶Figure 810-5

Note: See NFPA 780, *Standard for the Installation of Lightning Protection Systems* [4.8.3.1], for the application of the term "rolling sphere."

810.20 Antenna Discharge Unit

(A) Where Required. Each lead-in conductor from an outdoor antenna must be provided with a listed antenna discharge unit. ▶Figure 810-6

Radio and Television Satellite Equipment | **810.21**

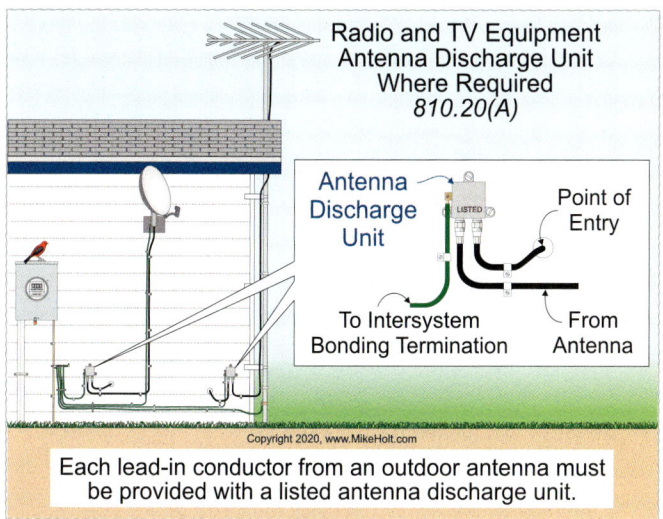
▶Figure 810-6

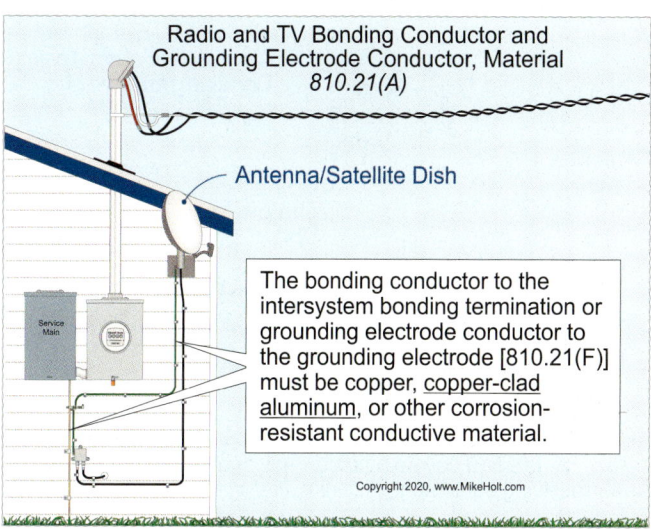
▶Figure 810-7

(B) Location. The antenna discharge unit must be located outside or inside the building, nearest the point of entrance, but not near combustible material or in a hazardous (classified) location as defined in Article 500.

(C) Grounding. The antenna discharge unit must be bonded or grounded in accordance with 810.21.

810.21 Bonding Conductor and Grounding Electrode Conductors

 Scan this QR code for a video of Mike explaining this topic; it's a sample from the videos that accompany this textbook. www.MikeHolt.com/20BGvideos

Bonding conductors and grounding electrode conductors must meet the requirements of 810.21(A) through 810.21(K).

(A) Material. The bonding conductor to the intersystem bonding termination or grounding electrode conductor to the grounding electrode [810.21(F)] must be copper, copper-clad aluminum, or other corrosion-resistant conductive material. ▶Figure 810-7

(B) Insulation. Insulation on bonding conductors or grounding electrode conductors is not required.

(C) Supports. The bonding conductor or grounding electrode conductor must be securely fastened in place.

(D) Physical Protection. Bonding conductors or grounding electrode conductors must be mechanically protected where subject to physical damage; and where installed in a metal raceway, both ends of the raceway must be bonded to the bonding conductor or grounding electrode conductor.

Author's Comment:

▸ Installing the bonding conductor or grounding electrode conductor in PVC conduit is a better practice.

(E) Run in Straight Line. The bonding conductor or grounding electrode conductor must be run in as straight a line as practicable.

Author's Comment:

▸ Lightning does not like to travel around corners or through loops, which is why the bonding conductor or grounding electrode conductor must be run as straight as practicable.

(F) Electrode. The bonding conductor or grounding electrode conductor must terminate in accordance with (1), (2), or (3).

(1) Buildings with an Intersystem Bonding Termination. The bonding conductor for the antenna mast and antenna discharge unit must terminate to the intersystem bonding termination [Article 100] as required by 250.94. ▶Figure 810-8

810.21 | Radio and Television Satellite Equipment

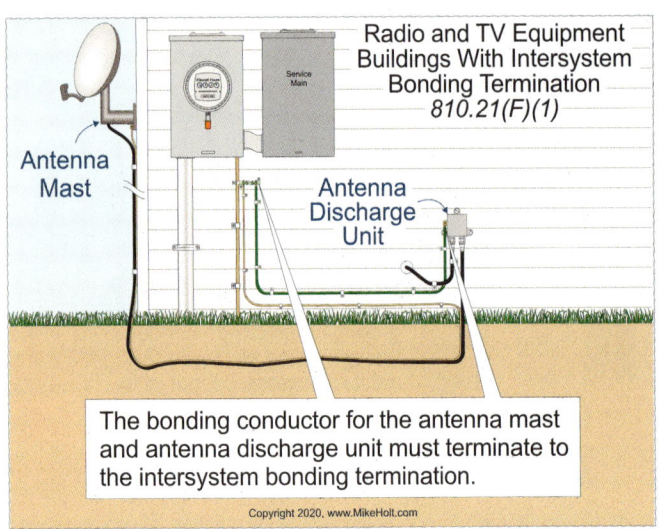
▶Figure 810–8

(2) In Buildings Without Intersystem Bonding Termination. The bonding conductor or grounding electrode conductor for the antenna mast and antenna discharge unit must terminate to the nearest accessible: ▶Figure 810–9

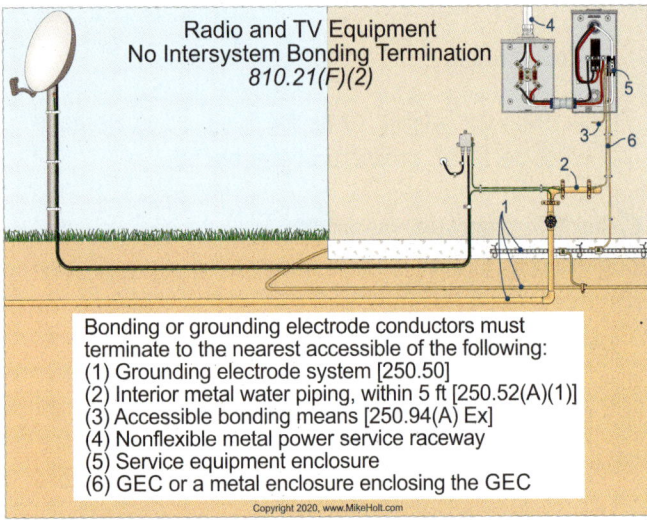
▶Figure 810–9

(1) Building grounding electrode system [250.50].

(2) Interior metal water piping system, within 5 ft from its point of entrance [250.52(A)(1)].

(3) Power service accessible means external to the building as covered in 250.94, including the exception.

(4) Nonflexible metal power service raceway.

(5) Service-disconnect enclosure.

(6) Grounding electrode conductor or the grounding electrode conductor metal enclosure.

(3) In Buildings Without a Grounding Means. The grounding electrode conductor for the antenna mast and antenna discharge unit must be connected to a grounding electrode as described in 250.52.

(G) Inside or Outside Building. The bonding conductor or grounding electrode conductor can be installed either inside or outside the building.

(H) Size. The bonding conductor or grounding electrode conductor is not permitted to be smaller than 10 AWG copper or 17 AWG copper-clad steel or bronze. ▶Figure 810–10

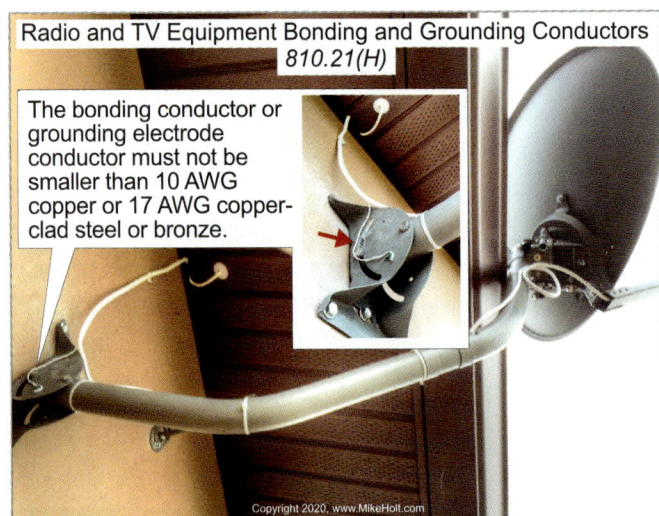
▶Figure 810–10

(J) Bonding of Electrodes. If a ground rod is installed to serve as the grounding electrode for the radio and television equipment, it must be bonded to the building's power grounding electrode system with a minimum 6 AWG conductor. ▶Figure 810–11

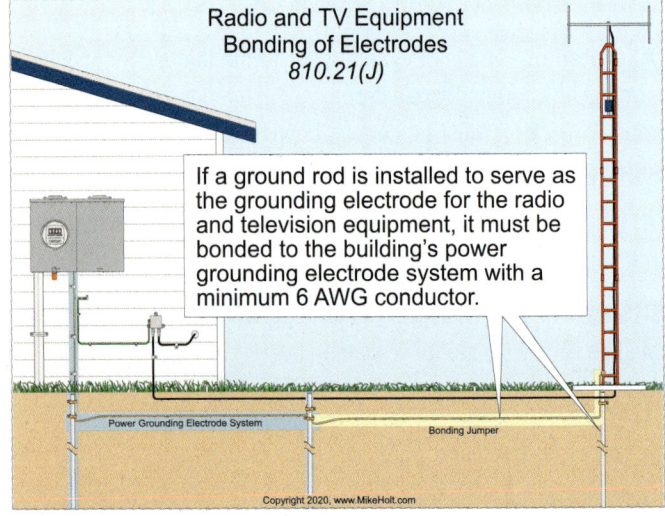
▶Figure 810–11

Author's Comment:

▸ A separate grounding electrode is not required for radio and TV equipment, but if it is installed it must be bonded to the building's power grounding electrode system with a minimum 6 AWG conductor.

▸ The bonding of electrodes together helps reduce induced voltage differences between the power and communications systems during lightning events. ▸Figure 810-12

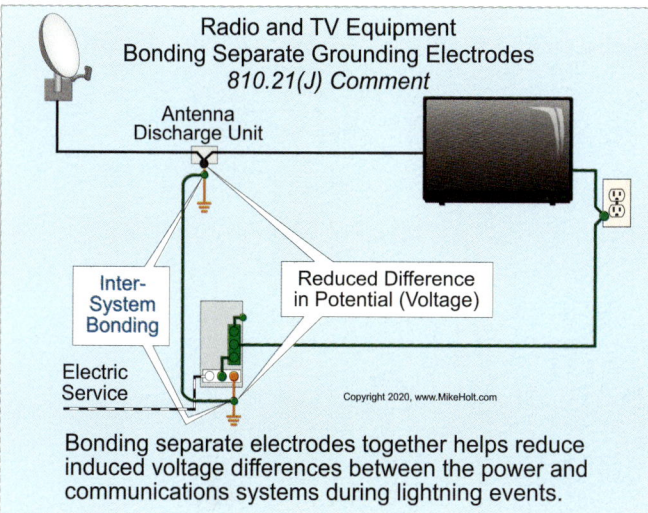

▸Figure 810-12

(K) Electrode Connection. Termination of the bonding conductor or grounding electrode conductor must be by exothermic welding, listed lugs, listed pressure connectors, or listed clamps. Grounding fittings that are concrete-encased or buried in the Earth must be listed for direct burial in accordance with 250.70. ▸Figure 810-13

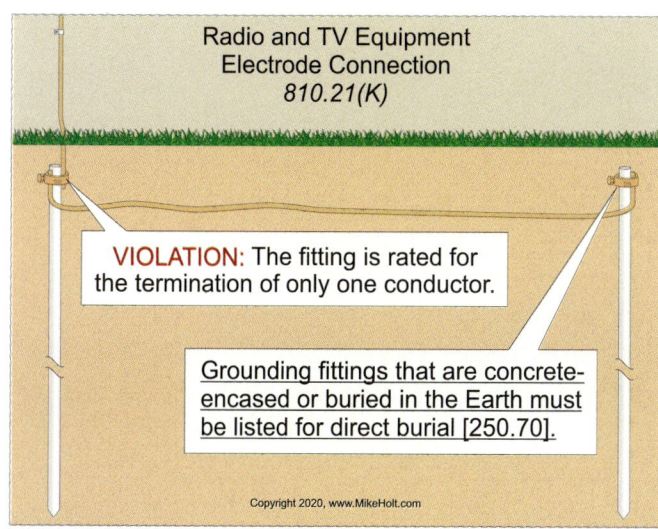

▸Figure 810-13

Author's Comment:

▸ Grounding the lead-in antenna cables and the mast helps prevent voltage surges caused by static discharge or nearby lightning strikes from reaching the center conductor of the lead-in coaxial cable. Because the satellite dish sits outdoors, wind creates a static charge on the antenna as well as on the cable to which it is attached. This charge can build up on both the antenna and the cable until it jumps across an air space, often passing through the electronics inside the low noise block down converter feedhorn (LNBF) or receiver. Connecting the antenna and satellite dish to the building's grounding electrode system (grounding) helps dissipate this static charge.

▸ Nothing can prevent damage from a direct lightning strike, but grounding with proper surge protection can help reduce damage to the satellite dish and other equipment from nearby lightning strikes.

Part III. Amateur and Citizen Band Transmitting and Receiving Stations—Antenna Systems

810.57 Antenna Discharge Units—Transmitting Stations

Each conductor of a lead-in for outdoor antennas must be provided with an antenna discharge unit or other suitable means to drain static charges from the antenna system.

Ex 1: Where the lead-in is protected by a continuous metallic shield that is grounded with a conductor in accordance with 810.58, an antenna discharge unit or other suitable means is not required.

Ex 2: Where the antenna is grounded with a conductor in accordance with 810.58, an antenna discharge unit or other suitable means is not required.

810.58 Bonding Conductors and Grounding Electrode Conductors—Amateur and Citizen Band Transmitting and Receiving Stations

Bonding conductors and grounding electrode conductors must comply with 810.58(A) through 810.58(C).

(A) Other Sections. All bonding conductors and grounding electrode conductors for amateur and citizen band transmitting and receiving stations must comply with 810.21(A) through 810.21(C).

(B) Size of Protective Bonding Conductor or Grounding Electrode Conductor. The protective bonding conductor or grounding electrode conductor for transmitting stations must be as large as the lead-in but not smaller than 10 AWG copper, bronze, or copper-clad steel.

(C) Size of Operating Bonding Conductor or Grounding Electrode Conductor. The operating bonding conductor or grounding electrode conductor for transmitting stations must not be less than 14 AWG copper or its equivalent.

ARTICLE 820

COMMUNITY ANTENNA TELEVISION (CATV) AND RADIO DISTRIBUTION SYSTEMS (COAXIAL CABLE)

Introduction to Article 820—Community Antenna Television (CATV) and Radio Distribution Systems (Coaxial Cable)

This article focuses on the distribution of television and radio signals within a facility or on a property via cable, rather than their transmission or reception via antenna. These signals are limited energy, but they are high frequency.

Article 800 defines the "point of entrance" for these circuits and provides the general requirements regarding installation methods for all types of communications wiring.

- Ground the incoming coaxial cable as close as practicable to the point of entrance.
- The bonding conductor must be connected to the intersystem bonding termination if there is one in, or at, the building.
- If a separate grounding electrode is used, a bonding jumper must be run to the power grounding system.

Part I. General

820.1 Scope

Article 820 covers the installation of coaxial cables for distributing high-frequency signals typically employed in community antenna television systems (CATV). ▶Figure 820–1

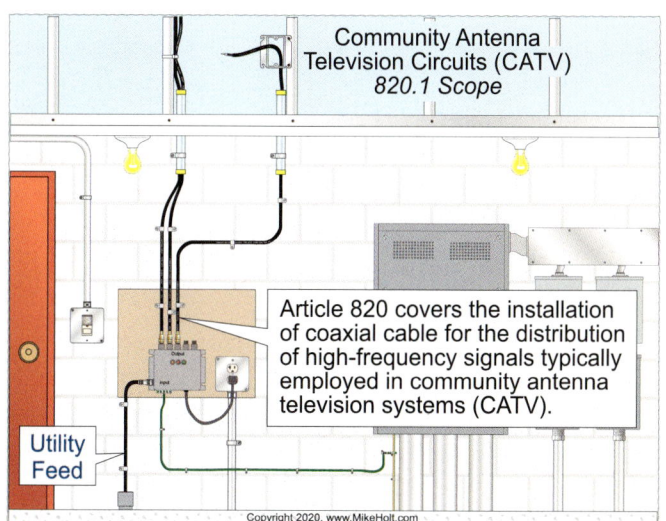

▶Figure 820–1

Author's Comment:

- Article 820 covers the installation of coaxial cable for cable television, closed-circuit television, security cameras, and radio and television receiving equipment.
- Coaxial cables that connect antennas to television and radio receiving equipment [810.3], and community television systems [810.4] must be installed in accordance with this article. ▶Figure 820–2

Part III. Protection

820.93 Grounding of the Outer Conductive Shield of Coaxial Cables

(A) Coaxial Cables Entering Building. Coaxial cables supplied to a building must have the metallic sheath members bonded or grounded as close as practicable to the point of entrance in accordance with 820.100. ▶Figure 820–3

Note: The grounding block location should be located to keep the bonding or grounding electrode conductor as short as practicable.

Mike Holt Enterprises • www.MikeHolt.com • 888.NEC.CODE (632.2633) | 321

820.100 | Community Antenna Television (CATV) and Radio Distribution Systems (Coaxial Cable)

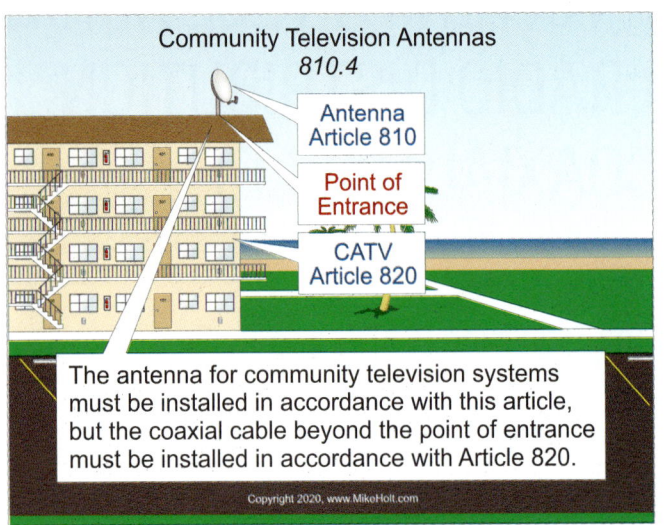

▶Figure 820-2

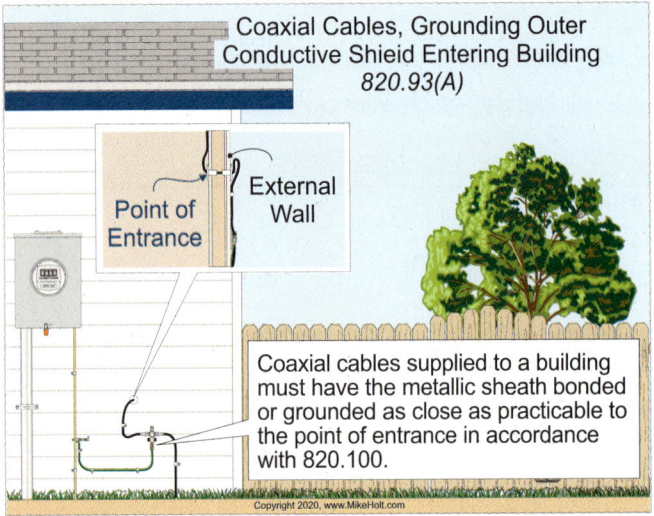

▶Figure 820-3

Part IV. Grounding Methods

820.100 Bonding and Grounding Methods

The outer conductive shield of a coaxial cable must be bonded or grounded in accordance with 800.100(A) and (B).

Ex: For systems using coaxial cable completely contained within the building (they do not exit the building) and isolated from outside cable systems, the shield can be grounded by a connection to an equipment grounding conductor as described in 250.118. This connection can be made through a grounded receptacle using a dedicated bonding jumper and a permanently connected listed device. Use of a cord and plug for the connection to an equipment grounding conductor is not permitted.

(A) Bonding Conductor or Grounding Electrode Conductor. The installation must comply with 800.100.

CHAPTER 8 PRACTICE QUESTIONS

Please use the 2020 *Code* book to answer the following questions.

CHAPTER 8—COMMUNICATIONS SYSTEMS

1. Article 800 general requirements apply to communications circuits, community antenna television and radio distribution systems, network-powered broadband communications systems, and premises-powered broadband communications systems, unless modified by Articles 805 and or _____.

   (a) Article 820
   (b) Article 830
   (c) Article 840
   (d) all of these

2. In one- and two-family dwellings, the primary protector bonding conductor or grounding electrode conductor for communications systems shall be as short as practicable, not to exceed _____ ft in length.

   (a) 5
   (b) 8
   (c) 10
   (d) 20

3. Limiting the length of the primary protector grounding conductors for communications circuits helps to reduce voltage between the building's _____ and communications systems during lightning events.

   (a) power
   (b) fire alarm
   (c) lighting
   (d) lightning protection

4. In one- and two-family dwellings where it is not practicable to achieve an overall maximum bonding conductor or equipment grounding conductor length of _____ ft for CATV communications system, a separate grounding electrode as specified in 250.52(A)(5), (A)(6), or (A)(7) shall be used.

   (a) 5
   (b) 8
   (c) 10
   (d) 20

5. Communications systems bonding conductors and grounding electrode conductors shall be protected where exposed to _____.

   (a) line voltage conductors
   (b) soil
   (c) physical damage
   (d) all of these

6. For community antenna television and radio distribution communications systems, where the building or structure served has an intersystem bonding termination established, 250.94(a) shall apply.

   (a) True
   (b) False

7. For buildings with a grounding means but without an intersystem bonding termination, the grounding electrode conductor for communications circuits shall terminate to the power service accessible means external to enclosures using the options identified in 250.94(a) Ex.

   (a) True
   (b) False

Chapter 8 | Practice Questions

8. Communications systems grounding conductor connections to grounding electrodes shall be made by _____.

    (a) listed lugs or clamps
    (b) listed pressure connectors
    (c) exothermic welding
    (d) any of these

9. Article _____ contains the installation requirements for the wiring of television and radio receiving equipment, such as digital satellite receiving equipment for television signals and amateur/citizen band radio equipment antennas.

    (a) 680
    (b) 700
    (c) 810
    (d) 840

10. Where radio or television equipment bonding or grounding is required, _____ used to connect a shield, a sheath, noncurrent-carrying metallic members of a cable, or metal parts of equipment or antennas to a bonding conductor or grounding electrode conductor shall be listed or be part of listed equipment.

    (a) fittings
    (b) clamps
    (c) lugs
    (d) devices

11. NFPA 780-2014, *Standard for the Installation of Lightning Protection Systems*, provides information for the application of the term "rolling sphere" as used in 810.15.

    (a) True
    (b) False

12. Antenna discharge units shall be located outside the building only.

    (a) True
    (b) False

13. Radio and television receiving antenna systems shall have bonding or grounding electrode conductors that are _____.

    (a) copper or other corrosion-resistant conductive material
    (b) insulated, covered, or bare
    (c) securely fastened in place and protected where subject to physical damage
    (d) all of these

14. The bonding conductor or grounding electrode conductor for a radio/television antenna system shall be protected where subject to physical damage, and where installed in a metal raceway, both ends of the raceway shall be bonded to the _____ conductor.

    (a) contained
    (b) grounded
    (c) ungrounded
    (d) largest

15. Article _____ covers the installation of coaxial cables for distributing radio frequency signals typically employed in community antenna television (CATV) systems.

    (a) 300
    (b) 430
    (c) 800
    (d) 820

16. For communications systems using coaxial cable completely contained within the building (that is, they do not exit the building) or the exterior zone of protection defined by a _____ radius rolling sphere and isolated from outside cable plant, the shield shall be permitted to be grounded by a connection to an equipment grounding conductor as described in 250.118.

    (a) 75-ft
    (b) 100-ft
    (c) 125-ft
    (d) 150-ft

FINAL EXAM A

SECTION II—STRAIGHT ORDER

Please use the 2020 *Code* book to answer the following questions.

1. A service is supplied by three metal raceways, each containing 600 kcmil ungrounded conductors. Determine the copper supply-side bonding jumper size for each service raceway.

   (a) 1/0 AWG
   (b) 3/0 AWG
   (c) 250 kcmil
   (d) 500 kcmil

2. When FMC is used where flexibility is necessary to minimize the transmission of vibration from equipment or to provide flexibility for equipment that requires movement after installation, _____ shall be installed.

   (a) an equipment grounding conductor
   (b) an expansion fitting
   (c) flexible nonmetallic connectors
   (d) adjustable supports

3. Metal enclosures and raceways containing service conductors shall be connected to the grounded system conductor if the electrical system is grounded.

   (a) True
   (b) False

4. Bonding conductors and grounding electrode conductors for television and radio communications systems, shall be _____ where exposed to physical damage.

   (a) electrically continuous
   (b) arc-fault labeled
   (c) protected
   (d) mechanically continuous

5. Outside of patient care vicinities, the equipment grounding terminals of isolated ground receptacles installed in branch circuits for patient care, shall be clearly _____ along the equipment conductor's entire length by green insulation with one or more yellow stripes.

   (a) listed
   (b) labeled
   (c) identified
   (d) approved

6. In health care facilities, isolated ground receptacles shall be installed in a patient care vicinity.

   (a) True
   (b) False

7. If the building or structure served has an intersystem bonding termination, the bonding conductor for an antenna mast shall be connected to the intersystem bonding termination.

   (a) True
   (b) False

8. Grounding electrode conductors of the wire type shall be _____.

   (a) solid
   (b) stranded
   (c) insulated or bare
   (d) any of these

9. The normally noncurrent-carrying metal parts of service equipment, such as service _____, shall be bonded together.

   (a) raceways or service cable armor
   (b) equipment enclosures containing service conductors, including meter fittings, boxes, or the like, interposed in the service raceway or armor
   (c) cable trays
   (d) all of these

10. Connections, taps, or extensions made from paralleled conductors shall connect to all conductors of the paralleled set.

    (a) True
    (b) False

11. In one- and two-family dwellings where it is not practicable to achieve an overall maximum primary protector grounding electrode conductor length of 20 ft, a separate communications ground rod not less than _____ ft shall be driven and it shall be connected to the power grounding electrode system with a 6 AWG conductor.

    (a) 5
    (b) 8
    (c) 10
    (d) 20

12. All conductors of the same circuit, including the grounded and equipment grounding conductors and bonding conductors shall be contained within the same _____, unless otherwise permitted elsewhere in the *Code*.

    (a) raceway
    (b) cable
    (c) trench
    (d) all of these

13. A single receptacle is a single contact device with no other contact device on the same _____.

    (a) circuit
    (b) yoke
    (c) run
    (d) equipment

14. The grounding conductor connection to the grounding electrode shall be made by _____.

    (a) listed lugs
    (b) exothermic welding
    (c) listed pressure connectors
    (d) any of these

15. Expansion, expansion-deflection, or deflection fittings and telescoping sections of metal raceways shall be made _____ continuous by equipment bonding jumpers or other means.

    (a) physically
    (b) mechanically
    (c) electrically
    (d) directly

16. The conductor used to ground the outer cover of communications cables such as a CATV coaxial cable shall be permitted to be insulated or bare and shall be no smaller than _____.

    (a) 14 AWG
    (b) 12 AWG
    (c) 10 AWG
    (d) 6 AWG

17. For ungrounded systems, noncurrent-carrying conductive materials enclosing electrical conductors or equipment shall be connected to the _____ in a manner that will limit the voltage imposed by lightning or unintentional contact with higher-voltage lines.

    (a) ground
    (b) earth
    (c) electrical supply source
    (d) enclosure

18. _____ shall not be used as grounding electrodes.

    (a) Metal underground gas piping systems
    (b) Aluminum
    (c) Metal well casings
    (d) Metal underground gas piping systems and Aluminum

19. Alternating-current circuits of less than 50V shall be grounded if supplied by a transformer whose supply system exceeds 150 volts-to-ground.

    (a) True
    (b) False

20. Bonding jumpers for service raceways shall be used around impaired connections such as _____.

   (a) oversized concentric knockouts
   (b) oversized eccentric knockouts
   (c) reducing washers
   (d) any of these

21. Outside of patient care vicinities, care should be taken in specifying a system containing isolated ground receptacles, because the _____ of the effective ground-fault current path is dependent upon the equipment grounding conductor(s) and does not benefit from any conduit or building structure in parallel with the equipment grounding conductor..

   (a) ampacity
   (b) resistance
   (c) effectiveness
   (d) impedance

22. For grounded systems, normally noncurrent-carrying conductive materials enclosing electrical conductors or equipment, or forming part of such equipment, shall be connected together and to the _____ to establish an effective ground-fault current path.

   (a) ground
   (b) earth
   (c) electrical supply source
   (d) enclosure

23. Where a shore power feeder supplies a remote panelboard, an insulated _____ conductor shall extend from a grounding terminal in the service equipment to a grounding terminal in the remote panelboard.

   (a) bonding jumper
   (b) equipment grounding conductor
   (c) grounding electrode conductor
   (d) copper conductor

24. Equipment not _____ for outdoor use or identified for indoor use such as "dry locations" or "indoor use only", shall be protected against damage from the weather during construction.

   (a) listed
   (b) identified
   (c) suitable
   (d) marked

25. Where an equipment grounding conductor is installed underground within an agricultural building, it shall be _____.

   (a) insulated
   (b) copper
   (c) bare
   (d) covered

26. Auxiliary grounding electrodes can be connected to the _____.

   (a) equipment grounding conductor
   (b) grounded conductor
   (c) earth as an effective ground-fault current path
   (d) any of these

27. Grounding electrode conductors shall be installed in one continuous length without a splice or joint, unless spliced by _____.

   (a) connecting together sections of a busbar
   (b) irreversible compression-type connectors listed as grounding and bonding equipment
   (c) the exothermic welding process
   (d) any of these

28. _____ alternating-current systems operating at 480V shall have ground detectors installed on the system.

   (a) Grounded
   (b) Solidly grounded
   (c) Effectively grounded
   (d) Ungrounded

29. An accessory, such as a locknut, intended primarily to perform a mechanical function rather than an electrical function best describes _____.

   (a) a part
   (b) equipment
   (c) a device
   (d) a fitting

30. Service raceways threaded into metal service equipment such as bosses (hubs) are considered to be effectively _____ to the service metal enclosure.

   (a) attached
   (b) bonded
   (c) grounded
   (d) secured

31. "Bonded" is defined as _____ to establish electrical continuity and conductivity.

    (a) isolated
    (b) guarded
    (c) connected
    (d) separated

32. Electrical continuity at service equipment, service raceways, and service conductor enclosures shall be ensured by _____.

    (a) bonding equipment to the grounded service conductor
    (b) connections utilizing threaded couplings on enclosures, if made up wrenchtight
    (c) other listed bonding devices, such as bonding-type locknuts, bushings, or bushings with bonding jumpers
    (d) any of these

33. The building or structure grounding electrode system shall be used as the _____ electrode for the separately derived system.

    (a) grounding
    (b) bonding
    (c) grounded
    (d) bonded

34. In completed installations, each outlet box shall have a _____.

    (a) cover
    (b) faceplate
    (c) canopy
    (d) any of these

35. Conductors with the color _____ insulation shall not be used for ungrounded or grounded conductors.

    (a) green or green with one or more yellow stripes
    (b) grey
    (c) black with a white stripe
    (d) white

36. This *Code* covers the installation of _____ for public and private premises, including buildings, structures, mobile homes, recreational vehicles, and floating buildings.

    (a) optical fiber cables
    (b) electrical equipment
    (c) raceways
    (d) all of these

37. Receptacles incorporating an isolated grounding conductor connection intended for the reduction of electromagnetic interference shall be identified by _____ on the face of the receptacle.

    (a) an orange triangle
    (b) a green triangle
    (c) the color orange
    (d) the engraved word "ISOLATED"

38. The grounding electrode conductor for an antenna mast or antenna discharge unit, if copper, shall not be smaller than 10 AWG.

    (a) True
    (b) False

39. Bonding conductors used for the bonding connections of the non-current carrying metal parts of signs shall not be smaller than _____ AWG.

    (a) 14 AWG
    (b) 12 AWG
    (c) 8 AWG
    (d) 6 AWG

40. Where circuit conductors are installed in parallel in multiple raceways or cables and include an EGC of the wire type, the equipment grounding conductor shall be installed in parallel in each raceway or cable, sized in compliance with 250.122 based on the overcurrent protective device for the feeder or branch circuit.

    (a) True
    (b) False

41. Alternating-current systems of 50V to 1,000V that supply premises wiring systems shall be grounded where supplied by a three-phase, 4-wire, delta-connected system in which the midpoint of one phase winding is used as a circuit conductor.

    (a) True
    (b) False

42. Conductors installed in nonmetallic raceways run underground shall be permitted to be arranged as _____ installations. The raceways shall be installed in close proximity, and the conductors shall comply with 300.20(B).

    (a) neutral
    (b) grounded conductor
    (c) isolated phase
    (d) all of these

43. If the building or structure served has no radio and television equipment intersystem bonding termination, the _____ conductor or grounding electrode conductor shall be connected to the nearest accessible location on the.

    (a) grounded
    (b) neutral
    (c) service equipment enclosure
    (d) bonding

44. Where a double-insulated water pool pump motor is installed where there is no connection between the swimming pool equipotential bonding means and the equipment grounding system for the premises, a solid 8 AWG copper bonding conductor shall be connected to _____.

    (a) a ground rod
    (b) the equipment grounding conductor of the motor circuit
    (c) 8 AWG bonding grid
    (d) any of these

45. Exposed noncurrent-carrying metal parts of an information technology system shall be _____.

    (a) GFPE protected
    (b) inaccessible to non-qualified personnel
    (c) GFCI protected
    (d) bonded to an equipment grounding conductor or double insulated

46. The word "Earth" best describes what *NEC* term?

    (a) Bonded.
    (b) Ground.
    (c) Effective ground-fault current path.
    (d) Guarded.

47. Internal parts of electrical equipment, including busbars, wiring terminals, insulators, and other surfaces, shall not be damaged or contaminated by foreign materials such as _____, or corrosive residues.

    (a) paint and plaster
    (b) cleaners
    (c) abrasives
    (d) any of these

48. Where branch-circuit wiring on the supply side of enclosures and junction boxes connected to conduits run to underwater luminaires are installed in corrosive environments as described in 680.14, the wiring method of that portion of the branch circuit shall be _____.

    (a) RMC or IMC
    (b) LFNC and PVC conduit
    (c) any wiring method
    (d) RMC/IMC or LFNC and PVC conduit

49. Electrical hazards often occur because the initial _____ did not provide for increases in the use of electricity and therefore wiring systems become overloaded.

    (a) inspection
    (b) owner
    (c) wiring
    (d) builder

50. If the grounding electrode conductor or bonding jumper connected to a single or multiple rod, pipe, or plate electrode(s), or any combination thereof, as described in 250.52(A)(5) or (A)(7), does not extend on to other types of electrodes that require a larger size conductor, the grounding electrode conductor shall not be required to be larger than _____ AWG copper wire.

    (a) 10
    (b) 8
    (c) 6
    (d) 4

51. Equipment grounding conductors of the wire type shall not be required to be larger than the circuit conductors.

    (a) True
    (b) False

52. The *Code* requires the installation of an equipment grounding conductor of the wire type in _____.

    (a) electrical nonmetallic tubing (ENT)
    (b) rigid metal conduit (RMC)
    (c) intermediate metal conduit (IMC)
    (d) electrical metallic tubing (EMT)

53. If a separate grounding electrode is installed for the radio and television equipment, it shall be bonded to the building's electrical power grounding electrode system with a bonding jumper not smaller than _____ AWG.

    (a) 10 AWG
    (b) 8 AWG
    (c) 6 AWG
    (d) 1/0 AWG

54. At existing buildings or structures, an intersystem bonding termination is not required if other acceptable means of bonding exists. An external accessible means for bonding communications systems together can be by the use of a(n) _____.

    (a) nonflexible metallic raceway
    (b) exposed grounding electrode conductor
    (c) connection to a grounded raceway or equipment approved by the authority having jurisdiction
    (d) any of these

55. Where a main bonding jumper is a screw only, the screw shall be identified with a(n) _____ that shall be visible with the screw installed.

    (a) silver or white finish
    (b) etched ground symbol
    (c) hexagonal head
    (d) green finish

56. The size of the grounding electrode conductor for a building or structure supplied by a feeder shall not be smaller than that identified in _____, based on the largest ungrounded supply conductor.

    (a) 250.66
    (b) 250.102
    (c) 250.122
    (d) Table 310.16

57. The conductors and equipment for delivering electric energy from the serving utility to the wiring system of the premises served is called a "_____."

    (a) branch circuit
    (b) feeder
    (c) service
    (d) service attachment

58. A buried iron or steel plate used as a grounding electrode shall expose not less than _____ sq ft of surface area to exterior soil.

    (a) 2
    (b) 4
    (c) 9
    (d) 10

59. The connection of the system bonding jumper for a separately derived system shall be made _____ on the separately derived system from the source to the first system disconnecting means or overcurrent device.

    (a) in at least two locations
    (b) in every location that the grounded conductor is present
    (c) at any single point
    (d) effectively

60. ENT is composed of a material resistant to moisture and chemical atmospheres and is _____.

    (a) rigid
    (b) flame retardant
    (c) fireproof
    (d) flammable

61. Buildings or structures supplied by multiple services or feeders shall use the same _____ to ground enclosures and equipment in or on that building.

    (a) service
    (b) disconnect
    (c) grounding electrode system
    (d) any of these

62. Article _____ covers the installation of portable wiring and equipment for carnivals, circuses, fairs, and similar functions.

    (a) 518
    (b) 525
    (c) 590
    (d) all of these

63. Metal boxes shall be _____ in accordance with Article 250.

    (a) grounded
    (b) bonded
    (c) secured
    (d) grounded and bonded

64. A bonding jumper not smaller than _____ AWG copper or equivalent shall be connected between the CATV communications system's grounding electrode and the power grounding electrode system at the building or structure served where separate electrodes are used.

    (a) 12
    (b) 8
    (c) 6
    (d) 4

65. Equipment, materials, or services included in a list published by an organization that is acceptable to the authority having jurisdiction are said to be "_____."

    (a) booked
    (b) a digest
    (c) a manifest
    (d) listed

66. Type NM cable shall be permitted in agricultural buildings.

    (a) True
    (b) False

67. Where electrical conductor material is not specified, the sizes given in the NEC shall apply to _____ conductors.

    (a) aluminum
    (b) copper-clad aluminum
    (c) copper
    (d) all of these

68. A separate bonding jumper to the building structural metal shall not be required if the metal frame of a building or structure is used as the _____ for the separately derived system.

    (a) bonding jumper
    (b) ground-fault current path
    (c) grounding electrode
    (d) lightning protection

69. A conducting object through which a direct connection to earth is established is a "_____."

    (a) bonding conductor
    (b) grounding conductor
    (c) grounding electrode
    (d) grounded conductor

70. The installed conductive path(s) that is part of a ground-fault current path and connects normally noncurrent-carrying metal parts of equipment together and to the system grounded conductor or to the grounding electrode conductor, or both, is known as a(n) "_____ conductor."

    (a) grounding electrode
    (b) grounding
    (c) equipment grounding
    (d) neutral

71. The armor of Type AC cable is recognized by the NEC as an equipment grounding conductor.

    (a) True
    (b) False

72. By definition, an equipment grounding conductor is considered to be a grounded conductor.

    (a) True
    (b) False

73. Areas where pool sanitation chemicals are stored, handled, or dispensed, and confined areas under decks adjacent to such areas, as well as areas with circulation pumps, automatic chlorinators, filters, open areas under decks adjacent to or abutting the pool structure, and similar locations are considered to be a _____.

    (a) hazardous area
    (b) restricted area
    (c) corrosive environment
    (d) wet location

74. The "patient care space" is any space within a health care facility where patients are intended to be _____.

    (a) admitted
    (b) evaluated
    (c) registered
    (d) examined or treated

75. Installations supplying _____ power to ships and watercraft in marinas and boatyards are covered by the *NEC*.

    (a) shore
    (b) primary
    (c) secondary
    (d) auxiliary

76. When a ground ring is used as a grounding electrode, it shall be installed at a depth below the earth's surface of not less than _____.

    (a) 18 in.
    (b) 24 in.
    (c) 30 in.
    (d) 8 ft

77. Where attachment to an equipment grounding conductor does not exist in the receptacle enclosure, a non-grounding-type receptacle(s) shall be permitted to be replaced with a grounding-type receptacle(s) where supplied through a ground-fault circuit interrupter and _____ shall be marked "GFCI Protected" and "No Equipment Ground," visible after installation.

    (a) the receptacle(s)
    (b) their cover plates
    (c) the branch circuit
    (d) the receptacle(s) or their cover plates

78. If a building or structure is supplied by a service or feeder with _____ or more disconnecting means in separate enclosures, the grounding electrode connections shall be made in accordance with 250.64(D)(1), 250.64(D)(2), or 250.64(D)(3).

    (a) one
    (b) two
    (c) three
    (d) four

79. For a grounded system, an unspliced _____ shall be used to connect the equipment grounding conductor(s) and the service disconnect enclosure to the grounded conductor of the system within the enclosure for each service disconnect.

    (a) grounding electrode
    (b) main bonding jumper
    (c) busbar
    (d) insulated copper conductor

80. When the term "exposed," as it applies to live parts, is used in the *Code*, it refers to _____.

    (a) being capable of being inadvertently touched or approached nearer than a safe distance by a person
    (b) parts that are not suitably guarded, isolated, or insulated
    (c) wiring on, or attached to, the surface or behind panels designed to allow access
    (d) being exposed to outdoor elements such as rain.

81. Metal enclosures shall be permitted to be used to connect bonding jumpers and _____, or both, together to become a part of an effective ground-fault current path.

    (a) grounded conductors
    (b) neutral conductors
    (c) equipment grounding conductors.
    (d) grounded phase conductors

82. Replacement luminaires are not required to be connected to an equipment grounding conductor if no equipment grounding conductor exists at the outlet box and the luminaire is _____.

    (a) more than 20 years old
    (b) mounted to the box using nonmetallic fittings and screws
    (c) mounted more than 6 ft above the floor
    (d) GFCI protected

83. Wiring shall be installed so that the completed system will be free from _____, other than as required or permitted elsewhere in the *Code*.

    (a) short circuits
    (b) ground faults
    (c) connections to the earth
    (d) all of these

84. Communications wiring such as telephone, antenna, and CATV wiring within a building shall not be required to comply with the installation requirements of Chapters 1 through 7, except where specifically referenced in Chapter 8.

    (a) True
    (b) False

85. Communications grounding electrodes shall be bonded to the power grounding electrode system at the building or structure served using a minimum _____ AWG copper bonding jumper.

    (a) 10 AWG
    (b) 8 AWG
    (c) 6 AWG
    (d) 4 AWG

86. The supply-side bonding jumper on the supply side of services shall be sized according to the _____.

    (a) overcurrent device rating
    (b) ungrounded supply conductor size
    (c) service-drop size
    (d) load to be served

87. In accordance with 517.13, the _____ assembly for branch circuits serving patient care spaces, shall itself qualify as an equipment grounding conductor in accordance with 250.118.

    (a) metal raceway system
    (b) metallic cable armor
    (c) metallic cable sheath
    (d) all of these

88. The _____ shall be bonded together and connected to an equipment grounding conductor on a branch circuit supplying the fountain.

    (a) metal piping systems associated with the fountain
    (b) metal parts of electrical equipment associated with the fountain water-circulating system
    (c) metal raceways, metal surfaces, and electrical devices and controls located less than 5 ft of the inside wall or perimeter of the fountain
    (d) all of these

89. Exothermic or irreversible compression connections, together with the mechanical means used to attach to fireproofed structural metal, shall not be required to be accessible.

    (a) True
    (b) False

90. A "neutral conductor" is the conductor connected to the _____ of a system, which is intended to carry current under normal conditions.

    (a) grounding electrode
    (b) neutral point
    (c) intersystem bonding termination
    (d) electrical grid

91. The outer conductive shield of a CATV coaxial cable entering a building shall be grounded as close to the point of entrance as practicable.

    (a) True
    (b) False

92. Chapters 5, 6, and 7 apply to special occupancies, special equipment, or other special conditions and may supplement or modify the requirements in Chapters 1 through 7.

    (a) True
    (b) False

93. Outside of patient care vicinities, the insulated equipment grounding conductor required in 517.13(B)(1) shall be clearly _____ along its entire length by green insulation, with no yellow stripes, and shall not be connected to the grounding terminals of isolated ground receptacles but shall be connected to the box or enclosure indicated in 517.13(B)(1)(2) and to noncurrent-carrying conductive surfaces of fixed electrical equipment indicated in 517.13(B)(1)(3).

    (a) listed
    (b) labeled
    (c) identified
    (d) approved

94. A cable tray is a unit or assembly of units or sections and associated fittings forming a _____ system used to securely fasten or support cables and raceways.

    (a) structural
    (b) flexible
    (c) movable
    (d) secure

95. The "_____" is the point of connection between the facilities of the serving utility and the premises wiring.

    (a) service entrance
    (b) service point
    (c) overcurrent protection
    (d) beginning of the wiring system

96. Cables and conductors installed exposed on the surfaces of ceilings and sidewalls shall be secured by hardware including straps, staples, cable ties, hangers, or _____ designed and installed so as not to damage the cable.

    (a) approved fittings
    (b) identified fittings
    (c) listed fittings
    (d) similar fittings

97. Type _____ cable is a factory assembly that encloses two or more insulated conductors within a nonmetallic jacket.

    (a) AC
    (b) MC
    (c) NM
    (d) NMJ

98. Masts and metal structures supporting antennas shall be grounded in accordance with 810.21, unless the antenna and its related supporting mast or structure are within a zone of protection defined by a _____ radius rolling sphere.

    (a) 75-ft
    (b) 100-ft
    (c) 125-ft
    (d) 150-ft

99. Liquidtight flexible metal conduit shall be permitted to be used as an equipment grounding conductor when installed in accordance with _____.

    (a) 250.102
    (b) 250.118(5)
    (c) 250.118(6)
    (d) 348.60

100. The largest size grounding electrode conductor required is _____ copper.

    (a) 6 AWG
    (b) 1/0 AWG
    (c) 3/0 AWG
    (d) 250 kcmil

FINAL EXAM B

SECTION II— RANDOM ORDER

Please use the 2020 *Code* book to answer the following questions.

1. Short sections of metal enclosures or raceways used to provide support or protection of _____ from physical damage shall not be required to be connected to the equipment grounding conductor.

    (a) conduit
    (b) feeders under 600V
    (c) cable assemblies
    (d) grounding electrode conductors

2. All PV system circuit conductors, including the equipment grounding conductor, shall be _____ when they leave the vicinity of the PV array.

    (a) installed in the same raceway
    (b) installed in the same cable
    (c) run with PV array circuit conductors
    (d) any of these

3. Agricultural buildings where corrosive atmospheres exist include areas where the following conditions exist _____.

    (a) poultry and animal excrement
    (b) corrosive particles which may combine with water
    (c) areas of periodic washing with water and cleansing agents
    (d) all of these

4. An important consideration for limiting imposed voltage on electrical systems is to remember that bonding and grounding electrode conductors should not be any longer than necessary and unnecessary bends and loops should be avoided.

    (a) True
    (b) False

5. Premises wiring includes _____ wiring from the service point or power source to the outlets.

    (a) interior
    (b) exterior
    (c) underground
    (d) interior and exterior

6. Where service-entrance conductors are installed in parallel in two or more raceways or cables, the size of the grounded conductor in each raceway or cable shall be based on the total circular mil area of the parallel ungrounded service-entrance conductors in the raceway or cable, sized in accordance with 250.24(C)(1), but not smaller than _____ AWG.

    (a) 1/0
    (b) 2/0
    (c) 3/0
    (d) 4/0

7. Wiring methods in healthcare facilities shall comply with Chapters 1 through 4 of the *NEC* except as modified in Article _____.

    (a) 511
    (b) 516
    (c) 517
    (d) 518

8. It is the intent of the *NEC* that factory-installed _____ wiring of listed equipment need not be inspected at the time of installation of the equipment, except to detect alterations or damage.

    (a) external
    (b) associated
    (c) internal
    (d) all of these

9. For grounded systems, the earth is considered an effective ground-fault current path.

    (a) True
    (b) False

10. The bonding conductor or grounding electrode conductor for an antenna mast or antenna discharge unit shall be run to the grounding electrode in as straight a line as practicable.

    (a) True
    (b) False

11. A splash pad is a type of fountain with a pool depth _____ in. or less, intended for recreational use by pedestrians.

    (a) 1 in
    (b) 3 in
    (c) 6 in
    (d) 12 in

12. When non-grounding-type receptacles are replaced by GFCI-type receptacles where attachment to an equipment grounding conductor does not exist in the receptacle enclosure, _____ shall be marked "No Equipment Ground."

    (a) these receptacles
    (b) their cover plates
    (c) the branch circuit
    (d) these receptacles or their cover plates

13. Type _____ cable is a fabricated assembly of insulated conductors in a flexible interlocked metallic armor.

    (a) AC
    (b) TC
    (c) NM
    (d) MA

14. The *NEC* does not cover electrical installations in ships, watercraft, railway rolling stock, aircraft, or automotive vehicles.

    (a) True
    (b) False

15. Each tap conductor to a common grounding electrode conductor for multiple separately derived systems shall be sized in accordance with _____, based on the derived ungrounded conductors of the separately derived system it serves.

    (a) 250.66
    (b) 250.118
    (c) 250.122
    (d) 310.15

16. Metal faceplates for snap switches, including dimmer and similar control switches, shall be _____.

    (a) bonded to the grounded electrode
    (b) bonded to the equipment grounding conductor
    (c) counted as one box fill volume allowance
    (d) replaced with nonmetallic switch cover plates

17. The grounding electrode conductor shall be made at any accessible point from the load-end of the service conductors and connected to the grounded service conductor at the _____.

    (a) load end of the service drop
    (b) load end of the service lateral
    (c) service disconnecting means
    (d) any of these

18. Article 645 covers _____ of information technology equipment and systems in an information technology equipment room that meets the requirements of 645.4.

    (a) equipment
    (b) power-supply wiring
    (c) interconnecting wiring
    (d) all of these

19. In patient care spaces, metal faceplates shall be directly connected to an insulated copper equipment grounding conductor by means of _____ securing the faceplate to a metal yoke or strap of a receptacle or to a metal outlet box.

    (a) ground clips
    (b) rivets
    (c) metal mounting screws
    (d) spot weld

20. Where attachment to an equipment grounding conductor does not exist in the receptacle enclosure, a non-grounding-type receptacle(s) shall be permitted to be replaced with a GFCI-type receptacle(s) where supplied through a ground-fault circuit interrupter; however, some cord-and-plug-connected equipment or appliances require an equipment grounding conductor and are listed in 250.114.

    (a) True
    (b) False

21. Alternating-current systems of 50V to 1,000V that supply premises wiring systems shall be grounded where the system is three-phase, 4-wire, wye-connected, with the neutral conductor used as a circuit conductor.

    (a) True
    (b) False

22. Limiting the length of the primary protector grounding conductors for community antenna television and radio systems reduces voltages that may develop between the building's _____ and communications systems during lightning events.

    (a) power
    (b) fire alarm
    (c) lighting
    (d) lightning protection

23. A service consisting of 12 AWG service-entrance conductors requires a grounding electrode conductor sized no less than _____ AWG.

    (a) 10
    (b) 8
    (c) 6
    (d) 4

24. Equipment or materials to which a label, symbol, or other identifying mark of a product evaluation organization that is acceptable to the authority having jurisdiction has been attached is known as "_____."

    (a) listed
    (b) labeled
    (c) approved
    (d) identified

25. The connection between the grounded circuit conductor and the equipment grounding conductor, or the supply-side bonding jumper, or both, at the service is the _____ bonding jumper.

    (a) main
    (b) system
    (c) equipment
    (d) circuit

26. A ground-fault current path is an electrically conductive path from the point of a ground fault through normally noncurrent-carrying conductors, equipment, or the earth to the _____.

    (a) ground
    (b) enclosure
    (c) electrical supply source
    (d) grounding electrode

27. Where the supplemental electrode is a rod, that portion of the bonding jumper that is the sole connection to the supplemental grounding electrode shall not be required to be larger than _____ AWG copper wire.

    (a) 8
    (b) 6
    (c) 4
    (d) 1

28. Listed FMC can be used as the equipment grounding conductor if the length in any ground return path does not exceed 6 ft and the circuit conductors contained in the conduit are protected by overcurrent devices rated at _____ or less.

    (a) 15A
    (b) 20A
    (c) 30A
    (d) 60A

29. When LFMC is used to connect equipment where flexibility is necessary to minimize the transmission of vibration from equipment or for equipment requiring movement after installation, a(n) _____ conductor shall be installed.

    (a) main bonding
    (b) grounded
    (c) equipment grounding
    (d) grounding electrode

30. _____ is a raceway of circular cross section having an outer liquidtight, nonmetallic, sunlight-resistant jacket over an inner flexible metal core.

    (a) FMC
    (b) LFNMC
    (c) LFMC
    (d) Vinyl-clad Type MC

31. For a separate building or structure supplied by a separately derived system when overcurrent protection is not provided for the supply conductors to the building/structure as permitted by 240.21(C)(4), the installation shall be _____ in accordance with 250.30(A).

    (a) AFCI protected
    (b) grounded and bonded
    (c) isolated
    (d) all of these

32. A device intended for the protection of personnel that functions to de-energize a circuit or portion thereof within an established period of time when the current to ground exceeds the values established for a Class A device, is a(n) "_____."

    (a) dual-element fuse
    (b) inverse time breaker
    (c) ground-fault circuit interrupter
    (d) safety switch

33. A "_____" is the total components and subsystem that, in combination, converts solar energy into electric energy for connection to a utilization load.

    (a) photovoltaic system
    (b) solar array
    (c) secondary source
    (d) standby source

34. Grounding electrode conductors that are not subject to physical damage can be run exposed along the surface of the building construction if securely fastened to the surface on which they are carried.

    (a) True
    (b) False

35. Where the main bonding jumper is a wire or busbar and is installed from the grounded conductor terminal bar or bus to the equipment grounding terminal bar or bus in the service equipment, the _____ shall be permitted to be connected to the equipment grounding terminal, bar, or bus to which the main bonding jumper is connected.

    (a) equipment grounding conductor
    (b) grounded service conductor
    (c) grounding electrode conductor
    (d) system bonding jumper

36. When LFNC is used, and equipment grounding is required, a separate _____ shall be installed in the conduit.

    (a) equipment grounding conductor
    (b) expansion fitting
    (c) flexible nonmetallic connector
    (d) grounded conductor

37. In the *NEC*, the word(s) "_____" indicate a mandatory requirement.

    (a) shall
    (b) shall not
    (c) shall be permitted
    (d) shall or shall not

38. Which of the following systems shall be installed and removed in accordance with the *NEC* requirements?

    (a) Signaling conductors, equipment, and raceways.
    (b) Communications conductors, equipment, and raceways.
    (c) Electrical conductors, equipment, and raceways.
    (d) all of these

39. Where a metal box is surface mounted, the direct metal-to-metal contact between the receptacle yoke or strap to the box is permitted to provide the required effective ground-fault current path provided that _____.

    (a) at least one of the mounting screw retaining washers is removed
    (b) the device is attached to the box with at least two screws
    (c) the raised cover mounting holes are located on a flat portion of the cover
    (d) all of these

40. By definition, an attachment fitting is different from an attachment plug because no _____ is associated with the fitting.

    (a) cable
    (b) fixture wire
    (c) cord
    (d) wiring compartment

41. Service conductors originate at the service point and terminate at the service disconnecting means.

    (a) True
    (b) False

42. Type _____ cable is a factory assembly of insulated circuit conductors within an armor of interlocking metal tape, or a smooth or corrugated metallic sheath.

    (a) AC
    (b) MC
    (c) NM
    (d) CMS

43. What is the minimum size copper equipment bonding jumper for a 40A rated circuit?

    (a) 14 AWG
    (b) 12 AWG
    (c) 10 AWG
    (d) 8 AWG

44. Handhole enclosure covers shall require the use of tools to open, or they shall weigh over _____.

    (a) 45 lb
    (b) 70 lb
    (c) 100 lb
    (d) 200 lb

45. Except as provided in 250.122(F)(2)(c) for raceway or cable tray installations, the equipment grounding conductor in each multiconductor cable shall be sized in accordance with 250.122 based on the _____.

    (a) largest circuit conductor
    (b) overcurrent protective device for the feeder or branch circuit
    (c) smallest branch-circuit conductor
    (d) overcurrent protective device for the service

46. For buildings with grounding means but without an intersystem bonding termination, the grounding electrode conductor for communications circuits shall terminate to the nearest _____.

    (a) building or structure grounding electrode system
    (b) interior metal water piping system, within 5 ft from its point of entrance
    (c) service equipment enclosure
    (d) any of these

47. An encased or buried connection to a concrete-encased, driven, or buried grounding electrode shall be accessible.

    (a) True
    (b) False

48. Listed liquidtight flexible metal conduit (LFMC) is acceptable as an equipment grounding conductor when it terminates in listed fittings and is protected by an overcurrent device rated 60A or less for trade sizes ⅜ through ½.

    (a) True
    (b) False

49. In accordance with Article 690, a solidly grounded PV system is often connected to ground through an electronic means internal to an inverter or charge controller that provides ground-fault protection.

    (a) True
    (b) False

50. Where an ac system operating at 1000 volts or less is grounded at any point, a(an) _____ shall connect the grounded conductor(s) to each service disconnecting means enclosure.

    (a) system bonding jumper
    (b) supply-side bonding jumper
    (c) main bonding jumper
    (d) equipment bonding jumper

51. When supplying a grounded system at a separate building or structure, an equipment grounding conductor shall be run with the supply conductors and connected to the building or structure disconnecting means and to the grounding electrode(s).

    (a) True
    (b) False

52. When PVC conduit extends from the pool light forming shell to a pool junction box for a wet-niche luminaire, an 8 AWG _____ bonding jumper shall be installed in the raceway.

    (a) solid bare
    (b) solid insulated copper
    (c) stranded insulated copper
    (d) solid or stranded insulated copper

53. _____ is an unthreaded thinwall metallic raceway of circular cross section designed for the routing and physical protection of electrical conductors and cables when joined together with listed fittings.

    (a) LFNC
    (b) EMT
    (c) NUCC
    (d) RTRC

54. When bonding enclosures, metal raceways, frames, and fittings, any nonconductive paint, enamel, or similar coating shall be removed at _____.

    (a) contact surfaces
    (b) threads
    (c) contact points
    (d) all of these

55. It shall be permissible to ground meter enclosures immediately adjacent to the service disconnecting means to the _____ circuit conductor on the load side of the service disconnect, if service ground-fault protection is not provided.

    (a) grounding
    (b) bonding
    (c) grounded
    (d) phase

56. The largest amount of current capable of being delivered at a point on the system during a short-circuit condition is defined as _____.

    (a) objectionable current
    (b) excessive current
    (c) induced current
    (d) fault Current

57. Listed flexible metal conduit or listed liquidtight flexible metal conduit that encloses the secondary circuit conductor from a transformer or power supply for use with neon tubing shall be permitted as a bonding means if the total accumulative length of the conduit in the secondary circuit does not exceed _____ ft

    (a) 6
    (b) 25
    (c) 50
    (d) 100

58. In health care facilities, _____ ground receptacle(s) installed in patient care spaces outside of a patient care vicinity(s) shall comply with 517.16(B)(1) and (2).

    (a) AFCI-protected
    (b) GFCI-protected
    (c) isolated
    (d) all of these

59. What is the minimum size copper supply-side bonding jumper for a service raceway containing 4/0 THHN aluminum conductors?

    (a) 6 AWG aluminum
    (b) 4 AWG aluminum
    (c) 4 AWG copper
    (d) 3 AWG copper

60. A building or structure(s) supporting a PV system shall utilize a grounding electrode system installed in accordance with Part III of Article _____.

    (a) 250
    (b) 690
    (c) 705
    (d) All of these

61. Equipment grounding conductors for motor branch circuits shall be sized in accordance with Table 250.122(A), based on the rating of the _____ device.

    (a) motor overload
    (b) motor over-temperature
    (c) branch-circuit short-circuit and ground-fault protective
    (d) feeder overcurrent protection

62. Where practicable, rod, pipe, and plate electrodes shall be installed _____.

    (a) directly below the electrical meter
    (b) on the north side of the building
    (c) below permanent moisture level
    (d) all of these

63. Metal conduit and metal piping within _____ ft horizontally of the inside walls of the pool shall be bonded unless separated by a permanent barrier.

    (a) 4
    (b) 5
    (c) 8
    (d) 10

64. For perimeter bonding, where conductive pool shell structural reinforcing steel is not available or is encapsulated in a nonconductive compound, a copper ring shall be utilized where _____.

    (a) a minimum 8 AWG bare solid copper conductor is provided and follows the contour of the perimeter surface.
    (b) only listed splicing devices or exothermic welding are used
    (c) the conductor is 18 to 24 in. from the inside wall of the pool and 4-6 in below the subgrade
    (d) all of these

65. Explanatory material, such as references to other standards, references to related sections of the *NEC*, or information related to a *Code* rule, are included in the form of Informational Notes.

    (a) True
    (b) False

66. Equipment grounding conductors for PV circuits having overcurrent protection shall be sized in accordance with _____.

    (a) 250.66
    (b) 250.102(C)(1)
    (c) 250.122
    (d) Table 250.122

67. Tap connections to a common grounding electrode conductor for multiple separately derived systems shall be made at an accessible location by _____.

    (a) a connector listed as grounding and bonding equipment
    (b) listed connections to aluminum or copper busbars
    (c) the exothermic welding process
    (d) any of these

68. When ungrounded circuit conductors are increased in size to account for voltage drop, the wire-type equipment grounding conductor shall be proportionately increased in size according to the increase in size of the ungrounded conductors using their _____.

    (a) ampacity
    (b) circular mil area
    (c) diameter
    (d) temperature rating

69. Steel or aluminum cable tray systems shall be permitted to be used as an equipment grounding conductor, provided the cable tray sections and fittings are identified as _____, among other requirements.

    (a) an equipment grounding conductor
    (b) special
    (c) industrial
    (d) all of these

70. A unit of an electrical system, other than a conductor, that carries or controls electric energy as its principal function is a(n) "_____."

    (a) raceway
    (b) fitting
    (c) device
    (d) enclosure

71. Where bonding jumper(s) are used to connect the grounding electrodes together to form the grounding electrode system, rebar is permitted to be used as a conductor to interconnect the electrodes.

    (a) True
    (b) False

72. The authority having jurisdiction has the responsibility for _____.

    (a) making interpretations of rules
    (b) deciding upon the approval of equipment and materials
    (c) waiving specific requirements in the *Code* and permitting alternate methods and material if safety is maintained
    (d) all of these

73. The bonding jumper used to bond the metal water piping system shall be installed in accordance with 250.64(A), 250.64(B), and 250.64(E) and the points of attachment of the bonding jumper(s) shall be _____.

    (a) readily accessible
    (b) accessible
    (c) enclosed
    (d) secured

74. An _____ is a mechanically and electrically integrated grouping of modules with support structure including any attached system components such as inverter(s) or dc-to-dc converter(s) and attached associated wiring.

    (a) inverter
    (b) array
    (c) dc-to-dc converter
    (d) alternating-current photovoltaic module

75. The _____ of a junction box, transformer enclosure, or other enclosure in the supply circuit to a wet-niche or no-niche luminaire and the field-wiring chamber of a dry-niche luminaire shall be connected to the equipment grounding terminal of the panelboard.

    (a) equipment grounding
    (b) grounded
    (c) grounding terminals
    (d) ungrounded

76. The receptacle grounding terminal of an isolated ground receptacle shall be connected to a(n) _____ equipment grounding conductor run with the circuit conductors.

    (a) insulated
    (b) covered
    (c) bare
    (d) solid

77. Examples of ground-fault current paths include any combination of conductive materials including _____.

    (a) equipment grounding conductors
    (b) metallic raceways
    (c) metal water and gas piping
    (d) all of these

78. In patient care spaces, an insulated equipment bonding jumper that directly connects to the equipment grounding conductor is permitted to connect the box and receptacle(s) to the equipment grounding conductor for other than _____ receptacles.

    (a) AFCI-protected
    (b) GFCI-protected
    (c) isolated ground
    (d) all of these

79. For circuits over 250 volts-to-ground, electrical continuity can be maintained between a box or enclosure where no oversized, concentric or eccentric knockouts are encountered, and a metal conduit by _____.

    (a) threadless fittings for cables with metal sheaths
    (b) double locknuts on threaded conduit (one inside and one outside the box or enclosure)
    (c) fittings that have shoulders that seat firmly against the box with a locknut on the inside or listed fittings
    (d) all of these

80. Listed or labeled equipment shall be installed and used in accordance with any instructions included in the listing or labeling.

    (a) True
    (b) False

81. Surface metal raceway enclosures providing a transition from other wiring methods shall have a means for connecting a(n) _____ conductor.

    (a) grounded
    (b) ungrounded
    (c) equipment grounding
    (d) all of these

82. In ungrounded systems, electrical equipment, wiring, and other electrically conductive material likely to become energized shall be installed in a manner that creates a low-impedance circuit from any point on the wiring system to the electrical supply source to facilitate the operation of overcurrent devices should a(n) _____ fault from a different phase occur on the wiring system.

    (a) isolated ground
    (b) second ground
    (c) arc
    (d) high impedance

83. Replacement luminaires shall be permitted to connect an equipment grounding conductor in the same manner as replacement receptacles.

    (a) True
    (b) False

84. Conductors in ferrous metal raceways or enclosures shall be arranged so as to avoid heating the surrounding ferrous metal by alternating-current induction. To accomplish this, the _____ conductor(s) shall be grouped together.

    (a) phase
    (b) grounded
    (c) equipment grounding
    (d) all of these

85. Connection of conductors to terminal parts shall ensure a thoroughly good connection without damaging the conductors and shall be made by means of _____.

    (a) solder lugs
    (b) pressure connectors
    (c) splices to flexible leads
    (d) any of these

86. A(n) _____ shall be used to connect the grounding terminal of a grounding-type receptacle to a grounded box.

    (a) equipment bonding jumper
    (b) grounded conductor jumper
    (c) equipment bonding jumper or grounded conductor jumper
    (d) equipment bonding jumper and grounded conductor jumper

87. The provisions of Article 690 apply to solar _____ systems, including inverter(s), array circuit(s), and controller(s) for such systems.

    (a) photoconductive
    (b) PV
    (c) photogenic
    (d) photosynthesis

88. The *NEC* requires that electrical equipment be _____.

    (a) installed in a neat and workmanlike manner
    (b) installed under the supervision of a licensed person
    (c) completed before being inspected
    (d) all of these

89. High-impedance grounded neutral systems shall be permitted for three-phase ac systems of 480V to 1,000V where _____.

    (a) the conditions of maintenance and supervision ensure that only qualified persons service the installation
    (b) ground detectors are installed on the system
    (c) line-to-neutral loads are not served
    (d) all of these

90. In order for a metal underground water pipe to be used as a grounding electrode, it shall be in direct contact with the earth for _____.

    (a) 5 ft
    (b) 10 ft or more
    (c) less than 10 ft
    (d) 20 ft or more

91. Article 600 covers the installation of conductors, equipment, and field wiring, retrofit kits, and outline lighting, regardless of voltage for _____.

    (a) electric signs
    (b) outline lighting
    (c) neon tubing
    (d) all of these

92. The common grounding electrode conductor installed for multiple separately derived systems shall not be smaller than _____ AWG copper when using a wire-type conductor.

    (a) 1/0
    (b) 2/0
    (c) 3/0
    (d) 4/0

93. Listed FMC and LFMC is permitted as an equipment grounding conductor at lengths, _____.

    (a) no greater than 2 ft.
    (b) no greater than 3 ft.
    (c) up to 6 ft.
    (d) up to 10 ft.

94. The following marina or dock items shall be connected to an equipment grounding conductor run with the circuit conductors in the same raceway, cable, or trench, metal boxes, cabinets, enclosures, and frames, and _____.

    (a) metal fencing
    (b) grounding terminals of grounding type receptacles
    (c) metal rails of piers and docks
    (d) metal ladders at piers and docks

95. For PV systems that are not solidly grounded, the equipment grounding conductor for the output of the PV system, where connected to associated distribution equipment connected to a grounding electrode system, shall be permitted to be the only connection to ground for the system.

    (a) True
    (b) False

96. The equipotential bonding requirements for perimeter surfaces contained in 680.26(B)(2) don\'t apply to a listed self-contained spa or hot tub installed above a finished floor.

    (a) True
    (b) False

97. Article 690 applies to solar PV systems, including _____.

    (a) array circuit(s), inverter(s), and controller(s) for such PV systems
    (b) interactive with other electrical power production sources or stand-alone or both
    (c) PV systems with ac or dc output for utilization
    (d) all of these

98. The arrangement of grounding connections shall ensure that the disconnection or the removal of a luminaire, receptacle, or other device fed from the box does not interrupt the electrical continuity of the _____ providing an effective ground-fault current path.

    (a) grounded conductor(s)
    (b) ungrounded conductor(s)
    (c) equipment grounding conductor(s)
    (d) all of these

99. The conductors and equipment required or permitted by this Code shall be acceptable only if _____.

    (a) labeled
    (b) listed
    (c) approved
    (d) identified

100. Handhole enclosure covers shall have an identifying mark or logo that prominently identifies the function of the enclosure, such as "_____."

    (a) "Danger"
    (b) "Utility"
    (c) "High Voltage"
    (d) "Electric"

INDEX

Description	Rule	Page

A

Agricultural Buildings
- Equipotential Planes — 547.10 — 269
- Wiring Methods — 547.5 — 268

Air-Conditioning and Refrigeration
- Grounding and Bonding — 440.9 — 243

Amateur and Citizen Band Transmitting and Receiving Stations
- Antenna Discharge Units—Transmitting Stations — 810.57 — 319
- Bonding Conductors and Grounding Electrode Conductors — 810.58 — 319

Armored Cable (Type AC)
- Equipment Grounding Conductor — 320.108 — 208

B

Bonding for Fault Current
- Bonding Communications Systems — 250.94 — 152
- Bonding Equipment Containing Service Conductors — 250.92 — 149
- Bonding Loosely Jointed Metal Raceways — 250.98 — 155
- Bonding Metal Parts Containing 277V and 480V Circuits — 250.97 — 154
- Bonding of Piping Systems and Exposed Structural Metal — 250.104 — 157
- Bonding Other Enclosures — 250.96 — 153
- Lightning Protection Systems — 250.106 — 161
- Neutral and Bonding Jumpers — 250.102 — 155

C

Cable Trays
- Equipment Grounding Conductor — 392.60 — 227

Carnivals, Circuses, Fairs, and Similar Events
- Equipment Grounding — 525.31 — 265
- Portable Equipment Grounding Conductor Continuity — 525.32 — 265

Class I Hazardous (Classified) Locations
- Grounding and Bonding — 501.30 — 253

Class II Hazardous (Classified) Locations
- Grounding and Bonding — 502.30 — 255

Class III Hazardous (Classified) Locations
- Grounding and Bonding — 503.30 — 257

Communications Systems
- Cable and Primary Protector Bonding and Grounding — 800.100 — 311
- Grounding Devices — 800.180 — 314

Community Antenna Television (CATV) and Radio Distribution Systems (Coaxial Cable)
- Bonding and Grounding Methods — 820.100 — 322
- Grounding Coaxial Cables — 820.93 — 321

E

Electric Signs and Outline Lighting
- Grounding and Bonding — 600.7 — 280

Electrical Metallic Tubing (Type EMT)
- Couplings and Connectors — 358.42 — 222
- Equipment Grounding Conductor — 358.60 — 222

Electrical Nonmetallic Tubing (Type ENT)
- Equipment Grounding Conductor — 362.60 — 223

Electrically Powered Pool Lifts
- Bonding — 680.83 — 298

Equipment Grounding and Equipment Grounding Conductors
- Equipment Connected by Cord and Plug — 250.114 — 162
- Equipment Grounding Conductor Installation — 250.120 — 168
- Identification of Equipment Grounding Conductors — 250.119 — 167
- Metal Enclosures — 250.109 — 162
- Restricted Use of Equipment Grounding Conductors — 250.121 — 168
- Sizing Equipment Grounding Conductors — 250.122 — 168
- Types of Equipment Grounding Conductors — 250.118 — 163

Index

F

Flexible Metal Conduit (Type FMC)
Description	Rule	Page
Equipment Grounding and Bonding Conductors	348.60	213

Fountains
Description	Rule	Page
Connection to an Equipment Grounding Conductor	680.54	297
Methods of Equipment Grounding	680.55	297

G

General
Description	Rule	Page
Bonding and Equipment Grounding	680.6	289
Bonding and Equipment Grounding Terminals	680.7	289
Clean Surfaces	250.12	110
Conductors	300.3	198
Connection of Grounding and Bonding Connectors	250.8	110
Definitions	680.2	285
Electrical Continuity	300.10	200
Equipment Grounding Conductor	410.44	242
Equipment Grounding Conductor Attachment	410.46	242
Induced Alternating Currents in Ferrous Metal Parts	300.20	200
Objectionable Current	250.6	106
Performance Requirements	250.4	100
Protection of Ground Clamps and Fittings	250.10	110

Grounding Electrode System and Grounding Electrode Conductor
Description	Rule	Page
Auxiliary Grounding Electrodes	250.54	139
Common Grounding Electrode	250.58	140
Connection to Grounding Electrodes	250.68	146
Grounding Electrode Conductor	250.62	141
Grounding Electrode Conductor Installation	250.64	141
Grounding Electrode Conductor Termination	250.70	148
Grounding Electrode Installation Requirements	250.53	134
Grounding Electrode System	250.50	131
Grounding Electrode Types	250.52	131
Sizing Grounding Electrode Conductor	250.66	145

Grounding Enclosure, Raceway, and Service Cable Connections
Description	Rule	Page
Other Enclosures	250.86	149
Service Raceways and Enclosures	250.80	149

H

Health Care Facilities
Description	Rule	Page
Equipment Grounding Conductor	517.13	260
Isolated Ground Receptacles	517.16	262
Wiring Methods	517.12	260

Hydromassage Bathtubs
Description	Rule	Page
Equipotential Bonding	680.74	297

I

Information Technology Equipment
Description	Rule	Page
Equipment Grounding and Bonding	645.15	283

Introduction to the National Electrical Code
Description	Rule	Page
Code Arrangement	90.3	52
Enforcement	90.4	53
Examination of Equipment for Product Safety	90.7	55
Mandatory and Explanatory Material	90.5	55
Purpose of the NEC	90.1	49

L

Liquidtight Flexible Metal Conduit (Type LFMC)
Description	Rule	Page
Equipment Grounding and Bonding Conductors	350.60	215

Liquidtight Flexible Nonmetallic Conduit (Type LFNC)
Description	Rule	Page
Equipment Grounding Conductor	356.60	219

M

Marinas, Boatyards, and Docking Facilities
Description	Rule	Page
Bonding of Non-Current-Carrying Metal Parts	555.13	271
Equipment Grounding Conductor	555.37	271

Metal-Clad Cable (Type MC)
Description	Rule	Page
Equipment Grounding Conductor	330.108	210

Methods of Equipment Grounding Conductor Connections
Description	Rule	Page
Attachment of Equipment Grounding Conductors in Boxes	250.148	178
Cord-and-Plug-Connected	250.138	173
Equipment Connected by Permanent Wiring Methods	250.134	172
Equipment Secured to Grounded Metal Supports	250.136	173
Frames of Ranges, Ovens, and Clothes Dryers	250.140	173
Neutral Conductor for Effective Ground-Fault Current Path	250.142	174
Receptacle Equipment Grounding Conductor	250.146	175

N

Nonmetallic Sheath Cable (Type NM)
Description	Rule	Page
Equipment Grounding Conductor	334.108	211

Description	Rule	Page

O

Outlet, Device, Pull, and Junction Boxes; Conduit Bodies; and Handhole Enclosures

Covers and Canopies	314.25	204
Handhole Enclosures	314.30	205
Metal Boxes	314.4	203
Nonmetallic Boxes	314.3	203
Sizing Pull and Junction Boxes	314.28	204

P

Pools Permanently Installed

Equipotential Bonding	680.26	292
Feeders	680.25	291
Junction Box, Transformer, or GFCI Enclosure	680.24	291
Pool Motors	680.21	289
Underwater Pool Luminaires	680.23	290

R

Radio and Television Satellite Equipment

Antenna Discharge Unit	810.20	316
Antenna Lead-In Protectors	810.6	316
Bonding Conductor and Grounding Electrode Conductors	810.21	317
Community Television Antenna	810.4	315
Grounding Devices	810.7	316
Metal Antenna Supports—Grounding	810.15	316

Receptacles and Attachment Plugs (Caps)

Connecting to Equipment Grounding Conductor	406.11	238
General Installation Requirements	406.4	236
Receptacle Faceplates	406.6	238
Receptacle Rating and Type	406.3	235

Requirements for Electrical Installations

Approval of Conductors and Equipment	110.2	83
Conductor Material	110.5	84
Conductor Sizes	110.6	84
Conductor Termination and Splicing	110.14	86
Deteriorating Agents	110.11	85
Suitable Wiring Methods	110.8	85
Use and Product Listing of Equipment	110.3	84
Wiring Integrity	110.7	85

Rigid Polyvinyl Chloride Conduit (Type PVC)

Equipment Grounding Conductor	352.60	217

S

Solar Photovoltaic (PV) Systems

Equipment Grounding and Bonding	690.43	301
Grounding Electrode System	690.47	303
Size of Equipment Grounding Conductors	690.45	303
Wiring Methods	690.31	300

Spas, Hot Tubs, and Permanently Installed Immersion Pools

Indoor Installations	680.43	296
Outdoor Installations	680.42	296

Surface Metal Raceways

Equipment Grounding Conductor	386.60	226

Switchboards and Panelboards

Equipment Grounding Conductor	408.40	239

Switches

General-Use Snap Switches, Dimmers, and Control Switches	404.9	233
Grounding of Enclosures	404.12	234

System Grounding and Bonding

Buildings Supplied by a Feeder	250.32	127
Generators—Portable and Vehicle- or Trailer-Mounted	250.34	129
Grounding	250.24	112
Grounding for Supply Side of the Service Disconnect	250.25	116
High-Impedance Grounded Systems	250.36	130
Main and System Bonding Jumper	250.28	117
Separately Derived Systems	250.30	118
Systems Required to be Grounded	250.20	111
Ungrounded Systems	250.21	112

T

Transformers

Grounding and Bonding	450.10	245

Notes

ABOUT THE AUTHOR

Mike Holt—Author

Founder and President
Mike Holt Enterprises
Groveland, Florida

Mike Holt is an author, businessman, educator, speaker, publisher and *National Electrical Code* expert. He has written hundreds of electrical training books and articles, founded three successful businesses, and has taught thousands of electrical *Code* seminars across the US and internationally. His electrical training courses have set the standard for trade education, enabling electrical professionals across the country to take their careers to the next level.

Mike's approach to electrical training is based on his own experience as an electrician, contractor, inspector and teacher. Because of his struggles in his early education, he's never lost sight of how hard it can be for students who are intimidated by school, by their own feelings towards learning, or by the complexity of the *NEC*. As a result of that, he's mastered the art of explaining complicated concepts in a straightforward and direct style. He's always felt a responsibility to his students and to the electrical industry to provide education beyond the scope of just passing an exam. This commitment, coupled with the lessons he learned at the University of Miami's MBA program, have helped him build one of the largest electrical training and publishing companies in the United States.

Mike's one-of-a-kind presentation style and his ability to simplify and clarify technical concepts explain his unique position as one of the premier educators and *Code* experts in the country. In addition to the materials he's produced, and the extensive list of companies around the world for whom he's provided training, Mike has written articles that have been seen in numerous industry magazines including, *Electrical Construction & Maintenance (EC&M), CEE News, Electrical Design and Installation (EDI), Electrical Contractor (EC), International Association of Electrical Inspectors (IAEI News), The Electrical Distributor (TED), Power Quality (PQ),* and *Solar Pro.*

Mike's ultimate goal has always been to increase electrical safety and improve lives and he is always looking for the best ways for his students to learn and teach the *Code* and pass electrical exams. His passion for the electrical field continues to grow and today he is more committed than ever to serve this industry.

His commitment to pushing boundaries and setting high standards extends into his personal life. Mike's an eight-time Overall National Barefoot Waterski Champion with more than 20 gold medals, many national records, and he has competed in three World Barefoot Tournaments. In 2015, at the tender age of 64, he started a new adventure—competitive mountain bike racing. Every day he continues to find ways to motivate himself, both mentally and physically.

Mike and his wife, Linda, reside in New Mexico and Florida, and are the parents of seven children and six grandchildren. As his life has changed over the years, a few things have remained constant: his commitment to God, his love for his family, and doing what he can to change the lives of others through his products and seminars.

Special Acknowledgments

My Family. First, I want to thank God for my godly wife who's always by my side and also my children.

My Staff. A personal thank you goes to my team at Mike Holt Enterprises for all the work they do to help me with my mission of changing people's lives through education. They work tirelessly to ensure that in addition to our products meeting and exceeding the educational needs of our customers, we stay committed to building life-long relationships with them throughout their electrical careers.

The National Fire Protection Association. A special thank you must be given to the staff at the National Fire Protection Association (NFPA), publishers of the *NEC*—in particular, Jeff Sargent for his assistance in answering my many *Code* questions over the years. Jeff, you're a "first class" guy, and I admire your dedication and commitment to helping others understand the *NEC*. Other former NFPA staff members I would like to thank include John Caloggero, Joe Ross, and Dick Murray for their help in the past.

ABOUT THE ILLUSTRATOR

Mike Culbreath—Illustrator

Mike Culbreath
Graphic Illustrator
Alden, Michigan

Mike Culbreath has devoted his career to the electrical industry and worked his way up from apprentice electrician to master electrician. He began by doing residential and light commercial construction, and later did service work and custom electrical installations. While working as a journeyman electrician, he suffered a serious on-the-job knee injury. As part of his rehabilitation, Mike completed courses at Mike Holt Enterprises, and then passed the exam to receive his Master Electrician's license. In 1986, with a keen interest in continuing education for electricians, he joined the staff to update material and began illustrating Mike Holt's textbooks and magazine articles.

Mike started with simple hand-drawn diagrams and cut-and-paste graphics. Frustrated by the limitations of that style of illustrating, he took a company computer home to learn how to operate some basic computer graphics software. Realizing that computer graphics offered a lot of flexibility for creating illustrations, Mike took every computer graphics class and seminar he could to help develop his skills. He's worked as an illustrator and editor with the company for over 30 years and, as Mike Holt has proudly acknowledged, has helped to transform his words and visions into lifelike graphics.

Originally from south Florida, Mike now lives in northern lower Michigan where he enjoys hiking, kayaking, photography, gardening, and cooking; but his real passion is his horses. He also loves spending time with his children Dawn and Mac and his grandchildren Jonah, Kieley, and Scarlet.

Mike Culbreath-Special Acknowledgments

I would like to thank Eric Stromberg, an electrical engineer and super geek (and I mean that in the most complimentary manner, this guy is brilliant), for helping me keep our graphics as technically correct as possible. I would also like to thank all our students for the wonderful feedback to help improve our graphics.

A special thank you goes to Cathleen Kwas for making me look good with her outstanding layout design and typesetting skills; to Toni Culbreath who proofreads all of my material; and to Dawn Babbitt who has assisted me in the production and editing of our graphics. I would also like to acknowledge Belynda Holt Pinto, our Executive Vice-President, Brian House for his input (another really brilliant guy), and the rest of the outstanding staff at Mike Holt Enterprises, for all the hard work they do to help produce and distribute these outstanding products.

And last but not least, I need to give a special thank you to Mike Holt for not firing me over 30 years ago when I "borrowed" one of his computers and took it home to begin the process of learning how to do computer illustrations. He gave me the opportunity and time needed to develop my computer graphics skills. He's been an amazing friend and mentor since I met him as a student many years ago. Thanks for believing in me and allowing me to be part of the Mike Holt Enterprises family.

ABOUT THE MIKE HOLT TEAM

Technical Writing

There are many people who played a role in the production of this textbook. Their efforts are reflected in the quality and organization of the information contained in this textbook, and in its technical accuracy, completeness, and usability.

Daniel Brian House

Brian House is Vice President of Digital and Technical Training at Mike Holt Enterprises and a permanent member of the video teams. He played a key role in editing this textbook, coordinating the content, and researching to assure the technical accuracy and flow of the information and illustrations presented. Brian also served as a member of the video team for the videos that accompany this textbook.

Editorial and Production

A special thanks goes to **Toni Culbreath** for her outstanding contribution to this project. She worked tirelessly to proofread and edit this publication. Her attention to detail and her dedication is irreplaceable.

Dan Haruch is the newest member of our technical team. His skillset and general knowledge of the *NEC*, combined with his work ethic and ability to work with other members of the production team, were a major part of the successful publication of this textbook.

Many thanks to **Cathleen Kwas** who did the design, layout, and production of this textbook. Her desire to create the best possible product for our customers is greatly appreciated.

Also, thanks to **Paula Birchfield** who was the Production Coordinator for this product. She helped keep everything flowing and tied up all the loose ends. She, **Jeff Crandall** and **Kirsten Shea** did a great job proofing the final files prior to printing.

Video Team

The following special people provided technical advice in the development of this textbook as they served on the video team along with author **Mike Holt** and graphic illustrator **Mike Culbreath**.

Scott Harding
Electrical Contractor
Rockville, Maryland

Scott Harding began his electrical career as an electrician's helper working part time in the family business. After graduating with an Electrical Engineering degree from Clemson University, he worked as an electrical engineer for RTKL Associates, a large design firm located in Baltimore, Maryland. After leaving RTKL, Scott went to work at F.B. Harding, Inc. an Electrical Contractor located in Rockville, Maryland where he's been for the last 31 years. He is a licensed Master Electrician in multiple jurisdictions and is the current President and CEO of F.B. Harding, Inc, making the family business a third generation company. Scott also serves on *NEC* Code-Making Panel Number 5 (Grounding and Bonding) and worked on the 2005, 2008, 2011, 2014, 2017, and 2020 cycles.

Scott lives in Maryland and is married with two kids.

Daniel Brian House
Mike Holt Enterprises
Leesburg, Florida

Brian House is Vice President of Digital and Technical Training at Mike Holt Enterprises, and a Certified Mike Holt Instructor. He began teaching seminars in 2000 after joining the elite group of instructors who attended Mike Holt's Train the Trainer boot camp. Brian was personally selected for development by Mike Holt after being named as one of the top presenters in that class. He now travels around the country to teach Mike Holt seminars to groups that include electricians, instructors, the military, and engineers. His first-hand experience as an electrical contractor, along with Mike Holt's instructor training, gave him a teaching style that is practical, straightforward, and refreshing.

Brian is high-energy, with a passion for doing business the right way. He expresses his commitment to the industry and his love for its people whether he's teaching, working on books, or developing instructional programs. Brian also leads the Mike Holt Enterprises apprenticeship and digital products teams. They're creating cutting-edge training tools and partnering with apprenticeship programs nation-wide to help them take their curriculum to the next level.

Brian and his wife Carissa have shared the joy of their four children and many foster children during 22 years of marriage. When not mentoring youth at work or church, he can be found racing mountain bikes with his kids or fly fishing on Florida's Intracoastal Waterway. He's passionate about helping others and regularly engages with the youth of his community to motivate them into exploring their future.

Jennifer Martin
Master Electrician/Instructor
Richland, Washington

Jennifer Martin is a third-generation wireman, IBEW Local #112 member that brings enthusiasm and charisma to the formal instruction and application of Electrical Codes and Safety Standards. She has been a vital part of the Volpentest HAMMER training facility within the Department of Energy (DOE). She provides her extensive experience in electrical instruction and consultation to local industries and generation facilities for ElecTrain while currently acting as the Electrical Administrator for Federal Engineers & Constructors (FE&C). She manages this workload all the while attending to her amazing children (six to be exact) ranging from twenty to six months of age. It goes without saying she is an incredibly busy woman.

Jennifer is a master electrician with electrical contractors' licenses in multiple states, a certified electrical safety professional (CESCP) and IEEE member, adding to her unbridled dedication to the electrical industry. Some may ask what she prefers to read for enjoyment; she usually responds with "Electrical codes and safety standards" followed by a sincere smile and slight giggle. Through her various industry memberships and representation of building trades there is always an opportunity for learning and sharing her passion with others.

Jennifer was introduced to Mike Holt by Eric Stromberg who she has worked with at DOE supporting Energy Facility Contractors Group (EFCOG); Electrical Safety Task Group for DOE Complex wide consistency and best practices. She most humbly accepted the opportunity to work with this unbelievable group of individuals and looks forward to the future adventures to come.

Jim Rogers
Inspector of Wires for Town of Oak Bluffs
Vineyard Haven, Massachusetts

James J. Rogers is currently the inspector of wires for the town of Oak Bluffs, Massachusetts, the owner/operator of Bay State Inspectional Agency, and an active instructor of the *National Electrical Code* on a national basis. Jim currently represents IAEI as the principal member and Chairman of CMP-4 and is a principal member of the NFPA 303 committee on boatyards and marinas. He's the Cape and Islands Chapter delegate and secretary to the Eastern Section, and serves on the Massachusetts Electrical Code Committee and the Massachusetts Electrical Interpretations Committee. Jim also conducts forensic investigations of electrical injury accidents and fire scenes and serves on multiple Underwriter's Laboratories, Standard Technical Panels representing enforcement.

On a personal note, Jim has been married to his wife Kathy for 40 years. They have two sons; Adam, a Fire Protection Engineer at Georgetown University; and Jeremie, a Police Officer for the town of West Tisbury. Jeremie is the proud father of Jim and Kathy's first grandson, Greyson Rogers.

When time allows, Jim's favorite hobby is playing golf and Kathy has now taken up the game as well.

Joel Sandel
Master Electrician, Engineer, Instructor
New York, New York

Joel Sandel is the president of JRS Consulting with his lovely wife Raizy as the CEO. He manages a team of expert and highly trained electrical engineers who conduct protective device coordination studies and arc flash studies, and design electrical power and fire alarm systems for many large projects. Joel also runs electrical and fire alarm and safety classes, serves on the NYC Electrical Code Committee, serves on the *NEC*'s Code-Making Panel 5, and is engaged with IEEE standards such as the color books and 1584 standard. He is a Licensed Master Electrician, an OSHA Authorized Safety Instructor, a NYS Licensed Electrical Instructor, and a member of IEEE, NYFAA, NFPA, IAEI, and FBECA.

Joel began his adult life working in his father's audio company where he learned to solve problems and get things done because as the saying goes, "the show must go on." That's where he had the opportunity to work with generators, temporary power, motors, and repairing electrical distribution systems and electronic equipment. Joel worked as a front of house (FOH) sound and systems engineer on several large events which were attended by as many as 35,000 people.

After that, Joel went to work for an electrical contractor in New York City where he worked in the field as a journeyman electrician for many years on residential, commercial, heath care, high-rise buildings, educational and industrial facilities, and retail projects. His duties included installing pipe and wire, large switchgear, electrical infrastructures, and fire alarm systems. He eventually began to do in-house engineering and training for the company to maintain the quality, safety, and code compliance which led him to his next endeavor.

Joel lives in Brooklyn, New York with his wife and three children. He volunteers on Sundays to play music to entertain the sick and elderly.

Eric Stromberg, P.E.
Electrical Engineer/Instructor
Los Alamos, New Mexico

Eric Stromberg has a bachelor's degree in electrical engineering and is a professional engineer. He started in the electrical industry when he was a teenager helping the neighborhood electrician. After high school, and a year of college, Eric worked for a couple of different audio companies, installing sound systems in a variety of locations from small buildings to baseball stadiums. After returning to college he worked as a journeyman wireman for an electrical contractor.

After graduating from the University of Houston, Eric took a job as an electronic technician and installed and serviced life safety systems in high-rise buildings. After seven years he went to work for Dow Chemical as a power distribution engineer. His work with audio systems had made him very sensitive to grounding issues and he took this experience with him into power distribution. Because of this expertise, Eric became one of Dow's grounding subject matter experts. This is also how Eric met Mike Holt, as Mike was looking for grounding experts for his 2002 Grounding vs. Bonding video.

Eric taught the *National Electrical Code* for professional engineering exam preparation for over 20 years, and has held continuing education teacher certificates for the states of Texas and New Mexico. He was on the electrical licensing and advisory board for the State of Texas, as well as on their electrician licensing exam board. Eric now works for a Department of Energy research laboratory in New Mexico, where he's responsible for the electrical standards as well as being a part of the laboratory's AHJ.

Eric's oldest daughter lives with her husband in Zurich, Switzerland, where she teaches for an international school. His son served in the Air Force, has a degree in Aviation logistics, and is a pilot and owner of an aerial photography business. His youngest daughter is a singer/songwriter in Los Angeles.

Save 25% On These Best-Selling Libraries

Understanding the NEC® Complete Training Library

This library makes it easy to learn the Code and includes the following best-selling textbooks and DVDs:

Understanding the National Electrical Code® Volume 1 Textbook
Understanding the National Electrical Code® Volume 2 Textbook
NEC® Exam Practice Questions Workbook
General Requirements DVD
Wiring and Protection DVD
Bonding and Grounding DVDs (4)
Wiring Methods and Materials DVDs (2)
Equipment for General Use DVD
Special Occupancies and Special Equipment DVDs (3)
Limited Energy and Communications Systems DVD

Product Code: 20DECODVD   List Price: ~~$599.00~~   Now only $449.25*

Electrical Estimating Training Program

Mike Holt's Electrical Estimating Training Program will give you the skills and the knowledge to get more jobs and to make sure that those jobs are profitable. This program gives you a comprehensive understanding of estimating and will also help you understand how electrical estimating software can improve your process.

Package includes:
Electrical Estimating Textbook
Electrical Estimating DVDs (4)

Product Code: EST2DVD   List Price: ~~$325.00~~   Now Only $243.75*

Solar PV Systems Training Program

Everyone in the solar industry needs to understand the NEC® rules governing Solar PV Systems. This content must be mastered by the designer, contractor, installer, inspector, and instructor.

As the market continues to grow, the rules governing solar installations continue to evolve. But don't be intimidated; Mike's textbook and videos will give you an edge because of the extra effort put forth to make the rules clear and explain how they should be applied in the field.

Package includes:
Solar Photovoltaic Systems Textbook
Solar Photovoltaic Systems DVDs (3)

Product Code: 20SOLDVD   List Price: ~~$299.00~~   Now Only $224.25*

---

* Prices subject to change. Discount applies to price at time of order.

Call Now 888.NEC.CODE (632.2633)
& mention discount code: B20NCT225